Moving Against the Stream

THE COMPLETE WORKS OF SANGHARAKSHITA include all his previously published work, as well as talks, seminars, and writings published here for the first time. The collection represents the definitive edition of his life's work as Buddhist writer and teacher. For further details, including the contents of each volume, please turn to the 'Guide' on pp. 575–83.

FOUNDATION

1 A Survey of Buddhism / The Buddha's Noble Eightfold Path
2 The Three Jewels I
3 The Three Jewels II
4 The Bodhisattva Ideal
5 The Purpose and Practice of Buddhist Meditation
6 The Essential Sangharakshita

INDIA

7 Crossing the Stream: India Writings I
8 Beating the Dharma Drum: India Writings II
9 Dr Ambedkar and the Revival of Buddhism I
10 Dr Ambedkar and the Revival of Buddhism II

THE WEST

11 A New Buddhist Movement I
12 A New Buddhist Movement II
13 Eastern and Western Traditions

COMMENTARY

MEMOIRS

POETRY AND THE ARTS

COMPLETE WORKS 23 **MEMOIRS**

Sangharakshita

Moving Against the Stream

EDITED BY KALYANAPRABHA

Windhorse Publications
17e Sturton Street
Cambridge
CB1 2SN
UK

info@windhorsepublications.com
www.windhorsepublications.com

First published in 2020.

Cover design by Dhammarati
Cover images: Front: Old Hall, Biddulph, © Clear Vision Trust Picture Archive. Back flap: Sangharakshita, Sherab Nangwa, Dhardo Rimpoche, Ventul Rimpoche and Terry Delamare. Kalimpong, 1966, © Clear Vision Trust Picture Archive.

Typesetting and layout by Tarajyoti
Printed by Bell & Bain Ltd, Glasgow

British Library Cataloguing in Publication Data:
A catalogue record for this book is available from the British Library.

ISBN 978-1-911407-49-2 (hardback)
ISBN 978-1-911407-50-8 (paperback)

CONTENTS

LIST OF ILLUSTRATIONS

FOREWORD

In Sangharakshita's memoir, *Moving Against the Stream*, there is a chapter about the 'secret life' based on a traditional Tibetan theory that the record of a life, be it biography, autobiography, or memoir, should cover not just the outer life of events but the inner life and the secret life as well. The idea is that this secret life, though held at bay for most of the time by the demands of the outer life, nevertheless slowly gathers momentum and periodically erupts into consciousness. Elaborating on this, Sangharakshita writes:

> It was as though I was living, on another level, a secret life that normally had no point of direct contact with my outer or even with my inner life.[1]

He instances such an eruption late on in the memoir when one day in Kalimpong, in 1967, it suddenly becomes clear to him that what is needed is a new Buddhist movement in the West. It comes like a flash of lightning, suddenly revealing possibilities that had 'hitherto been shrouded in darkness or perceived only dimly.'[2]

For me personally, being as it were in the right place at the right time, one significant consequence of that dramatic moment of illumination of his came when I made contact with the new Buddhist movement on the first retreat held by the Friends of the Western Sangha.[3] As I listened that week to the teacher's inspiring words when he was teaching the

Dharma or guiding us into the realm of meditation, I bathed for days in the bliss of Beginner's Mind. It all felt refreshingly new, yet at the same time uncannily familiar. Was my own secret life, after lurking so long in the shadow of some dim peripheral consciousness, at last breaking through the carapace of mundane events?

As is the case with most memoirs, Sangharakshita's main focus is on his 'outer life', from his arrival in England in the summer of 1964, after twenty years in India, up to the spring of 1969. The short *1970 – A Retrospect* which completes this volume of the *Complete Works* offers a few fascinating glimpses into the second kind of life, his inner life, including a dramatic near-death experience and a venture into the world of psychedelics. Though the historical range is short it covers a period that was significant not only in the life of the author but, through him, in the history of Buddhism in the West.

In those early years after his return from India, I wasn't the only one who felt a palpable air of magic surrounding Sangharakshita, an aura that faded as the movement gradually expanded. He seemed to have come from another world, a bit like Nietzsche's prophet descending from the mountain top to the market place with the good news. He had returned to the West after living many years in the foothills of the Himalayas, much of the time meditating, studying, and reflecting on the Dharma, and receiving initiations from some great Tibetan lamas. By the time he stepped off the plane at Heathrow, he had accumulated, in traditional Buddhist terms, an impressive stock of merit and wisdom, of which we were to be the early beneficiaries. But the allure didn't just come from his side. The times were propitious too: the counter-culture of the 1960s. Perhaps one couldn't go so far as to say with Wordsworth that to be young then 'was very heaven',[4] but there was for many of us a bracing sense of freedom in the air that came with the softening of the hard edges of a rigid conservatism, and gave rise to new possibilities. No longer 'square', we grew our hair! The zeitgeist also suited Sangharakshita's great spiritual project, the spreading of the Dharma in the West, especially after he had been released, albeit involuntarily, from the restraints of working at the Hampstead Buddhist Vihara.

The following pages are all about Sangharakshita at work and his reflections on the many activities he engages in. There is a pleasing flow to the enterprise; he works hard but it never comes across as graft or draining, which is surprising considering the amount of time he puts in. His first attendance at the Buddhist Society's summer school is fairly representative of the pace and variety of his work. In the course of a week he conducts six meditation sessions, delivers ten lectures, holds a question-and-answer meeting, participates in the school's concluding brains trust, and records two interviews for the BBC. Between times he also manages to do a lot of reading. He appears to sail through it all, even though, as the subtitle of the memoir indicates (The Birth of a New Buddhist Movement), his work often involved taking his stand against the prevailing trend in contemporary Buddhist circles. He has the courage and energy to move against the stream, the rather sluggish stream of Buddhism in England at the time, a Buddhism not without its merits and traditional core values, but marred by a serious conflict between its two governing bodies, the English Sangha Trust and the Buddhist Society. He is a moderating influence, listening patiently and making friends with people from both sides.

At the heart of the conflict – which the English Sangha Trust had invited him, as the seniormost English monk, to try and resolve – lay the traditional split between monastic and lay, a deep-rooted belief that the *bhikkhus* were the true Buddhists and the laity were there only to support them. At various points in the story we encounter Sangharakshita deliberately distancing himself from monastic formalism. Though still wearing his *bhikkhu* robes, he lets his hair grow longer than the regulation length, often eats after twelve o'clock, goes to the opera, and during mealtimes at the summer school insists on sitting not with the *bhikkhus* but with the rest of the retreatants, much to their delight but, no doubt, to the dismay of the establishment. These are not just indicators of his grasp of the vital distinction between rules and principles but of a significant reorientation in his understanding of the true Dharma and the way it should be practised. In an article for the local sangha newsletter he goes so far as to say,

> to the extent that they, too, have gone for refuge to the Buddha, the Dharma, and the Sangha, the laity are as much Buddhists as are the members of the Monastic Order,[5]

which must have come across in those days as at least startling if not revolutionary. Such are the initial sounding notes of what would eventually become the dominant theme of his teaching as it developed in later years, namely that it is essentially the Going for Refuge to the Three Jewels that makes one a Buddhist, or, to quote what became something of a slogan, especially in the early days of the FWBO, *commitment is primary, lifestyle secondary*. Ordination within the Western Buddhist Order was to be a unifying, not a divisive, factor.

In 1965 Sangharakshita gave a series of lectures at the Hampstead Buddhist Vihara on the nature of conversion in Buddhism. There he defines Spiritual Community, the third of the Three Refuges, as essentially communication which, in the context of Going for Refuge, is *a vital mutual responsiveness on the basis of a common ideal and a common principle*.[6] He goes on to say that this kind of communication is not limited to that between teacher and disciple but can also take place between those who are simply friends, or *kalyāṇa mitras*. Listening recently to recordings of these lectures I was struck again and again by the clarity and energy in his voice and how inspired he is to be passing on his fresh and penetrating insights into the nature of spiritual community. He was 'possessed by a passion for spreading the Dharma through the medium of the spoken word'.[7] His legacy to the Triratna Buddhist Community comes largely in the form of the spoken word and it is hardly surprising that giving talks and lectures is for many members of the Triratna Buddhist Order a major channel for the spreading of the Dharma. Another lecture that proved popular in the early days (he gave it live at that first retreat I attended and it was afterwards published as a booklet) is *Mind – Reactive and Creative*, an exploration of his teaching on the two basic types of conditionality in Buddhism, the cyclic and the spiral.[8] Coming as I did from a strain of religious conditioning that was quite definitely God-based, one in which one's soul after death would be eternally damned or saved, I remember the truth flooding in on me as I listened to Sangharakshita speaking – that I was now at last free to take control of my own life. The creative mind, he says,

> loves where there is no reason to love, is happy where there is no reason for happiness, creates where there is no possibility of creativity.[9]

From the start of his work in England, Sangharakshita was well aware of the need to restate spiritual truths in a language that was meaningful to Western Buddhists. To be a good translator of the Dharma from East to

West – for that is how he saw himself – Buddhism needed to be adapted to the realities of Western society without compromising the essential principles of the Dharma. In this sense he was an authentic Western Buddhist as distinct from being 'merely a Westerner who has adopted the Buddhism of Tibet, Japan, Burma or Thailand.'[10] It is important, both psychologically and spiritually speaking, that one does not completely renounce one's cultural roots as many Western Buddhist monks at the time felt it their duty to do, but rather to reclaim, as he puts it, one's cultural heritage. 'I wanted', he said, 'to immerse myself in Western culture'.[11] In the context of meditation practice the equivalent term for 'immerse' would be 'become absorbed'. What often struck me as I read through the memoir was Sangharakshita's extraordinary ability to become easily and totally absorbed in whatever he was interested or involved in, be it meditating, delivering lectures, reflecting more generally on the Dharma, or reading poetry or listening to music. When a young woman invites him to a performance of Wagner's *Ring* cycle, he sits in the train on the way back without uttering a word or glancing even once in her direction. She thinks he is angry with her for inviting him, whereas the truth is that he is still enthralled by the music he has just heard. Living in community with him many years later I experienced at first hand this aspect of Sangharakshita's make-up. If he happened to be in an intensive writing phase he would come down to lunch still very much in the world he had been steeped in at his desk. It was almost as if he sat alone in the room, totally oblivious of everyone else; till one got used to it this could be quite disconcerting. Yet looking at it from his side, and in view of the intensity of his concentration, the sudden switching between worlds could surely be jarring. He remarks how difficult he could find it at the end of a lecture he has just given to come down from the exalted state of consciousness he has been dwelling in.[12] This ability to become totally absorbed was an aspect of his exceptional mindfulness. I experienced many times the strength and continuity of his mindfulness, a quality that led quite naturally to concentration and absorption. 'The mindful person', says the *Dhammapada*, 'absorbed in superconscious states, gains ample bliss'.[13] In a letter he wrote not long after we met he told me he felt 'most of the time quite ecstatic, with a sense of the heavens opening,' so that when he spoke of the Spiral Path, I felt it was based on his own experience.

In the account of his European travels in the later chapters of *Moving Against the Stream* we see this talent for absorption combined with an impressive knowledge of Western art and culture, and a highly developed aesthetic sensibility. Sangharakshita revels in the wealth of cultural delights on offer. In Florence the architectural details of the numerous Renaissance palaces give him a 'particularly keen thrill of aesthetic delight'.[14] A week or two later, sitting on the upward slope of Apollo's theatre at Delphi, he recalls how he first read Chapman's *Homer* in his youth, 'in a state bordering on ecstasy'.[15] More generally speaking, this faculty for total immersion was key in helping him to achieve in his own inner life a level of integration between the religious and the aesthetic. This would eventually come to flower as one of the distinctive emphases of the Triratna Buddhist Community: the appreciation of beauty in nature and great art as a method of spiritual development.[16]

The last few chapters of the memoir centre on Sangharakshita's friendship with Terry Delamare. At the end of the questions and answers that follow his lecture on *Buddhism and the Problem of Death,* a tall young man who had been sitting in the front row assiduously taking notes approaches to say that he has himself experienced the white light that Sangharakshita has been talking about in connection with *The Tibetan Book of the Dead.* At the core of the friendship that quickly develops between them is the kind of mutual responsiveness on the basis of a shared spiritual ideal that earlier in the book Sangharakshita has defined as the essence of Spiritual Community. This friendship, he writes, 'was to have important consequences for the rest of my life and, through me, for the future of British Buddhism'.[17] Terry had a keen intellect and the exchanges between them in their long and intense discussions on matters philosophical and spiritual provided a vital stimulus to the development of Sangharakshita's thinking. They travel to India together for Sangharakshita's farewell visit before his moving permanently to the West. But the friendship has a tragic undertone. Terry was severely depressed, a condition which Sangharakshita constantly did his best to alleviate, time and again gently talking his friend out of his darker moods. He once told me that he would spend hour after hour pouring energy into Terry, but to no lasting effect. As Terry's own diary makes clear, his profound insight when he experienced the White Light had exposed the 'fiction of time', coupled with 'the crippling effects that personality has upon a person's true self.'[18] Seeing another possible way to dispel the dark clouds obscuring the pure light of the mind, Sangharakshita introduces him to the *sādhana* of Vajrasattva, a Tantric method of purification, which they practised together daily for a period. But the gap between insight and personality proved to be too wide for Terry, and the clouds obscuring the Light he had twice experienced eventually led to his tragic death.

Moving Against the Stream, together with *1970 – A Retrospect*, is the story of a remarkable man who founded a new Buddhist movement and steered it through its formative years, 'a unique figure', as one of his early followers puts it 'in the world of Buddhism – a man of undoubted and distinguished intellectual powers, of supreme efficiency and advanced spiritual awareness'.[19] It provides many a foretaste of his fully fledged vision of the Dharma expounded in the many hundreds of thousands of words of the *Complete Works*. Sitting with Terry at a table in the open-air tea rooms at Kusinara in 1967, he watches a few hippies, 'long-haired, emaciated, and half naked, and seemingly under the influence of drugs'. He thinks they do not look very happy, and

> though I could understand their rejection of conventional values, a rejection soon to become widespread among young people in the West, I also saw that because of their inability to replace those values by real ones they had lost their way and were simply drifting.[20]

Later that same year quite a few hippies started to drift down to his meditation classes in a tiny basement in Monmouth Street in the West End of London, the birthplace of the new movement. There he was able to offer them the highest value imaginable, the gift of the Dharma.

Abhaya
Brighton
January 2019

A NOTE FROM THE EDITOR

When first setting out to prepare Sangharakshita's memoirs for the *Complete Works* we had it in mind not to intrude on the flow of the text with any but the fewest notes. We received, however, a complaint: where were the explanatory notes that readers had come to expect from the *Complete Works*? In subsequent memoirs we have tried to make good this omission. There are cross references to earlier memoirs, and other works by Sangharakshita, for readers who want to find out more. There are explanations of cultural references – for Sangharakshita's readers come from all parts of the globe; and there will be readers in the future who will not be familiar with what today is common knowledge.

In the account of the tour of Italy and Greece told in chapters 36–9, Sangharakshita writes:

> Paintings were often without meaning for [Terry] because he was ignorant of the Bible stories or classical myths and legends on which they were based. Such ignorance was by no means unusual, and in years to come, when 'progressive' education policies had done their work, it would be widespread in Britain. Terry at least knew that he was cut off from his cultural heritage, and resented the fact. People in the future would hardly know there was a cultural heritage to be cut off from.

Imagining some readers may find themselves in a position similar to Terry's, when paintings or sculptures are referred to, or mention is made of the great names of Renaissance Italy and Ancient Greece, I have given a few extra points of information hoping they will encourage such readers to enter further into that bright world of cultural heritage, the world of painting and sculpture especially, but also the worlds of religion, history, and philosophy.

In compiling references to books read by Sangharakshita I have included a few words about their author, and often an indication of when the book was first published to give readers a sense of the diverse intellectual and literary world that was his.

The context for the events related in this volume – mainly Britain of the 1960s and 1970 – is a world that differs fundamentally from the one we are in today – and will be in tomorrow. I have attempted to augment in some endnotes the information in the text that evokes the world in which Sangharakshita set up a new Buddhist movement – a world of anti-psychiatry, *Honest to God*, the Peanuts Group, and the like.

In his work to bring the Dharma to the West, Sangharakshita gave many lectures, frequently mentioned in these pages. From early on they were recorded and can be accessed online at freebuddistaudio.com. Most are transcribed and will be included in *Complete Works*, especially in volumes 11 and 12.

This is the seventh and, due to deteriorating eyesight, last volume of the *Complete Works* that I will edit. I would like to record my deep appreciation and gratitude to Vidyadevi. For several years we were co-editors, working together to get the project off the ground. She is willing – and able – to take it forward and oversee its completion, a task of Herculean proportions – and surely the merit gained will be likewise. Perhaps only those who have done the work themselves can give full recognition to the task. My thanks to Shantavira, our copyeditor *par excellence*, who has worked on almost all Sangharakshita's books since the beginning and whose dedication, patience, and humour have enabled the project to come so far. I would like to acknowledge with gratitude Priyananda, Michelle, and the team at Windhorse Publications without whose care and dedication no publishing could have taken place; and my thanks to the volunteers who helped me personally in preparing the texts for publication.

During the course of the last year, on 30 October 2018, Sangharakshita died. He was 93. He had held in his hands eight of the volumes of his *Complete Works*, and knew a further four were well on their way to publication. May the bounty of his writings help many, many people to a deeper understanding and experience of the Dharma – the end to which his whole life was dedicated.

Kalyanaprabha
Great Malvern
June 2019

MOVING AGAINST THE STREAM

Sangharakshita's European Journey

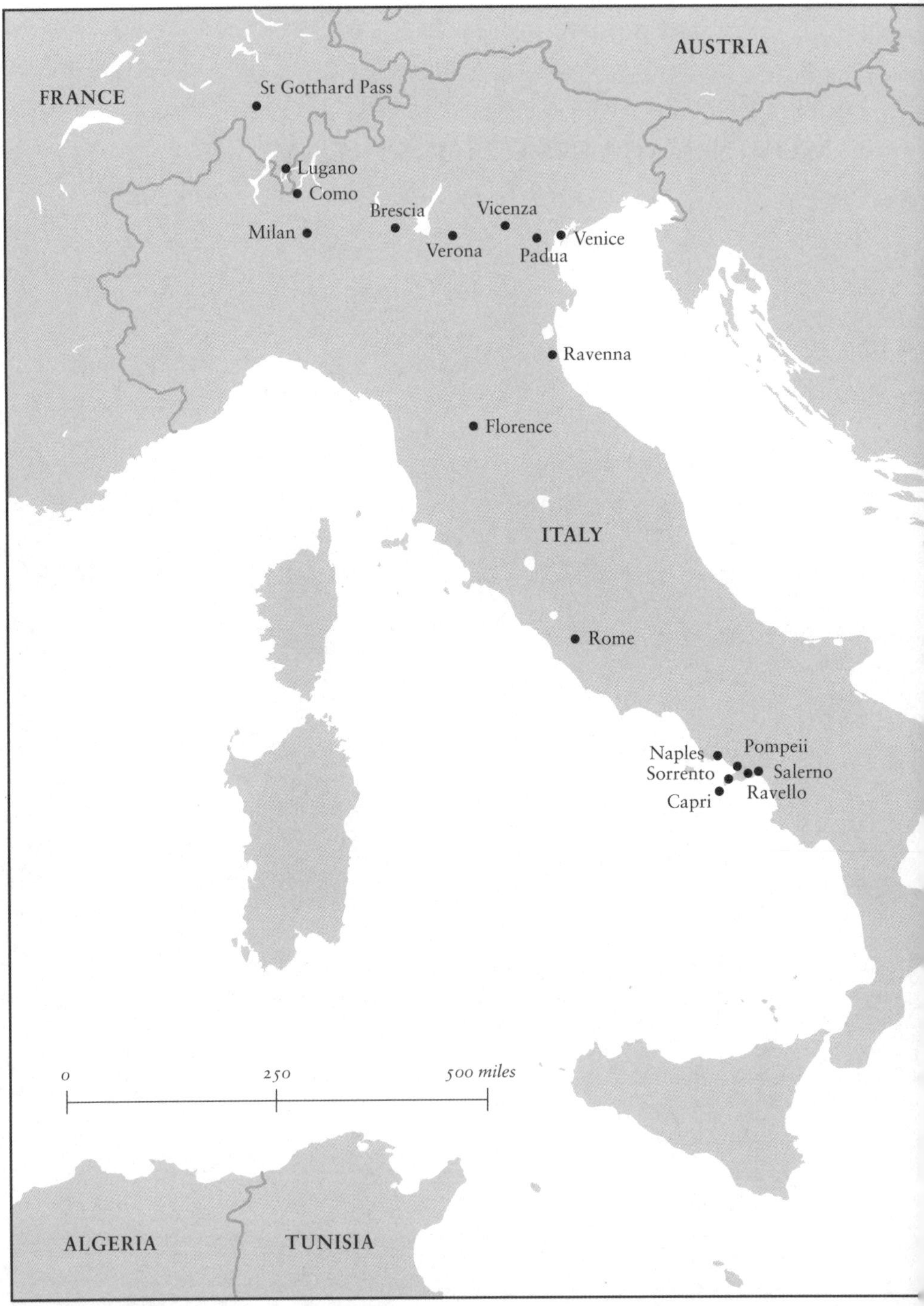

HUNGARY
RUMANIA
YUGOSLAVIA
BULGARIA
Brindisi
ALBANIA
GREECE
TURKEY
Igoumenitsa
Dodona
Arta
Naupactus
Delphi
Missolonghi
Eleusis
Corinth
Athens
Mycenae
Cape Sounion
Olympia
Epidaurus
Tripoli
Tiryns
Mistra
Argos

1
A COOL RECEPTION

Had I been keeping a diary at the time, my entry for the day would probably have read something like this: 'Wednesday 12 August 1964. Arrived Heathrow 2.00 p.m. local time. Raining. Met by Ananda Bodhi and Mrs Rauf and driven to the Hampstead Buddhist Vihara. On the way passed through St John's Wood. Sun came out. Little front gardens full of flowers.' Indeed I do not remember much more than that, even though I was returning to England after an absence of twenty years. I have no recollection of the flight from India, nor am I sure whether I boarded the plane at Bombay or Calcutta, though I think it was at Calcutta and I think I was seen off by a small group of friends and well-wishers.[21]

I do, however, remember that there was a stopover in Paris and that while stretching my legs in the brilliantly lit concourse I saw standing not many yards away two tall, elegant young women in identical sky blue uniforms and identical little sky blue hats. They were air hostesses, and they were engaged in conversation. As I watched, I saw first one man, then another, approach them with what was evidently a polite request for information or direction. To my astonishment, on each occasion the two haughty beauties not only failed to respond to him but carried on with their conversation as if totally unaware of his presence, so that after vainly repeating his question he was obliged to retreat nonplussed by their behaviour. Indian women in similar circumstances would never have behaved like that. What had happened while I was away? Had

European women become dehumanized? Certainly the two air hostesses, with their angular forms and studied gestures, were more like dummies worked by wires than creatures of flesh and blood.

The incident must have made an impression on me, for even now, thirty-three years later, in my mind's eye I can see the elegant, blue-clad figures standing there talking and see the way in which they treated the travellers who approached them. Perhaps it made such a strong impression on me because it gave me my first experience of Europe for twenty years and was a concrete reminder of the fact that Europe was not Asia and that the England of 1964, besides being very different from India, would be socially and culturally a different place from the England of 1944.

At Heathrow the sky was overcast and it was raining slightly. It was also strangely quiet, and there seemed to be hardly anyone about. Having been out of the country for twenty years, I was half expecting that the immigration officer would want to know where I had been all that time, and what I had been doing, but he returned my passport without a word and I was through. I was now officially back in the United Kingdom and I could see, waiting behind the glass doors, the figures of the tall, yellow-robed Western monk and the much shorter, white-haired Western laywoman who had come to meet me.

In the car there was no conversation that I can remember, though Ananda Bodhi must have asked me what the flight had been like. In fact I was aware of a feeling of constraint between us. I therefore spent much of the journey looking out of the window. We were now making our way through a part of London that was *terra incognita* to me (I had never been further north than Regent's Park), and as at Heathrow a strange quiet prevailed. Very few people were on the streets, and there was little traffic. By the time we reached St John's Wood (a name that was familiar to me from correspondence with Christmas Humphreys, who lived there) the sun had come out from behind the clouds and was shining on the slate roofs and neat little front gardens with their roses, delphiniums, and antirrhinums. The sight of those colourful little front gardens remains my most vivid memory of the whole journey. I have no recollection of arriving at the Vihara, or of the people who must have come to see me on that and the following day.

I do, however, remember having breakfast in the basement next morning with Ananda Bodhi and the three novices. There was a choice of four or five different hot drinks, and at the centre of the table, besides jam, marmalade, and honey, there were various spreads quite new to me. In my own monastery in Kalimpong we drank only tea, and jam had been seen there on only one occasion when, plums being unusually cheap that year, we had made a couple of dozen jars of it. As I was going upstairs to my room after the meal I heard the oldest of the novices ordering supplies on the phone. 'You've only *two* kinds of salmon?' he was saying. 'Then send the more expensive kind.'

Three days later I received an unexpected message from Ananda Bodhi, who was away visiting one of the provincial Buddhist groups. Would I give the Sunday lecture that afternoon, as he would not be back at the Vihara in time to give it himself? It was then nearly four-thirty, and the lecture was due to start at five. Though rather taken aback by the shortness of the notice, I had no objection to giving the lecture. Indeed I was glad to do so, though on second thoughts I decided not to give a lecture but to hold a question-and-answer meeting instead, as this would give me an opportunity of getting to know a cross-section of the Vihara's supporters and finding out how much – or how little – they knew about Buddhism. There were twelve or fourteen people in the meeting room, of various ages, and since nobody was there to introduce me I had to introduce myself. At first the questions were fairly routine, but then a young man suddenly demanded, 'Why have you come to England?' His tone was belligerent, even challenging, as if my presence was unexpected, even unwelcome, and standing in need of explanation. This gave me the opening I needed, and I therefore replied at some length, giving an account of my life and work in India, emphasizing that I appreciated *all* schools of Buddhism, and making it clear that I had come principally in order to bring British Buddhists together. My frankness seemed to give general satisfaction, and when the meeting ended there was a more relaxed and friendly atmosphere in the room than there had been at the beginning.

My work in the West had begun.

2
THE STORY SO FAR

Though north-west London was *terra incognita* to me I nonetheless was a Londoner, having been born in Stockwell and brought up in Tooting, not far from the famous Broadway. When I was eight I was diagnosed as suffering from heart disease and for the next two years was confined to bed, not being allowed even to sit up by my own efforts. I saw no one except my parents and the doctor and had nothing to do all day except read. Fortunately I was already something of a reader, having worked my way through Andrew Lang's *Fairy Books*,[22] and therefore devoured, during those two years in bed, whatever reading matter my hard-pressed parents were able to provide me with, from boys' papers like the *Wizard* and the *Hotspur*[23] to classic English novels such as *Pickwick Papers*, *Jane Eyre*, *Hypatia*, and *The Last Days of Pompeii*.[24] My biggest single resource was a complete set of Arthur Mee's *Children's Encyclopaedia*, the gift of a kindly neighbour, every one of whose sixty parts became as familiar to me as the owl clock on the wall, whose eyes clicked from side to side with the swing of the pendulum, or the nasturtium-and-trellis pattern of the wallpaper.[25]

I have more than once reflected that the two years I spent confined to bed, alone with a few books and the *Children's Encyclopaedia*, must have had a decisive influence on my character and thus on the course of my whole life thereafter. Until then, so far as I know, I had been just an ordinary boy, indistinguishable from other working-class Tooting boys. Like them I loved playing in the street, was not particularly fond of school, got into scrapes (and fights), and was overjoyed when I could go fishing with my father on a Saturday afternoon.[26] The discovery that I had heart disease put a stop to all that. From a lively, occasionally naughty eight-year-old I was transformed, overnight, into a bedridden invalid who was scarcely permitted to move his arms freely. Abruptly and drastically, the current of my youthful energies was dammed and redirected. Strange to say, I cannot recall ever resenting this, or even feeling frustrated or restless: perhaps I was sedated. I may even have been quite happy, in a way. Yet such a lengthy period of enforced immobility could not but have affected me radically.

From a distance of more than sixty years I can see it as having affected me in at least three ways. It forced my energies inwards, towards the world of thought and imagination, making me more introspective than was normal for one of my years or than I probably was by nature. Then the fact that I was scarcely permitted to move my arms freely meant that I was obliged to be conscious of what I was doing. This was even more the case when I came to graduate, at the end of the two years, from bed to wheelchair and when, later still, I started using my legs again. There was always a voice in my ear – my mother's or father's – warning me to be careful, or not to move so quickly, and I may have ended up internalizing that admonitory voice. This constant need to be aware of what I was doing had both a positive and a negative effect: while it made it easier for me, years later, to cultivate the Buddhist virtue of mindfulness, whether of bodily movements or mental states, it also tended to check any spontaneous physical expression of my feelings. Finally, my confinement to bed not only cut me off from contact with boys of my own age but made me feel separate and different. This feeling of separateness and difference persisted after my eventual return to school, for I was not allowed to take part in games or to play with my schoolfellows.[27]

The habit of reading that I had acquired during my period of enforced immobility remained with me even after my return to school. No sooner was I able to get out and about on my own than I started spending my pocket money in the woefully inadequate bookshops of Tooting, as well as carrying away from the Tooting public library every week the armful of books I had borrowed using my father's ticket. My principal interests were Ancient Egypt, the Italian Renaissance, and what Dr Johnson called 'the biographical part of literature',[28] and in all these fields I read as widely as I could. Later I added to the list philosophy, poetry, and painting, and the Greek drama. Fiction I hardly ever read and anything of a scientific nature I instinctively avoided.

On 1 September 1939 the air raid sirens sounded for the first time: the Second World War had begun, and eight or nine months later I was evacuated to North Devon. In the course of the next three years I left school, worked in a coal merchant's office in Torquay, returned to London in time to experience the last of the Blitz, and joined the staff of the London County Council as a clerical assistant. During this period I continued to read avidly, and after my return to London developed a passionate love for classical music and, though to a lesser degree, for the theatre. I also had a series of realizations that exercised a decisive effect on the whole subsequent course of my life. I realized there was no reason why I should confine myself to the literature of Europe; I realized that I was not a Christian; and I realized that I was a Buddhist and had, in fact, always been one. The first of these realizations came when I read Mme Blavatsky's *Isis Unveiled*, especially volume 2, *Theology*;[29] the second, when I read the *Diamond Sūtra*, of the ineffable truth of whose teaching I at once had an immediate apprehension.[30] The way for this last realization may have been prepared by certain experiences of a 'mystical' nature that had befallen me several years earlier.[31]

Three months after my eighteenth birthday I was called up, having been found fit enough for the army despite my history of heart disease. 'You can make yourself comfortable even in hell if you go about it in the right way,' says a Tibetan proverb. The Signals Unit in Surrey to which I was posted was certainly not hell, yet army life was so different from anything I had hitherto experienced that for the first two weeks I was in a state of shock. But youth is resilient, and eventually my numbed faculties revived. I made friends, went home on weekend leave, joined the London-based Buddhist Society, borrowed rare books on Buddhism from the Society's library, continued my practice of writing poetry, and in short led my own life to the extent that the army permitted me to do so. One weekend I arrived home to find my father contemplating what remained of our house, which half an hour earlier had suffered a direct hit by a flying bomb. Luckily no one was inside at the time. A few weeks later the Unit was ordered to India, and I celebrated my nineteenth birthday on a troopship bound for Bombay.[32] After three months spent at the Unit's headquarters in Delhi I was posted first to Colombo, then (at my request) to Calcutta, and finally to Singapore. While I was in Ceylon, Germany was defeated, Japan surrendered after the dropping of the first atom bomb, and the Second World War came to an end.

Wherever I happened to be, whether in Delhi or Colombo, Calcutta or Singapore, I spent much of my free time visiting mosques, temples, and viharas and making the acquaintance of Hindu swamis and Buddhist *bhikṣus*. I also bought books on Buddhism and Hinduism that were not available in England and experimented, at times with results I had not foreseen, with different methods of meditation. During my stay in Ceylon I saw less of Buddhism and Buddhists than I had hoped, though I was able to visit the Tooth Relic Temple in Kandy and pay my respects to the historic Tooth. But if I saw less of Buddhism and Buddhists than I had hoped, of Hindus and Hinduism I saw more than I had expected. In particular I got to know two Indian swamis belonging to the Ramakrishna Mission, and soon was spending several evenings a week at their ashram. My friendship with them led to introductions to their brethren in Calcutta, where I met my mother's youngest brother and his family, and these in turn led to my being introduced to the rich cultural and religious life of the city. In Singapore I met Sinhalese and Chinese Buddhist monks, and was a regular visitor to the newly revived lodge of the Theosophical Society, as well as to the local branch of the Ramakrishna Mission, which had somehow managed to function throughout the Japanese occupation. I also became a vegetarian, much to the amusement of the Unit's Indian cooks, wrote a good deal of poetry, and started giving public lectures.[33]

All this was good in its way, and my year in Singapore passed quickly enough. But the war was over. My twenty-first birthday had come and gone, and I wanted to get on with my own life. I wanted to be a monk and devote all my energies to the study and practice of Buddhism, and while still in Ceylon I had written to my parents informing them of my intentions. Initially I had assumed that after being demobilized in England, and spending some time with my family, I would be able to return to India and there don the saffron robe. I now discovered that this would not be possible, as the new Labour government was discouraging any drainage of manpower out of the country. The discovery gave rise to a feeling of desperation – a feeling that recent developments within the Unit did nothing to assuage. Discipline had been tightened up, and such things as parades and fatigues increased, as if to remind us that although the war might have ended we were still in the army and were not going to escape from it so easily. Not wanting any more of my life to be wasted painting rings on fire buckets or preparing for yet another inspection, I decided to take drastic action. I would apply for six weeks' leave in India, on the grounds that I had an uncle in Calcutta with whom I could stay, and that at the end of that period I would not return to Singapore. Instead, I would melt into the Indian background – and disappear. Technically I would be deserting, and could be court-martialled if ever I was caught. Convinced that what I was doing was morally justified, I was prepared to take the risk.[34]

In Calcutta I lost no time contacting Robin Banerjee, the idealistic young Bengali whom I had met in Singapore. He was there as part of the Congress Medical Mission to Malaya, we had become good friends, and on the Mission's return to India we had agreed that as soon as I was free we would meet in Calcutta and somehow work together. When my leave ended I therefore said goodbye to my uncle and his family, and Robin and I moved first to the Ramakrishna Mission Institute of Culture and then, a month or so later, to the Maha Bodhi Society. We were not very happy in either place. In neither of them did we find the sort of conditions that were, we believed, essential to our ethical and spiritual development. Moreover, towards the end of March, when we were staying at the Maha Bodhi Orphanage and looking after the boys, there occurred a renewal of the communal rioting of the previous year. Throughout the city Muslims attacked Hindus and Sikhs, and Hindus and Sikhs retaliated by attacking Muslims. Hundreds, perhaps thousands, were killed, and I witnessed more bloodshed and violence than I had ever seen while in the army. Calcutta was not a particularly healthy place to be just then. But the Maha Bodhi Society's headquarters, to which the orphans had been removed for their safety, was not a particularly healthy place either, morally and spiritually speaking, and the longer my friend and I stayed the more we became aware of this unpleasant fact. When I left Calcutta the following month to attend an inter-religious gathering in Ahmedabad, on the other side of the country, as a representative of Buddhism, it was therefore with the hope that I would be able to contact other Buddhists and make arrangements for us to join a more genuinely Buddhist organization.

At the week-long Dharma Parishad, which was dominated by Hindu holy men of various colourful persuasions, I met Pandit-ji, an aged

Bengali scholar of venerable appearance who had plans for the revival of Buddhism in India. He invited me to accompany him to Kishengunj in the UP,[35] I accepted, and not long after our arrival there we were joined by Robin. Pandit-ji had assured me that his plans had the approval and support of Anandamayi, the famous Bengali mystic, who was then staying at her ashram in Kishengunj with a band of devotees; but as the weeks passed it became obvious that Anandamayi, many of whose followers believed her to be a divine incarnation, had not the slightest interest either in Buddhism or in Pandit-ji's schemes. She was an orthodox Hindu who insisted on the strict observance of the caste system. But Pandit-ji refused to give up hope. When Anandamayi left for her ashram in Raipur we left for Raipur too, and when she left Raipur for Delhi he and Robin followed her there. I remained in Raipur, studying and meditating, and after a week or so Robin rejoined me. Eventually the three of us were reunited in Kasauli, a hill station in East Punjab where Anandamayi had stayed the previous year. Here Robin and I discovered that none of Pandit-ji's schemes (he now talked of starting a girls' boarding school in Anandamayi's name) had ever progressed beyond the fund-raising stage and that the old man was well known for his chicanery. Shocked and horrified, we decided we would have nothing more to do with religious organizations of any kind. We would give up the household life and go forth as homeless wanderers in search of Truth. Having shaved our heads and dyed our clothes saffron (I had already adopted Indian dress), on the morning of 18 August, three days after Independence Day, we accordingly left Kasauli on foot for the plains. The path of our descent was spanned by a series of double and even triple rainbows, through which we passed as though through a triumphal arch. It was an auspicious beginning.[36]

But the auspiciousness did not last. Our intention had been to study Buddhism in Ceylon and perhaps become monks there, but as we had no means of identification and refused to disclose our nationality (we had decided that as sadhus we had none) on our arrival at Colombo we were not allowed to land and had to return to India by the same boat. Disappointed but not downhearted, we therefore travelled to Cape Comorin, the southernmost point of India, and having paid a visit to the famous Kanya Kumari temple started walking up through what then was the princely state of Travancore, eventually settling at Muvattupuzha, a subdivisional town in the interior, where we took up our abode in a deserted ashram situated on a low ridge amid rice-fields.

We stayed in Muvattupuzha for about fifteen months. During that time we learned something of the history and culture of the state (now part of Kerala), and came to appreciate its distinctive character; we also picked up a little Malayālam. The reason for our settling in Muvattupuzha was that we wanted to deepen our experience of meditation, which we had not been able to do while on the move, and our day was organized accordingly. We meditated in the morning, rising before dawn, and again in the evening, sometimes sitting on until quite late. During the day we studied (Buddhism in my case, English in Robin's), paced up and down the veranda, or sat contemplating the view. We also experimented with periods of fasting and silence, and once or twice a month we went calling on the ashram's supporters, some of whom we got to know quite well. This arrangement suited me perfectly, but it soon proved too restrictive for Robin, who for a while therefore put his abundant energies into plans for starting an industrial school at the ashram, leaving me to my studies and literary work.

I was thus enabled to reflect on the Dharma uninterruptedly for long periods. Six years ago I had read the *Diamond Sūtra* and realized that I was a Buddhist. Since then I had delved not only into Buddhist but also into many Hindu scriptures, as well as into Western philosophy and Christian mysticism, and though my commitment to the Buddha and his teaching was basically unimpaired I needed to get the various spiritual and intellectual influences that had been impinging upon me into some kind of perspective, especially as I was now living in a predominantly Hindu environment. I needed to clarify my doctrinal position as a Buddhist. This I did with the help of the first fifty discourses of the *Majjhima Nikāya* or *Collection of the Middle Length Discourses*, Śāntarakṣita's encyclopaedic *Tattvasaṃgraha* or Compendium of Principles, and Mrs Rhys Davids' meaty little book on Buddhism in the Home University Library series.[37] I concentrated on three basic formulations of the Buddha's teaching: the doctrine of dependent origination (or conditioned co-production), the four noble truths, and the three characteristics of conditioned existence. Though all three formulations were well known to me, I had not previously given them much systematic attention; but at that juncture, as I have written elsewhere,

> they occupied my mind virtually to the exclusion of everything else. Besides reflecting on them during the day I meditated on them at night. Or rather, as I meditated, flashes of insight into the transcendental truths of which they were the expression in conceptual terms would sometimes spontaneously arise.[38]

By the time these 'sessions of sweet silent thought'[39] had come to an end, and Robin had switched his energies from plans for an industrial school to the intensive practice of hatha yoga, including *prāṇāyāma* or breath control, I had succeeded in clarifying my ideas on a number of important doctrinal issues. As a result, my approach to the Dharma changed, becoming as much a rational understanding of principles as an emotional response to an ideal.[40]

Our eighteen months in Muvattupuzha were followed by six weeks in Kanhangad, in North Malabar, with the famous Swami Ramdas,[41] and six weeks in Tiruvannamalai, in the Tamil country, with the still more famous Ramana Maharshi.[42] In Tiruvannamalai we stayed in a cave on the slopes of Arunachala, the Hill of Light, from which we had a panoramic view of the courtyards, shrines, and *gopurams*[43] of the great Shiva temple below. Once a day we descended to the town for alms, and every few days we walked round the hill to the ashram, in the hall of which the Maharshi sat giving *darshan* to sixty or seventy inmates and visitors. One night I had a vision. I saw Amitābha, the Infinite Light, the Buddha of the West. Ruby-red in colour, he sat cross-legged on an enormous red lotus and held up by the stalk a single red lotus in full bloom. The lotus on which he was seated floated on the sea, across which the light from the red hemisphere of the setting sun made a glittering golden pathway. Visions had come to me before, but this one was unique, and it stirred me deeply.[44] I took it to mean that our apprenticeship to the homeless life had come to an end, and that it was time for us to return to North India and seek ordination in one of the Buddhist centres there.

But we did not leave the South immediately. Friends we had met at Tiruvannamalai invited us to Bangalore, and from there another friend took us on a ten-day excursion into the heart of what then was the princely state of Mysore. We drove through vast sandalwood forests, visited marvellously beautiful Hindu temples, and spent a night at an important centre of Jain pilgrimage, where a sixty-foot nude statue of

Gommateshwara towered against the sky. We even penetrated into the Sringeri Math, the Vatican of Hinduism, and met the Shankaracharya. In Bangalore itself we made the acquaintance of Yalahankar Swami, a one-eyed guru with highly unconventional methods of dealing with his disciples' egos, who was reputed to be 600 years old. At his suggestion we spent some time in the nearby mountains, where we found shelter in a ruined temple that at night was surrounded by leopards. We then left for Bombay.[45]

In Bombay we stayed with a devotee of Swami Ramdas, who besides taking us to see the Kanheri Caves, an ancient Buddhist monastic complex, also bought us tickets for our journey to Benares. From Benares, after spending a few days sightseeing, we walked out to Sarnath, where the Buddha had first taught the Dharma and where we hoped to be ordained. We were disappointed. The Sinhalese monks of the Maha Bodhi Society wanted nothing to do with the two barefoot, penniless strangers (since leaving Kanhangad we had not been handling money), and we therefore decided to walk up to Kusinara, where the Buddha had died, and seek ordination there. It was the worst time of year to be doing so. The hot wind was blowing, the temperature was 120°F or more,[46] and people were dropping dead from the heat. But there was no alternative. Doing as much of our walking as we could in the early morning, and at night staying at temples and ashrams, we covered the distance in ten days.

The Burmese senior monk in Kusinara received us kindly, ordained us as *śrāmaṇeras* or novice monks on Vaiśākha Pūrṇimā Day, the anniversary of the Buddha's Enlightenment, named Robin Buddharakshita and me Sangharakshita (previously we were Anagārikas Satyapriya and Dharmapriya), and told us to go and preach the Dharma to his disciples in Nepal. Up through the jungles of the Terai we therefore went, still on foot, but now carrying bowls with which to go for alms in the traditional Buddhist manner. We spent two months in Nepal, in the course of which we visited Lumbini, the birthplace of the Buddha, and ministered as best we could to the spiritual needs of the tiny Buddhist communities in Butaol and Tansen. Longer we could not stay, as the autocratic Rana regime was still in power and our unauthorized presence aroused the suspicions of the local police.[47]

Buddharakshita and I therefore returned to Benares. Here we parted company. Buddharakshita left for Ceylon, while I went to live with

Bhikkhu Jagdish Kashyap at Buddha Kuti, his cottage on the campus of the Benares Hindu University, where he was professor of Pāli and Buddhist philosophy. I was sorry to lose my friend, but also relieved. The practice of *prāṇāyāma*, which on Ramdas's advice he had given up, had inflamed his naturally hot temper, and relations between us were at times strained. I stayed at Buddha Kuti for nine months, studying Pāli, Abhidhamma, and logic, and making extensive use of the University library. With a monk from Sarnath, I went on pilgrimage to Bodh Gaya, the scene of the Buddha's Enlightenment. When spring came, Kashyapji showed me the Buddhist holy places of his native Bihar, after which we travelled up to Kalimpong, a cosmopolitan little hill station in the eastern Himalayas, not far from Darjeeling and within sight of Tibet.

In Kalimpong my teacher left me, with the parting injunction that I was to stay there and work for the good of Buddhism.[48]

I stayed in Kalimpong for the next fourteen years, working for the good of Buddhism as best I could, getting to know the local people, both Buddhist and Hindu, and being uplifted and inspired by the sight of Mount Kanchenjunga, the third highest peak in the world, dazzlingly white against the blue sky. In the course of my first seven years in the town I founded a Young Men's Buddhist Association; started a monthly journal of Himalayan religion, culture, and education called *Stepping-Stones*; was ordained as a *bhikṣu* or full monk by an international sangha; organized a public reception for the relics of the Buddha's two chief disciples, then touring India amid scenes of wild popular enthusiasm; found a kindred spirit in Lama Govinda, the German-born artist and scholar; re-established contact with the Maha Bodhi Society (conditions at its headquarters had recently changed for the better); and became well known as a lecturer not only in Kalimpong and the surrounding area but also in Calcutta, Bombay, and Bangalore.[49]

But if I was not to work for the good of Buddhism at the expense of my own good, spiritually speaking, I needed to have a means of uniting the two. I found this in the bodhisattva ideal, especially as presented in Śāntideva's *Śikṣā-samuccaya* or Collection of Teachings: the ideal of the one who strives for Enlightenment not just for his own sake but for the sake of all living beings.[50] It was not that the bodhisattva literally gave up the prospect of Nirvāṇa for himself in order to remain in the world and help others achieve Nirvāṇa, as in the popular version of the ideal, but rather that he saw no difference between striving for his own Enlightenment and striving for theirs. He saw no difference because he had transcended the dichotomy of 'self' and 'others'; and it was this very dichotomy that was the real obstacle to Enlightenment. Some years later I affirmed my allegiance to the bodhisattva ideal by taking the bodhisattva ordination. I took it from Dhardo Rimpoche, a Tibetan incarnate lama who had arrived in Kalimpong shortly before I did, whom I gradually got to know, and whom I came to revere as a living embodiment of the bodhisattva ideal.[51]

During those first seven years in Kalimpong I operated from a succession of borrowed or rented premises. In March 1957 the generosity of friends enabled me to buy a small hillside property on the outskirts of the town and there establish the Triyana Vardhana Vihara, the Monastery Where the Three Yānas Flourish. It was the year of the Buddha Jayanti or 2,500th anniversary of Buddhism, a year that was important for me on a number of counts. Besides establishing the Triyana Vardhana Vihara, I toured the Buddhist holy places as a guest of the Government of India together with Dhardo Rimpoche and fifty-odd other 'Eminent Buddhists from the Border Areas'; took part in the official Buddha Jayanti celebrations in Delhi; met the Dalai and Panchen Lamas; and had the satisfaction of seeing my book *A Survey of Buddhism* published to widespread acclaim. Most important of all, perhaps, I became involved with the movement of mass conversion of so-called 'ex-Untouchable' Hindus to Buddhism.[52]

This historic movement had begun in Nagpur, where Dr B. R. Ambedkar, the leader of the ex-Untouchables, had embraced Buddhism with 400,000 of his followers.[53] Six weeks later he died suddenly in Delhi. I happened to arrive in Nagpur less than an hour before the news of his death was received there, and that night I addressed a condolence meeting attended by 100,000 grief-stricken and demoralized new Buddhists. Ambedkar was not dead, I assured my audience. He lived on in them, and his work – especially the work of conversion – had to continue. In the next four days I visited practically all the ex-Untouchable ghettoes in the city, made more than forty speeches, and initiated 30,000 persons into Buddhism. By the time I left for Calcutta I had addressed altogether 200,000 people, and given them renewed confidence in their future as Buddhists. Leading members of the community declared that I had saved Nagpur for Buddhism. That may or may not have been true. I had certainly forged with the Buddhists of Nagpur, and indeed with all Ambedkar's followers, a link that was destined to endure.[54]

In the course of my second seven years in Kalimpong I developed the Triyana Vardhana Vihara as a centre of interdenominational Buddhism. Thai, Vietnamese, and Tibetan monks came to stay with me, and there was even the occasional Western Buddhist. Much of my time when I was actually in Kalimpong was spent at my desk, and my literary output during this period included the books later published as *The Three Jewels* and *The Eternal Legacy*.[55] At the suggestion of a friend I also started writing my memoirs.[56] When not in Kalimpong I was usually to be found either in Calcutta, editing the Maha Bodhi Society's monthly journal, or touring central and western India preaching to the followers of Dr Ambedkar. The fourth and longest of my preaching tours lasted from October 1961 to May 1962. In those eight months I visited more than half the states of India, gave nearly 200 lectures, and received 25,000 men and women into the Buddhist community.

But there was another thread running through the fabric of my life, during that second seven-year period: the colourful thread of the Vajrayāna. Since the invasion of Tibet by the Chinese in 1950, there had been a steady trickle of refugees into Kalimpong, and in 1959, when the Dalai Lama himself fled to India, the trickle became a flood. A number of the refugees were incarnate lamas. Naturally I got to know these, and between 1957 and 1964 received from some of the most distinguished of them various Vajrayāna initiations. Among my Vajrayāna gurus were Dilgo Khyentse Rimpoche and Dudjom Rimpoche, both of whom subsequently became well known in the West. The Vajrayāna being nothing if not practical, I naturally came to devote more and more of the time I spent in Kalimpong to deity yoga and to the Four Foundation Yogas, especially to the Going for Refuge and Prostration Practice centred upon the figure of Padmasambhava, to whom I had felt strongly drawn ever since my arrival in the Himalayan region. As though in recognition of my connection with him, in the course of one of my initiations I was given the name Urgyen, Padmasambhava being known as the Guru from Urgyen or Uḍḍiyāna.[57]

In 1963 the English Sangha Trust invited me to spend a few months in England.[58] Prior to that I had not thought even of visiting the West: my life and my work lay in India. Two considerations induced me, eventually, to accept the invitation. The first was that my presence might help resolve the differences that had arisen between the two principal Buddhist organizations in London; the second, that my parents were growing old and I ought to see them. After several delays and postponements, and one more visit to western India, in August 1964 I therefore returned to England after an absence of twenty years.[59]

3
THE EMBROIDERED CUSHION

The Hampstead Buddhist Vihara was situated on Haverstock Hill, opposite a public house and within easy reach of Belsize Park Underground Station. It was a narrow, three-storey terrace property with a basement, and it was permeated by a peculiar smell which I subsequently identified as that of a combination of dry rot and boiled cabbage.

At the time of my arrival the Vihara's only occupants were Ananda Bodhi and the three novices. The latter had all been ordained by Venerable Saddhatissa, the incumbent of the Sinhalese vihara at Chiswick (Ananda Bodhi as a junior *bhikkhu* was not competent to ordain), but it was Ananda Bodhi with whom they actually lived. Two of the novices were English and one was German (Ananda Bodhi himself was a Canadian), and all three wore dark brown habits girt about the waist with a cord, so that they looked more like Franciscan friars than Buddhist monks. When they went out they donned voluminous cloaks of the same colour, as did Ananda Bodhi whenever he did not want his yellow robes to be seen.

As none of them spent much time at the Vihara I usually saw them only at breakfast and lunch (there was of course no evening meal),[60] and not always even then. On those occasions when we did eat together neither Ananda Bodhi nor the novices made the slightest attempt to include me in the conversation, or to let me know what was going on, and any question I put received no more than a perfunctory reply. The novices were totally

At the Hampstead Buddhist Vihara

wrapped up in Ananda Bodhi, and Ananda Bodhi clearly was wrapped up in himself and in his own schemes. Considering that I was a senior monk, their behaviour was a gross violation of monastic etiquette: it was deplorable even by the most elementary standards of decency; but I said nothing, kept my ears open, and bided my time.

One day the conversation over lunch was more than usually animated. Ananda Bodhi and the novices were all wildly excited; even the rather saturnine orderer of the more expensive kind of salmon was affected by the general mood. I gathered that they had spent the morning at Hampstead Town Hall, where an international psychiatric congress was being held that week. It was not clear in what capacity Ananda Bodhi himself had been present (he was not a psychiatrist), but he had intervened in the morning's debate, apparently speaking from the gallery, and after criticizing the current methods of treating schizophrenia had confidently assured the assembled psychiatrists that the condition was curable and that it could be cured by means of Buddhist meditation. The kind of meditation he had in mind was the highly controversial Burmese 'insight meditation', his teaching of which was a principal cause of the differences that had arisen between the Sangha Association, as represented by him, and the Buddhist Society, as represented by Christmas Humphreys – differences with which I would soon be having to deal. How the psychiatrists had responded to the intervention – whether with interest, or astonishment, or amusement – did not transpire. Ananda Bodhi obviously was elated by what he had done, while the three novices gazed at him more admiringly than ever. The Master had spoken, their shining eyes seemed to say, and a new era was about to dawn for the world.

In the midst of the jubilation the telephone rang, and Ananda Bodhi answered it. The caller was Beth, whose name I had already heard bandied about. It seemed she telephoned the Vihara frequently, sometimes twice or thrice a day, to ask if she had the permission of 'the Sangha' to open a window, or wash her hair, or do one of a number of other quite ordinary things. Whether or not she was a schizophrenic, and whether or not Ananda Bodhi was treating her, I do not know, but the novices regarded poor Beth as a great joke, and talked about her in the most unfeeling manner. Later I inherited her, so to speak, and the telephone calls turned into a series of long, rambling letters that eventually petered out.

More than once, during those first few days of mine at the Hampstead Buddhist Vihara, the conversation at mealtimes revolved round various schemes of Ananda Bodhi's. These were referred to, as often as not, in an allusive manner that was obviously intended to keep me in the dark as to what was going on, but I gathered that Ananda Bodhi had purchased, or was about to purchase, a large country house in Scotland. The project was being funded by one of his supporters, an elderly spinster, and the place was to serve as his personal headquarters and be quite separate from, and independent of, the Hampstead Buddhist Vihara. I also gathered that two other members of the English Sangha (or rather, of the Sangha in England) would shortly be arriving in England. They would be arriving from Burma, where they had been undergoing training as meditation teachers.

Mangalo and Vimalo were much more friendly than Ananda Bodhi, and much more communicative, so that I soon had a better understanding of what was going on, not only at the Vihara itself but also within the wider British Buddhist movement. Like Ananda Bodhi, both were considerably junior to me, in years as well as in respect of monastic ordination, and like Ananda Bodhi both were, of course, Theravādins. Mangalo was English, and evidently from an upper middle-class family. He was tall and thin, with a round, monkey-like head and protruding ears, and though not really ill-natured he was much given to indulging in ridicule. As I afterwards discovered, he had given up a promising career at the Foreign Office – and left a fiancée – in order to become a Buddhist monk. Vimalo, who was German, presented a more robust appearance. Pink-faced and smiling, he bore himself stiffly, and was somewhat slow of speech. I never learned anything about his background, but he had a twin brother who also had become a *bhikkhu* and who for a while had lived at the Vihara with him and Mangalo. This brother had returned to Germany, where he had disrobed and married and was now a yoga teacher.

Different though the English and the German *bhikkhu* were in character and background, they had much in common. Both of course were monks, and both were Theravādins, in addition to which both were inclined to attach more importance to the practice of meditation than to doctrinal study. Their position to this extent was unexceptionable; but they also shared, unfortunately, an attitude that I later on found to be characteristic of a certain kind of Western Theravādin, whether member of the monastic order or lay supporter. While unsympathetic and even hostile to the Mahāyāna, they at the same time were strongly drawn to Christianity, especially in its more mystical aspects. Theravāda Buddhism and Christianity, they seemed to believe, had more in common with each other than had Theravāda Buddhism and the Mahāyāna. It was as though one could be a Theravādin Buddhist without ceasing to be a Christian, whereas if one was a Theravādin it was not possible for one to be a Mahāyānist or even to accept the Mahāyāna as a genuinely Buddhist tradition. My own position was clean contrary to this. For me, theistic Christianity and non-theistic Buddhism were radically incompatible, so that it was impossible for a Buddhist to be at the same time a Christian, or a Christian a Buddhist, even though it might be possible for them to appreciate some of the more peripheral features of the religion to which they did not belong. During the period of my acquaintance with Mangalo and Vimalo (we were never close friends) the three of us therefore had some interesting discussions, and the differences between me and my two colleagues sometimes had amusing consequences.

I once happened to refer to the fact that for orthodox Christians the dogmas of Christianity were true in the literal sense, citing as an example their belief that Christ ascended *bodily* into heaven after his death on the cross. Mangalo emphatically denied this. According to him, the ascension was a purely spiritual event; its significance was symbolic, and no Christian believed otherwise. To this I replied that the doctrine of the bodily ascension of Christ was one of the Thirty-nine Articles of the Church of England. But this too Mangalo refused to accept, declaring that it was just another example of the way in which I misrepresented Christianity. Fortunately in the Vihara library there was a copy of *The Book of Common Prayer* bound up in one volume with the *Bible*. Turning to the Thirty-nine Articles, I read out Article 4, Of the Resurrection of Christ:

> Christ did truly rise again from death, and took again his body, with flesh, bones, and all things appertaining to the perfection of Man's nature; wherewith he ascended into Heaven, and there sitteth, until he return to judge all Men at the last day.[61]

For once Mangalo 'had not what to say'. On another occasion I returned from a short stay at the Sangha Trust's meditation centre at Biddulph, in Staffordshire, to find people expressing their dissatisfaction with the previous Sunday's lecture, which I had asked Vimalo to give in my place. All the German *bhikkhu* had done, they complained, was to read out a series of extracts – more than thirty of them – from the writings of Meister Eckhart.[62] 'We come to the Vihara to hear the Dharma,' some of them told me, 'not to learn about Christian mysticism.' The two incidents lay in the future, but I mention them in this place, partly because they revealed something about the state of Buddhism in Britain at the time and partly because Mangalo and Vimalo play little further part in my story. (Mangalo disrobed a few years later and became an Anglican priest.) Meanwhile the two of them were there at the Vihara with me, and shortly after their arrival we agreed that since four Western *bhikkhus* were now living under the same roof we ought to hold a chapter meeting.

We met in the front room on the first floor, where lectures were held and where a green-and-gold Thai shrine, complete with shining brass Buddha image, stood against the far wall. To the left of the shrine, and to the right, two chairs had been placed, and on one of the chairs next to the shrine there was an embroidered cushion. When Ananda Bodhi at last swept in, he straightway plumped himself down on the chair with the embroidered cushion, as if it were his by right. Vimalo at once objected. 'We ought to let Venerable Sangharakshita sit there,' he said bluntly, 'as he is senior to us.' Whereupon the Canadian monk vacated the chair with a very ill grace, I took my seat on it, and our meeting began. I do not remember what we discussed. Probably it was on this occasion that it was agreed between us that during the winter Mangalo and Vimalo would take it in turns to live for a month at a time at the Biddulph centre and be available for individual instruction in meditation. Ananda Bodhi took very little part in the proceedings. His being compelled to relinquish the seat of honour had shaken him badly, and he may have been thinking that the incident represented a deposition from the throne of his hitherto unquestioned supremacy at the Vihara and within the English Sangha Association. Whether this was actually the case or not, I noticed that whereas when surrounded by the admiring novices he was bumptious in the extreme, in the presence of his fellow *bhikkhus* he was like a pricked balloon. No wonder he avoided our company as much as he could! I also noticed that Vimalo did not take him very seriously, and at times spoke of him slightingly.

After the chapter meeting none of us saw much of Ananda Bodhi. When in London he usually stayed at the English Sangha's old home in Swiss Cottage, the lease on which had not quite run out. I therefore took possession of his room at the Vihara. It was situated on the second floor of the building, immediately above the meeting room, and was known as 'the abbot's room'. Beside the bed I found a crystal ball, together with half a dozen yards of black velvet.

4
FAMILY REUNIONS AND A BIG DISAPPOINTMENT

My parents had separated during the war, when I was still living at home. Later they were divorced, and each remarried. Once I had melted into the Indian background and disappeared, for prudential reasons I stopped writing to them (I did not want the army to be able to track me down, supposing it was minded to do so), and once I had gone forth as a homeless wanderer I naturally thought it incumbent upon me to sever all earthly ties. It was not that I did not love my parents, but that I loved the Dharma more, and wanted to devote my whole life to it; and devoting my life to the Dharma, I had concluded, meant becoming a monk, with all that this entailed in the way of separation from society and the family. Whenever I thought of my parents, and I certainly did think of them from time to time, it was with unalloyed affection, and gratitude for having given me a happy childhood. In any case, while in Ceylon I had told them that I was thinking of becoming a monk in India after demobilization and they had, in effect, given me their blessing.

At the time the English Sangha Trust invited me to England I had been a *bhikṣu* for nearly fourteen years, during which period a change in my attitude to the monastic life had taken place. Though continuing to value *real*, as distinct from merely formal, monasticism, I no longer saw monastic life and spiritual life as virtually identical, which is the strict Theravādin position, nor did I any longer see monastic life as necessarily involving an austere aloofness from the world. I therefore accepted the Trust's invitation, not only because I might be able to help resolve the differences between the English Sangha Association and the Buddhist Society, but also because it would give me an opportunity of seeing my parents.

My mother was living in Rayleigh, in Essex, and within a week of my arrival in England I had caught the train at Liverpool Street and was on my way to see her. She had written to me some months earlier, having obtained my address from Christmas Humphreys, who had informed her that I was expected in the country shortly. This I had immediately confirmed, thus giving her plenty of time to get used to the idea of seeing me again. Our meeting was a joyful one. I would not have been surprised if my mother had become emotional and shed a few tears, or even if she had reproached me for having kept her without news of my whereabouts for so many years, but she did neither. She simply was overjoyed to see me, and it was clear from her demeanour that the only thing that mattered to her was that I was actually there at last. She had been a widow for three years and lived alone, though John, her elder grandson, who was nineteen and whom she had brought up, still had a room at the bungalow. News having been exchanged over a cup of tea, I gave her the presents I had brought. They included a set of six silver teaspoons, of ornate Newar workmanship, each one of which was set with a turquoise. The following day she took me with her when she went out shopping, and proudly introduced me to the numerous friends she met on the way. What they made of my shaven head and yellow robes I could not tell, for they were much too polite to show any surprise at them and behaved as though meeting a Buddhist monk in the high street was an everyday occurrence.

In outward appearance my mother was very little changed. Though she had grown a trifle stout, her expression was still youthful and her step light. But mentally there had been a change, though perhaps it was not so much a change as a development, a maturation, of qualities already present in her. She seemed more confident and self-assured than I remembered her to have been. I attributed this to the fact that during the seventeen years of her second marriage she had travelled abroad a lot with her husband, an inspector of school supplies whose official duties frequently took him to conferences in Europe. Her favourite countries, she told me, were Switzerland and Austria. They were so clean!

Sangharakshita's mother (l) and friend

But if there had been little change in the outward appearance of my mother, the years had not dealt quite so kindly with my sister, who came to see me on the second or third day of my visit, my mother not having allowed her to come any earlier as she wanted to have me entirely to herself for a while. Joan was fifteen months younger than me, but already there were silver threads in her dark brown hair and it was soon apparent that she was a habitual smoker. She had been a young girl when I left England; now she was a haggard-faced woman on the verge of middle age. As my mother afterwards told me, she had led an adventurous – even a hectic – life, had married more than once, had given birth to three children and now was expecting a fourth, and for several years had lived – to my mother's horror – in a real gypsy caravan, as she had an aversion to the city, to houses, and to ordinary domestic life. She was nevertheless of a placid, easygoing disposition, as I well knew, and I gained the impression that my mother worried about Joan much more than the latter worried about herself. That same day I met John, a shy and reserved youth, as well as his eleven-year-old brother David, who bombarded me with questions about India and wanted me to 'talk Hindu'. I may also have met Joan's husband Eddie, who was ten or twelve years her senior and whose entire working life had been spent with Ford Motors.

My father was living in Southfields, not far from Wimbledon Common, in the ground floor flat of the terrace house that had belonged to my grandmother. She had lived there with Aunt Helen, my father's unmarried younger sister, and the place was hardly less familiar to me than my own home. On the outside it was unchanged. There was the same privet hedge, the same neat front garden, the same balustraded porch, the same dark green front door with the stained glass panels, and the same polished brass letter box which, as a very small boy, I had loved to rattle to announce my arrival. Within, much had changed. Gone from the walls of the entrance hall were the big Chinese painting and the ceremonial swords, gone from behind the front door the Tibetan ritual bell I had so loved to ring, and gone all the old-fashioned mahogany furniture that my grandmother had polished with such loving care. Gone, even, were the well-known portraits of my grandmother's two deceased husbands and the photograph of my parents with me as a baby in long clothes, that used to hang in the living room. The living room itself was relatively unchanged, though it seemed smaller and narrower. There I gave my father and his wife their presents, and there the three of us had tea. My father's present was a bowl from Bhutan, carved from the excrescence of an apple tree and lined with silver. (When I was a boy he had bought me many a 'curio', and it was fitting that now I should be giving him one.) To his wife I gave a set of Indian handmade place mats. No introduction to her had been necessary; she was already well known to me, and had been no less glad to see me than had my father. She was the sister of Auntie Hilda, the first wife of my mother's brother Jack, and as a girl had often acted as my nursemaid.

Though my father was glad to see me, I soon observed that there was something on his mind. It related to my grandmother. I was certainly not surprised to learn she had been dead for some years, but it came as a shock when my father told me she had committed suicide. She had been living with them at the time (or they with her), there in Elborough Street, and one morning Florrie had returned from the shops to find her with her head in the gas oven. They had been shocked and distressed beyond words, and from the heartfelt way in which my father spoke of the unhappy event I could tell that it still distressed him even to think about it. I also had the impression that he was anxious I should not think that he and Florrie had neglected my grandmother in any way or made her feel she was a burden to them. They had done everything for her they could, he assured me. Nothing had been too much trouble. I had no difficulty believing him, as he had always been an affectionate and dutiful son. But I also knew that my grandmother was a strong-minded, independent old lady, who would not have enjoyed being dependent on others, however close to her they were, and however happy they may have been to look after her.

My grandmother's death had not been the only one within the immediate family. Uncle Charles, my father's stepbrother and his junior by ten or more years, had died prematurely of a heart attack. He had inherited the Chinese painting and the ceremonial swords, together with the other curios and antiques his father had collected, which explained why they were not in their usual places. Like the rest of his estate, they were still the subject of litigation between his ex-wives. Aunt Helen had not been seen for many years. She had turned strange, as my father put it. Strangest of all, having inherited my grandmother's house, she had sold it over their heads without consulting them, so that he and Florrie had woken up one morning to find they had a new landlord. This astonished me greatly, as Aunt Helen had always been conspicuously devoted to my father, and Florrie had for many years been her best friend.

Before I left my father handed me my Post Office Savings book, which I had entrusted to him twenty years earlier, on the eve of my embarkation for India. I had forgotten all about it. But my father had not forgotten. He had religiously sent the book in every year for the interest to be made up, with the result that I now had £120 to my name. I also had entrusted to my father the various notebooks containing my poems, together with the manuscript of my novel and the hundred or more books that had not been destroyed when our house was bombed. These I certainly had not forgotten. I was looking forward to the opportunity of casting a critical eye over my early literary efforts, especially the poems. But when I asked my father about them he looked blank. 'Oh yes,' he responded at length, passing his hand across his brow as he tried to remember, 'there were a few poetry books. I think your cousin Ezalda took them.' I was deeply disappointed.

5
AT THE SUMMER SCHOOL

The Buddhist Society's summer school was the highlight of the British Buddhist year, and had been so for more than a decade. It lasted a week, and was held at High Leigh, a conference centre on the outskirts of Hoddesdon, a small town in Hertfordshire. People came to it from all over the country. They came to meet fellow Buddhists and sympathizers with Buddhism, to attend lectures and classes, and to buy books on Buddhism and other Eastern religions that were not easily obtainable outside London.

That year I was the principal teacher, and as such was kept fully occupied. According to a report later published in *Sangha*, the monthly journal of the Buddhist Sangha Association, in the course of the week I conducted six meditation sessions, delivered ten lectures, held a question-and-answer meeting, participated in the School's concluding brains trust, and recorded two interviews for the BBC. As the report went on to say,

> The Ven. Sthavira's experience at the Summer School, where he contacted a representative cross-section of English Buddhists, besides meeting old friends, was a great help to him in assessing the present position of the Buddhist movement in England.[63]

One of the old friends I met was the author and translator John Blofeld, who four or five years earlier had spent three weeks with me

Buddhist Society Summer School. l–r: John Blofeld, Dr Malalsekara, Stella Coe, Sangharakshita, Ven. Piyadassi, Trungpa Rimpoche, a Sinhalese bhikkhu

in Kalimpong. He was not only a friend but a fellow disciple, the two of us having received the Vajrasattva initiation together from Dudjom Rimpoche.[64] Another report, which appeared in the *Middle Way*, the quarterly journal of the Buddhist Society, spoke of me as combining the three approaches of the Hīnayāna, Mahāyāna, and Vajrayāna, and as showing how the seeds of the last two are found in the first, and how the later developments grew without losing the fundamentals of the earlier approach. At the morning study classes, according to the same source, I outlined the Theravāda and Tibetan schools.[65]

Thirty-three years later I have little or no distinct recollection of all this, which is why I am having to rely on the two journals for an account of what was, nevertheless, my first important assignment on my return to England. But although I have no distinct recollection of what I did at my first summer school, in the way of delivering lectures and conducting meditation classes, a few vivid, if unconnected, impressions still remain, one of them sufficiently striking for me to have wanted to set it down in my notebook shortly afterwards. There also survives an article I wrote for the *Middle Way* on 'Twenty Years After: Impressions of Buddhism in England'. In this article I commented on the fact that a high proportion of Western Buddhists seemed interested in meditation. I also gave an account of an experiment in guided meditation, as I called it, that I conducted at the morning meditation sessions.[66]

The dining room at High Leigh was occupied by rows of long tables, with seating on either side. There were separate tables for vegetarians and non-vegetarians. At breakfast the first day I joined the vegetarians, among whom were Maurice Walshe, the chairman of the English Sangha Trust, and his wife Ruth, both of whom had already been to see me at the Vihara. In previous years, monks attending the summer school had always eaten by themselves, thus reinforcing the rigid Theravādin separation between monks and the lay community, and the fact that I chose to do otherwise occasioned a certain amount of astonishment. But it also gave rise to a good deal of pleasure, so that I still have a vivid impression of the satisfaction and delight with which people received me when I sat down at their table that morning and the joy with which they hastened to serve me. Christmas Humphreys and his entourage, I noticed, were not vegetarians.

Anne Lobstein may or may not have been part of the entourage. She was a short, fresh-faced woman of about forty who, I afterwards learned, had written an article that the editor of the *Middle Way* refused to accept, on the grounds that it contained, besides an account of the writer's mystical experiences, revelations concerning her love life. At the summer school she took the morning study class in Zen, and it was this class I decided to sit in on as part of my programme of informing myself about the current state of Buddhism in Britain. When I walked in, the class was pleasantly surprised, but Anne looked shocked. 'Oh no!' she cried, 'This is not fair.' 'In Zen everything is fair,' I retorted, as I took my seat, and the poor woman had no alternative but to proceed. There would be a short period of quiet reflection, she at length announced, in an unsteady voice, presumably so that she would have time to compose herself. When we had sat with closed eyes for ten or fifteen minutes she gave a confused, rambling talk about the trees and the flowers and the butterflies, and about the blue sky and the bright sunshine (and indeed it was a glorious August day outside), and about how it was all One, and how *that* was Zen. Years later, when we were better acquainted, she told me that the episode had caused her deep embarrassment. She was then new to Zen, and had never taken a Zen

With Christmas Humphreys, Buddhist Society Summer School

class before, but Mr Humphreys had asked her to do so, and as she regarded him as her teacher (she was a member of his Zen class at the Buddhist Society) she felt unable to refuse.

Humphreys himself spoke more than once that week, his principal contribution in this regard being the evening lecture he gave on 'A Buddhist Travelogue'. In this lecture he compared the spiritual life to climbing up the side of a mountain, and at one point described the spiritual mountaineer as 'hacking off great bleeding lumps of self' in the course of his ascent. The violent image made me shudder at the time, and it makes me shudder still. Of my own lectures I remember nothing. I do, however, remember an incident that took place immediately before one of them. Christmas Humphreys was to take the chair. On arriving at the lecture hall I found him waiting impatiently outside the door. 'You're two minutes late,' he observed disapprovingly, looking up at the clock above the lintel as though for confirmation of his words. I could hardly explain that in India I was accustomed to meetings beginning two hours late, and murmured something about not having a watch. The upshot was that the following day he sent me into Hoddesdon with Muriel Daw, his meetings secretary, to choose a watch for myself at the local jewellers. The day being my birthday, it would be a birthday present to me from him and the Buddhist Society. At the jewellers I unwittingly selected what I afterwards came to know was a quite expensive watch, but it lasted me a long time, and served to remind me that I was now living in a different culture, with a different set of values, one of which was punctuality.

The impression that was sufficiently striking for me to want to set it down in my notebook, once I was back at the Vihara, related to the demonstrations of *ikebana*, the Japanese art of flower arrangement, that were given towards the end of the week by Stella Coe and her pupils. Stella Coe was a leading *ikebana* teacher, so I gathered, and a regular visitor to the summer school. Some of the flower arrangements appeared to have a therapeutic effect. This was particularly the case with an arrangement representing a thoroughly selfish person carrying 'a heavy coil of knotty karma', the work of a stout, middle-aged woman in a blue dress. As my notebook entry went on to ask:

> Did the almost hysterical laughter of the audience represent a release of tension brought about by the recognition, in consciousness, of the dark side of themselves? Does the traditional Japanese art have this therapeutic effect, or is it merely aesthetic? Or are the two not inseparable? Miss Coe and her pupils (except the young man, a comparative beginner) had a peculiarly radiant grace and kindliness which might, perhaps, be the result of continually evoking, through the flower arrangements, images of beauty from the unconscious and incorporating – even assimilating – them into consciousness.

Whatever the explanation may have been, the grace and kindliness of Stella Coe and her three women pupils was very evident, and it gladdened my heart to see such a high degree of emotional positivity.

The differences that had arisen between the Sangha Association and the Buddhist Society were connected with the teaching of a particular form of meditation. I was therefore concerned to find out what place meditation occupied in the lives of British Buddhists, and in my article 'Twenty Years After' I touched on the subject. A high proportion of Western Buddhists seemed interested in meditation, and it was significant that at the summer school there were four different meditation sessions a day, all of them well attended. In view of the alarmingly high incidence of mental strain and disorder this interest was natural, I observed, adding that it was always to be borne in mind that the significance of Buddhist meditation was not merely psychological but primarily spiritual: its goal was Enlightenment. The article continued:

> Some people at the Summer School, however, regretted that a wider range of meditation practices were not available. As one of them told me, 'We aren't attracted by Zen, and we don't like Vipassanā, and there doesn't seem to be anything in between.' Actually there is very much 'in between'. At the 9.30 meditation sessions I conducted an experiment in what I [afterwards] called Guided Meditation, the class progressing from one stage to another of Mettā Bhāvanā (Development of Love) practice as directed at five-minute intervals by the voice of the instructor. Verbal directions were gradually reduced to a minimum until, in the last session, transition from one stage to the next was indicated merely by strokes of the gong. The experiment seemed successful, and it may be possible to apply the same technique to the teaching of other types of meditation. In any case, I feel strongly that there is a great need, among English Buddhists, for a wider and more intensive practice of the 'classical' systems of meditation, such as Mettā Bhāvanā and Ānāpāna Sati (Respiration-Mindfulness), which are common to all Yānas and which constitute the indispensable foundation of the more advanced techniques. I also feel that less attention is paid than might be to the devotional side of the Buddha's Teaching. As the formula of the Five Spiritual Faculties reminds us, Faith (śraddhā) and Wisdom (prajñā), Energy (vīrya) and Meditation (samādhi) must be in perfect equilibrium: Mindfulness (smṛti) 'is always useful'.[67]

The *vipassanā* that some people at the summer school didn't like was the controversial Burmese 'insight meditation' that Ananda Bodhi had been teaching, about which I shall have something to say later on. My experiment in guided meditation was an experiment in the sense that I had not taught meditation in this way before, and as the experiment was successful it did prove possible to apply the same technique to the teaching of types of meditation other than *mettā bhāvanā*. Guided group meditation, as I now called it, came to be the standard way in which I taught *mettā bhāvanā* and *ānāpānasati* to beginners in meditation both at the Vihara and elsewhere. This served to encourage the practice of the 'classical' systems of meditation among English Buddhists, some of whom were inclined to hanker after more 'advanced' methods of development.

6
RUSTLE OF AUTUMN

During the war, meetings of the Buddhist Society were held at its two-room headquarters in Great Russell Street, not far from the British Museum. I attended a number of them, as well as once or twice participating in the Wesak celebration that was held each year in this or that Bloomsbury hotel, and made several friends among the other members. The most important of these new friends was Clare Cameron, the pixie-like editor of *Buddhism in England* (as the *Middle Way* was then called), who read my latest poems, invited me to tea at her Bayswater flat, and took me walking in Kensington Gardens.[68] Though following my departure from England we corresponded for a while, it was only after I had settled in Kalimpong that a regular exchange of letters became possible. Clare was a good correspondent, so that I learned, in the course of the years, about *Here and Now*, the little magazine she had bought from the poet and mystic Derek Neville, about the magazine's failure a few years later, about her growing interest in the teachings of Sri Aurobindo and J. Krishnamurti, about her association with Thomas Henry Hamblin ('an English saint in an ordinary serge suit') and his *Science of Thought Review*, about her becoming editor of the review, and, most recently, about her moving, on the death of Hamblin's widow, into Bosham House, where she now lived and worked and where, one early autumn day, I visited her.[69]

Bosham House backed on to the Sussex Downs, and from the front lawn, where we had tea, there was a view out over the waters of Bosham

Creek. Clare was not greatly changed. Her hair was still cut in pageboy style, though it was grey now, her face wore the same enigmatic smile, and she was still a chain-smoker, albeit an apologetic one. As I knew from our correspondence, she had long since drifted away from the Buddhist Society, though she remained on friendly terms with Christmas Humphreys, but I was dismayed, even so, at the extent to which she had lost herself in the clouds of a vague, universalist mysticism. What was more, she assumed that after twenty years in the spiritual East I must be lost in them too and would, therefore, be in agreement with everything she said. 'As you, with your great wisdom, of course know,' she kept saying, by way of preface to some New Age platitude, blandly producing it as though it embodied the wisdom of the ages. Poor Clare! I felt deeply sorry for her; sorry that she had lost her way so badly; sorry she had not fulfilled the promise that shone so brightly in the pages of *Rustle of Spring*, the story of her East End childhood, which she had given me in the early days of our acquaintance.[70] Much as I was glad to see my old friend again, my meeting with Clare was therefore a disappointment. It was a disappointment in more ways than one. Before leaving for India I had entrusted to her the thick black notebook containing my most recent poems, together with three books I particularly prized: the original, Shanghai edition of the *Sūtra of Wei Lang*; *Tao, the Great Luminant*, a version of the works of Huainanzi, bound in blue silk and likewise published in the Far East; and the Bohn translation of Hegel's *Philosophy of History*.[71] But when I enquired after these precious volumes Clare only looked mystified. She had no recollection of them whatever.

Another old Buddhist Society friend was Claire Maison, who lived down the road from the Vihara, in a block of luxury flats. Like Clare Cameron, she was nearly seventy, and either because the two women were of the same age or because their Christian names were virtually identical I had always bracketed them together in my mind. Though Claire lived so near the Vihara, and was a member of the Buddhist Sangha Association, she was rarely well enough to attend meetings and once we had established contact I usually saw her in her own home. She was obviously a very sick woman, and even if I had remembered what she looked like twenty years earlier she now was so emaciated, and her deeply lined face had such a cadaverous look, that I probably would not have been able to recognize her. Besides often being in great pain, she was subject to moods of black despair, and in the course of some of my visits I had to spend time talking her out of them and into a more positive mental state. At times this was quite hard work, but I never minded, and Claire was always intensely grateful for whatever help I was able to give.

Though I had never known her so well as I had known Clare Cameron, or spent so much time with her, there was an incident from our wartime Buddhist Society days that had remained sharply etched on my memory. One night, after a meeting, Claire and I had walked together to Tottenham Court Road Underground Station, and while we stood waiting on the deserted platform she told me she was collecting material for the biography of Ananda Metteyya she was planning to write. Ananda Metteyya, who was English by birth, was one of the first Westerners to become a Theravādin Buddhist monk in the East, and the first Theravādin monk of any nationality to visit Britain or, for that matter, the West. He therefore occupied an important place in the history of Western Buddhism and a biography was a great desideratum.[72] But when I asked Claire, in the course of one of my visits, if she had been able to carry out her plan, she admitted, sadly, that she had not. She had not even been able to collect much in the way of materials for the work. Later, she gave me a few pamphlets written by Ananda Metteyya and a framed photograph of him, taken when he was a monk.

When I hung the photograph in the lecture room the resemblance between me and my predecessor was remarked on by a number of people. Some of them in fact took it, at first, for a photograph of me. Others thought I must be the reincarnation of Ananda Metteyya. Strange to say, not only had I been born two years after he died, I also drew my first breath not far from where he had drawn his last. Not that I had any memories of my previous existence, whether as Ananda Metteyya or anyone else. Yet if I had no memories of past lives, there were those within the British Buddhist movement who did. Christmas Humphreys believed he had been an officer in Pharaoh's bodyguard, with a gold breastplate of which he was immensely proud. But he also once told me that he knew at least seven or eight women who claimed that in a previous life they had been Cleopatra.

7
HEALING THE BREACH

The idea of forming a Sangha Sabha or Council of Buddhist Monks of Great Britain was not mine but Venerable Ratanasara's, though it was I who called the meeting at which that body came into existence. Ratanasara was a Sinhalese monk of a type with which I had become familiar in India as a result of my connection with the Maha Bodhi Society. Portly, urbane, and voluble, and my senior in both years and ordination, he was working towards a Ph.D. in the University of London with a thesis on Pirivena Education in Ceylon.[73] Though there was little of the monk about him except his robes (he wore a long overcoat over them when he went out, while his shaven head was concealed by a beret), and though he regarded meditation as frankly a waste of time, he was good-natured and sociable, and since I was used to his type, and did not expect much from him, spiritually speaking, I did not find it difficult to get on with him. We met at his lodgings in South Kensington, and at the Vihara, where on occasion he could be found sitting at our dining room table in the basement, puffing away at a big cigar, and jovially presiding, through clouds of tobacco smoke, over a meeting of his Buddhist Studies Trust.

One day he told me that being newly arrived in England I was in duty bound, as a monk, to report my arrival to the Sangha and seek their cooperation. Thinking this a good idea, I made arrangements for a meeting of the Sangha to be held at the Sinhalese vihara in Chiswick on the next full-moon day. Seven monks in all attended, the seniormost being Chao Kun Rajasiddhimuni, a leading member of the Thai ecclesiastical establishment who later became Sangharaja or Supreme Patriarch. He had been in England since June or July, teaching 'insight meditation' and conferring with his embassy about the temple the Thai government planned to build in London. I had met him once or twice before, when he spent a few days at the Vihara, where a few weeks earlier I had been welcomed with a warmth that was in marked contrast to the coldness of my reception at the Hampstead Buddhist Vihara. Phra Maha Vichitr, who was junior to me in years and monastic ordination, was the Chao Kun's interpreter, besides being a teacher of 'insight meditation' in his own right. Plump and self-satisfied in appearance, he always reminded me of a well-fed cat. When the Chao Kun returned to Thailand, a month or so after the formation of the Sangha Sabha, he stayed on at the Vihara for a year or more, though not without making it clear that he was *not* part of the Vihara and had nothing to do with the English Sangha. On the door of his room he hung a sign announcing, in large letters, 'Office of Thai Sangha'. In the room itself he installed an enormous executive desk, quite the biggest I had ever seen, behind which he sat when receiving visitors. His standoffishness saddened me. In India, in recent years, Thai monks had been among my closest friends within the monastic order. They had stayed with me in Kalimpong, and accompanied me on my lecture tours, and it seemed strange that in England one of their compatriots should behave in such an unfriendly fashion. Besides Ratanasara, who in respect of seniority came between Sumangala – the *bhikkhu* in charge of the Chiswick Vihara – and me, the remaining members of the meeting were Vimalo and Mangalo, the two juniormost in ordination. Ananda Bodhi did not attend.

After I had reported my arrival to my brother monks, and explained that we needed to discuss ways and means of ensuring the continuance and expansion of Buddhism in Great Britain, the meeting got down to business and a number of resolutions were passed. I was formally recognized as Head of the English Sangha and incumbent of the Hampstead Buddhist Vihara, and the establishment of the London Buddhist College, by the Buddhist Studies Trust, was 'highly commended' and given the meeting's wholehearted support. It was also resolved that those present should constitute themselves into an organization known as the Sangha Sabha or Council of Buddhist Monks of Great Britain, with Venerable Sayadaw U Thittila as president and Venerable Sthavira

Sangharakshita as secretary. U Thittila was the first Buddhist monk I had ever set eyes on. It was from him that I took the Three Refuges and Five Precepts at a Wesak meeting in London, during the war, and I was glad to be once again associated with him. A fine Pāli scholar, he now lived outside London with an elderly English couple, his supporters, and was engaged in editing an Abhidhamma text for publication by the Pali Text Society.[74]

The fact that I had been formally recognized as Head of the English Sangha and incumbent of the Hampstead Buddhist Vihara naturally strengthened my position, both at the Vihara and within the wider British Buddhist movement. As I realized only later, this had not by any means been Ratanasara's sole objective. His principal objective, in reminding me of my duty as a monk, and getting me to call a meeting of the Sangha, was to secure the Sangha's backing for his London Buddhist College, which was due to open the following month at the Vihara, in whose premises the classes would be held for the time being. It was in fact Ratanasara who had directed discussion at the meeting, who had drafted all the resolutions, and who had persuaded the rest of us to agree that novices should be encouraged to take advantage of the College, as he tactfully put it, and it was clear that in his eyes, at least, my cooperation with him in his plans for the College was no more than a *quid pro quo* for the part he had played in my recognition as Head of the English Sangha and incumbent of the Hampstead Buddhist Vihara. When I was obliged, later on, to oppose certain of those plans because of their implications for the Sangha Trust's finances he therefore felt that I was not keeping my side of the bargain. For my part, I was unaware of any bargain having been struck. When I supported his plans I supported them on principle, and when I opposed them I did that, too, on principle. Ratanasara seemed quite unable to understand this. At the same time, he was too shrewd a person to quarrel with me; we remained on friendly terms, and when he found himself without anywhere to live (he was not welcome over at Chiswick) I offered him a room at the Vihara.

Whether or not I had Ratanasara to thank for it, I was certainly in a stronger position after the holding of the Sangha Sabha, and could start thinking of establishing personal contact with the dozen or so little Buddhist groups that had sprung up outside London, some of whose members I had met at the summer school, and of how best to heal the breach between the Sangha Association and the Buddhist Society. I had already conducted a meditation class in Hastings and given a lecture in Leeds, where I stayed with the secretary of the Leeds Buddhist Society, Rosa Taylor, with whom I had exchanged letters while still in Kalimpong. As Rosa was not on the platform to meet me when my train arrived, as I expected she would be, I went and waited for her outside the station entrance. Two porters were talking to each other. As they were standing quite near me, and had loud voices, I could not help overhearing their conversation, but it was only after a few minutes that I realized I did not understand a word of what they were saying. I was in the North of England! I was in Yorkshire!

A less amusing experience awaited me in Staffordshire, at the meditation centre at Old Hall, which the Sangha Trust had bought the previous year. Not much of the original building was still standing, the greater part of it having been reduced to ruins by Cromwell's cannon during the Civil War.[75] There were only eight or nine habitable rooms, two of them quite big, and I quickly perceived that a good deal of work would have to be done on the place. This did not worry me. What worried me was the tense, strained atmosphere of the place. I do not remember who was in charge at the time, or if a formal course was in progress, but I noticed that the seven or eight meditators then in residence all had a remote look. They were disciples of Ananda Bodhi and were practising 'insight meditation'.

As tiny, white-haired Mrs Rauf drove me back to London, crouching over the wheel as we hurtled down the M1 at a speed to which I was unaccustomed, I had a lot to think about. 'Insight meditation', at least in the extreme form taught by Ananda Bodhi, in conjunction with the Canadian monk's brash and arrogant personality, had been responsible, at least in part, for the breach between the Sangha Association and the Buddhist Society. If that breach was to be healed, and if more people were not to be turned into zombies in the name of Buddhist meditation, then the teaching of the controversial Burmese technique at the Vihara by Vichitr and Nai Boonman, a Thai layman, would have to be phased out and the more traditional methods taught instead. This would have to be done circumspectly. In recent years many members of the Sangha Association had come to identify meditation with 'insight meditation', and in the eyes of some of them not practising 'insight meditation' was tantamount to not meditating at all. It also had to be borne in mind that in the case of some people, at least, a moderate practice of the technique had proved beneficial. But even if the teaching of 'insight meditation' was phased out at the Vihara this would not by itself be enough to ensure that relations between the Sangha Association and the Buddhist Society were harmonious and cooperative. There were other, broader differences between the two organizations to be resolved, some of which were rooted in their respective histories.

The Buddhist Society had been founded in 1924 as the Buddhist Lodge of the Theosophical Society,[76] from which it separated two years later as a result of the Krishnamurti debacle,[77] and members and friends would soon be celebrating its fortieth anniversary. Christmas Humphreys, the president ('Toby' to his intimates within the Society), was Britain's best-known Buddhist and his best-selling Pelican *Buddhism* had probably introduced more people to the Buddha and his teachings than had any other book since the publication of Sir Edwin Arnold's *The Light of Asia* in 1879.[78] Perhaps because of its origins in the theosophical movement, and Humphreys' personal sympathies (he believed Buddhism and theosophy to be complementary), the Buddhist Society's approach to the Buddha-Dharma was not sectarian but ecumenical. Besides running its own classes and holding the summer school, it provided a platform for visiting Buddhist teachers of all traditions, and was the central body to which what London-based Buddhists called 'the provincial groups' were loosely affiliated. Since the appearance of Dr D. T. Suzuki's writings in the fifties,[79] Christmas Humphreys' special interest within the field of Buddhism had been Zen, and his 'Zen class' (the scare quotes indicate its admittedly non-traditional status) was in effect the Buddhist Society's equivalent of the Theosophical Society's esoteric section. Other members of the society had a special interest in the Theravāda and it was one of these who, as the Bhikkhu Kapilavaddho (formerly William Purfurst), had in 1956 been mainly responsible for forming the Sangha Trust and, I think, the Sangha Association, with the object of creating in Great Britain a monastic community for Westerners.

Kapilavaddho was by all accounts an eccentric, charismatic figure who oscillated between the cloister and the hearth, asceticism and hedonism, and who tended to go to extremes in both directions. After spending less than a year in Thailand, and achieving what he seems to have thought was Enlightenment, he had returned to England, spent not much more than a year in a whirlwind of activity, and then abruptly given up the robe in order to marry and run a public house. 'I like my beer and women,' he had told the press, according to a cutting sent to me at the time. Kapilavaddho was succeeded by Paññavaddho, who despite his youth and inexperience, and the fact that he had been a full monk for only six months, nobly rose to the occasion and carried on his teacher's work for the next five years. All the English Buddhists to whom I spoke praised him warmly for his simplicity, his sweetness of character, and his conscientiousness. In 1961 he went to live permanently in Thailand and his place was taken by Ananda Bodhi. At first all was well. Both Kapilavaddho and Paññavaddho having worked in harmony with Christmas Humphreys and the Buddhist Society (Humphreys had originally hailed Kapilavaddho as 'the modern Milarepa'), there appeared to be no reason why Ananda Bodhi should not do likewise. The Buddhist Society had accordingly made him welcome, invited him to teach under its auspices, and published a portrait photograph of him in the *Middle Way*.[80] It was not long before his 'insight meditation' evangelism, coupled with what he himself called his 'hell-and-brimstone' style of lecturing and his abrasive personality, not only helped to bring about a split between the Sangha Association and the Society but also alienated a number of the Sangha Association's own members, many of whom resigned. There was an exchange of letters between Maurice Walshe, who was both a vice-president of the Society and a loyal supporter of Ananda Bodhi, and Christmas Humphreys, in the course of which the latter had spelled out his objections to Ananda Bodhi's teaching. This was more than a year before my arrival on the scene, and since then the breach between the Buddhist Society and the Sangha Association had been complete.

I had no wish to take sides in the dispute. I wanted to be fair to both parties, and despite the fact that my first few days at the Vihara had given me an unfavourable impression of Ananda Bodhi's character I was prepared to recognize that he was not without good qualities and had done much for the Sangha Association and, indeed, for the cause of Buddhism in Britain. He was active and enterprising, and possibly on account of his Canadian background was not afraid to break fresh ground or to do things in an unconventional manner. It was he who, the Sangha Trust having received a large donation, bullied the reluctant trustees into buying first the two adjacent properties on Haverstock Hill, one of which was now the Vihara, and then, a year later, Biddulph Old Hall. I was also prepared to recognize that both parties may have been at fault to an extent, and that in respect of certain of Ananda Bodhi's proceedings opponents and supporters alike may have over-reacted. The incident of the bowl of jelly was a case in point. I was told about this incident by many people, some of whom had been present at the time. It had taken place in Cambridge, at a meeting of the Cambridge University Buddhist Society, among whose undergraduate members the controversial monk had an enthusiastic following, and had generated an enormous amount of excitement. Ananda Bodhi had walked into the lecture hall carrying a bowl of jelly and a large spoon with which he proceeded to flick the jelly over the audience until the bowl was empty. His disciples were beside themselves with delight and admiration. Once again Ananda Bodhi had demonstrated his unique greatness as a teacher. Flicking jelly was an absolute masterstroke. It was a profound teaching, even an initiation of sorts. Others were less impressed.

When I first heard about the jelly-flicking I could not help smiling to myself. To me it seemed amusing at best, at worst childish and in poor taste, and I was surprised to learn that it had provoked such over-reactions. But I quickly perceived that, as symptomatic of a tendency to polarization within the British Buddhist movement, such over-reactions were in reality no laughing matter. Ananda Bodhi's teaching of the Burmese 'insight meditation', itself a controversial variant of an important traditional practice, may well have been dangerously one-sided, and his supporters within the Sangha Association may well have gone to extremes in their enthusiasm for the technique, but Christmas Humphreys and Ananda Bodhi's other opponents at the Buddhist Society and elsewhere had also gone to extremes, albeit in the opposite direction. 'Insight meditation' stood accused of concentrating on the development of the *iddhis* or lower psychic powers of which the Buddhist Society's theosophical heritage had taught it to be so afraid. Some of its members went so far as to throw away the meditation baby with the '*vipassanā*' bathwater. Meditation was 'dangerous'! I could perhaps have resolved the conflict, at least to an extent, by speaking to Ananda Bodhi and persuading him at least to teach 'insight meditation' in a more traditional manner, but he was no more willing to discuss matters with me than he had been to discuss them with Christmas Humphreys, and shortly after the formation of the Sangha Sabha he left for Canada. Better to be the first man in a village than the second in Rome! His departure left me free to start phasing out the teaching of 'insight meditation' at the Vihara. It also made it easier for me to heal the breach between the Buddhist Society and the Sangha Association and, perhaps, resolve some of the broader differences between them.

The first thing I did was to make myself equally available to both organizations. On Sunday afternoons I lectured at the Hampstead Buddhist Vihara and on Friday evenings at the Buddhist Society's premises in Eccleston Square, near Victoria Station, to which it had moved seven or eight years earlier. I also started visiting the provincial groups on a regular basis and giving talks for societies and clubs of various kinds in and around London, besides officiating at funerals, speaking at the Buddhist Society's fortieth anniversary celebrations at Caxton Hall, and organizing an innovatory three-day Christmas Buddhist Seminar for fifty persons at the Vihara. In this way I got to know quite a number of people, especially in London. After my weekly lecture at the Buddhist Society ten or twelve of us would adjourn to the Jiffy Bar, where those who had come to the lecture straight from work would have a meal or a snack, I would have a cup of tea, and where a lively discussion would generally take place, either on a point arising out of the lecture itself or on some unrelated Buddhist topic. Several of the participants told me that they enjoyed these informal gatherings even more than the lectures themselves and actually learned more about Buddhism from them. After meetings at the Vihara, if no one wanted to see me privately, as was often the case, I would invite two or three people up to my room for a chat. Some faces I saw both at the lectures I gave at the Buddhist Society and those I gave at the Vihara. In fact I encouraged members of the Sangha Association to join the Buddhist Society and attend its meetings and members of the Buddhist Society to join the Sangha Association and take part in its activities both at the Vihara and at the Biddulph meditation centre. Many were happy to do this, though there were a few diehards on both sides who wanted to have nothing to do with the rival organization.

Several of the faces I saw both at the Buddhist Society and at the Vihara were to become very familiar to me. They included the morose and radiant faces belonging, respectively, to Maurice and Ruth Walshe;

In the garden of the Hampstead Buddhist Vihara. l–r: Maurice Walshe, Mike Hookham, Terry Delamare, Alf Vial, Sangharakshita, Jack Ireland, with a visiting Japanese Buddhist (front)

the jovial, worried-looking, and smiling faces of the Vihara's 'Three Musketeers' – Alf Vial, Mike Hookham, and Jack Ireland; and the plump, cheerful face of Anna Phillips, who had a car and had already constituted herself my driver. They all, in their different ways, played a part in my life during the next two years, and even beyond, and I shall later on have to attempt a portrait – or at least a sketch – of each of them.

8
'THE WORLD OF PUBLISHING'

In India I had been accustomed, when not on tour, to devote my mornings to literary work. At the time of my departure for England I was engaged on a five-part 'Heritage of Buddhism', which had kept me busy for the last two years and was still far from complete. As I did not want to stop working on it, in accepting the Sangha Trust's invitation to spend a few months in England I had stipulated that I should have my mornings to myself. I had not been at the Vihara many weeks before it became obvious that I would be spending more time in England than I had expected and that there was no question of my mornings being my own. There were always people to see, lectures to prepare, correspondence to attend to – and the telephone kept ringing. In these circumstances there was little hope of my being able to produce more than the occasional article. But if it was not possible for me to carry on working on my 'Heritage of Buddhism' I could at least prepare the first part of it for publication in separate book form and write a short preface.

The 'Heritage' had begun as a series of articles for the *Oriya Encyclopaedia*, but I soon realized – my enthusiasm for the Dharma having carried me far beyond the number of words required – that I was writing not a series of articles but a book or books. I therefore started looking for a London publisher, and at Lama Govinda's suggestion wrote to Gerald Yorke, the reader for Rider & Co., then the leading English publisher of books on Buddhism. He replied promptly, and after a few more letters had passed between us an agreement was signed. As it happened I met him at the summer school, which he was in the habit of attending in quest of new authors.

Gerald Yorke was a cheerful, communicative man of sixty or more, in a tweed jacket, and with a brier pipe which he waved around when talking. At the summer school he was to be found of an evening in the Oak Room, where he would hold forth to some of the younger men until quite late, reminiscing about his experiences in China in the thirties and sometimes telling, so I gathered, stories that were not fit for the ears of monks. Not least because I was one of his authors, he took a fatherly interest in me, and in the course of the next few years I saw quite a lot of him and his wife, both at their London flat and at Forthampton Court, their country house near Tewkesbury, in Gloucestershire. During one of my stays at Forthampton Court, once a residence of the abbots of Tewkesbury, Gerald showed me the house library, which had been started in the eighteenth century by one of his ancestors and contained a number of leather-bound volumes that I took the opportunity of perusing. He also showed me his personal library, which was of a very different character. In his younger days he had been a disciple of the black magician Aleister Crowley, 'the Wickedest Man in the World', and the collection was rich in books and, I think, unpublished manuscripts, by that strange and complex being, besides other memorabilia. Perhaps because he wanted to see how shockable – or unshockable – I was, Gerald at one point drew from the shelves a slim, blue-covered volume and asked me to read the little work. It turned out to be a long stanzaic poem by Crowley in praise of the Virgin Mary, and it had been published by Burns, Oates & Washbourne, publishers to the Holy See. It was a rather beautiful poem, I thought, and showed that the celebrated Satanist possessed, among his other talents, an admirable command of metre and rhyme. But before I could finish reading it my host, with a chuckle, drew my attention to the fact that the first letter of each line of verse, read downwards, spelled out a string of obscenities very much at variance with the professed character of the work. Crowley had been delighted with the success of his stratagem; Burns, Oates & Washbourne, deeply embarrassed, had hastily withdrawn the book from circulation.

Jack Austin, a Westminster Bank employee and whilom leading member of the Buddhist Society, had certainly not been a disciple of Aleister Crowley; but he shared the black magician's tastes in at least one respect. He had a marked fondness for what has been called, in disparagement, 'ecclesiastical millinery'. In his case the millinery was of Japanese provenance, and almost the first thing he did when I visited him at his home in Banstead, in Surrey, where he lived with his wife and two young children, was to fling open the doors of his wardrobe and show me his collection of brocade robes. There must have been several dozen of them, of various colours and designs and degrees of sumptuousness, and Jack not only explained to me, enthusiastically and at great length, who had presented each robe to him and in what circumstances, and when he was entitled to wear it, but paraded back and forth in his favourite items so that I could see how he looked in them. Had he lived in the previous century he would probably have been a Ritualist curate, very much preoccupied with surplices and chasubles, genuflections and incense. Instead he was a Mahāyāna Buddhist living at a time in the history of Western Buddhism when the only robes with which the average English Buddhist was at all familiar were the yellow cotton robes of the Theravādin monk, such as I was wearing, and when the only kind of ordination of which he (or she) had any real knowledge was monastic ordination.

As I knew from our long correspondence, the topic of ordination was a very sensitive one with Jack. He did not want to be a monk, but he desperately wanted to be an ordained person. He wanted to be a Buddhist *priest*, and exercise priestly functions, conducting services, marrying and burying (or cremating) people, sitting on interfaith committees as the Buddhist 'representative' and, of course, giving public lectures on Buddhism, of which he had a good general knowledge. Over the years he had sought ordination in various quarters, at one time receiving from Robert Stuart Clifton, founder of the short-lived Western Buddhist Order, what he believed – wrongly, as it turned out – was a Sōtō Zen ordination.[81] It was on the strength of this ordination that he styled himself, and insisted on being styled by others, the Reverend Jack Austin. But while he was comparatively well known outside the British Buddhist movement, his position within it was ambiguous. He had always ploughed a lonely furrow, and even though this was more by choice than necessity it was impossible not to admire the energy and pertinacity of his ploughing. In particular I admired the way in which, year after year, he brought out *The Western Buddhist*, his little magazine of Mahāyāna Buddhism. Bringing out a Buddhist magazine was not easy, as I well knew. Though now living in England, I was still having to edit the *Maha Bodhi*, the monthly journal of the Maha Bodhi Society of India, which was printed and published in Calcutta and which I had edited for the last ten or eleven years.[82]

Fortunately I had the assistance of Mrs A. A. G. Bennett. In her capacity as the *Maha Bodhi*'s Representative in Europe and the Americas (a post I had created specially for her) she had assisted me for many years. Besides writing for the journal herself, and providing news of Buddhist activities in the West, she had translated a number of scholarly articles from German and French, thus helping to give the *Maha Bodhi* a more international flavour. Though she had assisted me for such a long time, and we had exchanged hundreds of letters, relations between us, though cordial, had remained rather formal (her letters were always signed 'Adrienne Bennett'), and I knew little more about her than what she had revealed in a biographical note which, at my request, she wrote in 1954 for a special number of the *Maha Bodhi*. The note read:

> Editor of the Bulletin of the Standing Conference of the Theological and Philosophical Libraries of London. Studied Mathematics and Physics. Later changed to Painting, exhibiting frequently in London. Lived for 14 years in India and China. 1939–45 war, engaged in linguistic work; then on a history of the Development of Religious Thought. Librarian of the Buddhist Society, London, 1949–52. Editor of the Middle Way, 1951–52.[83]

Her association with the *Middle Way* – and the Buddhist Society – had not ended happily. Her efforts to upgrade the magazine intellectually had been frustrated by Christmas Humphreys' determination to keep it popular. According to Jack Austin, at that time a regular correspondent, there had been a stormy Council meeting at which Humphreys spoke to her so brutally that she left the room in tears.

The *Middle Way*'s loss had been the *Maha Bodhi*'s gain, and since it had been my gain too I was anxious to establish personal contact with our faithful representative in Europe and the Americas and get to know her personally. On visiting her at her flat in Holland Park, shortly after my return to England, I found a haggard-faced woman of sixty or thereabouts, wearing heavy make-up and with henna-dyed hair, who was bursting with nervous energy that evidently needed an outlet. It being our first meeting we naturally talked shop. I was particularly interested in the translation of the *Bodhicaryāvatāra* on which she was then engaged, and encouraged her to persevere with it, despite the difficulty of the work.[84] At that time there was only one English translation of Śāntideva's classic celebration of the bodhisattva ideal in print and this, though very readable, unfortunately was incomplete.

The chapter of the *Bodhicaryāvatāra* that had been giving Mrs Bennett most trouble was chapter 9, on the Perfection of Wisdom, which Lionel Barnett, the previous translator, had chosen to leave in the obscurity of the original Sanskrit. The Perfection of Wisdom was the principal subject matter of the Prajñāpāramitā or 'Perfection of Wisdom' *sūtras*, an important body of Mahāyāna canonical texts that had been translated, almost in their entirety, by Dr Edward Conze, who had devoted twenty years of his life to the project, thus putting all English-speaking Buddhists very much in his debt. With him too, therefore, I was anxious to establish personal contact.

We met in Oxford, that famous 'home of lost causes',[85] when the Oxford University Buddhist Society invited me to give a lecture under its auspices that autumn. I spoke on 'The Spiritual Ideal in Buddhism'. Dr Conze was in the audience, and afterwards the two of us met. This was the first of a number of meetings, at his home and at Manchester College, where he taught, and where I once heard him speak on the Madhyamaka School to no more than twenty people – a pitifully small audience for so great a Buddhist scholar. Though he was reputed to have a ferocious temper, and people were said to be terrified of his caustic tongue, I never saw the least sign of either. He struck me as being a kindly, even compassionate, person. Common friends to whom I mentioned my impression disputed this, but I remained convinced that that was what he was really like. If it is true that 'As fire drives out fire, so pity pity,'[86] then it could have been that his compassion for people's spiritual ignorance at times got the better of his pity for their mundane sensitivities. His, perhaps, was the healing knife, that wounded only to cure.

Be that as it may, Edward Conze struck me as being not only a kindly person but also quite a sad one, and indeed he was not very happy at Oxford. When I naively asked him, during our first meeting, if there was not a good deal of interest in Buddhist philosophy at Oxford, now that he was there, he replied, gloomily, that there was no interest in it whatever. Oxford philosophers were interested only in linguistic analysis, which was not philosophy in the traditional sense at all. Buddhist philosophy was a lost cause, it seemed, even in the home of lost causes.

There were other reasons for Dr Conze's unhappiness. Academic Oxford was an exclusive, conventional, and snobbish place, and it was not above humiliating a social and intellectual outsider in mean and petty ways. As Freda Wint and other Buddhist friends there told me, since Dr Conze held only continental degrees he was listed in the university calendar as plain Mr Conze, and since the lady with whom he was living was not his legal wife the authorities refused to recognize her existence and she was not included in invitations to official functions. So far as the university was concerned, Mr Conze was a bachelor.

I met Mrs Conze (as she truly was in Buddhist eyes) more than once. The first time was when I had lunch with them at their flat and Dr Conze introduced her in what I thought was rather an offhand manner, simply saying, as she walked into the room, 'This is Muriel.' Did he feel embarrassed? Or was he unsure what my attitude would be? Whatever the explanation, it pained me to think that a man of his eminence and distinction should be placed by society in such an invidious position. Years later, having eventually succeeded in obtaining a divorce from his first wife, Dr Conze married his Muriel. But by that time he had long severed his connection with Oxford.[87]

9
LONDON TWENTY YEARS AFTER

In recent years people have sometimes asked how long it took me to adjust to living in England, after my twenty years in the East. In fact it took me no time at all. I might even say that the idea that one needs 'time to adjust' to a new situation, or set of circumstances, and has just to sit there 'adjusting' for a few weeks or months before being able to do anything, was meaningless to me, not to say absurd. There was not such a great deal of difference between arriving in London and taking up residence at the Hampstead Buddhist Vihara and arriving in Calcutta or Bombay or Poona and going to stay at one of the local monasteries or with friends. Of course this did not mean that there were not differences between London and the various Indian cities I was accustomed to visit. Obviously the differences between them were enormous, but for me there was no question of my having to make a psychological 'adjustment' to those differences as distinct from my familiarizing myself with them and learning to take them into account when it was necessary to do so. There was no question of my being given an emotional shock by the new situation and no question, therefore, of my needing time to recover from that shock.

One of the biggest differences between London on the one hand and the Indian cities on the other was a singular one I had noticed on the very day of my arrival. Compared with Calcutta and Bombay, and even Poona,[88] London was a very quiet place. The traffic rolled smoothly through the streets making hardly a sound; and it all kept, miraculously, to the side of the road to which it was supposed to keep. There were no bullock carts or wandering cows getting in the way, or sweating coolies pushing barrows piled high with tins of kerosene or sacks of flour. What was hardly less strange, London was practically deserted. There were no streets aswarm with men, women, and children, and the few people who were about behaved in an orderly fashion; no one walked in the road, or squatted to urinate in the gutter, and there were no beggars. Compared with what I was used to when I left my mountain retreat to travel the plains of India, London was '*luxe, calme et volupté*' as the lands to which Baudelaire, in a famous poem, invites his faithless beloved to accompany him.[89]

The one place that was neither *luxe*, nor *calme*, nor *volupté* was Haverstock Hill, or at least that part of it on which the Hampstead Buddhist Vihara happened to be situated. A busy arterial road, it was so noisy that one had a long way to go before finding a noisier. Traffic, especially lorries, roared and thundered up and down it incessantly, from early morning until late at night, or rather, until the early hours of the following day, so that one had only a few hours' respite from the din. Sometimes the traffic was so heavy, even on a Sunday afternoon, that the whole building shook with the vibrations and the windows rattled. On the opposite side of the road stood the Haverstock Arms, and on Friday and Saturday nights, especially, the shouts and cries of revellers could be heard above the noise of the traffic. In the whole of north-west London there could hardly have been a less suitable spot for a Buddhist monastery.

What, then, had led Ananda Bodhi and the Sangha Trust to fix on 131 Haverstock Hill as the new home of the English Sangha and the venue of its teaching activities? The reason was that Haverstock Hill, together with its continuation Rosslyn Hill, ran straight through the then London borough of Hampstead, bisecting it along its north-south axis, and Hampstead was reputed to have more intellectuals to the square mile than any other part of the metropolis. As Buddhism was an intellectual religion, and could therefore be expected to have a special appeal for Western intellectuals, what better location for a vihara could there be than in the area where the potential interest was greatest? Western intellectuals, who had no faith in meaningless rites and ceremonies, and who relied solely on reason, were already more than halfway to Buddhism. Let them only hear the Dharma, in its pure

Theravādin form, from the lips of a Theravādin Buddhist monk, and they would be sure to embrace it immediately.

I had long been familiar with this line of argument. It was a favourite one with Western-educated Eastern Buddhists like Narada Thera, the doyen of the English-speaking monks of Ceylon, who had visited Europe on more than one 'mission of mercy' and who seemed to believe, judging by the reports he wrote, that inasmuch as 'the intellectual Westerners' had listened attentively to his lectures and applauded politely at the end he had made converts of them on the spot. No doubt there were a few who really did think of Buddhism as an early Indian form of Rationalism and to whom it appealed for that reason, and no doubt they had their representatives within the British Buddhist movement in London and elsewhere, but so far as I could make out Western intellectuals in general were more likely to embrace scientific materialism and scepticism, or even cynicism and nihilism, than a spiritual, transcendentally-oriented teaching such as Buddhism. Apart from Maurice Walshe, who was a minor academic rather than an intellectual, during my tenure as incumbent of the Hampstead Buddhist Vihara I did not, to my knowledge, see even one of the famed Hampstead intellectuals at my Sunday afternoon lectures. They preferred to play chess at Prompt Corner in South End Green.

People have also sometimes asked me, in recent years, if I ever missed India, especially Kalimpong, the little town in the foothills of the eastern Himalayas where I had lived for fourteen years and where I had several teachers and many friends. Did I not miss them particularly badly during those first few months after my return to England? So far as I remember I did not miss them at all, if by 'missing' one means pining for them and regretting that I was not there in India, and especially in Kalimpong, instead of being where I actually was. This is certainly not to say that I never thought of them. I thought of India, and of Kalimpong in particular, every now and then, and with great fondness. I thought of the crowded, colourful bazaars, of the green rice-fields, of the great rivers, of the mighty snow-capped mountain ranges. I thought of my peaceful hillside hermitage, where in latter years I had been wont to spend the three or four months of the rains reading, writing, and meditating, and hearing no other sound than that of the rain drumming on the roof and the occasional soothing tinkle of the wind-bells on the veranda outside my window. Above all, perhaps, I thought of (and sometimes found time to write to) my kind teachers, particularly Dhardo Rimpoche, and to my affectionate friends, of whom I had many in Calcutta, Bombay, Poona, Ahmedabad, Nagpur, Jabalpur, and Delhi, and other parts of the country.

I have sometimes wondered why, after my return to England, I did not miss my Indian friends at least to a small extent, especially as I was now having to live and work with people who almost without exception were perfect strangers to me. But unless memory plays me false, I did not miss them, did not, that is to say, pine for them or regret I was not in their company. In this connection I recall what one of them once told me, after I had spent some three weeks in Poona giving lectures for the benefit of my ex-Untouchable Buddhist friends. 'We have all become very fond of you,' he said, 'and we are extremely sorry to see you go, but *you* do not seem to be at all sorry to be leaving *us*.' Whether these words expressed admiration for my detachment as a monk or disappointment at my indifference as a friend, or even a mixture of both, I do not know, but they made an impression on me at the time and gave me food for thought afterwards. Detachment, in the sense of freedom from self-interest, was one thing, indifference, in the sense of a lack of concern for other people, quite another. While the former was perfectly compatible with true friendship, the latter made any kind of friendship impossible. Did my not feeling sorry to be leaving my friends in Poona, and my not missing my Indian friends after my return to England, mean that I was detached, or did it mean that I was indifferent? Was there, I even wondered, a general lack of emotion in my make-up?

In the end I came to the conclusion that I was neither without concern for other people nor lacking in emotion generally. But my feelings were to a great extent buried. They were buried beneath layers of reticence and reserve through which it was difficult for them to break. For this there were, so far as I could see, a number of reasons. Besides my cultural conditioning as an Englishman, which had probably given me a stiff upper lip without my realizing it, there was the fact that the natural expression of my feelings had been inhibited by my being obliged, from an early age, to be constantly aware of what I was doing. Then again, I was a Buddhist monk, who was expected to be always calm and controlled, and at the time of my arrival at the Hampstead Buddhist Vihara I had been a monk for fourteen years – longer, if my period as a freelance wandering ascetic is included. But there were other, more positive reasons for my apparent coldness. If my feelings strove to break through the layers of reticence and reserve less urgently than they might have done, it was partly because they had an alternative outlet. This outlet was poetry, which I had written since I was a boy and in which I could express my feelings freely. Similarly, if I did not miss my Indian friends at all, my not missing them was partly due to the fact that I possessed a vivid imagination, so that whenever I thought of them it was as though they were, in a manner of speaking, actually present and I could see them. In other words, I did not miss them in the ordinary sense of the term, because they were not really absent – at least not when I was thinking of them.[90]

Not that I very often felt the need to think of them and, as it were, enjoy their company. My life was a full one, and I was kept very busy, not infrequently until late at night and even into the early hours. I had the management of the Vihara to attend to, besides which there were lectures to prepare, provincial Buddhist groups to visit, people to see – and my immediate environs to explore. During my first few weeks in England explorations were limited to the Belsize Bookshop and the nearer reaches of Hampstead Heath, but later I refamiliarized myself with central London, which I had known very well during the war, visiting the second-hand bookshops in Charing Cross Road again, renewing my acquaintance with the Egyptian mummies in the British Museum, and once more walking past County Hall, where I had worked for two years before being conscripted.[91] As I made my way around I realized that London was not only different, in so many ways, from the major conurbations of India; it was also different from its own former, wartime self. Red double-deckers still plied the major London routes, but the bone-shaking trams and swift, silent trolley buses had gone, and there were more motor cars on the roads. Launderettes and Indian restaurants had sprung up and become, apparently, an integral part of people's lives, TV aerials sprouted from rooftops, and men no longer raised their hats when passing the Cenotaph in Whitehall. I also noticed that people were much better dressed and had, as it seemed, more money to spend (there were certainly more consumer goods in the shops for them to buy), so that I could not but recall the ignoble slogan 'You've never had it so good', with which Harold Macmillan and the Conservative Party were said to have won a general election and which, when the echo of it reached me in distant Kalimpong, had almost made me ashamed of being British.

But though much had changed much had remained unchanged. Besides the red double-deckers, red telephone kiosks and red pillar boxes were still to be seen; policemen wore the same kind of helmets as before; the Underground was as stuffy, crowded, and convenient as ever; and in the City there were still a few bomb sites, grim reminders of the Blitz, from whose rubble-heaps there rose clumps of pink-flowering willowherb.

10
A PORTRAIT IN OIL – AND A FEW SKETCHES

Portraits can be executed in oils, in water colours, and even in charcoal. A portrait of Maurice O'Connor Walshe – Reader in German at Bedford College, vice-president of the Buddhist Society, chairman of the Sangha Association, etc. – would doubtless have to be executed in oils, for only in that rich and expressive medium would the artist be able to do justice both to his mottled complexion and his complex, contradictory character. A portrait of him in words, even one that is no more than a sketch, must be executed in the literary equivalent of oils. I have described the expression on Maurice Walshe's face as morose and that on his wife Ruth's as radiant. Both epithets are only approximations, as single epithets as applied to human beings unavoidably are. Maurice Walshe looked morose only when he was comparatively relaxed, as he sometimes was after attending a lecture or a meditation class. At other times his expression could range from the belligerent to the sullenly obstinate. Most often, though, and perhaps most characteristically, the face that looked out from beneath the stiff grey hair and prominent brow was that of an angry child.

In his capacity as a member of the Sangha Trust (he was not then its chairman, I think), I had been in correspondence with him for several months prior to my departure from India, and after my arrival at the Vihara we naturally became personally acquainted. He and Ruth Walshe

With Maurice and Ruth Walshe

lived just round the corner from the Vihara, down a tree-lined side street a little further up Haverstock Hill, though whether Mohammed had gone to the mountain or the mountain to Mohammed I never discovered. The summer school had not been long over before they invited me to tea, and soon an afternoon visit to their comfortable upstairs flat in Howitt Road was a regular feature of my week. These visits usually took place on the days I was lecturing at the Buddhist Society when, the three of us having had tea together, Maurice and Ruth would take me down to Victoria and to the Society's premises in Eccleston Square. After the lecture – and our usual session in the Jiffy Bar – they would bring me back to the Vihara. I was not used to being escorted and accompanied in this ceremonious manner, but it seems my predecessors had insisted on it. Some of them, indeed, had always taken taxis when a private car was not available, as travelling by public transport was thought to be incompatible with monastic dignity. Kapilavaddho in particular, I was told, had cost the Trust hundreds of pounds in taxi hire for himself and his attendant.

While Ruth always chattered gaily on our journey into central London, Maurice was usually morose and silent, and I was therefore not surprised when, on the grounds that he had work to do, he eventually stopped accompanying us. Tea being over, he would withdraw into his study, leaving Ruth with the responsibility of getting me to the Buddhist Society in good time for my lecture (or meditation class, as the case might be) and returning me safely to the Vihara afterwards. Occasionally he came to the Society straight from college, arriving just before the lecture was due to begin. On those days I did not have tea at Howitt Road and Ruth called for me at the Vihara.

That I no longer had Maurice's morose company on my shuttlings between the rival Buddhist establishments (as they still were to an extent), but only that of his more cheerful and communicative wife, certainly did not mean that I saw him only when the three of us had tea together. Living as he did just round the corner, it was easy for him to call in at the Vihara, which he did at all sorts of odd times. At first he came simply to see how I was settling in, or if there was anything I needed, but after a while it was in order to confer with me on this or that item of Sangha Trust or Sangha Association business. I thus had many opportunities of observing him, even of studying him, at close quarters. Clumsy in manner and awkward in demeanour, he usually appeared ill at ease, whether in my own company or that of other people, and he often fidgeted and grimaced as though torn by violent conflicting emotions. When engaged in conversation, he would study the floor, or glance from side to side of the room – anywhere but in the face of the person to whom he was speaking. All this tended to give him a shifty, untrustworthy look, as if he had something to hide, or was ashamed of himself, or felt guilty. I also noticed that when something went wrong, or if there was an emergency, Maurice either became flustered and threshed about helplessly, not knowing what to do, or else panicked and acted precipitately, without thinking. He moreover was extremely forgetful, being in this respect the typical 'absent-minded professor' of popular belief. Once he forgot the key to the Buddhist Society, with which he had been entrusted since he was chairing my lecture that evening, and had to go back to Hampstead for it while we all waited outside. Later on he repeatedly forgot to send notices of my 'outside' lectures to the press, with the result that there was a smaller attendance than usual. He forgot so often that I could have been forgiven had I wondered whether his forgetting was not a Freudian slip.

Though he always treated me with respect, even consideration, and seemed pleased that I was staying in England longer than I had originally intended, and though for my part I appreciated his scholarly knowledge of Buddhism, the fact was that we never really became well acquainted. The reason for this, questions of personal chemistry aside, was that he knew I had serious reservations about the Burmese-style 'insight meditation', which he himself had been practising under the guidance of Ananda Bodhi and which he continued to practise under the guidance of Vichitr, with whom he had a weekly 'meditation interview' in the 'Office of Thai Sangha' whenever the plump, self-satisfied Thai monk happened to be in residence. He also was aware that I was taking steps to phase out the teaching of 'insight meditation' at the Vihara, at least where the public classes were concerned, and replace it with more traditional methods – a process that in the end took me six or seven months to complete. Thus although we could regularly discuss – and agree upon – Trust and Association affairs, and although we could sometimes exchange views on points of general doctrinal interest, Maurice Walshe and I were never able to touch upon anything of a more personal nature, least of all on anything that had a bearing on the practice of meditation. Had I attempted to take the initiative in this connection, and especially if I had attempted to raise with him the question of the validity or otherwise of 'insight meditation', the result, I suspect, would have been an explosion.

Maurice's original instructor in the controversial Burmese method was, of course, Ananda Bodhi, and I gathered that he had loyally supported the Canadian monk throughout the latter's dispute with Christmas Humphreys and the Buddhist Society, even though he himself was one of the Society's vice-presidents. He supported him loyally still. In the course of his chairman's report at the Association's annual general meeting, which was held at the beginning of December, he made a point of paying 'heartfelt tribute' to Ananda Bodhi, speaking of his great qualities as a teacher and his wonderful work. Yet for all his loyalty, and despite the public eulogy, from time to time there escaped from him, almost against his will, a caustic comment, or acerbic aside, that suggested there was an element of ambivalence in his attitude towards his former teacher.

There was certainly an element of ambivalence in his attitude towards Christmas Humphreys. It might not be too much to say that his entire attitude towards the founder-president of the Buddhist Society was one of ambivalence. Publicly he sang his praises, just as he did those of Ananda Bodhi, but in private he rarely spoke of him without disparagement. At the Vihara, and in his own home, he was in the habit of referring to the older man as 'the Pope of Eccleston Square', a sobriquet which in view of Humphreys' high-handed, even dictatorial, way of running the Buddhist Society was not entirely inappropriate. But those who bestow sobriquets must beware lest they are similarly honoured. One of the more waggish, and perhaps better read, members of the Sangha Association had nicknamed Maurice himself 'the Mock Turtle' ('Mock' for short), after Lewis Carroll's famous character, as depicted by Tenniel – either because of the way in which our chairman held himself when he stood up to speak at meetings, or because in the figure of the Mock Turtle the author of *Alice's Adventures in Wonderland* had satirized the academics of his day. Personally I thought that with his baggy suit, dangling flipper-like arms, and disconsolate air, he looked much more like Tenniel's Walrus, in *Through the Looking-Glass*, despite the absence from his upper lip of that oyster-loving creature's drooping moustache.[92]

Had I then been better acquainted with psychoanalytic theory, I might have been tempted to conclude that Maurice had a problem with authority, for it was obvious that he tended to behave towards anyone higher up than himself in the organizational, religious, or social hierarchy with a mixture of respect and resentment, deference and defiance, submission and rebellion. This was all the more the case when the authority figure in question happened to be, as Christmas Humphreys was, an older man. Whether Maurice's father had been a theosophist I do not know, but his mother certainly was one. She was a member of the Hastings Buddhist group, and once told me that Maurice had had a difficult childhood. Difficult childhood or not, he had been brought up as a theosophist, and perhaps it was not without significance that the favourite target of his criticism, so far as Humphreys was concerned, should have been the latter's marked theosophical leanings. Beside bestowing on the Society's president the sobriquet of 'the Pope of Eccleston Square', he had dubbed the latter's unique mixture of Buddhist and theosophical teachings 'Christmas pudding'. This was by no means unfair. Humphreys was as much a theosophist as a Buddhist. He indeed believed – and loudly proclaimed – that as expressions of the same Ancient Wisdom Buddhism and theosophy were fundamentally identical. In his pantheon, Mme Blavatsky – a large photograph of whom dominated the Society's library – occupied a place that in effect was practically on a par with that of the Buddha. Though I was ready to acknowledge the part played by the theosophical movement in making the Enlightened One and his teaching known in the West, I no more believed that Buddhism and theosophy were identical than Maurice did. I could, therefore, agree with many of the criticisms he levelled against Humphreys on that score. I only regretted that on Maurice's caustic tongue those criticisms, objectively valid though they were, should have had an emotional edge to them that was far from objective. Perhaps it was the angry child speaking.[93]

Apart from the fact that she, too, was a Buddhist, Ruth Walshe was as different from her husband as it was possible to be. Not only was her expression as radiant as his, usually, was morose. She was as gracious in manner as he was clumsy and awkward, and as much at ease with people as he was ill at ease with them. Possessing a delightful laugh, as compared to the sardonic grin that was all he could manage, she spread sweetness and light rather than the sourness and gloom he tended to dispense and was a popular figure with the members of both Buddhist organizations, whereas Maurice, while not exactly unpopular, was few people's favourite British Buddhist. How two persons of such very diverse characters had ever come to meet and marry was a mystery of which the popular theory that 'opposites attract' seemed a quite inadequate explanation. But they had met, and they had married, and appeared to jog along together beneath the matrimonial yoke as contentedly as most married couples. I noticed, though, that Maurice rarely mentioned Ruth's name in her absence, and even then only in passing. Ruth, on the other hand, spoke of 'dear old Maurice', as she always called him, quite frequently.

In appearance Ruth was undistinguished. She was of medium height, rather slightly built, and probably had not been very pretty even as a girl. Her only remarkable feature, apart from her expression, was her hair, which was deep ginger in colour and so heavily permed as to resemble a wig. I had been writing to her, as to Maurice, while still in India, and since the correspondence was in this case of a personal rather than an official nature we were in a sense acquainted even before we actually met. But although the acquaintance was commenced at the summer school, and over the cups of tea I had with her and Maurice at their flat, it was only when Maurice stopped giving us his company on lecture days, and Ruth and I travelled down to the Buddhist Society without him, that acquaintance started developing into something like friendship. We both enjoyed these trips. Except in very bad weather, when we were glad to take advantage of the Underground, we walked up to the South End Green bus terminus and there boarded one of the red double-deckers that were usually waiting. We sat upstairs, at the front of the bus, and as the journey to Victoria took forty minutes there was plenty of time for conversation.

Ruth naturally was eager to know more about my life and work in India, and about my teachers, and I was happy to satisfy her curiosity. So far as I can remember, I never asked her about herself, as quite early in our acquaintance I had gained the impression that she did not like having to recall the past. Since she was of Austrian Jewish extraction and had, I believe, come to England as a refugee, this was hardly surprising. Her curiosity regarding my life and work in India, and my teachers, having been satisfied, our bus-top conversations were generally concerned with matters of Buddhist interest nearer home, and in this way I came to learn much about recent events with the Buddhist Society and the Sangha Association, as well as about some of the more prominent personalities involved. But communicative, even talkative, though she was, Ruth was no gossip, and I never heard from her lips an unkind word about anyone. She certainly did not share Maurice's ambivalent attitude to Christmas Humphreys. On the contrary she liked and admired the man, was tolerant of his theosophical leanings, and was a leading member of his Zen Class, Zen being the form of Buddhism to which she was most attracted. She was not attracted to the Theravāda, at least not to the kind of Theravāda that was virtually identical with Buddhist monasticism, and I gathered that she distrusted Ananda Bodhi and disliked his teaching. At the same time, she was aware of her husband's loyalty to his old teacher and of the extreme importance that 'insight meditation' had come to have for him. On one occasion, when we had become good friends and were able to confide in each other, she spoke to me frankly about this, saying, with great earnestness, 'Bhante, *please* don't criticize the *vipassanā*. Maurice's whole emotional security is bound up with it.' Unfortunately, it was difficult for me to avoid criticizing the controversial Burmese method, however tactful I tried to be. Though I never criticized it in my lectures, people often asked me what I thought of it, both publicly and privately, and in honesty I could not conceal my real views.[94]

Among those whose emotional security was *not* bound up with 'insight meditation' were the Vihara's 'Three Musketeers', jovial Alf Vial, worried-looking Mike Hookham, and smiling Jack Ireland. Alf, who was the leader of the trio, or at least its most vocal member, was a pink-faced, fair-haired man in his early or middle forties who for many years had been a communist and a shop steward. He worked as a cashier, spoke with a decidedly cockney accent, and was proud of the fact that he and his two teenage children were Bethnal Green's only Buddhists. Both Mike and Jack were somewhat younger and both were bachelors. Mike had a background in science and was engaged in scientific work of some kind. Though knowledgeable, he was a colourless sort of person, so that I find it difficult to give even a sketch of his character. Jack was quiet and unobtrusive, and like the Cheshire Cat was at times little more than a grin. All three Musketeers were great admirers of *A Survey of Buddhism*, and referred to it constantly.[95] But while Alf and Mike were strongly inclined to the Mahāyāna, particularly in its Tibetan form, and were always questioning me about the Yogācāra and the Madhyamaka, and about lamas and Tantric initiation, Jack on the other hand tended to favour the Theravāda and wanted to know about Pāli texts and translations.

Anna Phillips's plump, cheerful face had not long been in evidence at the Vihara, her effective discovery of Buddhism having more or less coincided with my own arrival on the scene. Middle-aged, and a divorcee, she was a strong, active, sociable woman for whose character 'impulsive' was probably the most appropriate single epithet, though 'good-hearted' and 'generous' would have done almost equally well, while terms such as slapdash, erratic, and reckless, would not have been entirely out of place. Since her car was at my disposal, together with herself as driver (a confident rather than a careful one), I saw quite a lot of her, and since she did not stand much on ceremony I did not find it difficult to get to know her.

11
MONKS AND LAYMEN

In 1965 I started keeping a diary. My entry for Friday 1 January began with a summary of my reflections as I faced the New Year, then went on to record the principal events of the day, which apart from the fact that there were no lectures, no classes, and no travel, was a fairly representative one. The entry was as follows:

> After twenty years in the East, I find myself, at the beginning of 1965, in England, where I have now spent more than four and a half months. Not unexpectedly, this has been a busy period, though an interesting one, and, I feel, so far as the Buddhist movement in this country is concerned, a time of crucial importance. On my arrival I found the whole British Buddhist community, practically, split as a consequence of Ananda Bodhi's almost pathologically conceited and arrogant behaviour, to say nothing of his mischievous and misleading teaching, with its dabblings in the pseudo-occult, and its irresponsible application of questionable meditation techniques (to date three persons driven insane, including one who is permanently confined to an institution, to say nothing of scores of mentally injured, alienated, or antagonized). Now, Ananda Bodhi is out, and (we hope) peace and harmony have been restored. During 1965 may I progress towards Supreme Enlightenment, and with the blessings of all the Buddhas, bodhisattvas, dharmapalas, and dakinis may the Dharma continue to spread in England!

Rose at 6.15 and attended puja in the Shrine Room with Ven. Dhammaloka (Ceylon), Ven. Maha Vichitr (Thailand), Ven. Vimalo (Germany), Rev. Kassapa (England), and Kenneth (USA) who, with Ven. S. as incumbent and Head of the English Sangha, make up our community at the Hampstead Vihara. Spent the whole morning in puja and reflection, reading the Bodhisattva Śīla and going through the various meditation texts translated from the Tibetan. Pleasantly interrupted by a phone call from Holland, from Rechung Rimpoche, whom I last saw in Kalimpong more than three years ago. Said his colleague, a Tibetan monk I probably met in India, would be coming to England for a few weeks and would like to stay with me, if convenient. In the afternoon a long talk with Mr Revill about the affairs of the London Buddhist Vihara, Chiswick. All by no means well, it seems. Read latest 'New Statesman'. Very peculiar behaviour by Vimalo; had to speak to him strongly, almost harshly. In the end he saw his mistake and apologized but the incident left me disturbed, as it showed he was not psychologically balanced, and that I would have to give attention to his spiritual development, whereas I had thought before that he was sufficiently advanced to be able to get on without my interposition. No one seems really normal. Mrs Phillips came. Discussed various people. She gave me, as a New Year present, the material for a Tibetan jacket. In the evening a long talk, about Buddhism, with Abraham's friend Ruben, who did not leave till 10.30.

Ananda Bodhi had indeed done a lot of damage. A few weeks after making this entry I met the Jungian psychiatrist Dr E. Graham Howe, author of *Invisible Anatomy* and founder of the Open Way venture, who was an old friend of the Buddhist Society and often lectured under its auspices.[96] How we came to meet I do not remember. Probably Christmas Humphreys put us in touch with each other. In the course of a pleasant and useful discussion, mainly about Buddhist meditation and the Buddhist movement in England, he told me that Ananda Bodhi had a messianic complex and that he had done untold harm to those who had come into contact with him. Ananda Bodhi's mental state had certainly given cause for concern even among his supporters.

Megalomania or no megalomania, there was little doubt that he had an exaggerated idea of his own importance, and little doubt that he had done enormous harm to at least some of those who had come into contact with him. His 'insight meditation' retreats at Biddulph involved the observing of complete silence, except for the daily ten-minute interview with the teacher, himself, and the systematic reduction of sleep to a maximum of four hours a night. Even without a form of 'walking insight meditation' that led to the unhealthy mental state for which I subsequently coined the term 'alienated awareness',[97] such a regimen, with its lack of ordinary human communication and lack of sleep, together with long periods in the same posture, was sufficiently demanding to cause nervous breakdowns and even, in the case of those who were so predisposed, to precipitate full-blown psychotic episodes.

There were also serious doctrinal misunderstandings. Sensations of pain in meditation, the meditator was told, was a sign that insight – transcendental insight – was being achieved. Experience of the *fact* of suffering thus was confused, simply on account of its occurring within the framework of meditation, with the experience of transcendental insight into the Buddha's noble *truth* of suffering – a very different thing. Moreover, the achievement of transcendental insight being equivalent to breaking one or more of the fetters binding to mundane existence, the meditator was encouraged to think that he had attained, or was in process of attaining, Stream Entry, the first stage of the transcendental path leading directly to Nirvāṇa. I had encountered misunderstandings of this kind before, in India. A Buddhist friend who had attended an 'insight meditation' course in Burma, the original home of the method, returned with a certificate stating that he had completed the course and attained Stream Entry. The certificate was signed by Mahasi Sayadaw, the leading monastic (as distinct from lay) 'insight meditation' teacher of his generation.[98]

Ananda Bodhi did not hand out certificates, so far as I know, but the fact that it was he who authenticated – or did not authenticate – the spiritual achievements of his disciples was sufficient to invest him, in their eyes, with tremendous authority, an authority which the formal 'insight meditation' interviews, with their repeated threefold prostrations, tended to reinforce. It also made the more susceptible of them dependent on his advice and approval even in quite minor matters.

But if I thought that I now had little more to learn about Ananda Bodhi, I was greatly mistaken. I in fact had a lot more to learn, as I was to discover less than a month later, when light was suddenly thrown upon him and his activities from a totally unexpected quarter.

The latter half of my diary entry introduces several new characters. Dhammaloka was a simple, scholarly monk who at Ratanasara's invitation had come from Ceylon to teach Pāli at the London Buddhist College, which as yet was no more than a weekly class or two held in the basement of the Vihara. After his arrival it transpired that Ratanasara had promised his old friend that he would meet all his travel expenses, provide him with board and lodging, and pay him a handsome monthly salary. Or rather, he had promised that the Sangha Trust would do so. As the Trust had not authorized him to make these promises on its behalf, and as it was in any case not in a position to pay anyone a handsome salary (the figure Ratanasara had mentioned was ludicrously high, especially for a monk), there was the inevitable showdown, first between Ratanasara and the Trust, and then between Ratanasara and Dhammaloka. In the end the latter, who was much less worldly-minded than his colleague, agreed to teach at the College in return for board and lodging plus a reasonable amount of pocket money. He was therefore accommodated in the house next door, which the Trust also owned and which had been divided into flats that were its principal source of income. During the time of his stay with us he proved to be a conscientious teacher, as well as a friendly and helpful member of our little community.

Kassapa was the elder of the two English novices and the one I had heard, on my first morning at the Vihara, ordering supplies on the phone and asking for the more expensive kind of salmon to be sent. I have already characterized him as saturnine. Forty or more, of medium height, and formerly a civil engineer, he moved slowly, and said very little. Occasionally, for no apparent reason, he would let out a low chuckle. As Ananda Bodhi had left him on my hands without telling me anything about him, it was only later that I came to know he had been quite ill and suffered from some form of mental illness. His GP warned me that if Kassapa stayed at the Vihara he would have to be kept under constant observation as he was suicidal and might throw himself out of the window. In fact, he added, it would be better if he did *not* stay there. He was not only suicidal but homicidal, and was more likely to kill another person than himself. In consultation with

Saddhatissa, his official preceptor, I therefore made arrangements for him to disrobe and return to lay life and, I hoped, proper medical care.

Kenneth was one of the handful of men who, during my incumbency, spent a few days or a few weeks at the Vihara, either because they were in search of peace of mind or because they wanted to have a taste of community life. I remember no more about him than I remember about Abraham's friend Ruben, who is mentioned at the end of my diary entry. Abraham himself I remember only as a youngish man with problems, who talked a lot, and who sometimes kept me up until very late at night.

As my reference to him suggests, Rechung Rimpoche was an incarnate lama whom I had known in Kalimpong.[99] Born into the aristocratic Pheunkhang family, at the age of thirteen he had been recognized as the fourteenth reincarnation of Rechung, the gifted but wayward disciple of the great yogi Milarepa and author of the famous biography of his master.[100] Like other lamas who had arrived in India in the aftermath of the Chinese occupation, he had eventually been offered employment in the West, and was now working with a Dutch scholar in Leyden. In Kalimpong he had lived with his two brothers, one of whom was also an incarnate lama, the other being the husband of the eldest daughter of the Maharaja of Sikkim. Pheunkhang-se, the married brother, was already a friend of mine, and Rechung and I were soon acquainted. During his years in the hill station he was a frequent visitor to my monastery, studied English with me, and was always ready to collaborate with me in my Buddhist activities there. By the time he left for the West he had become my closest friend among the incarnate lamas, so that when he phoned me from Holland I was glad to hear his familiar voice.

Like Kassapa, William Revill had been a civil engineer (he was now retired), but unlike Kassapa he was cheerful, talkative, and very long-winded. A white-haired, ruddy-faced bachelor who lived with his mother in one of the remoter suburbs, he often spent the whole day at the Vihara, bringing his sandwiches with him in a small attaché case that also contained an assortment of tools and copies of his most recent correspondence. Originally he came to complain about the monks attached to the London Buddhist Vihara, as the Sinhalese Buddhist centre at Chiswick was officially styled. None of them understood him, he declared, and they had treated him very badly. He was particularly critical of Vinita, a young monk with whom he had struck up a friendship which, if Revill was to be believed, was being undermined by the monk's obtuseness, intellectual dishonesty, and inability to admit that a *bhikkhu* might commit a mistake in relation to a layman. As evidence of Vinita's shortcomings, and the correctness of his own position, he produced from his attaché case copies of the letters they had exchanged over the last few months. His own were of considerable length, written in a crabbed hand with many underlinings, and so obscure and tortuous in expression that it was difficult to make out what he was saying except that he was in the right and his friend in the wrong. Vinita, a pleasant, good-natured monk whom I had met once or twice and who clearly was out of his depth dealing with someone like Revill, had confined himself to typewritten general expressions of good will and esteem that the obstinate, eccentric old man found highly unsatisfactory.

Some months later Vinita and a Sinhalese monk whom I had come to know in Calcutta, while staying at the headquarters of the Maha Bodhi Society, left England to teach at the Washington Buddhist Vihara, then the principal Theravādin centre in the United States. One day they went out together for a walk – and were not seen again. At least, they were not seen again for many months and not in America. When eventually they did resurface it was in Japan, two years later, by which time both had disrobed and married. Had they been as much out of their depth with American Buddhists as Vinita had been with William Revill, I wondered, and had this had anything to do with their dramatic disappearance from the scene?

12

THE PENALTIES OF SUCCESS

The Dharma, in the sense of the Buddha's teaching, has been described in a number of different ways. The Buddha himself described it as a raft and as a path.[101] It was a raft inasmuch as it was something to be made use of and then left behind, and a path inasmuch as it consisted of a series of steps or stages that had actually to be traversed.

Probably the best-known formulation of the path is that in which it is described as eightfold, as consisting of Perfect View, Perfect Motivation, Perfect Speech, Perfect Action, Perfect Livelihood, Perfect Effort, Perfect Mindfulness, and Perfect Meditation. Perfect View is view that is in accordance with reality, while Perfect Motivation and the rest are perfect to the extent that they are in accordance with that view. Perfect View is not easily achieved. It is achieved only with the help of, or on the basis of, right view, which is the mundane counterpart of Perfect View in the sense of being the expression of that view – or better, that vision – in conceptual terms, Perfect View or Vision itself being of the nature of a supra-conceptual, transcendental, transforming insight or gnosis.[102]

The development of right view, and therewith the abandonment of wrong view (views that are not in accordance with reality) thus is of crucial importance. Without right view it is difficult to make progress on the mundane eightfold path and without systematic progress on the mundane eightfold path it is extremely difficult to achieve Perfect Vision and thus to make progress on the transcendental path and attain, ultimately, Nirvāṇa or Enlightenment.

Right view can be expounded, and wrong views exposed as such, through the medium either of the spoken or the written word. The spoken word, by virtue of its more immediate impact, is often the more effective medium, and much of my time was therefore spent giving lectures. Besides lecturing regularly at the Vihara and at the Buddhist Society, I gave talks to the members of the provincial Buddhist groups, and on different occasions addressed divinity students, young Jews, philosophers, farmers, and theosophists. I always prepared my lectures, at least mentally and in outline, and they always contained a strongly doctrinal element. I also enjoyed giving them. In giving them I was communicating the Dharma; I was sharing my own deepest convictions and insights. But much as I enjoyed giving lectures whatever the nature of my audience, I most of all enjoyed lecturing at the Vihara and at the Buddhist Society, particularly at the Vihara. There were several reasons for this. Apart from the circumstance that in both places my audience consisted mainly of Buddhists, or at least of persons sympathetic to Buddhism, there was the fact that I lectured at both of them regularly. This meant that I got to know my audience, and they got to know me, so that as the weeks and months went by, and one lecture succeeded another, a definite rapport was established between us. It also meant that in every lecture I was able to build, at least to an extent, on all the lectures that had gone before, knowing that certain topics had already been dealt with and that the larger, more regular part of my audience was already familiar with them. This was particularly the case when I gave a whole series of lectures, as I did that winter at both the Vihara and the Society, speaking at the one on 'The Bodhisattva Ideal and the Six Pāramitās' every Sunday and at the other on 'The "Developed Buddhism" of the Mahāyāna' on alternate Fridays. Other lectures were on such subjects as the Middle Way, Tantric Buddhism, and Buddhist meditation.[103]

Many of the lectures, including those that made up the two series, covered ground that was covered in a more detailed and scholarly manner in *A Survey of Buddhism*. This made it possible for the more studious, or more inspired, members of my audience to follow up the topic of the week's or fortnight's lecture by turning to the relevant section of my book. The *Survey* itself, of course, had grown out of a series of lectures. I had given the lectures ten years ago, in Bangalore, to a mainly Indian, predominantly Hindu, gathering. I had given them without making any concessions to my audience, and now that I was speaking to a mainly English, predominantly ex-Christian audience in London I made no more concessions than I had made then. On both occasions I beat the drum of the Dharma, and blew the conch shell of the Dharma, vigorously and without compromise, and on both occasions my efforts met with a positive response, the only difference being that in England people expressed their appreciation in a more restrained fashion.[104]

There was one lecture that did not meet with a very positive response. This was an independent lecture, that is, a lecture that did not form part of a series. It was on 'The Pure Land'. I gave it at the Buddhist Society, and like the lectures that made up the two series it covered ground that was more adequately covered in the *Survey*. In Bangalore, so far as I can remember, my exposition of the Mahāyāna conception of the Pure Land, the archetypal realm where Enlightenment is more easily attained than on earth, had met with as positive a response as the rest of my lecture on the Mahāyāna schools, of which it formed part; but in London it fell flat, probably because the subject was new to my audience and, perhaps, confusing.

Not all the lectures I gave covered ground that was covered in the *Survey*, either at that time or later on. In some I explored aspects of the Dharma I had not explored before, at least in lectures, while in others I gave expression to recent developments in my thinking. The first time I did either of these things systematically, in a series of lectures, was when I gave four lectures on 'The Meaning of Conversion in Buddhism'. In these lectures, given at the Hampstead Vihara, I dealt with conversion to (and within) Buddhism in terms of Going for Refuge, Stream Entry, the arising of the will to Enlightenment, and turning about in the deepest seat of consciousness.[105] The immediate cause of my giving thought to this question was that some English Buddhists spoke of their having been converted to Buddhism (some even claimed to have converted themselves), though the fact that I had until recently been involved in the movement of mass conversion of ex-Untouchable Hindus to Buddhism must also have played a part. Short as the series was, compared with the two others I had given, it was an important one. In it I not only gave expression to some of the ideas that had come to me as a result of my realization, over the years, of the central importance in the Buddhist life of the act of Going for Refuge; I also paved the way, with the help of the concept of conversion, for the further development of those ideas. In particular I paved the way for what I have elsewhere described as 'that radical reduction of Stream Entry and the arising of the will to Enlightenment – and even of turning about in the deepest seat of consciousness – to Going for Refuge which characterized my later Buddhist thinking'.[106]

Success is not without its penalties. The fact that I was giving so many lectures, and that more and more people were coming to hear me (though they still came in their dozens, not in their hundreds), gave rise to certain problems. There was a problem of logistics, for instance, and there was a problem of space. The logistical problem was due to the fact that I lectured both at the Hampstead Vihara and at the Buddhist Society, as well as elsewhere, and that the programmes of the two establishments had to be co-ordinated. Usually Muriel Daw, the Society's black-browed, rather intense meetings secretary and I did this between us. But whenever there were arrangements for the joint celebration of a festival to be agreed upon, or a common policy on some matter of general Buddhist concern, Christmas Humphreys came instead. The first time this happened he drew from his briefcase a list of proposals which he proceeded to run through at top speed, prefacing each proposal with 'I'm sure you'll agree that ...' and ticking it off and passing on to the next one before I had a chance to say anything. When five or six proposals had been dealt with in this way I interrupted him with 'Wait a minute, Toby, I'm not sure if I agree with that,' whereupon he looked up from his list with undisguised astonishment. Evidently he was accustomed to having his proposals accepted without demur, and the possibility of my actually wanting to discuss any of them had not occurred to him. But though inclined to be dictatorial he was no fool. By the time our meeting ended he had realized I was not to be steam-rollered into agreement and had changed tack accordingly. At our subsequent meetings, therefore, agreement was always preceded by discussion, in the course of which a proposal – whether his or mine – might be amended or even dropped.

It was at one of these meetings, I think, that there arose the question of my place in British society. Just how it arose I do not remember, but at one point Christmas Humphreys told me, in all seriousness, that I ought to regard myself as being the Buddhist equivalent of the Vicar of Hampstead. If I could do that, he seemed to think, I would be doing very well for myself, besides bringing credit to British Buddhism. Though I had yet to meet the Vicar of Hampstead, who for all I knew was a very worthy gentleman, I did not relish the idea of being the Buddhist equivalent of a Christian cleric, Anglican or otherwise, nor did I see why the area of my jurisdiction should have to correspond with his. Britain was my parish, and I had no intention of allowing myself to be confined to any one part of it.

Space was a problem only at the Vihara, for whereas the Buddhist Society's meeting room held between ninety and a hundred people, the Vihara's, which doubled as the shrine-room, could hold little more than half that number. At first this did not matter, but as the weeks went by, and as attendance at my Sunday lectures gradually increased, difficulties arose. People had to sit on the floor on either side of the green-and-gold shrine, on the landing outside the door, and even at the top of the stairs, from which position it fortunately was still possible to hear my voice and follow what I was saying. Obviously, if we wanted to continue holding lectures at the Vihara the meeting room would have to be enlarged. As we – the Sangha Association committee members and I – definitely did want to go on holding them there, the Sangha Trust agreed that the partition wall between the meeting room and a second, smaller room at the back should be demolished and collapsible doors installed. This would give us an L-shaped room capable of seating ninety people that could be divided, whenever necessary, into two. While the work was being done lectures would be held amid the eighteenth-century splendours of Burgh House, in the heart of old Hampstead.

On my recommendation the contract for enlarging the meeting room was given to a young builder called Krishna Gamre. One of a small group of Indian Buddhists, all followers of Dr Ambedkar, who sometimes came to see me, he was badly in need of work and I wanted to help him. Though I was now living in England, I had not forgotten my ex-Untouchable friends in central and western India, many of whom were still suffering at the hands of the caste Hindus, and spoke about them and Dr Ambedkar and the movement of mass conversion to Buddhism whenever I had an opportunity. Earlier in the year I had spoken about them at Linacre House in Oxford, when I addressed the Hammarskjöld Society on 'What Buddhism has done for the Untouchables in India'.[107] But words were not enough. I wanted to give some practical help, on however small a scale, and the least I could do, now that I was at the Hampstead Buddhist Vihara, was to urge the Sangha Trust to give the contract to Krishna Gamre. It did not take him and his labourers – all immigrant Indian Buddhists – long to demolish the partition wall. But that was the easiest part of the job. Soon it became evident that there was much more to demolishing a wall than demolishing a wall. It also became evident that Krishna Gamre had had much less experience of building work than, in his eagerness to secure the contract, he had led me to believe, and that he was in fact quite out of his depth. I therefore had to become personally involved and ended up virtually supervising the project. There was the District Surveyor to be consulted, floorboards to be taken up, the number of joists doubled to take the weight of ninety people. Above all, there was a twenty-foot steel girder to be inserted beneath the ceiling where the partition wall had been and across the whole width of the building. As it was too long to be manoeuvred up the narrow stairs, we had to hire a crane and swing it in through the window. Miraculously, not a single pane of glass was broken. Maurice became almost ill with anxiety during this exercise, and even I felt a little worried, since I knew no more of building work than Krishna Gamre did and had only my common sense to guide me. But eventually the job was done. The collapsible doors having been hung, and the carpet relaid, I was able to go down to Camden Town and buy the additional wooden folding chairs that would now be needed. Krishna Gamre had estimated that the work of enlarging the meeting room would take altogether two weeks. In the event it had taken more than six.

Besides my ex-Untouchable friends in central and western India, there were my Nepalese and Tibetan friends in Kalimpong. I had not forgotten them either. In particular, I had not forgotten my servants and disciples at the Triyana Vardhana Vihara, the interdenominational monastery I had established on the outskirts of the town seven or eight years earlier, who continued to be financially dependent on me, as did the Vihara itself.[108] Previously I had supported them out of the donations I received and from my remuneration for articles and book reviews, but now I was living in England these sources of income had dried up. If I was not to have no alternative but to return to India I would have to find a way of raising funds where I was. Having sounded out Anna Phillips, Alf Vial, and a few others, all of whom were anxious to keep me in England, I set up a small, informal organization, the Friends of the

Triyana Vardhana Vihara, the members of which all contributed a small monthly sum towards the upkeep of the monastery and the support of its inmates. Among the two dozen members (no greater number was required) were the president of the Buddhist Society and the chairman of the Sangha Association.

Though I was the principal speaker at the Hampstead Vihara I was not the only one. Mangalo and Vimalo also spoke there occasionally, when they were in London, as did some of the more knowledgeable members of the Sangha Association. Since the lay speakers had a poor delivery (not that Vimalo was a shining example in this respect), besides being deficient in other ways, I launched the speakers' class, as it was called. Membership was open to all who were willing to prepare and give a fifteen-minute talk which would then be collectively criticized by the other members of the class. There was no honorary membership. We met every other week, initially at the Vihara but subsequently (at Christmas Humphreys' invitation) also at the Buddhist Society, and at each meeting there were three or four talks. Subjects (given by me in advance) included 'Practical Buddhism', 'The Three Jewels', 'Faith in Buddhism', 'The Message of Buddhism', 'The Symbolism of the Stupa', 'Right Action', and even 'A Teenager's View of Buddhism', the teenager in question being Alf Vial's sixteen-year-old daughter Christine. Soon the speakers class was not only improving old speakers but producing new ones, so that the Sangha Association was in a better position to respond to the growing demand for talks from schools, women's clubs, and other groups. Our 'star performers', by general consent, were Ruth and Alf, whose talks later appeared in the Association's journal *The Buddhist* (formerly *Sangha*), which I now edited.[109] Maurice either spoke very well or spoke very badly – there was no middle way. Probably because he was in the habit of doing so at college, he always spoke extemporaneously, and if he got into the right track straight away he could be brilliant and even witty. If this did not happen, he very soon lost his way and floundered from one inconsequential point to another until he dried up and had to sit down. All the time he would be frantically twiddling a pencil or fiddling with his bottom waistcoat button.

My Sunday lectures at the Hampstead Vihara were generally followed, both before and after the enlargement of the meeting room, by a little quiet socializing. People talked with one another or came up to me and introduced themselves. One evening I was approached by a young woman. She was a nurse, she said, but she also had a kind of second sight that enabled her to 'see' when someone was suffering from cancer. She was sorry to have to tell me that I had cancer of the stomach, and that I should see a doctor as soon as possible. Her words naturally gave me quite a nasty shock, especially as she obviously believed what she said and was deeply concerned for me. I therefore consulted Maurice and Ruth, both of whom strongly advised me not to go to an 'orthodox' medical practitioner but to an acupuncturist. The acupuncturist was Mr van Buren, from whom Ruth herself had been receiving treatment for some time. As a result of this treatment, so she assured me, she felt much better and was bringing up enormous quantities of mucus. (A tendency to dwell on this unpleasant subject was one of Ruth's few weaknesses.) To Mr van Buren I accordingly went. He could find no trace of cancer but said I needed treatment for my heart. He would give me a 'little prick' then and I could come for the 'big prick' in June or July (it was now mid-February), summer being the best time for the treatment of heart conditions.[110] I little knew that when I visited him for the second time, five or six months later, I would have one of the strangest experiences in my life.

13
ENTER THE SPECIAL BRANCH

One afternoon early in February I received a visit from the Special Branch. The visit was not unexpected, it being the result of a telephone call I had received that morning from Christmas Humphreys. The Branch wanted to talk to someone in the Buddhist movement about Ananda Bodhi, and he had suggested they should talk to me, as the person most likely to be able to help them with any enquiries. Would I be willing to see one of their people and tell him what I knew about Ananda Bodhi and his activities? As it seemed I did not really have much choice in the matter I agreed, and thus it was that Detective-Inspector Ginn came to be sitting in my room at the Hampstead Buddhist Vihara that February afternoon.

In the event I learned much more about Ananda Bodhi from him than he, so far as I could tell, learned about the Canadian monk from me. He was in fact extremely communicative, even chatty, possibly in order to encourage communicativeness on my part. Ananda Bodhi had recently been in Scotland, so my visitor informed me, and while there he had given a talk to a Buddhist group. (Whether or not this was the group that met at Johnstone House, the newly acquired mansion in Dumfriesshire, was unclear.) In the course of this talk he had spoken in such a way as to convince at least one member of the group, herself a Buddhist, that he was not a Buddhist monk at all but a communist who, under the cloak of Buddhism, was engaged in propagating the gospel according to Marx and Lenin. Horrified, she had written to the

Special Branch denouncing him and demanding an investigation. On their looking into the matter, Detective-Inspector Ginn continued, they had made the interesting discovery that Bhikkhu Ananda Bodhi was none other than their old friend Leslie Dawson, of whom they had lost track four or five years earlier when he suddenly 'disappeared'. Now he was again under surveillance, it seemed, for Ginn added that according to reports they had received he did not behave like a Buddhist monk. What exactly this meant I thought it best not to enquire. Except for his disregard of monastic etiquette, I had witnessed no un-*bhikkhu*-like behaviour on his part, nor had I ever heard him talk in a way that suggested he might be at heart a communist. But then, I had seen very little of him, and he had shown no sign of wanting to take me into his confidence even to a small extent. There was only one circumstance that could be regarded as being at all suspicious. This, as I explained to my visitor, was the fact that he and two of his staunchest supporters, a youngish married couple based in the West Country, had first met in Moscow, when the three of them were attending an international communist students' conference.

A few days later Mangalo told me that the previous evening while I was away at the Buddhist Society taking a meditation class, Ananda Bodhi had been to see him. In the course of the visit he had declared, in his usual dramatic fashion, that he was now trying to 'tear people away' from Buddhism as it was 'too stultifying'. How seriously were these words to be taken? Neither Mangalo nor I really knew, but if Ananda Bodhi had been indulging in that kind of talk in Scotland, and perhaps also giving expression to left-wing political views, it was not surprising that people should have started doubting his *bona fides* as a Buddhist monk or have even become convinced, in the case of at least one person, that he was not a Buddhist monk at all but a crypto-communist.

Though I found it difficult to believe that the brash, controversial Canadian monk was truly a Buddhist (as distinct from being simply the purveyor of a mixture of 'insight meditation' and psychotherapy), I found it no less difficult to believe that he was a paid-up member of the Communist Party who had become a Buddhist monk in order to propagate the gospel according to Marx and Lenin under the cloak of Buddhism. The fact that he had first met two of his staunchest supporters in Moscow, at an international students' conference, did not really amount to much. Many young people went through a vaguely 'idealistic', left-wing phase, and Ananda Bodhi, in his days as Leslie Dawson, may well have been one of these. At the same time, I could not ignore the fact that this troubled world of ours, halfway through the sixties, was still in the grip of the Cold War, with the Soviet Union and Eastern Europe ranged on one side of the great ideological divide and the United States and Western Europe on the other. Three years earlier the Cuban missile crisis had brought the world to the brink of nuclear war, but although Khrushchev had drawn back at the last minute the Soviet Union had not yet awoken from its dream of a world dominated by totalitarian Communism. As I knew from my own experience in India, its strategy included such activities as subsidizing fellow-travellers, setting up front organizations, and infiltrating cultural bodies (not to mention government departments, trade unions, and the media), and it was not inconceivable that the British Buddhist movement, tiny as it was, had been thought worthy of the KGB's attentions. The Indian Buddhist movement had certainly been infiltrated, as had a section of the Theravādin monastic order in Ceylon. I could not, therefore, altogether rule out the possibility that Ananda Bodhi was in fact a crypto-communist, or, at the very least, more of a communist than a Buddhist.[111]

Despite the Cold War, and the fact that the British Buddhist movement might have been infiltrated by communists, I took little interest in politics. Least of all did I take interest in British party politics. I knew, of course, that there had been a change of government in the autumn, but I was no more enthused by Harold Wilson's talk of the white heat of technological revolution than I had been, in India, by Harold Macmillan's talk of Britain never having had it so good.[112] But if I was not interested in British party politics I was interested in the opportunity of meeting a British politician, especially one who was a famous journalist and an author to boot. The politician was Tom Driberg, the Labour MP (and future Chairman of the Executive Committee of the Labour Party), with whose lively 'William Hickey' column I had been familiar during the war. We met in the Lobby of the House of Commons, the meeting having been arranged by Anna Phillips, who had once worked for him and who had told him that I liked his book *The Mystery of Moral Re-Armament*, a copy of which she had given me, and was planning to review it in a Buddhist magazine. So far as Anna was aware, he knew little or nothing about Buddhism, but years later I discovered, on reading his autobiography, that he wished he had kept more of his parents' Indian 'curios' – for instance, a Tibetan prayer-wheel.

At the time of our meeting Driberg was a tall, well-preserved man of sixty, with rugged features and a non-existent hairline. He received us with what was even then being described as 'old-fashioned courtesy', but when Anna, with misplaced flirtatiousness, attempted to rally him on his having neglected her for the last few months he repressed her promptly and without mercy, and I perceived that there was a streak of brutality in his composition and that he was not a man with whom it was wise to take liberties. Naturally we talked about the book, and about Dr Frank Buchman, the leader of the Moral Re-Armament Movement,[113] about whom my Bombay friend Dr Dinshaw Mehta had often spoken to me, the American evangelist's ideas on divine guidance having influenced his own.[114] As Driberg was well known for his championship of the underdog, I took the opportunity of telling him about the plight of the ex-Untouchables, and about Dr Ambedkar's movement of mass conversion to Buddhism, as well as about the visit that B. K. Gaikwad, one of the political leaders of the new Buddhists, was proposing to make to England. Our host listened with what appeared to be genuine interest and sympathy, and expressed his willingness to help with newspaper publicity in connection with Gaikwad's visit.

When the three of us had talked for half an hour Driberg obtained passes and showed Anna and me to the Distinguished Strangers' Gallery, where we spent the next half hour and more listening to the debate. We heard two short speeches, one by Quintin Hogg (the former Viscount Hailsham) and one by Anthony Crosland. Hogg was a Conservative, and thus spoke from the opposition benches, and as the Distinguished Strangers' Gallery faced these we had a good view of him as he spoke. He spoke extremely well, in the sense that his delivery was excellent and his language polished. What the debate was about I no longer remember, if indeed I ever knew. Of Crosland's speech I have no recollection whatever. But what drew my attention even more than the two speakers was the historic Chamber itself. It was much smaller than I had expected it to be, and much more 'Gothic' in style. Indeed, with its abundance of elaborately carved woodwork and heraldic reds and blues and golds it looked less like the home of a modern legislative body than a royal chapel – which is what it was originally. As I looked round at the place, and thought of the great issues that had been debated there, it was as though the fretted roof still echoed with the oratory of Canning, Cobden, and Bright, of Gladstone and Disraeli, of Lloyd George and Winston Churchill.[115]

Churchill had died the previous month, so that it was not difficult to imagine that bulky, cigar-smoking figure rising to address an anxious House in the darkest days of the war. Happening to drive past the Parliament building on a grey January afternoon, I saw the long dark lines of mourners silently waiting to pay their last respects to the great man as he lay in state in Westminster Hall. At least, I think I saw them. Vividly as the picture of Big Ben and the Houses of Parliament in the gathering dusk, the lines of mourners, the drizzle, and the occasional black-caped policeman, presents itself to my mind's eye, I may only have seen it in the newspaper the following day.

Not that I was a great reader of newspapers. I sometimes looked at the conservative *Daily Telegraph*, of which I had been a regular reader during the war, as well as at the weekly *New Statesman*, the left-wing house organ of the Hampstead intellectuals, and that was about all. In those days the press hardly ever carried material of specifically Buddhist interest. When it did so the item related, more often than not, to the Hampstead Buddhist Vihara. In the weeks following my return to the country I was in fact interviewed several times. One reporter, from a popular women's magazine, apparently thought that Buddhist monks were something to do with the Trappists.[116] Was I allowed to speak to people, she asked, or to leave the Vihara? Another wanted to know who had sent me to England, as though somewhere in the East there was a central Buddhist authority, rather like the Pope, who sent out missionaries in all directions.

But my most interesting encounter with the press came when I was interviewed by a journalist from a leading Scottish daily. He could not have spent more than half an hour with me, yet in his article, which appeared under a pseudonym, he described at length how he had asked if I would ordain him, how I had agreed, and how he had spent the weekend at the Vihara wearing the yellow robes and fasting and meditating. Apart from me, he informed his readers, he had seen nobody during that time, and the silence of the place had been uncanny.

14
A STARTLING CLAIM

The College of Psychic Science was situated down a side street in South Kensington, not far from the Underground. A product of the wave of interest in spiritualism that had struck mid-Victorian England, it offered a programme of lectures on various aspects of the paranormal as well as demonstrations of mediumship under controlled conditions. I had no special interest in either the lectures or the demonstrations, for though I knew from my own experience that things for which there was no scientific explanation did happen, and was willing to believe that not all mediums were frauds, for me such matters had no direct bearing on the living of the spiritual life. What interested me about the College of Psychic Science was the fact that its lecture room was for hire at a reasonable rate, and that the College itself was located in a part of London to which I was keen to extend the Sangha Association's activities. True, I was already giving a weekly lecture at the Hampstead Vihara, and fortnightly lectures at Burgh House and the Buddhist Society, besides occasional lectures elsewhere, but at that time I was possessed by a passion for spreading the Dharma through the medium of the spoken word. Socially and economically, South Kensington was a very different kind of place from Hampstead, and a series of lectures there might be expected to attract a correspondingly different kind of audience.

Beginning in the middle of March I therefore travelled, every alternate Wednesday, from Belsize Park down to South Kensington and to the rather gloomy premises of the College of Psychic Science. The lecture room, which was situated at the front of the building, on the first floor, seated about sixty people, and thanks to its big windows was fairly well lighted. Entrance hall, staircase, and first floor landing and passages were on the contrary all dimly lit, though not so dimly that one could not make out, through the gloom, the framed examples of spiritualist art with which the walls on either hand were entirely covered – an art of crepuscular colours in which mysterious robed figures floated through vast cathedral-like interiors. The atmosphere of the place was not exactly spooky, but one sensed that something out of the ordinary went on there.

My first lecture, on 'Buddhism and Humanism', was poorly attended, Maurice having forgotten to advertise it, and the second, devoted to 'Buddhism and Mental Health', fared only a little better; but for the third in the series we had a full house, the subject on this occasion being 'Buddhism and the Problem of Death'.

What had led me to speak on such a topic I cannot say. Perhaps I thought it might attract some of the people who attended the College's own lectures. There certainly were a lot of unfamiliar faces in the audience that evening, as well as those of Anna Phillips, Bill Revill, and Ruth, and the rest of the little contingent from the Vihara that manned the bookstall, tape-recorded my lecture, and stood at the door with the *dāna* bowl at the end of the meeting. Death was not something about which I had thought very much. Awareness of the inevitability of death had played no part in my becoming a monk, any more than it had in my realization that I was a Buddhist. I knew that I would die, but the knowledge did not go very deep until the day I heard the young English monk Khantipālo (then known as Sujiva)[117] speak on the subject at a training course I had organized for new Indian Buddhists in Poona.[118] Khantipālo said nothing I had not heard, or read, many times before. I could have been giving the talk myself. But on this occasion the familiar words took on a vital new meaning and sank deep into my heart. I *knew* that I would die. That was three years ago. Khantipālo was now in Thailand, but we were still in touch, and it perhaps was a letter from him which, by reviving memories of that day, had led me to speak on 'Buddhism and the Problem of Death'.

I began by denying that the subject was a morbid one. Far from being morbid, thinking about the fact of death was realistic, even though people who liked to think of themselves as realistic tended to be unrealistic in this regard. To speak of death in euphemistic terms, to have gloomy funerals, and to hide the dead body in a wooden box – *this* was what was really morbid. It was morbid because it represented a refusal to accept the fact of death, and it was this refusal – not death itself – that constituted the problem. The reason we refused to accept the fact of death was that we clung to 'self', and saw death as signifying loss of selfhood. We therefore feared death. Indeed, so terrible to us did loss of selfhood appear that we were unable to contemplate even the bare idea of it. This suppressed – or repressed – fear of death was the cause of much psychological disturbance. We were unable to come to terms with life – were unable to live happily – because we had not faced the fact of death. Haunted, as it were, by suppressed fear of death, we were like the man who sees a ghost but pretends it isn't there.

The problem could be solved, I declared, if we first learned to face the facts, and the recollection of death practice, one of the group of forty traditional Buddhist meditation exercises, could help us do this.[119] Having described the practice at length, I pointed out that if we bore the fact that we will die one day constantly in mind, and oriented our lives accordingly, many things now regarded as important would become unimportant. Quarrels would cease, and funerals instead of being gloomy would be relatively cheerful affairs, as they were in the Buddhist countries of Asia. Besides teaching the recollection of death practice, Buddhism studied the phenomenon of death in detail, paying greater attention to the psychological and spiritual dimensions of the process than was usual in the West. According to Buddhism death takes place in five stages. The physical senses withdraw from their respective objects, so that the external world is no longer perceived; the breath ceases; heat departs from the body; the dying person swoons; and, finally, consciousness is completely dissociated from the physical organism. Buddhism also taught that at the time of death various experiences of a hallucinatory nature could occur. One might see oneself performing past actions, whether skilful or unskilful, or see signs indicative of one's place of next rebirth.

All this was common ground to the different forms of Buddhism, I said, but Tibetan Buddhism investigated the death process in greater detail than any other school. In particular it investigated what happened in the *bardo* or 'intermediate state', the period between the ending of one life and the beginning of another. Having explained that in fact there were three *bardos*, I went on to describe each of them in turn, following the account given in the so-called *Tibetan Book of the Dead*.[120] I described how in what was termed the *bardo* of the moment of death one is suddenly confronted by the pure white light of the Void, the light of ultimate reality, and how, if one does not shrink back from it in terror, and is able to recognize it as being one's own mind in its primordial state, one achieves Liberation from the cycle of repeated births and deaths. Such an achievement was within the reach only of those who, during their lifetime, had been advanced practitioners of meditation. Next I described how in the *bardo* of (glimpsing) reality those who had been unable to achieve Liberation in the *bardo* at the moment of death are faced by a succession of glorious visions – visions of archetypal Buddhas and other divine beings; and how, if one has meditated on them during one's lifetime, and neither shrinks from their dazzling radiance nor is attracted by the duller light proceeding from the corresponding sphere of mundane existence, one attains Buddhahood in the archetypal realm. Finally, I described how in the *bardo* of seeking rebirth those who had neither achieved Liberation nor attained Buddhahood see a vision of the five (or six) spheres of mundane existence, and how, if they are attracted to the human sphere, as usually is the case, they see their future parents copulating, try to get between them, and fall into a swoon, whereupon there follow conception and, eventually, rebirth.

While I was describing the three *bardos* the audience was especially attentive, and there prevailed in the room an atmosphere the intensity of which relaxed only slightly when I went on to speak of the post-mortem rituals of Tibetan Buddhism and to draw attention to the correlation between the three *bardos* and the deep sleep, dream, and waking states, and the three *kāyas* or 'bodies' of Buddhahood. I concluded by saying that death was a problem only when it was ignored, or seen out of context. If life was understood, death was understood, and vice versa. Life and death were the two sides of the same coin. Once this was realized there was no 'problem' but only a great opportunity for which we had to prepare ourselves *now*.

After the lecture, which lasted nearly an hour and a half, several members of the audience came and spoke to me, as people often did on such occasions. The last person to come was a tall young man in a dark three-piece suit who had been sitting in the front row making notes and whom I had, I thought, seen once or twice before. 'I just wanted to tell you,' he said, 'that I have seen the pure white light.' Had almost anyone else made such a startling claim I would have been inclined to think he was either crazy or a charlatan, but so unassuming was the young man's demeanour, and so frank and trustful his gaze, that it was impossible for me not to believe that he spoke the truth. What reply I made I do not remember. Probably I simply acknowledged his communication in a way that showed him I took it seriously.

The following month he was at the Vihara for my Sunday afternoon lecture on right livelihood, and I invited him to come and see me one evening. This he shortly afterwards did, and we had a long and interesting talk, lasting until nearly midnight, in the course of which he told me his entire history. 'Quite an exceptional person,' I commented in my diary. After my next lecture at the College of Psychic Science, which this time was on 'Buddhism and Mysticism', he offered me a lift in his Volkswagen caravan, Anna's little car not being available. Not wanting to trouble him unnecessarily, and thinking that perhaps he could drop me at a convenient Underground station, I asked him how far in the direction of the Vihara he was willing to drive.

'I can drive you as far as you like,' was the cheerful response.

'Could you drive me to India?' I asked, the words springing unpremeditated to my lips.

'Yes,' he replied, his face lighting up, 'I could.'

Thus began a friendship that was to have important consequences for the rest of my life and, through me, for the future of British Buddhism.

15
THE HISTORY OF A DEPRESSIVE

Terry Delamare was ten years younger than me, and like me he was a Londoner born and bred. On the spear side he was partly of Huguenot descent, his father being a nephew of the poet Walter de la Mare, who had died as recently as 1956 but whom Terry had never met. More than once I wondered what would have happened had the two been able to meet and whether the aged author of 'The Listeners' and 'Peacock Pie' would have understood his sensitive great-nephew.

Terry's father clearly did not understand him, any more than his hypochondriacal mother did. A butcher by trade, and a Freemason who had once had the honour of welcoming a member of the royal family to his lodge, he was a stern, harsh man of decidedly Victorian views who believed that to spare the rod was to spoil the child, and the rod had certainly not been spared in Terry's case, either literally or metaphorically. One of Terry's earliest memories was of his father catching him, at the age of three, 'playing' with another little boy and thrashing him, in the interest of his morals, very severely. Whether he told me about the incident in the course of our first talk I do not remember, but I know he spoke of it, whether then or later, on only one occasion, probably because the subject was so painful. This thrashing may have prevented him from making friends with other boys at school. An only child, he grew up lonely, anxious, and withdrawn, his main concern being to guard himself against the encroachments of the outside world.

Terry

Not that he could guard himself against those encroachments completely. In particular he could not guard himself against them on Saturday mornings, when he had to help his father in the shop. The smell of blood and the sight of carcasses and sections of carcasses hanging up was bad enough. What was worse was the fact that his own special job was to kill the rabbits. If Terry did not speak of his school life (and I do not remember him speaking of it even once), uncongenial as this must have been, it probably was because the unhappiness of weekdays was quite eclipsed, in his memory, by the horror of those Saturday mornings, about which he spoke several times. He hated having to kill the rabbits, but was much too afraid of his father to refuse to do the work or even to think of refusing. Once, when we had known each other for two or three years, I suggested he tried writing about the rabbits and how he felt about having to kill them, as writing could have a cathartic effect, and he eventually made the attempt. It was not very successful. After describing how before killing the rabbits he had cuddled and talked to them, telling them how sorry he was and trying to soothe their fears, he broke out in a cold sweat and started trembling and shaking so violently that he had to stop.

The strength of his reaction was hardly surprising. He had been shown how to kill rabbits when he was ten or eleven, and had carried on killing them week after week, except when on holiday with his parents at the seaside, until well into his teens. Naturally the experience of having to do something so utterly repugnant to his feelings, and having to do it repeatedly for so many years, traumatized him deeply. But of this his parents knew nothing. They were quite oblivious to the fact that 'a soul raged in their child' – a soul which, being unable to communicate the pain it felt or even to grasp it consciously, simply shrank back into itself. Quiet and obedient, and physically healthy, Terry gave them no trouble, and they assumed he was happy. When years later, as a man of thirty-three, he tried to tell them, in a carefully-worded letter, that his childhood had not been a happy one, they were incredulous, and his mother wrote back saying, *inter alia*, 'We always thought we three got on so well together.' According to *their* lights they had been good parents. Terry had always been well fed and well clothed and had, in fact, wanted for nothing, and they were puzzled to think what had gone wrong.

Having to kill rabbits on Saturday mornings was not the only cause of Terry's later resentment against his parents, though it was perhaps the most important one. He was also bitter because they had allowed him to leave school at fifteen. His bitterness was due not so much to his having liked school as to his conviction that, having received only an elementary education, he was at a serious disadvantage when mixing with people more educated and knowledgeable than himself, whether at his place of work or socially. Such people made him feel inferior and inadequate and, therefore, nervous and tongue-tied.

Terry's place of work, at the time we met, was the New Bond Street offices of a well-known advertising agency. How he had managed to get into the highly competitive world of commercial advertising, then as popular a career choice for ambitious young men as television and computing would be in future years, he never thought it worthwhile to tell me, but I gathered that his having been 'good at art' when at school had opened a door. Once in the advertising world he had stayed in it and without actually reaching the top of the tree had done quite well, eventually joining his present firm and becoming a chief designer there. The reason for his success, he believed, was that unlike some designers he did not think of himself as an artist *manqué* and did not try to be 'creative'. He simply followed the client's instructions. Much of his work was concerned with motor vehicles, especially trucks, and his photographs of the latest model appeared regularly on the front covers of leading trade magazines.

There had been only one interruption to his career. This was when he was doing his two years' National Service, an experience that did him no harm and perhaps some good. He worked in the company office, was popular with his colleagues, and was away from the repressive and deadening influence of home. A year after leaving the army, when he was twenty-one and back at work, he married the daughter of a Jewish solicitor. They had a church wedding, and her father gave them, as a wedding present, two houses in north-west London, one to live in and one as a source of income. Terry never told me how he had met Gillian, or why he had chosen to marry her rather than any of the other women he knew, though I gathered he had not been 'in love'. What he did tell me, more than once, was what he had thought marriage would be like. It would be like living in paradise. Indeed, it would be paradise itself. It would be a supremely blissful state of perfect harmony and fulfilment that left nothing further to be desired. How he had arrived at such a conception of marriage was not clear. He could hardly have believed his parents to be living in paradise, unless he was as ignorant of their real feelings as they were of his, and it is unlikely that he had been influenced by Renaissance love poetry like that of Spenser or – at the other end of the literary scale – by modern popular romantic fiction like that of Barbara Cartland.[121]

Tennyson claimed that the peace of God came into his life when he married, and Dean Inge made a similar claim.[122] Both men married when they were over forty, after a lifetime of celibacy, and the peace of which they spoke evidently was not St Paul's 'peace of God which passeth all understanding'[123] but the peace of sexual fulfilment after a long period of abstinence and frustration. In Terry's case there had been no such period of frustration, and the peace Tennyson and the Gloomy Dean claimed to have experienced did not enter into his life at this time. Marriage nevertheless brought him a measure of sexual fulfilment (Gillian had been his first girlfriend), though he had never responded to women in a purely physical way and considered himself to be lacking in male aggressiveness. The fulfilment, such as it was, proved to be short-lived. Terry soon discovered that Gillian was a very frigid woman who found sex distasteful and who regarded copulation as an unpleasant marital duty to be got over as quickly as possible. The discovery left him more emotionally traumatized than ever. He was unable to give free rein to his feelings, and sexual intercourse, never satisfactory, became a repulsive and degrading exercise that brought on headaches and a feeling of stuffiness that gave him what he called a cotton-wool mind. Gillian herself he eventually came to despise. Though a nice person and an excellent housewife, she was naive, with many adolescent enthusiasms, and no more capable of responding to him intellectually than she was of responding sexually. That Terry should have realized this so late in the day suggests that he could not have known Gillian very well before their marriage and had, perhaps, been so convinced of the paradisal nature of marriage as to think that who one was actually married to hardly mattered.

However that may have been, for Terry domestic life was becoming unbearable. He and Gillian never argued. Perhaps it would have been better had they done so. Between them lay what has been called the silence of marriage – the silence not of mutual understanding but of mutual estrangement. To make matters worse Gillian was pregnant, and when the child came Terry felt more tied down than ever. So tied down did he feel that his attitude towards the new arrival was one of indifference, though later he grew very fond of his little daughter. Not only did he feel tied down; he felt he was spending the best years of his life simply dissipating his energies, besides which he realized how emotionally and intellectually deprived he had been as a teenager and how lacking in freedom. Eventually he came to loathe everything connected with marriage and the home. In deciding to get married, he concluded bitterly, he had acted immaturely and now was having to suffer the consequences.

At this juncture he encountered Vivien, a Chilean girl who also worked in advertising. Though in his opinion she lacked the capacity to be creative or original, he found talking nonsense with her, as he termed their light-hearted exchanges, a pleasant relaxation from his debilitating everyday experiences. Just when the friendship developed into a sexual relationship, whether shortly before or shortly after Terry left his wife, I do not know, but at the time he and I met Vivien was still his girlfriend, though they did not live together and apparently had never done so. Perhaps it was not without significance that the first time I saw her sitting primly beside Terry at one of my Sunday afternoon lectures I was uncertain if she was his wife or his sister. Despite her South American origins she was light-complexioned, with auburn hair, cold blue eyes, and full flushed cheeks, and though she was slightly built, and small in the waist, when she stood one saw that her legs were remarkably thick, almost like tree-trunks. If his friendship with her had turned into a sexual relationship while he was still living with Gillian Terry must have felt extremely guilty, for he certainly felt guilty about it after leaving the marital home, and continued to do so for some time. In his own eyes he was committing adultery, and adultery, he had been brought up to believe, was a sin. Divorce was unthinkable.

It was therefore with some trepidation that he eventually told his parents that his marriage had broken down irretrievably, and that he and Gillian were thinking the unthinkable. Though shocked and upset beyond measure, they were in no doubt as to who was to blame for the catastrophe. The culprit was Vivien. She was the fatal 'other woman' who had wrecked their son's marriage and no words were too bad for her. Thereafter she was always 'that South American bitch' or simply 'that bitch' and they refused to meet her. So far as Terry was concerned Vivien was only a minor factor in the breakdown of his marriage, but he could not tell his parents this without telling them what the major factors were, and this it was psychologically impossible for him to do. He could not speak of the chronic emotional frustration he had experienced with Gillian (sex had always been a taboo subject at home), nor could he tell them of the revelation that had finally brought matters to a head.

The revelation had come without warning, like a flash of lightning from a clear sky. There was a telephone call from Gillian to Derek at the office, as a result of which Terry was told that the two of them were having an affair. Derek was not only Terry's colleague. He was his best – in fact his only – friend, the only friend he had ever had, and he owed a lot to him. It was Derek who had taught him how to handle money, Derek whose influence had made him less self-conscious in social situations, Derek who had helped him get through many a bad weekend. And now.... Terry felt, in his own phrase, that everything had been blown sky high. At the same time, he felt free – free to tell Gillian about Vivien, and free to see Vivien herself as often as he wanted.

The fact that he was free to see Vivien as often as he wanted did not mean that all was well. On the conscious level he had no qualms about seeing her, but deep down it was another story, and each morning he woke exhausted by the conflict. He was particularly concerned for the future of his daughter Fiona, now three years old, and though annoyed with Gillian for her 'foolishness' (he used no stronger term) in becoming involved with Derek he therefore felt obliged to point out the implications, for both her and the child, of the situation in which she had landed herself. Derek was loose-living and erratic, as he well knew, and it was unlikely that she would be able to rely on him for long. With Derek, to whom he still felt a basic loyalty, he was no less frank, warning him what he had to look forward to where Gillian was concerned. Derek soon found this out for himself. Within a few months he was complaining to Terry about Gillian's lack of individuality, and the way her views fluctuated, and before long the wretched affair was over.

For some time afterwards Terry was undecided what to do. Life was proving too much for him, and initially he was tempted to creep back into the shell from which, with Derek's help, he had emerged not many years earlier. But he resisted the temptation. Instead of withdrawing, he would on the contrary face the problems that had arisen and try to understand them. The biggest of these problems was his continued lack of sexual responsiveness. In fact the problem haunted him, and convinced that unless it was sorted out his emotions could not be unblocked he sought the advice of Dr David Cooper, an associate of R. D. Laing. Cooper, with whom he was to be in contact, on and off, for the rest of his life, advised him to postpone any decisions. This advice Terry had rejected. Far from postponing any decisions, he had proceeded to abandon all interests and activities other than his job, had stopped trying to patch up his marriage, and finally had broken to his parents the news that he and Gillian were thinking of getting divorced.

The next four years – the years immediately preceding his appearance at my lecture on 'Buddhism and the Problem of Death' – was a period of psychological exploration and adjustment, mystical experience, and widening intellectual horizons. The psychological exploration took place at the London Clinic of Psychoanalysis, to which David Cooper had given him a referral. He was a patient of the Clinic for two and a half years, attending each day for fifty minutes, five days a week (except when on holiday), and paying eight shillings a session for treatment. As the Clinic was situated in New Cavendish Street he was able to get there in the morning on his way to work. Psychoanalysis freed him up sexually and, in consequence, emotionally too to an extent, and he ceased to suffer from a lack of sexual responsiveness. But sex was not everything, and in any case, even at its most satisfactory he never experienced the 'erotic glow' he had sometimes felt as a child. When he had been attending the London Clinic for two and a half years he therefore again sought the advice of David Cooper, who this time recommended that he become a short-term patient at Villa 21.

Villa 21 was an experimental therapeutic unit for young schizophrenic patients in the Shenley Mental Hospital in Hertforshire, just north of London. Cooper had started the unit in 1962 (it lasted until 1966), and it was experimental in the sense that it dealt with schizophrenic patients according to the 'family-oriented' ideology of R. D. Laing and A. Esterson.[124] That he should have thought Terry might benefit from treatment in the unit did not mean that he regarded him as suffering from schizophrenia, but only that he thought he exhibited some of the characteristics on account of which a person was labelled as schizophrenic by his family and members of the medical profession. For Cooper such terms as 'schizophrenic', 'patient', and 'treatment' were mentally to be placed within single inverted commas, and in a book published in 1971 he was to define schizophrenia as

> a micro-social crisis situation in which the acts and experience of a certain person are invalidated by others for certain intelligible cultural and micro-cultural (usually familial) reasons, to the point where he is elected and identified as being 'mentally ill' in a certain way, and is then confirmed (by a specific but highly arbitrary labelling process) in the identity 'schizophrenic patient' by medical or quasi-medical agents.[125]

Terry's parents may not have actually labelled him a schizophrenic, but they certainly regarded his evident dislike of what he called 'the stereotyped living of suburbia' as a sign of mental illness or, at least, of there being something seriously wrong with him.

The treatment Terry was given at Villa 21 was simple and, in a sense, drastic. He was given ether. There were two sessions, and on both occasions the ether was administered by a certain Dr Caple. As he wrote shortly afterwards,

> As Dr Caple administered the ether so my mind seemed to ascend one level of understanding after another. Time was the first fiction to be exposed coupled with the crippling effects that personality has upon a person's true self. As my awareness increased the frequency at which my mind seemed to function was fantastic and in contrast to that of my surroundings. I was irritated by Dr Caple's ignorance of my experience and longed for her to stop questioning me as it was time-consuming and inane. I became reluctant to talk and wished only for silence.

Presently he transcended time and the feeling he had was one of exquisite fineness – a fineness he at one stage described as the point of the point of the point of a needle. Yet knowing that there was the climax of 'no point' still to come he waited and observed. Whereupon he experienced a sensation of 'standing *in* pure knowledge' – a moment of total comprehension – that represented a human being's perfect and total development. But even this moment of 'no point' contained a subtle experience of knowing. It therefore was not the absolute experience, which was.... But what it was Terry was never able to say. Or rather, he gave different accounts of it at different times. It was a state of total oblivion, a fluorescent darkness (a description that reminded me of Dionysius the Areopagite's 'deep but dazzling darkness')[126], and even, on one occasion, an experience of being back in the womb. In his discussions with me he usually spoke of it, borrowing the language of the *Tibetan Book of the Dead* (with which he seems to have been familiar even before meeting me), as the pure white light or, more simply, as the ether experience or ether abreaction.

At both of his two sessions of treatment the experiences Terry underwent followed much the same pattern. On both occasions, ether having been administered, there was the same immediate rapid ascent through successively more refined levels of consciousness, and on both occasions, unfortunately, the same irritating questioning by Dr Caple. At one point in the second session he was so exasperated by her continual bombardment that he decided to satisfy, for a moment, her desire that he should become aggressive, and in the course of so doing demonstrated – presumably in relation to the attendants who were restraining him – 'incredible strength'. Having thus dispensed what he termed the appropriate shock treatment he returned to lying on his back and allowed the process of ascent to continue. At no stage of the ascent, on either that or the previous occasion, were there any LSD-type visionary experiences, and on both occasions the climactic moment – the moment of total oblivion – occurred simultaneously with the descent back into ordinary consciousness. The moment of 'death' was also the moment of 'birth'. But despite his having returned to ordinary consciousness it seemed to him, again on both occasions, that silence was imperative, and he attempted to remain quite mute. At the same time, coupled with a feeling of detachment and serenity, there was an intense love for, and understanding of, all the people around him, including the insensitive and talkative Dr Caple.

The ether experience had a permanent effect on Terry's thinking. It left him convinced that for human beings there were two possible approaches to reality. They could either develop an understanding of themselves and their environment over scores of lifetimes, and experience reality as the reward of their creative effort to evolve; or they could simply see that the truth, pure and unadulterated, was and always had been available and that it moreover was capable of being experienced here and now, whether by means of fasting or meditating or as the result of a drug abreaction such as he had undergone. He also realized that in the course of a lifetime a human being had to put in what seemed an unbelievable amount of effort and discipline, and this 'hideous, self-imposed struggle' he found so upsetting, when recovering after his first session of treatment, that he burst into tears. He also felt compelled to tell Dr Caple, in this connection, that she could not help him, for while her drugs were extremely potent he now knew that for him the best psychotherapy was a prolonged and sincere attempt to dispel the clouds that were obscuring the pure light of the mind.

That attempt could not be made in an ideological vacuum. It had to be made within the context of a particular philosophy, and with the help of that philosophy's special disciplines. Terry therefore started attending the meetings of a number of different organizations, from the Fabian Society to the Personalist Group, and from the Gurdjieff

Society to the College of Psychic Science.[127] He did not look for what he was seeking in any of the Christian churches, nor did it ever occur to him to look for it there. This was partly because he had not been brought up to be religious (his parents, though puritanical, had no time for religion), and partly because conventional Christian piety nauseated him. Even after he had come to regard himself as a Buddhist he saw Buddhism as a philosophy rather than as a religion, and though by no means lacking in a spirit of reverence (a phrenologist would have said that his bump of reverence was a big one) he was disinclined to join in acts of corporate worship such as pujas.

The organization whose meetings Terry attended most regularly, and whose teachings he took most seriously, during the difficult time that followed his ether experience, was the School of Economic Science. In the summer of 1965, when our paths started to converge, he was still attending classes at its premises in the Haymarket (he was to attend them until the end of the year), and in the early days of our friendship the organization and its teachings was one of the topics of discussion between us. I knew nothing about the School of Economic Science, though the name was quite familiar to me. Like many others, I had seen on the walls of various London Underground stations – usually from the other side of the track, while waiting for the train to come in – the big black-and-white posters advertising the School's courses. Later I learned it was the front organization, so to speak, for a curious amalgam of Western Esoterism and brahminical Advaita Vedanta. The Western Esoterism derived from one of the numerous Gurdjieff-Ouspensky splinter groups, while the brahminical Advaita Vedanta derived from the Maharishi Mahesh Yogi[128] and, subsequently, from Swami Shantananda Saraswati, one of the four principal Shankaracharyas[129] and a fellow disciple of the Maharishi. The School's teachings were therefore sufficiently broad, not to say eclectic. Students moreover were encouraged to read the philosophical and religious classics of both East and West. In particular, it seems, they were encouraged to read Plato, and Terry was already familiar with several of the dialogues, including *The Republic*.[130] Contact with the School of Economic Science had, in fact, widened his intellectual horizons, and he had much to be thankful to it for. But 'much' was not 'everything'. There was still something lacking....

Which was why he had started coming to my lectures at the College of Psychic Science.

16
STRANGERS HERE

What was lacking at the School of Economic Science was communication. At least, communication was one of the things that were lacking albeit perhaps the most important. The teaching given out at the classes was undoubtedly interesting and helpful, at times even stimulating, but there was no room for discussion, and Terry's soul panted for discussion as much as the Psalmist's hart panted for the water brooks.[131] He desperately wanted to be able to engage, with a sympathetic friend or two, in the kind of intellectual exchange of which the Platonic Dialogues were the supreme example. Discussion, however, was something 'School' frowned upon. Teaching was given very much *ex cathedra*, and students were not expected to ask questions or air doubts, or even to talk much among themselves during the coffee break. Communication thus was entirely one way, which meant it was not communication at all in the full sense of the term, and it was not surprising that the tutors (as the class instructors were called) should have been in Terry's opinion rather too conscious of their position.

He therefore was pleased when I asked him to come and see me one evening, and still more pleased to have the opportunity, when he took up the invitation shortly afterwards, of telling me his entire history. Two days later came my lecture on 'Buddhism and Mysticism' and our exchange about India. I had been only half serious when I asked him if he could drive me there, for I was undecided whether to go back that year or not, but an hour or two later, when we were in my room at the

Vihara, he confirmed that he was ready to accompany me there. This time, too, he stayed until nearly midnight, and I confided to my diary, 'As before, had an extremely interesting exchange of thoughts. Find he brings out what is best and deepest in me.' Thereafter our friendship developed rapidly. Usually we met once or twice a week, more often than not after Terry had driven me back to the Vihara from either a lecture at the College of Psychic Science or a lecture or meditation class at the Buddhist Society. On one such occasion, being loth to stay indoors, we went for a walk on Hampstead Heath, and despite two showers of rain (it was early July) sat on Parliament Hill talking and looking down on the lights of London until somewhere a clock struck twelve. We then drove to an Indian restaurant in West Hampstead, where Terry had a meal and I a coffee, after which he returned me to the Vihara and I gave him a copy of the *Sūtra of Wei Lang*.

Most of our conversations were *à deux*, but whenever Vivien accompanied Terry to the Sunday afternoon lecture, as she occasionally did, they would both come up to my room afterwards, and one Sunday Terry was accompanied by his younger colleague Alan who wanted to meet me. Though I knew now that Vivien was Terry's girlfriend, I was not surprised that I had at first been uncertain whether she was his wife or his sister, for they behaved more like good friends than lovers and it was obvious she had a life of her own apart from Terry and did not expect him to spend all his evenings and weekends with her. What was more, she too was looking for a philosophy, and may have attended classes at the School of Economic Science for a while. She had certainly been given a mantra, either there or at the School of Meditation (both organizations taught the so-called Transcendental Meditation introduced by the Maharishi Mahesh Yogi) and in the course of the next couple of years she was to visit me independently of Terry a few times in order to discuss her practice. Though Terry still thought she lacked the capacity to be creative or original, and though there was no question of her being the ideal partner of his youthful dreams – the partner he once hoped Gillian would be – he remained fond of her, in a detached sort of way, and was grateful for the companionship she had given him over the years.

If Vivien was more like a friend than a lover, then Alan was more like a disciple than a colleague – at least outside office hours. An unsympathetic observer might even have described him as Terry's sidekick. Short and stocky, with a square, pallid face and dark hair, and an expression at once good-natured, earnest, and puzzled, he evidently hero-worshipped Terry and hung on every word that fell from his lips. In his own way he must have been looking for a philosophy, or at least for something more than a career in advertising could give, but he had little capacity for abstract thought and I noticed, at both that and our few subsequent meetings, that he received the scraps of Gurdjieff and Plato that Terry fed to him from time to time with the same mixture of awe and incomprehension with which the average ancient Greek must have received the pronouncements of the Delphic Oracle. I also noticed that Terry adopted towards Alan an attitude that was distinctly didactic, even a shade patronizing, and that he was less open with him than he was with me or even Vivien.

The truth was that Alan did not know Terry very well. He knew nothing of the unhappy childhood, the problems with Gillian, or the two and a half years of psychoanalysis. Least of all did he know about Terry's ether experience or the effect this had had on him. In Alan's admiring eyes Terry was a young man who, besides being remarkably well versed in philosophy and psychology, had a good job in advertising, an account at the fashionable Berkeley Square branch of Lloyds, an attractive girlfriend, a Volkswagen caravan the office had jocularly christened 'the sex wagon' (Terry himself was known as 'Golden Balls' on account of his supposed success with women), and a bachelor flat in NW3.

Terry indeed was all that, but he was very much more. What Alan and others saw was only his persona, the mask he had learned to don for social purposes or, in the more radical language of an author to whose writings we were to give a good deal of attention in days to come, only the 'character armour' he had developed in order to protect himself initially from his parents but afterwards from a hostile world.[132] Behind the persona, beneath the armouring, there existed the lonely frightened child who was forced to kill rabbits, the lover who never experienced an erotic glow, the 'schizophrenic' for whom the moment of total oblivion – the moment of seeing the pure white light – was also the moment of a return to a world which, in comparison with *that*, was hell, and the desperate seeker after a philosophy within whose context he could attempt to dispel the clouds that were obscuring the natural radiance of the mind. Looking at Terry's relaxed figure as we sat talking in my room, and listening to his measured speech, it was difficult for me not to believe, as Alan and others did, that the mask *was* the man, and that the history Terry had related to me on our first evening together was a tale of 'old, unhappy, far-off things'[133] that now belonged to the past. Only gradually did I come to realize, in the course of the months and years that followed, that the account he had given me was as much synchronic as diachronic, and that my friend's past was very much part of his present reality, indeed was steadily encroaching upon it. Even his experience of the pure white light, euphoric as it had been, had left him with an existential problem to solve.

Though our conversations were interesting and worthwhile even with other people present, Terry and I found them most stimulating when there were only the two of us, which usually was the case. After these more intimate exchanges my diary for the day would include such entries as 'Felt very strong affinity', 'Long talk until 2.00 [in the morning]', 'Good quiet discussion for an hour', and 'Deep mutual exchange'. Apart from the one on Hampstead Heath, these early discussions all took place in my room at the Vihara, in the evening, and they invariably lasted a long time. But stimulating though they were, and crucial to the development of our friendship, I have no recollection of their actual content, except that I know we talked about some of the Gurdjieffian ideas Terry had acquired from 'School', and about Timothy Leary's recently published *The Psychedelic Experience* (an updated version of the *Bardo Thödol* or *Tibetan Book of the Dead*),[134] into which I had dipped at Terry's suggestion, and that I once spoke about the late great Jamyang Khyentse Rimpoche, from whom I had received a number of Vajrayāna initiations in 1958.[135] My capacity for reproducing a conversation or discussion verbatim has always been limited, so that it is not surprising that at a distance of more than thirty years, and with only a few laconic diary entries to help me, I should be able to give no more than a general idea of the kind of things Terry and I talked about at the time.

Not that this really matters a great deal. What the two of us talked about was less important than the fact that we did talk, and that our talk was of such a kind as to bring us closer together and, in this way, to forward our friendship. The key to the nature of that friendship was perhaps to be found in the word affinity, which I had used in one of my diary entries, and in a dream I had a couple of months after Terry and I met. The affinity was a spiritual, even a transcendental one. Terry had seen the pure white light and I, at the age of seventeen, had awoken to the truth of the teaching contained in the *Diamond Sūtra*

– described by Dr Conze as one of the sublimest spiritual documents of mankind – and in the words of my earlier memoirs had 'at once joyfully embraced it with an unqualified acceptance and assent. To me the *Diamond Sūtra* was not new. I had known it and believed it and realized it ages before and the reading of the *Sūtra* as it were awoke me to the existence of something I had forgotten.'[136] Neither Terry nor I had been able to remain permanently on that higher level. Both of us had been forced to descend and devote ourselves to the task of what he called dispelling the clouds obscuring the pure light of the mind and what I, more Buddhistically, thought of as self- and world-transformation in accordance with Perfect Vision.[137] But though both had descended it was as though we had descended on either side of a veil, a veil that was sufficiently transparent for us to be able to communicate with each other through it without too much difficulty.

The dream, according to my diary, was both curious and impressive. '[I] was seated round a table,' I wrote,

> with a number of other people (as at last night's meeting). In front of me, on the table, [there was] a collection of jewels, of all sorts of beautiful shapes and colours. Apparently I had been away somewhere and had brought the jewels back with me. In the dream [I] felt rather sad because no one was interested in the jewels or even wanted to look at them. Suddenly, [my teacher] Dhardo Rimpoche appeared on my left, smiling, and looked at the jewels, whereupon I felt happy and awoke.

Jewels, and objects made of jewels, often figured in my dreams, and the beautiful ones about which I had dreamt the previous night were all the Buddhist teachings I had brought back to England with me from India and which I was trying to communicate to the people attending my lectures and classes. No one appreciated those teachings at their true value, the dream seemed to be telling me. Between me and my auditors, too, there was a veil, but *this* veil was a thick and opaque one, through which it was difficult for me to make myself heard. The 'last night's meeting' was a meeting of the Sangha Trust. The meeting had been a stormy one (probably it was the one at which the Trust eventually decided, by a majority vote, to rescind its support for the London Buddhist College), and the fact that tempers had been lost and harsh words spoken must have disturbed me and left me with the impression that the Dharma was the last thing anyone really wanted to know about. Deep down I must have felt that I was 'a stranger here', a metaphysical Outsider (I had read Colin Wilson's famous book in Kalimpong),[138] so that when I came across Hans Jonas's *The Gnostic Religion* some years later I felt I was in familiar territory and that I understood what had led the ancient Gnostics to formulate their doctrine – or create their myth – of the Alien whose true home is Elsewhere and who sojourns on earth as in a foreign land.[139]

But if I was spiritually a stranger in my present environment, and an outsider, Terry was equally a stranger and an outsider in his. Inasmuch as we had both 'descended' we were in a similar predicament, and just as two exiles in the literal sense are overjoyed when they happen to meet and at once feel at home with each other, so Terry and I, recognizing that we were both citizens of another realm, were able to communicate without too much difficulty and to develop, before many weeks had passed, a friendship such as neither of us had experienced previously. I did not feel I had known Terry in a former earthly existence, nor did he entertain any such idea with regard to me. Our affinity was beyond time, so to speak, not within it. Neither did I feel that in Terry I had miraculously found my Platonic – or rather Aristophanic – other half (I have never felt that way about anyone),[140] though Terry still hoped to find the ideal partner who would enable him to experience himself more fully and function more effectively. Not that he was actively in quest of her; he was only too happy, for the present, to concentrate on developing his friendship with me.

That friendship soon was disembarrassed of any remnants of formality. Due partly to his strict and repressive upbringing, Terry in any case tended to dislike formality, preferring that human relations should be conducted on an informal basis. This did not mean that he treated people casually, much less still took liberties with them, but only that he sought to relate to them simply as fellow human beings rather than in accordance with their social or economic position. Me he never treated as a monk in the way others did; the fact that I wore a yellow robe, and was Head of the English Sangha, meant nothing to him. He even took to addressing me not as Bhante or 'Your Reverence', as everybody else at the Vihara and the Buddhist Society did, but by my Christian name, a fact that scandalized one or two good lay Buddhists when they came to know of it. I did not mind him addressing me in this way (had he thought I minded, he certainly would not have done so), even though I had never liked my Christian name and had been glad when eventually it was superseded by a Buddhist monastic one. Indeed I rejoiced that such a degree of intimacy and mutual confidence could exist between us, and that I was in contact with at least one person who was able to relate to me not as layman to monk, or even as disciple to master, but as friend to friend in the highest and fullest sense. We even talked of one day working together, though it was difficult for us to imagine what form this would actually take. Terry had his job, and a seven-year-old daughter whom he saw every other weekend; I had the incumbency of the Hampstead Buddhist Vihara, as well as my work in India, especially among the newly converted ex-Untouchable Buddhists. For the time being, therefore, we collaborated just intellectually and spiritually, by way of our late-night discussions, and did what we could for each other in small practical ways. Terry was particularly anxious to be of service to me as a designer and as the driver of a Volkswagen caravan, and towards the end of July I was able to afford him the opportunity of functioning in both these capacities.

The publishers of *A Survey of Buddhism* had written a few weeks earlier informing me that they were planning to bring out a third edition of the work, printing double the number of copies, and enquiring if I wanted to write a new preface or make any corrections. When I told Terry this he at once volunteered to design a new dust jacket for the book. I therefore let the publishers know that I would be sending them not only a new preface and a list of corrections but the draft design of a new cover too, a professional designer who was attending my lectures in London having agreed to do the work for nothing. When we had decided, after a good deal of discussion, that the cover should feature not the Buddha's whole form, as the old one did, but simply his face, Terry and I went to see Claire Maison who, I recollected, possessed a fine, rather mysterious-looking image of Sino-Japanese provenance. Terry thought the image would photograph well, Claire had no objection to him keeping it at his flat for a couple of days, the publishers signified their approval of the draft design he soon produced, and a year or so later the third edition of the *Survey* came out. Not everyone liked the black and red cover, with its simple white lettering, but Terry and I liked it, and my friend was pleased that his skills as a designer had been of use to me.

Despite having been out of England for twenty years, since my return I had done very little in the way of sightseeing. I had been to

Inside the Little Bus

Hampton Court, and had taken a young Indian visitor, the son of my old friend Dr Mehta of Bombay, to see the Tower of London, and that was about all. When Terry one day asked me if there was any place in England I particularly wanted to see, and offered to drive me there in his Volkswagen one weekend, I naturally jumped at the opportunity of seeing a little more of my native land. But was there a place I particularly wanted to see? There were so many places I had not seen, and that I would have liked to see. In the end I decided on Stonehenge. I had not seen the famous megalithic monument before, it was less than a hundred miles from London, and if I was to start contacting my roots (then a growing preoccupation in some quarters), it was surely the best place for me to begin. One Friday evening, therefore, towards the end of July, we took the M4 to Windsor and thence headed for the south-west.

It was the first time Terry and I had travelled outside London together. I usually left town only when I had a lecture to give, or a class to take, at one of the provincial Buddhist groups, but on this occasion there was no lecture to give, no class to take, and I felt freer than I had done for a long time. Probably Terry, too, felt free. He was certainly glad to be driving not just from one part of London to another, through heavy traffic, but from one part of the kingdom to another, along an open road on which it was possible to maintain a decent average speed. He was also glad that there lay ahead of us several hours of uninterrupted discussion, and lost no time coming up with one of his usual philosophical questions. This led to a small disagreement – the first we had ever had. With me it was axiomatic that a driver should keep his eyes on the road, especially when driving at speed, and that it was impossible to drive safely and carry on a serious conversation at one and the same time. Terry however thought otherwise. Two quite separate areas of the brain were involved, he explained, and in any case he had been driving since the age of sixteen and had never had an accident. Though not entirely satisfied by these arguments I allowed myself to be convinced (later I came to have complete faith in Terry's ability to keep his eyes on the road *and* carry on a serious conversation), and for the remainder of our journey the time passed all the more quickly for our being deep in discussion.

It was ten-thirty when we reached Stonehenge. To my astonishment it was surrounded by a barbed wire fence (I had not realized that vandalism was a problem) up against which several cars were parked. We parked alongside, and in the light of the headlamps were able to see the grey shapes of the Stones. Probably because they were some distance away, and because there was no object beside them – no human figures, no tree – by which to estimate their real dimensions, they looked disappointingly small, and rather forlorn, huddled together there in the middle of the desolate Wiltshire plain like so many fallen Titans.

The following morning I woke early, while it was still dark, and as soon as dawn broke sat up and looked out of the window at the Stones. I looked at them, on and off, for an hour or more, and when Terry eventually woke he looked at them too. There had been rain the previous evening, but now it was wonderfully bright and clear, without

At Stonehenge

a cloud in the blue sky, and the venerable Stones, as they stood bathed in the early morning sunshine, appeared more gold than grey. The gate did not open until nine-thirty. We therefore had time for a walk, after which Terry prepared breakfast, for the Little Bus (as he called the Volkswagen) was of the Dormobile type, and besides being capable of sleeping four persons contained a miniature kitchen and sundry other conveniences. Once inside the fence we wandered in and out among the gigantic Stones, some of which were fallen or broken, and Terry took photographs. Most impressive of all were the three trilithons, twenty or more feet in height, which stood within what remained of the great outer circle of stone uprights. Chauvinistic Indian friends (mostly upper-caste Hindus) had been fond of pointing out that India was highly civilized at a time when Britain was still sunk in barbarism, but as I looked around me that bright Saturday morning, and reflected on the skill and knowledge that must have gone into the shaping and positioning of these enormous sarsens, more than four thousand years ago, I found it difficult to believe that the builders of Stonehenge had been quite such barbarians as my Indian friends supposed.

As the place was aswarm with visitors, some clambering over such Stones as were fallen or in fragments (evidently the weekend was not the best time to see the monument), we did not stay long at Stonehenge, but drove back to Salisbury, through which we had passed the previous night. According to my diary, I thought Salisbury Cathedral the most beautiful cathedral I had yet seen, by which I probably meant that I thought it more beautiful than either Norwich Cathedral or Chichester Cathedral, those being the two episcopal seats with which I was then most familiar. But beautiful as its cathedral was we did not stay long in Salisbury either, and having left the city behind us we managed to find our way to a delightful spot by the river. Here we lay for more than an hour in the sun and here, having slept for a while, Terry made tea and we had lunch. We also had '[an] exceptionally deep exchange, perhaps our deepest so far', but regarding the nature of that exchange my diary, once again, is silent. Perhaps I was contacting my roots in more senses than one.

On our arrival back at the Vihara Terry telephoned his friend Ivan. As I already knew, Ivan was infatuated to the point of obsession with a young woman colleague of theirs who, unfortunately for Ivan, refused to have anything to do with him, and Terry was concerned for his friend's mental balance. The news was not good. Ivan had attempted to commit suicide, and Terry spent the best part of an hour talking to him and trying to persuade him not to repeat the attempt. He then signalled to me to take over from him, as he needed a break. I had not met Ivan, but Terry told him who I was and that I would like to talk to him. The minute I took over I felt I was struggling with the powers of evil. He was determined to commit suicide, Ivan said. But it was not what he said that horrified me so much as the way he said it. He sounded desperate, possessed. I had the impression I was talking not to a human being but to a demonic entity which, thanks to the state of intense, overwhelming craving into which Ivan had allowed himself to fall, had been able to enter into him and was now speaking through his lips. After Terry had talked to Ivan a second time there seemed to be an improvement in his condition, and he said he might call back before twelve. Terry therefore went to sleep in my armchair, while I told my beads, but the telephone remained silent and at twelve o'clock Terry went home, though not before we had arranged that I should let him know if Ivan called back. Fifteen minutes after he had left the telephone rang. It was Ivan, with a message for Terry. I passed the message on, and at two o'clock my friend telephoned to tell me that he had just finished talking to Ivan and hoped that everything would now be all right.

At noon next day, when I was making notes for the Sunday lecture, Terry telephoned again, this time with the news that Ivan had committed suicide. He had gassed himself, apparently during the night. I was not surprised, though I had not expected the sad and shocking event to happen so soon.

A few hours later Terry came to see me, and we discussed Ivan's death, and arranged to visit the Brighton Buddhist group together the following evening. Terry also told me that he had broken the news of Ivan's death to Nicki, the girl at the centre of the tragedy, and had brought her along to the Vihara with him to hear me speak. The lecture dealt with the arising of the will to Enlightenment, and was the third in the series 'The Meaning of Conversion in Buddhism'. Nicki sat in the front row, with Terry and Vivien – a dark-haired, white-faced figure in black that was probably not mourning. After the lecture Terry took her home, and I did not see her again.

17
VISITORS FROM EAST AND WEST

During the months that I was lecturing at the College of Psychic Science and developing my friendship with Terry Delamare I was occupied in a number of other ways too. Besides running the Vihara, visiting provincial Buddhist groups, and editing two Buddhist magazines (one of them published from Calcutta),[141] I met, and spent time with, people I had known in Kalimpong, or who had been to see me there. I also had one of the strangest experiences in my life, led three meditation retreats at Biddulph Old Hall, the last of which Terry attended, and ordained one person as an eight-precept lay Buddhist – the first time I had ordained anyone in England.[142]

Kesang Dorje was the younger daughter of Raja S. T. Dorje of Bhutan and his Sikkimese wife Rani Chuni, sister of the then Maharaja of Sikkim. Our acquaintance dated from 1950, when we met at her parents' house on the outskirts of Kalimpong, shortly after my arrival in the town. A few years later she married the King of Bhutan, Jigme Dorje Wangchuk. Apparently the union was not a happy one. At least there were serious tensions within it. The Dorje family was the second most powerful family in Bhutan, and reputedly even wealthier than the royal family itself, and the marriage between Kesang and the young ruler had been arranged, it was said, in order to consolidate the family's influence in the kingdom. Kesang's eldest brother Jigme Dorje, whom I had also known, was the (non-elected) 'Prime Minister' of Bhutan, while her astute sister Tashi sometimes represented Bhutan in its dealings with the

Indian Central Government in New Delhi. Jigme had been assassinated a year ago, when I was still in Kalimpong, and I well remembered the sensation the news of his death had caused throughout the surrounding area and the rumours to which it had given rise. One rumour attributed the assassination to a Nepalese whose brother Jigme Dorje had shot the previous year; another, to friends and supporters of the King acting, perhaps, with the connivance of the King himself. Whatever the truth may have been, Bhutan was for months in a state of turmoil and Kesang, finding herself in an increasingly difficult position, had for a time taken refuge in Calcutta. Now she was in London and had asked Christmas Humphreys to arrange a private memorial service on the anniversary of her brother's death and Toby, as he usually did on such occasions, had invited me to conduct the ceremony.

Whether by accident or design, however, he had omitted to tell Kesang this, so that when she and her younger brother Lhendup arrived at the Buddhist Society they were pleased and surprised to find that the monk who would be conducting the ceremony was the same English monk whom they and their family had known in Kalimpong. The memorial service took place in the Society's library, which I had previously made ready for the occasion. Only Kesang and Lhendup were present, together with Kesang's elder son Jigme, the future king, then nine or ten years old. After chanting the appropriate *suttas* I gave a short talk in the course of which, besides referring to Jigme's assassination, I spoke of the shortness of human life, of the inevitability of death, and of the importance of practising the Dharma while one was still in a position to do so. No doubt Kesang and Lhendup remembered, as I did, the occasion when, thirteen years ago, I had jointly conducted a similar service over the dead body of their father and had spoken in much the same vein to the grief-stricken family.[143] After I had given my talk and concluded the ceremony by chanting verses invoking on the bereaved brother and sister the blessing of the Three Jewels, Mrs Humphreys and the three women who worked in the Society's office brought in tea and soon a lighter atmosphere prevailed. Later on in the afternoon Lhendup and I were able to have a private talk, and he gave me his version of what had happened in Bhutan the previous year. He also spoke about the political situation in Sikkim, where the position of the new Maharaja, his cousin, was becoming increasingly untenable. As he did so, I could not help thinking how greatly he had changed since our last meeting. Then he had been a strapping young man whose principal interest, apart from women and drink, was football. Now he looked as though he had suffered a lot, his once stalwart frame appeared to have shrunk, and it was evident that all his old confidence was gone. Kesang, on the other hand, had changed very little, and I was glad to see she was still her sweet and gentle self. When the time came for us to part both she and Lhendup expressed a wish to see me again, and in Kesang's case, at least, the wish was fulfilled.

Four weeks after the memorial service Toby and Puck (as Mrs Humphreys was familiarly known) invited me to lunch. The Queen of Bhutan would also be coming, I was told, as would my old friend Marco Pallis.[144] This time Kesang was accompanied not by Lhendup but by Tashi, who was the elder of the two and still unmarried. As Marco Pallis (or Thubden Tendzin, as he preferred to be called) had lived in Kalimpong for several years and had known both

Luncheon party for the Queen of Bhutan, London 1965. l–r: the Queen – Kesang, her sister Miss Tashi Dorje, Marco Pallis, Sangharakshita, Mrs Humphreys

sisters, as well as their parents and other members of the Dorje family, the occasion had something of the character of a happy reunion. I myself had seen Marco only once since my return to England, and had formed the impression that he was not anxious to keep up the connection, either because he had no time to spare from his musical activities or, what was more likely, because he disapproved of my failure to adhere to the strict 'traditionalist' principles he had imbibed from René Guénon, the French Sufi master.[145] Unfortunately I had to leave early, as that evening I was giving a lecture in Birmingham. Before my departure Kesang presented me with three lengths of Bhutanese hand-woven cloth.

We met for the third and last time two weeks later, when she and Tashi attended the Buddhist Society's Wesak celebrations, which took place in Caxton Hall, Westminster. This was my first Wesak since I returned to England, and as the thrice-sacred day was the highlight of the Buddhist year I had been looking forward to it. In the event I was disappointed. Things were much the same as they had been the last time I attended the Society's Wesak celebrations, some twenty years earlier.[146] Toby was in the chair, there were speeches and a reading from the scriptures, and that was about all. The audience had not changed much in the interval either, whether numerically or in respect of its composition. There could not have been more than a hundred people in the hall, not all of them Buddhists, and including a sprinkling of colourfully attired Asian nationals. The big difference, so far as I was concerned, was the fact that twenty years ago I had been a humble member of the audience, 'taking *pansil*' from a Burmese monk and listening to the various speeches, whereas now I was on the platform, a monk myself, leading the audience in a (rather ragged) recitation of the Three Refuges and Five Precepts and giving the opening speech after being warmly welcomed by the chairman. In a way it was unfortunate that I spoke first. Back in India I had preferred to speak last on such occasions, so that if any of the previous speakers, who often were orthodox Hindus, happened to misrepresent the Dharma, I would have an opportunity of correcting them. This time there were no previous speakers to be corrected. Rather was it a question of stirring up the audience, which seemed to be in anything but a celebratory mood. I therefore spoke vigorously, reminding my listeners that what we were celebrating that day, above all else, was the supreme fact of the Buddha's Enlightenment; that by following his teaching we could achieve what he achieved; that whether followers of the Theravāda, the Mahāyāna, or any other tradition, as Buddhists we were all one in the Dharma, and that Buddhism in Britain was not going to be confined to any one school. According to a report appearing in the *Middle Way* I went on to say that I had noticed in the East that when people celebrated Wesak they were remarkably joyful, whereas in the West there was generally an atmosphere of gravity and seriousness. 'Surely when we come to a meeting like this we can concentrate our hearts on the one fact of the Buddha's Enlightenment,' I concluded, 'which should mean so much to all of us.'[147]

My words were not altogether without effect, but that effect, such as it was, was soon nullified by the other speakers. White-haired Douglas Harding, who was known to many of the Society's members through his book *On Having No Head*, lost himself and his audience in his very personal brand of 'Zen' mysticism,[148] Toby's speech was very flat, and though Marco Pallis rightly emphasized the importance of devotion in the spiritual life he did so in such a pedantic, 'old-maidish' way that few people could have been inspired by what he said. The decade had yet to learn that 'the medium is the message'.[149]

What Kesang and Tashi thought of our English way of celebrating Wesak I do not know. In Bhutan and Sikkim, as I was only too aware, the major Buddhist festivals were celebrated in a highly elaborate and colourful manner, and in Tibet this was still more the case – or had been until recently. Even in Kalimpong, where Buddhists were a minority, albeit a substantial and influential one, Buddha Jayanti – as Wesak was generally known in India – was celebrated not just with speeches but with pujas and processions and the singing of devotional songs. When I spoke to the sisters afterwards I did not, therefore, ask them what they thought of the meeting. Had I done so, they no doubt would have been far too polite to express anything save warm appreciation of our efforts. But they must have been disappointed. Certainly I was disappointed. I felt I had hardly celebrated Wesak at all, and was glad that two days later we would be celebrating the thrice-sacred day at the Vihara in what I hoped would be a very different manner. Two days later, therefore, we celebrated it not for an hour but for the greater part of the day, and not just with speeches but with a morning devotional meeting, an afternoon at-home for members and friends, and a ceremonial flower-offering by the younger devotees at the commencement of the evening public meeting.

If lawyer Christmas Humphreys was the best-known English Buddhist at the time, then probably poet Allen Ginsberg was the best-known American Buddhist. Three years earlier, when he was not even a name to me, he had come to Kalimpong in search of Tantric initiation and one afternoon had unexpectedly appeared on the veranda of my hillside monastery – a dirty, hirsute, and dishevelled figure. I had taken him to see my Chinese friend and teacher the hermit Yogi Chen, and Yogi Chen had directed him to the celebrated Dudjom Rimpoche.[150] Since then I had not seen or heard anything of the poet, and it was only when some young men came to see me that I learned, quite by chance, that he was in London. They were from the printers, the young men explained, and had come to enquire what a thousand-petalled lotus looked like. They wanted a picture of one, together with a Sanskrit *oṃ*, for the programme of the poetry reading Allen would be giving at the Royal Albert Hall in a few days' time.[151] I gave them a note for Allen, and a week later he came to see me – still hirsute, but this time clean and tidy.

We spent the whole afternoon talking, and Allen told me all about his experiences in India after leaving Kalimpong. Having visited Sikkim and met the Karmapa, the head of the Karma Kagyu school of Tibetan Buddhism, he had rejoined his 'wife' Peter in the plains and for months the two of them had lived in cheap rooms in Calcutta and in Benares, associating with ganja-smoking holy men, watching bodies being burned at the ghats, reading and writing poetry, and – eventually – being harassed by the CID. Allen had loved India, even though he had not succeeded in obtaining Tantric initiation and his guru was still William Blake. He did not play his finger cymbals and sing 'The Tyger' that day (as he did the next time we met, a decade later), but before leaving he presented me with a copy of *Reality Sandwiches*, from which he had read at the Albert Hall, and I took the opportunity of asking him what had really happened on that historic occasion. According to the press, the poetry reading had been a rowdy affair. Allen did not beat about the bush. 'I was drunk,' he said.

A few months later there was a sequel to my meeting with the Beat icon. Among the people Allen had got to know in London that summer was a young poet called Dick Wilcocks. Dick was secretary of the

Peanuts Group,[152] and Allen, the born facilitator, had told him about me and urged him to invite me to give the group a Buddhist poetry reading. This he eventually did, with the result that on the evening of 5 November – Guy Fawkes Day – Terry drove me from the staid Victorian ambiance of the Buddhist Society, where I had just spoken on 'The Schools of Tibetan Buddhism',[153] to the King's Arms public house near Liverpool Street Station, where, in an upstairs room with a bar at the other end, I read poems by Milarepa and Hanshan to an audience of about fifty people.[154] This was the first public poetry reading I had given, but the occasion was a great success, and Terry and I did not get away much before eleven o'clock.

Before my return to England I had been keenly following developments in South Vietnam, where persecution of the Buddhists by the Roman Catholic oligarchy headed by President Ngo Dinh Diem had led, towards the end of 1963, to the overthrow of his much hated regime.[155] I had been kept abreast of those developments not only by the newspapers but by my Vietnamese monk friends. The chief of these was Thich Minh Chau, who was studying at the then Nava Nalanda Mahavihara with my own teacher, Jagdish Kashyap,[156] and sometimes spent the hot weather with me in Kalimpong. One afternoon in June, the day before my meeting with Allen Ginsberg, I received a visit from the South Vietnamese ambassador. Dr Thich Minh Chau would shortly be arriving in England, he informed me. In fact my old friend did not arrive until the middle of August. He stayed with me at the Vihara for four days, and in that time did a good deal of sightseeing. With me for guide, he visited various places of historic interest in London, including Westminster Abbey, St Paul's Cathedral, and the Tower, as well as spending a few hours in Oxford, where he was particularly impressed by the Ashmolean Collection and by the 'monastic atmosphere' – it not being term time – of Christ Church and St John's.[157]

The second day of his stay happening to be a Sunday, a special meeting in his honour could be held at the Vihara instead of the usual lecture. After I had introduced him to the gathering, he spoke at length on Buddhism in Vietnam, dwelling especially on recent developments in that unhappy country, and answering questions put to him by members of the audience. What struck people most about his talk, I think, was the fact that, as he made clear, Vietnamese Buddhism was characterized by a harmonious combination of the contemplative Buddhism of the Thien or Chan school and the devotional Buddhism, centred on the figure of the 'archetypal' Buddha Amitābha, of the Pure Land school.

18
SHADOWY FIGURES AND A STRANGE EXPERIENCE

The Sangha Trust was a rather shadowy body. Or perhaps I should say the members of the Trust were rather shadowy figures. The only one I could be said actually to know was Maurice Walshe, with whom I had been in correspondence previous to my return to England. Indeed it was Maurice who, on the Trust's behalf, had invited me to spend a few months at the Hampstead Buddhist Vihara. Whether he was at that time its chairman I do not know; he was certainly chairman at least from the early days of my incumbency. He was also chairman of the Sangha Association, and in this double capacity was often to be seen at the Vihara, especially when there was an organizational crisis, at which time he would rush round from his home in a panic and generally succeed in making matters worse. Withold Stepien, an amiable but excitable Pole, was the treasurer of the Trust. He was a friend of Ratanasara, and a supporter of the latter's plans for a London Buddhist College, and it was he who, without consulting his fellow trustees, had allowed the ambitious Sinhalese monk not only to invite his old friend Dhammaloka to teach Pāli at the College but to promise him that the Trust would meet all his travel expenses, provide him with board and lodging, and pay him a handsome salary. Stepien's loyalty was to the London Buddhist College rather than to the Sangha Trust, and I knew him much less well than I knew Maurice, even, especially as he took little part in the activities of the Vihara and was seen there only occasionally – usually in the company of Ratanasara. The most shadowy figure, among the trustees, was Marcus – so shadowy that I cannot recall his first name. Marcus was a solicitor. Though not a Buddhist or even interested in Buddhism, he had been brought into the Trust in his professional capacity, and was its longest-serving member. He was seen at the Vihara, very briefly, only on the rare occasions when the Trust met, and I could not have spoken to him more than once or twice.

But though two of the three current trustees were such shadowy figures, the Trust itself was not really a shadowy body, in that it was a registered charity and controlled by statutory requirements and limitations. It was the Trust that owned the Vihara and the house next door, as well as Biddulph Old Hall, and it therefore was the Trust that, in point of fact, allowed the Sangha Association (and, latterly, the London Buddhist College) to use the Vihara premises for its activities and that invited monks to come and stay there. It was the Trust, too, that appointed the resident caretaker of the house next door, the rents from which constituted the Trust's only regular source of income.

The caretaker, Bernie Whitelaw, was a lean, hyperactive man in his late thirties, with a thin, haggard face, grey-blue eyes, and an expression that was both startled and worried. He lived with his cats in the next door basement, all the other flats in the building, with the exception of the one occupied by Dhammaloka, being let furnished to short-term tenants of various nationalities and varying degrees of rectitude. Besides the actual caretaking, Bernie had the unenviable task of advertising vacancies, interviewing prospective tenants, keeping existing tenants happy, collecting rents, and making sure nobody fell into arrears or did a moonlight flit. It was also his duty to come and see me every Saturday morning and give me, out of the rent money, the fifteen pounds the Trust allotted me each week for the housekeeping and other expenses of the Vihara. (I had no personal allowance from them.) On such occasions Bernie liked to stay for a little chat, and as he was a talkative soul I learned quite a lot about the idiosyncrasies of his tenants, the trouble they gave him with their unreasonable demands, their squabbles, and their reluctance – in some cases – to pay their rent on time. I also learned a lot about the previous occupants of the Vihara. Monks and novices, like the tenants who were their next-door neighbours, had come and gone over the years, but Bernie and his cats, in their snug basement abode, had remained a permanent fixture, and as his confidence in me increased he expressed himself about them, and their predecessors at the old Sangha House in Swiss Cottage, more and more freely.

From all this I gathered that Bernie did not have a very high opinion of the trustees, either past or present, nor view with unmixed approval what had been going on at the Vihara previous to my arrival on the scene. Though he was loyal to the Trust in his caretaking capacity, and served it conscientiously, his real connections were with the Buddhist Society rather than with the Vihara and the Sangha Association. He was an ardent admirer of Christmas Humphreys, and a faithful member of his Zen Class. His most fervent admiration, however, was reserved for the police, whose praises he sang even more frequently than he sang those of the Society's lawyer president. 'They've got this fantastic *loyalty*!' he would exclaim, his eyes shining. It did not surprise me that Bernie's best friend was a policeman. Gordon was a large, slow-moving, blond young man who, since he lived (with his wife) in a distant suburb, sometimes stayed overnight with Bernie after attending the Zen class, of which he too was a regular member. Lest there should be any misunderstanding on my part, Bernie was at pains to assure me that although he and Gordon shared the same bed on such occasions their friendship was a platonic one. Whether Toby was aware of his acolyte's enthusiasm for the force, or what he would have thought of the way Bernie distributed his praises, I do not know. I do however remember an incident which, though slight, may not have been without significance. Toby was paying me a visit, and we were standing by the window of my room talking. On happening to look out, we saw a black police car draw up outside the house next door and three or four uniformed officers get out and go inside. I knew the officers were friends of Bernie's, probably dropping in for a cup of tea and a chat, but Toby's eyes narrowed, and he watched the car for some time, apparently in order to satisfy himself that there was nothing wrong.

What Bernie had told me about the Sangha Trust, particularly its failure to submit returns to the Charity Commissioners, disturbed me. I therefore spoke about the matter to Maurice, who had already been made uneasy by the extent to which Stepien, under Ratanasara's influence, had in effect been siphoning funds belonging to the Trust into the London Buddhist College. Partly as a result of my intervention, and partly due to tensions within the Trust itself, there was a showdown, the upshot of which was that Stepien resigned as a trustee and George Goulstone was elected in his place. There was also talk of inviting Alf Vial to join the Trust, and both he and Mike Hookham in fact did join it some months later.

So far as I remember I had not heard of Goulstone before. He certainly had not been attending lectures or classes at the Vihara, even though he lived only a few hundred yards up the road. Like Marcus he was a solicitor, and Maurice, who seems to have known him socially, may well have invited him to join the Trust in his professional capacity. Unlike Marcus he was a Buddhist, of sorts. At least he had installed an image of the Buddha in the garden of his weekend cottage, so I was told, and was sponsoring a young Tibetan refugee, an incarnate lama, who had recently arrived in Oxford. I never had the opportunity of verifying the first report, but a few weeks after his joining the Trust Goulstone, a short middle-aged man who sported an imperial and dressed in black, invited me to accompany him and his wife to Oxford to meet the new Rimpoche, whom they would be seeing for the first time themselves. We reached the towery city by midday, after a pleasant drive, collected the Rimpoche, and took him to the Randolph Hotel for lunch. Throughout the meal Mrs Goulstone, a tall handsome woman I had not met before, was very gay and lively, even flirtatious, and I could not help wondering what the Rimpoche, who seemed a decent, serious young man, thought of her behaviour. As he knew Hindi, we were able to have a good discussion, and I presented him with a set of Tibetan monastic robes I had brought with me from Kalimpong and never used. From the hotel we returned him to the flat where he was living with two other incarnate lamas, Trungpa and Akong, both of whom were already known to me.[158] Trungpa and I had met in India, not long after his arrival there in 1959 as a refugee. He was only nineteen then and did not know a word of English. Since that time he had acquired a reasonably good command of the language, and I had invited him to speak at the Vihara's Wesak celebrations.

The day I accompanied the Goulstones to Oxford it was very hot. It had been hot all that week, and was getting hotter, and the fact served to remind me of what Mr van Buren the acupuncturist had said, back in February, about my needing treatment for my heart and about summer being the best time for treating that organ. In mid-July I therefore went to him for the 'big prick', as he had called it. There in fact were two pricks, one in the little finger of my right hand, the other in my right wrist. The instant he gave me them there surged up my arm, and from the depths of my trunk, a current of energy which, hitting the brain, knocked me right out of the body. I found myself located, as it seemed, fifteen or twenty feet above my own head, a little to the right. I felt quite unperturbed, as though what had happened was the most natural thing in the world. Moreover, even though I was out of the body I still had a body – a body that was in all respects identical with my ordinary physical body. (Presumably this was the *manomaya-kāya* or 'man-made body' of Buddhist tradition.) Looking down with the eyes of this body, I could see van Buren frantically massaging my legs. When I 'came to' my heart was beating faster than usual, I felt slightly sick, and I was bathed in perspiration. I also had a feeling of physical well-being such as I had never experienced before – a feeling that lasted several days.

Before I left him van Buren told me that for thirty or thirty-five minutes I had been technically dead. With this statement I was not in a position either to agree or disagree, since while looking down at myself, so to speak, I had no awareness of the passage of time. So far as I was concerned, the experience could have lasted two minutes or it could have lasted two hours. Years later medical friends assured me that van Buren was mistaken in thinking I had actually been dead. At the time of death there might well be an 'out of the body' experience, they pointed out, but it did not follow from this that an 'out of the body' experience was an experience of death. Whatever the truth of the matter, the experience I had in van Buren's consulting room, that hot July afternoon in 1965, was certainly one of the strangest in my life.

After the acupuncture I went to a tea shop with the friend who had accompanied me, and sat drinking tea outside in the sunshine feeling like one new-risen from the dead. From the tea shop we walked to Oxford Circus, and from Oxford Circus through Soho to the Charing Cross Road, where I bought a copy of P. W. Martin's *Experiment in Depth*, a Jungian work popular at the time, and where my friend left me. Having looked in a new Chinese shop and bought a small porcelain figure of Guanyin for my mother, whom I would be visiting the following month, I made my way to Cambridge Circus and so up St Martin's Lane to Monmouth Street. Here I found a shop selling Japanese arts and crafts, and on going inside found that the proprietor, a cheerful man of about forty with big, bulging eyes, had been attending my lectures at the Vihara. The name of the place was Sakura, and in years to come the obscure little Japanese shop – or rather its basement – was to play an important part in my life and in the history of British Buddhism.

19
MEDITATING AMONG THE RUINS

In Kalimpong I had been accustomed to start the day with puja and meditation, rising at dawn for this purpose and repairing to the shrine-room as soon as I had drunk a cup of tea. For the first six or seven years I spent in the town my principal practice was *ānāpāna-sati* or 'respiration-mindfulness', as it had been during my years of wandering, but from 1957 onwards there was a change. In that year, and the years that immediately followed, I received from Chattrul Sangye Dorje and other leading Tibetan lamas, including Dilgo Khyentse Rimpoche and Dudjom Rimpoche, a number of Vajrayāna initiations, as a result of which an increasing amount of my time came to be devoted to such practices as deity yoga and the Four Foundation Yogas, especially the Going for Refuge and Prostration Practice centred upon the awe-inspiring figure of Padmasambhava.[159] After my return to England I soon found that my duties as Head of the English Sangha and incumbent of the Hampstead Buddhist Vihara left me with as little time for personal meditation as for literary work. Not that I minded overmuch. For me, communicating the Dharma through the medium of the spoken word was an important spiritual practice, and one that sometimes left me, at the end of a lecture, in an exalted state of consciousness from which it was not always easy to come down. Nonetheless it was with a feeling akin to relief that one morning towards the end of May, with Ruth and the Vihara's 'Three Musketeers' for travelling companions, I left Euston for the first of the three meditation retreats I was to lead that summer for the benefit of members of the Sangha Association and other friends.

The first and second of these retreats each lasted a week, while the third lasted a whole fortnight. All three were held at Biddulph Old Hall, the Sangha Trust's meditation centre on the Staffordshire-Cheshire border. I had last visited the place early in March, when the countryside was covered in snow. Now it was spring, and since spring not only 'comes slowly up this way'[160] but stays later than it does in the south, the grounds of Old Hall were gay with clumps and banks of daffodils, the brilliant yellow of which contrasted admirably with the green of the turf and the grey of the ruins that once had been part of the original building. In India I had occasionally given instruction in meditation to individuals, but I had not led a meditation retreat for a group of people

With the Three Musketeers. l–r: Jack Ireland, Alf Vial, Sangharakshita, Mike Hookham

before, so that the first thing I had to do, on my arrival at Old Hall on that first day of the first of my summer meditation retreats, was to decide what kind of programme we should follow. As the retreat and its two successors were billed as *meditation* retreats, the practice of meditation, in the form of *ānāpānasati* and *mettā bhāvanā*, naturally had to predominate, but for obvious reasons I did not want to adopt the 'insight retreat' type of format, in which up to twenty hours of so-called *vipassanā* practice a day, combined with a complete lack of normal human communication, tended to reduce the retreatant to the zombie-like state I had observed on my very first visit to Biddulph. I therefore devised a more balanced, 'mixed' type of programme. There were altogether five sessions of guided group meditation a day, one in the morning after breakfast, three in the afternoon after an early lunch, and one in the evening. The morning and evening sessions were preceded by the performance of the Sevenfold Puja, while for the first four days the last afternoon meditation was followed by a session of the speakers' class, at which Ruth, Alf, Mike, and others spoke on different aspects of the Dharma. The atmosphere of the retreat is well conveyed in an article by Ruth that appeared in the Sangha Association's journal a few months later under the title 'Meditating Among the Ruins':

> It is difficult to convey the atmosphere of complete relaxation and, at the same time, of complete alertness. We really lived every minute of these days in such harmony with everyone and everything around us, as I had never experienced before. There was a constant two-way stream of understanding and friendship between the members of the group and, simultaneously, between teacher and pupils. And the animals were included too. The two Siamese cats who used to be so wild and destructive during their short stay at the Hampstead Vihara, that the neighbours complained bitterly, were now quite tame and part and parcel of the meditation-family....
>
> Our week passed quietly and swiftly in the routine of Buddhist practice. The day started with the sounding of the gong at 6.30 and soon after breakfast our group silently crept up the stairs leading to the Ven. Sthavira's tower-room where we always had our meditation. We were usually joined by Anna who is staying at Biddulph all the year round practising serious meditation as well

> as helping the wardens in the running of the centre. At the weekend Margaret managed to join us too and even Douglas popped up from time to time when neither the kitchen nor the garden was calling him.
>
> We always started and finished the day with puja – a little devotional Mahayana service, which included the taking of the three refuges and the five precepts. In the morning we usually had just one hour meditation – on watching breathing. The rest was spent in walking quietly amongst the shrubs and bluebells in the extensive grounds of the centre, or studying....
>
> Early lunch – the last meal of the day – and then extensive meditation on watching breathing and loving kindness with always one hour break after each hour of meditation. We could help ourselves to cups of tea, coffee or soup in our own little pantry during our off-time and if the pangs of hunger were too strong, someone might even take a chunk of bread and a little cheese. There was no 'you must not!' uttered or written on notice-boards – but, instead, it was left to each of us to decide how much of the monastic discipline he was willing to take.
>
> In the evenings in the Great Hall under the supervision of our beloved Sthavira, we had miniature speakers' training classes where we lectured on practically all the schools of Buddhism. The staff happily joined us on these occasions and once even a Buddhist couple from Manchester came along to listen in. This was so nice about Biddulph – all the people who came to work and meditate there, were practising Buddhists.[161]

I had forgotten the bluebells and the Siamese cats, but I remember Ruth and the other retreatants creeping silently up the stairs to the tower room every morning after breakfast and meditating with me there. I had already meditated on my own earlier having risen at dawn in order to do so. In between the day's sessions I gave personal interviews, discussed repair and reconstruction work with a local builder, and tape-recorded the Three Refuges and Five Precepts in Pāli for Douglas, the centre's youthful warden, who though wary of me at first (he was a disciple of Ananda Bodhi) soon realized I was not as bad as he and Margaret, his wife, had been led to believe. I also finished reading Rodney Collin's *The Theory of Eternal Life* and started on his *Theory of Celestial Influence* and on Iamblichus' *The Egyptian Mysteries*.[162] After a few days of this peaceful routine I felt almost as though I was back in Kalimpong in my secluded hillside monastery, where during the rains-residence I would concentrate on meditation and study, see only my resident students and the occasional visitor, and go no further than the garden gate.

When we were four days into the retreat I received an unwelcome reminder of the existence of the outside world. There was a telephone call after breakfast from an agitated Maurice, who told me, in his usual panicky fashion, that there was a 'crisis' at the Vihara and that immediate action was required. On my contacting Victor, the young man who was about to join our little community, he assured me that all was well, and I therefore asked him to go and see Maurice and try to sort things out. Later that morning, during the pre-lunch break, I telephoned our easily-alarmed chairman, whom Victor had by that time seen. There had been no crisis. All that had happened, it transpired, was that there had been no bread for breakfast, and that Ratanasara, instead of sending his personal attendant out to buy a loaf, had used the fact that there was no bread as an excuse for making various complaints of the 'hardship' and 'difficulty' he was experiencing at the Vihara. I was so disgusted by his total lack of the spirit of renunciation that I could not forbear speaking about the matter to Mangalo, who was then at Biddulph, though not taking part in the retreat, and he agreed with me that when it came to spreading the Dharma in England worldly-minded South-East Asian monks were useless. Nor was this the only time Ratanasara gave me cause to regret I had ever invited him to stay with us. On another occasion I returned to the Vihara to find that, in my absence, he had run up a bill for ninety-two pounds at the local delicatessen – a bill I had to pay. Small wonder that Victor, who was a shrewd judge of character, should have christened him 'King Rat'!

The fifth day of the retreat was a day of silence (there had been no talking during breaks from the third day), and instead of the speakers' class there was an extra session of meditation. A very good atmosphere prevailed, and as I had no personal interviews, and the weather was fine, I was able to spend some time strolling in the garden and grounds. The programme the following day – our last full day at Biddulph – was somewhat less demanding. We meditated as usual, but people could talk during the breaks, and in the evening there was a special Buddhist version of that old BBC favourite *The Brains Trust*.[163] I divided the retreatants into what I hoped were two evenly matched teams, which then took it in turns to ask and answer questions on the Dharma. The puja before the final meditation was more elaborate than usual.

Next morning, when we had all meditated together for the last time, those of us who were returning to London left for Congleton station. We had spent a week bathed in a special kind of atmosphere, and in the words with which Ruth concluded her article, 'this Biddulph atmosphere of calm and quiet happiness, greatly deepened through our prolonged meditation, we carried away with us when we faced the turbulent waters of the outside world once more.'[164] For me those waters, as I encountered them on my return to the Vihara that afternoon, were not so much turbulent as stagnant. It was evident that during my absence the meeting-room shrine, with its brass Buddha image, had been shamefully neglected. There were no candles, and the flowers in the vases were all withered. Having settled in, and had a talk with Victor, I went for a walk over Hampstead Heath, taking Victor with me. As it was Saturday afternoon, and the weather was fine, there were rather a lot of people about – a fact of which I was all the more conscious for being fresh from the silence and calm of the retreat. On the way back to the Vihara I bought a packet of candles and some flowers, sadly reflecting, as I did so, that Ratanasara was mindful enough of food but not, it seemed, at all mindful of the Buddha.

The second retreat took place four weeks later, and apart from the fact that there was no speakers' class it followed the same 'mixed' type of programme that I had devised for its predecessor. This time I travelled up to Biddulph not by train but by car, and thus could pay a short visit to Lichfield, which as the birthplace of Dr Johnson was to me an important place of literary pilgrimage. I had become an ardent Johnsonian at an early age, after borrowing Birkbeck Hill's six-volume edition of Boswell's *Life* from the Tooting Public Library, and in the course of the next few years managed to read practically everything the Great Lexicographer had written. Even in India I did not neglect his works completely, and once back in England had returned to them with renewed zest. It was therefore with great delight that, after visiting the fine old cathedral, I explored the four-storey corner house, now a museum, where Johnson had spent the first eighteen years of his existence, and which contained many interesting relics of his life and work. Before leaving I purchased a brass paper-knife as a souvenir, the handle of the knife being in the form of the bewigged head of the Doctor. The souvenir lies beside me on my desk as I write. Since purchasing it I have visited Lichfield more than once, and seen the corner house on the market square turn from a rather shabby museum into a smart information centre and from an information centre back into a (well maintained) museum, complete with comprehensive Johnsonian bookshop. I have also seen, seated high above the awnings of the market stalls and facing the birthplace, the massive, brooding figure of Johnson, which I do not recollect having seen on my original visit.[165]

Partly because of the weather, which was inclement for the time of year, in comparison with the first retreat the second was a little dull, though with two people, at least, I had some interesting discussions, one of them being on Jung's psychology with particular reference to the anima and animus archetypes.[166] As before, the penultimate full day of the retreat was 'peak day', as I called it, with silence being observed practically the whole time. For me the silence – and the peace – was broken by Mangalo, who, having returned earlier in the day from a trip to London, came to see me that evening full of the gossip and backbiting he had heard there. Ratanasara, he said, had not only asked him to cooperate in 'ousting' me; he had also told him that Alf Vial ought not to be a member of the Sangha Trust as he was a Mahāyāna Buddhist! It was the last straw. Such interference was not to be tolerated. On my return to London, I discussed the situation with Maurice and with Alf, and a few days later, at the same stormy meeting at which it rescinded its support for the London Buddhist College, the Trust decided that Ratanasara should be asked to leave the Vihara. The following afternoon I had a frank talk with him and communicated the Trust's decision, for which he apparently had been prepared by Stepien. According to my diary, '[It was] interesting to observe his change of tactics.' What those tactics were I have long since forgotten, but 'all ended well, and he swore eternal friendship', and I was pleased and relieved at the way things had turned out.

The third and last of the three summer meditation retreats was in point of fact two separate retreats, even though a few people from the first retreat had stayed on and joined the second. Among those who stayed on was Anna Phillips, who, as Ruth mentioned in her article, was living at Biddulph all the year round. With characteristic impulsiveness, Anna had plunged into Buddhism at the deep end. Not satisfied with attending all my lectures and classes, and being a member of the Sangha Association committee and secretary of the Friends of the Triyana Vardhana Vihara, she had persuaded her trustees to allow her to sink what remained of her capital in the purchase of a terrace property in Camden Town where she would live and create a Buddhist community. She had also asked me to ordain her as a lay sister, and I had agreed to do so on condition that she spent a year at Biddulph deepening her experience of meditation and studying the Dharma. This she was now doing, and the ordination ceremony was due to take place on the peak day of the second of the two weeks that, between them, comprised the last summer meditation retreat. Part of my time during the first week was therefore spent going through the stages of the ceremony with her, and impressing upon her the significance of the step she was taking, as well as in giving meditation interviews to her and the other retreatants, among whom there were several who had not been to Biddulph before.

Terry was one of these. Though entitled to three weeks' summer holiday, he had already made arrangements to spend the second and third of those weeks with Vivien in the south of Spain, where they in fact went every year, driving down in the Little Bus and camping. However, he was free to devote the first week to Biddulph and meditation, and we both had been looking forward to a longer period of continuous personal contact than it so far had been possible for us to have. We drove up to Old Hall via Coventry, where neither of us was impressed by the new cathedral, and that evening, after the guided group meditation, I took him through the visualization and mantra-recitation practice centred upon the figure of Vajrasattva, the embodiment of Primordial Purity.[167]

In this practice the meditator imagines a stream of milk-white nectar falling from the heart of Vajrasattva upon the crown of his head, whence it descends through the median nerve, permeating his entire being, and washing away all the defiling passions that obscure the innate purity and radiance of the mind. Terry already thought of the spiritual life in these terms. As a result of his ether abreaction, he had realized that the truth, pure and unadulterated, could be experienced here and now, and that for him – as he had told Dr Caple – the best psychotherapy was a prolonged and sincere attempt to dispel the clouds that obscured the pure light of the mind.[168] In the philosophy of Buddhism he had found a context within which, he thought, it would be possible for him to make that attempt, and I judged that the spiritual practice which would enable him to do this in the most direct and effective manner was the one centred upon the figure of Vajrasattva. We did the practice together every morning before breakfast, and in the afternoon Terry did it alone in his room while I talked with some of the other retreatants, one of whom, a young man who had been coming regularly to the Vihara for the last few months, wanted to become a *śrāmaṇera* or novice monk under my direction.

The fact that Terry and I were doing the Vajrasattva practice together, as well as meditating for five or six hours a day with everyone else, gave to our friendship a new dimension, and created between us a field of spiritual energy that was almost tangible. It was as though within the lake of silence and stillness that was the retreat (that is, the retreat at its best) there was a charmed area of intenser silence and more vibrant stillness that we alone occupied. In these circumstances communication between us naturally deepened. Besides a mysterious 'mutual revelation of loneliness', there were exchanges my diary, in its usual laconic fashion, characterizes as being, respectively, 'profound and poignant', 'intense', and 'serious and important'. There are also a few references of a more specific nature – references to a discussion on affinity, arising out of notes Terry had made earlier in the day (he was an inveterate maker of notes and filler up of notebooks), to a talk we had about his daughter Fiona, and to a long walk in the course of which we touched on 'deepest themes'. One of those themes was his ether abreaction, and I think it was only then that I fully appreciated the effect the experience had had on him and the extent to which it determined the way he thought about himself and about the spiritual life. By the end of the week I was not only well satisfied with the progress of our friendship but felt I understood Terry better than before. I also realized there was a qualitative difference, so to speak, between him and the rest of the people on the retreat, genuine as their interest in Buddhism and meditation may have been, up to a point. Victor and certain of the other young men (not excluding the one who wanted to become a novice monk) were capable of behaving, on occasion, in a crude and insensitive fashion, but Terry was invariably mindful, invariably well-mannered, and invariably sensitive to the feelings of others, besides being possessed of a depth of seriousness which they entirely lacked.

On the last day of the retreat Terry and I slipped out after the evening puja and meditation and drove to Rudyard Lake. Having walked round it, and explored the picturesque countryside nearby, we found a quiet spot at the edge of a field and there passed the night in the Little Bus. The weather next day was exceptionally fine, and it was with reluctance that, around noon, we returned to Biddulph, having spent the morning in serious talk. Before leaving the place we said our goodbyes, in case we should not be able to do so in private at the meditation centre, and I hung my rosary round Terry's neck and asked him to wear it while he was away. We both were much affected by the thought of our impending separation. After lunch I saw Terry and others off, and a little later found myself being taken by bubble car to Manchester, where I met the members of the Manchester Buddhist Society at the home of Connie Waterton, the secretary of the group, and gave a public lecture in a hired hall. Having stayed up late several nights running I was feeling extremely tired, even after two or three cups of tea, but an energy from deep within came to my rescue and the lecture, which was on Tibetan Buddhism, was pronounced a great success.

20
AN IMPORTANT MILESTONE

Ordination was a subject that had preoccupied me for some time. In 1959, five years before my return to England, I had written an article entitled 'Ordination and Initiation in the Three Yanas', the purpose of which was to distinguish, firstly between ordination (*saṃvara*) and initiation (*abhiṣeka*), and secondly between the different kinds of ordination. The three *yānas* in question were the Hīnayāna, the Mahāyāna, and the Vajrayāna, representing the three successive phases of historical development through which Buddhism passed in India, as well as the three successive stages of spiritual ascent through which the individual Buddhist, according to the late Indo-Tibetan tradition, passes on his way to supreme Enlightenment. Speaking of the difference between ordination on the one hand and (Tantric) initiation on the other I pointed out that according to that tradition the rite of admission to the status of lay brother (*upāsaka*), no less than to that of novice monk (*śrāmaṇera*), full monk (*bhikṣu*), or bodhisattva, was termed a *saṃvara*, literally 'restraint', 'control', 'obligation', or 'vow'.[169] This was an important discovery. As I wrote many years later in *The History of My Going for Refuge*,

> The fact that admission to *upāsaka*, *śrāmaṇera*, *bhikṣu*, and *bodhisattva* status was in each case termed a *saṃvara* or 'ordination' meant that the differences between the various grades of religious persons were of far less significance than they were

> sometimes thought to be. In particular it meant that the difference between the monk and the layman was not a difference between the ordained and the unordained. Both monks and laymen were ordained persons and both monks and laymen were, therefore, full members of the Buddhist spiritual community. This came very close to saying that *saṃvara* or ordination was a unifying rather than a dividing factor in Buddhism, and therefore very close to saying, as I afterwards did say, that ordination and Going for Refuge were in fact synonymous and that Going for Refuge was a unifying factor in Buddhism – indeed, that it was *the* unifying factor.[170]

In latter-day Theravāda Buddhism, as this had developed in Ceylon and the other Buddhist countries of South-East Asia, ordination was definitely *not* a unifying factor. In those countries ordination was identified exclusively with monastic ordination, whether as a novice monk or as a full monk, with the result that the difference between monks and laymen was a difference between the ordained and the unordained. Until quite recently the handful of monks living and teaching in England had all been Theravādins, and they had introduced into British Buddhism, as a matter of course, the rigid separation of the monks from the laity which was so prominent a feature of Theravāda Buddhism and which they tended to regard as part of the natural order of things. Monks did not eat with the laity, for example, and the fact that at the Buddhist Society's summer school I chose not to adhere to this convention, as monks attending previous summer schools had done, was the occasion of a certain amount of astonishment – and a good deal of pleasure. Broadly speaking, the Buddhist Society, which provided a platform for all schools of Buddhism, preferred not to emphasize the division between monks and lay people (though monks were always treated with respect), whereas the Sangha Association, whose allegiance was to the Theravāda and which described itself as 'supporting a community of Buddhist monks', not only emphasized the division but like the Sangha Trust, its sister body, in fact had that division for its constitutional basis and *raison d'être*. This was one of the reasons for the tensions that had developed, in recent years, between the Society and the Association – tensions which Ananda Bodhi's abrasive personality, and his assumption that he, as a monk, was the sole authority on what was Buddhism and what was not had increased to the point where there was an open breach between the two organizations. In these circumstances it was not surprising that a year before I returned to England Christmas Humphreys should have written to me, apropos of my expected arrival, that there could be no question of a red carpet welcome at the start, the Buddhist Society being, at that moment, frankly 'sick to death of the word "Bhikkhu"!'

During the year that had passed since my return I had been able to heal the breach between the Buddhist Society and the Sangha Association, to an extent, as well as to convince at least some people that the division between monastic order and laity was less great than they had supposed. In an editorial on 'Sangha and Laity', published in the February issue of *The Buddhist*, I went so far as to assert that 'to the extent that they, too, have gone for refuge to the Buddha, the Dharma, and the Sangha, the laity are as much Buddhists as are the members of the Monastic Order', and that monks and nuns, lay brothers and lay sisters, 'together form one great spiritual family'.[171] Knowing that most Theravādin monks would reject as ridiculous, even blasphemous, the idea that the laity were *as much Buddhists* as were members of the monastic order, I was careful to add that in so far as between the monk and the layman there was a difference of commitment there was traditionally also a difference in their respective duties, the monk being expected to study, practise, and disseminate the Dharma and the lay disciple to give material support to the sangha (i.e. the monks) and fulfil at least the basic ethical requirements of the Buddhist way of life. Nonetheless, in the concluding paragraph of the editorial I observed:

> At this stage in the development of the Buddhist movement in England it is unlikely that the traditional pattern of Sangha–laity relations will be perpetuated in the extreme form that it has taken in some parts of the Buddhist world, and perhaps undesirable even if it were possible. The few bhikshus present in this country have, inevitably, to be more deeply involved in organizational problems than they might care to be, while the laity – as witness the newly formed Speakers' Class – are obliged to take a more active part in the propagation of the Dharma than they might feel really qualified for. Nevertheless, if without confusing their distinctive functions this development helps to bring Sangha and laity closer together, and strengthens their common devotion to the Three Jewels, it will be fully justified.[172]

In ordaining Anna Phillips as a lay sister I was actually doing more than just bringing Sangha and laity closer together: I was demonstrating that the two bodies overlapped. They overlapped by virtue of the fact that the ceremony in which Anna became a lay sister was not merely a simple lay 'precept-taking' ceremony, such as was customary in Theravādin countries, but a *saṃvara* or rite of (lay) *ordination* – a rite that registered as definite a commitment to the spiritual life as did that of monastic ordination. In a report that appeared in *The Buddhist* Anna's ordination was therefore correctly described as 'an important milestone in the development of Buddhism in this country.'[173] It was a milestone not because it was the first time a particular Eastern Buddhist ceremony had been performed in the West, for in the East, as represented by the Theravādin countries of South-East Asia, lay ordination, as distinct from the taking of the lay-disciple precepts, was quite unknown. It was a milestone – and an important one – because it served to make British Buddhists aware of the fact, of which they had not been aware before, that there was such a thing as lay ordination, and that the ordained lay person was as much a member of the Buddhist spiritual family as a monk or nun. Anna's ordination as a lay sister thus constituted a milestone on the road that led me, eventually, to the crucial realization that 'commitment (to the Three Jewels) is primary, lifestyle secondary.'[174]

Though in my address on the occasion I made it clear that Anna was being *ordained*, probably not one of the twenty people who witnessed the ceremony had even an inkling of what this signified. (It was years before I realized its full significance myself.) Most of the twenty were already at Old Hall on retreat, following the 'mixed' type of programme I had devised earlier and working their way up to peak day and Anna's ordination, and of these the majority were not people who had stayed on from the previous week but new arrivals. Among the new arrivals were Gerald Yorke and Jack Ireland, who this time came without his brother Musketeers, a Swedish youth, an Austrian Buddhist from Vienna, a young man who was mixed up with the black arts, and an elderly Frenchwoman. The elderly Frenchwoman was Antoinette Willmott, who was married to an Englishman, who lived with him in France, who attended my lectures whenever she was in London visiting her daughter, and who was to become a lifelong friend and supporter.

The ordination took place in the Great Hall, which was decorated for the occasion. After the gathering had taken the Three Refuges and

Five Precepts in the traditional manner, and Mangalo and I had chanted the *Karaṇīyamettā Sutta* or 'Discourse on Loving-Kindness',[175] Anna came forward and kneeling before me asked me to give her the Three Refuges together with the Eight Precepts of the lay disciple. She made the request using the traditional Pāli formula, which she had learned by heart, whereupon I asked her if she realized the seriousness of the step she was taking and if she was free of such other obligations as would interfere with the discharge of her responsibilities as a lay sister. To both questions she replied in the affirmative. A short catechism followed. What were the four noble truths? What were the steps of the Noble Eightfold Path? What were the three categories of the training? To these questions, too, Anna gave satisfactory answers. She then left the room, returning after a few minutes wearing a Tibetan-style gown (she had cropped her curly brown hair some time ago) and followed by two women attendants bearing flowers, candles, and incense. I then gave her the Three Refuges and Eight Precepts of the lay disciple and announced that henceforth she would be known as Amritapani or 'Nectar-in-Hand'; after which she offered the flowers, candles, and incense at the shrine as a sign of her commitment to the Three Jewels; Mangalo and I chanted verses of blessing; and amid the congratulations of the gathering the 'solemn and impressive ceremony', as *The Buddhist* afterwards called it, came to an end.[176]

But solemn and impressive as the ceremony was, I detected in the celebratory atmosphere of the retreat that morning an element that was not quite Buddhistic. On reflection I realized that this was due to the fact that some of the women present, quite unconsciously, responded to the ceremony emotionally as though they were witnessing not an ordination but a wedding. They even referred to the two older women who acted as Anna's attendants and who accompanied her to the altar, so to speak, as her 'matrons of honour'. It was as though they somehow felt that Anna was 'taking the veil', with all that the phrase suggested in the way of union with a heavenly bridegroom. Anna – or rather Amritapani – herself appeared to be untouched by any such feeling, and I was confident that in becoming a lay sister she had genuinely committed herself to the Three Jewels. Whether she would be able to sustain that commitment through the years to come was another matter.

By the following morning, the morning of our last full day at Old Hall, the atmosphere of the retreat had changed from the celebratory to the deeply peaceful, and it remained deeply peaceful up to the time of our departure the next day. Like most of the retreatants I left Biddulph soon after breakfast, though not without first having a final word with Amritapani. I was glad that in the course of the summer I had been able to spend four weeks on retreat, one of them together with Terry, and glad that it had been possible for me to devote more time than usual to meditation. I was also glad that I had not only gone through the Vajrasattva visualization and mantra-recitation practice with Terry but taken it up again myself, and resolved that after returning to London I would continue to do it every morning before breakfast.

Since I returned to find myself caught up in a busy weekend (it was the weekend of Minh Chau's visit), this was more easily resolved than done, though it *was* done, at least for a few weeks. The ensuing fortnight was no less busy. During that time I gave lectures and took classes, compiled an issue of *The Buddhist*, saw the Three Musketeers and sundry other people, at least two of whom were mentally disturbed, and spent my fortieth birthday at Rayleigh with my mother.

Marking as it does the beginning of the inevitable decline into old age, one's fortieth birthday is generally supposed to be a time of serious reflection, but in my own case I do not recall having had any particularly serious thoughts in connection with the anniversary. My diary certainly records no such thoughts. As it was a year since I had seen my mother, I travelled down to Rayleigh two days before the actual date, so that we would have a little more time together.[177] She was very glad to see me, I gave her the white porcelain Guanyin I had bought on the day of my 'out of the body' experience, and we spent the rest of the day very quietly, going for a walk in the afternoon and watching television in the evening – the first time I had watched it. The following afternoon we took the bus into Southend, where we sat in deckchairs on the front for a while, enjoying the sunshine and the sea breeze, and where we had tea. In the evening we spent an hour with my sister Joan and her husband Eddie, who since my last visit had moved to Rayleigh, and I gave Joan and David, her younger son, the presents I had bought for them in Southend. David, now twelve, was much quieter than he had been before, and obviously devoted to his baby sister, who had arrived at the beginning of the year and whom I was asked to name. I named her Kamala, or 'Lotus', which years later, as a teenager, she chose to reduce to Kay.

Next day was my birthday, but after lunch I was obliged to bid my mother an early goodbye. The Buddhist Society's annual summer school was due to begin the following afternoon, and I had much to do at the Vihara before leaving for High Leigh.

21
THE DIVINE EYE AND DIALECTIC

While it is possible to fall in love instantly ('Whoever loved, that loved not at first sight?'),[178] friendship requires time for its development and even for its recognition as being such. Though I had taken seriously what Terry told me, after my lecture on 'Buddhism and the Problem of Death', about his having seen the pure white light, and though I had commented in my diary, after hearing his entire history, 'A quite exceptional person', I cannot say I felt particularly drawn to him in a personal way at that time or that I envisaged a friendship developing between us. As we got to know each other, however, a friendship did develop – and develop rapidly. We discovered we had a spiritual, even a transcendental, affinity, and communication between us accordingly deepened. At Biddulph it had deepened still further, with the result that by the end of Terry's week there with me I was not only well satisfied with the progress of our friendship but felt I understood him better than before.

Perhaps I understood myself better too. It was not simply that I was well satisfied that the friendship between Terry and me was making good progress. I realized that Terry himself had come to occupy an extremely important place in my life and that if anything untoward was to happen to him I should feel I had suffered an irreparable loss. Until I received the letter in which he informed me that he and Vivien had arrived safely at their destination in the south of Spain, after a non-stop twenty-four-hour drive, I therefore felt increasingly anxious about him, imagining all sorts of dangers and disasters. The long-awaited letter came on my birthday (the postal service between Spain and England was very slow), and the extent of my relief – and the nature of my expectations – is evident from what I wrote in my diary. 'He is all right. Big load off my mind. Can hardly imagine what future may bring.' A few days later, in the middle of the summer school, Terry telephoned me to say he was back in England. As it happened, I had promised to perform a name-giving ceremony at the Vihara the following afternoon, and we therefore arranged to meet there shortly afterwards.

The name-giving ceremony was for the infant son of Ken Pardoe, a burly, bearded young Midlands Buddhist who was attending the summer school. After collecting Olive and the baby from Eltham we drove through the dense rush-hour traffic to Hampstead, I performed the ceremony in the meeting room, before the green-and-gold shrine, and bestowed on the little boy the three names his parents had chosen for him, the middle name being a Buddhist one. In India I had performed scores of name-giving ceremonies, most of them for children of the newly converted followers of Dr Ambedkar, but this was the first time I had performed a name-giving ceremony in England. Though I was happy to oblige Ken and his wife on this occasion, my feelings about such ceremonies were mixed, and I certainly had no wish to see performing domestic rituals for the lay community becoming a regular part of the duties of a British Buddhist monk. On leaving the meeting room I spoke briefly to Ratanasara, who happened to be visiting the Vihara, and a few minutes later Terry arrived.

For some time we could hardly speak, and we realized – if we had not realized it before – how deep a feeling we had come to have for each other. To me it was almost as though Terry, after being dead for three weeks, had been miraculously 'restored to life and power and thought'. Eventually we found our tongues, and with an intermission at our usual Indian restaurant in West Hampstead, where Terry had a meal, we talked until half-past four in the morning. Whether on account of the stimulating and refreshing character of our exchange, or simply because we were glad to be together again, neither of us felt in the least tired, and before parting we arranged to visit the Brighton group in a few days' time and Maidstone and John Hipkin the weekend after that. Though I did not get to bed until nearly five o'clock, I rose at half-past seven, roused Ken, who had slept in the meeting room, and at eight o'clock, after drinking a cup of tea, left the Vihara with him for High

Leigh. We arrived in time for breakfast, after which I led the morning session of guided group meditation, attended Toby's talk on Zen, and in this way eased myself back into the whirl of activities that was the Buddhist Society's summer school.

As it was my second summer school, and as it followed much the same programme as before, my impressions of it are less vivid than those of my first, and I have few distinct recollections of what I did that week. The Recording Angel, in the form of the Notes and News section of the October *Buddhist*, credits me with having delivered fourteen lectures and talks, and conducted twelve guided group meditation classes and three devotional meetings, besides participating in the brains trust and giving many personal interviews.[179] Such recollections as I do possess relate to the violent toothache I suffered for two days as a result of an abscess, which eventually burst, and to the evening devotional meetings I conducted in the Oak Room on the last three days of the school. In the course of the devotional meetings the participants made offerings of flowers, lighted candles, and incense at the improvised shrine, and recited verses expressive of reverence for the Three Jewels. I remember these meetings because they were very much an innovation, and because Christmas Humphreys had doubted whether more than a handful of people would want to attend them – nine or ten at the most, he thought. In the event, practically the whole summer school attended on all three days, only Toby and his immediate entourage remaining aloof, which suggested that some British Buddhists, at least, understood that in order to achieve a balanced approach to the spiritual life it was essential to cultivate the spiritual faculty of faith (*śraddhā*).

The Brighton Buddhist group was run by Carl and Violet Wragg, a white-haired, septuagenarian couple who had become interested in Buddhism only a few years previously, after a lifetime of involvement with spiritualism. As theirs was one of the provincial groups I visited regularly, I had come to know both of them quite well, and indeed regarded them as friends. Terry knew them too, as he had accompanied me on more than one of my Brighton visits and once, when I was on retreat at Biddulph, had actually gone and led the guided group meditation class on my behalf. On the occasion of the visit that had been arranged at the time of our reunion, a few days before, we met beneath the indicator at Victoria Station as usual and caught the six-thirty train. We were soon deeply absorbed in discussion, so deeply that we were astonished when we saw rising sheer on either side the white chalk-cliffs that showed we had reached our destination. A member of the group was there to meet us and drive us to the month's venue, the group's meetings being held sometimes at the treasurer's house and sometimes in a rented room above the Tatler restaurant. Later they were always held at the Wraggs' house in nearby Hove, in a downstairs room whose doors opened into the garden and where a permanent shrine had been set up.

The name of the Tatler restaurant has remained lodged in my memory, not on account of the number of times we met on its premises, but because of an experience Violet had there during one of my lectures, an experience about which she told me some time afterwards. While I was speaking, she said, she saw standing behind me a strange figure, rather larger than life, who appeared to be overshadowing me and inspiring me. He was clad in a red robe and wore a curiously shaped red hat, and although his features were of a decidedly oriental cast they were neither Indian nor Chinese but somehow both. From this description I had no difficulty recognizing Padmasambhava, the Greatly Precious Guru, whose form I had been accustomed to visualize as part of the Going for Refuge and Prostration Practice. Neither Violet nor Carl had even heard of him before. They knew nothing of Tibetan Buddhism, and had only a limited acquaintance with Buddhist doctrine and history. Their interest in Buddhism was practical rather than theoretical, and Violet, whom I knew to be psychic, was a serious meditator. A few years later there was to befall me, in the Wraggs' own sitting room, an experience in connection with Violet no less remarkable than the one that had befallen her at the Tatler restaurant in connection with me.

John Hipkin was a personable, confident, and highly articulate young man who lived at the Blue House, a sixteenth-century farmhouse located about seven miles out of Maidstone. He lived there with his wife Bronwyn and his friends John and David, who like himself were teachers. John Eliot – 'the other John' as he was called – was his best friend, and in so far as the four young people – the married couple and the two single men – shared the expenses of the place it could be regarded as a commune. I do not remember when or where John Hipkin and I first met, but it must have been either at Eccleston Square or at a meeting of the Cambridge University Buddhist Society (Cambridge was his Alma Mater and he was, or soon would be, a Fellow of King's), for he had no connection with the Hampstead Buddhist Vihara at that time and joined the Sangha Association only later at my suggestion – an act which was to have consequences that could not then have been foreseen. Wherever it was we met, we had taken to each other, and at the beginning of the year I had spent a couple of days at the Blue House with him and the other members of the commune. Naturally we discussed Buddhism, and as 'the other John' was a Methodist lay preacher and one of the friends who dropped in was preparing for the Methodist ministry (another was an ex-*śrāmaṇera*!), the question of the relation of Buddhism to Christianity in general and to Methodism in particular, as well as to psychology and existentialism, inevitably arose. Though discussion was at times very lively, it was both serious and friendly, and I confided to my diary, 'Very much impressed by the spirit of these young people.' John Eliot seemed particularly open-minded, and he evidently had read quite widely in Buddhism. John Hipkin, though no less open-minded, had read much less widely, and on the second day of my stay we therefore visited the new County Library and I selected for him, from the rather good section on Buddhism, some half a dozen books to read. This would be his 'homework' for the next three weeks, I told him. Since then we had kept in touch, our most recent meeting having taken place at the summer school. Probably it was on that occasion that John had suggested Terry and I pay him a visit some time during the weekend after next.

As I was free that weekend (except for the Sunday afternoon meeting at the Vihara), my friend and I did not drive straight to Maidstone. Instead, we made an extensive detour, spending two nights on the road and taking in Rochester, Canterbury, Ashford, and Tenterden. In Canterbury we looked round the cathedral. 'Very much impressed,' my diary recorded. 'Like projection of contents of own mind.' Whether both of us were impressed, or only I was (on a subsequent visit Terry was decidedly not impressed by the 'ecclesiastical goings-on', as he called them), and what I could have meant by the comment that the interior of the vast Gothic structure was like a projection of the contents of my own mind, I am now quite unable to remember. What I do however recall is the atmosphere of the place, which was quite unlike the atmosphere of any of the cathedrals I had hitherto visited or was to visit in years to come. But distinctly as I recall it, I can find no words to describe that atmosphere, though such epithets as 'warm and golden' and 'harmonious and gracious' may give an indication of the kind of effect it had on me both at the time and subsequently.

It was on a gloriously fine Sunday morning that Terry and I arrived at the Blue House, there to be welcomed by John and Bronwyn and the others. Not long after our arrival a pure white bird – either a dove or a pigeon – came and settled on the roof of the garage, where it stayed for half an hour. The bird had not been seen before, and its appearing when it did seemed like a good omen – an omen that portended the success of our visit. Good omen or not, the visit certainly was a success. Terry got on well with the Johns (owing to his high standards he did not always find it easy to get on well with people), and in the discussions which we had with them and with the various friends who dropped in both before and after lunch he acquitted himself admirably. It was not just that he had a good mind. He was a formidable dialectician who invariably succeeded in driving his opponent, step by relentlessly logical step, into a corner from which there was no possibility of escape.

I use the word 'opponent' advisedly. For Terry, anyone with whom he became locked in serious discussion (myself alone excepted) represented a threat. He was *dangerous*. He was dangerous because he was powerful and because, being powerful, he might want to harm Terry, or even destroy him. He therefore had to be *defeated*, for an opponent defeated was an opponent rendered powerless and, therefore, incapable of harming one. Consciously or unconsciously, Terry regarded discussion as being like a game of chess, in which one picked off one's opponent's pawns, bishops, and other inferior pieces until his king was left defenceless and could be immobilized and checkmated. The only difference was that Terry played not to win so much as to prevent the other person from winning; he had no wish to harm his opponent, but wanted only to make sure his opponent could not harm *him*.

His dialectical method was in a way Socratic, for like the Socrates of at least some of the Socratic dialogues he was concerned not to advance any thesis of his own but simply to undermine whatever thesis might be advanced by his interlocutor. In this he was often highly successful, at times leaving his opponent totally nonplussed and on the verge of an existential crisis, much as Socrates sometimes left a respondent feeling as though he had been stung by an electric ray whose touch temporarily paralyses.[180] On future occasions Terry was to give John Hipkin – himself no mean debater – a taste of this kind of treatment, thus earning his deep respect, but in the present discussions he made no attempt to press home his advantage over either of the two Johns, though leaving them in no doubt as to his dialectical ability. He therefore was no less satisfied with our visit to the Blue House than I was, and when the time came for us to set out for London we both regretted having to leave.

Though now living in Kent, John Hipkin kept up his connections with Cambridge (he and Bronwyn were soon to move there), especially his connections with King's College. It was in a room at King's that I had addressed the Cambridge University Buddhist Society back in April – eight months after my arrival at the Hampstead Buddhist Vihara. The reason for the delay was that Ananda Bodhi had quite a following among the undergraduate members of the society, some of whom were strongly opposed to my being invited to speak, the Canadian monk having told them – as it seems he had told everybody else – that I had been 'thrown out' of the Hampstead Buddhist Vihara. The leader of this group was one Lance Cousins, a pretty, effeminate-looking youth who besides being a member of the Cambridge University Buddhist Society was also a member of the Sangha Association, and who shortly after my arrival in England came to see me at the Vihara. The opposition had eventually been overcome with the help of Dr Carmen Blacker, the lecturer in Japanese at the University, who I believe was then either senior chairman or senior treasurer of the Society, and John Hipkin himself may well have played a part. He certainly played a part some two years later, when Lance Cousins and his supporters again tried to prevent my being invited to speak by the Society and were again defeated.[181]

Not all Ananda Bodhi's followers were as blindly devoted to him as young Lance. Some of them, much as they might have benefited from his 'insight meditation' teaching, or have relished his 'hell and brimstone' style of lecturing, were by no means unaware of the fact that their hero's character was deeply flawed, and could even make jokes at his expense. Maurice Walshe, who in any case was more devoted to the so-called *vipassanā* than to Ananda Bodhi himself, and in whose attitude to his old teacher there lurked (as I had noticed quite early on) a distinct element of ambivalence, was one of these. Clare Sampson was another. At the time of my arrival on the scene she was secretary of the Sangha Association, and having been re-elected to the post a few months later worked with me, quite happily, for the whole of the ensuing year. Svelte and sophisticated, and the daughter (so I was told) of a titled woman, twenty-year-old Clare to the best of my knowledge was the Association's sole socialite member. At first she came and consulted with me at least once a week, wearing a black sheath dress and a string of pearls and with her blonde hair dressed in the fashionable 'beehive' style. Though she took her duties as (honorary) secretary of the Association seriously, and was helpful to me personally in a number of ways, she never attended my meditation classes, or went on retreat with me, and was hardly ever seen at lectures – least of all when they took place at the Buddhist Society. Like Maurice, she had practised 'insight meditation' under the guidance of Ananda Bodhi, and after the Canadian monk's abrupt departure had continued, like Maurice himself, to practise it under the guidance of Vichitr whenever the plump Thai happened to be in London. Unlike Maurice she had little or no interest in Buddhism, and when she relinquished her post in order to have more time for her social life (she was said to have set her cap at Jeremy Thorpe, the future leader of the Liberal Party) I was not greatly surprised.

22
AN INQUISITIVE PRINCESS

The British Buddhist movement was very small – much smaller than I had imagined it to be when I was still in India. Because it was so small, it felt it needed to keep up its connections with the wider Buddhist world, and the Buddhist Society, as represented by Christmas Humphreys, had long made a point of laying on a reception for any prominent Asian Buddhist who happened to be visiting, or passing through, London, regardless of whether they were monk or layman, and regardless of the school of Buddhism to which they belonged (before my arrival the Sangha Association had honoured only Theravādin monks in this way). I was therefore not surprised to learn, towards the end of September, that the president and council of the Society were giving a reception to two leading Thai Buddhists who were then in town and that I was among those invited to attend the function.

The two visitors were Princess Poon Diskul, a cousin of the King of Thailand, and Mr Aiem Sanghavasi, president and honorary secretary respectively of the World Fellowship of Buddhists, and the reception was held at the Society's premises in Eccleston Square. Princess Poon was no stranger to London. As she reminded her hosts and the other guests, when replying to Christmas Humphreys' words of welcome, she had first visited the Society in 1930 with her late father, Prince Damrong, while her uncle, the late King Chulalongkorn, had been a patron of the original Buddhist Society of Great Britain and Ireland in 1907.[182] Toby was obviously gratified by these references to the (present)

Buddhist Society's history, as he had a strong sense of tradition, and was particularly proud of the Society's links with the Thai royal house. What the purpose of her present visit was Princess Poon did not say, but knowing that she and Sanghavasi were already preparing for the Fellowship's next conference (conferences were held every two years, each time in a different Asian country) I assumed the pair were in London to consult with Christmas Humphreys, who I believe was one of the vice-presidents of the Fellowship, about the choice of venue.[183]

The World Fellowship of Buddhists had been founded at Kandy, Ceylon, in 1950, by Dr G. P. Malalasekera, the distinguished author of the *Dictionary of Pāli Proper Names*, who some years later became the Ambassador for Ceylon in the USSR, where he had persuaded the State Publishing House (so he once proudly told me) to print 40,000 copies of a Russian translation of the *Dhammapada*. Short, plump, and amiable, Malalasekera invariably dressed – at least when abroad – in traditional Sinhalese costume, consisting of white sarong, long white overshirt, and a sort of embroidered stole. He and I had corresponded during my Kalimpong days, when we were both being violently attacked in the pages of the fanatical, but mercifully short-lived (Theravādin) Buddhist paper the *Buddhist World*, but it was not until our paths happened to cross in England that we actually met.[184] I do not remember all the grounds on which the paper's fiercely 'orthodox' and (as I afterwards discovered) alcoholic editor attacked Malalasekera, but one of them certainly was that he was sympathetic to the Mahāyāna and had by inviting the 'heretical' Mahāyānists to join his organization in effect recognized them as genuine Buddhists, despite their not being followers of 'the pure pristine Dharma', as the editor and his associates were pleased to term the Theravāda. Malalasekera was what I called a liberal Theravādin (I had no quarrel with the Theravāda as such, if by Theravāda one meant simply the teaching of the Buddha as contained in the Pāli canon), and there were many issues on which we were in hearty agreement, though I suspect he would have been dismayed by some of the later developments in my thinking, had he lived to see them.[185]

To date there had been seven conferences of the World Fellowship of Buddhists, the last having taken place towards the end of 1964. It had taken place at Sarnath, near Benares, where according to tradition the Buddha spent the rainy season after his Enlightenment explaining to his five former companions in asceticism the Middle Way he had discovered.[186] Toby and Puck attended as delegates of the Buddhist Society, and a brief mention of the conference appears in the former's autobiography, *Both Sides of the Circle*. 'We listened to the reports of the delegates, and the splendid speeches,' Toby wrote, 'and I played my part in the work of the committees. There was much talk of what should be done but little of who would do it, or how and when.'[187] In the 'official' account he produced at the time for the *Middle Way* he was less dismissive, though even here he spoke of 'tedious messages from Heads of State' and resolutions that were 'so many pious platitudes'.[188]

I did not attend the conference, and probably would not have attended it even if I had been in India at the time instead of being newly arrived in England. I had not attended any of the Fellowship's previous conferences, though often urged to attend by friends who thought it would be worth my while to do so. It was not that I disagreed with the Fellowship's 'ecumenical' objectives, or that I was not happy to meet brother and sister Buddhists from different parts of the Buddhist world. Such was far from being the case. But experience had convinced me that gatherings of this sort were more or less a waste of time, and that I, for one, was better occupied getting on with my own work, of which in any case I had more than enough to keep me busy. As for meeting Buddhists from different parts of the Buddhist world, living in India as I did I met them anyway, either at the Maha Bodhi Society's Calcutta headquarters or at one or other of the places of Buddhist pilgrimage. Some of them even made their way up to my hillside hermitage in Kalimpong.[189]

Despite my conviction that conferences were a waste of time, I might have been less disinclined to attend the Fellowship's Sarnath conference, had I still been in India, if I had not known that earlier conferences had been little more than talking shops. After the third conference, held in Burma in 1954, the delegate of a North American Buddhist group had written, in some bewilderment,

> I had supposed that there would be considerably more attention to devotional practices, including periods of meditation. My friends in asking about the conference almost invariably bring up this suggestion. The relatively small space given to devotions constituted a surprise. Am I merely betraying my occidental and

> Christian background in saying that world-wide Buddhism as a vital force will never come into existence until there is a spiritual basis more concrete than mere acceptance of a common faith?

I did not think the writer was betraying any bias. Buddhists, in fact, by virtually excluding devotional practices from the programme of their conferences, showed a bias which was distinctly non-Buddhist and non-oriental. The suggestion that we needed 'a spiritual basis more concrete than mere acceptance of a common faith' put a finger on one of the weakest points in the modern Buddhist movement of revival. It put a finger, indeed, on one of the weakest points – perhaps *the* weakest point – in much of traditional Buddhism, and years were to pass before I was able to identify the act of Going for Refuge to the Three Jewels, considered as the central and definitive Act of the Buddhist life, as the concrete spiritual basis that was needed if Buddhism was to be a vital force in the modern world.[190] Meanwhile, in the fifties and sixties, conferences of the World Fellowship of Buddhists continued to follow the type of programme of which my North American Buddhist had complained. Reviewing the official report of the Fellowship's fifth conference, held in Thailand in 1958, and attended by 199 delegates, visitors, and observers from eighteen countries including the host country, I wrote in the *Maha Bodhi*:

> There were five Plenary Sessions, five business meetings, one for each subject committee, and an Executive Council meeting, besides a wide variety of religious, educational and social engagements. Despite the criticism which has been so often levelled against the practice, the Plenary Sessions were as in previous years mainly occupied with the reading out of Messages. The committees all passed a number of praiseworthy resolutions but without making any concrete suggestion as to how they could be implemented. As with the reports of the previous General Conferences, the reader is apt to get the impression of a week of hectic sightseeing by representatives of various Buddhist organizations or of none followed by two years of complete inactivity. The present report, for instance, comes out two years after the conclusion of the Conference.

Having dealt with the last conference, I turned to the next:

> The WFB, which claims to be the global organization of the Buddhists, has been in existence for ten years. Apart from its excellent magazine World Buddhism, published from Ceylon, it appears to have no permanent achievement to its credit. Work on the Buddhist Encyclopaedia, we understand, has practically come to a standstill. This reviewer suggests that if there is still enough life in the WFB to hold the Sixth General Conference – due to meet next month, though the venue is not yet known – all concerned would be well advised to give most serious thought to the future of the organization.[191]

The conference did *not* meet the following month. It met more than a year later, in Cambodia, and a month before it did so I returned to the attack in an editorial in the *Maha Bodhi*. Having pointed out that a Buddhist organization was not something imagined to exist in its own right above and beyond the individuals who composed it, but simply the means of their fruitful communication with one another, I continued:

> In view of the very nature of Buddhism it is impossible that the Fellowship, or any other Buddhist organization however widespread, should develop into a kind of super-body which would control its constituent and affiliated groups in a dictatorial manner and think, speak, and act on their behalf. Yet surely more is expected of the WFB, after more than a decade of existence, than simply to assemble every two or three years for the purpose of sightseeing in the host country, listening to messages of greeting, and passing resolutions that it is powerless to implement.
>
> No thinking person needs to be reminded that we live in critical, even dangerous times, when the continued existence of the human race itself is at stake. In circumstances such as these it is imperative that the Buddhist point of view should be powerfully projected in the world and the pacific moral influence of the Buddha's Teaching brought massively to bear on contemporary issues. This year's Conference should give its most serious attention to the question. The WFB urgently needs a permanent headquarters, an efficient secretariat, and a really first-class journal: makeshift arrangements will no longer suffice. It must devise ways and means of bringing about a much

> closer understanding and more active co-operation between the Buddhists of the world than at present obtains. Unless such steps as these are taken without delay the WFB will never be a force to reckon with in the world of Buddhist affairs, much less still a vital factor in the much wider, more complex and more dangerous world of the Cold War and the Atom Bomb.[192]

These steps were not taken, least of all at the WFB's sixth conference, held as this was in the Cambodia of Sihanouk Varma, the playboy prince, and the organization never became either a force to reckon with in the world of Buddhist affairs or a vital factor in the wider world of international relations and power politics. Nevertheless I continued to support the Fellowship's 'ecumenical' objectives, little as these were realized in practice, and was glad to attend the Buddhist Society's reception and to meet Princess Poon and Aiem Sanghavasi, neither of whom I had met before. Two days later they came to see me.

Princess Poon was a tiny, bird-like woman with a round, moon-like face framed by an abundance of grey curls. She wore Western dress, as did Aiem Sanghavasi, a rather small, youngish man who did not look comfortable in his dark, ill-fitting lounge suit. The princess took the lead in the conversation, her companion merely supporting her with an intervention from time to time. Every now and then they consulted together *sotto voce* in their own language. After we had discussed Buddhist affairs in general for a while, and I had given them a brief account of the present state of Buddhism in Britain, so far as this was known to me, Princess Poon started asking me about the activities of the Vihara and about the relations between its various resident members. In particular, she wanted to know how well Vichitr and the Thai monk who had recently joined him there had fitted in and whether their behaviour had given me cause for complaint in any way, and I began to realize that my visitors had come with a definite purpose in view and that there was something they wanted to find out.

Truth to tell, neither Vichitr nor his companion had fitted in very well. They had not made the slightest effort to fit in. Of Vichitr it could even be said that all his efforts had been directed to *not* fitting in, and to making it clear to everyone that although temporarily based at the Vihara he belonged to the *Thai* Sangha, not to the English Sangha. To an extent I could understand their position and even sympathize with them. So far as they were concerned, they were living in a kind of *bardo* or intermediate state, waiting for the moment when they would be able to move to the temple the Thai government was building in Wimbledon, and probably saw no point in trying to adjust to a situation in which they had no personal interest and would be leaving soon. Consequently they tended to treat the Vihara very much as a hotel, where they ate and slept when in London (Vichitr was often away), and where they received people, but with the running of which they had nothing to do. But even a hotel has its house rules, and Vichitr and his companion did not always observe the rules of the Vihara. The rule they most frequently flouted had to do with food. Though the Vihara was vegetarian, I would often return from visiting one of the provincial groups to find in the refrigerator the remains of whole chickens they had ordered from the local delicatessen.

Yet little as the Thai monks had fitted in, and much as their behaviour had given me cause for complaint, I was reluctant to apprise Princess Poon of the true state of affairs. The very idea of informing in this way on my two guests, who after all were fellow monks, was repugnant to me. Besides, though Princess Poon was clearly anxious to know how well Vichitr and his companion had fitted in, and whether their behaviour had given me any cause for complaint, why she should want to know this was not clear at all. Were she and Sanghavasi trying to find out what kind of attitude I had towards their monks? Or were they looking for a handle against the monks themselves, whether because they came from a monastery that was out of favour with them, or because they belonged to a different faction within the Thai Buddhist establishment? Thai Buddhist politics were, as I knew, extremely complicated; there were wheels within wheels within wheels. There was also the question of 'face' to be considered. 'Face' was no less important to the Thais than to the Chinese, and if it was known that I had complained about them to two such prominent and influential people as Princess Poon and Sanghavasi the two monks might suffer a serious 'loss of face', both in their own eyes and in the eyes of their compatriots. These thoughts all flashed through my mind in an instant, and I therefore simply gave my visitors to understand that the Thai monks had fitted in reasonably well and that I had no complaints regarding their behaviour.

Though I must have known many of the guests at the Buddhist Society's reception, the only people I actually remember meeting there, apart from Dr Malalasekera, are Maurice and Ruth Walshe. I remember meeting them because they had just spent five weeks in Japan and I had not seen either of them since their return. At that time few English Buddhists had visited Japan, or knew very much about Japanese Buddhism (apart from Zen!), and Maurice soon wrote for *The Buddhist* a lively and informative article entitled 'Not All is Zen in Japan'.[193] Ruth did not write about their experiences, but she talked to me a lot about them. In particular she spoke about the visit she and Maurice had paid to the Sōtō Zen monastery where Peggy Kennett, a former member of the Buddhist Society, was staying and practising Zen and where they had a long discussion with her teacher. Kind-hearted Ruth was very concerned for Peggy. Her teacher, who was the abbot of the monastery, had seemed very displeased with his English disciple. 'He kept *scolding* her in front of us!' Ruth exclaimed, in shocked tones. What she and Maurice had not realized, and I think never did realize, was that the abbot was scolding not Peggy but *them*. He was scolding them for their wrong views about Zen – views which *she*, supposedly, was 'mirroring' for their benefit. 'Mirroring' played an important part in Japanese education and culture. Basically it consisted in reflecting a child's or a disciple's misbehaviour or misunderstanding back to him by mimicking it in such a way that he was shamed into conformity. Four or five years later, when she returned to the West as Jiyu Roshi, Peggy's attempts to introduce this typically Japanese technique into the culturally very different world of British Buddhism had some amusing consequences.[194]

23
CHANGES AT THE VIHARA

By mid-November I had been incumbent of the Hampstead Buddhist Vihara for well over a year, and during that time my work had increased to such an extent that it was hardly possible for me to do more than I was already doing. Indeed, I needed to do less. During the summer months I had suffered, on and off, from an extremely painful gumboil (with me always a sign of physical strain), which I took to be a warning that I was doing too much work on too little nourishment, for I was still following the rule of taking no solid food after midday and did not always eat properly even before then.[195] Besides all my regular lectures and classes at the Vihara and at the Buddhist Society, and my lectures at the College of Psychic Science and elsewhere, I had *The Buddhist* to edit and produce, the provincial groups to visit, correspondence to deal with, visitors to receive, personal interviews to give, and the everlasting telephone to answer. There was also, of course, the Vihara itself to run, with all that this entailed in the way of caring for the shrine and meeting room and making arrangements for such mundane things as shopping, cooking, and cleaning.

After returning from the summer school I therefore started sounding out Maurice and Goulstone regarding the possibility of the Trust providing me with full-time paid secretarial help. I already had an agency shorthand typist coming and taking dictation whenever I had an unusually large number of letters to answer, but this ad hoc arrangement (paid for, I think, by the Association) was not very satisfactory. The same person was not always available, sometimes I did not get the finished work back for a week or more, sometimes it contained mistakes, and sometimes the shorthand typist herself – usually an elderly woman – arrived in so depressed and tearful a state that I was obliged to spend the time listening to her troubles and counselling her instead of giving dictation. Though I explained all this to Maurice, and though he was aware of the extent to which my work had increased, his initial reaction when I sounded him out on the subject of full-time paid secretarial help was one of alarm. The Trust couldn't possibly afford it, he protested. It simply didn't have the money. Goulstone was more sympathetic. As Treasurer of both the Sangha Trust and the Sangha Association, he had a better understanding of the needs of the situation. He knew that Clare Sampson would not be around much longer, and that it would not be easy for the Association to find a new honorary secretary, especially one who could help him in the way Clare sometimes did. The upshot was that the trustees agreed, after weeks of discussion, that the Trust could, in fact, afford to meet the expense of a full-time secretary, that Goulstone and I would share her services, and that it would be up to me to find the right person.

I found her with the help of Kathy Phelps, the blonde, voluptuous young cockney woman who was soon to become general secretary of the Buddhist Society in succession to staid, elderly Joan Pope, who had occupied the post for longer than most members of the Society could remember. She had a friend who was looking for a job with a religious organization, Kathy told me in the society's office one afternoon over a cup of tea. This friend had spiritual interests, was working on a book on occultism, and might well be just the sort of person I wanted. Could she ask her to come and see me? She certainly could. A few days later, therefore, the friend presented herself at the Vihara. I saw and liked her, as did Goulstone, and three weeks later, when November was almost over, despite last-minute objections from Maurice, our new full-time secretary started work in the ground floor front room that Vichitr and his companion fortunately had just vacated. Instead of 'Office of Thai Sangha' the sign on the door now read 'Reception'.

Francoise Strachan, brown-haired and simply dressed, was a quietly spoken young woman of average looks and rather more than average intelligence. Within a few weeks she had created a proper office, probably the first either the Trust or the Association had ever had, and had started relieving me of all kinds of minor but time-consuming tasks. Besides typing articles meant for publication in *The Buddhist*, she dealt with routine correspondence, received casual visitors, answered the telephone, passed on messages, went to the post office, and bought flowers for the shrine, all of which enabled me not only to devote more time to my own real work but to have a little time to myself. Goulstone found her no less useful than I did. Formerly he had rarely been seen at the Vihara, usually only when there was a meeting of the Association committee or, more recently, of the Trust; but now, wearing his black opera cloak and smelling of whisky and cigars, he was to be seen there almost every weekday morning, generally spending at least half an hour closeted with Francoise before going on to his legal practice. Despite his increased interest in the Vihara, he did not start attending lectures and classes, and on Sunday afternoons and weekday evenings I saw no more of him than I had done before Francoise's arrival.

That we now had a full-time secretary working in our ground floor front room, with all that this entailed for me in the way of reduced workload, was not the only change to take place at the Vihara that autumn. Our little community saw various comings and goings both before and after the departure of the Thai monks. Most of these were of young men who wanted, or thought they wanted, to become monks, and whom I invited to stay at the Vihara for a while and have at least a 'tongue-tip taste' of monastic life. Only three of them lasted for more than a couple of weeks (one or two did not even manage to pluck up the courage to accept my invitation), and they therefore remain, for the most part, shadowy figures whose names I have long since forgotten. The three exceptions were Victor, who had moved into the Vihara when Ratanasara moved out; the young man who, after coming to the Vihara regularly for some months, had been on retreat with me at Biddulph, and whom I had recently ordained as Vajrabodhi; and – the one who lasted longest – Eric, whom I was to ordain as Viriya.

Eric was a pink-faced, sandy-haired young man of twenty-five or twenty-six whose slightly aquiline nose was wrinkled up, more often than not, in an expression of disgust. I do not remember where we first met, but it must have been either at a meeting of the Brighton Buddhist group or at the Buddhist Society's summer school, probably the latter. Wherever it was, he was soon coming to see me regularly; we had a number of serious discussions, and one early September afternoon, in the course of a particularly good exchange, he asked me to accept him as a probationer. I remember that afternoon very well, though not so much on account of Eric's request itself, which was not entirely unexpected, as because of what followed. Eric had a girlfriend called Elizabeth, whom I had not met, and he had asked her to come to the Vihara two hours after his own arrival there, by which time, as he knew, he would have made his request and, he hoped, been accepted as a probationer. No sooner had she entered my room, and been introduced, than he drew a deep breath and told her, with evident emotion, 'Liz, I'm going to become a monk.' However much she may have been aware of her boyfriend's intentions, this abrupt announcement must have come as a shock to Elizabeth, but she took it well, and Clare having joined us for a cup of tea we all spent the rest of the afternoon together pleasantly enough. A week later Eric moved into the Vihara.

A new broom sweeps clean, says the proverb, and so far as the domestic arrangements of the Vihara were concerned Eric proved to be every inch a new broom. He swept and cleaned the kitchen and dining room, turned out cupboards, threw away junk, burned stacks of old magazines, mowed the lawn at the back of the house, and weeded the overgrown little front garden. Within a month of his arrival the Vihara was looking neater and tidier than it had done for a long time. So much of a new broom was Eric that eventually he swept out of the Vihara both Victor and Vajrabodhi, whose untidy ways, and lack of care for the place, caused his nose to wrinkle up in an expression of deeper disgust than usual. Victor, who in any case was not really a probationer, having asked for ordination in a rash moment and then regretted it, had been showing signs of restlessness for some time. After spending three weeks in North Africa, and a week in his home town of Nottingham, he moved into Amritapani's community in Camden Town, where his girlfriend was already staying. Subsequently, as a result of his being involved in an incident there, he had to leave the place in a hurry and was not seen for a year or more. As for Vajrabodhi, he left the Vihara in a huff after he and Eric had clashed in the kitchen. His departure may have had something to do with the fact that I had reprimanded him for allowing a sixteen-year-old girl to come to his room for private lessons in the Dharma, as he most unwisely had been doing. He left without telling anybody, and some weeks later I heard that he and the girl had gone to stay with friends of the Vihara in Gloucestershire and that the girl was pregnant.

Eric's passion for cleanliness and order was not simply of the utilitarian kind but possessed a decidedly aesthetic dimension. He had a great interest in Japanese art and culture, was learning the Japanese language, preferred chopsticks to a knife and fork, and when not actually working wore a blue and white patterned kimono about the house. Before long he struck up a friendship with Emile Boin, the proprietor of the Japanese shop in Monmouth Street, and Emile's partially deaf wife Sara, and at Eric's suggestion Emile presented me with a yellow silk kimono. So far as I remember, Eric had no particular interest in Zen, but naturally he was interested in meditation, and therefore was happy to join me in my morning sessions 'on the cushion'. Sometimes we went for a walk on Hampstead Heath before meditating, for like me he was an early riser and liked to be up and about before dawn. Sometimes, indeed, we were out so early that it was still dark when we got back, and then Eric would take up his guitar and in his pleasant, rather nasal tenor voice sing, to his own accompaniment, plaintive country-and-western ballads (as I suppose they must have been) until the clock struck seven and it was time to meditate. Terry usually joined us for our morning sessions, after which the three of us would have a cup of tea and a chat together and he would leave for work.

The appearance at the Vihara of a full-time paid secretary, and the comings and goings of various members of our little community – especially the arrival of Eric on the scene – were important changes, and they made a big difference to me. But there also took place around this time another important change, and one that made, in the long run, an even bigger difference to both me and Terry. On 19 November Terry left his job. Or rather, he told the advertising agency for which he worked that he would be leaving at the end of the year. He also moved, earlier that same week, from his old quarters in Chalk Farm to a bigger flat nearer the Vihara.

Terry's decision to leave his job was not a sudden one. It was a step he had been contemplating for some time, even before meeting me. Though good at his (well-paid) design work, and popular with his colleagues, he nonetheless felt, in the competitive, manipulative world of advertising, out of place to the point of alienation, and indeed had developed for its shallow, materialistic values a loathing that at times made him physically ill. During the last few months he had been finding it increasingly difficult to carry on, though he kept up a cheerful front and nobody in his office – not even the faithful Alan – had the least idea how he really felt. From time to time he was the victim of moods of depression out of which I did not always find it easy to talk him.

These moods were not entirely due to the kind of work he was doing. His visits to Ilford also played a part. Every other week he collected Fiona from her mother and took her to his parents' place for the weekend. These weekends under the parental roof were a sore trial to Terry. Besides reminding him of his solitary, unhappy childhood, and thus reviving all his old feelings of resentment towards his parents (feelings he was forced to conceal), they tended to confirm his impression that his daughter was being subjected, at the hands of her mother and grandmother, to influences of the same repressive and deadening kind that had had such a disastrous effect on his own emotional life. As an instance of this, he once told me that by the time she was three they had conditioned Fiona into refusing to be undressed, or given a bath, in front of her father or grandfather. What was an even greater trial to him, his parents had never told their friends and neighbours about the breakdown of his marriage, the whole subject being in their eyes too painful – and too shameful – to be mentioned. If anyone asked after Gillian Terry had to say she was quite well, thank you, as though the two of them were still living together – a piece of pretence that revolted his honest and truth-loving nature. He therefore returned from his visits to Ilford tired and depressed, and in need of a good deal of encouragement and reassurance.

The flat to which Terry had moved was situated in Lancaster Grove, conveniently equidistant from Belsize Park and Swiss Cottage Underground stations, and not far from the Hampstead Public Library. It was bigger than his old flat only in the sense that it comprised not a single but a double room one corner of which had been partitioned off to form a kitchen. Terry had moved there not only because his flat in King Henry's Road was small and dark, and not at all the sort of place he wanted to spend his days as well as his nights in once he had stopped working, but also because he was concerned to provide me with a quiet place to which I could retire whenever I needed a brief respite from the busy life of the Vihara. The upstairs, eastward-looking front room at 3 Lancaster Grove was certainly quiet – much quieter than my own room on busy Haverstock Hill. It was quiet partly because Lancaster Grove was a side street, so that hardly any noise penetrated from outside even when the windows were open, and partly because the various occupants of the other flats in the building, a substantial Victorian property, were out most days of the week and even when they were in made little or no sound and kept out of each other's way. During the six or seven months that Terry (and I, sometimes) lived there, the only people we actually saw, apart from the landlady, were the two women, apparently mother and daughter, who occupied a room on the same floor as us and whom, to their embarrassment, we occasionally surprised tiptoeing along the passage towards the common bathroom. The landlady herself, who lived in the rather gloomy basement flat, we saw only when Terry paid the rent. Like many landladies, old Mrs Hartmann was a suspicious soul (rightly so, if even half the stories Bernie Whitelaw told me about his tenants were to be believed), and Terry had not won her confidence immediately. On his going to see her about the room and explaining that he would be sharing it, occasionally, with a friend who was a Buddhist monk, she had insisted on seeing me before accepting him as a tenant. As she only wanted to make sure I was not an Indian, the interview passed off successfully, and two weeks later Terry moved in.

From the middle of November, therefore, I had nearby a place of retreat. I had only to walk a little way up Haverstock Hill, turn left into Belsize Avenue and then, having continued along it for a few hundred yards in the direction of Swiss Cottage, turn left again into Lancaster Grove. As I did so, the noise of the traffic would gradually die away, then cease altogether, and when, fifteen minutes after leaving the Vihara, I entered Mrs Hartmann's domain, it would be to find myself enveloped in a profound silence – a silence I could guarantee would be broken, over the next few hours, only by the occasional flushing of a distant toilet.

While Terry was still working I tended to make use of the flat only at weekends and late in the evening, sometimes staying there overnight when I had a lecture to think about the following morning. Since we were free from interruptions (we took no telephone calls, and received no visitors), our discussions could last as long, and go as deep, as we pleased, without the necessity of our going away for the weekend in the Little Bus. It was at this time, I think, that the subject of energy first arose and was discussed, at great length, between us. How it arose I no longer recollect. Probably it was in connection with the 'sexo-yogic' practices of the Vajrayāna, as described to me in Kalimpong by Yogi Chen,[196] or Wilhelm Reich's highly controversial ideas about energy, character armour, and orgasm, or, what is most likely, in connection with both. Terry was particularly interested in the relation between sexual energy and spiritual energy, especially so far as this has a bearing on the practice of celibacy. Fond as he was of Vivien, he was finding the sexual side of their relationship increasingly repugnant. Her orgasms, so he told me, were becoming 'more and more primitive', and when they had intercourse he felt as though a fine thread was being drawn from his brain. Whether he ever communicated his repugnance to Vivien I do not know, but it was she who, in effect, solved the problem, around this time, by embarking on a Freudian analysis one of the requirements of which was that she should abstain from sexual activity while it was in progress. As Terry was not interested in finding a new girlfriend, this meant a period of abstinence for him too, and he in fact remained celibate for the next two years or more. But although not interested in finding a new girlfriend, he was certainly interested in finding a *ḍākinī*. A *ḍākinī*, in Tantric tradition, is a woman or a goddess who, as the embodiment of a current of spiritual energy, has the effect of arousing the dormant energies of the practitioner by whom she is taken, in fact or symbolically in meditation, as a *paredra* or consort. Terry had first heard about *ḍākinīs* from me, when I told him, quite early in our friendship, about Jamyang Khyentse Rimpoche, perhaps the most eminent of my Tibetan teachers,[197] whose own *ḍākinī* – and chief disciple – was a young woman remarkable alike for her beauty, her intelligence, and her devotion. At the time he showed little interest in the subject, and in our discussions on energy it was touched on only incidentally; but during the months that followed the ending of his sexual relationship with Vivien he became increasingly interested, not just in *ḍākinīs* in general, but in the idea of finding that unique, magical person who, by being *his ḍākinī*, would grant him the kind of ideal fulfilment he had expected to find in marriage. It was an idea that eventually came to preoccupy him virtually to the point of obsession and which, in the end, proved to be no more than a will-o'-the-wisp leading him deeper into the morass of disappointment, frustration, and despair.

That development was then many months away. Meanwhile, not all our time together at the flat was spent in discussion. Terry had a record player, and sometimes we listened to music last thing at night.

Our favourites were Mozart, Chopin, and Grieg, especially the piano concertos of all three composers, and, in my case at least, Haydn and the Elgar of the *Enigma Variations*. As a teenager I had been passionately fond of music, and had listened to symphony concerts on the radio whenever I had the opportunity. For me music was not the brandy of the damned but the ambrosia of the blessed, and swept me up to heights of ecstasy in a way that even poetry could not do.[198] In India I was rarely able to listen to music – that is, Western classical music. Such music was not easy to come by, and in any case, as a (Theravādin) Buddhist monk I was expected to observe the rule of abstaining from 'dance, song, instrumental music, and improper shows'. This rule I had long understood as applying only to music of the cruder and more vulgar kind, such as must have been no less popular in the Buddha's day than it is in our own, and I was therefore able to listen to Mozart and the rest of my – and Terry's – favourites with a clear conscience. The School of Economic Science, which Terry had recently left, indeed regarded the music of Mozart, in particular, as having a positive, spiritualizing effect on the mind.

What the 'School' thought of Wagner I do not know. The composer was by no means a favourite of mine, though as a teenager I had enjoyed the overtures to *Lohengrin* and *Tannhäuser*, but when a member of the Sangha Association offered, that autumn, to take me to see all four constituent parts of *The Ring* cycle at Covent Garden I was glad to accept.[199] Wendy was a tall, angular woman of thirty or thereabouts who worked at Coutts in the Strand and was a keen practitioner of judo. Her angularity was not only physical but mental. There were all sorts of sharp corners and edges to her personality, and while she could be warm-hearted and generous (as her offer to me demonstrated) she was morbidly quick to take offence and was, in truth, of so prickly, indeed so spiky, a disposition, and so extremely sharp-tongued, that I called her – to her great amusement and delight – Kūṭadanta or 'Sharp Tooth', after an old brahmin mentioned in the Pāli scriptures.[200] Had I then been as familiar with modern psychology and its jargon as I afterwards became, I would probably have said that Wendy-Kūṭadanta found it difficult to accept herself as a woman (in India the women had appeared to experience no such difficulty). She certainly resented being treated as a woman, and the fact that I accepted her offer to take me to see *The Ring* cycle pleased her immensely, for since monks were not supposed to go out and about with women my acceptance meant I was not treating her as a mere woman but as a man. So pleased was she that she dressed for our opera-going in a striking, Chinese-style outfit of yellow satin, heavily embroidered, which besides giving her a distinctly oriental look made her appear much more feminine. I of course had on, over my robes, the long fawn-coloured cloak I always wore outside the Vihara. We must have been an odd-looking pair. The first time we made our way to the Royal Opera House, through Covent Garden market, one of the porters called out to his companion, with true cockney wit, 'Look, mate, 'ere comes Julius Caesar and Cleopatra!' Neither of us could help laughing, and Wendy, strange to relate, seemed not at all displeased to think that she looked like the royal Egyptian *femme fatale*. As for me, for a moment it was as though Caesar's laurel wreath encircled my brow.

An incident that occurred on our way back from Covent Garden one night was definitely *not* a laughing matter at the time. I do not remember which part of the cycle we had just seen (probably it was *Götterdämmerung*, the concluding part), but whichever one it was, so overwhelmed was I by the experience that during our journey back to Belsize Park I sat speechless, unable to utter a word. Unfortunately, Kūṭadanta completely misunderstood my silence. She thought I was silent because I was angry with her, and that I was angry because I had not enjoyed the performance and blamed her for being responsible for my having wasted a whole evening. This was enough to throw her into a state of emotional turmoil in which she blamed herself for taking me to the opera, blamed me for allowing myself to be taken, hated me for being angry with her, and hated herself for hating me. The misunderstanding was cleared up only some days later when, having recovered the use of my tongue, I thanked her warmly for giving me the opportunity of seeing the complete *Ring* cycle and assured her I had thoroughly enjoyed the whole experience.

Towards the end of November, when Terry had been settled in the new flat for less than a fortnight, we spent two days in Cambridge. The reason for the visit was that the University Buddhist Society had invited me to speak on 'Practical Problems of the European Buddhist' – problems with which I was beginning to be well acquainted. The lecture was to have been given by Marco Pallis (the subject was of his own choosing), but as he was ill I was asked, at short notice, to take his place, even though I had addressed the Society only a few weeks earlier, on 'The Spiritual Community in Buddhism'. On our arrival in the city we met John Hipkin for lunch, and at his suggestion went to see the Russian *Hamlet* at the local Arts Cinema. Both Terry and I enjoyed this black-and-white version of the famous play, and though thirty-four years have passed since I saw the film, the appearance of the murdered king's ghost on the castle battlements, amid swirling mist, remains a vivid memory. It was also at John's suggestion – indeed, on his warm recommendation – that we saw Peter Brook's production of Peter Weiss's controversial *Marat/Sade* at the Aldwych.[201] Neither of us enjoyed it very much, though not because it could be regarded, from a strict Theravādin point of view, as being an 'improper show'. Improper or not, I was in any case beginning to be less rigid in my observance of the rules relating to such matters as taking solid food after midday, listening to music, and wearing robes, at least when I was at the flat with Terry.

24
NORTH OF THE BORDER

Most of the ten or twelve provincial Buddhist groups were situated in the southern part of Britain, and so far my pastoral excursions had carried me no farther north than Newcastle, whose chairman, the bluff, rationalistic Bill Halford, had introduced himself to me at my first summer school and invited me to pay them a visit.

The visit did not take place until the following April. Having travelled up by the *Flying Scotsman*, and caught a glimpse of York Minster and of Durham Cathedral and Castle on the way, I was met at the station by Bill and by him driven some miles out of town to a small lake in the moors known, so he informed me, as the Duckpond. The trip served a double purpose. It enabled my host to tell me about the book he was writing about Newcastle Buddhist affairs (the group had eight or nine regular members, all men), and what he thought of Ananda Bodhi, about whom he was not very complimentary, as well as to show me the moors, of which he seemed rather proud, but which, seen through a thin veil of rain, beneath a leaden sky, to me appeared bleak and desolate in the extreme. In the evening I gave personal interviews to members and friends, and conducted a meditation session, at the Quaker meeting house where the Newcastle group usually met. Bill and others then escorted me to the station, where I caught the Pullman back to London after what according to my diary had been a very worthwhile visit. As I settled into my little compartment I could not help thinking how comfortable and convenient the sleeping arrangements were, especially when compared to the conditions under which I had been accustomed to travel in India.

Since that visit to the Newcastle group I had penetrated no farther north than Biddulph. Later in the year, however, I received an invitation from Glasgow. The invitation came not from a Buddhist group – at that time there was no Buddhist group in Glasgow – but from Glasgow University as represented by its lecturer in the Philosophy of Religion, the Reverend E. H. Pyle. Glasgow being the second biggest city in Great Britain, and its university an old and distinguished one, naturally I was happy to accept, and after a further exchange of letters it was agreed that my visit should take place during the first week of December. At ten o'clock one Sunday morning I accordingly left for Glasgow from Euston, Terry accompanying me. Luckily we had the compartment to ourselves, so that we could talk freely and I was able to work on my lecture notes while my friend either read or dozed. Terry was visiting Scotland for the first time, but I had been there once before. It was from Glasgow that, twenty years earlier, I had embarked for India, and I had vivid memories of the docks, of the crowded quayside, and of how my khaki-clad comrades and I had filed up the gangway into the bowels of the enormous grey troopship without knowing where we were, where we were really going, or how long we would be away.[202]

At Queen Street station Terry and I were met by Ernest Pyle, a short, balding man of about my own age, and an Indian student who was the president of the International Society. Our train having arrived two hours late, they took us straight to the university and straight to the meeting room where, after a cup of coffee, I addressed the members of the International Society on 'The Buddhist Way'.

I explained that way in terms of the twelve positive *nidānas*, beginning with 'in dependence upon suffering arises faith' and concluding with 'in dependence upon liberation arises knowledge of the destruction of the defilements.'[203] Not that I plunged straight into my subject. After giving an outline of the Buddha's early life, and describing his attainment of Enlightenment, I explained how that Enlightenment or Vision of Reality found conceptual expression, for purposes of communication, in the principle of conditionality, and how conditionality itself was of two kinds, cyclical and spiral, or reactive and creative, and how the Buddhist way was based on the second kind of conditionality. Only when I had prepared the ground in this manner did I launch into an extended account of each of the positive *nidānas* in turn.[204]

The lecture was attended by about 170 students of all nationalities, and I was given an enthusiastic reception. Many questions were asked, and there was much vigorous discussion.

The following afternoon I addressed a much smaller gathering, consisting mainly of Ernest Pyle's own students, on 'The Nature and Development of Buddhism'. As I wanted to leave plenty of time for discussion, this lecture was shorter than the previous one, besides being more technical and less systematic. In it I dealt, initially, with various questions of interpretation, as I called them. *Śīlavrata-parāmarśa*, the third of the ten fetters binding to mundane existence, was not 'dependence on rites and ceremonies' (the usual translation) but 'attachment to moral rules and religious observances' as ends in themselves.[205] Nor had the Buddha 'borrowed' this or that idea from his Upanishadic predecessors, or from popular Indian religion, as alleged by some scholars. He had simply used the language of his time and place to communicate his own unique vision, and in so doing had given a new meaning to such key terms as *brāhmaṇa* and *vasala*.[206]

This led me to explore the nature of the relation between a founded (or universal) religion like Christianity, Buddhism, and Islam, and an ethnic religion like Judaism and Hinduism,[207] and this, in turn, to what I called the phenomenology of Buddhism, that is to say, the fact that its history comprised the three great phases of development known, respectively, as the Hīnayāna, the Mahāyāna, and the Vajrayāna. Having briefly characterized each of these phases, I addressed myself to the question of the supposed 'deification' of the Buddha in the Mahāyāna, insisting that the Buddha was neither 'God' nor 'man'. He belonged to a third category, for which there was no equivalent in Western thought – that of *Enlightened* man.[208] In conclusion I reminded my hearers that we should be careful how we applied Western categories to Eastern religions, a point that was well taken and one which, in particular, gave rise to a number of questions in the lively and prolonged discussion that followed.

The actual giving of my two lectures occupied only a fraction of the time Terry and I spent in Glasgow, but thanks to Ernest Pyle our programme nonetheless was a full one. On the Monday morning he came to the University Guest House, where we had spent the night, and took us on a sightseeing trip into the city centre. 'We went by bus,'

I noted in my diary that evening. 'Everything very grim and grimy. Victorian Gothic. Not so cold as had expected.' After visiting a second-hand bookshop, where I bought a nice edition of Bishop Butler's *Works*, in two volumes bound as one,[209] we went to see the River Clyde, on whose dull, polluted waters we gazed down from an iron bridge and which I thought, in the words of my diary, 'quite picturesque'. At one point we bumped into our guide's teenage son. Down the side of the youngster's face ran the scarlet line of a recently healed wound. He had been standing outside a cinema one evening, his father explained, when someone had suddenly appeared out of the darkness and slashed his cheek with a razor. The notorious razor gangs were, it seemed, still operating in Glasgow.[210]

Back at the University we took coffee with the Professor of Divinity and the University Chaplain, lunched with Ernest Pyle and the young lecturer in Logic, met the Professor of Zoology and his wife, and saw the university library. We then had tea with our host in his study, where a number of people came to see me, including the Chaplain for Overseas Buddhists, and where we were kept talking until it was time for me to give my second lecture. After the lecture and the ensuing discussion Ernest Pyle took us round to his own place for tea and from there, after more talk, to the station and the Pullman in which we were to travel back to London that night.

It had been an interesting visit, and we had much to talk about and, indeed, to reflect upon. My visits to Oxford and Cambridge had been at the invitation of their respective Buddhist Societies, which were student organizations, so that my contacts within those twin seats of learning were largely confined to that tiny section of the undergraduate population which, for various reasons and in varying degrees, was attracted to Buddhism. In the case of Glasgow, my visit took place at the invitation of the University itself, and I addressed not only one of the bigger student organizations but Ernest Pyle's class in the Philosophy of Religion. I also had the opportunity of getting to know Ernest Pyle himself and of meeting, through his good offices, representatives of some of the University's different faculties. Thus although my visit to Glasgow was a short one, I had there a range of contacts that was wider, intellectually speaking, than I had at either Oxford or Cambridge, or than was available to me at the Hampstead Vihara and the Buddhist Society. My exchanges with representatives of the various disciplines from Divinity to Zoology, limited as those exchanges may have been, in fact gave me a better understanding of the nature of the challenge to which Buddhism in Britain would have to rise if it was to exert a real influence on the spiritual and intellectual life of the nation. Perhaps new ways of presenting the Dharma would have to be found. We might even be able to learn something from other spiritual groups. Only the previous month Terry and I had investigated an Ouspensky group with this possibility in mind. The group met in a hired room in Victoria, in the shadow, so to speak, of the Buddhist Society. Including the speaker, there were four people present besides ourselves, and the talk, which was devoted to Ouspensky's teachings, was the poorest I had heard since leaving India. It was certainly poorer than any I had heard at the speakers' class, and Terry and I did not bother to visit the group again.

We did not visit Glasgow again either (in the following decades I was to visit it many times on my own), though Ernest Pyle and I continued to correspond. The correspondence came to an end only some years later, when the friendly, broad-minded Congregational minister transported himself and his family to the other side of the globe and took up a teaching appointment at an Australian university.

25
A SECRET LIFE

A biography or an autobiography – even a set of memoirs – can deal with the particular human being who happens to be its subject in a variety of ways. It can skate more or less lightly over the surface of his life, describing circumstances and chronicling outward events, or it can seek to penetrate beneath the surface and to explore in greater or less depth attitudes and motivations that are not immediately apparent and which may even have been concealed. It can also do both, either balancing narrative and psychological analysis or giving more weight to one or other of them in accordance with the inclinations of the author and the kind of life his subject has led.

Tibetan Buddhists have long recognized that inasmuch as a human life is lived on a variety of levels a biography should take account of all of them. The biography of a saint or a great teacher is therefore often divided into three parts, one giving his outer, one his inner, and one his secret biography. The outer biography covers such matters as the saint's birth, parentage, secular education, doctrinal studies, monastic ordination, and travels, while its inner and secret counterparts deal, respectively, with his spiritual practices and his transcendental attainments and realizations. It thus is a multi-layered work, reflecting in its highly organized formal structure the storeyed complexity of the saint's or great teacher's experience as he lived his life.

Though the ordinary person's experience will be much less comprehensive in range, it is similarly stratified. Besides the outer world of work and play, there is the inner world of more or less conscious thought and emotion, great as the extent to which thought and emotion are bound up with external objects and events may be. There is also the world of dreams, recollections of which sometimes mingle with the stream of waking consciousness only, more often than not, to be quickly forgotten.

In my own case I have always been aware that I lived on different levels. Though neither a saint nor a great teacher, I too had an outer, an inner, and a secret life (secret in the Tibetan Buddhist sense) and had, therefore, in principle, not only an outer and an inner biography but a secret one as well. When I came to write the first volume of my memoirs, on which I started – rather light-heartedly – in 1959, there however was no question of my structuring them in accordance with the time-honoured Tibetan model, about which, in any case, I may not have known at the time. My life was far too complex to be divided up in any such way, besides which there were levels on which I dwelt only intermittently, so that no connected account of them was possible. Indeed it is doubtful whether it ever is possible for *all* the experiences of a person's lifetime to be included in a single narrative line, greatly though such inclusiveness may be desired, and doubtful, therefore, whether any biography can really be considered complete.

In my memoirs I had a good deal to say about my outer life, rather less about my inner life, and very little about my secret life (again in the Tibetan Buddhist sense), so that the three divisions of traditional Tibetan biography were by no means equally represented. This was due partly to the fact that I happened to have a strong visual memory and enjoyed describing the scenes through which I had passed and the people I had met (I was definitely one of those for whom 'the visible world exists'),[211] and partly to the fact that, especially when working on my second and third volumes of memoirs, I could rely on reports of my activities that had appeared, over the years, in the pages of the *Maha Bodhi*, as well as on old letters, odd diary leaves, and my published writings on Buddhism. For my secret life there was no comparable record, save for a handful of poems of a more personal nature and the occasional cryptic reference in notebook or diary.

A reference of this kind occurs at the beginning of the entry I made in my diary for Monday 6 December 1965 – the second day of my visit to Glasgow. It reads, 'Slept very little. Feverish most of the night.

Mental state very clear. Extraordinary experience of Transcendental, such as have not had since leaving Kalimpong. Terry had experience of intensely heightened state of awareness.' That is all. The entry goes on to speak of the arrival of tea (presumably brought by one of the guest house staff), breakfast, and the coming of Mr Pyle to settle our programme for the day.

Perhaps the most remarkable feature of this 'experience of the Transcendental', as of similar experiences of mine in the past, was its complete and utter discontinuity with any of my immediately preceding experiences. True, I had been speaking, only a few hours earlier, about the Buddha's Vision of Reality, and about how that vision found expression, for purposes of communication, in the principle of universal conditionality, but even though I had felt very much in tune with my subject, as I usually did on such occasions, this fact alone did not suffice to account for the abrupt appearance, or descent, of an experience of such a totally different order. It was as though I was living, on another level, a secret life that normally had no point of direct contact with my outer or even with my inner life, and that by the time of my visit to Glasgow this secret life had reached a point where its accumulated energy, no longer able to confine itself to its own level, so to speak, had suddenly burst through into the two lower levels. The sleeplessness, the feverishness, and the greatly enhanced mental clarity that accompanied the experience of the Transcendental were, as I well knew, all symptoms of that bursting through, and as such they could be seen as the infinitely remote repercussions of that experience in my physical and mental being.

That my experience of the Transcendental that night should have been such as I had 'not had since leaving Kalimpong' was hardly surprising. The life I had been leading for the last sixteen months, with its continual round of lectures, classes, personal interviews, and travel, was very much an outer life, and although there was an inner life too this was subordinated, to a great extent, to the requirements of the outer life. Of secret life there was none, or rather, that life was left to look after itself in its own mysterious way on its own level, where it continued to accumulate energy and from whence, during my Glasgow visit, it suddenly broke through into the lower levels on which I normally dwelt. It was not the first time such a thing had happened to me. In India, too, there had been times when my life was one of lectures, classes, personal interviews, and travel for months together, and during these periods too (as during quieter periods of retreat) there had been experiences which served to remind me that I had a secret as well as an outer and an inner life and that this secret life continued almost regardless of what was happening on the two other levels.

I was reminded of the existence of this secret life not only by the occasional irruption of the Transcendental but also by dreams, or rather by the appearance in a number of different guises of what was essentially one and the same dream. In these dreams there were always two buildings. Sometimes the buildings were like a monastery or a hermitage, sometimes like an ordinary house, but whatever their appearance, and regardless of whether they were large or small, one was always either situated on a higher level than the other or tucked away somewhere behind it, the two structures being connected by a secret path or, as in at least one dream, by a flight of stone steps cut in the mountainside. The building standing on a lower level, or alternatively in front of the other one, was open to the public; much frequented, it was a busy place, and it was here that (in my dreams) I usually stayed. The other building was private; it could not be seen from the one open to the public, and few people were even aware of its existence. Occasionally I would find myself making my way to it, either alone or with two or three friends. In other dreams, again, it would be derelict, or deserted, or I would realize that I had not visited it for a long time or even had forgotten that such a place existed and that it belonged to me.

When Terry moved to the flat in Lancaster Grove and I started spending part of my time there, it was as though the dream that had haunted me for so many years had, in a manner, come true. Once again there were two buildings, one public and one private, and once again, only this time in full waking consciousness, I found myself making my way from the former to the latter – from the Hampstead Buddhist Vihara to what Eric, more truly than he realized, jocularly referred to as the Other Vihara. But there was an important difference. In my dreams I had visited the private monastery or hermitage only occasionally, and at times had even forgotten about it completely. The Other Vihara, on the contrary, I visited at least once or twice a week, and I was always very much aware that by walking a couple of miles I could transport myself to an atmosphere rather different from the one by which I was usually surrounded. But though I spent much less time in Lancaster Grove than I did at Haverstock Hill, the truth was that at this time my centre of spiritual gravity had begun to shift from the Hampstead Buddhist Vihara to the Other Vihara, or rather, to that for which the Other Vihara, as the outward embodiment of the private monastery or hermitage of my dreams, had come to stand. This shift was eventually to have far-reaching consequences, not only for me but for the Buddhist movement in Britain, even for Western Buddhism as a whole. Those consequences would not begin to be felt for a year or more. In the meantime there awaited me more work, many important new impressions, and an experience of treachery such as I had never expected to have to face.

26
RESTORING THE BALANCE

My diary entry for 1 January 1966 was very different from my entry for the corresponding day of the previous year. This time there was no summary of my reflections on the recent history of British Buddhism, no expression of my hopes for the future, and no invocation of the blessings of the Buddhas, bodhisattvas, and *ḍākinīs*. There was only a record of the principal events of the day, as indeed there had also been in my entry for the last New Year's Day. *That* New Year's Day I had spent at the Hampstead Buddhist Vihara. It was a fairly typical day, in the course of which I had attended puja in the shrine-room with the rest of our little monastic community, received an unexpected telephone call from an old friend, and seen members of the Sangha Association. *This* New Year's Day I spent with Terry at the flat, where I had in fact passed the night. The day was by no means a typical one, either for my friend or for me. My diary entry reads:

> Got up at about midday, having spent the morning talking. At about 1 o'clock went and had lunch at the Indo-Pak. First time I had been out in civilian clothes. Then down to George Cummins, where Terry collected a box of stuff from his former office. Looked down the Charing X Rd for a jacket for me, but finally decided against getting one. Walked round Soho. Had a coffee. Did our shopping for the week, some of it in a street market. Stopped at Chalk Farm, where Terry collected his laundry. Looked round

> a second-hand bookshop. Terry bought a couple of paperbacks. Back to the flat. Terry found he had lost a black address book and thought it might still be at the office. Went back and searched, but without any success. Terry left a note for Alan. On returning to the flat discovered the address book in a camera case. Spent the evening reading, talking, and listening to records. Terry still depressed on account of the circumstances of yesterday's 'farewell'.

There are several points here that require explanation. To begin with there is the fact of my not getting up until about midday. By nature, I was (and still am) an early riser, and except for the rare occasions when I was ill I had not spent a whole morning in bed since I was a teenager. Terry was an early riser too, though in his case this was due not so much to personal inclination as to the fact that for many years he had had a nine-to-five job. Now that he had stopped working he saw no reason why he should not spend the morning in bed if he wanted to, and I saw no reason why I should not follow suit. In both cases there was an element of conscious rejection of a particular conditioning. What Terry was rejecting, in effect, was the Protestant work ethic in which he had been brought up, which was an integral part of a system and a way of life he had come to loathe, and according to which such minor indulgences as spending the morning in bed were not just wrong but positively sinful. In my own case I was rejecting the idea that as a Buddhist, and especially as a monk, it was necessary for me always to be leading a strictly disciplined life, as I had done for the last so many years. Not that I was disposed to question the value of discipline. Leading a disciplined life, working methodically, and following a regular routine, were things that came easily and naturally to me, so that I was all the more aware of the danger of their becoming matters of fixed habit and of my becoming incapable, eventually, of functioning in any other manner. Discipline was a means to an end, not an end in itself. From time to time it was therefore necessary to go, prophylactically, to the opposite extreme, at least in small harmless ways.

Thus it was that on that New Year's Day I did not get up until about midday, after Terry and I had spent the morning talking to each other across the room from our respective beds. Thus it was, too, that it was not until about 1 o'clock that we drove across to West Hampstead and had lunch at our favourite Indian restaurant. According to the Vinaya, it was an offence for a monk to partake of solid food after midday.[212] In India I had observed this rule strictly for a number of years, and it was 'official policy' at the Hampstead Vihara. During the last few years of my stay in India, however, I had adopted a more flexible attitude, especially when on tour among the newly converted Indian Buddhists, though I continued to observe the 'twelve o'clock rule', as some of my *bhikkhu* friends jocularly called it, during the four months of the rains-residence, when I immersed myself in study, meditation, and literary work and did not go beyond the gate of my small hillside monastery. But regardless of whether I did or did not partake of solid food after midday, it was clear to me that the principle, as distinct from the rule, was *moderation in eating*, and that this was a principle to be honoured by monk and layman alike.

Though it was an offence for a monk to eat after midday, it was a very minor offence, and one that could be expiated by formal confession to a fellow monk. Theravādin lay folk, who generally were ignorant of the Vinaya, tended to regard the offence as a serious one, sometimes even going so far as to equate it with the infinitely more serious offence of engaging in sexual intercourse with a woman, which automatically entailed permanent expulsion from the monastic community. Had a Theravādin layman, especially one of the older generation, happened to see me eating in the Indo-Pakistan restaurant that afternoon he (or she) would have been deeply shocked. He would have been still more shocked to see me wearing civilian clothes. That is to say, he *would* have been shocked had it been possible for him to believe the evidence of his senses and not think, as he was almost bound to think, that it was a case of mistaken identity on his part. Back in his own Sri Lanka, or Burma, or Thailand, it was unthinkable that a monk should ever wear civilian clothes. There a monk was one who wore the yellow robe, and one who wore the yellow robe was a monk, so that despite what the Buddha says in the *Dhammapada*, verse 142,[213] one who was *not* wearing the robe could not possibly be a monk and therefore the person seen in the restaurant, in this particular instance, could not possibly have been wearing civilian clothes *and* have been the Venerable Sangharakshita.

In India I had not once thought of wearing civilian clothes, that is, not since my going forth into the homeless state, and especially not since my formal ordination as a Buddhist monk.[214] I always felt quite at home in the yellow robe, and in any case, in the socio-religious context within which I was then living and working, the question of my wearing anything other than the robe simply did not arise. People may have been somewhat surprised, initially, to see a Westerner wearing the yellow robe of the renunciant, but they at least knew what the robe signified, so that even though it happened to be a stranger who was the bearer of the message the message itself was a perfectly familiar one and communication between us could, therefore, be easily established. In England – in Great Britain – the situation was entirely different. There the yellow robe did not signify anything, though the shaven head (if one did not wear a beret in public, as Ratanasara did) might convey a suggestion of something vaguely medieval and ascetic. My mother's friends had shown no surprise at my yellow robe, not only out of English politeness but because she had already told them all about me; but this was exceptional. Even in cosmopolitan London I had to put up with some strange looks, even with the occasional rude comment, when travelling by bus or tube, especially if I happened to be on my own. Some people seemed to think I was in fancy dress; others, that I was wearing a sari underneath my cloak, or even that I was a transvestite.

Thus it was with a distinct feeling of relief that, for the first time in nearly twenty years, I went out in civilian clothes. It was a relief to be able to walk down Charing Cross Road and round Soho, and to have a cup of coffee, without being stared at or feeling that I was being looked at out of the corner of somebody's eye. I have known Western Buddhist monks who did not mind being intruded on in this way and who, in the case of one or two of them, not only enjoyed being the object of so much attention but flaunted themselves and their yellow robes in a manner that was calculated to attract it. I was of a very different temperament from such exhibitionists. Far from wanting to attract attention, I sought to avoid it as much as possible. I wanted to be free to go about my occasions without being taken particular notice of by anybody. I wanted to be inconspicuous, to be lost in the crowd, to be the observer rather than the observed.

I was certainly inconspicuous that afternoon, as I walked round central London in my civilian clothes. I was wearing a pair of grey flannel trousers I had bought in Cambridge a few weeks earlier, together with a tweed sports jacket belonging to Terry. The jacket fitted me perfectly, as did the shirt (complete with sober tie) that went with it, for my friend was narrow-shouldered for his height, which was well above average. Terry was pleased to see me in civilian clothes, for he was one of those who believed that such oriental trappings as yellow robes had nothing to do with the actual study and practice of the Buddha's teaching and could, in fact, be an obstacle to its being taken seriously by intelligent people. For my part, I felt less strange in civilian clothes than I had expected to be, given the length of time that had elapsed since I last wore them, and soon I felt as much at home in jacket and trousers as I did in robes, besides being more comfortable in them when it was a question of going out and about. Not that I very often went out in civilian clothes. I went out in them only occasionally, and even then only with Terry, and more often than not we would be driving around in the Little Bus rather than walking or using public transport.

Nobody at the Hampstead Vihara knew that I sometimes wore civilian clothes, with the possible exception of Eric, whom I may have told. Had the more decidedly Theravādin members of the Sangha Association known they would have been scandalized, for thanks to the efforts of a succession of Sinhalese, Thai, and Thailand-returned *bhikkhus* the minds of a section of the British Buddhist community were already imbued with the formalistic notions that prevailed in the Buddhist countries of South-East Asia. As for the other members of the Association, most, I suspect, would not have objected to my wearing civilian clothes sometimes, any more than most members of the Buddhist Society would have done. According to Christmas Humphreys the true Buddhist was one who 'wore the yellow robe within' (a favourite phrase of his), and probably he and his colleagues at the Society would have preferred to see Western monks wearing ordinary Western dress rather than going about in what the average Englishman, and even the average English Buddhist, could not but regard as outlandish costume.

My finally deciding against getting myself a jacket, when Terry and I looked down Charing Cross Road for one, was certainly not owing to any shortage there either of clothing shops or jackets. Rather was the opposite the case. There were several such shops, and in each shop there were so many jackets, of so many different sizes, colours, materials, styles, and prices, that in the end, unable to make up my mind which one to choose, I decided to put off the whole perplexing business to another day, with the result that several years were to pass before I actually bought myself a jacket. My indecisiveness was due, in part, to the fact that as a monk I was not used to buying my own clothes (one's yellow robes were provided by the laity, and were always of the same traditional pattern), in part to the fact that I had been away so long that I had no idea what sort of clothes would be suitable for someone of my age and position (or lack of position), and neither Terry nor the shop assistants were able to give me much help in this connection.

While I had experienced no difficulty in adjusting psychologically to being back in Britain, the truth of the matter was that living, as I did, in the esoteric enclave that was the Hampstead Buddhist Vihara, I had little knowledge of what life in the workaday world outside was really like. Not only did I have no idea what sort of clothes to buy. Doing the week's shopping and collecting laundry, as Terry and I did after walking round Soho and having a coffee, were novel experiences for me, the more especially as some of that shopping was done in a crowded and noisy street-market and I had not set foot in a launderette before. To my friend, of course, such tasks as shopping and collecting one's laundry were only too familiar, and it was thanks to him that, as the weeks and months went by, these and a hundred other concomitants of modern living became familiar to me – or became less unfamiliar. It was Terry more than anyone else, in fact, who enabled me to make the transition to living in England (as distinct from living at the Hampstead Buddhist Vihara), just as twenty years ago it had been the then Robin Banerjee who enabled me to make the transition to living in India, and for me, at least, this was an important element in our friendship.[215]

The last point that requires explanation, in my diary entry for New Year's Day, relates to the fact that in the evening Terry was still feeling depressed. He was depressed, as the entry itself indicates, on account of the circumstances of the send-off his colleagues at the advertising agency had given him the previous evening. This had been a boisterous, alcoholic affair; he had not looked forward to it, and returned to the flat slightly drunk and wanting to talk. It was not the boisterousness, or even the freely flowing alcohol, that had disturbed him, so much as his being there on what he felt were completely false pretences. Though he had worked for the agency for a number of years, and was regarded as a popular figure, none of his colleagues really knew him, so that the 'good old Terry' who was the recipient of their hearty, if alcoholic, good wishes for the future was not he but a totally different person. They knew nothing of his problems, nothing of his aspirations, and did not understand why, at the age of thirty, he was leaving a well-paid job in order, apparently, to study philosophy.

Another source of Terry's depression was the fact of his having been unable to make a short speech acknowledging his colleagues' good wishes, as was customary on such occasions. He had made a few notes beforehand, and indeed tried to speak, but after stammering out a few words he was so overcome by anxiety, and was sweating so profusely, that he was obliged to stop and sit down. He sat down amid applause, his colleagues thinking he had simply had too much to drink. But Terry knew better. For him, therefore, his failure to rise to the occasion was a deeply humiliating experience, and one that served to reinforce the inferiority and anxiety he often felt in social situations.

27
CIRCLES WITHIN CIRCLES

Although there was no summary of my reflections on the recent history of British Buddhism, and no expression of my hopes for the future, as there had been in my diary of a year ago, this did not mean that I had no plans for the coming months or that I did not have a tolerably clear idea of the nature and present extent of our tiny British Buddhist movement or of my own place within that movement. It was as though there was a series of concentric circles, and that the bigger these circles were the greater was the number of people they contained. I occupied the innermost circle. With me in that circle there were only two other people, Terry and Eric, though we were shortly to be joined by a fourth, in the person of Thich Thien Chau, a scholarly Vietnamese monk of about my own age who had often stayed with me in Kalimpong and who was one of my closest friends within the monastic order.[216]

The second circle, which was not very much larger than the first, contained the Three Musketeers, Amritapani, Ruth, Beryl Jenks, and, perhaps, Bernie Whitelaw. The Three Musketeers saw me regularly, and few weeks passed without my having a lengthy discussion with all three or with one or two of them. Alf and Mike continued to be strongly inclined to the Mahāyāna, especially in its colourful Tibetan form, and under their influence Jack, too, had begun to incline to it, though the Theravāda remained his favourite form of Buddhism. Amritapani saw me rather less often. Having left Biddulph before her year of meditation and study was up, she was struggling to create a community in the terrace property which, with the reluctant agreement of her trustees, she had bought in Camden Town, and which she liked to think of as an outpost of the Hampstead Vihara. Ruth (and of course Maurice) still lived just round the corner; we still travelled down to Victoria together by bus or tube whenever I had a lecture or class at the Buddhist Society, or at least did so on those occasions when Terry was not free to drive all three of us there in the Little Bus. Besides being one of the stars of the speakers' class, she was now able to teach basic meditation, and I had already started handing over some of my classes to her. Beryl Jenks, a tiny, ginger-haired South African, was a former Scientologist. She was also a former actress, as well as being a drama teacher and a speech therapist, and it was by virtue of this combination of talents that she had quickly become my right-hand man at the speakers' class. Lean, haggard-faced Bernie Whitelaw came to see me every Saturday morning, when it was his duty (unless I happened to be out of London at the time) to hand me the Vihara's housekeeping money for the week and his pleasure to stay for one of those little chats from which I learned so much about his tenants and about the previous occupants of the Vihara.

The third circle was not only bigger than the second but very much bigger. It comprised about two hundred persons, of whom the majority were people who regularly attended my lectures and classes, whether at the Hampstead Vihara or at the Buddhist Society. The rest were people like Christmas Humphreys, Muriel Daw, Kathy Phelps, Maurice Walshe, and even George Goulstone, with all of whom I was in fairly regular contact by virtue of the fact that they were office-bearers in one or other (or in Maurice's case both) of the two Buddhist organizations which, ever since my arrival in England, I had been trying to bring together, namely, the Buddhist Society and the Sangha Association. Most of those attending my lectures and classes left straight afterwards, but a few of them, especially at the Vihara and especially after the Sunday lecture, stayed on either to talk with one another in the basement over a cup of coffee or to have a personal interview with me. On Sunday evenings there might be half a dozen people standing in the passage outside the door of the abbot's room or sitting on the stairs, all patiently waiting their turn. Of all ages, both sexes, and varying degrees of cultivation, they were probably representative of the kind of audiences I had for my lectures (far more people came to lectures than to classes), at least there at the Vihara. Some of them wanted to ask my advice about a personal problem, others to discuss this or that point of Buddhist doctrine, and yet others simply to ask which book on the Dharma they ought to read next. Occasionally there would be a young man who wanted to be a monk, or an evangelist who wished to convert me to Christianity, or rather, to his own particular brand of that religion. But whatever the reason for their coming to see me might be, few of them, as I gradually discovered, thought of themselves as Buddhists or indeed could be regarded as such, so that the actual number of those attending my lectures, or even my meditation classes, was not a reliable indication of the real strength of the Buddhist movement in Britain.

Most of the people who came to see me in the abbot's room are now not even names to me. Even those whose names survive in my diary are, in many cases, no more than names. The few exceptions relate to people who were unusual in some way or who had a strange story to tell. One of these was a young man of nineteen whose father was in prison for committing incest with his daughter, the young man's elder sister. The case had attracted a good deal of publicity (I could well imagine how the gutter press had revelled in the details), and he and his mother and sister had been forced to change their name and move to another part of the country. All this had happened some years ago, he said. His father would be in prison for a few more years, and in the meantime he was visiting him every week and trying to share with him whatever he himself had learned about Buddhism. I was greatly struck by the young man's sincerity and decency, as well as by his loyalty to his father in these painful and even traumatic circumstances. Eventually, when we had met a few times, he brought his mother and sister to see me, and it was then that I heard the strangest part of the story. His sister, who was now married, and who was the older of the two by five or six years, said little or nothing; but the mother had a good deal to say, and indeed seemed relieved to have found someone outside the family to whom she could speak freely. The relationship between father and daughter had lasted for several years, coming to an end only when the girl reached the age of sixteen, when she started going out with boys. This made the father very jealous, so jealous, in fact, that whenever she went out with a boy there was a furious row, and in the end, exasperated by his behaviour, she had told her mother the truth. Daddy didn't want her to go out with boys because he was jealous, and he was jealous because.... The mother had been thunderstruck. At the same time, she told me, she realized, to her horror, that she *had known what was going on all along*.

Veronica was certainly an unusual person. She was a witch. How she came to be present at my Sunday lectures I no longer recollect, if indeed I ever knew, but before long it became obvious that she was interested less in Buddhism than in me. Of medium height, blonde, and in her mid-thirties, she habitually wore a black sweater and black leggings that fitted as closely as a bathing costume and revealed every detail of her decidedly curvaceous figure. Naturally she was an object of intense masculine interest, and I was not surprised to learn, later on, that she could not travel on the Underground without exciting what Dr Johnson would have termed the amorous propensities of her male fellow passengers.[217] In the meantime she had joined the queue outside the door of the abbot's room, and was even coming to see me during the week, usually bringing some charm or amulet for me to wear. Perhaps she was trying to cast a spell on me. I certainly seemed to have cast a spell on her. In front of me she either stood absolutely rigid, as if transfixed by my gaze, or trembled and looked down in confusion as if totally overpowered by my presence. I was unable to make up my mind whether I really did have that kind of effect on her or whether it was just an act she put on in order to flatter my masculine – or spiritual – vanity and in this way wheedle herself into my good graces. Years later I remembered that my friend Dr Mehta of Bombay had once told me, after giving me a medical examination, that I had 'a high sex potential'.[218] Could Veronica, I wondered, have sensed this (untapped) potential and wanted to utilize it for her own magical purposes? It was well known that magic, especially of the darker kind, often depended on the deployment of sexual energy, whether individual or collective.

Whatever the reason may have been for her behaving in front of me in the way she did, that behaviour had no effect on me, and I was in no danger of succumbing to whatever designs she may have had on the potential of which Dr Mehta had spoken. Her antics amused me, like those of a kitten playing on the hearthrug, and when she invited me to tea at her flat in Putney, where she lived with her ten-year-old son, I had no hesitation in accepting the invitation. I arrived just as another person was leaving – a tall, thin young man wearing a green dress and heavy make-up. That was her friend Daphne, Veronica explained, as though young men in green dresses and heavy make-up were part of everyday life. She was much more at ease in her own surroundings than she ever was at the Vihara, and much more talkative, and before long I was being regaled with an account of the activities of the various black magic groups to which she and her friends belonged. One of these friends was Gerald Yorke, whom she seemed to know quite well. Though aware that in his youth Gerald had been a disciple of the notorious Aleister Crowley, I was under the impression that his involvement with black magic was very much a thing of the past, but it now appeared this was not the case. Not that I was really surprised. Gerald's fondness for telling smutty stories in the Oak Room indicated there was a 'dirty old man' side to his character, and this may well have found an outlet in some of the activities Veronica described. So far as I knew, he was the only Buddhist (for such he regarded himself as being) who had anything to do with black magic, but a few months later there came to see me a young Adonis with a Yorkshire accent who combined a fascination for black magic with an interest in Buddhism, and who besides attending my Sunday lectures wanted me to teach him the black magic practices he was convinced I must have learned in India. In vain I protested I had learned no such practices, whether in India or anywhere else. He continued to press me, and one day brought his girlfriend to meet me. She was Irish, and a Roman Catholic, and after our meeting told him – so he reported – that she had felt terrified and was convinced I was the Devil. But black magic is not a subject on which it is desirable to dwell, and I had better pass on to the fourth and last of my circles.

This contained all the people who attended the summer school and the various provincial Buddhist groups I visited from time to time, especially those I visited on a regular monthly basis. As some of the people attending the summer school also came to my lectures and classes at the Hampstead Vihara or the Buddhist Society, or at one or other of the provincial groups, some of the people contained in the third circle were also contained, temporarily, in the fourth. People whom I met only during the ten days of the summer school, or in the course of a flying visit to a provincial group, I obviously could not get to know very well, though there were exceptions, at least in the case of some of the provincial groups. Among the exceptions were white-haired Charles Williams in Hastings, the Wraggs, and lame, loyal Jim Martin in Brighton, much-married Derek Southall in Birmingham, and bald, bespectacled little Cyril Petitt in Northampton, who despite being a victim of polio and having to run about on all fours when at home, had a wife and two children and functioned as the very efficient secretary of the group.

My fourth circle could be regarded as also containing people who, though I knew them quite well, I did not see very often. These included John Hipkin at the Blue House near Maidstone, Adrienne Bennett, whose husband was dying of cancer, Clare Cameron, still editing the *Science of Thought Review* down in Bosham and still a chain smoker, and the various Sinhalese *bhikkhus* at Chiswick, the seniormost of whom was the Venerable Saddhatissa, who at Ratanasara's insistence had been elected vice-president of the Sangha Sabha *in absentia*. Tall, scholarly, and inclined to be sardonic, Saddhatissa had been known to me in India, having in fact participated in my *bhikkhu* ordination at Sarnath in 1950.[219] Shortly after his arrival in England I went to see him at the Sinhalese Vihara, as the London Buddhist Vihara was commonly designated. I found him wriggling into the long, narrow tube that one could make with the upper robe by rolling its two shorter edges together, after which one pulled the top of the tube well down, thus freeing one's head, then wound the upper portion of the roll round one's left shoulder and so down into one's left hand, which had to keep a tight grip on the end of the roll if the whole arrangement was not to come undone. It was a style much in favour with the 'orthodox', probably because of the way in which the monk's imprisonment within his yellow cocoon was suggestive of a strict observance of the Vinaya on his part. 'Do you know *why* I am doing this?' Saddhatissa demanded, as his head emerged from the drapery. No, I did not know. 'I am doing it,' he said slowly and emphatically, 'in order ... to *please* ... FOOLS.' The fools in question, as I well knew, were the conservative Sinhalese lay folk who would soon be coming to offer Saddhatissa and his fellow monks a ceremonial meal.

Though few of the people attending the summer school and the various provincial Buddhist groups were well known to me, after sixteen months in England I was sufficiently well acquainted with most of them to understand just where they stood in relation to Buddhism. As was the case with those attending my lectures and classes in London, few of them thought of themselves as Buddhists or could be regarded as such. Some were Spiritualists, some theosophists, some Vedantists, while others subscribed to this or that brand of universalism. More than once, at the summer school, I overheard a group of elderly women comparing the merits of the different summer schools they had already attended that year, it apparently being their custom to pass the summer months going from one to another of these. As one of them remarked, it was cheaper than staying at a hotel and one met more people. At a meeting of the Northampton group I met a stout, obviously uneducated woman who, it transpired, was a professional medium. Who was my spirit guide, she wanted to know. I explained that Buddhist monks did not have spirit guides. My reply greatly astonished her. She had a spirit guide, she assured me, volubly. He was a little boy, all dressed in blue. She saw him every day, and he told her what to say. If I did not have a spirit guide, how did I know what to say when I gave a lecture or when people asked me for advice? It therefore was not surprising that my experience at the summer school and the provincial groups should have led me to conclude, as I had concluded from my experience of the people I saw at the Vihara, that the actual number of those attending lectures and classes was not a reliable indication of the real strength of the Buddhist movement in Britain.

British Buddhists still numbered hundreds rather than thousands, though from time to time one heard more optimistic estimates. Nor was the British Buddhist movement simply a very small one. It was also a highly diluted one. It was diluted in the sense that even those who regarded themselves as Buddhists, and they were few enough, tended to combine their Buddhism with elements that were incompatible, in some cases, with the basic principles of the Dharma. When asked how many Buddhists there were in Britain, I was apt to reply, if in provocative mood, that there were altogether two and a half. There was myself, reckoned as one whole Buddhist, while the combined membership of the Buddhist Society, the Sangha Association, and the provincial groups, made up the remaining one and a half Buddhists. This was a gross exaggeration, or rather minimization, of the actual position, but I wanted people to ask themselves what it meant to be a Buddhist and whether they were really justified in regarding themselves as such.

Though it was with spiritualism, or theosophy, or Vedanta, that many of them sought to combine their Buddhism, Christianity was the biggest diluting agent. This was only natural. Christianity, in one form or another, was the national religion, most people had been brought up in it, and much as they might appreciate the ethical teachings of Buddhism, or value meditation, they did not always find it easy to give up their belief in God or to accept the fact that Buddhism was a non-theistic religion. Some of them found it quite impossible to do this, even going so far as to maintain, despite the evidence of the scriptures, that the Buddha had *not* denied the existence of God.[220] In India I had encountered this perverse attitude time after time (Mahatma Gandhi had famously argued that all great spiritual teachers believed in God, and that since the Buddha was a great spiritual teacher he too must have believed in God, whatever his latter-day disciples might say to the contrary),[221] and it was disappointing to find the same attitude so prevalent in England. It was disappointing, indeed, that the Buddhist movement in Britain should be so small, and so diluted, even though I could not but recognize that it took people a long time to become accustomed to unfamiliar ideas, and that in the meantime their views might well be an odd mixture of the old and the new. Perhaps an entirely fresh impetus was needed. More than once I wondered if I ought not to start giving lectures and holding classes outside the orbit of the Hampstead Vihara and the Buddhist Society, though without relinquishing my existing activities and responsibilities, and even discussed the feasibility of my so doing with the Three Musketeers and Eric (Terry had no interest in the Buddhist movement as such), all of whom were as wholeheartedly Buddhist as anyone within any of my four circles. There was no question of starting another Buddhist organization. We already had two of these, the Buddhist Society and the Sangha Association, and in any case, had I not been trying, ever since my arrival in England, to bring the Society and the Association together, and did not much work still remain to be done in this connection?

Just how much work remained to be done was borne in on me quite early in the New Year, when Maurice told me that the less we had to do with the Buddhist Society the better – 'we' meaning the Sangha Association, the Vihara, and, I supposed, the Vihara's present incumbent, who was still giving lectures and taking meditation classes regularly at the Society's Eccleston Square headquarters. What prompted him to say such a thing I do not know. Perhaps he was going through one of his periodic bouts of antagonism towards the Society's president. Perhaps he had quarrelled with Ruth on account of her loyalty to Toby and his Zen Class. (It was difficult to imagine *her* quarrelling with *him*.) Or again, perhaps he was unhappy at the extent of my own involvement with the older and better-known organization, of which, after all, I had been a member during the war and to which I still felt a certain loyalty. Whatever may have been the reason for his wanting us to have less to do with the Buddhist Society, I strongly disagreed with him. We ought to have more to do with the Society, I declared, not less, so that there took place between us what my diary terms 'rather a clash', after which he left to take the first of the Vihara's Tuesday Theravāda study classes.

It was not simply that I disagreed with Maurice. I was profoundly shocked. Besides being chairman of the Sangha Trust and the Sangha Association, he was one of the vice-presidents of the Buddhist Society, and one would have thought that as a matter of common honesty – not to speak of Buddhist principle – he would not have urged upon me in private a policy which, as he well knew, he could hardly have advocated publicly without being accused of trying to split British Buddhism. It also shocked me to recall how at the last Annual General Meeting of the Sangha Association, held a few weeks earlier, he had taken a very different line from the one he took with me. Speaking in his chairman's report (which I published in the January issue of *The Buddhist*) of the past year's very extensive programme of lectures and other activities, he referred appreciatively to how the speakers' class and the guided group meditation classes had been held alternately at the Vihara and at the Buddhist Society's headquarters in Eccleston Square, adding 'relations between the two organizations have undoubtedly become closer recently' as though he thoroughly approved of this development.[222] As I was beginning to realize, Maurice had a Machiavellian side to his character, and a month after our clash I caught another glimpse of it. Mangalo having decided to leave Biddulph for good, the Sangha Trust had decided to dispose of the property and make plans for a meditation centre nearer London. Maurice had been one of the parties to the decision. However, at the beginning of February I discovered that he had been playing a double game, having secretly instigated the Midlands Buddhist Group, as the Birmingham group was officially known, to get up a petition opposing the sale of Biddulph. Though well aware that Maurice was difficult and irascible, I had not realized he could be duplicitous, and the realization gave me cause for disquiet.

28
NEWS FROM SIKKIM

The way in which I spent the first day of the New Year was far from being typical of how I spent the whole month. But although January was a busy time for me, it also happens to be one of those times my recollection of which is decidedly patchy. In itself this is not surprising. What is surprising is that I should have no memory whatever of the very event which, of all the events of the month, might reasonably be expected to have made the strongest impression on me and of which, therefore, I might be thought to have the clearest and most vivid recollection. This notable event was the memorial meeting held for Lal Bahadur Shastri, the Prime Minister of India, who had died suddenly a few days earlier and which, according to my diary, I attended with Terry.[223] The entry for Friday 21 January reads (in part), 'Reached Albert Hall soon after 7 and took our seats on the platform. Speeches by Prime Minister [Harold Wilson], Lord Mountbatten, Selwyn Lloyd, Lord Sorensen and Jeremy Thorpe. Lord Attlee, Kingsley Martin, Dame Sybil Thorndike, Arnold Toynbee, etc. also present. All over by 8.30.'[224] Whether I spoke to anyone, or anyone spoke to me, either before or after the meeting, I do not know, but I must have surveyed this gathering of the nation's great and good with considerable interest and have been more than a little pleased, perhaps, to find myself – probably thanks to friends in the Indian High Commission – occupying a seat on the platform as sole representative of Buddhism.

But if I have no memory of the Albert Hall meeting I have a distinct recollection of what Terry and I did straight afterwards. 'Then round to Clare's,' my diary continues, in its usual laconic fashion. 'Fitted my cloak. Left at 9.15.' The Clare in question was the elegant, well-groomed Clare Sampson. Though she was no longer secretary of the Sangha Association, we were still in touch, as she had offered to make me a winter cloak to replace the light summer one that had been stitched for me, shortly after my arrival in England, by Upāsikā Jhanananda, the elderly Russian nun who had been a disciple of the notorious Chao Kung, alias Trebitsch-Lincoln,[225] and who lived alone in a flat not far from the Vihara on a stipend from the Sangha Trust. Clare being a much less experienced needlewoman than the old *upāsikā*, my winter cloak had been a long time in the making, and it was only now, more than halfway through January, that Terry and I found ourselves visiting her in her basement flat in Victoria for my fitting. The cloak was of a thick woollen material, dark brown in colour, and so voluminous that it hung down round me in a multiplicity of folds. It was also very heavy, and very hot, so that when it was at last finished I wore it only when the weather was exceptionally cold – or used it as a blanket. In its very different way, my brown woollen cloak proved to be no less inconvenient a garment than Saddhatissa's yellow cotton tube.

Victoria was the scene of another visit that month. This time I paid it on my own, and not to a tiny basement flat but to a spacious apartment in the vicinity of Westminster Cathedral. The apartment had been rented from a relative of the Queen by Palden Thondup Namgyal, the Maharaja of Sikkim, who was paying a short visit to London with his American second wife, the former Hope Cooke, and their small son.[226] I had known the Maharaja since the early fifties, when he was still Crown Prince, and had several times been his guest in Gangtok, the principality's 'village capital', when I went there to lecture on the Dharma.[227] Indeed I believe I was his guest in Gangtok, and delivered lectures there, not long before my departure for England. Politically, Sikkim (population about 200,000) was a protectorate of India; constitutionally, it was a diarchy, in that some powers were vested in the Maharaja, who exercised them through his *diwan* (actually an Indian appointee), and some in the elected representatives of the people. There were a number of political parties, as well as a representative of the Government of India, known as the Political Officer, who like his British predecessors was the real power in the land. The situation was further complicated by the fact that the ruling family and the landowning aristocracy were of Tibetan Buddhist stock, while the rest of the population was mainly Hindu and mainly of Nepalese immigrant origin. I was in the uncomfortable position of being on friendly terms both with the Maharaja and with Kazi Lhendup Dorje, the Maharaja's main political opponent, who lived in Kalimpong and who with his formidable European wife was committed to the overthrow of the Namgyal dynasty and the establishment of full parliamentary democracy in Sikkim.[228]

The Kazini, as she was universally known, was the Maharaja's *bête noire* on account of the campaign she was conducting against him in the correspondence columns of the English-language Calcutta dailies, and whenever we met he would be sure to complain bitterly to me about her latest attacks. The present occasion was no exception. After we had discussed the state of British Buddhism, and the current political situation in Sikkim, the Maharaja proceeded to launch into his customary diatribe against the Kazini, a diatribe that his painful stutter did not make it easy for him to deliver. Since he and the Kazini were both Buddhists (he was president of the Maha Bodhi Society, she a personal disciple of mine), I had always sought to pour oil – the oil of the Dharma – on these very troubled waters, and if I could not bring the two of them together at least persuade them to moderate their hostility. Hitherto I had been unsuccessful, and in London, so far as the Maharaja was concerned, unsuccessful I continued to be.

Palden Thondup Namgyal was not the only Sikkimese friend who was in town that month. One afternoon I received a visit from diminutive, quietly-spoken Sonam Topgay, who was a nephew of Kazi Lhendup Dorje, a member of the Political Officer's staff, and a disciple of Dudjom Rimpoche, one of my own Vajrayāna gurus, and who had been the means of my meeting more than one eminent Tibetan lama.[229] Sonam's visit was not without a purpose. As I already knew, the Political Officer had placed his services at the disposal of the Dalai Lama, and he had come to ask me if I would help correct the English of a book His Holiness was writing on Tibetan Buddhism. Naturally I agreed, though Sonam was unable to say how long it would be before the first draft of the book was ready. The rest of our time together was spent exchanging news of common friends, talking about the Dalai Lama and the Karmapa, and discussing, at considerable length, the important Buddhist doctrine of the so-called 'two truths', namely, the relative truth and the absolute truth or – to translate the Indian terms more literally – the conventional truth and the ultimate truth.[230] More than my meeting with the Maharaja, my contact with Sonam Topgay brought with it memories of my life in the foothills of the eastern Himalayas, with their views of the distant snow peaks, their colourful local people, and their no less colourful festivals and processions. As we talked, I could almost hear the deep, rumbling sound of the Tibetan trumpets, almost smell the acrid perfume of the juniper incense.

From the foothills of the eastern Himalayas to the suburbs of South London is a far cry, and it did not take long for my memories of the one to be obliterated by my far older memories of the other when, a few days after Sonam's visit, Terry and I drove down to Southfields to see my father and Auntie Florrie (as I still thought of her). I had seen my mother a few weeks earlier, when she told me of the death of my Auntie Jessie, who had been a kindly presence in my early childhood,[231] and now it was time for me to see my father. Of my actual meeting with him and Florrie I remember only that he showed Terry some photographs of me as a child, but I have a vivid recollection of the journey to Southfields. From central London we drove down across Westminster Bridge to Kennington, and from Kennington down through Oval, Stockwell, Clapham, Balham, and Tooting Bec to Tooting Broadway, where we turned right into Garratt Lane. Garratt Lane – formerly known as Defoe Road, after the author of *Robinson Crusoe*, who once lived there – took us to Earlsfield, where we turned left at the station, made our way through the side streets, and so arrived at my father and Auntie Florrie's door. Balham, Tooting Bec, and the Broadway were the heart of working-class south London. They also happened to be the scene of the first eighteen years of my life, and as we drove through them I looked out of the window of the Little Bus with more than just idle curiosity. Much had changed. Balham Hill was no longer dominated by the giant green dome of the Hippodrome, traffic had increased tenfold, and there were no swaying, clanging trams rattling along. The biggest change, however, was in the population. Two-thirds of the people thronging the streets of Balham and Tooting Bec were Asian, and some, the women especially, wore traditional dress. In Upper Tooting High Street many of the names above the shops were Punjabi, Gujarati, and Bengali names, while the windows of the shops themselves, more often than not, displayed either crimson, emerald green, and mustard yellow saris or pyramids of Indian sweetmeats covered with silver foil. One could almost have fancied oneself in Bombay. The South London of 1966, it seemed, was an altogether more crowded, lively, and colourful place than the South London I had known in the thirties and forties.

Towards the end of the month Terry and I saw several films, only one of which I remember at all clearly. This was the famous screen version of *Henry V*, with Laurence Olivier in the title role, which according to my diary I enjoyed very much, though I thought the sets 'a little crude'.[232] Terry had now more or less recovered from the depression into which the circumstances of his send-off had plunged him, and which had lasted for several days, and we spent much of such time as we were able to spend together listening to music and discussing the books we were then reading, which in my case included D. T. Suzuki's *The Zen Doctrine of No Mind*[233] and in Terry's *The Heart of Man* by Erich Fromm.[234] We also visited Bristol, where I addressed the members of the University's International Society on 'Buddhism and Western Civilization' and where, taking advantage of the opportunity, we looked round the cathedral, including the particularly impressive Norman chapter house, and saw the church of St Mary Redcliffe (the fairest parish in England, according to Elizabeth I), with its poignant associations with Chatterton, 'the marvellous boy'.[235] On the way back to London we stopped first at Bath, where we saw the Abbey, then at Oxford, where, having spent an hour at the Ashmolean, we called on Trungpa Rimpoche, who was happy to accept my invitation to conduct a few meditation courses at Biddulph.

29
BUDDHISM AND THE BISHOP OF WOOLWICH

During my years in India I had become increasingly aware that the Christian missionaries, both Roman Catholic and Protestant, were not only anxious to make converts but none too scrupulous about how they made them, and my knowledge of this fact had given me a decided animus against Christianity.[236] I had not always had that animus. The reading of *Isis Unveiled* at the age of fourteen may have liberated me from the burden of Christian belief,[237] but I was not antagonistic to Christianity, and even when, two years later, I read the *Diamond Sūtra* and the *Sūtra of Wei Lang* and realized I was a Buddhist and always had been,[238] I continued to appreciate such works as St Augustine's *Confessions* and Dionysius the Areopagite's *Mystical Theology*.[239] While still in the army, and stationed in Singapore, I happened to come across a little book called *The Practice of the Presence of God*, a collection of the sayings and letters of Brother Lawrence of the Resurrection, the seventeenth-century French Carmelite mystic, and was so taken by the work that I wrote an article on certain aspects of its teaching for the *Vedanta Kesari*, one of the English-language monthly organs of the Ramakrishna Math and Mission.[240]

It was only some years later, when I had settled in Kalimpong, and had come to know what kind of methods the missionaries, with few exceptions, were employing to 'win souls for Christ', that I developed that animus against Christianity of which I have spoken. The methods in question were both direct and indirect. They ranged from providing free, or virtually free, education and medical treatment to offering direct financial inducements, as when the moneylending priests of the local Roman Catholic mission offered to write off the debts of the poverty-stricken inhabitants of a Lepcha village not far from Kalimpong if they agreed to be baptized. This anxiety of the missionaries to make converts, and their total lack of scruple about how they made them, was at no time more nakedly apparent than in the months immediately following the Lhasa uprising of 1959, when there was a dramatic increase in the number of Tibetan refugees pouring into the little Himalayan township and when it seemed as though evangelists were flocking vulture-like from the four quarters of the globe to feast on what they thought was the dead body of Tibetan Buddhism. More than once, during the next few years, did I see preachers compelling hungry refugees to listen to a sermon, or read a tract, before they would give them a few spoonfuls of rice. But that was not the worst. Children taken from parents who were unable to feed them would be kept incommunicado within the mission compound and subjected to intensive indoctrination. Nonetheless, my animus against Christianity did not prevent me, during this period, from reading a certain amount of Christian literature, especially once I had accepted the Sangha Trust's invitation and agreed to spend a few months in England.

Three books were of special interest to me: Geoffrey Faber's *The Oxford Apostles* and the two Penguin volumes on, respectively, Methodism and the Orthodox Church. The central figure of Faber's study was John Henry Newman, whose life was traced in detail up to the point at which, as all England held its breath, he made the fateful decision to leave the Church of England and become a Roman Catholic. It was a dramatic story, and I too held my breath as the future cardinal nerved himself to take the final step. In my teens I had read Newman's *Arians of the Fourth Century* and the two volumes of his *Essays Critical and Historical* and had greatly admired his beautiful, Ciceronian prose style, but now I empathized with him as he agonized over his religious difficulties, and shared his relief as he emerged from the darkness, as it was for him, of his doubts, into the light of certainty.[241] Of the volume on Methodism I remember only its leaving me with the impression that the religion of John Wesley was a very different thing from the

Methodism with which I had been familiar in my boyhood, albeit to a very limited extent, and that there was in it an experiential element which was almost Zen-like in its intensity. Timothy (later Bishop Kallisto) Ware's *The Orthodox Church* was quite another matter. I had read Stanley and Arseniev's works on the subject[242] around the time of my reading Newman's writings, while I was still in the *bardo* between my two realizations, namely, that I was *not* a Christian and that I *was* a Buddhist, but Ware's book was a new one, and not only gave a detailed and comprehensive account of the great Eastern branch of Christendom but was the means of introducing me to the highly significant concept of *sobornost*, most inadequately translated as 'collegiality', of which I was to be reminded, many years later, when attempting to give adequate expression to my understanding of the real nature of the Buddhist spiritual community.[243]

After my return to England I continued to read Christian literature. The Hampstead Vihara's little library, which I was not slow to investigate, contained a number of popular and scholarly books on Christianity, including translations of some of the classics of Christian mysticism. The proportion of works dealing with Christianity, especially as compared with the proportion of those dealing with Buddhism, was indeed astonishingly high, a fact the significance of which I came to understand only later. Among the classics of Christian mysticism were two volumes of selections from the *Philokalia*, the Orthodox Church's great collection of writings on the ascetic and contemplative life, and these I read with avidity. Though there were fundamental doctrinal differences, I sensed a greater affinity between Buddhism and Orthodoxy, spiritually speaking, than there was between Buddhism and Roman Catholicism. In the Hampstead Public Library I came across more books on Orthodox spirituality, including one about the monks of Mount Athos. My most important discovery in this field, however, was *Lectures in Godmanhood*, by Vladimir Solovyov, the nineteenth-century Russian philosopher, mystic, and poet, who had researched the Indian and Gnostic philosophies at the British Museum and was a friend of Dostoyevsky and Tolstoy. Later I read other works of his, and came to develop an admiration not just for his thought but for his life, which was one of exceptional integrity and courage.[244] Both the Hampstead Public Library and the Vihara Library contained accounts of the Second Vatican Council,[245] as well as a number of books on matters of current religious debate, and it was not long before I came upon a modest paperback volume, published the previous year, which had sold hundreds of thousands of copies on both sides of the Atlantic and been the centre of a good deal of controversy.

This was *Honest to God*, by the Bishop of Woolwich, John A. T. Robinson.[246] Echoes of the controversy surrounding the book had reached me even in distant Kalimpong, and I had looked forward to being able to read it on my return to England. I was not disappointed. It was an honest book, and one that was of more than academic interest even to a Buddhist, and I therefore decided to give a lecture on it under the title 'Buddhism and the Bishop of Woolwich'. After all, I told my audience at the time, the Bishop was trying to come to grips with a problem that was common to all religions, and which they all had to face: the problem of the restatement of spiritual truths in a language that was meaningful to contemporary humanity. In the case of Christianity the problem was perhaps more acute than it was in the case of some other religions, and the Bishop's efforts to come to grips with it were therefore of particular interest.

As it was not possible for me to deal in a single lecture with all the issues he had raised, I confined myself to two or three major ones that were of special interest to Buddhists. The most important of these was the issue of God. Historically speaking, Christianity was a form of theism, but in modern times theism had come increasingly under attack; even religious people felt it to be unsatisfactory. The Bishop's great merit was that he had faced up to the fact. Chapter 2 of *Honest to God* was entitled 'The End of Theism?' Despite the interrogative, the reader was not left much in doubt that he thought traditional theism was finished. Moreover, in Appendix 1 of *The New Reformation* (published a few weeks earlier) he had not only asked 'Can a truly contemporary person *not* be an atheist?' but had conceded that God was intellectually superfluous, emotionally dispensable, and morally intolerable. Where did all this lead? It led, in my opinion, to the idea of non-theistic religion – even to the idea of non-theistic Christianity. Though the Bishop was quite aware of this, he seemed not to be aware of the fact that the idea of non-theistic religion was a very ancient one, and that there existed a whole family of non-theistic religions of which Buddhism was the perfect example. The significance of the Bishop of Woolwich for Buddhists consisted in the fact that he represented a movement, within the Church, towards a non-theistic form of religion, and Buddhists might not always agree with him, but he certainly commanded their sympathy and respect.

Chapter 4 of *Honest to God*, entitled 'The Man for Others', dealt with the issue of Christ. According to tradition Christ was God incarnate, but if there was no God, then who or what was Christ? Though the Bishop rejected the traditional view, he did not go to the opposite, humanistic extreme of regarding him simply as an exceptionally good human being. This fact was of great interest to Buddhists, I pointed out. For Buddhists, the Buddha was neither God nor an exceptionally good human being: he was an *Enlightened* human being, and the Bishop seemed to be struggling towards some such conception of Christ. In Bonhoeffer's phrase, Christ was 'the man for others',[247] and it was in concern for others that transcendence was to be experienced. This was certainly a very noble conception, but the fact of his having lived for others did not make Christ unique, as it seemed the Bishop still wanted to think. He might, of course, say that Christ had *died* for others (that is had died to redeem mankind), but this idea was part of the doctrinal structure he was trying to abandon, and in any case, Socrates could equally be said to have died for others, as could Edith Cavell and the Vietnamese monks who had burned themselves to death a few months previously.[248] There was also the issue of prayer and worship. If there was no God, then to whom did one pray, whom did one worship? The Bishop seemed not to give serious consideration to meditation, so that the religious life appeared to be reduced to various forms of social service. However, I did not want to criticize the Bishop, I said in conclusion. He had introduced an important catalyst into the Church of England, and one could only hope that, as this did its work, Christianity would gradually become less theistic, both in theory and practice. If that was to happen, then in my opinion it would cease to be Christianity in any recognizable sense. One could appreciate that the Bishop was attached to Christianity, but it seemed to me that the logical outcome of his position was Buddhism. Whether he would ever take the next step and recognize this remained to be seen.

I had given the lecture back in May, at Burgh House, and Bill Revill, who liked to style himself Honorary Recording Engineer-in-Chief to the Hampstead Buddhist Vihara, had recorded it. Bill had been very excited by the lecture, which he was convinced would make history. So excited was he, and so convinced, that he was determined that the Bishop should listen to the tape recording he had made. His first move was to write to the Bishop inviting him to come to the Vihara and hear the tape. I did not see the letter, but having had some experience of Bill's epistolary style I wondered what the Bishop would make of it and whether he would reply. In the event he did reply, but through his secretary who, after explaining that there was no need to address the Bishop as 'My Lord Bishop' as Bill apparently had done, went on to inform him that swamped as the Bishop was with correspondence arising out of *Honest to God* he was unable to come to the Vihara and listen to the recording, but that if a copy was ever made he would be glad to have it. In those days of the cumbersome old reel-to-reel machines it took a long time to copy a tape. At least it always took Bill a long time (I often found him sitting on the floor of the lecture room surrounded by miles of tape), and it was not until November that a copy of 'Buddhism and the Bishop of Woolwich' was finally dispatched to the Bishop's residence in Blackheath, pending his return from Majorca. Within twenty-four hours of his listening to the lecture he had telephoned Bill to say he was in the district and would like to pay him a visit. Whether the district in question was Hampstead or the suburb where Bill lived, and whether the Bishop saw Bill at the Vihara or at the latter's home, I do not remember, but the visit was paid and the Bishop made three requests. He wanted to hear the question-and-answer session that had followed the lecture; he wanted to hear my lecture on 'Buddhism and Mysticism', and he wanted to meet me. Thus it was that one evening early in the New Year, seven months after I had given my 'historic' lecture, I found myself being driven down to Blackheath in the snow to meet the Bishop of Woolwich.

Though I had allowed Bill to write to the Bishop (it would have been difficult to stop him), I had not really expected his efforts to meet with the success they did. Least of all had I expected them to lead to my actually meeting the Bishop. I may even have been a little wary of meeting him, for though impressed by *Honest to God* I was aware that meeting the author of a book one admired could be disappointing, and besides, my last encounter with a representative of the Church of England had not been an entirely happy one. The encounter had taken place exactly a year previously, when before an audience mainly of very young people I had a discussion at the Arrowline Club, Hampstead, with the Rev. Joseph McCullough, the Rector of St Mary-le-Bow in the Strand. Joseph McCullough was a theological pugilist, being well known for his lunchtime debates with leading public figures, when the two contestants occupied pulpits on opposite sides of the famous City of London church. The theme of our discussion was 'Buddhist and Christian Attitudes to the World'. Each of us spoke briefly in turn (I spoke first), after which we responded to each other's remarks and finally the audience were invited to ask questions. To my amazement the Rector agreed with practically everything I said. The doctrine of karma and rebirth? It was found in Christianity. Nirvāṇa? It too was found in Christianity. And so on. I realized that my interlocutor's object was to 'contain' Buddhism (a tactic with which I had been familiar in India, where it was a favourite one with orthodox Hindus), for if everything taught by Buddhism could be found in Christianity it followed that there was no need for a Christian to become a Buddhist. Probably Buddhism was being 'contained' in this unceremonious manner for the benefit of our youthful audience, but even so I felt that in having recourse to such tactics the Rev. Joseph McCullough was being disingenuous, not to say intellectually dishonest, and this saddened me. As the Arrowline Club was connected with the Hampstead Parish Church, our discussion was preceded by drinks (in my case orange juice) at the Vicarage, where I met the portly, rubicund old Vicar of Hampstead, whose Buddhist equivalent Christmas Humphreys had once seriously told me I should regard myself as being. There was also a bevy of curates, as Trollope might have called them, elegant young men dancing attendance on the Vicar's fashionably dressed wife and daughters, all of whom wore black fishnet stockings. 'I like to see a nice pair of legs on a woman,' declared the Vicar over his port.

Sitting beside Terry in the Little Bus, on the way to Blackheath, I remembered that evening with the Arrowline Club. Though I felt reasonably certain that the Bishop of Woolwich would not be at all like the Vicar of Hampstead, I was not so sure that he might not be at least a little bit like the Rector of St Mary-le-Bow. I need not have worried. Within minutes of our arrival at the episcopal palace, as Bill would probably have called the Bishop's modest suburban residence, I realized that Dr Robinson was no more like the pugilistic Rector than he was like the rubicund, port-drinking Vicar. Unfortunately my diary is as laconic on the subject of our meeting as on everything else. 'Got lost at Lewisham,' the entry for the day records (in part). 'Arrived at Manor Way 10 minutes late. Welcomed by Bishop of Woolwich and his wife and son. Long and interesting discussion. Nothing very deep, though. Found him more "donnish" than I had expected. Spoke about my work in India among the ex-Untouchables. Said he would put me in touch with a friend interested in Eastern religions. Left at 10.30.' Had Bill been there to tape-record that 'long and interesting discussion', the tape would have been a useful aide-memoire, as I have no recollection of what was actually said on the occasion, but neither the Bishop nor I wanted our words to be tape-recorded, and in any case the Vihara's Honorary Recording Engineer-in-Chief was of an argumentative disposition and would have found it difficult not to butt in and put us right whenever he thought we were wrong.

As the Bishop had told Bill that *he* wanted to meet me I had assumed, perhaps rather literal-mindedly, that he meant just that, and that such discussion as there might be would take place *à deux*. I had forgotten that Anglican bishops had wives, and that wives do not like being left out of things. Ruth Robinson was no Mrs Proudie,[249] but she had no intention of being left out of the discussion between me and her husband (Terry and their son were content simply to listen). The discussion was therefore a three-cornered one, which probably accounts for the fact that although it was long and interesting 'nothing very deep' in the way of communication took place. This lack of depth was not necessarily due to Ruth Robinson's being a woman. Communication is always likely to be less deep and intense when the parties to a discussion happen to be more than two in number.

Though I have no recollection of what was actually said that evening, I do remember noticing that Ruth Robinson's religious views were even more unorthodox than her husband's, or it may simply have been that she expressed them more freely. Dr Robinson himself, being not only a bishop but a theologian and New Testament scholar, chose his words carefully, and in the course of our three-cornered discussion he did not, I think, go much beyond the position with which I was already familiar from my reading of *Honest to God*. Probably it was this careful choice of words, together with the air he had of a man more at home in the senior common room of a college than in a cathedral cloister, that was responsible for my finding him, in the words of my diary, 'more "donnish" than I had expected.' He was certainly more don than bishop, if by bishop one meant a mitred 'reverend father in God' of the traditional type, so that I was not surprised to learn, years later, that he had resigned his bishopric in order to devote himself to New Testament scholarship, and that Ruth Robinson, more unorthodox than ever, was attending meetings of Don Cupitt's Sea of Faith group.[250]

What effect listening to my lecture on his book, and meeting me, had on Dr Robinson's thinking I do not know. Perhaps none at all. For my own part, reading *Honest to God*, and spending an evening in discussion with the author (and his wife), made me realize, more clearly than I had done before, that not all Christians were like the missionaries whose methods of making converts had been responsible for my developing, while in Kalimpong, an animus against Christianity. During the twenty years I had been away a change had taken place. Among sincerely religious people – which is to say, mostly among Christian people – there was now a good deal of interest in non-Christian religions, perhaps especially in Buddhism. Some Christians had written about Buddhism not only sympathetically but with a degree of understanding. One such more open-minded Christian was the friend of whom Dr Robinson had spoken and with whom he had promised to put me in touch. This friend, so it transpired, was George Appleton, author of *On the Eightfold Path*, a copy of which the publishers sent me on Dr Robinson's instructions a couple of months after our meeting. George Appleton, now Archbishop of Perth, had worked in Burma for twenty years and had known many Buddhists. The little paperback book was a study in the Three Jewels and the four noble truths based, mainly, on Theravādin sources, and though not entirely free from errors and infelicities it was on the whole a reasonably faithful account of the essentials of the Buddha's teaching. As one might have expected, the author compared and contrasted Buddhism and Christianity and concluded, what might no less have been expected, that Christ's Way went beyond the Eightfold Path, even as Christianity itself, with its vision of an Eternal God who is Creator and Redeemer, went beyond Buddhism. Nonetheless, he considered that Christianity needed to learn from its worldwide encounter with Buddhism and this attitude, after my experience with the missionaries, gave me food for thought.

If Christians could study Buddhism, and even write sympathetically about it, then it ought to be possible for Buddhists to study Christianity. I did not have either the leisure or the facilities to study it systematically and in depth, but at least I could read Christian literature from time to time, as I had been doing for the last year or more, and in this way make myself at least as well acquainted with Christianity as I was with Hinduism, which I had studied enthusiastically in my early years in India. The reading of such literature was all the more necessary if, as now seemed likely, I would be staying in England indefinitely and having, therefore, more and more contact with people who, if they were not actually Christians, had a Christian background of some kind. In the years to come I was to read many of the classics of Christian spirituality, as well as histories of Christianity and studies of Christian thought, and though I continued to be critical of many aspects of the religion, and to disagree with its fundamental doctrines, my animus against Christianity gradually disappeared.

30
AN IMPORTANT ANNIVERSARY AND A TYPIST'S NIGHTMARE

Thursday 24 February was a rather full day, though perhaps no more full than were most other days at the time. In the afternoon, Francoise having been given her work and visitors dealt with, Terry and I drove to Mildmay Hospital to see Alf Vial's fourteen-year-old son, who had had his tonsils out and was still recovering. (My own tonsils had been removed when I was six, and remembering the unpleasantness of my stay in hospital on that occasion I could sympathize with the boy.) Alf was already there, and after the three of us had spent half an hour with David, and I had given him a big picture of a Buddha-image and a bundle of incense sticks (he regarded himself as a Buddhist), the most vocal of the Three Musketeers took us to his flat in nearby Bethnal Green, where we had tea with him and his wife and his daughter Christine, who was already known to me as a member of the speakers' class. I had not been in the East End before and little suspected that one day I would be very familiar with Bethnal Green and that it would occupy an important place in my history. From Bethnal Green Terry and I drove to Red Lion Square, Holborn, and to Conway Hall, where we attended a meeting of the Personalist Group and heard a lecture by Dr E. Graham Howe, a psychiatrist whom I had met a year earlier, author of *The Invisible Anatomy* and founder of the Open Way venture, who was an old friend of the Buddhist Society. The lecture was followed by a discussion, after which my friend and I made our way up to West Hampstead where, by way of celebration, we had a meal at the Indo-Pakistan restaurant.

We were celebrating because 24 February was an anniversary. It was the anniversary of the day on which he and I first saw each other. This had been when Terry happened to attend, and I happened to be chairing, a talk by Mangalo on 'Buddhist Meditation'. The talk was given at the College of Psychic Science, South Kensington, where two months later I gave my lecture on 'Buddhism and the Problem of Death', and where, after the lecture, Terry came up to me and told me he had seen the pure white light. Since then a lot had happened, culminating in Terry's giving up his job at the end of the year, after moving to the bigger, brighter flat in Lancaster Grove where much of our time together was now spent. Believing as we did that the moods of depression to which he was subject were due partly to the nature of his job, we had assumed, perhaps naively, that once he stopped working and was free to study and meditate there would be an improvement in his condition, but this proved not to be the case. In the New Year he became more depressed than ever, so that years afterwards, when I reflected on this development, I was led to wonder if his having to hold down a job he loathed, besides being a cause of his depression, had not also sometimes been the means of his keeping the blacker moods of it at bay. He also started having nightmares, from which he awoke sweating and trembling and in need of reassurance, so that I had to stay overnight at the Other Vihara more frequently than I might otherwise have done. Some of the nightmares were not only horrific but bizarre. In one of them he was a baked bean, trapped inside a Heinz tin with hundreds of other beans.

Happily it was not a state of affairs that lasted. After a couple of weeks the nightmares ceased, and with them the moods of depression from which, as I had soon learned, Terry periodically suffered. For the remainder of the month, and for the whole of February and March, he in fact was more consistently cheerful than I had ever known him to be or than he was ever to be again. During that period I did not have to write in my diary, as I had had to write so often before, 'Terry a little low', or 'Terry depressed', or 'Terry upset'. Thus there was a welcome respite, and though it was Terry who had been suffering from the moods of depression it was almost as much a respite for me as for him. Having to spend time talking him out of these moods had on occasion been something of a strain, especially when I also had people to see, lectures to prepare and give, correspondence to deal with, and the affairs of the Vihara and the Sangha Association to oversee and direct, all of which made heavy demands not only on my time but on my energy. The situation was made more difficult by the fact that Terry was obsessively anxious that no one should know he suffered from depression or, indeed, suspect that he was anything other than the positive and well-adjusted, if rather reserved, young man he appeared to be. This meant that I was never able to talk freely to anyone about him, and had to make excuses for him when he was too depressed to turn up for a lecture or class as expected.

But now those days were over, at least for the time being. Terry was able to devote his morning hours to study and meditation as originally planned, I no longer had to spend time talking him out of his moods of depression or make excuses for his non-appearance, our friendship blossomed anew, and we fell into a routine that lasted, with few interruptions, until April came and with it the Easter meditation retreat at Biddulph. The routine varied a little according to whether or not I had spent the night at the flat. If I had spent the night there, Terry and I would meditate together, after which I would spend the rest of the morning working on my next lecture, while he studied and made notes, and then go back to the Vihara after lunch. Otherwise I would try to be at the flat for part of the evening and we would talk and listen to music. On some days Terry would come round to the Vihara early and join Eric and me and, later, Thien Chau and Robert, the new postulant, as well, for our morning puja and meditation and for breakfast. Thus my time was usually divided, during those months of welcome respite, between the Vihara and the flat, between periods of external activity and shorter periods of withdrawal, reflection, and deeper communication. It was divided, in other words, between the two places that had come to embody, respectively, the public and the private – the lower and the higher – monasteries or hermitages of my dreams.[251]

Sometimes Terry and I would spend the afternoon in town, either visiting the bookshops or seeing a film. So far as I remember we never visited the National Gallery or any other of London's great art collections, probably because Terry had little interest in the visual arts for their own sake. He did however have a favourite painting, or perhaps I should say there was one painting he liked, and of which he possessed a postcard. This was the work by Bronzino known as *An*

Allegory or, alternatively, as *An Allegory of Time and Love*, with its smooth, marmoreal bodies, its predominance of cold whites and blues, its touches of rose and pale green, and its enigmatic meaning.[252] Despite his lack of interest in the visual arts, Terry was happy to photograph a small soapstone Buddha-image for the Sangha Association's Wesak card, as well as to design the card and get it printed – a task that took up more of his time and energy than either of us had expected. There were also visits to the provincial Buddhist groups. Some of these visits involved an evening meditation class or lecture, and one of my most vivid memories of that whole period is of Terry and me driving down the eerily deserted motorway afterwards and my watching, fascinated, as the long rows of overhead sodium lights in front of us appeared to twist and turn with every turning of the road and every change of altitude. At such times I experienced a deep sense of contentment, with myself, with my surroundings, and with the work I had just done.

The only thing that disrupted Terry's cheerfulness was his fortnightly visit to Ilford, when he took Fiona there for the weekend. Though these sojourns under the parental roof with his harsh, tyrannical father and hypochondriacal mother continued to be a trial to him, they affected him much less badly than before and he recovered from them much more quickly. This was all the more remarkable in that his parents now had, as they thought, more cause for complaint than ever. Not only was it no longer possible for them to conceal from friends and neighbours the shameful fact of the breakdown of their son's marriage. They now had to come to terms with the no less shameful fact that he had given up his well-paid job in order to study philosophy, whatever that might be, and that sooner or later friends and neighbours would have to be informed of this too. From what Terry told me, I gathered his parents were as little able to understand his giving up his job as they were of understanding his desire to study philosophy (he dared not say anything about studying Buddhism). The only explanation they could think of, apparently, was that his interest in philosophy had affected his brain, and that it was because his brain was affected that he had given up his job. Now that he was studying philosophy full-time he was bound to get worse.

Terry did indeed get worse, though not in the sense they meant, and his getting worse was certainly not due to philosophy. The immediate cause was the decisive change that took place in his relations with

Gillian – a change for which Gillian herself was responsible. The change related not to their divorce, which was about to be made absolute, but to some of the consequences of that divorce. I had met Gillian in November, Terry having taken me with him when he went to collect a few belongings from the former marital home in Harrow. Tall, dark, and slim, she was, as Terry had reported her to be, a nice person and, obviously, a good housekeeper. During the half-hour we were there she and Terry conversed amicably enough, and anyone observing them together would have thought they were a well-matched couple. But now, as March passed into April, there came from that quarter a succession of blows from which, perhaps, he never really recovered. The gist of the matter was that Gillian was planning to marry again, that she and her husband-to-be would be moving to Cornwall, and that the latter had stipulated, as a condition of the marriage, that Fiona should live with them and be brought up as his daughter.

Terry was shocked, hurt, angry. Unfortunately, he was quite unable to express his anger, even in a controlled way. To express anger and aggression was to invite violence (here the butcher father of his boyhood cast a dark shadow), and of violence he was so afraid that any expression of anger, whether in speech or writing, was for him a psychological impossibility. Consequently whenever he replied to a letter from Gillian, or wrote to his solicitor, there was a severe conflict between what he felt like saying and his fear of actually saying it, so that his drafts and redrafts were a typist's nightmare of false starts, corrections, and interlineations. Had he expressed himself too strongly? Could the same point not be made more moderately? Was a qualification needed? Sometimes the struggle would go on for hours, even days, leaving him feeling exhausted and depressed, and with nothing to show for his pains other than a stilted statement of his position that could have been written for him by someone with no personal interest in the matter and which, dissatisfied with it though he might be, he had no alternative but to sign and send.

Much as I sympathized with Terry there was little I could do to help, apart from offering advice and reassurance and typing his letters for him when he was too tired or too depressed to do so himself. Though I have no recollection of the precise content of these letters, I remember being left with the distinct impression that strong as his position might be, morally speaking, legally it was quite weak. Whether out of old-fashioned gentlemanliness, or naivety, or a feeling of culpability, he had allowed himself to be cast in the role of the guilty party (after his separation from Gillian her father had put two private detectives on his – and Vivien's – trail) and as the divorce laws then stood this circumstance probably counted against him so far as custody of, or access to, Fiona was concerned. Be that as it may, one of the consequences of the divorce was that when, in the late spring or early summer, Gillian moved to Cornwall with her new husband, Fiona went with them and Terry saw his little daughter no more.

31

GIVING THE THREE JEWELS A FINAL POLISH

In accepting the Sangha Trust's invitation to spend a few months in England I had stipulated that I should have my mornings free for literary work, just as I did in India when not on tour. That in the event this proved impracticable was not the Trust's fault. It was not anybody's fault. So much was there to be done, almost from the very day of my arrival, that for upwards of a year there was no question of my ever having time to produce anything more than a short article or book review. Not that I really minded this. To borrow an image from Śāntideva, I was no less happy to meet the demands of the new situation than the tusker is to plunge in hot weather into the next pool he comes across.[253]

Since Francoise's appearance on the scene towards the end of November, and Terry's giving up his job and moving to a bigger flat, there had been a change. I now had more time to myself, which meant I had more time for writing. There consequently appeared in the April 1966 issue of *The Buddhist*, under the heading 'Ven. Sthavira's Literary Work', the following item of Vihara news:

> Since the beginning of the year the Ven. Sthavira Sangharakshita has been devoting himself to literary work, neglected since his return to this country. Last month he completed The Three Jewels: An Introduction to the Study of Buddhism, the greater part of

> which was written before he left Kalimpong but which had to be laid aside owing to the great pressure of lectures and other work, particularly the reorganization of the Vihara activities. During the last two or three months he has, therefore, been less available at the Vihara for personal interviews than previously, but it is hoped that through the written word he will be able to reach a larger number of people than through the spoken word. The Three Jewels will be published by Rider before the end of the year. The Ven. Sthavira has also revised his well-known work A Survey of Buddhism, the third edition of which is now in the press.[254]

The Three Jewels was not published before the end of the year (it did not come out until the beginning of 1968), and the third edition of the *Survey*, the black and red dust jacket of which had been designed by Terry and printed in England, remained 'in the press' in Bangalore for many more months. So far as I remember, I completed *The Three Jewels* at that time only in the sense that it was then that I gave the work a final polish, checked my references, and wrote a preface, all the actual writing having been done in Kalimpong.[255] Though *The Buddhist* did not mention the fact, I had a third work in the pipeline. This was the work that was eventually published, in 1985, as *The Eternal Legacy: An Introduction to the Canonical Literature of Buddhism*.[256] In a sense it was a continuation of *The Three Jewels*, with which, together with three other works, one partly written and two as yet unwritten, it was to form part of a projected five-part series entitled *The Heritage of Buddhism* – a series I was never able to complete. Since I was not expecting to be away from Kalimpong for more than four months I had left the manuscript of *The Word of the Buddha*, as *The Eternal Legacy* was originally called, in a cupboard in my hillside hermitage. But four months had become six, and six a whole year, and as it now seemed likely that I would be staying in England indefinitely I had arranged for the manuscript to be retrieved from my cupboard and sent to me at the Vihara, where Francoise was currently typing it for me.

The business of giving *The Three Jewels* a final polish, and checking my references, must have been both laborious and time-consuming, for apart from the preface I did not, I think, do any *original* writing during the months to which the item in *The Buddhist* referred or indeed for a long time afterwards. I did not even write fresh editorials for the

Sangha Association's little monthly journal, which I was still editing, as I had occasionally done before. Instead I reproduced some of the editorials I had written fourteen or fifteen years earlier for *Stepping-Stones*, the little monthly journal of Himalayan religion, culture, and education I had published from Kalimpong, which, since they dealt with themes of fundamental Buddhist concern, were as relevant now as they had been then.[257] I also started serializing my essay 'The Meaning of Orthodoxy in Buddhism: A Protest', which had first appeared in 1957, in the Buddha Jayanti issue of the quarterly *France-Asie*, and which remains one of the most important literary products of my India period.[258] The essay was a critique of the claim that the Theravāda was 'certainly the most orthodox school of Buddhism' and a systematic inquiry into the real nature of 'orthodoxy'. Its appearance in the pages of *The Buddhist* scandalized a few people, as its appearance in *France-Asie* had done a decade and a half earlier, the more especially as the claim that the Theravāda was 'certainly the most orthodox form of Buddhism' had been made by the eminent, if rather dry, Pāli scholar Miss I. B. Horner,[259] whose work Adrienne Bennett, herself a Pāli scholar, had once characterized, in memorable phrase, as 'the last ounce of dust in desiccation'. Maurice Walshe was not exactly scandalized by my essay, but he was perturbed, and wrote an article on 'Orthodoxy and Fundamentalism' which I printed in a subsequent issue of *The Buddhist*. Though admitting that Miss Horner's remark of several years ago was probably incautious, he also thought that there was a certain amount that could and should be said on the other side. On the whole his article was sensible and balanced, and there was much in his discussion of some of the points I had raised with which I agreed. He also scored a palpable hit at (some) students of Mahāyāna. Though fundamental Buddhist doctrine was found in Mahāyāna sources, this was not realized because the doctrine was so wrapped up in glorious and extraneous trappings as to become much less noticeable. The result, in his opinion, was that students of Mahāyāna were often inclined 'to lick off the jam and avoid swallowing the pill'.[260]

Limited as my literary activity then was to polishing what I had already written, checking references, and reprinting old material, the early months of 1966 were among the least productive of my whole life. I had in fact written very little for the last year or more, and nearly a decade was to pass before I was able to achieve anything like the degree of productivity that I had habitually enjoyed during my days in Kalimpong. In the course of my first two years back in England I produced only one poem, whereas previously few weeks had passed without my writing one or two. That solitary poem of mine was written – or rather composed – in Berkeley Square, as I sat in the Little Bus waiting for Terry while he transacted some business at his bank. It was spring, and the green shoots that had started to appear on the branches of the aged trees moved me in the way that, in Kalimpong, I had been moved by the scarlet crowns of the poinsettias, the ink-blue foliage of the pines, and the distant spectacle of the gleaming white masses of the eternal snows. London itself was beautiful that calm, sunlit morning, and for a few moments, at least, I did not regret that for the time being my lot was cast not among the foothills of the eastern Himalayas but in the midst of one of the biggest conurbations in the Western world.[261]

But productivity is not just literary. Though I was less available for personal interviews than previously, and was devoting myself to literary work, I continued to lecture regularly at the Vihara and at the Buddhist Society, as well as occasionally to groups outside London, and this lecturing activity of mine was in principle no less a way of being productive than was writing itself. It was as though the creative energies that formerly had gone into literary work were now going into the business of lecturing. Besides continuing my fortnightly lectures at the Buddhist Society on 'Tibetan Buddhism',[262] with the New Year I started a new series of Sunday lectures at the Vihara under the general title 'Introducing Buddhism'. Each lecture, I announced, would be self-contained, so that those who for any reason missed any of the lectures need not be afraid of being unable to follow the later ones in the series. Among my February lectures, which like their predecessors were very well attended, there was one in particular which, according to a report appearing in the March issue of *The Buddhist*, gave rise to comment and discussion. This was the lecture on 'Evolution – Lower and Higher', in which I attempted, for the first time, to situate Buddhism, as a spiritual path, within a broader, 'evolutionary' context. In later years the idea that the path to Enlightenment was also the path of the Higher Evolution was to play an increasingly important role in my thinking. As I wrote in 1971, summarizing my position,

Science revealed how far man had come. This was the lower evolution. Buddhism, as the Path, showed how far he still had to go. This was the higher evolution. Though not strictly continuous the two phases between them constituted the halves of a single process. Science and religion, the lower and the higher evolution, were comprehended in one gigantic sweep.[263]

32

ORDINATIONS ON THE EASTER RETREAT – AND A BIRTHDAY

Thich Thien Chau arrived at the Vihara in the middle of March, and after my experience with Vichitr and Ratanasara – and even with Mangalo and Vimalo – I was glad to have living and working with me a monk who was already a close friend, who had been a student of one of my own teachers, who as a Mahāyānist shared my 'ecumenical' views, and who moreover was easy to get on with. I had come to know him through his mentor Thich Minh Chau. Like Minh Chau he was then studying at the Magadh University in Bihar, where he was later to take his MA in Pāli, and like Minh Chau he used to spend the summer months with me at the Triyana Vardhana Vihara, thus exchanging the scorching heat of the plains for the comparative cool of the hills. Last year, too, he had spent the summer there, in my absence organizing the Vihara's usual Vaiśākha celebrations. Now he was in London where Minh Chau had arranged for him to read for his Ph.D. at the School of Oriental and African Studies.

In appearance and character he could hardly have been more different from Minh Chau. Both were quite short, but whereas Minh Chau was short and stout Thien Chau was short and slender. So short and slender was he that what with his smooth cheeks (neither he nor Minh Chau needed to use a razor) and piping voice he could easily be mistaken for a youthful novice, though he had been a monk for almost as long as I had and was my junior by only five or six years. Minh Chau, energetic and efficient, was very much the scholar-administrator (he was Rector of Van Han University in Saigon), whereas Thien Chau, quiet and retiring, was very much the scholar-poet. The one, though not unkindly, was brusque and decisive, the other gentle, sensitive, and affectionate.

Once my old friend had succeeded in tracking down the elusive Professor Henderson, his supervisor at the University of London, and I had taken him to see the British Museum and a few other places of interest, he soon settled in at the Vihara and started making friends. Terry and Eric both took to him, in their different ways, Terry on account of his gentleness and sensitivity, Eric because he knew classical Chinese and could help him with his Sino-Japanese studies. Much as Eric liked Thien Chau, however, his slightly aquiline nose was often wrinkled up in disgust at what he regarded as the latter's sentimentality. The reason for Thien Chau's sentimentality, if sentimental he really was, was the plight of his native land, where the United States was increasing its military involvement and where thousands of men, women, and children were being killed or horribly maimed every month. 'My country, my country!' the tender-hearted little monk would sob, the tears trickling down his face, whenever the news from Vietnam was particularly bad.[264] On such occasions Eric was sometimes so unfeeling as to mimic him, but Thien Chau never took it amiss, apparently considering Eric had as much right to mock his grief as he himself had to feel it. Ruth, too, took to Thien Chau, for much the same reasons as Terry, he and I having taken the new arrival round to her place for tea one afternoon, after which we all drove down to the Buddhist Society, where he met Christmas Humphreys and sat in on my meditation class.

Back in Kalimpong Thien Chau had always helped me in whatever way he could, and now that he was again staying with me, this time not at my quiet hillside hermitage but in London, at the noisy Hampstead Buddhist Vihara, he was as helpful as ever. Indeed he was more than just helpful. Convinced that I worked too hard, that I was not taking proper care of myself, and that my health was suffering, he saw it as his duty to look after me, especially as nobody else at the Vihara, so far as he could see, was doing any such thing. Perhaps with traditional Chinese medical notions at the back of his mind, he was particularly concerned that I was expending so much energy in lectures. No sooner had I finished giving my Sunday lecture, therefore, and was sitting down, than he would hurry up to me with a little pot of Vietnamese tea and two tiny cups on a tray and gently urge me to swallow at least four or five cupfuls of the beverage. As the cups were not much bigger than thimbles I had no difficulty doing this, though the tea was always piping hot and made me catch my breath. All the time Thien Chau would be standing over me, smiling approvingly and filling one tiny cup as fast as I emptied the other. Before many weeks had passed he and his little teapot were a familiar sight at the Vihara on Sunday afternoons, and my drinking the ritual four or five tiny cupfuls of Vietnamese tea after the lecture was as much an accepted part of the regular proceedings as the lecture itself.

By the time Easter came, and with it the Easter retreat, Thien Chau was well settled at the Vihara and I was therefore able to leave for Biddulph knowing that he and Eric would be looking after the place

With Terry, Biddulph Old Hall

and that in my absence activities would be continuing more or less as usual. Spring was early that year, I think. Terry and I, through the open windows of the Lancaster Grove flat, had already heard the nightingales singing in a neighbouring garden, nightingales that were perhaps descended from the very bird that had inspired Keats's ode,[265] and on our arrival at Old Hall I was glad to see that the brilliant yellow daffodils were more plentiful than they had been the previous year and that the pink rhododendrons were out. I was less glad to find the retreat centre itself in a very dirty, untidy, and neglected condition, though Mangalo was still lingering there (he left the following day, after being critical of vegetarianism) and though Douglas, the young warden, lived on the premises with his wife and was supposedly looking after the place. My friend and I had arrived a few days earlier than the other retreatants, partly because we wanted to have some time to ourselves before the retreat began and partly so that I could spend my last free afternoon and evening with the members of the Midlands Buddhist Group. By the time we returned from Birmingham, which was not until well past midnight, everybody who was expected had arrived, and after breakfast the following morning I led the first guided group meditation of the week, Terry and I having already meditated together before breakfast, in my room.

There were altogether twelve or fourteen people attending the retreat, including Ruth, the Three Musketeers, Terry's friend Alan, and a bright-eyed, red-cheeked woman of uncertain age called Phyllis Turner, who though not herself a medium had a personal spirit guide, known to her simply as Chang, whose instructions she implicitly followed. The programme was of the more balanced, 'mixed' type that I had devised for the retreats of the previous year, though I think there was less meditation and more discussion this time, and in the evenings we had either a live talk by Ruth or a tape of one of my lectures on 'The Meaning of Conversion in Buddhism'. The biggest difference was that each day I devoted a disproportionate amount of my time to the same three people, namely, to Alf, Mike, and Jack, the Vihara's Three Musketeers. All three were deeply interested in Tibetan Buddhism, especially Alf and Mike, and in the course of the last seven or eight months I had not only shared with them the texts of some of the practices into which I had been initiated but had promised that next time they came on retreat with me I would explain the four *mūla* or 'foundation' yogas of the Vajrayāna, take them through certain forms of deity yoga, and give them the bodhisattva ordination. This promise I was now keeping, while Ruth, acting as my deputy, took the meditation class or led the discussion. I gave the bodhisattva ordination, the taking of which marks one's commitment, at least in principle, to the Mahāyāna ideal of Enlightenment not for one's own sake only but for the sake of all beings, on the penultimate full day of the retreat, which was a day of silence and the one on which we listened, most appropriately, to my lecture on 'The Arising of the Will to Enlightenment'.[266]

The following day was Ruth's birthday. Terry and Alan had made a birthday card and this, together with a big bowl of pink rhododendrons, was put in front of her place at the breakfast table. I had asked the others to come and sit down *before* the bell rang, so that Ruth should come in at the end, by herself, when we were all seated. She was delighted with the card and the flowers and her artless joy was reflected in the faces of all around her. Joy was indeed the keynote of the whole day, especially as the weather had changed and it was now fine and sunny. In the afternoon Terry and Alan took group photographs out in the garden, after which I had a lengthy final session with the Three Musketeers, saw a distraught and tearful Phyllis, and talked for a few minutes with Mangalo, who had been staying nearby with a married couple who were, or had been, supporters of Ananda Bodhi. The day ended with puja, meditation, and my lecture on 'Parāvṛtti – the Turning About in the Deepest Seat of Consciousness'.

Despite there having been no actual 'turning about' on the part of any of the retreatants, at any rate not in the deepest seat of consciousness, the retreat must have had a strong effect on all of them, for the following morning everybody turned up at six-thirty for the concluding Sevenfold Puja. Thereafter Terry and I had only to pick daffodils and rhododendrons for the Vihara shrine, have breakfast, and then make the journey back to London with Ruth sitting with us in the front of the Little Bus and Alf, Mike, and Alan sitting behind. Having had lunch at the Vihara with Thien Chau, Eric, Alf, and Mike, we drove with them and Ruth down to the Buddhist Society, where the Society's Wesak party was in progress and where I talked with Toby, Carmen Blacker, Jack Austin, a Japanese Sōtō Zen bishop, the rigidly Theravādin Mrs Quittner (just back from Ceylon, and looking quite ill), Kathy Phelps, and the Parsi universalist Phiroz Mehta, whom I had first met many years ago in Bombay when he was in the middle of a nervous breakdown. As it was a warm day, and there were nearly a hundred people at the party, the atmosphere gradually became hot and stifling, and after a couple of hours I was glad to leave, glad to get out into the fresh air, glad to be back in the silence and comparative coolness of the flat. By this time I was feeling very tired, and I had a headache. After talking briefly with Terry, and listening to a little Mozart, I therefore went to bed early. Tomorrow was Sunday and there would be a lecture to prepare.

33
PREPARING FOR GREECE

A year or two before my departure for England one of my friends in Kalimpong had given me a copy of Henry Miller's *The Colossus of Maroussi*. I had not read anything by Miller before, and his books may not even have been generally available in India at that time. This one was the result of an eight-month trip through Greece in 1939, and though I did not find Katsimbalis, the 'Colossus' of the book's title, as attractive a character as the author himself evidently did, the book as a whole impressed me deeply and gave me a liking for Miller's writing at its lyric, improvisatory best that lasted for many years. I was particularly struck by his account of his visit to Delphi which, seen on the afternoon of his arrival through a strange twilight mist, seemed even more sublime and awe-inspiring than he had imagined it to be. The following day after wandering about amid the broken columns, he and his friends had ascended the tortuous path to the stadium on high.

> The setting is spectacular [he wrote]. Set just below the crest of the mountain one has the impression that when the course was finished the charioteers must have driven the steeds over the ridge and into the blue. The atmosphere is superhuman, intoxicating to the point of madness. Everything that is extraordinary and miraculous about Delphi gathers here in the memory of the games which were held in the clouds.[267]

Evocative as were such passages as this, I was struck less by Miller's description of the sights of Delphi than by the fact that his visit had affected him so deeply. The oracle may have ceased long ago, but it was evident that Delphi was still very much a sacred place, and though there seemed little likelihood then of my visiting England, much less still Greece, there arose in me as I read those enthusiastic pages a desire to see Delphi with my own eyes.

I must have spoken to Terry about this desire of mine quite early in our friendship, and in the course of the next few months we must have talked quite a lot about Greece and about the possibility of our visiting it together. It was not until late summer or early autumn, however, that we eventually decided to make the trip, and not until February, when Terry was no longer working, that we were in a position to start actually planning our journey. Less than a year earlier, after one of my lectures at the College of Psychic Science, I had asked Terry how far in the direction of the Vihara he was willing to drive me. As far as I liked, he had replied. Could he drive me to India? Yes, he could. In retrospect the exchange seemed significant, even prophetic. The possibility of our visiting Greece together had been first mooted in connection with the idea that Terry might accompany me to India, for by this time it had become obvious that my work now lay in the West, and that sooner or later I would have to pay a farewell visit to the land of the Buddha and take proper leave of my friends, disciples, and teachers there. We would drive all the way to the subcontinent in the Little Bus and visit Greece – and see Delphi – on the way! This was by no means impossible, but we soon realized the impracticability of the plan which in fact was really never anything more than a dream. Instead of going overland to India we would go overland to Greece! We would leave England for the Continent in the middle of June, and be away for two months. The India visit would take place separately, probably in the autumn or winter. By the time we returned from the Easter retreat, therefore, our Greek adventure was only five weeks away. They would be five busy weeks. Not only were there the final arrangements for our journey to be made. There was the Festival of Wesak to be celebrated, a retreat to be attended, parents and friends to be visited, and the details of the Vihara's programme for July and August to be finalized.

The Wesak celebrations followed much the same pattern as those of the previous year. There was a public meeting at Caxton Hall,

Westminster, under the auspices of the Buddhist Society, at which the speakers were me, Dr Malalasekera, and Christmas Humphreys, who as president of the Society was, of course, also in the chair.[268] Probably fewer people attended than last time, but this year there was, I thought, a happier atmosphere. There was certainly a happy atmosphere at the devotional meeting I conducted at the Vihara late that night, as well as at the Vihara's own Wesak celebrations a few days later. The public meeting began with a little procession consisting mainly of the children of members bringing in flowers. After I had placed the flowers on the green-and-gold shrine, where candles and incense were already burning before the image of the Buddha, there were speeches by Trungpa Rimpoche, Dr Malalasekera, Maurice, Thien Chau, and me. There were also readings from the scriptures by Beryl and Jack, and the proceedings concluded with a vote of thanks by Alf, who had recently taken over from Maurice as chairman of the Sangha Trust. After the meeting Maurice, Ruth, and I, together with other members and friends, talked at length with an important guest who had turned up unexpectedly. This was Dr Manzen Nakada, the Sōtō Zen bishop whom I had met at the Buddhist Society's Wesak Party the previous week. In the course of discussion he intimated that an invitation to come and teach in England for a while might not find him unresponsive.

Though the Wesak celebrations themselves followed the usual pattern, on the morning of the thrice-sacred day there took place at the Vihara a ceremony that marked, according to *The Buddhist*, 'a turning-point in the history of the English Sangha'.[269] This ceremony was the ordination of Eric as a *śrāmaṇera*, and it marked a turning point in the history of the English Sangha in that it represented 'the first time that an English novice monk had been ordained, on English soil, by an English-born *sthavira* or Elder.' Apart from the fact that the ceremony was conducted in Pāli (with a running commentary in English), that I was assisted by Thien Chau, and that I gave Eric the name Viriya, I remember little or nothing of the proceedings. There does, however, survive a group photograph that was taken in front of the shrine after the ceremony. I am standing nearest the camera, with Thien Chau behind me to my right. I am wearing a Tibetan-style shirt and jacket beneath my Theravādin robes and my hair, I notice, is rather longer than it used to be in India. Viriya is standing behind me to my left, his head freshly shaved for the ceremony. In front of him, further to my left, stands his adoptive

Viriya's ordination. l–r: Thich Thien Chau, Sangharakshita, Viriya's adoptive father, Viriya, Viriya's adoptive mother, Mr and Mrs Lawrence

mother and behind Thien Chau his adoptive father. Behind Viriya and his adoptive mother stand Viriya's friends Mr and Mrs Lawrence. She is wearing an enormous fur hat shaped rather like an inverted bucket, that comes down almost below her eyes. Mr Lawrence is something in the City, and Mrs Lawrence is second or third cousin to someone who is, or was, private secretary to the Queen. For reasons I was never able to fathom, Viriya idolizes the Lawrences and spends quite a lot of time in the company of them and their three teenage daughters. We all look rather serious, except for Viriya's adoptive mother, who attempts a brave smile but who, I know, is afraid that Viriya may have become a Buddhist monk because she and her husband have failed him in some way. Light comes from the window to our right, highlighting the right side of my face, as well as that of Viriya and his adoptive mother, and leaving everyone else's faces in the shade.

In my speeches at the two public meetings, at Caxton Hall and the Vihara, I had spoken of the significance of Wesak in general terms, reminding my audience that it was the anniversary of the Buddha's attainment of *Enlightenment*, and emphasizing that we, too, could attain Enlightenment if we followed the Buddha's path of ethical conduct, concentration and meditation, and transcendental wisdom, as many in the West were already doing. My editorial in the May issue of *The*

Buddhist struck a similar note, besides which I pointed out that Vaiśākha (the Sanskrit equivalent of the more familiar Sinhalese 'Wesak') should be a time of moral and spiritual stocktaking, of ruthless self-examination. This stocktaking was not only individual but collective, and since at this time of year Buddhist groups in some parts of the Buddhist world surveyed the progress made during the previous twelve months I proceeded to do a little stocktaking on behalf of the Sangha Association. I also ventured a prediction.

> While complacency would be out of place, the English Buddhist movement as centred on the Hampstead Buddhist Vihara can look back over the past year with a feeling of sober satisfaction. Systematic teaching of the Dharma, together with the regular practice of guided group meditation, attendance at the Speakers Class, and participation in the devotional meetings, have between them not only built up membership of the Association but helped to create the nucleus of a spiritual community of people who, taking Enlightenment as exemplified by the Buddha as their ideal, His Dharma as their way of life, and the members of the Sangha as their guides, are gradually coming to constitute a living presence of Buddhism in Great Britain. Various Buddhist traditions have contributed to this development. Theravāda, Mahāyāna, Tibetan Buddhism, and Zen are all honoured at the Vihara. If anything has become clear during the last year it is the fact that while English Buddhism, or British Buddhism as some prefer to call it, will draw gratefully on all Buddhist traditions, it will not confine itself exclusively to any one of them. Indeed, it is clear that a distinctive Western Buddhism, a Buddhism adapted to the spiritual needs of the West, is already in process of emergence.[270]

Like my essay 'The Meaning of Orthodoxy in Buddhism: A Protest', the 'ecumenical' views expressed in the concluding sentences of this extract scandalized a few people. They gave particular offence to those Theravādins who believed that Buddhism in the West should be simply a transplanted Sinhalese or Thai Buddhism, cultural trappings and all, and to whom the idea of a distinctive Western Buddhism was anathema.

The retreat came two weeks after Wesak and was, I think, a smaller and quieter affair than the Easter retreat. Terry was on it with me, while among the other retreatants were Antoinette, Mrs Mills, Emile Boin, and two elderly married couples. The programme was of the same 'mixed' type as before, the only difference being that this time there were two tape-recorded lectures a day, one in the morning and one in the evening, an arrangement some people preferred. I did not attend the lectures, which in any case were ones I had given myself. Instead, I stayed in my room clearing up arrears of correspondence while Terry conducted proceedings downstairs. At most other times I was with the retreatants. Besides leading all the meditation sessions, I saw them at meals and was available for personal interviews. Mrs Mills, who confessed to having a problem with repressed anger, and who came to see me more than once, was a schoolteacher. She was also the mother of Bhikkhu Khantipālo, who had once spent a few months with me in Kalimpong before moving on to Thailand[271] and to whom, as it happened, I was then writing to ask if he would come to England for a while during my absence in India. Emile Boin, who came to see me on the last day of the retreat, and whom I strongly suspected of also having a problem with repressed anger, was the proprietor of Sakura, the Japanese shop in Monmouth Street upon which I had stumbled the previous summer. As one might have expected, he was interested in Zen, though he never attended any of my meditation classes and had not been on retreat with me before. He was constant in his attendance at my Sunday lectures, however, besides being a lively, if controversial, contributor to the pages of *The Buddhist*. His pseudonymous ('M. Eel') article 'Sentimentality, Samurai, Violence, Vegetarianism', with its blunt assertion that 'Buddhism is not beamed at a little group of sentimental old women, but at mankind as a whole,' and its caustic reference to 'the old girl shedding a tear for her deceased cat, while relishing a leg of lamb', prompted an immediate rejoinder from Maurice which, in its turn, led to a whole series of letters to the Editor of the Association's little monthly journal.

The fact of the matter was that Emile was an idealist, and if he had a problem with repressed anger it was because he was a frustrated idealist. He was an idealist in that he had an ideal, the ideal being the mental picture he had formed of what a British Buddhist movement ought to be like, and he was a frustrated idealist in that this ideal had found no concrete embodiment. It was not that he was critical just of the sentimentalized, emasculated pseudo-Buddhism of the type he had handled so roughly in his article. He was critical, indeed bitterly critical, of the Sangha Association as it had been before my arrival and of the Buddhist Society as it had been, was now, and according to him always would be. Walshe he regarded as an old woman, Humphreys as a fraud, and though he faithfully attended my lectures at the Vihara (the Society he eschewed) he was far from believing that the problems facing British Buddhism could be solved simply by healing the breach between the two rival organizations, a breach which, despite my efforts, still existed to an extent. What Emile really wanted, I suspect, even at that time, was a new Buddhist movement, a movement that would make a quantum leap to the next stage of the development of Buddhism in Britain, leaving both the Sangha Association and the Buddhist Society far behind. But of such a movement there was no sign.

Shortly after our return from Biddulph Terry and I spent an evening in Southfields with my father and Auntie Florrie, whom we found concerned about the war in Vietnam. This was followed, a few days later, by an afternoon and evening in Rayleigh – and Southend – with my mother and sister and my sister's two youngest children, twelve-year-old David and eighteen-month-old Kamala. We also paid a visit to Veronica, who seemed rather upset. She was upset, it later transpired, because she had been under the impression that the following week we, too, would be leaving for India, not for Greece, and that she would be meeting up with us in Calcutta. How the misunderstanding arose I do not remember, if I ever knew, but in recent months it had become increasingly obvious that I featured in Veronica's plans much more than she featured in mine. I had one old friend who had close ties with both Greece and India. This friend was, of course, Marco Pallis, of whom I had seen little or nothing since sharing the platform with him at the Buddhist Society's Wesak meeting the previous year. A fortnight before the meeting with Veronica, however, I lunched with him and his friend Richard Nicholson at their Knightsbridge flat, where we talked at length about our much-loved Kalimpong, to which I would soon be paying a farewell visit, and about the friends we had in common both there and in neighbouring Sikkim and Bhutan. There were other reminders of my Indian past about this time. One of them was a visit I received from Rechung Rimpoche, who showed me his translation of the first part of a Tibetan medical text.[272] Another was a visit from amiable, scholarly Mother Fiske, an American Roman Catholic nun I had met in Poona, where she was doing research into the meaning of 'religion' and 'Buddhism' among what she termed India's New Buddhists.

Thus the days between our return from Biddulph and our departure for Dover passed quickly, both for me and for Terry. Not only were visits paid and received. We had trips to make to the AA,[273] to the bank, and to the bookshops, where we stocked up on classical authors, besides which I had my usual classes to take and lectures to deliver. I also hosted a reception at the Vihara. About sixty people turned up, including representatives of some of the provincial Buddhist groups, so that it was fortunate that the weather was fine and we were able to get out into the garden. In the course of the afternoon I managed to talk for a few minutes with everyone present, which left me feeling a little exhausted, though after a short outing to Kenwood[274] with Terry, Alan, and Paul, the young Adonis with the Yorkshire accent, I was sufficiently refreshed to be able to have a long talk with Alf and his family, Mike, and Jack and, after they had left, with Terry, Alan, and Viriya.

The last few days passed quickest of all. We were to leave on the Sunday, in the evening. On Wednesday, after lunching with Antoinette, I checked the dummy of the June issue of *The Buddhist*, which included the Vihara's programme for July (the June programme had appeared the previous month), and saw a young man who had embarked on a fast. Thursday Terry and I spent packing and clearing up at the flat, which we were vacating. On Friday, our packing done, we took several boxes of Terry's belongings round to the Vihara and stored them in my cupboards, after which I left Terry to finish moving out of the flat while I went and took my meditation class at the Buddhist Society. On Saturday, Terry having left for Ilford, I spent the morning clearing my desk and the afternoon attending part of the Society's weekend Conference of Provincial Buddhist Groups. Sunday was of course lecture day at the Vihara. I spent the morning writing my notes, talking with Viriya, Bill, and Alf in the afternoon, and at five-thirty gave what for the time being would be my last lecture. It was entitled 'Buddhism and "The New Reformation"', and was by way of being a successor to 'Buddhism and the Bishop of Woolwich'. After the lecture I spoke to a few people, Terry returned from Ilford, and half an hour later, after I had given Viriya some final instructions (Thien Chau was away in Paris), we left in the Little Bus. 'Both very happy to be off,' my diary records. 'Headed south.'

34
BOYHOOD HAUNTS

Shoreham-by-Sea, six miles to the west of Brighton, was the scene of some of the happiest days of my childhood, for it was in this quiet, unfashionable resort that the family had its annual summer holiday.[275] Having spent Sunday night in the vicinity of Worthing, camped beside a cornfield, on Monday morning Terry and I drove back along the coast into the old seaport, where we parked the Little Bus opposite the same unremarkable terrace house where I and the rest of the family had stayed and where we always occupied the upstairs back rooms overlooking the river Adur, with its miscellaneous shipping, its gulls hovering and crying, and its broad expanse of brown mudflat when the tide was out. We were in Shoreham partly because we were not due to leave Dover until Wednesday the fifteenth, as I had a meditation class to take in Brighton the previous evening, and partly because I was desirous of revisiting some of my old haunts and showing them to Terry.

Our first stop was the parish church, a grey Norman structure with a square tower and a truncated nave. Dedicated to St Mary the Virgin, it was commonly known as St Mary de la Haura (or de la Havre – accounts differed), Shoreham having been a flourishing harbour town throughout much of the Middle Ages. In the churchyard, after a short search, I found something I particularly wanted Terry to see. This was the tombstone of a man who, if the inscription on the weathered tombstone itself was to be believed, had died at the age of 146. I used to visit the churchyard every time we were on holiday in Shoreham, and in the family album there was a photograph of me standing beside the tombstone, taken by my father, which I used to show to the sceptical as proof I was not romancing and that in Shoreham there really was a tombstone with such an inscription on it. From the churchyard we walked to the beach, which meant having to cross to the other side of the Adur by means of the iron former toll bridge. It was a fine, fresh morning, and as Terry and I plunged down the pebbly foreshore I was glad to have sight of the sea again, glad to have the sound of the waves in my ears and the smell of the ozone in my nostrils. There was a strong wind blowing, and after plodding along the beach for a few hundred yards we took shelter under a breakwater, sitting with our backs against it and legs stretched out. It could well have been one of the very breakwaters in the crevices of whose rotting, seaweed-clad timbers I had once hunted for crabs. As we sat there eating bananas the sun came out and it grew quite warm. Shoreham had not changed much, I reflected. The principal difference was that Bungalow Town had expanded, that there were more chalets, and that there now stood, at the very edge of the beach, an ugly, incongruous, high-rise block.

The afternoon was spent up on the Downs behind Shoreham. We were parked beside a field of barley, and in the distance we could see the silver windings of the Adur and, away to the north-west, the neo-Gothic splendours of Lancing College. While Terry was busy inside the Little Bus, stowing away books, clothes, and tinned goods in their proper places, I sat outside on the grass preparing a salad lunch. Having driven down to the south of Spain many times and camped there, my friend had a good idea what we needed to take with us. We would not be away for only two weeks, however, as he and Vivien had always been. We would be away for two months, and would therefore be needing a proportionately bigger stock of certain items. Thus it was that we had on board sixty tins of minestrone, as well as sixty tins of condensed milk, of which Terry was particularly fond and which he always took in his tea. After lunch I read Euripides' *Iphigenia in Tauris* and *Hecuba*, having started working my way through the two volumes of the Everyman translation of the Greek dramatist's plays more than a week before. I had read the whole of Aeschylus and Sophocles (and Aristophanes) in my teens, but so far as I remember all I had read of Euripides was the *Bacchae*, in Gilbert Murray's translation, and it seemed appropriate that as part of my preparation for visiting Greece I should make good the deficiency and make myself better acquainted with 'sad Electra's poet'.[276] While I was absorbed in Iphigenia's joy and Hecuba's sorrow Terry was deep in the mysteries of the *Laṅkāvatāra Sūtra*.

We could not have had a more pleasant, peaceful afternoon. There were larks singing in the sky, tiny specks that soared higher and higher until, lost in the living blue, they became 'sightless songs'. In my boyhood I had often heard the larks. I had heard them on Wimbledon Common, on the Sussex Downs, and in Norfolk, and now, as I lay in the sun reading Euripides, I was hearing them once again. It was the first time I had heard them since my return to England, so far as I remember, for the lark was a rarer bird than it had been twenty years earlier (thirty-five years later it is rarer still). I must not only have heard the larks in my boyhood but have been greatly moved by those distant ecstatic trillings, for my first poem, written when I was eleven or twelve, was about the lark. The poem has not survived (it was in one of the poetry notebooks left with my father in 1944), but I remember the first verse, which ran:

> The lark rose singing from the ground
> Singing with all its might;
> No sweet singer might be found
> To equal the lark in flight.

Shortly afterwards I discovered Shelley's 'To a Skylark', which became for me, as perhaps it was for him, a symbol of the upward aspiration of the human spirit – an aspiration whose principal expressions were literature and the fine arts, friendship and the spiritual life.[277]

The Brighton Buddhist group was still holding its meetings at the Tatler restaurant, and it was there that I took the meditation class that evening, Terry and I having driven into the resort a little earlier and taken a stroll along the seafront. After the class we chatted with people for a while, then drove along the coast to Hastings, and from there inland in the direction of Battle, near which we passed the night. The following day was spent in Hastings, where we explored the second-hand bookshops, visited the Fishermen's Museum, and walked along the beach. It was a fine hot day; both sea and sky were intensely blue, and we saw several hovercraft skimming the waves. In the evening we drove to Dover, stopping only at Brookland to see the thirteenth-century church, which was remarkable for its belfry, a three-storeyed, conical wooden structure standing separate from the main building.

That night we camped on the Downs. In the morning, having done a little shopping in the town, called at the AA office, and had a good walk along the front, we drove up to Dover Castle and established ourselves in a corner of the car park. The castle was much more extensive than we had imagined, and in the afternoon it took us a couple of hours to look round the massive keep, from the top of which there was a fine view, and round the ancient fortress to drive down to the dockside, where I passed the hour and a half we had to wait before boarding the ferry reading Plutarch's *Lives* (the Greek ones, not the Roman!).[278] Once on board, we went and sat in the saloon. At midnight on 15 June the ferry left for Ostend. During the crossing Terry and I spent some time on deck. It was a little cold, and there was a strong wind blowing. I read the *Life of Aristides*.[279] We were on our way to Greece.

35
OVER THE ALPS

In Brussels we had our first experience of culture shock. We arrived in the Belgian capital at six in the morning, having driven there via Ghent in dull weather through flat, uninteresting countryside. After admiring the ornate, gilded façades of the town hall and other buildings in the Grand Place, and seeing the rather tawdry interior of a church that may or may not have been the cathedral, we made our way to the market. It was here that we received our culture shock. We had just bought some fine cherries and strawberries and a few vegetables, and were about to leave, when I happened to see a stall at the back of which was a row of plucked chickens. This was not surprising. What was surprising – indeed deeply shocking – was that in front of the chickens there were rows upon rows of tiny plucked songbirds – among them, in all probability, larks that less than twenty-four hours earlier had been singing in the sky. There were several such stalls, all with their pathetic rows of tiny naked victims of human barbarity and greed. This was my first intimation of the fact that songbirds were a feature of continental cuisine. Nor was this the worst. In France and Italy, as I was to discover a few years later, the shooting of small birds constituted a favourite national sport, millions of them being destroyed annually by the guns of so-called sportsmen.[280]

Even had we experienced no culture shock there, we would have felt little inclination to linger in Brussels. The city presented a somewhat shabby appearance, and having done our shopping we drove straight out. Or rather, we attempted to drive straight out. Getting in had been easy, but owing to the complicated one-way system and poor signposting getting out proved difficult and it was half an hour before we found the right exit and were on our way to Namur. I navigated, using the route plans Terry had obtained from the AA in London, which were both detailed and accurate and which were to stand us in good stead throughout our journey. From Namur we followed the course of the River Meuse to the picturesque little town of Dinant, through which we drove after crossing the historic bridge. Dinant! The name rang a bell for me, and eventually I recollected having read somewhere about a certain David of Dinant, a medieval scholastic who had narrowly escaped death for his heretical views.[281] After Dinant came the Ardennes, under whose green eaves we were glad to stop for lunch, and after the Ardennes the city of Luxembourg, capital of the Grand Duchy of that name. In Luxembourg we stayed only long enough to visit the Cathedral of Notre Dame, where there were fifteen or twenty people praying in the sunlit nave of the building. Their prayers were directed to the statue of the Virgin Mary standing on the altar at the far end, and to judge from the expressions and attitudes of the supplicants their prayers were real prayers. So real were they that I could actually see them winging their way through the air to their objective. The atmosphere of devotion was more intense than any I have experienced in a church before.

From Luxembourg we drove through the Moselle Valley to Metz. We were now in France. First we saw the church of St Segolene (a saint of whom I had not heard before), where a woman showed us round and where there was a quantity of fine stained glass, some of it damaged in war. In which war it was damaged was unclear, for in the course of the last four or five centuries Metz and its fortress had been much fought over. Originally a free town of the Holy Roman Empire, it was part of France for two hundred years, part of Germany for fifty, and was now again part of France. The damage to the stained glass may of course have been done during the Second World War. Though I did not realize it at the time, the beautiful Ardennes had been the scene of the Battle of the Bulge, when the Germans attempted to halt the eastward advance of the Allied forces and huge losses were sustained on both sides. There was fine stained glass in the cathedral too. By the time we found ourselves standing in front of that building, however, it was evening, and I was feeling extremely tired, so that I have only a vague, dreamlike recollection of our climbing the steps to the entrance of the great Gothic structure looming up in the dusk, and of our cautiously opening the heavy iron door. Inside we were at once enveloped by a mighty, rolling volume of sound which, proceeding majestically from an invisible organ, entirely filled the vast space of the deserted church and continued to fill it, rising and falling, for the greater part of our visit. Whether it was Bach or Buxtehude that was being played, or simply the organist improvising, I do not know, but the sound was the most magnificent I had ever heard and one that transported me, despite my tiredness, to the seventh heaven of delight. We were still looking at the stained glass when a young man quietly descended from the organ loft and slipped out by a side door.

Having left Metz by one of its ancient gates, we pressed on as far as Nancy, where we pulled up on the roadside and there spent the night. We had driven 320 miles that day, had not slept for thirty-six hours, and were now eighty miles from the Franco-Swiss border.

In the morning we drove south-east through Épinal to Remiremont, where there were many public fountains, and from Remiremont to Mulhouse, passing on the way wooded hills and picturesque villages. At the border we stopped and bought picture postcards (I sent one to Viriya, Terry one to his parents), then drove on through Basel, and from Basel, still heading south-east, to Olten. The more direct route to Olten being blocked, we were obliged to make a wide detour. This turned out to be a blessing in disguise, for it took us – after we had been briefly caught in a hailstorm – through some exceptionally beautiful wooded ravines we would otherwise have missed. Here we halted for lunch, heating minestrone and brewing tea on our portable Calor gas stove. For reasons of economy, but also because Terry tended to feel anxious in unfamiliar restaurants and cafés, we had decided that we would buy provisions along the way as we needed them and we adhered to this decision throughout our journey. From Olten we drove through thirty or forty miles of beautiful countryside to Lucerne, the scenery becoming more mountainous with every turn of the road. Switzerland, we could not but notice, was much better kept than either Belgium or France, and I remembered my mother telling me that her favourite holiday destinations were Austria and Switzerland. They were so *clean*, she said. But Switzerland was not only clean. It rejoiced in picturesque old wooden houses, carefully cultivated fields, and what my diary terms 'thoughtful arrangements for tourists'.

As we approached Lucerne we had our first glimpse of the snows and soon were inside the town walls and looking for a parking spot. Having eventually found one, we spent a couple of hours walking round the place, which obviously depended very much on the tourist trade, bought a few souvenirs, and then drove via Brunnen to Altdorf, skirting the Lake of Lucerne on the eastern side and passing through several small tunnels. A mile or two past Altdorf we left the main road and found a pleasant spot beside the River Reuss, the noise of whose fast-flowing waters we could hear in the darkness. Owing to the different nature of the terrain, as well as to our having been obliged to make a detour between Basel and Olten, we had covered only half the distance covered the day before, but we were well content with our progress and slept soundly.

The third day of our journey saw us crossing the Alps. The famous mountain chain was more than a fact of geography, more than a white patch on the map. For centuries it had been a barrier separating Italy and Northern Europe psychologically as well as physically, so that crossing the Alps, far from being simply a stage in the journey south, possessed significance that was psychological and cultural and even spiritual. It was a significance of which travellers from the north were often aware, at least subliminally – an awareness of which, in modern times, the Goethe of the *Italienische Reise* is the prime example.[282] Crossing the Alps meant emerging from grey skies, fog, and mist into a world of blue skies, brilliant sunlight, and vivid colours – emerging from numbing cold into bone-penetrating warmth. It meant leaving primeval forests of fir and oak for orange groves and olive gardens. It meant exchanging the Gothic for the classical, Christianity for paganism, religion for art, melancholy for joy. Small wonder, then, that poets and artists from England and Germany, especially, should not only have celebrated the splendour of those immaculate peaks but have felt, as they crossed the Alps, that they were about to enter a new world, perhaps begin a new life.

What Terry and I felt as we crossed the Alps there is now no means of telling. I have no recollection of what I myself felt then, and my diary is silent on the subject. But I must have enjoyed the unfamiliar landscape, and have looked forward to seeing Italy, for in my teen years I had had as great a love for Renaissance Italy as for Classical Greece and Ancient Egypt – especially after reading John Addington Symonds' *Renaissance in Italy*, the seven volumes of which I borrowed from the

Tooting Public Library.[283] Silent as it is about feelings, my diary is fairly circumstantial regarding facts. In relying on those facts, however, no doubt I would do well to bear in mind what Dr Johnson has to say, in *Idler* no. 97, on those narratives of travellers in which 'nothing is found but such general accounts as leave no distinct idea behind them, or such minute enumerations as few can read with either profit or delight.'[284] Probably there have been more than enough of these minute enumerations already in this account.

Be that as it may, on the morning of the day we crossed the Alps Terry and I rose to find the mountains flecked with snow. We also found the waters of the fast-flowing Reuss icy cold. The crossing took much less time than we had expected. Hardly had we left the pleasant spot where we had passed the night than the road started becoming steeper and the scenery more and more impressive. In less than two hours we were at the head of the St Gotthard Pass (6,926 feet above sea level), having driven through Wannen, where we did some shopping, and the popular mountaineering resort of Andermatt. Both places reminded me of hill stations I had known in India; there were the same narrow streets, the same wooden houses, the same cheerful faces and, above all, the same buoyant, exhilarating atmosphere. In the course of ascent we saw great patches of hard, unmelted snow, patches through which the road cut from time to time. The air was very thin, so that I experienced a slight nausea; the weather was cloudy, and there were several showers of rain. Rather to our surprise, traffic was heavy all the way, for at that time of year there was little danger of the road being blocked by snow and the route was a popular one, as we ought to have known. After the St Gotthard Pass came a succession of hairpin bends, thirty-seven in number, that dropped us down via Airolo and Faido to Bellinzona (761 feet above sea level), from where it was only a short drive to Lugano.

In Lugano, having lunched in a quiet spot with a fine view of the lake and the mountains, we explored the shopping arcades, visited the fifteenth-century cathedral, and looked round what I think must have been the cathedral shop, where we found a remarkable variety of modern Catholic art, some of it of a very high standard, especially the carved wooden figures of the Virgin Mary and other saints. We then continued on our way skirting Lake Lugano for several miles, passing through the Swiss and Italian customs, where there was a short delay, and arriving in Como late in the evening.

Finding a secluded spot in which to pass the night proved difficult, and in the end we simply parked at the side of the road near the lake. Como was quieter than either Lucerne or Lugano, and when we went for a walk along the shore before darkness fell we found it deserted. The air was very still, and there was a pleasant view across the waters. That night Terry and I had a long talk. It was our first real talk since leaving England, but regarding the content of the talk my diary is, as usual, silent.

36
RECLAIMING A HERITAGE

Venice was about 150 miles from Milan, at least as the crow flies. We could easily have covered the distance in a day, but our route lay through three historic north-Italian cities, all of some cultural significance, and it therefore took us the better part of three days to complete this stage of our journey. On each of the two nights we parked in a lay-by on the autostrada. This was probably illegal, but no one took any notice of us, and we reckoned we could be safer there than parked somewhere in town. Italy was not Switzerland, or even France.

Milan did not detain us long. We arrived there from Como around midday, having driven down the autostrada, and found the city centre without any difficulty. At the far end of the Piazza del Duomo rose the vast bulk of the cathedral, the third largest in Europe, its triangular west front positively bristling with crockets and pinnacles. As there was a High Mass in progress we were unable to see much of the building's interior, but we could see the archbishop in his red skull-cap and hear the priest who, in highly declamatory style and with much waving of arms, was holding forth from a pulpit on the opposite side of the nave. Though I knew no Italian, from the constant recurrence of the word *comunismo*, often to the accompaniment of a vigorous shaking of the speaker's fist, I had little difficulty concluding that the worthy priest was engaged in denouncing the godless creed for the benefit of the assembled faithful. The faithful themselves were quiet and attentive, though people were coming and going all the time in a way that would have been unthinkable in England.

There were other differences between the colourful Roman Catholic ceremony and the more sober Anglican services I had attended as a boy. What those differences were I cannot now recall in any detail, but I distinctly remember finding the whole atmosphere much more 'pagan' than anything with which I was familiar. It was therefore possible for me to understand the reaction of a Protestant who, witnessing a Roman Catholic service for the first time, and seeing its images and altars, its candles and incense, its tonsured priests in gorgeous vestments, its worship of relics, its elaborate rituals, its chantings and blessings, should have concluded that Roman Catholicism was in truth little more than a pseudo-Christian version of the old Mediterranean paganism. Such had been the conclusion of the genial superintendent of the Baptist Sunday school I attended for a while who, on his return from a business trip to Rome, solemnly described to some of the older boys the abominations he had personally witnessed in St Peter's.[285]

From the cathedral and the Piazza del Duomo we walked the length of the Via Dante to the Sforza Castle. On the way we had our second experience of culture shock – or rather I did. Having located a *gabinetto*, and made sure I was following the signs that read *signori* or 'gentlemen' and not the ones reading *signore* or 'ladies', I descended the stone steps briskly. At the bottom of the steps, to my astonishment, sat a *woman* – a stout, elderly woman in a tight-fitting black dress and black cotton stockings. But apparently I had *not* made a mistake. On seeing me the woman rose to her feet with a welcoming smile and, hurrying on ahead of me with every expression of delight, flung open the door of a cubicle, gave the toilet seat an energetic dusting, and having thrust a wad of tissues into my hand finally ushered me in with bows and smiles that were evidently meant to wish me a successful outcome to my visit. These ministrations were not entirely disinterested, as I quickly discovered when, in my ignorance of *gabinetto* etiquette, I attempted to 'return, and gain the cheerful skies'[286] without according them the customary recognition. Evidently Benign Mother could easily become Terrible Mother! Reflecting afterwards on this my second experience of culture shock it occurred to me that perhaps the average Italian male did not feel comfortable unless there was a sympathetic and encouraging maternal figure close at hand on such occasions.

The Sforza Castle was extensive without being impressive. On our arrival we found that the museum and art gallery that were housed within its walls, and which we had been hoping to visit, were both closed. We therefore walked back to the Little Bus and drove first to the twelfth-century church of Sant'Ambrogio, then to San Lorenzo Maggiore, with its colonnade of reused sixth-century Corinthian columns, and finally to the Monastery of Santa Maria delle Grazie. All three were closed, to our great disappointment, for we had not yet grasped the fact that in Italy the afternoon hours were sacred to siesta and that during this period even the saints were not to be disturbed. We were particularly disappointed that the Monastery of Santa Maria delle Grazie was closed, for this was the building that contained, painted on the wall of the former refectory, what was the most famous, even as it was probably the greatest, of all Milan's artistic treasures: Leonardo da Vinci's *The Last Supper*.[287]

Having found our way back to the autostrada, we therefore drove on to Brescia, turning aside into a service area when we were a few miles short of our destination in order to improvise a belated lunch. Fields of ripe wheat and half-grown maize lay golden and green all around us, while away to the north and west, each on its separate hill, there were dotted four or five little towns, one walled, and all of them with red-tiled houses and red-tiled churches. Some of the churches, as was apparent even from where we sat, were in a sad state of dilapidation, and the little towns themselves, I thought, had a desolate and deserted look, many of their inhabitants no doubt having left to work in the factories of Milan, which far from being just a treasure-house of centuries-old art and architecture, as one might have thought, was one of the major industrial centres of modern Italy. Despite the proximity of the filling station, it was pleasant and peaceful there amid the fields, beneath a clear blue sky, and within sight of the foothills of the Alps. So pleasant and peaceful was it that Terry and I not only lingered over our lunch but sat contemplating the scene for so long afterwards that we did not reach Brescia until six o'clock. In Brescia we spent the evening exploring the city on foot, but although the names of the churches and other buildings we saw are noted in my diary, these are now little more than names, and I have no distinct recollection of any of them.

Such is not the case with regard to Verona, where we spent the whole of the following day. In connection with this city there come crowding upon me recollections of ancient bridges over the fast-flowing River Adige, Romanesque churches of pink brick, the statue of Dante in the Piazza dei Signori, ornate polychrome porches whose pillars were supported by winged lions, paintings by Pisanello, Mantegna, Titian, Tintoretto, and Veronese,[288] and the unobstructed view we had, after climbing up to the Castel Vecchio, of the red-tiled roofs, the campaniles, and the domes of the unspoiled old city, the sunlit pinks and reds of which were relieved, here and there, by the dark spires of the cypresses. Three recollections stand out with particular vividness. The first finds us in the Basilica of San Zeno, standing before Mantegna's altarpiece, *Enthroned Madonna and Child with Saints*,[289] perhaps the most magnificent of all the many paintings we saw that day, of which it has been said, 'Considering the brightness of the colours and of the gold, the power of the architectural masses, the sharp definition of forms, and the consistency of the spatial formulation, the illusion of reality – a higher reality – within the frame is overpowering.' My next recollection is of our coming, quite by chance, upon what according to local tradition – and the city's tourist department – was Juliet's House, complete with the very balcony from which the lovely daughter of the Capulets listened to the pleadings of the lovesick scion of the Montagues. I had forgotten that the scene of Shakespeare's *Romeo and Juliet* was laid in fourteenth-century Verona.[290] Finally, there is a recollection of Terry and myself arriving late that afternoon at the entrance of the great Roman amphitheatre, said to have seated 25,000 people, only to find the gates already closed for the night. We did not greatly mind, for our impression on looking through the bars was one of what my diary describes as 'massive brutality'. The impression was as much psychic as aesthetic, for like the Colosseum in Rome the amphitheatre had been used for fights between wild beasts, and between wild beasts and men, as well as for gladiatorial contests of various kinds.

The sixth day of our journey began unpropitiously. We woke early, and it was a fine morning, but Terry admitted he was feeling rather depressed, and this necessitated our having a long talk before we could drive on to Vicenza. He had not felt depressed for several weeks, the last time having been around the middle of May, when he was still coming to terms with the knowledge that he might never see his daughter again. This time his depression had a quite different cause. It was due, as I eventually discovered, to all the sightseeing we had been doing the last few days. It was not that he had any objection to sightseeing, or that he was not almost as keen as I was to visit the famous and interesting sights of the places through which we passed. But so much of what we saw had no meaning for him. This was particularly true of the paintings. Most of them were of a religious nature, and they illustrated stories with which he was unfamiliar, depicted personages whose very names were unknown to him, and were replete with symbols to the significance of which he had no clue. The more he saw of such paintings, as well as those of a historical or mythological character, the more acutely he felt his lack of education, and the more acutely he felt his lack of education the more he was reminded how much he was at a disadvantage with people more educated and knowledgeable than himself and how inferior and inadequate such people made him feel. Terry laid the blame for his lack of education at the door of his parents, who had allowed him to leave school at sixteen, and his depression that morning, as on so many previous occasions, was due largely to the anger and resentment he felt towards them on this account. Had it not been for his lack of education, the places we had visited and the paintings we had seen would have had meaning for him, he believed, and he would not have felt so cut off from an important section of the great heritage of Western culture.

My own position in this respect was quite different from my friend's. Though I had received even less formal education than Terry, in my teens I had read as widely as I could in the fields of European literature, art, and philosophy, both ancient and modern, and even during my twenty years in the East I had not entirely lost contact with Western culture, at least to the extent that this was represented by English poetry. For me our present journey, and the sightseeing we were doing along the way, represented a renewal, and a deepening, of that contact. The places we visited, and the paintings we saw, had meaning for me. Through them I was reconnecting with my cultural roots, reclaiming my cultural heritage, for although I was a Buddhist I was a Western Buddhist, and could not afford, psychologically and even spiritually, to cut myself off from those roots, or to renounce that heritage, as some misguided Western Buddhists thought they were obliged to do. Now that I had the opportunity, I wanted to immerse myself in Western culture. I wanted to stop at every historic city, to visit every church, castle, and palace there, to look at every painting and sculpture. At the same time, I was aware that for Terry much of what we saw was without meaning, though he dutifully consulted such guidebooks as we possessed and asked me questions from time to time. Paintings were often without meaning for him because he was ignorant of the Bible stories or classical myths and legends on which they were based. Such ignorance was by no means unusual, and in years to come, when 'progressive' education policies had done their work, it would be widespread in Britain. Terry at least knew that he was cut off from his cultural heritage, and resented the fact. People in the future would hardly know there was a cultural heritage to be cut off from.

How I talked Terry out of his depression I do not remember, but a few hours later we were in Vicenza and looking at paintings by Mantegna, Tiepolo, Memlinc,[291]and others in the Chiericati museum and art gallery. Among the works we saw (I forget by whom) were a remarkable *Herodias with the Head of John the Baptist*, a beautiful *St Sebastian*, and an impressive *Ecstasy of St Francis*.[292] We had already visited the cathedral which, having been practically destroyed during the war and then rebuilt, was not only spacious but uncluttered. Palladio's Basilica,[293] which was not a church but the town hall, appeared to have suffered no damage, but it had a shabby and neglected air, and we were surprised to find that there were shops downstairs and that the great hall upstairs was being used for basketball. Despite its many Renaissance palaces, Vicenza was on the whole a much less attractive place than Verona and we were not altogether sorry when the time came for us to leave for Venice. We did not leave without seeing Palladio's last work, the famous Teatro Olimpico, a classical Renaissance theatre with fixed perspective scenery in and out of which, the building being open, we were able to wander at will. Our evening was spent in a campsite on the seashore near Mestre, the industrial suburb of Venice. There were many caravans parked on the grass among the trees, and the place had a pleasant, relaxed atmosphere. Terry and I walked for a while on the beach, which was strewn with shells, then bought a few provisions at the site shop, cooked ourselves a meal, and read, my own choice of reading matter being *Selected Poems of D. H. Lawrence*.[294]

There was a lot to see in Venice. So much was there to see that after spending the whole of the following day in the city sightseeing Terry and I decided to spend an extra half day there, which meant staying a second night at the campsite. Venice was not to be seen from the comfort of a motor vehicle, whether public or private. Twice crossing the causeway linking Mestre and Venice, and each time leaving the Little Bus in the car park, in the course of our day and a half in the city we saw, either on foot or travelling in one of the *vaporetti* that plied up and down the Grand Canal, the sights that millions had seen before us and that thousands, perhaps, from Goethe and Byron to Ruskin and Frederick Rolfe, had celebrated in verse and impassioned prose.[295] There were streets that were only alleys between high walls, tiny bridges over canals a few feet wide, a fruit and vegetable market that was the finest we had seen in Italy, and an enormous number of shops selling the famous Venetian coloured and gilded glassware. Above all, there were the glories of the Byzantine St Mark's Cathedral and the grandeurs of the Venetian-Gothic Ducal Palace, both of which we visited on our first morning in the city; the Gallery of the Academy, which we visited on our second morning and where we saw Giorgione's mysterious *Tempest*;[296] and Veronese's sumptuous *Feast in the House of Levi*;[297] and the palaces that stood on either side of the Grand Canal, their façades reflected in the dull waters. But though we saw many buildings, many paintings, and many people (most of them tourists), what most impressed me was the *tout ensemble* of Venice itself. It was enough simply to be there, to walk round in the brilliant sunshine, to sit a while in the Zen Chapel, to eat our sandwiches in the little secluded garden. It was enough simply to enjoy the gay, almost festive atmosphere of the place, to feel the breeze coming off the lagoon, and to have the sense that Venice was open to the sea and, through the sea, open to the world. Thus it was not surprising that the Doges should have 'wed the sea with rings',[298] or that it should have been from Venice that Marco Polo set out on his travels – travels that were to take him, eventually, to the court of Kublai Khan.[299] Venice had her back to Europe, and looked towards the East. Venice was Europe's gateway to the East.

On the direct route between Venice and Brindisi, from where we were to take the car ferry to Greece, there were only three cities of cultural importance: Padua, Ravenna, and Rimini. In Padua, to which we drove after spending the morning in Venice, we had time to see only the Basilica of St Anthony, the Eremitani Church, and the Arena Chapel. The Basilica was a monastic church, the first one we had visited, and on entering it we found the monks, all in black habits, chanting in the choir. St Anthony of Padua, to whom the Romanesque-Gothic structure was dedicated, was the most celebrated of the followers of St Francis of Assisi (legend represented him as preaching to the fishes, just as St Francis had preached to the birds), and the chapel containing his bones was evidently the object of much popular devotion. Richly ornamented with carved marbles of various colours, it was hung with scores, perhaps hundreds, of *ex votos* of the different limbs and organs that had been healed thanks to the intercession of the saint. In Greece we were to discover that this pious practice had very ancient roots. Popular devotion was also very much in evidence in the cloisters of the Basilica, where there was a large shop selling an amazing variety of cheap souvenirs, all in the worst possible taste and all decorated with, or incorporating, however incongruously, a picture or figure of St Anthony. Five or six monks ran the shop, serving customers and operating the cash registers with remarkable speed and efficiency. Outside the Basilica, on the piazza, was Donatello's fine equestrian statue of the Venetian general Erasmo da Narni, sitting relaxed and thoughtful on his great charger.[300]

The Eremitani Church, rebuilt after the Second World War in the original Romanesque style, was a simple and impressive building. It was famous for its frescoes by Mantegna. Some of these had been destroyed during the fighting, but I have neither record nor recollection of our seeing those that survived and they may not have been on view. Fortunately the Arena Chapel, which stood nearby, had suffered no damage, and its inner walls were still resplendent with the blues, reds, greens, and browns – especially the blues – of Giotto's frescoes depicting the life of Christ and the Last Judgement, all largely intact and all very little faded. In Verona we had seen a painting that may or may not have been by Giotto, but here was a whole series of works that were undoubtedly from the hand of the master and from that hand at the height of its powers. Though the life of Christ was depicted in strict accordance with the traditional narratives, and though symbolism was by no means absent, so naturalistic was Giotto's style, so dramatic his treatment of each episode, so vivid his characterization of the personages involved, and so great his capacity to represent the emotions they were experiencing, that many of the frescoes could have meaning – at least a simple, humanistic meaning – even for those who, like Terry, were unfamiliar with the gospel stories and the dogmas with which those stories were associated.[301]

From Padua we drove to Chioggia and from Chioggia down the coast to Pomposa, where we decided to stay at the campsite near the Lido. Our intention was to stay only one night but in the event we stayed three. The reason for this change of plan was that towards the end of the following afternoon, when we should have left for Ravenna, I started running a temperature and had to go to bed, where I passed a feverish night, sleeping only fitfully and perspiring a lot, and where I woke late next morning feeling better but rather weak. The fever may have been due to malaria, from which I had suffered in India, or, what is more likely, to the fact that it being a fine day, with a clear blue sky, Terry and I had spent much of our time on the beach, where he went swimming and I took a few dips in the pleasantly warm water. Whatever the cause of the fever may have been, we decided to stay where we were until I was fully recovered. This enabled us to catch up on our reading. I dipped again into *Selected Poems of D. H. Lawrence*, began and finished *The Bostonians*, probably my favourite Henry James novel (not that I know them all),[302] and read Plutarch's *Life of Pericles*.[303]

Ravenna was only a few miles from Pomposa. We arrived in the small, compact city soon after ten o'clock and spent the next four or five hours visiting the Basilica of San Vitale, the Mausoleum of Galla Placida, the Neonian (or Orthodox) baptistery, the cathedral, the Basilica of Sant'Apollinare Nuovo, and the cloisters of the National Museum, where there was an exhibition of books and manuscripts relating to Dante, who had died in Ravenna and was buried there. Except for the eighteenth-century cathedral, all the churches belonged to the fifth and sixth centuries and contained mosaics of the same period. These mosaics gave me one of the most intense aesthetic experiences of my life. 'Mosaics of quite unearthly beauty', I commented in my diary that evening, adding that they were 'incomparably better' than the ones we had seen at St Mark's in Venice. The mosaics of San Vitale, which we visited twice, were remarkable for richness and harmony of colour, variety of subject matter, and historical interest; those of the Mausoleum of Galla Placida for the depth and intensity of their blues, especially the blues of the elaborately decorated vaulting; and those of S Apollinare Nuovo for their long, rhythmical processions of white-robed Martyrs and gold-robed Virgins, one occupying the right-hand side of the nave, as the spectator looked towards the altar, the other the side on the left.

But the most beautiful mosaics were those in the Basilica of S Apollinare in Classe, which was situated three or four miles south of Ravenna, amid fields, and which we saw on our way to Rimini. As in S Apollinare Nuovo, the nave was flanked by two rows of marble columns, but apart from the very late series of portraits on the side walls the mosaic decoration was confined to the choir and the semidome of the apse. In the semidome, his arms held up in prayer, stood the figure of St Apollinare, the first bishop of Ravenna. He stood in a wide green valley, a valley filled with all manner of trees and shrubs, while from either side there advanced towards him a row of white lambs, each separated from the next lamb in the procession by a spray of white lilies. Above the saint, within an enormous blue medallion, was a jewelled golden cross, and above the cross a sky of gold streaked with cloud. Combined as they were with the symbolism of the shepherd and his sheep, the predominant greens, browns, and whites of the lower half of the semidome created a sense of harmony and peace reminiscent of Bach's 'Sheep May Safely Graze' or the pastoral interlude in *Messiah*.[304] This sense of deep peacefulness was enhanced by the silvery hues of the Corinthian columns, by the quality of the light filling the place, and by the fact that during our visit we had the whole building to ourselves.

Among the trees depicted in the apse, in highly stylized form, was the umbrella pine, and indeed there extended not far from the Basilica what was left of the ancient pine forest Byron admired and in which he was accustomed, during his residence in Ravenna, to ride and shoot. We did not venture into the forest, but drove straight to Rimini, where we were content to view the ruined Castle of Sigismondo from a distance, and then on via Pesara to Fano.

That night we stayed in a small new campsite, the Verde Luna. The following day we drove to Pescara in the morning, and in the afternoon from Pescara, where we stopped for lunch, all the way to Campomarino. Our route lay between the mountains and the sea. On our right were the foothills, many of them crowned with towns and castles; on the left, the Adriatic, in colour an intense green-blue and with rollers of white foam. In the course of the day's journey we saw vineyards and cornfields and, eventually, olive groves, which we had not seen before, and which to judge by the gnarled and twisted trunks of the little trees with the silver-green foliage must have been very old. There were also broad sandy beaches, with fewer and fewer people on them the further south we penetrated. Near Campomarino we found a campsite. It was small and scruffy, but it was situated on the seashore, it was deserted, and there was a fine view, and we were delighted with the place. So delighted were we that we stayed there not just that night but for the greater part of the following day. For the first time since

Terry and the Little Bus

leaving England I felt truly 'away from it all'. We had nothing to do but cook, wash a few clothes, and read about Greece. Above us was only the blue sky, before us only the green-blue sea, behind us only the low-lying range of mauve foothills. There was no sound but that of the wind and waves, no sign of life but the lizards darting about in the wiry grass and the black scarab beetles which, the afternoon of that second day, I watched trundling their balls of dried dung over the hot sand. We were in a different world. It was a world of intense heat, the world of Hyperion and Apollo, almost the world of Aton and Ra.[305]

It was certainly a different world through which we drove during the next twenty-four hours, on the last lap of our journey from Venice to Brindisi. It was a world of small towns where people sat in their doorways and where there prevailed an atmosphere of complete inertia. It was a world of long cypress avenues and untidy commercial centres, of streets strewn with litter and squares filled, late at night, with people, and of glaring contrasts between the old and the new, the traditional and the modern. In many respects, it was a world that reminded me strongly of India. It was a world in which, when we reached Bari, there was only a rather dirty campsite wherein to pass the night, but it was a world, also, of clear, bright mornings, and a coastal road that ran past beautiful bays and curious rock formations and from which we could see giant prickly-pear cacti, stone 'beehive' huts in the middle of fields, and grove after grove of olive trees with trunks fantastically contorted.

In Brindisi we discovered there was a car ferry leaving for Igoumenitsa that afternoon, but decided not to take it as there was some uncertainty about sleeping accommodation. Having booked a passage on a ferry that would be leaving next day, we therefore found a campsite, had a meal, and read. That night there was a very strong wind, and I had a strange dream, in the course of which I drew forth the life-essence of a number of demons and cast them into the fire. Like many dreams, it appeared to have no connection with my waking thoughts and I was at a loss to understand where it had come from and what it might mean.

Terry and I spent our last day in Italy – our last for the time being, at least – cleaning out the Little Bus, replenishing our stores, and seeing what we could of Brindisi. Though we turned up at the dockside on time, we were unable to board until ten o'clock, and the *Egnatia* did not sail until an hour and a half later. We wandered round the ship, which was much bigger and more luxurious than we had expected, cashed travellers' cheques, drank tea, and did not retire to our berths until two o'clock. Before retiring we went up on deck. It was a clear night, the sea was calm, and there was a nearly-full moon shining on the waters.

37
THE ROAD TO DELPHI

Though we had gone to bed so late the previous night, Terry and I rose early, and on going on deck soon afterwards found hardly anyone about. It was a fine, clear morning, the sea could not have been more calm, and we were sailing between the mainland and some four or five small, widely separated islands. Despite the muffled hum of the ship's engines, and the occasional muffled shout coming from the swimming pool, there was a breathless hush in the air, and as I gazed out over the dark blue waters it was as though time stood still, as though nothing had changed, and that I was seeing what Homer – had he not been blind – might have seen three thousand years ago.[306] I felt much as D. H. Lawrence must have felt when he wrote, as he passed that way:

> Now the sea is the Argonauts' sea, and in the dawn
> Odysseus calls the commands, as he steers past those foamy
>   islands;
> wait, wait, don't bring me the coffee yet, nor the pain grillé.
> The dawn is not off the sea, and Odysseus' ships
> have not yet passed the islands, I must watch them still.[307]

I don't remember if Terry and I were brought any coffee that morning or any *pain grillé*, but we had swallowed a cup of tea before going on deck and probably were still standing at the rail when the ferry reached Corfu, the largest of the Ionian islands, where a few passengers disembarked.

Two hours later we were in Igoumenitsa, and after a delay in the customs found ourselves on the road to Yannina, the provincial capital, sixty-four miles away.

It was exciting to be in Greece at last, exciting that a dream had come true and we were actually on our way to Delphi. The countryside through which we were passing was brown and desolate, while above a certain altitude the sides of the mountains were entirely devoid of vegetation. Presently we saw a few miserable stone huts, though little evidence of any cultivation. As we approached Yannina, however, we started to see extensive fields of what I eventually recognized as tobacco, which I had not known was produced in Greece. There were also people on donkeys, and standing in a dusty yellow field, evidently just harvested, two bearded Orthodox priests in black gowns and cylindrical headgear could be seen bending and straightening up as between them they lifted bundles of what seemed to be hay on to the back of a donkey. They moved slowly and stiffly, in a way that combined the laboriousness of the peasant and the dignity of the priest. The scene could well have been painted by the Millet of the *Angelus*, and it moved me deeply.[308] Immemorially pastoral and immemorially patriarchal, it was reminiscent of the time when farmer, priest, and father were one and the same person, and when the powers of earth served religion and the forces of religion blessed the earth.

There was nothing pastoral about the filling station at which we stopped shortly before reaching the town, and nothing patriarchal about the voluble Shell agent we encountered there.[309] Petrol was expensive, though whether because it was more heavily taxed in Greece than in the countries through which we had passed, or because it was a case of the wily Greek taking advantage of the innocent foreign travellers, we had no means of telling. In Yannina we parked beside an extensive lake, over the waters of which there was a view of the domes and minarets of what appeared to be a mosque. Epirus had been part of the Ottoman empire for 500 years, and Turkish cultural influence was still very much in evidence. While we were resting after lunch three inquisitive Greek boys appeared, one of whom proceeded to catch and dismember a crayfish, though whether with a view to cooking and eating it or out of sheer devilment was unclear. From the lake we drove to the town centre, where we strolled round what I could not help calling the bazaar, and where the shops were as poor and shabby as those of small-town provincial India.

In one of these shops I bought a black-and-green pottery wall plate of the head of Achilles, not realizing that in the course of our three weeks in Greece we would be seeing scores, even hundreds, of souvenir shops, and tens of thousands of cheap, mass-produced souvenirs of every kind. Achilles and the events of the Trojan War had been familiar to me since my boyhood, initially from a little book called *The Story of the Iliad*, which my father had given me, and later from the *Iliad* itself, in Chapman's translation, a second-hand copy of which I picked up in Bideford, during the war, and which I read in a state bordering on ecstasy.[310] I was particularly delighted with the episodes in which the gods and goddesses appear, whether it was Hera whipping up the celestial horses and driving herself and Pallas Athene down from the heights of Olympus to the earth, the axle of the chariot groaning beneath the combined weight of the two goddesses, or Aphrodite being wounded in the hand by the Greek hero Diomedes as she removes her son Aeneas from the fray, or Thetis rising from the depths of the sea, stealing up to the throne of Zeus, and prevailing upon him to give victory to the Trojans until the Greeks gave due honour to her son, the 'valiant and glorious' Achilles, who was fated to die young.

Zeus was king of the gods, and his oracle at Dodona claimed to be the eldest of the oracles of the Hellenic world. We arrived there from Yannina early in the evening, having turned off into the green, peaceful valley from the Arta road, and spent a couple of hours looking round the archaeological area, where except for the partly restored theatre there was little to be seen other than the exposed foundations of various ancient buildings. Whether on account of the bare mountains by which it was shut in, or because of the lingering influence of the feeling of awe with which visitors must have approached the sacred site, there was a strange quietness in the atmosphere of the valley, a quietness that was more than mere absence of sound. In classical times the oracle was regarded as having its seat in the leaves of an oak, the whisperings of which communicated the god's responses to the questions put to him. Originally, however, the place seems to have been the seat of a dream-oracle, the dreams coming to the attendant prophets, the Selloi, as they slept on the bare ground. There is an allusion to Dodona and the Selloi in the *Iliad*, in the speech in which Achilles prays to Zeus for the victory and safe return of his friend Patroclus, whom he has sent to fight against the Trojans in his place.

High Zeus, lord of Dodona, Pelasgian, living afar off,
brooding over wintry Dodona, your prophets about you
living, the Selloi who sleep on the ground with feet unwashed.
Hear me.
As one time before when I prayed to you, you listened
and did me honour, and smote strongly the host of the Achaians,
so one more time bring to pass the wish that I pray for.[311]

Within the archaeological area there stood a big old tree, more trunk than branch, that may or may not have been an oak, and may or may not have been the lineal descendant of the tree in whose leaves the oracle had had its seat. Probably because there was no wind, we heard no whisperings from the scanty foliage above our heads, neither did we see any trace of the Selloi, though at ten o'clock the site's young Greek attendant came to lock up for the night, so to speak. He was friendly and inquisitive, as were two young Greeks who had turned up earlier and who came and visited us at the Little Bus the following morning.

Such visits were to be a common feature of our journey through Greece, especially when we were in the more out-of-the-way places. No sooner had we settled down for the night, or simply stopped for a meal and a rest, than one or two young men – usually two friends – would appear from nowhere and approach us, sometimes after loitering for a while in our vicinity. In France and Italy such a thing had not happened even once. Communication often began with the young men smilingly asking, 'You have cigarette?', the question being put in a way that did not quite amount to a request but was more than just a simple enquiry. Terry and I would thereupon be forced to explain that we were non-smokers and had no cigarettes, and as our visitors had little English, usually no more than the three words already spoken, and we had no Greek, we had no alternative but to shake our heads vigorously, spread our fingers wide, and shrug our shoulders, and hope they would understand what we meant. Probably they did understand, for they never took offence at our failure to produce any cigarettes and remained as friendly as before. Their inquisitiveness was directed as much to the Little Bus as to Terry and me. They walked round it slowly and admiringly, peered through the windows, and were evidently much taken by the way it was fitted out within. One young man, after peering inside, turned to us in surprise, saying, 'No women?' The most common enquiry, after 'You have cigarette?' was 'German or English?' In certain places the latter was indeed the initial enquiry, and no smiles would be forthcoming until the question of our nationality had been cleared up. The Germans had attacked and overrun Greece in 1941, and the wounds of war were taking a long time to heal. Once the young men had satisfied their curiosity they would drift away, disappearing as quietly as they had arrived on the scene. They appeared to have nothing to do, and may well have been unemployed.

Rather to my surprise, Terry seemed not to mind these intrusions upon our privacy. Sometimes he appeared almost to welcome them. This was only partly due to the obvious inoffensiveness of the intruders, if such they could really be called. It was also due to the fact that, as could be safely assumed, they were not more educated and more knowledgeable than he was and that there was no question, therefore, of his being at a disadvantage with them. Even had they happened to be more educated and knowledgeable, in the absence of a common language this would not have become apparent. Thus there was no danger of my friend being made to feel inadequate and inferior, as sometimes was the case in England, and he could meet the advances of our friendly, inquisitive young visitors in a natural, easy manner. The truth was that Terry really liked people, and became anxious, and therefore stiff and reserved, only when he felt threatened by their superior education and knowledge. There were times when I thought he felt threatened even by me, though the fact that in certain fields he was the more knowledgeable of the two should have been enough to rule out any feelings of this kind. I might know more about religion and philosophy, but he knew more about the practicalities of modern urban living. If I was to stay on in the West indefinitely, as I had now decided to do, I would need to know more about those practicalities. I already knew a little about them, thanks to Terry, and could expect that in time I would know as much as he did. In that case there would be an imbalance between us; he might feel threatened, and this could affect our friendship. But that was all in the hypothetical future, and it was best not to speculate. Now we were at Dodona, within sight of the big old tree that may or may not have been an oak. The two young Greeks had just paid their second visit, Terry seeming not to mind the intrusion, and it was time for us to leave.

We left at ten o'clock, not without regrets, driving back through the green, peaceful valley and rejoining the highway. 'Many wild flowers,' notes my diary. 'Along banks of Lauros River, through fine mountain scenery, to Arta.' Lauros! The name conjures up a vision of crystal-clear waters – waters that wound their rapid way between smooth grey boulders and were half hidden by overhanging trees. So beautiful was the river, and so mysterious in its flow, that it was not difficult to believe, as an Ancient Greek would have done, that it was the haunt of nymphs and that one might, if one was lucky, catch a glimpse of two or three of them sporting in the water. In Arta we stayed only long enough for Terry to photograph some storks. We had seen storks in Yannina, nesting on the chimney tops, but here a pair of them had built their big untidy nest on the top of a tall, rather ornamental church tower, and the opportunity was too good to miss. With an eye to the lucrative travel brochure market, Terry had already taken shots of the Grand Canal in Venice, and of divers – tiny figures silhouetted against a sky of ultramarine – about to plunge from a huge rock on the Adriatic coast, but I suspected his heart was not really in the work, reminiscent as it was of the job he had so recently quitted. At Amphilokhia we stopped again, there being a magnificent view over the Gulf of Arta, and Terry took a few more photographs. We then headed for Stratos, the old capital of the area, which was just off the main road, in the hope of finding there a place to park during the hot afternoon hours. On the way we passed three lakes, one large and two small. Though pleasant to look at, the large lake smelt badly, and it was very windy. In Stratos our hopes of finding somewhere to park were quickly dashed. The place turned out to be no more than a tumbledown village plus a few ruins, and we decided to press on to Agrinion. Unfortunately, we missed the town, probably bypassing it, and in the end simply drove into a convenient field and parked beneath a tree.

Here for the next four hours we camped, on this occasion without any friendly, inquisitive young men intruding on our privacy. We had lunch, and I read Euripides' *The Madness of Herakles*.[312] In years to come the figure of this the greatest of the Greek heroes, with his lion skin and his club, was to occupy a special place in my imagination and be the subject of one of my longer poems.[313] That Herakles (or Hercules, as he is called in the poem) was not so much the boisterous, brutal Herakles of popular legend as the altruistic Herakles whose *might* was at the service of *right* and who for centuries had been the patron saint, so to speak, of the Stoic philosophers of Greece and Rome. Traces of this altruistic Herakles were to be found even in the oldest legends. In Euripides' play itself the Chorus of Theban elders, having lamented the passing of youth, breaks out in praise of Memory and of the greatness of Herakles, singing:

> Proud theme hath minstrelsy, to sing mine hero's high achieving:
> He is Zeus' son, but deeds hath done whose glory mounts, far-
> leaving
> The praise of birth divine behind,
> Whose toils gave peace to human kind,
> Slaying dread shapes that filled man's mind with terrors ceaseless-
> haunting.[314]

Since Herakles' toils (no doubt a reference to the famous Twelve Labours) 'gave peace to human kind', and thus were of an altruistic character, their glory surpasses the praise due to the hero as son of the king of the gods. Indeed, it is altruism itself that is the true divinity, and Herakles is to be praised, even worshipped, not on account of his supposed divine paternity, but as the embodiment of altruism. Embodying as he does the principle of altruism he exemplified, for the Stoics especially, a definite ideal, an ideal that may be regarded as representing, on its own ethical level and within its own Greco-Roman cultural context, the transcendental altruism that is exemplified, for Buddhists, in the idea of the infinitely wise and boundlessly compassionate bodhisattva who, in the words of the *Devotion to Tārā*, 'labours for the weal of all beings'.[315]

Euripides' play was still giving me food for thought when, shortly before six o'clock, we struck camp and drove coastward to Missolonghi. It was in this nondescript little town that Byron had died in 1824, at the age of thirty-seven, the victim (it has been said), as he was the author, of his own legend.[316] One of our books on Greece described Missolonghi as being situated on the edge of a wide, stagnant lagoon, only navigable by flat-bottomed boats, but we saw nothing of either the lagoon or the boats, and very little of the town itself other than the fat brown pipes of the new sewerage system. All the roads having been dug up for laying them, it was difficult to get around, and we therefore had to drive on without seeing the museum or the statue of Byron. Between Missolonghi and Naupactus, as if to compensate us for any disappointment we may have felt, there was a fine view of the Gulf of

Patras to the south and west. Naupactus, renamed by the Venetians as Lepanto, was situated further along the coast, on the Gulf of Corinth. As Lepanto, the town had given its name to the great sea battle of 1571 in which the combined Christian forces under Don Juan of Austria, the half-brother of Philip II of Spain, had inflicted a crushing defeat on the forces of the Ottoman Empire. From the Christian point of view it was a famous victory, and one that G. K. Chesterton celebrates with his usual gusto in his poem 'Lepanto', which I had more than once encountered in anthologies of twentieth-century poetry.[317] Since we were hoping to reach Delphi that night, we drove straight through Naupactus, as it was again being called, without stopping to see the remains of either Venetian or Turkish occupation.

For the second time that day our hopes were dashed – this time in a more serious manner. Our route lay through the mountains, and we were not long out of Naupactus before we hit a fifteen-mile stretch of extremely bad road. To make matters worse night fell, and as there was no moon we had to find our way by the light of our headlamps as best we could. The road evidently was being widened. Rocks had been blasted and trees felled on either side of it; in places it was impassable, and the little detours that had been created were no more than the roughest of rough tracks. Driving was not only difficult but dangerous. More than once we found ourselves on the edge of a precipice, and more than once we had to cross what appeared to be a ravine by means of a bridge that was no more than half a dozen tree trunks laid edge to edge and covered with a layer of dirt. Progress was therefore painfully slow, and it was only after at least three hours of anxiety that we were clear of the roadworks and again on tarmac. Before long we saw in the distance the lights of the little mountain village of Mornos. The lights shone brightly, but no sound was to be heard, as though no one was living there. So many and so bright were the lights, and so profound the silence, that it was positively eerie, and I was reminded of old tales in which a wandering knight, lost in the depths of the forest, at midnight sees lights glimmering among the trees and rides towards them not knowing if they are those of a king's castle, a hermit's chapel, or a sorcerer's magically created palace. As there was no campsite in Mornos we drove straight through the strange little place without stopping and eventually, the road having descended, out of the mountains and into a small valley.

In this valley we spent the night – the last night of the outward part of our journey. It was Delphi we had come all this way to see, and once we had seen Delphi we would be homeward bound, however wide a detour we might thereafter make and whatever else of importance or interest we might happen to see on the way back. Delphi was the perihelion of the orbit of our journey. It was the point at which we would be spiritually nearest to the mysterious force that for the Ancient Greeks was embodied in the great and glorious figure of Apollo, god of the sun, music, poetry, and prophecy.

Henry Miller wrote about Delphi within a year of his visiting the place.[318] I am having to write about my own visit thirty-four years after it occurred, so that despite the help provided by a few diary notes there is no question of my being able to write about my impressions of the sacred site with the freshness and immediacy – not to mention the genius – of the author of *The Colossus of Maroussi*. Having passed a quiet night in the small valley, in the morning Terry and I drove over the hills into another valley in which there were tens of thousands – perhaps hundreds of thousands – of olive trees, all growing so close together that from a distance it was as though the floor of the valley was covered by a sea of silver-green foliage. At our approach the sea divided, so to speak, and we drove on through Bonnichora and Amphissa, after which several miles of straight road took us, through more olive groves, up to Chruson. From Chruson, which must have been several thousand feet above sea level, there was a view back over the Gulf of Corinth that my diary is content to describe as 'magnificent' and which must have been truly so.

At nine o'clock in the morning, on Sunday 3 July, we reached our destination.

Henry Miller had 'come upon' Delphi at four o'clock in the afternoon, after driving up from Athens. It was midwinter, there was a mist blowing in from the sea, and seen in that strange twilight mist the ancient site had seemed even more sublime and awe-inspiring than he had imagined it to be. Later it rained. Terry and I arrived early in the day, at the height of summer, and instead of mist from the sea there was only a slight haze. Unlike Henry Miller, I had not imagined Delphi to be sublime and awe-inspiring or, in fact, anything else, so that whether the place exceeded my expectations or fell short of them was not a question that could arise. Such imaginings were in any case utterly irrelevant.

The last bend of the road once turned, the prospect that lay before us was one in which there was a perfect harmony of the sublime and the beautiful, of the work of nature and the creations, now fragmentary and ruined, of the human brain and hand. Delphi was situated on the steep lower slope of Mount Parnassus, in a kind of natural amphitheatre, with the Phaedriades or Shining Rocks rising high above it to the north and with a view southward across the Pleistus gorge to the mountain range beyond. The sacred precinct, within whose walls the great temple of Apollo had once stood, occupied what appeared to be the centre of the amphitheatre. On the mountainside, and here and there among the ruins, grew olive, fig, and pomegranate trees, as well as slim, dark cypresses, all bathed in the calm morning sunshine beneath a sky intensely blue.

Deeply impressed though I was by the sublimity and beauty of the scene, what I felt most strongly about Delphi was that it was a holy place. I had been in holy places before, notably in Bodh Gaya, Sarnath, and Kusinara, and other Buddhist holy places of northern India. These sites were holy by virtue of their association with events in the life of the Buddha. In Bodh Gaya he had attained supreme, perfect Enlightenment, in Sarnath he had taught his first five disciples, and in Kusinara he had died, and each of these places had its distinctive atmosphere. That of Bodh Gaya was intense and powerful, that of Sarnath joyful and expansive, that of Kusinara solemn and mysterious, and so on. Delphi was different. It was not holy by virtue of its association with a particular event, at least not of the historical order. Delphi was itself holy. It was not a holy place simply because it was there that Apollo's temple and oracle were located. Temple and oracle were located at Delphi because Delphi was a holy place. It was as if the very earth was holy, and as if this holiness penetrated the rocks and the trees and permeated the air, so that one felt it in the warmth of the sun and drew it in with every breath. Though the temple was in ruins, and though the oracle had been silent for more than a thousand years, Delphi was still a holy place and its influence could still be felt. I certainly felt that influence during the two days Terry and I stayed there, despite the noisy tourists, of whom there were quite a few wandering among the ruins even at nine o'clock in the morning and who arrived by the coachload throughout the day.

Our first visit was to the two temples of Athene Pronoia and the Tholos, which stood with a few smaller structures on a terrace below the road, well away from the sacred precinct. All three were, of course, in ruins, three fluted Doric columns with a section of entablature being practically all that survived, more or less intact, of the Tholos, a mysterious circular structure the purpose of which is unknown. From the sanctuary of the Marmorea, as the place was called, we made our way round to Kastri, the small town or large village adjacent to Delphi though out of sight, so far as I remember, of the sacred precinct and the other ancient sites. What we took to be the principal street was lined with souvenir shops and we spent some time looking at reproductions of the various types of ancient pottery – red, red-and-white, black, and black-and-green in colour and of every imaginable size, shape, and decorative style. Almost without exception they were extraordinarily graceful, and the thought that the ancient originals were for the most part articles of everyday household use gave rise to some very Ruskinian reflections not all favourable to modern civilization. Having already bought a wall plate in Yannina, I did not buy anything, but Terry bought two hand-woven bags, one for his mother and one for Vivien. Souvenir shops not being the only ones in Kastri, we were able to buy a loaf of good Greek bread and a pot of good Greek yoghurt, both of which we had already come to appreciate, sometimes making a meal of the latter.

In the afternoon, having lunched back at the Little Bus, we visited the Castalian spring, which was situated half a mile to the east of the sacred precinct and was dedicated to Apollo and the Muses. Earlier in the day we had seen it running down the hillside and through the olive groves near the Marmorea. Now we were at its source. The cold, clear water came gushing from a deep cleft in the Phaedriades and poured into the court of an artificial grotto. Bending down, we scooped a little of it up in our hands and drank. Originally, people had purified themselves at the Castalian spring before approaching the oracle, but in later, post-classical times the waters came to be regarded as a source of poetic inspiration. Purified and inspired, or at least refreshed, we then made our way down to the ruins of the gymnasium complex, with its double running track, one indoor and one outdoor, its Greek and Roman baths, and other buildings, which stood on a terrace a little higher than that on which stood the ruins of the Marmorea. Much of the site was overgrown, besides being surrounded not so much by groves as by a whole forest of olive trees, so that few tourists ventured there. In the welcome shade of a cluster of the bushy-headed old trees, with their silver-green foliage, we sat down and read. I read an interesting but confused book on the history and mythology of Delphi, Terry a book on Zen by D. T. Suzuki, to whose writings and the *Laṅkāvatāra Sūtra* he remained faithful for much of our journey. After a while I became aware that my friend was feeling very depressed, so that I laid aside my book (he had already laid aside his) and we had what my diary terms 'a little talk'. Apparently he was depressed because Delphi was far more crowded than we had expected it to be, depressed because some of the tour groups were quite rowdy, and depressed, most fundamentally, because our being surrounded by the remains of an ancient civilization and culture about which he knew very little served to remind him of his lack of education and thus to trigger those feelings of inferiority and inadequacy that were never far from the surface.

Just what I said to Terry I do not remember. I never attempted to argue him out of his depressions, or to convince him that since there was no *reason*, objectively speaking, for his depression, he *ought not* to be feeling depressed. Much less still did I ever urge him to 'snap out of it'. Usually, after acknowledging that he felt depressed and empathizing with him (not having suffered from depression myself, I did not find this easy), I would gradually change the subject and start talking about something which was of interest to both of us and calculated to evoke a positive response from him. This served to divert his attention from the depression which, as he became more and more engrossed in the topic under discussion, would little by little subside of its own accord. Probably this is what happened that hot afternoon, as we sat in the shade of the olive trees, among the ruins of the gymnasium complex. In any case, as a result of our little talk, Terry regained his cheerfulness, at least for the time being, but as it was now four o'clock we repaired to the Little Bus to partake of 'the cups that cheer but not inebriate',[319] generously laced with condensed milk, though in view of the classical nature of our surroundings

> a beaker full of the warm South,
> Full of the true, the blushful Hippocrene,[320]

would no doubt have been more appropriate. Thus fortified, we spent the rest of the afternoon, and the early part of the evening, visiting the temple of Apollo, the theatre, and the stadium, and then the museum.

The temple was one of the glories of the ancient world. Now all that could be seen of it, apart from the numerous fragments strewn around, were the five or six weather-beaten Doric columns, only one of them of full height and with a capital, that stood on the north-eastern end of the temple's rectangular plinth and had probably been put together from scattered drums by archaeologists in the late nineteenth century. The theatre, which seated 5,000 people, was situated higher up the hillside, in the north-west corner of the sacred precinct, and had for backdrop a view of the temple and the valley beyond. It was in a much better state of preservation than the temple, which being a place of pagan worship had been first vandalized and then destroyed by the Christians, and seats, staircases, and orchestra were all more or less intact. From the theatre a steep path wound through pine trees up to the stadium, the tiers of seats on the north side of which had been cut out of the hillside just below the Amphissa road. After the cluttered, uneven terraces lower down the sight of the bare, perfectly level track – two hundred yards long and thirty wide – on which the games had been held, and could still have been held, was strangely soothing. Unlike Henry Miller, I had no impression of charioteers driving their steeds over the ridge and into the blue, much less still did I find the atmosphere 'superhuman, intoxicating to the point of madness'.[321] Instead, all was silence, solitude, and peace.

The exhibits in the museum were all from Delphi and the surrounding area. Most of them belonged to the period from the seventh up to and including the fourth century BCE, and many were only fragments. There were inscriptions in Greek and Latin, mosaics, bronze dedications, metopes, Corinthian capitals, and grave goods of various kinds, from weapons to bracelets and fibulae. Above all there were the free-standing sculptured figures, of which I particularly remember the Charioteer, the Two Brothers, and the statue of Antinous. The Charioteer stood erect, looking a little to his right, the vertical folds of his long racing costume, the *xystis*, serving to accentuate the uprightness of his posture. In his right hand he grasped the reins (most of the left arm was missing); his gaze was intent but calm. 'Severe in youthful beauty' he stood there,[322] having won the chariot race, and being about to take part, apparently, in the triumphal parade that was held after the race.

Whereas the Charioteer was of bronze and belonged to the fifth century BCE, the colossal figures of the Two Brothers, which were of marble, must have antedated it by at least a hundred years. Cleobis and Biton were two young Argives, the sons of a priestess of Hera, who when the oxen failed to arrive and their mother was in danger of being late for a festival, harnessed themselves to the wagon and drew her from Argos all the way across the plain to the temple. For this service they were honoured above all other men by their fellow Argives and their statues, carved in the chunky style considered by some scholars to be characteristic of the Peloponnese, were set up in Delphi, where they remained until their discovery in modern times. One of them had an arm and a hand missing, and the faces of both were slightly damaged; otherwise the two colossi were more or less intact. They stood side by side in the room bearing their name, as they must have stood for centuries in the place where they were originally installed, the clenched fists of the less damaged brother suggesting that the sculptor had depicted them in the act of performing the service for which they were honoured. According to one of the books on Greece I was reading at the time, the broad faces, wide open eyes, and naked bodies of the Two Brothers were fixed in 'an almost Egyptian rigidity'. Almost Egyptian, too, were the wig-like braids, three on either side, that hung down over their broad shoulders from behind their ears. What struck me most about these two massive archaic statues from the Peloponnese was not, however, their rugged strength and dignity, great as these were, so much as the fact that they had been set up in Delphi, the holiest of all the holy places of ancient Greece, by way of giving public recognition to an outstanding act of filial piety. If the Charioteer bore witness to the ancient Greeks' love of sporting contests, and their enthusiastic admiration for the qualities of skill and courage such contests helped promote, the Two Brothers bore witness to the high esteem in which they held a virtue we tend to associate less with Ancient Greece than with Confucian China.

Antinous was the favourite of the emperor Hadrian, and after his death in mysterious circumstances the afflicted monarch caused statues of the beautiful youth to be set up – even temples to be dedicated to him – in cities throughout the Roman world. One such statue, evidently, had been set up in Delphi, where it was found, still standing, when a room in a building within the Sacred Precinct was cleared of earth and rubble in the course of excavations. Belonging as it did to the second century CE, it was in a style very different from that of the Charioteer, and still more different from that of the Two Brothers, even as Antinous himself represented a type of masculine beauty that differed markedly from that of either the upstanding winner of the chariot race or the hefty young Argives who had harnessed themselves to their mother's wagon. It depicted him as the divine *ephebe*, broad-shouldered, but with thick, luxuriant curls, and a thoughtful, almost melancholy expression. Both forearms of the statue were missing, and with them the hands, and the nose was slightly chipped. Otherwise it was complete and one could not but admire the harmonious proportions and full contours of the young favourite's magnificent physique. With his very individual physiognomy and style of beauty it indeed was Antinous, not Keats's Psyche, who was

> the latest and the loveliest vision far
> Of all Olympus' faded hierarchy.[323]

He was an unforgettable figure. I certainly did not forget him, and when we encountered busts and statues of him in Athens and other places in the course of our homeward journey I recognized him immediately.

What kind of impression the Charioteer, the Two Brothers, and the statue of Antinous made on Terry I cannot say. He undoubtedly felt much more at home with the art of Ancient Greece than he did with Christian art, especially as so much Greek sculpture, whether of the archaic or the classical period, was devoted to the representation of the human figure, and could be appreciated for its formal and expressive qualities without that knowledge of sacred history and religious symbolism that was often essential to a proper understanding of Christian art. Nonetheless, despite his having appeared to enjoy the sculptures in the museum, it was not long before Terry was again feeling depressed and not long, therefore, before we were having another of our little talks. We had it not sitting in the shade of the olive trees but parked beside a rubbish tip outside Kastri from which, by way of contrast, there was a fine view of the Gulf of Corinth. This time I was more successful in my efforts to cheer him up, and some days were to pass before he again felt depressed. So successful was I that in the morning, the two of us having gone down to the Tholos, he was happily taking photographs of the mysterious circular structure just as the rays of the rising sun struck the tops of the three remaining Doric columns.

That day was perhaps the best day of our holiday so far. Such is the testimony of my diary, at least. Not that we did a lot of sightseeing. In fact we did none at all. Having breakfasted we found a sheltered nook above the theatre and there spent the greater part of the day, returning to the Little Bus only in order to bring a flask of tea and something to eat up to the spot where we had established ourselves. Above our heads, there was nothing but blue sky; immediately below our feet, only the theatre descending the hillside in tier after semi-circular tier to the level on which stood the temple all around, and as far as the eye could see the landscape was steeped in clear, bright, invigorating sunshine which, as the sun ascended, threw shorter and shorter blue shadows. Probably because it was a weekday, there were far fewer people than the day before, and the sounds that came up from the little groups of tourists wandering among the ruins reached our ears but faintly. In the course of the morning I read Euripides' *Ion*. It was no coincidence that I was reading this particular play in this particular place, for the scene of the play was Delphi, in the forecourt of the very temple of Apollo on which Terry and I were then looking down, and I had deliberately postponed the reading of the work to this moment.

Ion is an attendant in the temple, at the entrance to which he was found as a baby. Now grown to manhood, he has been made treasurer of the god and 'steward of all trust', and when we first see him he is busy decorating the portals of the temple with garlands of bay leaves, sprinkling the pavement with water from the Castalian spring, and scaring birds away from the offerings with his bow and arrows. Among those approaching the oracle is Kreusa, Queen of Athens. She and her husband Xuthus, king-consort of Athens, are childless, and she wants to know if they will have issue. From the exchange that takes place between her and Ion we learn that she wishes to question the oracle secretly, on behalf of a friend, and that she does not want her husband to know of this. The question concerns the fate of the child whom this friend, without her father's knowledge, bore to Apollo some years ago and then abandoned. Their conversation is interrupted by the arrival of Xuthus, who has been consulting the oracle of the hero Trophonius. While not presuming to forestall the utterance of Apollo, Trophonius has assured the king that neither he nor his wife will return home from Delphi childless. Having broken the joyful news to Kreusa, Xuthus exits to the inner temple where Apollo speaks through the lips of the Pythia, leaving Ion to wonder why Kreusa should seem to rail upon the god, and Kreusa's attendant handmaids, who form the Chorus, to sing the praises of the virgin goddesses Pallas Athene and Artemis, Apollo's sisters, as well as to celebrate the joy of having sons to continue the family line and inherit the ancestral wealth, and to lament the fact that the offspring of the gods by mortal women are never happy.

The sound of their voices has hardly died away before Xuthus is back (dramatic time and real time do not coincide). Apollo has spoken. He has told Xuthus that the first man he meets on leaving the inner temple is his truly-begotten son. As it happens, the first man he meets is Ion. Initially Ion refuses to believe that Xuthus is his father and angrily repulses him. But eventually he is convinced, Xuthus having admitted, under questioning, that in his younger days he had visited Delphi at the time of the nocturnal Bacchic orgies and taken part in them in the company of the local girls. Ion must be the fruit of that visit and father and son, overjoyed, fall into each other's arms. Kreusa is far from overjoyed. On learning from the Chorus that Apollo has given Xuthus a son, while *she* remains childless, she is distraught with anger and grief, and when a loyal old servant offers to kill Ion while he and Xuthus are feasting she gives him a deadly poison with which to do the deed. On no account will she allow her husband's bastard to inherit the throne of Athens! A timely omen having frustrated the plot at the last moment, the old servant confesses everything, the rulers of Delphi condemn Kreusa to death for attempted murder within the sacred precinct, and Ion comes with a band of armed men to carry out the sentence. He finds Kreusa sitting on the altar in front of the temple, where she had taken refuge, and a fierce altercation takes place between them. At this point the Pythia enters, bearing the ark in which, as a baby, Ion was found at the entrance to the temple. Kreusa recognizes the ark, and without seeing them is able to describe the objects it contains – objects which she herself once placed there. She has found her son, and Ion has found his mother. Mutual hate is transformed into mutual love, and both are beside themselves with joy. But who, Ion wants to know, *is* his father? Is it Apollo, as Kreusa maintains, or is it Xuthus, as Apollo himself, apparently, has declared?

He is about to go and ask the god when there appears high above the temple, in a blaze of light, an awe-inspiring figure. It is Pallas Athene in her chariot. She has come from Athens with a message from Apollo. He is indeed Apollo's son by Kreusa, she tells Ion, and Kreusa is to take him with her to Athens and seat him on the throne of her fathers.

He will have four sons, who will give their names to the four Athenian tribes, the descendants of whom will spread overseas and be called Ionians. Kreusa and Xuthus, too, will have offspring, but Xuthus is to be kept in ignorance of Ion's true parentage. Apollo has done all things well, the goddess tells Kreusa in conclusion. Having given her an easy delivery, he caused Ion to be brought up in his own temple, and has saved him from death by means of a timely omen. Kreusa thankfully acknowledges this, and the play ends with the Chorus hailing Zeus and Apollo and affirming their belief that those who despite adversity continue to honour the divine powers 'at last attain their right'.

Ion was an enthralling work. It was based on a story of deep human interest, and with its sudden reversals of fortune, its violent confrontations, its eloquent speeches, its dazzlingly beautiful lyric flights on the part of the Chorus (flights that could be appreciated, to an extent, even in English translation), and its daring exploration of the mystery of divine justice, it was proof that Euripides fully deserved his place as one of the three master tragedians of Ancient Greece, little as he may have been appreciated, in his own day, in comparison with his two great rivals. As I read the play that morning in our nook above the theatre, every now and then raising my eyes from the page to look down at the remains of the temple in whose forecourt the action took place, it was as though I could see the drama unfolding before me. Indeed, it was as though I saw not buskined actors but living human beings moving and speaking there. I saw Ion decorating the portals of the temple, saw the arrival first of Kreusa and then Xuthus, saw Ion repulsing and finally embracing his (supposed) father, saw Kreusa give poison to the old servant, saw her taking refuge on the altar in front of the temple, saw the Pythia enter with the ark, saw mother and son reunited at last – even saw high above the temple roof, in the midst of the blue sky, the majestic figure of Pallas Athene, helmeted and carrying a spear and with her breast covered by the aegis.

In Euripides' *Andromache* too, which I read that afternoon, the Delphic oracle plays a crucial role, though the scene of the play is the temple of Thetis in Phthia, a town of Thessaly. All the principal cities and people of Ancient Greece appear to have maintained close relations with Delphi and its presiding deity, as was evinced by the little temple-like state treasuries – or their ruins – that could be seen lining the Sacred Way, much of it still paved, that wound up through the Sacred Precinct to the temple. Delphi and Athens, Apollo and Pallas Athene, enjoyed particularly close relations, and it was therefore fitting that at seven o'clock that evening, having paid a second visit to the souvenir shops without my buying anything, Terry and I should have left Delphi for Athens, following the very route via Lebadeia that Ion, Kreusa, and Xuthus had followed in the distant, legendary past.

38
ATHENS AND THE PELOPONNESE

Athens was both extremely crowded and extremely hot, and instead of its ancient 'violet crown' it wore a dun-coloured mantle of modern industrial smog. Terry and I arrived in the city shortly before midday. We had spent the night at a spot a few miles on from Labadeia, once the seat of the oracle of Trophonius, and having crossed the Boeotian plain, with its newly harvested wheatfields, had made our way over range upon range of low mountains to emerge, eventually, into the plain of Attica, where we were at once surrounded by the silver-green of the olive – Pallas Athene's gift to the people of Athens. Soon we were driving past Eleusis, and as we approached the coast we could see not only a skyline disfigured by tall factory chimneys but also, through the haze, the vision of a white rock on which stood a pure white temple – the Acropolis and, crowning it, the Parthenon.

Parking proved to be a matter of some difficulty, but after driving around for a while, and incidentally enjoying a view of the Parthenon from the west, we managed to find a spot. According to my diary we found it near 'Onomia', by which I must have meant Omonia – or Concord – Square, for my diary further records that we explored the area a little on foot and ate some 'rather sickly' Greek sweetmeats. We also looked in some of the bigger souvenir shops, but to our disappointment the reproduction pottery was inferior in quality to what we had seen in Delphi. At three o'clock we decided to find a campsite. Unfortunately, we took the wrong road out of Athens and found ourselves down at the

Athens, before the Parthenon

harbour of the Piraeus, so that, having re-entered the city and found the right road, it was four o'clock before we booked in at Athens Camping, as the site was called. Here we spent the rest of the day, as we felt too tired to do more than make a few purchases at the camp shop and go for a little walk.

In the same way that Delphi meant the temple and oracle of Apollo, so for me Athens meant the Parthenon, where the great chryselephantine statue of the Virgin Goddess had once dominated the inner sanctum, and the following morning Terry and I lost no time driving into the city centre through the thick haze – the product less of car exhausts than of the countless smoking chimneys – and then round to the western slope of the Acropolis. Here we parked the Little Bus, and having climbed up to the Boule Gate and followed the zigzag ramp through the forest of ruined Doric and Ionic columns that was the Propylae at last attained the summit of the Acropolis, 512 feet above the surrounding city. Before me, planted firmly on the highest point of the great limestone rock, with nothing behind it but the bluest of blue skies, there rose dazzlingly white in the brilliant morning sunshine the miracle that was the Parthenon. Though time, vandalism, and war had damaged the structure badly (there was nothing left of the roof, or the walls of the *cella*), most of the fifty or more enormous, fluted Doric columns were still standing or had been restored, and Terry and I wandered among them admiring their beautiful proportions. Except for the Erechtheum, famous for the Porch of the Caryatids, and the Sanctuary of Zeus, both of which we also explored, much of the area surrounding the Parthenon was a waste of white marble fragments from which the sunlight was reflected so dazzlingly as almost to hurt the eyes. Such sculptures and carvings as had survived more or less intact, and were not in the Berlin Staatliche Museen, the British Museum, or the Louvre, were housed in the Acropolis museum, which was situated in the south-east corner of the citadel and into whose coolness and gloom we were glad to escape from the growing heat outside. Though the rooms contained much that was memorable, I recollect only the enigmatically smiling Norai or Maidens; a Calf-bearer that could well have been the prototype of Early Christian representations of Christ as the Good Shepherd; and a calmly beautiful bas-relief of Pallas Athene leaning on her spear.

Before leaving the Acropolis we stood and gazed down for a while at the urban sea which, spreading in all directions, lapped against the tree-girt lower slopes of sharply-pointed Mount Lycabettus a mile or so away to the north-east. Beyond Lycabettus, on the horizon to the north, there extended the shadowy blue shapes of the mountains where ancient Athens had obtained the marble from which the Parthenon was built. Sweating profusely in the intense heat, we walked back to the Little Bus, and from the Little Bus to the Pnyx, the hill on which the Athenian democracy met, and then to the ancient central Agora or market place, which were situated west and north-west, respectively, of the Acropolis. The Agora was dominated by the Doric so-called Theseum, said to be the best-preserved Greek temple in the world, it having been used, successively, as a Christian and as a Muslim place of worship. Like the bigger and slightly later Parthenon it was surrounded by a waste of white marble fragments – fragments that had once been part of the various administrative and religious buildings which then occupied the area. Near the Theseum stood an Orthodox church, but although we ventured inside I remember nothing of what we saw. I do, however, recollect the little wayside chapels – in themselves miniature churches – that we saw here and there in the bustling modern city. Some were hardly bigger than a good-sized doll's house, but all were complete with the traditional round-arched doors and windows, triangular gables, and red-tiled domes.

On our way back to the Little Bus we decided to visit Cape Sounion, the southernmost point of the Attic peninsula. Why we decided to visit it I cannot say. Perhaps we wanted to get away from people, by whom we seemed to be always surrounded, even on the steps of the Parthenon and in the Acropolis museum. Perhaps we wanted to escape from the polluted atmosphere of twentieth-century Athens and breathe the ozone-laden air of the coast. Or perhaps, again, we simply wanted to see the famous temple of Poseidon. Whatever the reason for our decision may have been, we left for Cape Sounion straight away, driving first down to the Piraeus via Omonia, and from there following the scenic coastal road south.

We spent three days at the coast, camping one night near the fishing village of Lagonissa and one night in the vicinity of the Cape. During the day we explored the little rocky bays and inlets, where pebbles of many beautiful hues could be picked up, wandered along the fine, sandy beaches, washed clothes, brewed tea, and heated up can after can of minestrone. Terry spent a good deal of time swimming in the warm, sunlit coastal waters, the colour of which ranged from pale turquoise near the shoreline to cobalt blue farther out. While he was thus disporting himself I sat on a nearby rock reading, on different occasions, Plato's *Apology of Socrates*, *Ion*, and *Meno*, and Euripides' *Bacchae*, all of which I had read before but never in such propitious surroundings. One afternoon we drove a few miles up the other side of the peninsula to a stretch of coast known, according to the guidebook, as the Green Coast. Why it was so called was a mystery. Though the view over the Saronic Gulf was a sufficient recompense for the journey, there was not a scrap of vegetation to be seen. There was only naked rock and sun, and no shade, consequently, in which to park, so that we were obliged to turn round and drive on until we found, back on the eastern side of the peninsula, a line of what I took to be tamarisk trees. Tamarisks or not, they were certainly trees, and we were glad to take advantage of their scanty shade.

The most rewarding part of our little excursion was the visit we paid to the temple of Poseidon, god of the sea, or rather, which we paid to the twelve white Doric columns that were practically all that was left of the imposing fifth-century BCE structure. The temple stood on a headland, and commanded a fine view of the Myrtoan Sea, whose calm waters were dotted, here and there, with the dim shapes of islands. According to the guidebook, Lord Byron had written his name on one of the columns. We did not see the signature, but if the noble lord had indeed committed such an act of vandalism he had set later visitors to the site a bad example.

That evening – the evening of the day on which we paid our respects to the trident-wielding god of the sea – Terry admitted to feeling rather depressed, which indeed was obvious. Though the attack was not a serious one, it necessitated our having a long talk and we were late getting to bed. In the morning my poor friend was still feeling depressed, but as the day wore on the dark cloud lifted and by the time we returned to Athens, in the late afternoon, he was quite cheerful. Fortunately the cloud remained lifted, and except for the occasional minor relapse he stayed cheerful for the remaining weeks of our tour.

In Athens we drove straight to the Acropolis, where Terry took photographs and we watched the sunset, and from there to Athens Camping. That night we had a problem to discuss – a problem that might have caused us serious inconvenience and even disrupted our travel plans. On the way back to Athens we had become aware that the Little Bus had developed engine trouble and was in danger, perhaps, of breaking down. What were we to do? We could not do anything that night, but early the following morning we drove – very gingerly – into Athens in search of information and advice. The Greek Automobile and Touring Club was not very helpful, but eventually, after we had walked around for two or three hours (and cashed travellers' cheques, posted cards, and bought a new cylinder of Gaz), we succeeded in locating the Volkswagen repair centre. They would not be able to do anything until Monday, they told us (it was now Friday), but if we took the Little Bus in early on Monday morning they would give the engine an overhaul and with this we had to be content. Sunday was perforce a day of rest, for not wanting to risk having a breakdown on the way we did not go anywhere. Instead, we spent the whole day at the campsite, where I read Plutarch and Aeschylus and started on *The Pelican History of Greece*.[324]

As we did not know what was wrong, exactly, with the Little Bus's engine, nor how much time it would take to put it right, Monday was a day of some uncertainty. It was also a day of disappointment, in one respect at least. Having left the Little Bus at the repair centre we walked via Euripides Street and America Street (piquant juxtaposition!) all the way to the National Archaeological Museum, our idea being to spend the rest of the morning in its galleries. We arrived there punctually at the usual opening time, only to discover that it was closed on Mondays. Fortunately, the museum gardens were open, and still more fortunately on our way through America Street we had called in at the English bookshop and added to our stock of classical authors. Instead of spending the morning with the masterpieces of Greek sculpture, therefore, we spent it with Richard Lattimore's *The Odes of Pindar*, Benjamin Rogers's translation of five comedies of Aristophanes, and *The Essential Works of Stoicism*.[325] Though both he and I dipped into all three volumes, Terry, I think, spent more time with the philosophers and I with the poets.

We had been told that the Little Bus might be ready for collection by two o'clock. Having had our fill of poets and philosophers, at least for the time being, at eleven-thirty we left the museum gardens and set out for the Volkswagen repair centre, stopping on the way only to buy some Greek sweetmeats and sit in one of the squares eating them. Though the Little Bus was not ready for collection by two o'clock, it was ready an hour or so later, and we were able to take delivery of it knowing that its engine was now in perfect working order and that there was no danger of our travel plans being disrupted by an untimely breakdown. We therefore returned to Athens Camping in high spirits – high spirits not untouched by a feeling of relief. We were glad to have the Little Bus back with us. We were glad to have it back, not simply because it was our means of getting from place to place. It was also our home, at least for the duration of our tour, and if we were obliged to be without it for any length of time, as had been the case that day, we felt naked and exposed, rather like a tortoise without its shell. With his extreme sensitiveness to other people, and especially to crowds, Terry felt such exposure more than I did. He also was quite attached to his convenient, comfortable Dormobile. In fact he was quite fond of it, and in the course of our travels I, too, became fond of the particoloured vehicle, half red and half white.

Tuesday was our last day in Athens. Having decided to leave for Corinth and the Peloponnese by midday we spent the morning in the

National Archaeological Museum, the doors of which now stood wide open and which was full, unfortunately, of parties of noisy tourists being shepherded from room to room by vociferous guides-cum-lecturers. Though the museum covered all the periods of ancient Greek civilization, pride of place appeared to belong to the Bronze Age treasure from Mycenae. The treasure itself was not of bronze but of gold, which probably accounted for the fact that the room in which it was displayed was the most crowded part of the museum, the majority of visitors no doubt being drawn to the artefacts less on account of their artistic refinement, which was of a high order, than because they were made of *gold*. Such was the crush that Terry and I caught only a glimpse of the gold masks that had covered the face of the dead, the gold bracelets and earrings and the gold cups. We had a better view of the various *kouroi*, once known as 'archaic Apollos', as well as of the famous bronze statue of Poseidon on the point of hurling his trident, the graceful Praxitelean bronze boy, his eyes inset, I seem to remember, with white stone and coloured glass, and above all – though only a Roman copy – the marvellously posed Discobolus or Discus-Thrower. Whether gods or mortal men, they were all represented nude, as were the other male figures in the museum's collection, whereas the female figures were usually draped, and the more I contemplated them the more I was inclined to think, with Goethe, Schopenhauer, and others, that the male human form was more beautiful than the female.[326] Hardly less impressive than the statues, in their own way, were the funeral *stelae*, with their reliefs of an old man and his hunter son, a girl taking incense from a small box, and other scenes of a tender, domestic nature. There was also the famous bas-relief from Eleusis, depicting the youthful Triptolemus between Demeter and her daughter Persephone. Demeter, the goddess of agriculture, was shown giving Triptolemus the first grain of corn. According to the myth, she also gave him a winged chariot harnessed with dragons, and bade him travel the world spreading the benefits of agriculture among all men.

It was in honour of Demeter and Persephone, together with Dionysus, the god of wine, that the Eleusinian Mysteries – the most famous mysteries of antiquity – were celebrated. They were celebrated in the Telesterion or Hall of Initiation at Eleusis, fifteen miles from Athens, and it was in Eleusis that Terry and I found ourselves half an hour after leaving the National Archaeological Museum. A small, independent city state before it came into the Athenian sphere of influence in the sixth century BCE, it was now an industrial town. Writing in the year of our own visit, one traveller described it as 'singularly unattractive'. Not only had the Goths and time wrought their usual destruction, but the foundations of the great hall and the scattered blocks of marble were surrounded by the smoking chimneys of several factories, so that he found it hard to imagine how such a scene of desolation could once have inspired the master of irreverence, Aristophanes, who wrote:

> To us alone, initiated men,
> Who act aright by stranger and by friend,
> The sun shines out to light us after death.[327]

This 'sun' was the light which blazed forth when, at the supreme moment of the initiation, the doors of the Anaktoron or King's House, which stood within the Hall of Initiation, were suddenly opened to reveal the Hiera or Sacred Objects. On the far side of the archaeological area there was a museum. Much of the statuary in it was Roman, but it also contained small scale models of the temples and other structures that had occupied the sacred precincts, and these gave us, between them, a good idea of how ancient Eleusis must have looked. But no models, however accurate, could revive the atmosphere of the place. Though tens of thousands, perhaps millions, of people had received there the deepest spiritual experience of their lives, no trace of that atmosphere remained. Unlike Delphi, the Eleusis of the Mysteries was spiritually dead, and it was therefore with thoughts not untouched by sadness that Terry and I left the once sacred site on the next stage of the day's journey.

Corinth was situated at the foot of the isthmus connecting the Peloponnese with mainland Greece. Having joined the Italian-style motorway and driven south-west along the coast, we reached it in the middle of the afternoon. Or rather, we reached *them*, for there were *two* Corinths, the Old and the New. Our business was with Old Corinth, a quiet, pleasant little town, hardly bigger than a village, but not so small as not to have several souvenir shops, in which we looked before visiting the archaeological area and the museum that stood on its outskirts. The archaeological area was a waste of ancient ruins from the midst of which there rose, relatively intact, the seven squat, monolithic Doric columns that were all that remained of the sixth-century BCE temple of Apollo, while in the museum there was little of interest except the Roman mosaics. We then drove to the Acro-Corinth, the great rock on the south which towered to a height of some 1,800 feet above Old Corinth. Commanding as it did the approaches to the Peloponnese, the citadel had been fought over not only by Greeks and Romans but also, in more recent times, by Franks, Venetians, Byzantines, and Turks, all of whom had occupied it for a while and all of whom had left their mark on the place. Terry and I did not climb to the top, but we climbed as far as the third gate, which was flanked by high towers and from which there was a fine view of the surrounding countryside.

We spent five days in the Peloponnese, visiting Mycenae, Tiryns, Nauplia, Epidaurus, and Argos in the east, Sparta in the south, and Olympia in the west – all of them names no less redolent of myth, legend, and history than were Dodona, Delphi, and Athens. My companion and I had not been long on the road out of Corinth, heading for Mycenae, before we noticed that there was more vegetation here than in the Attica region. A good deal of tobacco was being grown, and there were olive gardens and vineyards, as well as plenty of wild thyme, the agreeably pungent scent of which filled the air. It was beside a field of tobacco, with the scent of thyme in our nostrils, that we slept that night, and before we left in the morning I picked some of the aromatic herb. Though I had already bought an Achilles pottery plate, and was to buy a small handmade rug, the real memento of my visit to Greece was those sprigs of wild thyme, which I kept in a small pot on my desk for many years and whose fragrance served to remind me not just of the days I spent in the Peloponnese with Terry but of our whole Greek experience.

On arriving at Mycenae we were dismayed to find several coachloads of tourists already there and streaming up to the citadel. Following in their wake, we soon found ourselves standing in front of the famous Lion Gate and gazing up at the massive lintel and the triangular bas-relief above. This relief depicted two lions confronted, resting their forelegs on the edge of a low, altar-like structure on which was a pillar which stood between them. Within the gate, surrounded by a double circle of stone slabs, were the shafts of the royal tombs in which Heinrich Schliemann, in 1876, had discovered the Bronze Age gold treasure that was now in Athens. Here we sat for a while consulting our guidebooks before ascending the broad, graded road that led to the summit of the acropolis and so to the terraces on which had once stood the palace of

Agamemnon – the palace to which he had returned in triumph from the sack of Troy only to be murdered by his adulterous wife Clytemnestra.[328] Ruins lay all around – ruins not only of the palace and of the Doric temple which, more than a thousand years later, was superimposed on its remains, but also of the many houses that had surrounded the royal residence in its days of glory. From the acropolis there was a view southward over the fertile Argolis plain.

Back at the circle of stone slabs we sat down and tried to read, but the chattering tour groups and loud-voiced lecturers in French, German, and English made it impossible for us to do this, and we therefore took refuge in one of the less important of the beehive tombs outside the Lion Gate. Here I read the *Agamemnon* of Aeschylus, the action of which takes place in the very palace whose ruins we had just been visiting. This was the first Greek play I ever read, and its grandeur inspired me, in my fourteenth or fifteenth year, with a wholehearted admiration for the genius of the great Attic tragedians, and for Aeschylus in particular, that I was never to lose.[329] On my finishing the work we visited the 'Tomb of Clytemnestra' and 'Aegisthus' Tomb', as the two beehive structures had been known since the time of their discovery, though the period to which they belonged was not that of the adulterous queen and her paramour but a much earlier one, that of the sixteenth century BCE. The biggest of the beehive tombs was the so-called 'Treasury of Atreus', also known as the 'Tomb of Agamemnon'. According to the guidebooks this was a very grand affair, and well worth a visit, but so great was the number of people trying to get in that we decided to give it a miss and press on to Epidaurus.

Between Mycenae and Epidaurus lay Argos and Tiryns, the former being – it was said – the oldest continuously inhabited town in Europe. It was a pleasant little place, and apparently flourishing, even if not to the extent that it had flourished during the spacious days of the Heroic Age. We halted there only long enough to buy provisions, telling ourselves that we would see the archaeological area and museum on our way from Epidaurus to Tripoli, which for reasons I no longer recollect we failed to do. Tiryns was remarkable for its massive 'Cyclopean' walls, so called from the Cyclopes, the race of one-eyed giants who the ancient Greeks believed had built the city for the legendary king Proetus. Some of the blocks used in its construction were 17 feet long and 7 feet high, and Hercules himself could hardly have moved them from their place.

Tiryns had, in fact, a close connection with Hercules. It was to Tiryns that the Delphic oracle had sent the hero to serve for twelve years under King Eurystheus, in expiation for the crime of having killed his own children in a fit of madness, and it was Eurystheus who had imposed on Hercules his famous Twelve Labours. As in Mycenae, there was an acropolis and the remains of a Bronze Age royal palace, both of which we saw, but so gloomy and oppressive was the place that we did not stay long in Tiryns. The very name of Tiryns, I thought, had a sinister sound, as if echoing down the corbelled stone galleries that ran within the thickness of the outer walls.

Dodona, Delphi, and the Parthenon to an extent, all had their distinctive atmospheres. Epidaurus, too, had its atmosphere – one that was immediately perceptible. It was a calm, healthy, harmonious atmosphere, as though a blessing rested upon the place, and it was not surprising that for a thousand years the sanctuary of Asclepius at Epidaurus should have been renowned as a centre of physical and mental healing. Terry and I arrived there towards evening, after a pleasant drive through low, pine-clad hills, and past orange orchards and lemon orchards, and whitewashed stone dwellings half hidden by olive trees. On our arrival we parked at the edge of the archaeological area, in a grove of pines. It was a peaceful spot, and when I had read the *Chosphori* or 'Libation Bearers', the second part of the great trilogy of which the *Agamemnon* is the first, and we had eaten, the two of us set out for the ancient theatre, in which there had been accommodation for 17,000 spectators, and which Pausanius, the second-century geographer, had described as the most beautiful theatre in Greece.[330] A rehearsal of Euripides' *The Trojan Women* was in progress. The play was being performed, as we soon realized, not in the original language, or even in modern Greek, but in French. Nonetheless, with a sprinkling of other visitors we sat and watched for a while, the semicircles of stone seating rising tier upon tier behind us. The tragedies of Aeschylus, Sophocles, and Euripides, and the comedies of Aristophanes, were regularly performed there during the summer months, we gathered, for though nothing remained of the stage buildings, the greater part of the auditorium had survived more or less intact and had needed little in the way of restoration.

In the morning we looked round the museum, where a plaster model of the buildings that had formed the nucleus of the sanctuary enabled us to imagine what the place had been like in its heyday in the fourth century BCE. There was the temple of Asclepius, the god of healing, the much smaller temple of Artemis, the maiden goddess of the hunt and the wild, and the mysterious Tholos, with its two concentric circles of columns, an outer Doric circle and an inner Corinthian one. Most interesting of all, perhaps, was the Abaton, or Porch, where patients spent the night and where they received, in their dreams, indications as to the kind of treatment they should be given by the establishment's priest-physicians. Such treatment must often have been effective. In the museum there were *stelae* inscribed with descriptions of miraculous cures, as well as *ex votos* in the form of replicas of different limbs and organs, such as we had seen in the Basilica of St Anthony in Padua. The beliefs and customs of pagan Greece had been inherited by Roman Catholic Italy. St Anthony was the direct descendant of Asclepius. To me, Asclepius was the more attractive figure of the two. Indeed, he was one of the most attractive figures in the Greek pantheon. I do not recall seeing a statue of him in the little museum (the temple's famous chryselephantine statue had long since disappeared), but his lineaments, as represented in ancient sculpture, were in any case familiar to me. He was represented standing, dressed in a long cloak, with bare breast, and grasping a club-like staff round which coiled a serpent. Himself the son of Apollo, he was sometimes accompanied by Telephorus, the boy genius of healing, and his daughters Hygeia, the goddess of health, and Panacea. As Terry and I left the museum, and as we wandered round the archaeological area, it was not difficult for me to imagine that the benign spirit of the divine physician still brooded over his ancient sanctuary.

According to the traveller who had described Eleusis as 'singularly unattractive', the remains of the temple and other buildings at Epidaurus were of archaeological rather than artistic interest, and in this he was probably right. Still, it was pleasant, in the morning sunshine, to wander in and out of the great piles of marble blocks and slabs, and past the rows of truncated columns, the whiteness of which contrasted very agreeably with the green of the pines and of the slimmer, darker cypresses. It was pleasant to breathe the same thyme-scented air that we had breathed on the road to Mycenae and which was a feature, so it appeared, of much of the Peloponnese. The only remains that were readily identifiable were those of the Tholon, the beautiful carvings from which we had seen in the museum, and those of the temple of

Asclepius, and once we had surveyed them we returned to the Little Bus to read our classics, eat, and write postcards. Having written our postcards, we naturally wanted to buy stamps and post them; but by then it was siesta time and everyone was either absent or asleep, and not caring to wait until they resurfaced we were soon on the road to Nauplia and Argos.

Nauplia had been a seaport since ancient times, but it was the Venetians who, in the seventeenth century, had fortified the Palamidhi rock and developed the town. Driving round the place, now very much a tourist centre, we had a fine view of the fortifications, as well as of the tiny fortified Bourtsi Island a few hundred yards out in the bay. The road between Nauplia and Argos was on the level, but from Argos our way lay over a high mountain range, which meant that we had many hairpin bends to negotiate and made a fairly rapid descent on the other side. Soon we saw large flocks of curly-horned goats and sheep, and small, irregularly shaped fields bordered by low stone walls. There were also hundreds of little piles of stones, usually three or four to a pile, and all whitewashed. What might be the significance of these rude monuments, if monuments indeed they were, we could not tell, and we were still wondering about them when we reached Tripoli. Located practically at the geographical centre of the Peloponnese as it was, Tripoli was a town of some importance, but it was a modern town, and we stopped only to buy provisions before heading south, in the direction of Sparta. By this time we were both rather tired, and half an hour after leaving Tripoli we found a place to camp. It was below the road, in a ravine in which grew an abundance of giant thistles. Here we cooked a meal, read, and slept – in Terry's case only fitfully.

Next day we set out quite early. It was a fine morning, and having driven over a low-lying range of mountains, and crossed the thin silver trickle that was the river Eurotas, we were in Sparta by seven. The town was situated at the foot of the mighty Taygetus range, which towered to a height of 8,000 feet above it to the west. Though it occupied the site of the famous ancient city of the same name – the city of Lycurgus and Leonidas[331] – Sparta, like Tripoli, was a modern town, and we therefore drove straight on, past olive gardens and orange groves, to Mistra, five miles away, and soon were in another world.

To me Greece meant *ancient* Greece. It meant the Greece of Hesiod and Homer, of Pindar and the Attic dramatists, of Socrates, Plato, and

Aristotle, of Herodotus and Thucydides, Demosthenes and Pericles, Phidias and Myron.[332] It meant, what for me was no less significant, the Greece of pagan myth and legend. It meant the Greece of Zeus, Pallas Athene, Apollo, and the rest of the immortals, and of the shrines that had been dedicated to their worship. It was *this* Greece I had come to see, especially what for centuries had been the spiritual centre of the Greek world – the temple and oracle of Apollo at Delphi. I was not interested in modern Greece, or even, at that time, in ancient Greece's heir in certain respects, the Orthodox-Christian Byzantine Empire. Culturally and spiritually speaking, therefore, the visit Terry and I paid to Mistra that morning represented an interlude in our tour of the Peloponnese; for Mistra, perched on a spur of the Taygetus, was a Frankish and Byzantine city, and had no classical remains.

We arrived at the gate of the old city only to find it did not open until eight. We therefore made our way round the ramparts up to the gate of the thirteenth-century Frankish castle. The castle was situated on the topmost part of the spur, high above the city, and from the gate – also closed – there was a fine view over the Eurotas valley. By this time the lower gate was open, and on entering it we found ourselves in what was virtually a city of the dead. Not that it was a city of ruins only. Some of the Byzantine buildings, especially the churches and monasteries, were still standing, or had been restored recently, and one was actually inhabited. This was the fifteenth-century convent of the Pantanassa, where two or three decrepit, black-habited nuns moved noiselessly from chapel to frescoed chapel lighting lamps in front of the icons. The atmosphere of the place, as of the other churches and monasteries we saw there, was serene and peaceful – a serenity and peace that whitewashed walls and window-boxes of bright flowers served only to enhance. From the ruins beyond there was direct access to the interior of the castle, and before long we were surveying what was left of the buildings surrounding the vast central courtyard, where pines and a solitary cypress grew, and looking down at the red-tiled roofs and domes of the city below. In the last days of the Byzantine Empire cosmopolitan Mistra with its 40,000 inhabitants had been second only to Constantinople, the capital, in prosperity and importance. Moreover, it had been a centre of culture and intellect, as well as of freedom of thought, and it was from Mistra that, in 1438, the philosopher Gemistos Plethon, 'the last of the Hellenes', had travelled to Italy, there to teach Greek, pioneer the revival of Platonism, and inspire Cosimo de' Medici to found the Platonic Academy at Florence, thereby contributing significantly to the Renaissance. Mistra therefore had played an important part in the cultural history of western Europe, and three centuries later perhaps it was his appreciation of this fact that had led Goethe, in the second part of *Faust*, to represent the union of Faust and Helen of Troy – that union of the spirit of the Middle Ages with the spirit of ancient Greece that had given birth to Romanticism, as embodied in the figure of their child Euphorion – as taking place in the richly decorated inner courtyard of the castle of Mistra.

To what extent these were my actual reflections as Terry and I looked down on the red-tiled roofs and domes of the deserted city I cannot say. Certainly I was in a thoughtful mood as we left Mistra and drove back to Sparta. After visiting the museum, in which there was a sculpture of Helen of Troy between her twin brothers Castor and Pollux, we set out for the coastal town of Kalamata, our intention being to drive from there up the western side of the Peloponnese to Olympia. To get to Kalamata we had to cross the Taygetus range. Hardly were we into it, however, than we found the road closed for repair. It would be opened at twelve, we were told, but not being sure if we could rely on this we decided to return to Tripoli via Sparta and drive to Olympia from there. Two hours later, therefore, we were in Tripoli again. This time we walked round the town, and looked into the nineteenth-century church, so that it was not until early afternoon that we were clear of Tripoli and on our way to Olympia. There were thousands of grasshoppers on the road, and however carefully Terry drove it was impossible for us to avoid crushing some of the unfortunate little creatures. Exactly halfway between Tripoli and Olympia, in a clearing on the pine-covered hillside, we found a campsite. After we had rested and eaten, and Terry had read for a while, we walked over to the open-fronted little shop that stood opposite the campsite, on the other side of the highway. It was run by a young man in traditional dress, and was chock-full of the most beautiful handmade rugs and floor coverings we had so far seen, all made, the young man told us, by him and his mother and sister. For the equivalent of three pounds I bought myself, to use as a meditation mat, a rug with a soft green background. Later that night I read Euripides' *Helen*, and we had a long talk with a German who was also travelling in a Dormobile, in his case alone, and who had spent two years in India.

Our journey next morning took us over a range of mountains, through lush, sometimes hilly, country, and past villages so picturesque that Terry could not resist taking a few photographs. A lot of maize was being grown, but the plants were small and stunted, and bore little resemblance to the tall, leafy specimens I was accustomed to seeing in Kalimpong. Pines and cypresses dotted the landscape, and as we approached Olympia we saw olive gardens and orange orchards. There was an abundance of wild flowers. During the last stage of our journey the road ran for a while beside the river Alpheus, or rather, beside the dried-up bed of the river, which wound its grey, rock-strewn way through scenery of exceptional beauty. At eleven we reached Olympia. It was quite hot. After buying stamps and groceries in what my diary calls the Olympic village, we drove to the campsite, which was 'pleasant, but primitive', and where a rough table and benches stood invitingly beneath a tree. Here we spent the remainder of the day, except for a brief excursion into the village for the sake of the souvenir shops, and here I finished *Helen* and read Aristophanes' *The Clouds*. What was more to the purpose, I read Pindar's Olympian Odes, in which the 'Theban eagle', as Gray calls him, celebrates, in language of great power and beauty, and with many mythological allusions and digressions, the success of various victors in the great quadrennial games that Hercules, according to legend, had instituted at the site in honour of his father Zeus.[333]

Originally, of all the sites we visited in the Peloponnese Olympia must have been the grandest. Besides the temples of Zeus and Hera and the principal altars and votive offerings, which were all situated within the Altis or 'sacred grove of Zeus', as the sacred precinct was called, there were administrative buildings, state treasuries, guest quarters, gymnasia, and colonnades, as well, of course, as the stadium and hippodrome where the foot races and horse races, respectively, were held. Above all, in the temple of Zeus with its six frontal and thirteen lateral Doric columns, there was Phidias' chryselephantine seated statue of Zeus, one of the seven wonders of the ancient world. But these had all long since disappeared, and with them Olympia's former grandeur. When Terry and I drove to the archaeological area in the morning, we saw among the pines that had been planted in an attempt, apparently, to recreate the ancient 'grove of Zeus', only rows of truncated columns, scattered drums, and immense quantities of marble fragments. On the whole it was a mournful sight, and after walking round for half an hour we were glad to visit the museum. Here our spirits were revived by the well-known statue of Hermes carrying the infant Dionysus, the work of Praxiteles,[334] and by the quite substantial fragments of sculpture from the western pediment of the temple of Zeus. The latter represented the battle of the centaurs and Lapiths, and I was greatly struck by the upright, calmly majestic figure of Apollo, who stood with right arm outstretched and head turned in the same direction, apparently in the act of repulsing a centaur. Of that figure it has been said that it marks the final achievement of Greek sculpture before the full 'classical' naturalism of the Parthenon's sculpture. Nonetheless, standing before it that morning, there in the Olympia museum, I realized that although in the transition to naturalism much had been gained, something precious had been lost, and that certain archaic and early classical sculptures possessed a quality that affected me, for one, at a deeper level than did any of the masterpieces of the fully naturalistic period.

My attention was also drawn by a terracotta group of a bearded Zeus, looking rather pleased with himself, carrying off, tucked under one arm, an unresisting Ganymede, as well as by a metope of Hercules performing one of his twelve labours – that of bringing the golden apples from the garden of the Hesperides. According to one account, the hero persuaded Atlas to pick the apples for him while he, Hercules, supported the world on his shoulders, and the metope represented him doing just this. Immediately behind him, clad in a simple garment with straight folds, stood Pallas Athene, helping him take the weight with her *left hand*. There was a striking contrast between the bowed head and straining muscles of the hero and the calm, relaxed attitude of the goddess, who appeared to be making no effort at all. Her features, like those of the pedimental Apollo, were expressionless. Superhuman in power and beauty as they were, the immortal gods were untouched by the troubles of mortal men.

Olympia was the last ancient site we visited in the Peloponnese, and having left the museum we set out for Patras, driving through flat, well-cultivated countryside the monotony of which was relieved by a generous sprinkling of cypresses. Our intention had been to stay at the Kato Achaia campsite, but there being no sign of any such place we decided to stay – despite its name – at Villy's Park-Camping Bamboo, which was situated at the seaside, only a few miles from Patras. Both the beach and the water were dirty, and there were no bamboos, though there were several fine red oleanders. During the afternoon things were quiet, and I was able to read Sophocles' *Antigone* and ?Euripides' *Rhesus*,[335] but from seven o'clock onwards there was so horrid a din coming from the jazz band next door that we went for a walk in order to get away from it. The road was hardly less noisy, however, as well as being dusty, and we were soon forced to return to the campsite, where the din continued unabated far into the night. The result was that neither of us slept very well, so that when morning came we were glad to pay our bill and go.

In Patras we bought a box of Turkish delight as a present for Francoise, then drove to Rion, where there was a fine view over the Gulf of Patras. It was a very hot day, and we waited half an hour in the sun before boarding the car ferry to Antirion. Fifteen minutes later we were on the mainland and heading for Missolonghi.

From Missolonghi we travelled up to Igoumenitsa, following (in reverse) the route down which we had driven three weeks earlier, passing through Agrinion (the town we had missed before), Amphilochia, Arta, and Yannina, and spending three nights on the road. In the course of the journey we watched the sun go down over the mountains, were an object of curiosity to goatherds and small boys, read Pindar and the *Pelican History of Greece* (me) and Suzuki on Zen (Terry), stopped for meals beneath big, shady trees, and posted the last of the cards we would be sending from Greece. In Igoumenitsa we found the shipping office closed (it was siesta time). We therefore had to return and complete the formalities in the evening, after we had booked ourselves into a campsite near the beach. Next morning we were at the quayside soon after five-thirty, embarked at six o'clock, and half an hour later were on our way to Brindisi. It was a fine, sunny day. The sea was a deep, dark blue, and very quiet. Terry and I passed the time either walking round the deck or sitting in deckchairs at the side of the ship reading. My reading was Plato (the *Gorgias*)[336] and Walt Whitman, whose 'Passage to India' I had read the night before.[337] At four-thirty we reached Brindisi. There were no formalities of any kind, and after shopping in the supermarket we drove straight to the campsite.

39
NAPLES, ROME, AND FLORENCE

Terry and I spent two nights in Brindisi. During the second night there was a storm, with plenty of thunder and lightning. It also rained heavily, so that on our leaving for Taranto the following morning, in bright, clear weather, there was an agreeable freshness in the air and the olive gardens, vineyards, and tobacco fields of the flat countryside through which we passed had a rejuvenated look. Taranto, on the gulf of that name, was a modern town, and much larger than we had expected. But though it was a modern town, there were no signposts, and we found our way through it with difficulty, incidentally catching a glimpse of the sea and of the old town on its island.

Taranto behind us at last, we drove on through a number of much smaller towns – all the time gradually ascending. At Castellanetta there was a large, gaudy monument to Rudolph Valentino, the archetypal romantic hero of the Hollywood silent films,[338] and at Matera we found people living in what apparently were abandoned stone quarries. From Matera onwards the road became steeper. So much steeper did it become, and so numerous were the bends, that I was overcome by altitude sickness and we had to call a halt. Terry was unaffected, and while he ate a good lunch I started reading Aristotle's *Ethics*,[339] which I had begun a few days before, but soon fell asleep. We then pressed on through the mountains to earthquake-prone Potenza, 2,700 feet above sea level. The scenery was very fine, and with its wooded slopes reminded me of that of Switzerland. After Potenza there were more towns on peaks, and I had another attack of altitude sickness. This time we did not stop, except to buy grapes at Eboli, our descent being in any case slowed down by all the road-widening work that was going on. Soon we were out of the mountains and driving through Campania, past the British war cemetery and past field after field of tomato plants. When we were a few miles short of Salerno we turned off the main road to the Lido di Salerno campsite, where we arrived at seven-thirty, having driven more than 230 miles and crossed from one side of the Italian peninsula to the other. The camp was situated within a few yards of the sea, and before retiring we went for a stroll on the beach. There was a strong wind blowing. Though the sea was a little rough, with big breakers, to me the sight was very appealing.

Salerno was famous in medieval times on account of its medical school, the earliest in Europe. Now it was a popular holiday resort, and as Terry and I drove into the modern town via the coastal road we saw that the beaches were strewn with litter. Indeed, parts of them were being used as rubbish dumps. The town's principal monument, the eleventh-century cathedral, was a building of considerable interest. In front of it there was a spacious quadrangular courtyard, the arcades surrounding which were formed of ancient Corinthian columns that no doubt once belonged to a pagan temple. The bronze doors of the cathedral were of Byzantine workmanship. At the time of our arrival a prelate, perhaps the bishop himself, was celebrating morning mass for the benefit of a very small congregation; but we were able to see the apse mosaics, where a rather naturalistic Virgin Mary was the central figure, and the two inlaid marble pulpits. From Salerno we drove to the resort of Sorrento, situated round the tip of the peninsula of that name, following the scenic coastal road, and turning aside to visit Ravello on the way. Not that we had to make much of a turn. The little town, or village, clung to the face of the cliff, almost immediately above the road, so that the climb up to it – past orange trees and lemon trees and curious rock formations – was a steep one. At the top of the steps stood the cathedral. Built in the eleventh century (thus said our self-appointed guide) it had been 'modernized' at the end of the eighteenth, though the Corinthian columns that had then been enclosed were in process of being freed. In the shabby sacristy we found a fine, Sienese-style painting of the Virgin and Child, and some old vestments. We were not able to see the twelfth-century mosaics. Tomorrow the town would be celebrating the feast of the cathedral's patron saint, and the interior walls of the building were entirely covered with crimson draperies. Strings of coloured electric-light bulbs were still going up – a form of decoration not at all to my taste. Like those we had seen on the way, the shops outside the cathedral were selling the local handmade pottery. In one of them we were approached for alms by an elderly, respectable-looking nun in black, the first religious mendicant we had seen. Having myself lived on alms for a while, I wanted to give her something, but before I could do so the woman shopkeeper intervened with what was evidently a scolding for bothering us and she turned silently away.[340]

Driving on from picturesque Ravello (the hackneyed epithet is unavoidable), along the winding, rock-cut coastal road, we passed in quick succession through the no less picturesque Amalfi, Praiano, and Positano. Whitewashed houses, nestling amid orange trees and cypresses, climbed tier upon tier up the hillside on our right, and on our left fell tier upon tier down to the soft blue of the Tyrrhenian Sea. Little rocky peninsulas thrust themselves out into the calm waters, their every coign of vantage occupied by the colourful umbrellas and tiny thatched pavilions of the bathers. It was an idyllic, even a paradisaical scene, and one that in its opulent loveliness rivalled the more austere beauty of coastal Greece. But of course there was a serpent in this paradise, in the form of the slow-moving, pollutant-emitting stream of cars, coaches, and campers of which we were ourselves a part. So slowly did the stream move in the hot sun, at times crawling along bonnet to bumper, especially when we turned and crossed to the other side of the peninsula, that it was not until mid-afternoon that Terry and I reached Sorrento and found the campsite.

In the cool of the evening we went into the resort and walked round for an hour. Horse-drawn carriages were very much in evidence, and there were many souvenir shops. In one of the shops I bought two bookmarks, a copy of Axel Münthe's *The Story of San Michele*, and an illustrated guide to Pompeii, which we were planning to visit the following day, on our way to Naples. *The Story of San Michele* was a fashionable Swedish doctor's account of his life in Capri in the halcyon days before the First World War, and in particular of the creation of San Michele, the villa he had built there with his own hands, incorporating into it marble fragments from the ruins of the palace of Tiberius, the old Roman emperor having spent the last years of his life on the island.

I had read the book in Bombay, on the recommendation of my friend Arjundev Rashk, a Punjabi poet and scriptwriter of about my own age, and had enjoyed it greatly.[341] That was ten years ago, and I was glad not only that I had the opportunity to read it again, but that I had come across it – and could start reading it – in a place so close to Capri, which geologically was an extension of the Sorrento peninsula, and which we hoped to be able to see from Naples. The illustrated guide to Pompeii, with its photographs of the excavated remains of houses, shops, and public buildings, and its artist's reconstructions of what the city must have been like 2,000 years ago, helped prepare us for what we would be seeing – and not be seeing – on the morrow. In my own case, at least, the name of Pompeii had long been a familiar one. As a boy of eight or nine, confined to bed with what was believed to be heart disease, I had read Bulwer-Lytton's *The Last Days of Pompeii*, and his vivid account of the city's destruction had left an indelible impression on my mind.

From Sorrento onwards the road round the peninsula was relatively uninteresting, and after Castellammare di Stabia, equidistant from Sorrento and Naples, it passed through an area of an increasingly built-up and industrialized character. Owing to the bad signposting, we experienced some difficulty finding the way to Pompeii, a way which took us, eventually, through very dirty streets and past piles of garbage. On arriving at our destination we were surprised to find, not the reconstructed pagan temple one might have expected, but a big Roman Catholic church. The church was indeed a basilica, and judging by the fact that all the shops and stalls in the vicinity were selling cheap religious souvenirs it was a centre of pilgrimage. There was also a Pontifical Institute, in whose modest museum we saw an interesting series of old prints depicting all the eruptions of Vesuvius from the seventeenth century onwards, as well as various objects recovered from beneath the layers of volcanic ash which for centuries had covered Pompeii. Thus prepared, we made our way to the excavations, and there spent more than two hours treading the pavements of the old city and seeing the remains, in some cases very extensive, of the buildings which the spade of the archaeologist had exposed to view. We saw the spacious Forum or market place, with its lateral rows of truncated columns, the Basilica or hall of justice (some ancient churches so styled were originally public buildings of this type), the House of the Faun, named for the bronze dancing figure that had been found there and whose place was now occupied by a replica, the elegant House of Menander, in the atrium of which there were frescoes of the Sack of Troy, and the sad remains of the Temple of Isis, which I remembered as having featured prominently in *the Last Days of Pompeii* – together with much else that my diary lumps together under a terse 'etc.'

Many of the objects found at Pompeii were in private hands, but many were in the National Archaeological Museum in Naples, and as we were eager to see them we drove straight from the excavations to Naples and straight to the museum. The streets through which we passed were all incredibly dirty; piles of rotting garbage rose breast-high at regular intervals, and in Naples itself – an otherwise beautiful city, occupying one of the finest sites in the world – the same filth was to be seen, even in the principal thoroughfares. Were the municipal dustmen all on strike, then, or was this the normal state of affairs? We had no means of knowing. The museum, unfortunately, was closed, or rather, it closed just after our arrival, either because it was siesta time or because Monday was early closing day. Taking the coastal road, we therefore drove on to Pozzuoli, which was rather cleaner, and from Pozzuoli to the campsite at Solfatara. It was a big, quiet camp, with plenty of trees, and I spent much of the evening reading *The Story of San Michele*.

As we discovered the following day, the National Archaeological Museum contained not only frescoes, mosaics, and encaustic portraits from Pompeii and its sister in disaster, Herculaneum, but an astonishingly rich array of Greek and Roman antiquities of every kind. On entering the building we were confronted by a perfect forest of white marble statues in which it was easy, as one wandered from room to crowded room, to get lost. Besides the Farnese Hercules, the group of the Punishment of Dirce, the bronze Hermes in Repose, and a hundred other sculptures hardly less famous, there were portrait busts of Greek philosophers and Roman emperors, elaborately carved sarcophagi, and colossal statues of river gods. The object that made the strongest impression on me, whether because of its non-naturalistic character, its warmer colouring, or its more subliminal appeal, was the rigidly hieratic statue of the Ephesian Artemis. This was not the fleet-footed virgin goddess of the Greeks, but a deity of a very different kind. Apart from her outstretched hands, her most conspicuous feature were the rows of breasts – more recently identified as the testicles of bulls sacrificed in her honour – that adorned the upper part of her body, and the friezes of beasts that covered the mummy-like remainder. On her head rested a square mitre, and there were more representations of beasts within the flat disc of her halo. Her attitude was reassuring, her expression benign.

On our way into Naples that morning we had enjoyed a fine view of the splendid curve of the Bay. We had also encountered roads which, while they may have been wider than those of yesterday, were no less filthy. On emerging from the museum we therefore lost no time getting on to the Autostrada del Sole and heading for Rome. This twentieth-century equivalent of the Appian Way ran through mountainous, well-wooded countryside; at one point we saw, perched on a neighbouring peak, the famed abbey of Monte Cassino – unfortunately badly damaged during the Second World War. Three hours after leaving Naples we were in the Eternal City and looking for the Villa Ada campsite.

The first thing we did after having a meal was go to the camp shop and buy a guidebook. There was a lot to see in Rome – perhaps more than in all the places we had so far seen put together – and during the next five days we probably saw as much of the city and its monuments as could be comfortably seen in so short a time. Each morning we left the campsite straight after breakfast, and each day we spent the morning and much of the afternoon sightseeing. Since we did most of our sightseeing on foot, often in the open air, we were glad the weather was now cooler, and that there was an occasional sprinkling of rain. Evenings were spent at the campsite, where we cooked, washed clothes, read, studied our guidebook, and planned the following day's excursion.

On the first day we saw first the Forum of Trajan and the Colosseum, then the Roman Forum and the Palatine Hill. 'Walked round the whole area and saw everything,' my diary records with satisfaction, adding, 'Strong impression of greatness in size rather than in artistic conception. Everything seemed dark and heavy. None of the lightness of Greece.' We also visited the Capitoline Museum, among whose treasures were the Dying Gaul ('very fine') and the Spinarius or Boy With a Thorn. The second day began with a visit to the Pantheon ('simple but grand'), after which we saw St Peter's in Vincula, with the famous statue of Moses by Michelangelo ('rather smaller than I thought it was'), and the Basilica of St Clement, beneath which there was a much older underground church and, what was still more interesting, a Mithraic sanctuary. From St Clement's we drove to the Basilica of St John Lateran, on which my diary comments, 'Big and impressive, but cold. Typical papal triumphalism. Mosaics in apse beautiful, though. Sadly overpowered by rest of structure.' The day's excursion ended in the National Museum in the ruins ('stupendous') of the Baths of Diocletian, where we saw a marble copy of the Discobolus of Myron ('extraordinarily beautiful'), the Pugilist at Rest, and the famous relief of the Bath of Hera.

Our third day in Rome was devoted to St Peter's and to the Vatican Museums. Though I could not but agree that the dome of St Peter's – Michelangelo's dome – was one of the most beautiful in the world, I was disappointed by the interior of the vast building. It was magnificent, but it was cold. Walking round the nave, we saw the bronze statue of St Peter (people were kissing its toe) and Michelangelo's *Pietà*. We also saw, at the foot of one of the great piers, the altar and bodily remains, apparently complete – of St Josaphat. Could this be the Josaphat of the popular medieval legend of Barlaam and Josaphat, which scholars had shown to be based, ultimately, on a version of the life of the Buddha, Josaphat being a corrupted form of 'bodhisattva' and Barlaam of 'Bhagavan' or Lord?[342] In that case the bodily remains of St Josaphat, enshrined there at the very centre of Roman Catholic power and prestige, would be, if genuine, those of Gautama the Buddha. As it happened, the accidents of history had been responsible for no such irony. Years later I discovered that the St Josaphat whose remains reposed beneath the dome of St Peter's was a Polish bishop, martyred in 1623, who had devoted his life to reuniting schismatics with the Holy See. But I also discovered that both Barlaam and Josaphat had a formal place in the roll of Christian saints, and that special days in the calendar were set apart in their memory. In the Menology of the Greek Church, the commemoration of St Josaphat was on 26 August – my own birthday.

The Vatican museums were very much in the plural number. There were at least five separate museums, besides numerous galleries, rooms, courts, chapels, and loggias, all full of works of art of various kinds, from ancient Greek sculptures to Italian Renaissance paintings, and from Etruscan vases to medieval illuminated manuscripts. By the time Terry and I arrived the museums had been open for an hour or more, and the tourist season being at its height the place was uncomfortably crowded. 'Tremendous crush', my diary records. Working our way through the press, we managed to visit the museums and the Vatican library, as well as the picture gallery and most of the chapels and apartments. With so many people everywhere, it was at times difficult to get a proper view of the works of art, and the only ones of which I have a distinct recollection are the *Laocoön*, the *Apollo Belvedere* ('grey with dust, especially on the shoulders'), and Raphael's *School of Athens*.[343] The Sistine Chapel was particularly crowded, but we sat there for a while, gazing up at Michelangelo's frescoes of the Creation on the ceiling and at the frescoes of the Last Judgement on the wall behind the high altar.

Our next day's excursion took us, initially, to the semi-rural outskirts of Rome and to the catacombs of St Domitilla and St Calixtus. The former appeared to be the less well-known of the two. At any rate, Terry and I were the only visitors, and the young man who showed us round appeared to be the only guide there was. I had not realized that these Early Christian underground cemeteries were so extensive. The catacombs of St Domitilla were on four levels. At each level there was a network of galleries, the different levels being connected by flights of steps. Excavated from the dark volcanic rock, the galleries were only a few feet in width, and the walls on either side were lined from floor to ceiling with row upon row of horizontal burial-niches. There was also a small (restored) basilica, the upper part of which had originally projected above the ground. At the catacombs of St Calixtus there were a dozen or more visitors, and our guide was a well-informed young Canadian priest. There were between twelve and fourteen miles of galleries on four levels, he told us, before we followed him down the steps into the dimly-lit passages of the labyrinth below. The principal objects of interest were the Crypt of the Popes, which contained the sarcophagi of nine third-century pontiffs, and the Crypt of St Cecilia, where there was a marble copy of Maderno's recumbent statue of the martyred patroness of music.[344] In the afternoon, having cashed travellers' cheques in the Piazza di Spagna and looked in vain for affordable marble statuary, we drove to the Villa Borghese. It had just closed for the siesta, so taking the hint we went and had a siesta of our own back at the campsite, returning three hours later to view one of the choicest collections of sculptures and paintings we had so far encountered. There was Bernini's *David*, together with his *Apollo and Daphne,* and *Rape of Persephone*,[345] all of which I thought particularly fine, as well as Cranach's *Venus and Cupid*, Caravaggio's *St Jerome*, Dossi's *Circe*, and Titian's *Sacred and Profane Love*.[346]

Our fifth and last day in Rome happened to be a Sunday, and the streets through which we drove on our way to the Church of St Ignatius – the church of the Jesuits – were comparatively deserted. The interior of the imposing 'Jesuit-baroque' building was highly ornate, with gilding and coloured marbles very much in evidence. Mass was still in progress, the congregation being a fairly large one in which there were many nuns, all conspicuous in the black, white, blue, or parti-coloured habits of their respective orders. Afterwards we went and looked at the sumptuous polychrome marble altar of St Ignatius – said to be the richest monument in Rome – and gazed up at the famous *trompe l'œil* fresco of the triumph of St Ignatius in the cupola of the church. From the Jesú we walked the few hundred yards to Santa Maria sopra Minerva ('extremely beautiful and impressive', says my diary), the only large Gothic church in the city. It was a church of the Dominicans, and though I did not realize it at the time, in a marble sarcophagus under the high altar lay the body of St Catherine of Siena. Having sat through mass, celebrated for the benefit of a very small congregation, we walked round the building and saw the tomb of Fra Angelico and the chapel dedicated to St Thomas Aquinas.

Our next port of call was Santa Maria in Cosmedin. In order to get there we had not only to drive along the bank of the Tiber, but also to cross the river more than once, which meant that we had a good view of the famous boat-shaped island. Santa Maria in Cosmedin was a small church, and its ninth-century interior, unlike that of the Jesú, was simple to the point of austerity. Nearby stood the Temple of Vesta, where the Vestal Virgins had once tended the sacred fire. The principal object of the morning's excursion, however, was St Paul's Outside the Walls, which as its name suggested was situated beyond the walls that had surrounded the ancient city. Dating from the fourth century, this was a basilica-type church, and next to St Peter's the biggest church in Rome. 'More truly grand than St Peter's', my diary records admiringly, 'especially the interior.' The latter consisted of a nave and four aisles. From the alabaster windows of the clerestory a soft amber light fell on the long double rows of Corinthian columns, lit up the carved and gilded ceiling and the glittering mosaics of the chancel arch, and penetrated into the apse. The overall impression was one of peace and harmony. No less peaceful were the cloisters, round which Terry and I walked as soon as the sung mass was over and the congregation had dispersed. On our way back into the city we passed the Pyramid of Caius Cestius – Shelley's 'wedge sublime'[347] – and the Baths of Caracalla, and paid a second visit to the Colosseum, where Terry took photographs. Our last stop was at Santa Maria Maggiore, a fifth-century basilica church the interior of which my diary pronounces 'glorious', and where there was the biggest congregation we had seen that day.

During our five days in Rome, some monuments – and some works of art – naturally impressed me more deeply than others, but there were three monuments that must have made a particularly deep impression, inasmuch as for many years they occupied, in recollection, the forefront of my picture of Rome, everything else being relegated to the background. The three were the Colosseum, the Pantheon, and the Catacombs. In the case of the Colosseum it was not the actual building I remembered so much as the experience I had there. During which of our two visits the experience took place I do not know. Probably it was during the second, when I wandered off on my own while Terry was taking his photographs. Whichever it was, as I stood at the centre of the vast amphitheatre I became aware of all the blood that had been shed there – of all the human beings and animals that had been 'butchered to make a Roman holiday' on that spot.[348] I did not simply remember having read about such horrors in books. It was as though the pain and terror that had accompanied those countless dreadful deaths had left permanent traces on the atmosphere of the place and that I was picking up those traces. My memory of the Pantheon was of a very different kind. It was a memory not of the exterior of the second-century building, grand though this was, so much as its hemispherical interior. As I stood beneath the centre of the vast dome, looking up through the circular opening that was the principal source of light, it was as though I was standing on the surface of the earth and looking through a hole in the outermost crystalline sphere of the Ptolemaic universe – the sphere of the fixed stars – directly into the Empyrean.[349]

If in the Pantheon I ascended in spirit to the heights, in the Catacombs I descended into the depths. The descent was as much temporal as spatial. It was a descent not only into terrene depths but into the 'dark backward and abysm of time'.[350] From there one could see how vast was the difference between the splendour of the ornate, triumphalist structures of the Church's later days and the stark simplicity of those tomb-lined subterranean galleries. Christianity had changed radically in the course of its nineteen hundred years of history. In St Peter's one breathed a very different atmosphere, spiritually speaking, from that which one breathed in the Catacombs. Pagan temples may have been converted into places of Christian worship, but Rome was still Rome, and the Pope was the successor, in many respects, not so much of the Prince of the Apostles as of Caesar.

Back at the Villa Ada campsite we had a meal, rested, and read, and then at five o'clock left for Florence by the Autostrada del Sole. The countryside through which we passed was pleasant, but not very interesting, and except for Orvieto on its rock we saw nothing remarkable in the course of our journey. At eight-thirty we reached Florence, where we soon located the International, as the campsite was called. Though it was the best campsite we had seen in Italy, very few people were staying there, and we had the olive grove in which we were parked all to ourselves. When darkness fell, we could see the lights of the Certosa – the monastery of the Carthusians – glittering in the distance.

Our five days in Rome had left us with a multitude of impressions to digest, and it was perhaps for this reason that in the morning neither my friend nor I felt like going anywhere. We were content, instead, to stay in the olive grove and read. For the last few days I had been reading A. H. Armstrong's *An Introduction to Ancient Philosophy* and Karl Jaspers' *Way to Wisdom*, but I now put them aside in favour of Plato's *First Alcibiades* and the *Śvetāśvatara* and *Kaivalya* Upanishads.[351] Why I should have wanted to read the Upanishads there in Florence, or indeed have taken a volume of these ancient Hindu scriptures with me to Italy and Greece in the first place, I do not know. Perhaps I was unconsciously preparing for my forthcoming visit to India. During my first two or three years in the East I had studied the Upanishads intensively, and the *Śvetāśvatara* or 'White Horse' Upanishad was a great favourite of mine. I was particularly fond of its more poetical verses, such as those in which the inspired author of the Upanishad, addressing the god Rudra (a form of Shiva), exclaims, 'You are the dark blue bird, you are the green parrot with red eyes. You are the cloud with the lightning in its womb. You are the seasons and the seas.' The image of the green parrot with red eyes had stayed with me ever since.[352]

There were no green parrots in our olive grove. In view of the Italian sportsman's penchant for shooting anything that moved, there were probably no birds there at all. Birds or no birds, the grove was very peaceful, and Terry and I spent the best part of our first day in Florence happily absorbed in our books. At four o'clock, however, having completed a few chores, we both experienced a change of mood and decided to drive into the city. Half an hour later we were in the Piazza del Duomo. The huge cathedral with its red-tiled dome and polychrome marble facing, the tall, slim bell tower, and the octagonal baptistery, were all looking extremely beautiful in the rays of the setting sun, and formed between them what was perhaps the most harmonious complex of buildings we had seen in Italy. The interior of the cathedral was dimly lit and cavernous, that of the much smaller baptistery lined with coloured marbles and Byzantine mosaics. We were particularly drawn to Ghiberti's bronze-gilt east doors of the baptistery – the Doors of Paradise, Michelangelo called them[353] – and spent some time looking at the sculptured panels depicting biblical scenes and at the statuettes of prophets and sibyls. In the streets nearby there were several good bookshops, in one of which I bought Burckhardt's *Civilization of the Renaissance in Italy* for myself, as well as Luigi Barzini's *The Italians*,[354] and the Modern Library *Philosophy of Kant* for Terry, who at that time was reading Will Durant's *Outlines of Philosophy*. We also looked at various other shops. The level of craftsmanship was higher than anything we had found elsewhere in Italy, and Terry bought two cheap but attractive necklaces, one for Nicki and one for Vivien.

Unlike Rome, where the ancient and the modern existed in uncomfortable juxtaposition, Florence, the cradle of the Renaissance, had succeeded in relegating modern urban and industrial development to the hinterland of the old, historic city. Terry and I were made aware of this fact when we drove, the following morning, across the river Arno and up to the broad sunlit expanse of the Piazzale Michelangelo, in the centre of which there stood a monument dedicated to the great artist. As we looked from the balcony of the Piazzale, which commanded a panoramic view of practically the whole of Florence, we saw a perfect sea of red-tiled roofs out of which there rose, looking for all the world like a ship serenely riding waves made red by the rays of the sun, the great bulk of the cathedral. Where the red sea ended there stretched the smudged grey line of the more modern part of the city, while beyond the grey line there rose, tier upon tier, the green, gently undulant Tuscan hills. For some time we stood gazing down at the scene. The sun shone, the air was completely still, and not a sound came up to us from below. I felt much as Wordsworth must have felt when, crossing Westminster Bridge in the early morning, on his way to France, as he looked from the top of the coach at the city of London,

The river glideth at his own sweet will:
Dear God! the very houses seem asleep;
And all that mighty heart is lying still![355]

The Arno, no less than the Thames, may well have glided at its own sweet will, but as Terry and I quickly discovered on descending from the Piazzale and re-crossing the river, the houses of Florence were certainly not asleep that morning and its heart was far from still. Florence was a busy, bustling, crowded place, and nowhere was it more crowded than in the Uffizi Gallery, which we visited after going round the Palazzo Vecchio or Old Palace of the Signoria and looking at Cellini's Perseus[356] and other sculptures in the arcades of the adjacent loggia. There were more than forty rooms in the Uffizi. Only two or three of them were closed at the time, and despite the crush we managed to shoulder and squeeze our way into all the rest. How Terry felt about the paintings I do not remember, but for my part I particularly enjoyed the Botticelli Room, where the *Allegory of Spring*, the B*irth of Venus*, and other masterpieces from the hand of the same artist were on view.[357] By the time we left the Uffizi we were both feeling rather tired, though this was due not so much to our having been so long on our feet as to the fact that the gallery had been so uncomfortably crowded. After looking at the souvenir stalls in the market place, and buying a few provisions, we therefore headed back to our peaceful olive grove, where we spent the rest of the day by ourselves. I continued reading *The Italians*, while Terry made a start on Kant but did not find the philosopher very easy going.

For the remainder of our stay in Florence our daily programme followed much the same pattern. The morning was spent sightseeing, the afternoon and evening reading in the olive grove. In a way it was unfortunate that we were seeing Florence towards the end of our tour rather than at the beginning, for by this time we had seen so many cities, monuments, archaeological sites, and works of art that even I was beginning to feel fatigued and we were not, perhaps, in a position to appreciate the glories of Florence as much as we might otherwise have done. Moreover, Terry felt rather depressed after one of our forays, and one morning, on our way into the city, I felt sick and faint. Nonetheless, in the course of the next three days we visited Santa Maria Novella, San Marco, Santa Croce, and other churches, the Gallery of the Academy, and the Medici chapels, and besides sculptures by Michelangelo, including his David and various unfinished Captives, saw paintings by Fra Angelico, Botticelli, and Masaccio, as well as the tunic and girdle of St Francis, the allegedly miraculous veil of the Virgin, and in the crypt of San Miniato, situated on a hill above the Piazzale Michelangelo, what my diary describes as 'strange relics'. In the evenings we read. I finished *The Italians* and started on *The Civilization of the Renaissance in Italy*; Terry continued reading *Outlines of Philosophy*. On our last day in Florence I read Dante's *La Vita Nuova*, the Penguin translation of which I had bought that morning, when Terry and I were looking for presents for our friends – a search that took us as far as the shops on either side of the Ponte Vecchio or Old Bridge, which had been blown up by the retreating Germans in 1944 and subsequently restored. I had first read *La Vita Nuova* or *The New Life* when I was fourteen or fifteen, and it seemed fitting that I should read it again while staying in the city of the poet's birth.[358]

Though my friend and I were not in a position to appreciate Florence as much as we might have done, the overall impression that the city left on me, at least, was a distinctive one. The predominant note of Florence was beauty, even as the predominant note of Rome was grandeur. The city as a whole was beautiful (that is, the red-roofed historic city of which the cathedral was the centre), and it was full of beautiful things. There were beautiful churches, chapels, and palaces, and the churches, chapels, and palaces themselves were full of beautiful paintings and sculptures. Even the people seemed more beautiful than those in other parts of Italy. Certainly they were more smartly dressed, particularly the slim, elegant women, who more often than not were stylishly clad in fashionable black and left behind them a trail of delicate perfume. At the same time, I noticed that the beauty that was Florence's predominant note was, at its best, a sober, even an austere beauty. This was especially true of the Palazzo Vecchio, whose vast square bulk and solitary corner tower dominated the square of that name, as well as of the city's numerous Renaissance palaces, some of them now museums or art galleries, the severe horizontal lines and rusticated stonework of which gave me a particularly keen thrill of aesthetic delight.

I also noticed that Florence set great store by the memory of her great men, whose names were to be met with on every side. Dante, Giotto, Masaccio, Donatello, Verrocchio, Leonardo da Vinci, Alberti, Brunelleschi, Fra Angelico, Botticelli, Michelangelo, Cosimo and Lorenzo de' Medici, Savonarola, Marsilio Ficino, Galileo ...[359] the list seemed endless. Florence in fact valued her great men. She valued them because they were individuals and she valued individuality. It was therefore not surprising that Burckhardt, writing of biography in the Middle Ages and in the Renaissance and comparing the two, should have pointed out that the search for the characteristic features of remarkable men was a prevailing tendency among the Italians, and that this it was that separated them from other Western peoples, among whom the same thing happened but rarely, and in exceptional cases. What was true of the Italians of the Renaissance generally was true, it seemed, of the citizens of Florence in particular; and, as Burckhardt had gone on to observe, 'This keen eye for individuality belongs only to those who have emerged from the half-conscious life of the race and become themselves individuals.'[360]

Neither Terry nor I slept much that night. This may have been due to the fact that our last night in Florence was also our last night in Italy, and because we both knew that once we had left Italy our tour would be virtually over, for we did not think of Belgium and the other countries through which we had passed on our way to Italy and, eventually, to Greece, and through which we would be passing – in reverse order – on our way back to England, as forming part of our true itinerary. But though we had not slept much, and were feeling rather tired, we rose early, left the campsite at six o'clock as planned, and were soon on the autostrada to Milan. It was a fine, cool morning. The countryside through which we passed was at first rather hilly, with plenty of cypresses, but afterwards it became quite flat and remained flat for the rest of our journey. At Milan, which we reached four hours after leaving Florence, we picked up the autostrada to Como, where we halted for a while beside the lake, then drove on to Chiasso. Though the customs formalities took only a few seconds, so heavy was the traffic that we spent nearly an hour getting from one side of the Italian-Swiss frontier to the other. Once across, we drove on to Lugano, where we decided to halt, having by this time been on the road for nine hours. The two lakeside campsites were full, but eventually we found a site away from the town, on the bank of a small river, and there passed the night.

40
PICKING UP THE THREADS

The last time we had crossed the Alps there had been snow on each side of the road through the St Gotthard Pass. That snow had now melted, exposing the rock beneath, though the surrounding peaks glittered white and immaculate in the morning sunshine. As before, I experienced a slight nausea, and was glad when we began making the descent to Andermatt. From Andermatt, after a further descent, we drove on almost as far as Altdorf, pulling up for the night on a small side road when we were a few miles short of the town. The following day found us in Lucerne. On the way we had a fine view of the lake, which was misty, with rainbows overarching the grey waters. In Lucerne we walked around for a while, had a coffee, and did a little shopping, then drove on to Basel via Olten. By this time it was raining heavily, and shortly after three o'clock, having crossed the Franco-Swiss border, we pulled up at the side of the road beneath the sheltering eaves of a stretch of forest. Here we ate, and here, the weather continuing 'very dull and dismal' (to quote my diary), we spent the evening absorbed in our books.

For the last few days I had been reading two books. One was Ronald Segal's *The Crisis of India*,[361] the other Elmer O'Brien's *The Essential Plotinus*, a new translation of selected treatises from the *Enneads*.[362] What India's crisis was, according to Segal, I no longer remember, but now that Terry and I were on the last lap of our homeward journey, with our forthcoming visit to India very much in prospect, I must have felt the need to start making myself better acquainted with what had been happening in the subcontinent since my departure from its shores. The need that led me to read *The Essential Plotinus* was of an entirely different order. Segal's book dealt with matters temporal; the *Enneads* were concerned with what Carlyle called the Eternities.[363] I had been interested in Plotinus since I was sixteen or seventeen. At that time I was indebted for my knowledge of his philosophy, as of Neoplatonism in general, mainly to the writings of Dean Inge and Thomas Whittaker, for although I possessed the Bohn *Select Works of Plotinus*, as translated by Thomas Taylor,[364] so abstruse was the thought of those treatises, and so unfamiliar were the terms in which that thought was expressed, that I was able to make very little of them. There was, however, one exception. This was the famous treatise 'On Beauty', which according to Porphyry, Plotinus's disciple and biographer, was the earliest of the treatises.[365] I usually read the treatise in the translation made by the mysterious group known as the Editors of the Shrine of Wisdom,[366] a copy of which I also possessed, and I never read the slim blue volume without experiencing a thrill of delight, such as I experienced when reading the *Symposium* or Shelley's *Prometheus Unbound*.[367] Reading it more than twenty years later, in a new translation, I experienced that thrill again.

> Chiefly beauty is visual [the treatise began]. Yet in word patterns and in music (for cadences and rhythms are beautiful) it addresses itself to the hearing as well. Dedicated living, achievement, character, intellectual pursuits are beautiful to those who are above the realm of the senses; to such ones the virtues, too, are beautiful.[368]

Beauty was chiefly visual! This was certainly true of the beauty that was the predominant note of Florence. It was a beauty of form and colour, of symmetry and proportion, of the contrast between dark and bright, light and shade, and the fact that I had responded to that beauty so keenly told me something about myself. It told me I was a lover of beauty. But beauty was not only bodily. There was a beauty that was supersensible – the kind of beauty of which the Buddha had given Nanda a glimpse when he transported him to the paradise of Indra.[369] That beauty, too, I could see, however dimly; to that beauty, too, I responded keenly. It was this keenness of response, indeed, that had helped me to become a Buddhist, or rather, that had helped me to realize that I was, in fact, already a Buddhist and had always been one. According to Plotinus, just as it is impossible for one born blind to talk about bodily beauty, so it is impossible for one who has never seen it to talk about the beauty that is supersensible.

> Seeing of this sort is done only with the eye of the soul. And, seeing thus, one undergoes a joy, a wonder, and a distress more deep than any other because here one touches truth.
>
> Such emotion all beauty must induce – an astonishment, a delicious wonderment, a longing, a love, a trembling that is all delight. It may be felt for things invisible quite as for things you see, and indeed the soul does feel it. All souls, we can say, feel it, but souls that are apt for love feel it especially.[370]

I had experienced something of that *trembling that is all delight* while I was in Florence, whether looking at the harmonious complex of cathedral, bell tower, and baptistery, at the paintings of Botticelli, or at the sculptures of Michelangelo, and it was perhaps this feeling of delight that had led me to read *The Essential Plotinus*, in which the first of the 'representative treatises' translated happened to be the treatise 'On Beauty'. Be that as it may, the fact was that I had started reading Plotinus the night after our departure from Florence, when the spell of the city was still upon me, that I had continued reading him on the road between Andermatt and Altdorf, and that I now was reading him by a stretch of forest somewhere in France, with the rain dripping from the trees onto the roof of the Little Bus.

Despite the rain, both Terry and I slept well, and at ten o'clock, my friend having made tea and I having read a little more of Plotinus, we set out for Metz. It was a warm sunny day. In the course of our journey we passed through Mulhouse, Thonn, Col de Bussang, Remiremont, Épinal, and Nancy, stopping only twice on the way, once to do shopping, and once for a snack. From Épinal onwards the countryside was increasingly industrialized. At six o'clock when we were a few miles from Metz, we halted for the night, parking in a beautiful green meadow beside a river. Terry had been a little depressed when we arrived there, but after reading Durant's chapter on Schopenhauer he declared he was feeling better, the teachings of the so-called philosopher of pessimism having cheered him up considerably. That night I had several strange dreams. In one dream – perhaps a recollection of a previous life – I was attending a party in Greek or Roman times. In another I was in Gangtok with Kachu Rimpoche, one of my Tibetan teachers, from whom I had received the Padmasambhava initiation and the name Urgyen.[371]

Whether on account of these dreams, or simply because I had slept well, when I woke in the morning – the morning of our last full day on the Continent – I felt quite refreshed. It was a fine, sunny morning, and the countryside from Metz onwards, while not picturesque, was sufficiently pleasing to the eye. At midday, having driven through Thionville, Luxembourg, and Neufchateau, and thus crossed into Belgium, we pulled into the side of the road for lunch. It was a beautiful spot but every seven and a half minutes the quiet was disturbed by the sharp crack like that of a rifle – evidently fired automatically, and meant to scare the birds from the crops. Nevertheless we stayed on there, and after a meal that concluded, for once, with pastries (bought in Neufchateau), we settled down to an afternoon of reading. Before my departure from England the editor of the *Middle Way*, Muriel Daw, had given me a book for review. The book was K. Venkata Ramanan's *Nāgārjuna's Philosophy, As Presented in the Mahā-Prajñāpāramitā-Śāstra*, and to this I now turned. As I was already familiar with the author's views, having met him more than once in India, I read the work with particular interest, though so far as I remember I never found time to review it. His principal concern was to set forth the basic philosophical conceptions found in the *Śāstra*, which unlike some scholars he believed to be a genuine work of Nāgārjuna, and to show that those conceptions constituted, in any case, a continuation and development of the thought of the *Mūlamadhyamaka-kārikā* and other works universally attributed to the great Mahāyāna philosopher.[372] From this he concluded that Nāgārjuna's philosophy was not nihilistic, as some of its critics maintained, but in its ultimate import positive and affirmative.

> The main purpose of the negative arguments in the *Kārikā* was to expose the self-contradictions inherent in the position of the Sarvāstivādins who clung to the determinate as ultimate, the relative as self-contained. This is the error of misplaced absoluteness. The major function of the negative arguments in the *Kārikā* is to reveal the relativity of the mundane; the question

> of the ultimate reality constitutes a minor part. It is the error in regard to the mundane nature of things that needs to be cleared up first. With the revelation of the essentially conditioned, non-substantial, relative nature of things, the tendency to cling might again operate, tending to end in negativism. This is an error in regard to the ultimate nature of things and it is in regard to this error that the *śūnyatā* of *śūnyatā* has been taught. What is sought to be revealed thereby is the non-ultimacy of the relative in their relative nature; the conditionedness of the conditioned is not their ultimate nature. The unconditioned is again not anything apart from the conditioned. The ultimate truth about the conditioned is that it is itself the unconditioned reality, the Nirvāṇa. This is the basic teaching of the Madhyamaka.[373]

By the end of the afternoon Terry had taken in enough of Kant and Schopenhauer for the time being, and I enough of Nāgārjuna, and feeling the need for exercise we walked a mile or two up the road in the direction of Dinant, keeping to the narrow footpath between the roadway and the fields. On returning to the Little Bus we decided to drive further that evening, and were soon on our way.

From Dinant the road followed the course of the Meuse, and it was on the banks of this pleasant river that we spent the last night of our tour. In the morning we drove on to Namur, from Namur to Brussels, and from Brussels to Ostend. At half-past three we boarded the ferry, and half an hour later it left.

41
BACK TO THE VIHARA

The voyage from Ostend to Dover was a rather noisy one. This was due less to the ferry's engines than to the behaviour of some of the passengers, returning holidaymakers who, having come on board already a little worse for drink, had proceeded to take full advantage of the vessel's duty-free facilities. Terry and I kept as clear of them as we could. I read a little more of *Nāgārjuna's Philosophy*, and from time to time we walked round the deck. At eight-thirty we arrived in Dover. The customs gave us no trouble, and from Dover we drove straight to Canterbury, where we parked near the cathedral. Whether we were as happy to be back from our travels as we were to set out on them my diary does not record and I do not remember. Perhaps we could not quite believe that we really were back from those travels, for prior to settling down for the night we went and walked round the outside of the cathedral, as though we were still in Italy or Greece and still sightseeing. The vast Gothic pile was floodlit, and walls, roofs, buttresses, and towers showed golden against the darkness of the sky. There was no one about, and a deep silence reigned. In the morning we went there again, and spent half an hour looking round the glorious interior of the building. On our way back to the Little Bus I bought a *Telegraph* and a *New Statesman*,[374] as I liked to know what was going on in the world, and what people were thinking. (Terry never read the newspapers.) We then took the motorway to London.

During our two months away my hair had grown the longest it had been since my arrival in England in 1964, and did not look very monastic. We therefore stopped at Dartford so that I could get it cut. In India I had always shaved my head, but in England I had allowed my hair to grow a little, though not much beyond the regulation length, which was in any case a matter of dispute, or at least of disagreement in practice, among monks belonging to different schools. Even so, the length of my hair had been commented on unfavourably by some of the more rigid English Theravādins, as I well knew, one or two of whom professed to believe that the reason I was allowing my hair to grow was that I had decided to give up the yellow robe and return to lay life. Not that all such comment was unfavourable. As I also knew, some of the people who attended my lectures and classes, both at the Vihara and at the Buddhist Society, were pleased to see me looking more 'human' and less ascetic. George Goulstone's flirtatious wife, who occasionally attended my Sunday afternoon lectures, indeed went so far as to whisper in my ear, after one such meeting, 'I love your gorgeous sexy hair.' I did not know quite what to make of this declaration. I had never thought of myself as being 'sexy' in any respect, and was certainly not conscious of putting out the quasi-erotic 'vibes' that seemed to emanate from some charismatic Buddhist and Hindu teachers. The vast majority of English Buddhists, in London and in the provinces, came not for the sake of my hair, whether long or short, sexy or otherwise, but for the sake of the Dharma. Nevertheless, I did not want to upset the Theravādins unnecessarily, or give them too much of a handle against me, and the haircut I had in Dartford was therefore quite a short one.

Besides getting my hair cut before returning to the Vihara, I had to change back into my monastic robes. Just when I did this I do not remember, any more than I remember at what point I changed into civilian clothes after leaving the Vihara for Greece, though I probably changed into them somewhere between Dartford and London and in the privacy of the Little Bus. For the Theravādin Buddhists of South-East Asia it was even more reprehensible for a monk to wear civilian clothes than to let his hair grow beyond the regulation length. Indeed it was unthinkable. In their eyes a monk who wore civilian clothes, if only for a few hours, was no longer a monk. I did not share this view, any more than the majority of English Buddhists would have done, had they thought the matter worth bothering about. While not entirely agreeing with Christmas Humphreys that the true Buddhist was one who 'wore the yellow robe within', I certainly did not believe that it was wearing the yellow robe and shaving the head that made one a monk. I had not worn my robes for the whole two months of our tour, but I knew myself to have been no less a monk, and no less a Buddhist, when wearing civilian clothes and visiting Delphi and other ancient sites, than when wearing robes and giving lectures and leading classes in London. This did not mean that monastic robes did not have their place, or that changes that might upset people, or give rise to needless controversy, should be introduced without due preparation, and as we drove to London I was happy to get back into my own familiar robes.

The drive was both long and dreary. It was long on account of the heavy traffic and the frequent red lights, and dreary on account of the picture presented by much of the urban landscape, and I was glad when we reached central London and parked near Charing Cross Road. While I waited in the Little Bus, Terry went to Watkins and collected the copy of Wilhelm Reich's *The Function of the Orgasm* which he had ordered some months before, the works of the controversial Austrian psychoanalyst being then difficult to obtain. From central London we drove up to West Hampstead and to the Indo-Pak restaurant, where we had a meal and from where I telephoned Francoise at the Vihara to let her know we would soon be there. No doubt we could have eaten at the Vihara, but Terry and I were conscious that our tour was now definitely at an end, and we wanted to have a farewell meal together before we started picking up the threads of our former interests and activities. Not that we were really saying farewell. But for two months each had been the other's sole company; we had shared many experiences; and although we would still be very much in contact the fact that I, in particular, would be very busy, now that we were back in London, would surely make a difference.

On our arrival at the Vihara we found Viriya and David Vial working in the little front garden. Francoise, at her desk as usual, was obviously very glad to see us, as was the ever-solicitous Thien Chau. After a cup of tea and a chat with everybody Terry and I unpacked and settled in, my friend having decided to base himself at the Vihara for a few days before going to stay with his parents in Ilford. I then telephoned Alf Vial and Mike Hookham, learned that Christmas Humphreys was away on holiday, and had a long talk with Owen Jenkins, to whom I had entrusted the leading of one of the weekly meditation classes. Things had gone well during my absence, he reported. Activities had continued as usual, exactly as I had planned they should, and although attendance at the Sunday lectures had fallen off this had not been the case with any of the classes. As if in confirmation of his words, people were now beginning to arrive and gather in the all-purpose shrine-room downstairs, it being Friday, the day of the guided group meditation class. I did not take the class myself, but during the break I gave interviews to three or four people, one of them being Antoinette Willmott. The following day I saw – and telephoned – more people, all of whom were eager to hear about the tour. Ruth Walshe came in the afternoon with Phyllis, followed later by Maurice.

That evening I attended the Annual General Meeting of the Friends of the Triyana Vardhana Vihara, the informal organization I had set up as a means of providing support for my little monastery in Kalimpong while I was away in England. Alf Vial, Mike Hookham, and Jack Ireland – the Vihara's Three Musketeers – were all present, and after the meeting the four of us had what my diary describes as 'a good talk' about the future activities of the (Hampstead) Vihara.

Thus within forty-eight hours of my return from Greece I was back in the midst of my responsibilities as incumbent of the Vihara and Head of the English Sangha. I was also being reminded, as I sat listening to Alf's report as secretary of the Friends of the Triyana Vardhana Vihara, that Terry and I would soon be paying a visit to India and that the visit would be, for me, one of farewell.

42
JOURNEY TO INDIA

I find it difficult to say just when I decided that my future lay in the West and not, as I had hitherto supposed, in India. Perhaps it was not so much a question of a decision taken at a particular point in time as of a realization that dawned on me gradually, after I had been at the Hampstead Buddhist Vihara for a year or more. When I asked Terry, at our third or fourth meeting, whether he could drive me to India – he having offered to drive me anywhere I liked – the words that thus sprang unpremeditated to my lips, though they turned out to have been prophetic, were not seriously meant. At that time I had been in England for little more than six months, and though I was aware that I had already exceeded the length of time I had originally intended to stay, and though I still thought of myself as being based permanently in India, I had not yet fixed a date for my return to the subcontinent, nor decided how I should travel, whether overland or in any other way. Little by little, however, as my six months in England became a year, and my year eighteen months, my attitude had changed. I saw with increasing clarity that for the present, at least, I could 'work for the good of Buddhism' more effectively in England than in India.[375] By the time Terry and I left for Greece, therefore, I had decided that I would be returning to India only to pay my friends and teachers there a farewell visit, and to explain to them what my plans were. I would be leaving in mid-September, and be away for four months. Terry would be accompanying me, and we would go by air.

A number of factors contributed to my decision – or gradual realization – that my future lay in the West, and that I could 'work for the good of Buddhism' more effectively there than in India, and I find it difficult to say which of them carried most weight with me. Before my arrival on the scene the differences that had arisen between the Buddhist Society and the Sangha Association had widened into an open breach. I had sought to resolve those differences, to heal that breach, and had succeeded to an extent; but tensions still existed below the surface, and I knew that if the process of reconciliation was to continue I would have to remain in England. One of the ways in which I had sought to resolve the differences between the Buddhist Society and the Sangha Association was by making myself available to both organizations and giving lectures and leading meditation classes not only at the Hampstead Vihara but also at the Society's premises in Eccleston Square. The result was that some of the people attending those lectures and classes had come to regard themselves as my disciples, and to look to me for guidance in their study and practice of the Dharma, and I felt it would be irresponsible of me to abandon them. Considerations of a more personal nature also contributed to my decision that my future lay in England, though none of them was of sufficient weight actually to tip the scales. I wanted to engage more with Western culture; I wanted to see a little more of my parents (or rather, to enable them to see a little more of me); and I wanted to deepen my friendship with Terry – though had I decided to return permanently to India he probably would have elected to accompany me, especially as there was now little possibility of his ever seeing his daughter again.

Not that there were no disadvantages attached to my being based in England rather than in India. As I had soon discovered, my busy life as incumbent of the Hampstead Buddhist Vihara and Head of the English Sangha left me with little time for literary work, despite my having stipulated, in accepting the Trust's invitation, that my mornings should be my own. My only consolation was that *The Three Jewels*, the preface to which I had written the previous summer, was now in the press, and that while I was away on my travels Francoise had typed the manuscript of the work that was eventually published as *The Eternal Legacy*.[376] There was also the fact that Hampstead, and even Biddulph, was no substitute for Kalimpong, and that the view I had from the window of my noisy upstairs front room at the Vihara was very different from the one I had from the veranda of my peaceful hillside hermitage in the foothills of the eastern Himalayas. In London there were no deep blue skies. There was no sudden vision of the snows of Mount Kanchenjunga as one turned a bend in the road. But the biggest disadvantage – not to say deprivation – attached to my being based in England was that I would no longer be in regular personal contact with my teachers, especially Dhardo Rimpoche and Kachu Rimpoche, or with my friends in Calcutta, Bombay, Nagpur, Poona, and other places I visited from time to time. My teachers, of course, did not need me, even if I still needed them, but the friends I had made among the followers of Dr B. R. Ambedkar who had converted to Buddhism did need me, and had my work among them not reached something of an impasse due to the politicization of the conversion movement after Ambedkar's untimely death I probably would not have left them. One of the biggest concentrations of the newly converted Buddhists was in Bombay, and it was to Bombay that Terry and I would be flying. There, I hoped, I would be able to make contact with some of my friends among them and explain that although in future I would be based in England I would continue to be concerned for their welfare and would help them in whatever way I could.

But it would be six weeks before Terry and I were in Bombay, and meanwhile there was much to be done. Between the time of my arrival back at the Vihara and my departure for the Buddhist Society's summer school two weeks later I gave lectures and led classes, saw friends like Ruth, John Hipkin, and Toby, gave interviews, checked the typescript of *The Eternal Legacy*, wrote and dictated letters, spent time with Thien Chau and Viriya, and received a variety of visitors, from the Indian founder of the Asian Music Circle to a Vietnamese *bhikṣuṇī* who wanted to start a world organization of Buddhist nuns. I also met, at the Sinhalese Vihara in Chiswick, the famous 'political monk' Walpola Rahula who, having made Ceylon too hot for himself, was now studying in Paris. We had a lengthy discussion, and according to my diary I found him 'very liberal-minded'. At that time I had not read his *Bhikshuvage Urumaya* or 'The Heritage of the Buddhist Monk', the notorious essay in which, on the basis of certain historical precedents, he had argued in favour of the full participation of Buddhist monks in the political life of the Sinhalese nation. Had I then been acquainted with the work, as I was to be some years later, I might have thought that Walpola Rahula carried his liberal-mindedness rather too far, for among the historical precedents he cited were those of the sixty monks who had attempted to assassinate the king; the 'large number' who in the 'decisive battle for the liberation of Buddhism and the Sinhalese' accompanied the army and encouraged the warriors to fight; and the monks who in Ceylon's 1965 general election were 'again in the forefront' *on both sides*.[377]

While I was thus occupied Terry was busy seeing Vivien, Alan, and other friends and getting the photographs he had taken developed, for though he had gone to stay with his parents in Ilford he did not, it seemed, spend much time with them. Whenever he was in town he called in at the Vihara, and on two or three occasions we were able to go out together. Once we went to the Hampstead Public Library, where Terry selected books on Spinoza, Hegel, and Schopenhauer (my own reading at the time was principally Dean Inge's *The Philosophy of Plotinus*), and once to Kenwood where, since it was raining, we simply sat in the Little Bus and talked. Despite staying at Ilford my friend was not only looking very well; to my great relief, he was also in a much more positive frame of mind than he had been before our tour, which on the whole seemed to have had a tonic effect on him. He said nothing about his ex-wife or about his daughter, and I thought it best not to enquire. In the course of our tour he had more than once bought presents for Fiona, and I assumed he had found a way of getting them to her, perhaps through his mother, with whom Gillian had always got on well and with whom she was probably still in touch. My only cause for concern was Terry's increasing preoccupation with the subject of *ḍākinīs*. 'Do you think I shall meet my *ḍākinī* in India?' he one day wanted to know. Since it was from me that he had first heard about *ḍākinīs*, in connection with my telling him about Jamyang Khyentse Rimpoche and *his ḍākinī*,[378] I could hardly answer the question with a flat negative, as though *ḍākinīs* did not exist and were therefore not to be met with, even in India. At the same time I did not want to encourage any unrealistic expectation that he would meet there that unique, magical person who, by galvanizing his dormant energies, would grant him that sense of ecstatic fulfilment which he had experienced when he saw the pure white light and which he so desperately wanted to recapture. I therefore replied to my friend's question non-committally, saying it was not impossible that he should meet his *ḍākinī* in India.

The Buddhist Society's summer school began on Friday 26 August – my forty-first birthday. In the morning I attended to various odd jobs, and in the afternoon, after lunching with Thien Chau and Viriya, I gave a long interview to a woman from the *Observer* weekend colour supplement.[379] Terry came at four o'clock, and an hour later I left for Hoddesdon with him and Thien Chau, Viriya following with Mike Rogers, a cheerful mid-thirties bachelor who was among the more regular attenders at my lectures and meditation classes. It was my third summer school, and as it followed much the same programme as the previous two, from Toby's opening address on the Friday evening to my own 'Buddhist Conversation' with John Hipkin a week later, my impressions of it are even less vivid than are those of its immediate predecessors. At seven o'clock each morning, having drunk a cup of Chinese tea with Thien Chau, I went and called Terry, whose room was some distance from mine, and the two of us went for a walk in the grounds. After the walk came breakfast, and after breakfast began a continual round of devotional meetings, meditation classes, lectures, discussion groups, and personal interviews which more often than not kept me busy until quite late at night. The only intermissions were the two occasions when I went down to London for a few hours, once to give my usual Sunday afternoon lecture at the Vihara, and once, three days later, to lead the full-moon day celebrations there.

Yet although my impression of that year's summer school are so lacking in vividness, and although, in recollection, only a few individual events stand out separate from the rest, like hilltops from the surrounding mist, I nonetheless remember feeling, when Terry and I left at the end of the week, that it had all been very worthwhile. It had been worthwhile, from my point of view, not so much on account of the different organized events in which I had taken part, as because of the opportunity it had given me of exchanging at least a few friendly words with so many English Buddhists, most of whom I already knew. Indeed, many people were eager to speak with me – many more than in previous years. Such was the warmth by which I was surrounded, in fact, and so much did I feel myself to be now part of the English Buddhist scene, that my third summer school was for me the most enjoyable. In Terry's case it was his first summer school (it was also to be his last, as it was to be mine), and although he tended to feel uneasy in large gatherings he managed to get through the week without becoming depressed, largely because he already

Terry (l) with John Hipkin

knew several people, especially John Hipkin and Viriya, and was able to spend time with them when not attending my lectures and classes. I was therefore thankful he had been able to cope, for it was more than likely that in India we would find ourselves in the midst of gatherings not of a hundred or so Buddhists, as at the summer school, but of thousands.

India was in fact much in my thoughts, now that the day of our departure was so near, and it was therefore not surprising that my first Sunday lecture, after my return from the summer school, should have been on 'Religion and Caste in India'. Among those attending the lecture were a number of Indian Buddhist friends, all followers of Dr Ambedkar, and all colleagues of some of the friends I was hoping to meet in Bombay and elsewhere. On the following Sunday I spoke on 'Living Buddhism', and on the next, it being the eve of my departure, I led a question-and-answer meeting and a puja. Between whiles I attended to my usual work, visited the Brighton and Hastings Buddhist groups, spent an afternoon with my mother, had two sessions with a young Harley Street dentist I had met at the summer school, recorded a talk on 'Self-Denial and Self-Affirmation' for the BBC, the choice of subject being theirs, and wrote an editorial for the October issue of *The Buddhist*, which would be appearing shortly after my departure.

In this editorial I explained that I had decided to shift my working headquarters from India to England, that I would be in India until about 1 February, and that during my absence lectures and classes would continue as usual. Ven. Thien Chau, with the assistance of Sāmaṇera Viriya, would be looking after the Vihara, besides which he would be taking the guided group meditation classes, his deputies being Ruth Walshe for the classes held at the Buddhist Society, and Ruth Walshe, Jack Ireland, and Owen Jenkins for those held at the Vihara. Maurice Walshe would be in charge of the fortnightly discussion group (as the speakers' class had become), which would continue to meet alternately at the Vihara and at the Buddhist Society. For the Sunday afternoon lectures I had secured the cooperation of a number of well-known speakers, the names of four or five of whom I proceeded to enumerate. *The Buddhist* would be the joint responsibility of Mike Hookham and Jack Ireland, assisted by Francoise Strachan.[380]

All these arrangements had been discussed thoroughly with Thien Chau and Viriya, as well as with all the other people involved, including Toby, who was pleased I had decided to stay in England and who, no doubt remembering the way in which I had kept postponing my arrival two years earlier, urged me in the strongest terms to fix the date of my return well in advance *and stick to it*. There was no reason, I therefore felt I could assure my readers, why the Vihara should not only consolidate its position during the coming months but make fresh gains, and I appealed to them to extend their full cooperation to Thien Chau and Viriya and help to make this period one of the most successful in the history of the movement.

The last paragraph of my editorial struck a more personal note. After my return to England, I declared, I proposed to divide my time between London and Biddulph, spending the winter and spring at the Vihara for lectures and classes, and the summer and autumn at Old Hall for meditation courses, literary work, and contact with the Midland and Northern Buddhist groups. Though I may not have realized it at the time, this must have represented a determination on my part to create for myself in England a pattern of life and work similar to the one I had followed in India, where I spent half the year studying, meditating, and writing in Kalimpong, and half travelling and lecturing in the plains, especially among the newly converted Buddhists in central and western India. Not that study and meditation, at least, had been entirely neglected during my two years in England, even though this might have been the case so far as serious literary work was concerned. Even during the busy days that succeeded my return from the summer school I found time, according to my diary, to dip into Plotinus, Suzuki, and Jaspers, as well as to read Alan Watts' *Psychotherapy East and West*, Colin Wilson's *Beyond the Outsider* ('interesting, though rather shallow'), the anonymous classic of Russian spirituality *The Way of the Pilgrim*, with its sequel *The Pilgrim Continues His Way*, and the great fourteenth-century classic of English mysticism, also anonymous, *The Cloud of Unknowing*. The last three titles suggest that despite my having so much to do my mind was turned as much inward as outward, and indeed my diary entry for Friday 9 September concludes, 'Spent rest of evening peacefully reading, meditating'.

On Saturday 17 September the Sangha Association held a reception at the Vihara, thus enabling members and friends to say farewell to me prior to my departure. About sixty people attended, with most of whom I managed to have at least a short conversation. Sunday was spent preparing for the morrow's journey, giving final instructions to Viriya, visiting Claire Maison, and leading my last question-and-answer meeting and last puja, both of which were exceptionally well attended. Next morning Antoinette drove Terry and me to Victoria, where we boarded the coach for Heathrow, and where she, Thien Chau, and Viriya waved us goodbye. The plane left at ten o'clock. Two hours later, after a short stopover in Zurich, my friend and I were looking down on the Alps, through which we had driven six weeks ago. Stopovers in Rome and Cairo soon followed, after which the plane headed straight for Bombay.

43
A LETTER FROM INDIA

Frontier Mail,
7.10.66

Dear Members and Friends,

After a very smooth and pleasant flight by Air India, Terry Delamare and I reached Bombay on Tuesday 20 September, at 4.30 a.m. local time, the whole journey having lasted only thirteen and a half hours. Bombay is more easily accessible from London than from Kalimpong, it seems! Within hours of our arrival my old friends the ex-Untouchable Buddhists were on our doorstep, and in an amazingly short time a programme of meetings and lectures was arranged. In fact, it began the very next evening, and in six days I gave eleven lectures on different aspects of Buddhism, including one on Buddhism in England. Most of these meetings were held late at night in the chawls or slum tenements under the conditions which I have described in my lecture on 'What Buddhism has done for the ex-Untouchables'. Others were held at the Bahujana Vihara, Parel (a branch of the Maha Bodhi Society), at the Japanese Buddhist Temple, Worli, and at Siddharth College. Everywhere we were given a very warm reception, and my Indian friends were delighted to see, in the person of Terry, yet another English Buddhist. (Terry is making, incidentally, a photographic record of our trip from which we hope to obtain, on our return to London, a series of colour slides with which to illustrate a few lectures.) We also found time, the day after our arrival, for a trip to the famous Kanheri Caves, dating from the early centuries of the Christian era, with their hundred or more cells and assembly halls cut out of the living rock and thirty-foot-high standing images of the Buddha. As no transport was available from the nearest railway station, thirty-five miles out of Bombay, to the Caves, we had to walk the five-mile distance both ways in the sweltering heat of the late monsoon season. Within minutes, we were drenched in perspiration. However, the sight of the Caves was sufficient reward for our trouble. In fact, had we not been expected back in London Terry and I might have been tempted to stay there indefinitely, and not return to 'civilization' at all!

From Bombay we proceeded North to Delhi, stopping one night on the way at Ahmedabad, where the local Buddhists turned out in force to receive us at the railway station with flower garlands and bouquets. In Delhi we spent two comparatively quiet days, staying at the Buddha Vihara (another branch of the Maha Bodhi Society), where I have often lectured, and visiting the Red Fort and other places of interest. We also explored the handicraft shops for ivory and sandalwood figures of the Buddha, but with a few exceptions did not find anything of much artistic value. From Delhi we travelled still further north to Pathankot, the railhead for both Dharamsala and Dalhousie, both of which are about a thousand miles from Bombay. We were now in the hills. All the time, in fact, the landscape had been changing, from the fertile fields of Gujarat, through the arid plains of Rajasthan, to the green and pleasant land of the Punjab with its long tracts of snow-white elephant grass and stretches of water starred with myriads of tiny pink water-lilies.

The main purpose of our visit to Dharamsala, of course, was to meet His Holiness the Dalai Lama, whom I had not seen for several years, though we had been in correspondence.[381] We met him at his residence, 'Swargashram', on the second day after our arrival and had a long talk. In the course of conversation I told him about the progress of the Buddhist movement in England. He showed particular interest in the meditation classes and asked what methods of concentration we practised. I also told him about our meditation centre at Biddulph. He was very pleased, though genuinely astonished, that so many English lay Buddhists took such a serious interest in meditation and could, in the course of a week's retreat, put in so many hours of practice. He also enquired after Mr Christmas Humphreys, and was particularly glad to learn that the Buddhist Society and the Vihara were working in close collaboration. Perhaps with certain differences among his own people in mind, His Holiness emphatically declared that unity among Buddhists was absolutely essential. While in Dharamsala we also took the opportunity of meeting Ling Rimpoche, the Dalai Lama's Senior Tutor, whose mental alertness impressed us very much, and Radu Rimpoche, the head of His Holiness's personal ecclesiastical establishment, besides several old friends of mine from Kalimpong and Gangtok.

Dalhousie is not much more than a hundred miles by road from Dharamsala, but it took us the best part of a day to get there. Travelling by the ramshackle, bone-shaking public transport, we first came down to the plains to Pathankot, then climbed the 7,000 feet to Dalhousie up a dizzying succession of hairpin bends where awe-inspiring views were revealed at every turn. In Dalhousie our main objective was to meet Dorothy Carpenter, who came out last March to help the Tibetan refugees, and Keith Satterthwaite, who came out only three weeks ago. Before my departure from England eager, warm-hearted Dorothy had written several times saying that I must not think of coming to India without paying her a visit. So to Dalhousie we went. Dorothy was overjoyed to see us (our arrival took her completely by surprise), and we all had a very happy reunion. Keith, whom we had last seen at the summer school, seemed to have learned to find his way about Dalhousie very quickly. With him for guide, we were able to make the best possible use of the one day at our disposal. Indeed, without him I do not know what we should have done, as the bungalows are scattered up and down the pine-clad mountainside at great distances from one another. Our first call was on Panggang Rimpoche, for seven years head of the Gyudto or Upper Tantric College and one of the greatest living authorities on the Vajrayāna. Next we visited the College itself, and saw Dorothy 'in action' teaching her class consisting of about forty members of the College. By special permission of the Dalai Lama, she is the first person to teach English to this very select body of Tantric initiates – a great honour for Dorothy. She also gives special lessons to Panggang Rimpoche. On my return to London I shall have much to say about Dorothy and her work (as well as slides to show, I hope). The remainder of our time was spent at the Four Sect Monastery at 'Kailash', originally the Young Lamas Home School, and the Mahāyāna Nunnery. There was even time, just before our bus left, for a few minutes with Khamtul Rimpoche, whom I had known quite well in Kalimpong. Everywhere in Dalhousie, in fact, I met incarnate lamas and monks whom I knew, or who knew me – some from Kalimpong and Darjeeling, others from Gangtok. As I remarked to Terry, I felt as though I was back in Kalimpong already!

At the moment of writing we are in the Frontier Mail heading south via Delhi and Mathura for Baroda. We have already been in the train twenty-four hours and will be in it for another twelve. The weather is hot, though not very sultry, and the compartment is filled with clouds of fine dust which covers the seats, our clothes, books, and food, as well as the paper on which I am writing. From Baroda we have a two-hour journey to Ahmedabad, where our Buddhist friends are arranging a five-day lecture programme. After spending a night in Bombay, where I shall be speaking at Theosophy Hall, we shall go on to Poona for more lectures, travelling thence to Nagpur, in Central India, in time for the Vijaya Dasami celebrations on 23 October.[382] From Nagpur we shall be going up to Almora for a few days with Lama Govinda and Li Gotami and from there I hope to write my next letter.

Rather surprisingly, our tour has so far gone strictly according to schedule, and if things continue this way there is no reason why we should not be back in England punctually by the end of January.

Yours in the Dharma,
(sd.) Sangharakshita.[383]

Such was the letter I wrote in the train and posted to Francoise in Ahmedabad, and which appeared a few weeks later in the November issue of *The Buddhist*. According to my diary I spent much of the day writing it, the same brief entry recording that Terry was very depressed, 'quite desperate, in fact', and that I felt very concerned for him.

This was not the first time since our arrival in India that my friend had felt depressed. On our journey from the airport to Victoria Terminus, through Bombay's extensive industrial suburbs, he had been shocked not only by what his own, short-lived diary terms the 'dirty and extremely low atmosphere' but by the sight of hundreds of people sleeping on the pavements; and in the evening, when we took a stroll along Marine Drive, he had been no less shocked by the sight of 'much unpleasant poverty and twelve-year-old mothers begging'.

In the course of my years in India I had grown accustomed to such sights, but though I deplored them I had preferred to direct my emotional energies to the task of giving practical help to the poor and oppressed, especially by putting my shoulder to the wheel of Dr Ambedkar's movement of mass conversion to Buddhism, rather than wasting them in sentimental lamentations over sufferings I was powerless to relieve. At the same time I could understand how the spectacle of so much poverty and degradation could shock the newcomer to India (it had shocked me twenty years earlier), especially if the newcomer was as sensitive as Terry and liable, as he was, to be upset and depressed by any concrete reminder of the essentially painful and unsatisfactory nature of the unenlightened human condition.

Terry had not only been shocked by the sight of hundreds of people sleeping on the pavements and twelve-year-old mothers begging. He had also been startled, on our arrival at the spacious Malabar Hill flat where we would be staying, by the unusual appearance of our host, Dr Dinshaw K. Mehta, for many years Mahatma Gandhi's naturopathic physician. My old Parsee friend was then in his early sixties. Short and extremely corpulent, he was clad in flowing white garments and had a full white beard which reached almost to his waist and an abundance of white hair which fell to his shoulders and which, as I knew, he sometimes gathered up and twisted into a Buddha-like topknot. He was an impressive figure. For someone like Terry he was also an intimidating and even an alarming one. In the early fifties, shortly before I met him, he had founded an organization known as the Society of Servants of God. The activities of the Society were conducted in strict accordance with the 'guidance' that he received in meditation. This guidance, Dr Mehta

With Dr Mehta

believed, came directly from God, so that it was to be accepted implicitly and acted upon to the letter. Not to accept the guidance that came for one through the Servant of Servants, as my friend styled himself, was to disobey God, and because one disobeyed God on account of the ego the ego had to be crushed. 'They must be *made* to obey!' I had more than once heard him declare, when members or employees of the Society were unwilling to accept the guidance that had been given to them through him.

In the early days of my acquaintance with Dr Mehta such guidance had come for me, too; but I had declined to accept it, explaining that I was already being guided by the Buddha, through his teachings as recorded in the Buddhist scriptures, and had no need for any other guidance. Eventually, after a good deal of discussion, he had reluctantly conceded that this might be the case, and that I might indeed be 'guided' *in my own way*, (on his lips a rather damning phrase), though he at the same time felt obliged to warn me that the guidance that came from scriptures was much less reliable than that which came directly from God through his chosen instrument, the Servant of Servants. Our respective positions having been thus clarified, something like a friendship developed between Dr Mehta and me. I often stayed with him when I was in Bombay, and at his invitation often lectured on Buddhism under the auspices of the Society of Servants of God. He was also warmly supportive of my work among the followers of Dr Ambedkar. His authoritative, even dictatorial ways with his disciples and dependants notwithstanding, he was fundamentally a very kind man, and over the years I had grown very fond of him. During the week that Terry and I spent as his guests the authoritarian side of his character was very much in evidence, and I soon realized that my sensitive friend was uncomfortable in Dr Mehta's presence. So uncomfortable was he, indeed, that he sometimes found meals at the flat rather an ordeal, and was glad whenever we were invited out to lunch or dinner by other, less intimidating friends of mine.[384]

Fortunately Terry felt quite at home with the newly-converted Buddhists, some of whom were on our doorstep literally within hours of our arrival. The first to appear was Maheshkar, the sociable, enthusiastic, and hyperactive young Maharashtrian who for months together had been my travelling companion and faithful translator, and who, with his future wife, had organized scores, if not hundreds, of the lectures I gave in and around Poona in the late fifties and early sixties. The following night he was translating for me again. According to my diary there was a happy, friendly atmosphere at the meeting, which was held at Worli, in Chawl No. 86. What my diary does not record, and Terry's does, is that the meeting was held *in the corridor* of the chawl, and that he took many pictures and was garlanded. Terry's diary in fact shows that he was struck by much that was familiar to me and of which my own diary therefore makes no mention. Thus it records that most Bombay taxis were 'falling apart', and that at a meeting held in the open outside another chawl, about 150 people attended 'amongst chickens, pigeons, and insects'. At the Hampstead Vihara and the Buddhist Society I was accustomed to lecture under very different conditions: yet it was the same Dharma I was teaching. The entry for the following day speaks of our visiting a 'ramshackle' vihara on the main road and being taken in procession to a chawl and given an elaborate lunch in 'badly smelling quarters – dark and damp. Every doorway decorated with rice paste. Food eaten with hands. Cold rice and cold soup. Four speeches mine included. Garland and flowers received.' Entries for other days make mention of deformed beggars, red bananas, and cows that wandered on the platforms of suburban railway stations and in the streets. On our last day but one in Bombay I gave three lectures, two of them in the evening, and the difference between our respective diary entries illustrates the extent to which Terry was affected by sights which, while they were familiar to me, were totally unfamiliar to him. 'Two lectures – worst conditions so far,' his diary records. 'Moving through narrow alleys between shacks.' My diary simply states: 'At 7.15 went to Worli. Gave lecture on Buddhist Meditation. Gathering slightly restless. Then to Pathan Chawl. Spoke on Five Spiritual Faculties. Good quiet audience.'[385]

In 1966 the term 'culture shock' had not yet been invented, or at least was not yet in general circulation, but there is little doubt that during our week in Bombay, and even subsequently, Terry suffered from that 'feeling of disorientation experienced by a person suddenly subjected to an unfamiliar culture or way of life' that the word signifies. His introduction to India was thus not an easy one, especially as he had to cope not only with culture shock but also with the anxiety he experienced in the presence of Dr Mehta. His diary for these days bears poignant witness to his struggles – struggles of which I was not always cognizant. 'Bit brighter today,' reads one entry. 'I really must make more intense effort and yet inwardly feel very reluctant and experience this void-like apathy.' Sometimes he did manage to make that more intense effort, especially in connection with our meetings in the chawls, at which he was invariably called upon to 'say a few words'. Very much to his astonishment, he found it easier – or at least less difficult – to address a hundred or more poor, mostly illiterate Indian Buddhists than it had been for him, a year earlier, to make a farewell speech to his colleagues at the advertising agency. His speech was translated sentence by sentence (he soon learned to make a few notes on the back of an envelope beforehand), and at the end of each translated sentence there was a burst of applause that encouraged him to launch into the next. The experience of addressing a warmly appreciative audience did a lot to boost Terry's confidence, so that by the time we left Bombay for Dharamsala he was in a more positive emotional state – at least for the time being – than might otherwise have been the case.

With the Dalai Lama

The compound of Swargashram, the Dalai Lama's residence in Dharamsala, was surrounded by barbed wire, and there were soldiers on duty at the entrance, to whom we had to show our passports before being allowed inside. It was not altogether clear whether His Holiness was the honoured guest of the Government of India or its prisoner. At the time of our meeting the Tibetan hierarch was thirty-one, had lived in India as a refugee for seven years, and had not yet visited the West. It was not the first time we had met, meetings having taken place in both 1956 and 1957, when he and the Panchen Lama were in India for the 2,500th Buddha Jayanti celebrations, and subsequently, after his dramatic escape from Tibet in 1959, so that we were reasonably well acquainted already.[386] Unfortunately my diary has no more to say about that Dharamsala meeting than does my letter from India, except that it lasted from 10.20 to 11.15 in the morning, and that besides meditation we discussed 'translation of Tibetan texts etc.'. Afterwards Terry took photographs of us outside, and I noticed how uncomfortable the Dalai

Lama was feeling in the brilliant sunshine while we posed together, how he kept mopping his brow with the corner of his thick maroon robe, and how impatient he was to get back into the cool of the bungalow.

If our diaries are to be believed, Terry was in good spirits during the five days that we spent in the two hill stations. I was all the more surprised, therefore, that for much of the thirty-six-hour journey from Pathankot to Baroda he should have been so very depressed. Perhaps he was unhappy that – as the fine dust covering everything served to remind us – we were on our way back to the filthy, poverty-stricken cities of the plain. Or perhaps he was disappointed that he had not met his *ḍākinī* in the streets of the Dharamsala bazaar or among the shrines of Dalhousie, for, as I well knew, the hope of meeting that unique, miraculous being was never far from my friend's thoughts.

44
AMONG THE NEW BUDDHISTS

In the late fifties and early sixties my work among the new Buddhists – as the followers of Dr Ambedkar who had converted to Buddhism were sometimes called – had lain mainly in Bombay, Nagpur, Poona, Ahmedabad, and Jabalpur. The Ahmedabad Buddhist community was a comparatively small one, and of its adult members only a small proportion were actually practising the Dharma (as distinct from *not* practising Hinduism), while an even smaller number of them were attempting to extend the movement of conversion. Tiny though it was, this little band of youthful activists was divided into factions, and I was obliged to devote part of the time Terry and I spent in Ahmedabad, on our way to Delhi, to settling the various personal differences that had arisen since my last visit. Such differences, and the factionalism to which they so easily led, seemed to be endemic to the Ahmedabad Buddhist community. They had arisen more than once before, and if the activists and their friends did not take the teachings of the Buddha more to heart they would be sure to arise again.

During the five days that Terry and I spent in Ahmedabad on our way back to Bombay all was well, and everyone cooperated to make the visit a success. On our arrival from Baroda, at five-thirty in the morning, we were garlanded, given tea in the station restaurant, and shown the Gujarati handbill announcing my lectures, after which we were taken by taxi to the place where we were to stay. This was the home of Amritlal, a young unmarried railwayman who had once visited

Giving the Refuges and Precepts, Ahmedabad

me in Kalimpong – the only Gujarati Buddhist ever to do so. We were accommodated in a quiet and secluded, if rather stuffy, room, where I proceeded to write letters to friends in Bombay, Nagpur, and England and where we were visited, both before and after lunch, by many people. In the evening I gave my first lecture, when I addressed what my diary describes as 'a good gathering'. After the meeting many people came to Amritlal's place to see me, but as I was suffering from a bad cold and a sore throat, and moreover had not had much sleep the previous night, I insisted, so my diary records, 'on sleeping early'. Terry's two-line diary entry for the day concludes, 'Mice in room. Dung floor.' The mice did not disturb me. As for the dung floor, this was a common feature of an Indian home of the traditional type, a thin layer of semi-liquid dung being smeared over the beaten earth and allowed to dry. I was well accustomed to this form of interior decoration, which sometimes extended to the walls, and in fact rather liked it, as it was both cool to the touch and soothing to the eye. To Terry, of course, a 'dung floor' was a novelty, and in his mind it probably had all sorts of unpleasant farmyard associations.

In the course of the next few days I gave eleven lectures, in a variety of venues and to a variety of audiences. There were lectures in public halls and lectures at crossroads that had been closed to traffic for the occasion, lectures in chawls occupied by workers in the cotton mills, and lectures in the alleys between shacks, as well as lectures in a village outside Ahmedabad and a lecture at the University. The lectures were by no means attended only by Buddhists or potential Buddhists. At the Akhandanand Hall, for example, where I spoke on 'Buddhism and Humanism', there were many Jains in the audience. Like the lecture on 'Buddhism and the Modern World' that I gave at the University three days later, this was an 'English' lecture, that is, it was not accompanied by a running translation into Gujarati, the local language. All my other lectures were of necessity so accompanied, for a high percentage of those who came to hear me, especially the Buddhists, far from being English-educated, were not even literate in their own vernacular. My translator on these occasions was usually Yashodhara, an unmarried schoolteacher of mature years who had sometimes functioned for me in this capacity on my previous visits. She was a remarkable woman. A brahmin by birth, she had not only become a Buddhist but had thrown in her lot, spiritually speaking, with the youthful activists who were attempting to extend the movement of conversion in Ahmedabad and the surrounding area. Being an outsider, in that she came from another community – indeed, from the opposite end of the caste spectrum – she was sometimes able to exert a moderating influence on her faction-prone Ambedkarite colleagues.

Though we were staying at Amritlal's place we did not take our meals there, except for lunch on the day of our arrival. We did not even have breakfast there, arrangements having been made for us to take this meal, as well as our lunch and our afternoon tea, with a different family each day, so that in the course of our visit we saw the inside of more than a dozen Buddhist homes. This arrangement had the double advantage of spreading the expense (and the merit) of entertaining us more widely and of enabling us to have personal contact with as many people as possible. It did, however, mean that we spent a lot of time travelling from house to house. Ahmedabad, then the state capital, was a busy place. More often than not we found ourselves in the midst of a noisy, chaotic stream of motor cars, lorries, scooters, and carts, some of the carts being drawn by bullocks, some by camels, and some by sweating, half naked human beings. On one occasion we were stuck in a traffic jam immediately behind an elephant, and I have a vivid recollection of looking up from the cycle rickshaw in which we were travelling to see the wrinkled hindquarters of the great beast looming directly above me.

The fact that we took our meals in so many different places not only meant that we spent a lot of time travelling; it also meant that we spent a lot of time talking – both to our host and his family and to the friends and neighbours who came to see us after we had eaten. Sometimes, if it seemed appropriate to do so, I delivered a short 'sermon of thanksgiving' in the traditional manner. All this talking did my throat no good, especially as it was in addition to the lecturing I was doing and to the conversations in which I could not help engaging after each lecture, the 'English' ones in particular, when I would be quite overwhelmed by people wanting to speak to me. Nonetheless, I was glad we were able to have personal contact with so many people, and thus to learn something about them and about the difficulties they were having to face. Breakfast at Ganpatnagar, for example, was followed by a discussion with various residents of the locality, among them a Buddhist income tax inspector, in the course of which we had to listen to many complaints about the way in which the Scheduled Castes were discriminated against in matters of employment and education and how they lacked all manner of facilities. As I well knew, the complaints were fully justified, and would have been echoed by the millions of people who belonged to the Scheduled Castes or who had belonged to them prior to their conversion to Buddhism. At the same time I felt that the attitude of these particular complainants was more negative and defeatist, on the whole, than the situation really warranted. I therefore told them that they would have to stand on their own feet, and that they could expect no help from outside India, meaning by 'outside India' the Buddhist countries of Asia.

In between meetings and meals Terry and I managed to do a little sightseeing, most of it on our last day in Ahmedabad. On that day we visited the sixteenth-century Sidi Sayeed Mosque, where we admired the two windows of filigree marble work, the design of which has been described as 'an imitation of twining and interlaced branches, a marvel of delicacy and grace, and finer than anything of the kind to be found in

Agra or Delhi'. A third such window had been removed in the days of the Raj and taken to the Victoria and Albert Museum in London. From the Sidi Sayeed Mosque we went to the Sabarmati Ashram, whence Mahatma Gandhi had once directed the struggle for Indian independence[387] ('surroundings in terribly slovenly condition,' comments my diary), and from there, finally, to the nineteenth-century Hutheesingh Jain Temple, an extensive, rather magnificent structure, the white marble splendours of which testified to the wealth, and piety, of Ahmedabad's sizeable Jain community. The previous day two Jain businessmen had taken us to see a famous Jain scholar-monk, the eighty-seven-year-old Acharya Prem Suri, who lived in a monastery with twelve or fourteen other white-robed monks, most of them small boys. The Acharya himself did not say anything (he may have been observing a vow of silence), but we had nearly an hour's discussion with two or three senior members of the community, one of whom seemed to have read something about Buddhism, including Zen. Before we left they showed us, with understandable pride, the first four volumes of their venerable master's *magnum opus*, a Sanskrit treatise on the Jain doctrine of karma.[388]

Our arrival in Ahmedabad had been accompanied by a certain amount of publicity and it seemed that our departure would be similarly accompanied. On returning to Amritlal's place from the University, where my lecture on 'Buddhism and the Modern World' had been followed by tea with the staff, we found waiting there a reporter from one of the local papers. While he interviewed me, Terry packed, after which we left for the station – in rather a hurry, the interview having delayed us. Amritlal, Yashodhara, and other friends were there to see us off. The train left at six-fifty. Three hours later we had retired to our berths and were asleep.

As we had already spent a week in Bombay, and as I wanted to have at least a week in Poona, as well as to be in Nagpur by the twenty-third of the month, Terry and I passed only one night in the busy commercial capital of India. Having arrived at Bombay Central at five-thirty in the morning, we took a taxi to Dr Mehta's place. At ten o'clock, after I had spent a couple of hours with our host, and written letters and made telephone calls, we walked from Malabar Hill down to Chowpatty, and from there – still following the great curve of the Back Bay – to Marine Drive. It was a fine day, with a breeze blowing off the sea. The Taraporewalla Aquarium falling in our way, we spent half an hour admiring the tropical fish, some beautiful, some grotesque, then took a taxi to the grimy Gothic splendours of the Victoria Terminus. Here we had to queue for two hours before getting reservations on the Deccan Queen for the following afternoon. Relieved to have got them at least, we cashed some travellers' cheques and had lunch at a vegetarian restaurant I knew, by which time my throat was feeling painfully sore and I was quite hoarse. On our arrival back at Dr Mehta's place we found Maheshkar's friend Thorat waiting for us. He had come to take us to Worli, he announced. We were expected there for lunch. Though we knew nothing of this arrangement, owing to some misunderstanding on the part of the organizers – as it later transpired – Terry and I had no alternative but to accompany Thorat all the way to Worli. The result was that shortly after three-thirty we found ourselves sitting down to a traditional Maharashtrian meal in one of the chawls. Commenting on this episode, Terry wrote in his diary, 'T. just about coped. Evident that D. quite positive and determined. T. fearful, retiring, and resistant.' The misunderstanding over lunch was not to be the only one of the day, as we discovered that evening after my lecture on Tibetan Buddhist meditation. I gave this lecture at Theosophy Hall, the Indian headquarters of the United Lodge of Theosophists, speaking, with difficulty, for an hour and a half, after which my voice collapsed completely. It was then that we learned that two meetings had been arranged for us at Worli – an arrangement about which, too, we knew nothing. We went nonetheless. I was unable to speak, but Terry spoke, briefly, as did Bhikkhu Shivalibodhi, an old friend of mine, who happened to be present.

The following morning we did very little, as I could speak only with difficulty and moreover had a slight temperature. By midday, however, I felt better, thanks to a short but refreshing sleep, and we went to have lunch with Hilla Petit, an elderly Parsee friend of mine who lived not far away, on the other side of the Malabar Hill peninsula.[389] In the afternoon, after I had taken a dose of the homeopathic medicine Hilla had prepared for me, Terry and I took a taxi to Marine Drive and from there walked back along the front in the hope of finding something worth photographing. At 4.15 we left for the station, and less than an hour later, having been seen off by Thorat and a number of other friends, we were on our way to Poona. On my previous journeyings to Poona by the Deccan Queen I had invariably bumped into someone I knew, or who knew me, and this time it was no different. As we climbed up into the Western Ghats I was accosted by P. N. Rajbhoj, an opportunistic, publicity-hungry Buddhist MP who had once worked closely with Dr Ambedkar but who was now a member of the Congress Party.

At Poona station Terry and I were met by Maheshkar, his wife Karuna, Amrao, and other old friends of mine, who, as soon as the train stopped, all piled into the carriage and garlanded us. From the train we were taken to the station restaurant for tea, from the restaurant to the booking hall, where we were given a reception, with more garlands and many shouts of 'Jai! Victory!', and from the booking hall to the high school playground where I was to give my first lecture. As I still felt unwell, I spoke for only half an hour. Terry also spoke ('quite well', in his own estimation), after which, the other speeches being over, we were escorted to the Nature Cure Clinic and Sanatorium in Tadiwalla Road, just behind the railway station, where we were to stay, and where, on our arrival at eleven o'clock, Terry and I were warmly welcomed by Dr Mehta's wife Gulbehn.[390]

The Nature Cure Clinic and Sanatorium had been started by Dr Mehta in 1929, when he was in his mid-twenties, and over the years he had built up a clientele that eventually came to include Mahatma Gandhi and a number of other leading nationalist politicians. During the last three years of his life, in fact, the Mahatma had made the institution his home in Poona, staying with his entourage in the bungalow now occupied by Gulbehn, which had been named 'Bapu Kuti' in his memory. Since 1953, the year in which he founded the Society of Servants of God, Dr Mehta had devoted less and less time to naturopathy, though he still saw some of his old patients, and occasionally sent them for rest and recuperation to the Poona institution. By the time I made his acquaintance he had been living in Bombay for some years, and the roomy, high-ceilinged old sanatorium building was virtually empty, so that he was happy for me to use the place as my headquarters whenever I visited Poona. Thus it was that on the occasion of this my latest visit to the city of the Peshwas[391] I came to be staying there once again, this time with Terry, and thus it was that on our arrival at the Clinic that night my friend and I had been warmly welcomed by kind-hearted, hospitable Gulbehn, with whom, over the years, I had come to be quite well acquainted.

Since they had not seen me for two and a half years, my Buddhist friends were naturally anxious to make full use of me during my brief sojourn among them, and anxious, therefore, to arrange as many lectures and other engagements for me as possible. Though I was happy to be of use in this way, for the first three or four days that Terry and I spent among them I was unable to do as much as I would have wished, as I was still feverish and headachy, and felt generally unwell. During that time my friend and I stayed quietly in the big, cool sanatorium, having breakfast and lunch with Gulbehn over at Bapu Kuti, and going out only in the evening, when I gave my lectures. The first of these lectures was 'Buddhism in England'. I gave it in the lane next to Karuna's – or rather her father's – house, and it was accompanied by a running translation into Marathi by Maheshkar, as were all my other Poona lectures except the one I gave the following night at the Western India Club. This was a repeat performance, so to speak, of the one I had given in Ahmedabad on 'Buddhism and Humanism', and was likewise an 'English' lecture. In the course of the next two days I gave four more 'Marathi' lectures, one of them at Yerawada, a suburb of Poona, on 'Buddhism and Ambedkar'. According to my diary, this was a particularly well-organized and well-attended lecture, and my audience was delighted – as Buddhist audiences always were – to hear me speaking about their beloved leader, thanks to whose courage and vision they had been delivered from the 'hell of caste', as he once called it,[392] and led to the feet of the Buddha.

The feverishness and headache left me only on the fifth day of our visit, by which time I was already giving two lectures every evening and Terry and I had started going out a little during the day. One such excursion took us to Poona's leading English bookshop, where Terry bought a copy of the Pelican *Schopenhauer*, another to the Shaniwarwada or 'Saturday Market' square in front of the grim old fortress-palace of the Peshwas, of which there remained little more than the tower-flanked main entrance. The biggest excursion of our visit took us to Kirkhalwadi, a Buddhist village situated about thirty miles from Poona and consisting of a few dozen thatched huts, some of which were in a very tumbledown condition. We were not expected, and our arrival, with Maheshkar, occasioned a good deal of surprise and excitement. The men were working in the fields (it was mid-afternoon, and a fine day), but the colourfully clad women soon emerged from their dark doorways, many of them carrying children, and greeted us, once they had overcome their initial shyness, with evident delight. While Terry took photographs, Maheshkar and I spoke to a few of them, especially one toothless old woman in a green sari, nor were we allowed to leave until we had taken tea in three different huts. It was from villages such as this that tens of thousands of men, over the years, had migrated to the city, partly in order to better themselves economically, but partly, in the case of the then Untouchables, to escape from the virtual slavery of the caste system, which was particularly strong in rural areas.

That evening, shortly after our return from Kirkhalwadi, Gulbehn gave a tea party in our honour, concerning which my diary has the following entry:

> Back to the bungalow [i.e. the sanatorium] by 5. Rested and read. At 6 o'clock tea party. Mother Fiske, Prof. Driver, Alu Driver, Mrs Watchmaker, Mr Rupawate, the Maheshkars, Father Mascarenhas and others. Quite friendly, but long and unnecessary discussion between Alu Driver and Father M. which everyone else found rather tiresome. Father, indeed, seems to have lost his mental grip. Mother Fiske looked rather startled.

Adele Fiske was an elderly Roman Catholic nun from the United States who was doing research into the religious beliefs of the newly-converted Indian Buddhists. She later published a number of useful papers.[393] Of Professor Driver and his wife I do not have even the vaguest recollection. They must have been friends of Gulbehn, and like Mrs Watchmaker they must have been Parsees. (Quite a few Parsee families had adopted English, or English-sounding, surnames, some of them expressive of their ancestral callings.) 'Dada Saheb' Rupawate, a plump, jovial man of about my own age, was a prominent local politician. A Buddhist, and a member of the Republican Party, the party founded by Dr Ambedkar's lieutenants after his death, he later became a member of the Maharashtra State Government, and he remained a friend and supporter of mine all his life. The Maheshkars, of course, were my faithful translator and his short, energetic wife Karuna. They were both only a few years younger than me, and both before and after their marriage, which I had attended and blessed, they had between them organized many of my lectures in and around Poona.

Father Mascarenhas, Goanese by birth and about sixty years of age, was a Roman Catholic priest whose enormous paunch threatened to burst the buttons of his white tropical soutane. I had known him for some years, through our common association with Dr Mehta and the Society of Servants of God, where he was the Christian representative, so to speak (I was the Buddhist representative).[394] He was a learned man, with a penchant for theological speculation that had more than once brought him into conflict with the Church authorities and led, on one occasion, to his being suspended for a while from the exercise of his clerical duties. Now he was in trouble of another kind. As I had learned from Dr Mehta, our old friend had become involved with a local woman, which was why he was currently in Poona and not in Bombay. At the time of Gulbehn's tea party he must have been undergoing considerable emotional stress, which perhaps accounted for the 'unnecessary discussion' (I have forgotten what it was about) with Alu Driver and for the fact that he seemed to have lost his mental grip. He may even have been slightly tipsy, for according to Terry's laconic diary entry for the day there was sherry at the party and the good father may have imbibed a little too freely. No wonder Mother Fiske looked rather startled.

From the tea party Terry and I went straight to Camp[395] for a name-giving ceremony, at which I gave names to more than twenty children of all ages. This engagement was followed by the two lectures of the evening, held at two different venues. My diary conveys something of the flavour of such meetings:

> First meeting held at New Modikhana Vihara, where I presented and installed image 2½ years ago. Spoke on 'Buddhism and Meditation'. Good quiet gathering. Mother F. took photos, but did not stay long. Prof. Driver and Alu Driver stayed for lecture. Second meeting at Bhimpura. Very lively gathering. Religious songs. Spoke on 'Ten Duties'. Good response. Back at bungalow by 11.30.

Despite its name, the New Modikhana Vihara was not a monastery but a simple, one-roomed temple-cum-meeting-place, and the image I had installed was a handsome brass image of the Buddha in *bhūmisparśa* or 'earth-touching' pose which had been presented to me some years previously by a pious old Burmese couple. The 'Ten Duties' were the ten duties of the lay Buddhist, such as observing the precepts of morality, studying the Dharma, and going on pilgrimage to the sites associated with the four principal events of the Buddha's life.

On our last full day in Poona Terry and I did little, as I was again suffering from a sore throat. We had breakfast with Rupawate at his place, I read Plotinus, there was some discussion, in the evening, with the Maheshkars and half a dozen other visitors, and that was about all. For once we were able to retire early, though according to Terry's diary the rats made a lot of noise during the night.

In the morning, after I had seen a few people individually, including an importunate Rajbhoj, Terry and I went with Maheshkar and Karuna to look at a property in Tadiwalla Road which was for sale and which might, they thought, be suitable for a vihara. We then had lunch for the last time with Gulbehn, whom I was not to see again,[396] and shortly afterwards set out for the station, where a few dozen people had gathered to garland us and see us off.

> Left for Nagpur at 8.30 [reads Terry's diary]. Tearful goodbye. Miserable journey. Met by chattering colleague of D. D had to get out of train until midnight. Poor sleep.

The journey was miserable in that (according to my own diary) it was a hot and dusty one that evening and a hot and stuffy one the following morning. The chattering colleague was R. D. Pawar, like Rupawate a local politician, who joined us at Ahmednagar and travelled with us all the way to Nagpur. Plump and voluble, he was the kind of person who finds it difficult to stop talking even when he has nothing to say, and I could see that Terry found his presence in our compartment extremely trying. The reason for my having to get out of the train was that word of my being on it had travelled up the line and at every station there were new Buddhists waiting with garlands in their hands. At three or four stations, indeed, there were so many people that I was obliged not only to get down on to the platform but also to deliver a short speech. In this way I was kept busy until nearly twelve o'clock. The following morning, by contrast, the journey was very tedious. At one-thirty we reached Nagpur. There we were welcomed by my old lawyer friend Kulkarni and others and driven to Kulkarni's place at Dharampath, where we were to stay.

Nagpur occupied a special place in the history of the movement of mass conversion of Untouchables to Buddhism. It was there, on 14 October 1956, that Dr Ambedkar, himself an Untouchable by birth, had inaugurated that movement by reciting the time-honoured formula for 'going for Refuge' to the Buddha, Dharma, and Sangha, together with the five precepts, after a senior Buddhist monk, and then, a few minutes later, personally administering those same Refuges and Precepts to some 400,000 of his followers.[397] Unfortunately, my invitation having failed to arrive in time, I had not been present at the ceremony, but the following month I met Ambedkar in Delhi (it was our third meeting) and although he was then a very sick man, and very tired, he insisted on speaking to me at length about his hopes and fears – mostly fears – for the future of the movement he had started.[398] From Delhi I travelled to Bombay, and from Bombay to Nagpur, as I was eager to make the acquaintance of the new Buddhists, who in fact had invited me to spend a few days with them on my way back to Calcutta and give some lectures. An hour after my arrival in the city came the news of Ambedkar's death. He had died in Delhi, only six weeks after inaugurating the movement of mass conversion to Buddhism. In Nagpur, as in towns and villages throughout central, western, and north-western India, his followers were grief-stricken and, for the time being, completely demoralized. What would they do, now that their great leader was gone? From Nagpur thousands of them left immediately for Bombay, where the funeral was to be held. Those who remained in the city – some 100,000 of them – attended the hastily organized condolence meeting that I addressed that night. Dr Ambedkar was not dead but alive, I assured my sobbing and groaning audience. He lived on in them, and he lived on in them to the extent to which they were faithful to the ideals for which he had, quite literally, sacrificed his life. My words (I spoke for an hour or more) were not without effect. Ambedkar's stricken followers began to realize that it was not the end of the world, that there was a future for them even after their beloved leader's death, and that the future was not devoid of hope. During the next four days I visited practically all the Untouchable localities of Nagpur and made more than forty speeches, besides initiating about 30,000 people into Buddhism. Wherever I went I repeated, in one form or another, the message I had given at the condolence meeting: Ambedkar was not dead and his work – the work of conversion – must continue. By the time I left Nagpur I had addressed 200,000 people, and local Buddhist leaders assured me that my presence at such a critical juncture was a miracle and that I had saved Nagpur for Buddhism.[399] Whether or not this was the case, in the course of those five memorable days I had certainly forged a permanent link with the Buddhists of Nagpur.

Nagpur thus occupied a special place in my life, and I was therefore glad to be back in the city again, glad to be there for the tenth anniversary of Ambedkar's conversion, and glad that Terry and I were staying in the outhouse Kulkarni had built for himself in the yard behind his brother's residence, where I had stayed on all my subsequent visits to Nagpur. On the day of our arrival we had no engagements, but the following day was a busy one. At nine o'clock we were taken to see the Diksha Bhumi or 'Initiation Ground', as the eighteen-acre site of the 1956 mass conversion was called. Thousands of people were already there, many of them having spent the night on the spot. From the Diksha Bhumi we were taken to the Nagpur Central Jail where, Kulkarni translating, I spoke for an hour to a very quiet and attentive audience of about 500 prisoners, many of them Buddhists. After the talk came tea, which was handed round by our escort of 'trusties' (prisoners who were serving life sentences for murder), and there was what my diary describes as 'quite a grand reception'. The rest of the morning was spent at the Diksha Bhumi, where Terry and I went round the area with Kulkarni and a few others, despite the intense heat, and where Terry photographed the huge bust of Ambedkar – fifteen or more feet high with its pedestal – which marked the spot where he had stood and recited the Refuges and Precepts, as well as taking shots of unhygienic-looking tea stalls, turbaned vendors of fried snacks, displays of garish oleographs of politicians, film stars, and Buddhas, and families resting in the shade of the bullock carts that had brought them in from the surrounding villages.

On returning to Kulkarni's place we found Dr M. B. Niyogi, a former Chief Justice of the Nagpur High Court, waiting for us. I had met him a number of times, and knew him quite well. Kulkarni had invited him and several other members and ex-members of the Nagpur bench and bar to lunch, and these very elderly and very distinguished gentlemen all interrupted one another so often, and talked at such cross purposes, that I felt like Alice at the Mad Hatter's tea party[400] and was not sorry when lunch was over and I could spend some time talking with Terry and making a few notes for the lecture I would be giving in a few hours' time.

The meeting celebrating the tenth anniversary of Dr Ambedkar's historic conversion started at seven o'clock, but it was not until eight-thirty that I was called upon to speak. G. S. Talwatkar, of the People's Education Society,[401] translated for me, and I spoke for an hour. Afterwards I was told that 200,000 people were there that night, but as the only illumination came from the floodlights on the stage and the strings of feeble electric bulbs on the periphery of the vast gathering, I could see only a fraction of them. I have no recollection of what I said on the occasion, but I must have spoken about Ambedkar's achievements, about the significance of the movement of mass conversion inaugurated by him, about the importance of actually practising the Dharma, and about the need for unity, it being common knowledge that both the Republican Party and its religious counterpart the Buddhist Society of India had split into a variety of warring factions. Though I do not remember what I said that night, I have a vivid recollection of the vast blackness of the sky, of the faces of the thousands of men and women seated on the ground directly in front of me, and of the evident satisfaction with which my words were received.

The next two days were filled with interviews and visits, one of them to a nearby vihara, as well as two legal tea parties, and a little reading. On the morning of the third day (the fourth since our arrival in Nagpur) Terry and I were escorted to the bus by Kulkarni and a young monk of my acquaintance, and soon after seven o'clock we were on our way to Jabalpur. The journey was a long and bumpy one, in the course of which our 'luxury coach' (as Terry, in his diary, ironically terms the battered old vehicle in which we were travelling) stopped three times for tea and we saw monkeys, vultures, and a good deal of jungle. At two-thirty in the afternoon we reached Jabalpur, where we found a number of local Buddhists waiting at the bus station to receive us and where we spent two nights, one at a hotel and one with Taranath Bhagat and his family, with whom I had stayed once or twice before. During our short stay we were taken to see a vihara that was under construction and a small temple, both of which were picturesquely situated on hilltops on the outskirts of the town. The vihara was the scene of a small function, at which I made a speech, while at the temple I installed an image of the Buddha and gave a short address. Both at the hotel and at Bhagat's place we had many visitors, and though again suffering from a sore throat I was obliged to answer a host of questions. Most of the questions were quite inane, our visitors, with the exception of one bright young man, all being quite dull and unintelligent.

In the afternoon of our second day in Jabalpur Terry and I visited the Railway Hospital, where Bhagat now worked, and met Dr Chetty, the physician in charge, and an Indian Christian nurse married to a Chinese Buddhist. The nurse was evidently a woman of character. She had five children, she told us, and her husband worked in the circus. That evening she came to see us, and we talked with her and others until midnight. At twelve-thirty we left for the station, where she and Bhagat helped us get a two-berth compartment on the Kashi Express, when it at last arrived at two-thirty. We slept until seven, and at four-thirty in the afternoon, after an uneventful journey, reached Varanasi. Half an hour later we were in Sarnath.

45
ON PILGRIMAGE

According to the *Mahāparinibbāna Sutta*, the *sutta* of the 'great passing', the Buddha shortly before his death told Ānanda, his disciple and constant companion, that there were four places the sight of which should arouse emotion in the faithful. These were the place where he was born, the place where he attained supreme Enlightenment, the place where he 'set in motion the wheel of Dharma' or first taught the truth he had discovered, and the place where he finally passed beyond mundane existence.[402] During my years in India I had visited all four sacred sites, now known, respectively, as Rummindei,[403] Bodh Gaya, Sarnath, and Kusinara. The first and second I had visited twice, the third and fourth at least five or six times, so that my memories of both Sarnath and Bodh Gaya were of a composite nature and it was not always possible for me to tell what I had done, or whom I had met, on which visit.

In the case of Sarnath, however, blurred and blended though my memories of subsequent visits may have been, I had a vivid recollection of my first visit to the place – a recollection that was all the more vivid for the experience itself having been, in one important respect, so painful. The year was 1949, the month Vaiśākha (April–May), the hottest month in the Indian calendar. With my friend and companion Satyapriya (Robin Banerjee) I arrived in Sarnath one morning, the pair of us having walked all the way from Varanasi. The reason for our walking there, despite the intense heat, was that we were observing the rule of not handling money and therefore were not in a position to hire a taxi or cycle rickshaw. For the last two years we had been freelance wandering ascetics, living on alms, studying and meditating, and testing in various ways our readiness to take formal ordination as Buddhist monks. Convinced that we were, in fact, now ready, we had travelled from South India, via Bombay, to Sarnath. At Sarnath, we knew, there was a branch of the Maha Bodhi Society of India and a community of Theravādin Buddhist monks, and from these monks we hoped to receive ordination. We were cruelly disappointed. On our arrival, footsore and weary, we were received in an unfriendly, even hostile manner, grudgingly accommodated and fed, and refused ordination with flimsy excuses which, we later discovered, were no better than lies.[404] We were therefore forced to seek ordination elsewhere. But that is another story. During the next fifteen or sixteen years I visited Sarnath a number of times, and in this way came to know the Maha Bodhi Society monks reasonably well. There were five or six of them altogether, only one of whom was Indian, the rest being Sinhalese. Some of them later apologized for the way that they had treated Satyapriya and me. Hindus who only wanted to be financially supported were coming and asking for ordination all the time, they explained, and they could not be too careful. The first to apologize was the Venerable M. Sangharatana, the Maha Bodhi Society's *bhikkhu*-in-charge at Sarnath, who from the first had been less unfriendly than the other members of the little monastic community. Though impulsive to the point of rashness, and far too outspoken for his own good, he was a warm-hearted man, with a stronger feeling for the Dharma than most of his fellow monks, and over the years an increasingly cordial relationship had developed between us.[405]

As it happened, the first person Terry and I met on emerging from the taxi that had brought us to Sarnath and to the door of the Maha Bodhi Society was none other than lean, excitable Sangharatana. He was glad to see me, and at once showed us to our room in the big pink sandstone rest house where we were to stay. After we had settled in, and had taken a stroll in the pleasant, park-like area on the other side of the road, I went and paid my respects to the chief monk. This was the Venerable Sasanasiri, a corpulent, jovial, easy-going man of about sixty who occupied a room on the same floor of the building. I found him lying in bed. He was suffering from high blood pressure, he told me, and the doctor had ordered him to take complete rest. Though he spoke cheerfully, I noticed that his face had an ashen look, and that the monks who were caring for him seemed anxious. One of these monks was quiet, scholarly Dhammaratana, a colleague of mine on the editorial board of the *Maha Bodhi*, who was usually to be found in Calcutta. From him I learned that the Venerable Jagdish Kashyap, with whom I had studied Pāli, Abhidharma, and Logic, was now at Nalanda. This was good news, for I wanted not only to see my old teacher but also to tell him that I had decided that my future lay in the West. Nalanda, in any case, was one of the places Terry and I were planning to visit on our way to Calcutta and, eventually, Kalimpong, the little town in the eastern Himalayas where I had lived for fourteen years – a third of my life.

Terry and I spent nine or ten days in Sarnath, dividing our time mainly between explorations of the extensive archaeological area and expeditions into Varanasi. The principal object of interest in the archaeological area was the still-standing portion of the monolithic column on which was inscribed, in Brahmi letters, the edict in which the emperor Aśoka warns the members of the monastic community against schism. We also circumambulated the massive Dhamekh Stupa, which marked the spot where the Buddha sat to give his first teaching, thus 'setting in motion of wheel of Dharma'; visited the Sarnath Museum; saw the room in the Burmese Temple where I had received my ordination as a *bhikṣu*; and studied the Ajanta-style frescoes in the Mulagandhakuti Vihara, the pink sandstone temple built by Anagarika Dharmapala, the founder of the Maha Bodhi Society. In colourful, chaotic Varanasi there naturally was much more to see, though little or nothing of Buddhist interest or significance, the ancient city having long been a stronghold of orthodox Hinduism.

Like most visitors, we saw the Durga Temple, with its unfriendly mother monkeys, the beautiful, dazzlingly white marble mausoleum of Swami Bhaskarananda, a nineteenth-century Hindu ascetic, and the dusty, dilapidated Bharat Mata Mandir or 'Temple of Mother India', where the object of worship, so to speak, was a huge contour model of the subcontinent. On one occasion we hired a boat and spent a couple of hours being rowed slowly past the famous ghats or bathing places, on the crumbling steps of which brahmin priests sat performing rituals beneath huge, mushroom-like umbrellas, where dead bodies were being cremated, apparently with very little ceremony, where washermen were banging and slapping clothes and beggars soliciting alms, and from the safety of which pilgrims of all ages were taking their ceremonial dip in the sacred, sin-absolving waters. Wedged between the ghats were domed and pinnacled temples innumerable, some of them tilted at such a rakish angle, due to subsidence, that they looked as though they might slip or topple over into the Ganges at any minute. Once we stayed longer in the city than usual, so that by the time we left the moon had risen and we made the journey back to Sarnath by moonlight. It was a full moon, and so bright that Terry tried – unsuccessfully – to take a picture of it through the leaves of one of the wayside bodhi trees.

Most evenings I joined Sangharatana and the other monks for the six-thirty puja, as I was accustomed to do when staying at Sarnath. The puja took place in the sanctuary, as it might be termed, that occupied the far end of the Mulagandhakuti Vihara's single nave and was on a slightly higher level. We sat in a row in front of the white marble image-table, cross-legged, and in order of seniority, with the more senior in ordination on the right and the more junior on the left. Over the years I had moved up along the row, and more often than not there would be more monks sitting on my left than on my right. The puja consisted of the chanting, in Pāli, of the Three Refuges and the verses for offering flowers, lights, and incense, followed by the *Maṅgala*, *Karaṇīyamettā*, and *Ratana Suttas*,[406] and verses invoking the blessings of the Buddha, the Dharma, and the Sangha, as well as of the *devas* or 'shining ones'. I always enjoyed the chanting, especially when Sangharatana was present, for despite his emaciated appearance, his narrow chest, and his ever-troublesome liver, he possessed a magnificent bass voice to which the temple's acoustics did full justice.

The puja concluded with a short period of meditation, the length of which was determined, as was the chanting led, by the seniormost monk. We then sat quietly for a few minutes before dispersing. I always took the opportunity of gazing up at the great golden figure on the image-table, which except for the fact that it was gilded was an exact replica of a fifth-century sculpture in the Sarnath Museum. The Buddha was depicted seated, eyes half closed, and with hands exhibiting the *mudrā* of 'setting in motion of wheel of Dharma'. He had set that sublime wheel in motion – had first taught the truth he had discovered – here in Sarnath. It was at a spot only a few dozen yards away that he had addressed his first five disciples, who initially were unwilling to give him a hearing. These disciples, and the hundreds of others who became his disciples in the years that followed, passed on what they had learned to *their* disciples, they to theirs, and so on. In this way the Buddha's teaching had spread, first throughout the Indian subcontinent, then throughout the rest of Asia. Now, twenty-five centuries after the Buddha's *parinirvāṇa*, that same teaching was beginning to spread – the Dharma-wheel was beginning to roll – from the East to the West. I was part of the process. Having spent twenty years in the East, fourteen of them 'working for the good of Buddhism' in Kalimpong as directed by Kashyap-ji, I was about to return permanently to the West to work for the good of Buddhism there. What form that work would take I did not know. Little did I suspect, sitting there and gazing up at the golden Wheel-Turning Buddha, that there was even then in train a series of events that would have the effect, by the end of the year, of making clear to me what needed to be done.

The laity did not take part in the puja. They sat on the marble floor of the nave listening to the chanting of the monks or, with hands clasped together as though in prayer, recited verses of their own under their breath. Some prostrated themselves from time to time; others chatted quietly, or allowed their eyes to wander to the frescoes depicting episodes in the life of the Buddha that decorated the side walls. Most were pilgrims from the Buddhist countries of South-East Asia, and they came in family groups and accompanied by their own yellow-robed or brown-robed monks who, if there were not too many of them, were sometimes invited to join the resident monks in the sanctuary. More than once, in the course of the week, I was asked to give a talk for their benefit immediately after the puja, which I did in the traditional manner, that is, seated (on a higher level than my auditors), and concluding with the customary blessings. Terry did not always attend the evening puja. He had little interest in ritual, and in any case, during our stay in Sarnath he was often depressed, sometimes quite badly, and did not feel like seeing much of other people.

One evening only one or two of the resident monks turned up for the puja. All the others were with Venerable Sasanasiri, who was seriously ill. The following morning, on returning to the rest house from the deserted refectory, I learned that he had died the previous night, on the way to hospital, his very high blood pressure having resulted in a heart attack. The funeral procession left from the rest house at nine-thirty, exactly twelve hours after the chief monk's death. Before it left, I went along to his room to pay my last respects, and Terry, at Sangharatana's request, took photographs of the body for dispatch to the Sri Lankan papers, afterwards commenting in his diary 'Interesting but macabre.' Several hundred people took part in the procession, which was a colourful affair, including as it did not only the yellow-robed monks on and around the decorated vehicle carrying the corpse but also a number of red-robed Tibetan monks with their drums and other musical instruments, Sinhalese and Burmese pilgrims holding five-coloured Buddhist flags, and students from the Maha Bodhi High School. The cremation took place on a hillock near Sarnath railway station. Soon the flames were leaping up from the pyre and within minutes the heat was so intense that everyone had to withdraw to a distance of a dozen or more yards, especially as it was now midday, and to the heat of the flames there was added the scorching heat of the sun, which blazed down upon the scene from a sky of cloudless blue.

In the afternoon Terry and I went into Varanasi, where we walked along the riverside for a while, bought six rosaries of black seeds, and made up for having had no breakfast and only a very small lunch by treating ourselves to a meal at the Kwality Restaurant.

Besides exploring the archaeological area and going on expeditions into Varanasi, during our stay in Sarnath Terry and I visited the Tibetan gompa and the Ladakhi rest house, neither of which had been there a few years ago. Indeed, since the time of my earliest visits to the place a kind of cantonment had sprung up between the end of the road on which stood the Maha Bodhi Society's rest house and the new railway station. At the Ladakhi rest house I had a pleasant talk with the young monk-in-charge, who turned out to be a relation of Kusho Bakula, the incarnate lama who was present at my *bhikṣu* ordination in 1959.[407] I also met some of the Ladakhi boys who had once spent their summer holidays with me in Kalimpong, having been brought there by Lama Lobzang, their then mentor, another relation of Kusho Bakula's, and who now attended the Maha Bodhi High School. The Tibetan gompa and the Ladakhi rest house were not the only recent additions to the attractions and amenities of Sarnath. There was also a open-air tea shop. Terry and I patronized it more than once, sitting at one of the little tables, sipping our strong, sweet Indian tea, and contemplating the passing scene. At other tables sat Buddhist pilgrims of different nationalities, middle-class Hindu day trippers from Varanasi and, occasionally, a Western tourist or two. Once we saw four or five American hippies, one of them a woman with a baby. Long-haired, emaciated, and half naked, and seemingly under the influence of drugs, they moved mechanically from table to table soliciting alms. Some of the Indians they approached were evidently shocked to see white people begging, and gave, when they did give, as much out of embarrassment as generosity. For my part, I felt sorry for the poor hippies, the first I had seen. They did not look very happy, and though I could understand their rejection of conventional values, a rejection soon to become widespread among young people in the West, I also saw that because of their inability to replace those values by real ones they had lost their way and were simply drifting.

Though there was much for us to do and to see at Sarnath, Terry and I did not forget our friends in England. Many letters and postcards had been sent from Ahmedabad and other places along the way, and in Sarnath we wrote more of them than ever. Terry wrote to his parents, and to Vivien, Alan, Viriya, and other friends. I wrote to Thien Chau, Viriya, and Francoise, to my mother, to Maurice and Ruth Walshe, to each of the Three Musketeers, to Christmas Humphreys, and to sundry other members of the Sangha Association and the Buddhist Society. I also wrote to our hosts and other friends in Bombay, Ahmedabad, Poona, and Nagpur, thanking them for their hospitality and cooperation, as well as to friends I was expecting to meet in Bodh Gaya, Calcutta, and Kalimpong, alerting them to my impending arrival with Terry. Among those in Kalimpong to whom I wrote was Śramaṇera Thubden, one of the two young Tibetans whom I had left in charge of the Triyana Vardhana Vihara. He was of a very serviceable disposition, and as soon as he heard I was in Sarnath he came and joined me there in order to be of assistance, arriving from Calcutta two days before Terry and I were due to leave for Bodh Gaya.

The following day there was a ceremonial food-offering to the monastic order in memory of Venerable Sasanasiri. About thirty Theravādin *bhikkhus* were duly fed, and about fifty Tibetan monks, including Thubden. Among the *bhikkhus* who happened to be in Sarnath that day there were several from Thailand. One of them, Sukitti by name, was known to me, and after the meal I invited him and his companions to my room, where we talked for a while about the progress of Buddhism in the West.

On the morning of our last day in Sarnath Terry took a few pictures, we had our last cup of tea at the open-air tea shop, and I had a long talk with Sangharatana and Dharmarakshita, the only Indian member of the Sarnath monastic community. Both men were very worried, especially Sangharatana. For the last year or more the Varanasi-based Hindi press had been conducting against the Maha Bodhi Society monks, and against Sangharatana in particular, a campaign of systematic abuse and vilification. Hardly a day passed without allegations being made by one or other of the numerous Hindu-owned and Hindu-edited dailies and weeklies. What those allegations were Sangharatana did not say, but knowing the depths to which the vernacular press was capable of sinking I did not need to ask. In recent weeks the campaign had reached such a pitch that the Maha Bodhi Society's governing body in Calcutta, fearing that the organization's reputation and standing were being jeopardized, had started putting pressure on Sangharatana to leave Sarnath. He did not want to leave Sarnath, he told me passionately, almost in tears, but it was beginning to look as though he would be forced to do so. When I left for Bodh Gaya that afternoon, with Terry and Thubden, it was therefore with a feeling of sadness on Sangharatana's account and with the reflection that, now as in the Buddha's day, in their efforts to retard or roll back the wheel of Dharma Māra and his agents would stop at nothing.

In Bodh Gaya we stayed at the rather splendid Thai temple, built by the Thai government in traditional style a few years earlier. I had stayed there once or twice before, and was acquainted with several of the resident monks. Though I had not visited Bodh Gaya so often as Sarnath, my memories of the former, too, were of a composite nature, and I had a distinct recollection of only two visits. Naturally my first visit, which took place in the winter of 1949–50 in the company of Venerable Sangharatana, was one of these. On that occasion I had been deeply moved, and felt like bursting into a paean in celebration of the beauties of the great pilgrimage centre, as I actually did long afterwards when writing about the visit.[408] The other visit of which I have a distinct recollection took place about ten years later. I was travelling with Bhikkhu Vivekananda, my closest friend among the Thai monks,[409] and we had taken a cycle rickshaw from Gaya station to Bodh Gaya. We did not reach our destination until after midnight and found the place completely deserted. Even the roadside boutiques were closed and a profound silence reigned. As we neared the Maha Bodhi Temple, the central tower of which was silhouetted against the starry sky, to our astonishment we saw that in every niche of the great building, as well as on the numerous votive stupas by which it was surrounded, a little oil lamp was burning. There must have been thousands of lamps. So tranquil was the scene that it was not difficult to believe they had been placed there in worship of the Buddha not by any human agency but by the invisible hands of *devas*.

At the Thai temple a stricter discipline prevailed than at the Maha Bodhi Monastery in Sarnath. *Bhikkhus*, novices, and laymen were all rigidly separated. They were accommodated separately, and ate separately. This meant that Terry and I did not see each other at meals or in the evening. The rest of the day we passed together as usual, circumambulating the temple and paying our respects to the bodhi tree, to the *vajrāsana* or 'diamond throne' on which the Buddha gained Enlightenment, and to the life-sized image of the Master that dominated the gloomy, candlelit inner shrine. As it was winter, and the pilgrimage and tourist season was in full swing, the sacred site was a crowded and sometimes noisy place. Indeed, it was much noisier and more crowded than I remembered it as having been on any of my previous visits. Not only were there hundreds more pilgrims and tourists but in the interval many more boutiques and stalls had sprung up. During the two days that we were in Bodh Gaya Terry and I therefore spent less time in and around the Maha Bodhi Temple than on the shores of a nearby lake in which there grew many water-lilies. While Terry took photographs I contemplated the pink blossoms that rose, here and there, from among the dark green leaves. According to the scriptures the Buddha, shortly after his Enlightenment, had 'seen' such a lake – not, indeed, of pink water-lilies but of blue, red, or white lotuses. Some of the lotuses he saw throve in the water without coming out of it, some rested on the surface of the water, and some, coming right up out of the water, stood clear of the water, unwetted by it. So seeing, the scriptures relate, he saw

> beings with little dust on their eyes and with much dust on their eyes, with keen faculties and dull faculties, with good qualities and bad qualities, easy to teach and hard to teach, and some who dwelt seeing fear in the other world and blame as well.

Thus seeing, he decided not to remain silent, as hitherto he had been inclined to do, but rather to communicate the truth he had discovered. The Doors of the Deathless were now wide open, and those who heard him had only to put forth their faith.[410] Perhaps it was while he was walking or sitting on the shores of this very lake that the Buddha had decided to teach.

The Thai temple was not the only new building in Bodh Gaya. Besides the Maha Bodhi Society's modest rest house several other temples and monasteries had been erected there in recent times, that is to say since the restoration of the site by a British archaeologist towards the end of the nineteenth century.[411] One of these was the Tibetan gompa, the horizontal lines of which were in striking contrast to the more vertical lines of its colourful Thai neighbour. Here we met a lama who happened to know me, and were amused to see that in front of one of the images in the main chapel there had been placed for the enlightenment of tourists a sign which read 'GOD BUDDHA'. We also visited the Samanvaya ashram built ten years earlier by Vinoba Bhave, the veteran follower of Mahatma Gandhi, in order to 'increase the importance of Bodh Gaya in the eyes of the world'.[412] At this institution we met Munindra Barua, a practitioner of 'insight meditation', whom I had known since 1949 and with whom I had had more than one lively discussion about the merits of this controversial new Burmese technique. With him there were two Western novices, Yasa and Sariputta by name, the one German, the other Swiss. The pair had come to see me in Bombay and told me on that occasion that they had spent seven years in the East and that the experience had proved a disappointing one. Since then they had visited Kalimpong and were now, apparently, on pilgrimage in Bodh Gaya before finally returning to Europe.

Back at the Thai temple I talked about meditation with my room-mate and had a long discussion with the Lord Abbot, as he was styled, about the progress of Buddhism in England. I must have mentioned that many English Buddhists were vegetarians, for in the course of our exchange it transpired that the Lord Abbot was a decided opponent of vegetarianism, both the principle and practice of which he clearly regarded as being very unbuddhistic. His attitude did not really surprise me, for I knew that the vast majority of Thai monks were inveterate meat-eaters, and would go to any lengths of rationalization to justify their fondness for pork and chicken. At the Thai temple itself even the simplest dishes were mixed with meat, so that whether at breakfast or at lunch both Ekkapanno – the temple's sole resident vegetarian – and I found it difficult to get enough to eat. Since the Lord Abbot was senior to me in ordination, and I was moreover a guest, I made no attempt to defend the cause of vegetarianism, especially as I knew that in any case few Thai monks were open to conviction on the subject.

My most interesting encounter was with Venerable Dhammajoti, one of the Maha Bodhi Society monks who had been so unwilling to ordain Satyapriya and me all those years ago. Terry and I came across him in the course of one of our circumambulations. He was performing a puja beneath the bodhi tree, and had with him a small Sinhalese boy. The boy was a medium, Dhammajoti explained, and the late Anagarika Dharmapala, who had been reborn in one of the higher, heavenly worlds, spoke through him. Anagarika Dharmapala was, of course, the founder of the Maha Bodhi Society, and he had spent much of his life trying to wrest ownership of the Bodh Gaya temple from the mercenary Hindu *mahant* whose predecessors had gained possession of the site after it was sacked by the Muslim invaders.[413] Though he may indeed have been reborn as a *deva*, and though I did not altogether disbelieve in the possibility of mediumship, the idea of the *anagārika* communicating with his disciples in such a manner was somehow distasteful to me and I found it difficult to accept Dhammajoti's claim.

During our stay in Bodh Gaya Terry was consistently cheerful, and he remained cheerful at least for the next two or three days, in the course of which we concluded our pilgrimage to the sacred sites by visiting Rajgir and Nalanda. At Rajgir we saw the caves associated, respectively, with Mahākaśyapa, the most ascetic of the Buddha's disciples, and with the so-called First Council. We also climbed to the top of the Vulture's Peak, where according to tradition the Buddha had revealed the *White Lotus Sūtra*, one of the most important Mahāyāna scriptures. At Nalanda we explored the extensive and immense remains of the great Buddhist monastic university, visited the museum, and talked with the students and professors of the university's modest modern successor, the Nalanda Pali Institute, founded by Venerable Kashyap in the previous decade. Kashyap-ji himself was not at the Institute when Terry and I arrived, but he came some hours later, and that evening and the following morning my old teacher and I had a long talk. In the course of the talk he gave his blessing to my plan of returning permanently to the West and working for Buddhism there. He gave it all the more readily for his being very disappointed with conditions in India, where little remained of the idealism that had inspired the Independence movement, and for his being pessimistic about the future of the Dharma in the land of its birth. For my own part, I was glad to have seen Kashyap-ji again, and glad to have received his blessing as I entered upon the next stage of my life and work as a Buddhist.

Thirty-six hours later, having returned to Bodh Gaya for the night, my friend and I, accompanied by Thubden, left Gaya for Calcutta at eight-thirty in the evening by the Dun Express. Our little party reached Howrah station on the morning of 13 November, exactly twelve hours after leaving Gaya. Soon we were in a taxi and on our way to the Maha Bodhi Society's headquarters in College Square, where we were welcomed by my old acquaintance Venerable Jinaratana who, like Sarnath-based Sangharatana, was one of the society's two joint secretaries.

46
EDITORIAL INTERLUDE

Anagarika Dharmapala had started the *Maha Bodhi* in 1892, a year after founding the Maha Bodhi Society.[414] I was invited to join the Editorial Board in 1953, and since then had been virtually in charge of the magazine.[415] Normally I edited it from my hermitage in Kalimpong, the Society having agreed to this arrangement, though I had to bring out some issues in the course of my increasingly lengthy lecture tours among the new Buddhists. I also went down to Calcutta each year in order to edit the special Vaiśākha number of the journal, which was three or four times bigger than the average monthly number and contained, more often than not, articles by such distinguished Buddhist authors as Lama Govinda and Dr Conze. This visit invariably took place during April and May, that is, at the height of the hot season, when Calcutta could indeed be termed the City of Dreadful Heat, as well as the City of Dreadful Noise. Many were the days I had spent proof-reading in my room on the second floor of the headquarters building, with the perspiration trickling down my body and falling in great drops from my forehead on to the galleys spread out on the table before me.[416] This time, however, I was visiting the city not at the height of the hot season but in the middle of the so-called cold season. Though the weather was still hot by English standards at least during the day, it was not uncomfortably so, and Terry and I were able to get out and about without experiencing any discomfort on account of the heat.

My acquaintance with Calcutta went back to 1945, when I was still in the army, and when a friendly Hindu monk had taken me on a tour of some of the city's religious and cultural institutions, including the Maha Bodhi Society's headquarters in College Square.[417] Since then I had visited the sprawling former metropolis many times, especially after taking on the editorship of the *Maha Bodhi*, and had come to be familiar with the place. Indeed, I had grown quite fond of it, despite the heat and noise and congestion, and even had a few favourite haunts to which I was now soon taking Terry. Prominent among these favourite haunts of mine were the well-stocked English language bookshops in College Street, Chowringhee, and Park Street, all of which my friend and I visited more than once in the course of our ten days in Calcutta. We also spent more than one pleasant half hour poring over the contents of the second-hand bookstalls on the other side of the Square, where in past years I had picked up more than one bargain. Naturally I made several purchases. For Terry I bought Adler's *Understanding Human Nature* and Husserl's *Phenomenology and the Crisis of Philosophy*,[418] and for myself David Lack's *Evolutionary Theory and Christian Belief*, Julian Huxley's *The Living Thoughts of Darwin*, and George Bernard Shaw's *Back to Methuselah* sequence, the lengthy preface to which has been described as the wittiest summary of the Darwinian controversy ever written.[419] The reason for my wanting to read up on the subject of evolution was that earlier in the year I had given a lecture on 'Evolution – Lower and Higher', in which I sought to situate the Buddhist spiritual path within a broader, 'evolutionary' context, and this line of thought I wanted to pursue further. In 1969, indeed, two years after my return to England, I was to give a series of eight lectures under the title 'The Higher Evolution of Man'.

While Terry and I were getting out and about in the city, sometimes on foot, sometimes taking advantage of the crowded two-car trams, the little printing press round the corner was hard at work on the joint September-October number of the *Maha Bodhi*, with the result that from the fourth or fifth day after our arrival I was spending time correcting page proofs. 'Many mistakes,' my diary comments tersely. I also became drawn into some of the activities that were taking place at the headquarters building, as well as in the Sri Dharmarajika Vihara, immediately behind which the building was situated. Besides attending, in my editorial capacity, a meeting of the Finance Committee, I gave a lecture on 'Buddhism in England', spoke at the reception given in honour of the Crown Prince of Laos, and took part in the *kaṭhina* or 'difficult' ceremony that was held in the shrine-room of the Vihara. The *kaṭhina* or 'difficult' ceremony (there were various explanations of why it was so called) was the ceremony at which the laity offered fresh robes to those monks who had observed the *vassāvāsa* or rains-residence, and despite the fact that I had not observed it that year I, too, was given robes. As the lay people offering the robes were all from Calcutta's rather Hinduized Bengali Buddhist community, and as the gathering contained a large number of women and children, the ceremony was a noisy, disorganized affair, and my diary, with its customary succinctness, characterizes it as having been 'a shambles'.

Venerable Jinaratana attended the *kaṭhina* ceremony as well as the Crown Prince's reception, but otherwise I saw little of him. As usual he was busy, but I noticed not only that he seemed pleased with himself but also that he was much friendlier than before. I thought I knew the reason for this. An ambitious man, he had long hoped to succeed Devapriya Valisinha as general secretary of the Society, even plotting and intriguing to this end, and it now appeared that his hopes were about to be fulfilled. Amiable, contentious Devapriya-ji was lying in hospital,[420] a stroke having left him paralysed, and Jinaratana had been appointed acting general secretary by the Society's governing body. Jinaratana's only rival for the general secretaryship was Sangharatana, who like Devapriya-ji was a personal disciple of Anagarika Dharmapala; but my impulsive, warm-hearted friend was under a cloud and was soon to be banished to one of the Society's smaller, more remote centres. Four or five days after my arrival Devapriya-ji was brought back home from the hospital to his room on the second floor of the headquarters building. He was a pitiable sight, able to make only a few inarticulate noises, and I could do no more than sit with him in silent sympathy. His eyes had a tragic, haunted look, and it was impossible to tell what he was thinking and feeling as he lay there. On the day I left he was a little better, and while Terry finished packing I was able to talk with him and say goodbye. Nevertheless it was evident that he did not have long to live and that Jinaratana would soon be occupying the position he had coveted ever since I knew him. 'Within two years I shall be general secretary of the Society,' he had assured Satyapriya and me back in 1947.[421] In the event it had taken him not two years but twenty to reach his goal, but at last his hour had come, or was about to come, and it was not surprising that he should look pleased with himself.

There were few visitors to the headquarters building during our stay, and fewer still to the room Terry and I occupied on the second floor. Our first visitor was from the CIB. He came to see my passport but for some reason did not ask to see Terry's. Two days later came another reminder that my arrival in Calcutta had not gone unnoticed by the authorities. It came in the form of a visit from a certain Mr Gupta, a senior officer of the Central Intelligence Bureau whom I had met once or twice and who in Indian terms was therefore a friend. Presumably to indicate that the visit was a purely social one, he came not alone but with his wife and child, though I knew that a man in his position was never really off duty. 'A rather inconclusive, desultory talk,' my diary records. 'Told him about Veronica's letter to Jinaratana.' Veronica had left for India at the beginning of June, shortly before Terry and I left for Greece. She was now in Kalimpong and her letter told a strange story. A man from what she called 'the military court' had not only accused her of being an American spy but had questioned her repeatedly about me, saying that I had been asked to leave Kalimpong and was unwelcome there, as were all foreigners! I had not been asked to leave Kalimpong, as Gupta was certainly aware, and he promised to investigate and let me know who was responsible for spreading the rumour. The following morning I received a letter from the little witch myself. It contained the disquieting news that she had been so shamefully treated in Kalimpong – apparently by the authorities – that she was leaving for New Delhi and would be contacting the UK High Commission. I therefore rang Gupta, who came to see the letter the following day – this time on his own.

Veronica's letter was not the only letter I received in Calcutta, nor was it the only one to contain disquieting news. Though in the course of our journey across the subcontinent I had not heard from any of our friends in England, on our arrival in Calcutta Terry and I found a small pile of letters waiting for us, and others soon followed. Among them there were letters from Viriya and Francoise. Maurice Walshe and George Goulstone were trying to prevent my return to the Hampstead Buddhist Vihara, they both informed me. The news was not only disquieting but surprising, and all the more disquieting for being surprising. Neither Walshe nor Goulstone had given me the least reason to think that they were dissatisfied with my teaching or that they no longer wanted me to be the incumbent of the Vihara. Maurice had been present at the reception at which members and friends of the Sangha Association had said farewell to me on the eve of my departure. Like them, he had not only wished me a safe journey and a happy reunion with my teachers and friends in India, but had also made it clear that he looked forward to seeing me again in four months' time. What had induced him and Goulstone to change their minds – if they indeed had changed them in the way that Viriya and Francoise believed and were not simply giving expression to a passing discontent with the way I had been running the Vihara? As I well knew, Maurice was subject to irrational outbursts in which he said things he afterwards regretted, while under the influence of his morning tipple Goulstone sometimes talked rather loosely. Whatever the explanation might be, a cloud had appeared on the horizon. It was a small cloud, but as Terry and I prepared to leave for Kalimpong we wondered what further news awaited us there.

Before we could actually leave we were obliged to have one more contact with officialdom, though this time we went to it rather than having it come to us. The previous day Terry had gone to the security control with Thubden to collect the permit that would allow him to cross the Inner Line[422] and stay in Kalimpong for a week (my own residential permit was still valid), but owing to a confusion about the dates it had not been given to him. On our way to Sealdah Station, therefore, we called at the office and the permit was issued immediately. Only then were the three of us free to leave for our destination in the foothills of the Himalayas.

47
FRIENDS, TEACHERS, AND A LETTER FROM LONDON

Kalimpong was situated 4,000 feet above sea level. Here the air was thinner and clearer than in the plains, and the sky a deeper, darker blue. On most days of the year except during the rainy season one could see, high above the foothills to the north-west, the dazzlingly white shape of Mount Kanchenjunga, the second highest peak in the Himalayan Range. I had lived in Kalimpong for fourteen years, ever since the memorable day when Kashyap-ji had left me there with the parting injunction to stay and work for the good of Buddhism. During that time I had become an accepted part of the cultural and religious life of the cosmopolitan little town. Now I had come to say goodbye. I had come to say goodbye to my friends and teachers, some of whom I might never see again. I had come to say goodbye to my hillside hermitage, with its row of Kashmir cypresses, its flowerbeds and terraces, its hundred orange trees, its bamboo grove, and its solitary mango tree. I had come to say goodbye to the shrine-room where I had meditated for so many hours, to the study-cum-bedroom where I had started writing the first volume of my memoirs, and to the veranda up and down which, during the rainy season, I had paced deep in reflection. I had come to say goodbye to Kalimpong – goodbye to Mount Kanchenjunga and its snows.

But though I had come to say goodbye, my 'homecoming' was in many ways a joyful one. The first to welcome me back to the Triyana

Vardhana Vihara, or Monastery Where the Three Ways Flourish, were Hilla Petit and Maurice Frydman, who had been staying there for the last few days. Hilla was the elderly Parsee friend with whom Terry and I had had lunch in Bombay, and diminutive, big-headed Maurice was her long-term house-guest. I had first met the oddly assorted pair in Gangtok, when they were holidaying with our common friend 'Apa Saheb' Pant, the then Political Officer of Sikkim, and in later years I had more than once stayed with them at their comfortable Bombay flat. Both were keen followers of J. Krishnamurti, and soon Maurice and I were deep in one of our usual rather inconclusive discussions as to whether Truth was really a 'pathless land' that could be approached only by way of 'choiceless awareness'. Not that I had much time for such discussions that morning – at least not as much as Maurice probably would have liked. There were letters to be opened, other friends to be seen.

One of the first letters to be opened was from the English Sangha Trust. It was dated 1 November and was signed by George Goulstone in his capacity as one of the Directors of the Trust. After assuring me in the most fulsome terms of the Trust's deep appreciation of my services to the Dharma in England, he went on to inform me that in the opinion of the Trust and my fellow Order members my long absences from the Hampstead Buddhist Vihara, together with what he described as my extramural activities, were not in accordance with the Theravāda's high standards of discipline and ethics. Moreover, I had not comported myself in a manner fitting the religious office that I held in the Order. The Trust had therefore decided to seek elsewhere for an incumbent of the Vihara. As my work in India was so dear to my heart, the letter continued blandly, I might think that my allotted task was to remain and serve Buddhism in the East. Should I, on careful reflection, consider that my work lay in the East, this would be acceptable as a reasonable ground for my resignation, and notification to this effect would be made to the Buddhist authorities in the West. Should I not feel disposed to take this step, the trustees would feel regretfully obliged to withdraw their support from me. In so doing, they felt sure of having the agreement of the Sangha authorities in England.

'Do you know what this means?' I asked Terry, when I had finished reading the letter. 'It means a new Buddhist movement!' The words sprang spontaneously from my lips. It was as if the Trust's letter, coming as it did like a flash of lightning, had suddenly revealed possibilities that had hitherto been shrouded in darkness or perceived only dimly. Though I had long felt that the Buddhist movement in Britain might need a fresh impetus, and had even discussed with the Three Musketeers and Viriya the feasibility of my giving lectures and holding classes outside the orbit of the Hampstead Vihara and the Buddhist Society, I had certainly never considered the possibility of my taking a step so radical as that of starting a new Buddhist movement, whether in Britain or anywhere else. But I now saw that a new Buddhist movement was what was really needed, and that the Trust's letter had opened the way to my starting it. The movement I was to found some months later may have been born in London, but it was conceived there in Kalimpong on 24 November 1966, at the moment when I addressed to Terry those six fateful words.

Yet clearly as I saw that there would be a new Buddhist movement in Britain, I had no idea what form that movement might take. Nor did I need to have any idea. My immediate concern was with the reasons alleged by the Trust for their wanting to replace me as incumbent of the Hampstead Buddhist Vihara. A number of points struck me in this connection. There was the claim that my fellow Order members (who were they?) shared the Trust's opinion that my conduct had been unethical. What evidence was there that they really did share that opinion? According to the Vinaya or Monastic Code a monk could not be charged with an offence *in absentia*, much less charged, tried, and sentenced as the Trust was actually doing in my case.[423] He had to be charged face-to-face at a formal assembly of the monks. Either the Trust's claim was false or my fellow monks had acted in direct contravention of the Vinaya. In any case, the Trust's charges against me were couched in very general terms. What did they mean by extramural activities, and in what way had I failed to comport myself in a fitting manner? As for my long absences from the Vihara, there had been only one such long absence, when Terry and I were away travelling in Italy and Greece. Before we left Walshe and others had assured me that I deserved a holiday, though a 'holiday' was not quite what I had in mind. Moreover, the trustees seemed to have forgotten that in accepting their invitation to visit England I had stipulated that my mornings should be free for literary work and that, when this proved impracticable, far from minding I had gladly accepted the new situation. Finally, the Trust had overlooked the fact that on the eve of my departure from England I had promised my friends and supporters that I would be returning in four months' time. In suggesting I might on reflection consider that my work lay in the East they were proposing not only that I should break my word but that I should cover up the fact that I was breaking it with the downright lie that I had changed my mind. So much for the Theravāda's high standards of discipline and ethics!

Such were the points that occurred to me as I read the Trust's letter. They were all points which would have to be made, I thought, when I replied to Goulstone. But much as I felt like replying immediately, I decided not to do so. Better to wait a few days, and reply when I had had time to think things over and consult with Terry. Meanwhile, there were friends to be visited. Having finished reading my mail I took the rough track up the hillside that led from the Lower to the Upper Cart Road and thence, eventually, to Chakhung House. The modest bungalow so named was the residence of the Kazi Lhendup Dorje-Khangsarpa of Chakhung, a leading politician of Sikkim, and his formidable European wife. I had known them since 1957, the year of their marriage, rather late in life, in New Delhi. The Kazini had come bringing from a common friend at the UK High Commission a letter of introduction in which he asked me to help her should she meet with any difficulties in Kalimpong. She did meet with difficulties and I did help her, and this had led to the development of a friendship between the Kazi and Kazini and me. Though her husband was a leading player in the politics of the tiny Himalayan principality (he became Chief Minister some years later), the Kazini herself was not openly involved in them, but instead pulled strings behind the scenes, maintained contact with a variety of intelligence agencies, and was an unfailing source of information and gossip.[424] During my absence they had kept an eye on the Vihara for me, making sure that Lobsang Norbu and Thubden kept the place clean and tidy and aired my books from time to time, especially during the rainy season, when they were apt to become mildewed. Both were in when I called, and we had a happy meeting. I gave them their presents (the Kazini's was a political biography she had wanted), heard all the news, and stayed for lunch, and it was not until late afternoon that Kazi left for a political meeting in Gangtok and I for the Vihara and further inconclusive discussion with Maurice. That night I slept in the shrine-room as Hilla was occupying my own quarters. Thus passed my first day back in Kalimpong.

Hilla and Maurice left after breakfast taking with them for posting in Bombay the letters I had written first thing that morning. I did not

The Kazi and the Kazini

want to post them in Kalimpong, since they would then be read by the local branch of the Central Intelligence Bureau, as were all letters to and from foreigners living in the town, and might therefore take a long time to reach their destination. Besides writing to Gerald Yorke and Jack Ireland I sent to the *New Statesman* an advertisement to the effect that I would be returning to England as planned and continuing my lectures on Buddhism. Hilla and Maurice had no sooner left than I received a visit from Durga and Nardeo, two young Nepali friends who had once studied English with me. Durga was particularly close to me, and had more than once stayed at the Vihara while I was away on one of my preaching tours.[425] After I had talked for a while with the two young men, Terry and I went to see Dhardo Rimpoche, on the way stopping first at Chakhung House (Terry did not take to the Kazini, nor she to him) and then at the Frontier Office where I was given a cordial reception by Moitra, the Frontier Inspector, and his staff and where we obtained the application forms for a one-month extension of Terry's Inner Line permit.

Dhardo Rimpoche was an eminent *tulku* or 'incarnate lama' who had lived in Kalimpong since 1950. In 1954 he had started the Indo-

Tibet Buddhist Cultural Institute, under whose auspices he was soon running an orphanage and school for Tibetan refugee children. I was associated with these projects from the beginning and this had led to the development of a friendship based on mutual respect and liking and on the fact that we were both working, in our different ways, for the advancement of Buddhism. Our friendship was deepened in 1956, the year of the 2,500th Buddha Jayanti, when with fifty-odd other Eminent Buddhists from the Border Areas, as we were styled, the Rimpoche and I went on pilgrimage to the principal Buddhist holy places as guests of the Government of India. During those nine or ten days we saw much more of each other than usual. Indeed at times we were in each other's company uninterruptedly for days together. I do not know what kind of impression I made on the Rimpoche during this period of closer contact, but the impression he made on me certainly served to reinforce the very positive one I had already formed of him. Besides being always mindful and alert, in his dealings with others – fellow pilgrims, Indian officials, and railway staff – he was invariably kind,

Kalimpong, with Dhardo Rimpoche and Terry

patient, and good-humoured and, in short, exhibited all the qualities of a true tulku.[426] To such an extent was this the case, that I eventually came to revere him as a living bodhisattva, so that when I felt ready to give formal expression to my acceptance of the bodhisattva ideal by taking the bodhisattva ordination it was naturally Dhardo Rimpoche whom I asked to be my preceptor. He had given me the ordination in 1962, thus from a friend becoming a teacher, though without ceasing to be a friend.[427] While I was away he had moved his Institute, together with its orphanage and school, to their new home at the edge of the lower bazaar, and it was to this new home, on the other side of the saddleback on which the town was situated, that Terry and I made our way from the Frontier Office. Dhardo Rimpoche received us with his usual cordiality, and I presented him with the maroon and gold table clock I had bought for him in Zurich. Though he had aged a little, his eyes still sparkled with intelligence and good humour, and I saw that Terry was regarding him with a mixture of curiosity and respect. As was his custom when at home, Dhardo Rimpoche wore only a maroon monastic 'skirt' and a sleeveless Chinese style shirt of orange silk so that his arms were bare. After he and I had talked for a while and Terry had been properly introduced and his background explained, it was agreed that Terry and I should return next day and that my friend should take the Rimpoche's photograph. The following afternoon, therefore, we saw the Institute again, and Terry took photographs of the Rimpoche seated on his elevated Dharma seat, wearing full monastic dress, and with his *dorje* and bell on the table before him.

A few days later Terry photographed the children of the school, of whom there were a hundred or more of all ages. Many of them were poorly clad, but they all looked healthy and well cared for, and it was evident that their relationship with the Rimpoche was a very happy one. Sherab Nangwa, an elderly Tibetan whom I had ordained as a Theravādin novice, was present on this occasion, and when Terry and I took Dhardo Rimpoche back to the Vihara for lunch he accompanied us. The weather had been cloudy that morning, but in the afternoon it was bright and sunny, and after lunch the four of us were able to sit out in the garden. Before leaving the Rimpoche performed, in the shrine-room, a short ceremony of purification and blessing for the benefit of the Vihara and its occupants, scattering rice and ringing his ritual bell as he did so. In the course of the next few weeks he came to see me three or four times, and I visited him still more frequently, sometimes with Terry, but more often on my own. We spent much of our time together working on the translation of a Tibetan *sādhana* text entitled 'The Stream of the Immortality-Conferring Nectar of the Esoteric Oral Tradition of the Lama's Bestowal of the White Tārā Abhiṣeka'. We had started working on it some years earlier, after the Rimpoche had given me the White Tārā *abhiṣeka*, or consecration as it was sometimes called, and were still working on it at the time of my departure for England.[428] As our medium of communication was Hindi, interspersed with words in Tibetan and English, the task of translation was a difficult one, but we both attached great importance to the work and were determined that it should be completed before I left for England a second time.

Dhardo Rimpoche was not my only Tibetan teacher, nor was he the only one to visit the Vihara after my return. Kachu Rimpoche, who was abbot of Pemayangtse Gompa in Sikkim, also came, accompanied by his nephew and one of his lamas. As always, he arrived unexpectedly, just as Terry and I were finishing breakfast, so that I was all the more glad to see him. He was obviously no less glad to see me. Like Dhardo Rimpoche, he was a monk, besides being a tulku, and like Dhardo Rimpoche he wore the maroon monastic robes, but apart from the fact that both were men of rare spiritual attainments and deep commitment to the Dharma, there the resemblance ended. Dhardo Rimpoche belonged to the dominant Gelug, or 'Virtuous', school of Tibetan Buddhism, founded by the reformer Tsongkhapa at the beginning of the fifteenth century. Kachu Rimpoche, on the other hand, was a follower of the Nyingma, or 'Old Style', school inaugurated more than 600 years earlier by the Indian yogin and wonder-worker Padmasambhava in the course of his historic mission to the Land of Snows. The two incarnate lamas also differed in character and manner, as well as in their way of relating to me. If Dhardo Rimpoche was the more urbane and cultivated, Kachu Rimpoche was the more spontaneous and direct. While Dhardo Rimpoche had always responded positively to my requests and had invariably answered my questions with patience and good humour, so far as I remember he had never given me any direction or instruction of his own accord. Kachu Rimpoche had habitually done just that, and though not one to stand on ceremony he was always very much the guru. Thus he had urged me to ask the celebrated Jamyang Khyentse Rimpoche, his own guru, for the *abhiṣeka* of Mañjughoṣa, the Bodhisattva of Wisdom; had given me, as instructed by the Rimpoche, the *abhiṣeka* of Padmasambhava, together with that of Amitāyus, the Buddha of Infinite Life; had started me on the practice of the four *mūla* or 'foundation' yogas of the Vajrayāna; and had insisted, as a result of a vision, on our having a multicoloured 'banner of victory' on the roof of the Triyana Vardhana Vihara.[429] But now it was my turn to take the initiative. Kachu Rimpoche having had his photograph taken, at his own request, I asked him if he would mind Terry taking pictures of him demonstrating the eight offering *mudrās*, the eight hand gestures representing the flowers, lights, and other items which, in Tibetan ritual worship, were offered to the Buddhas and bodhisattvas. To this he readily agreed, and the pictures were accordingly taken out in the garden, in the sun, and against the background of a white sheet. Next day he came for lunch, as did Sherab Nangwa. After the meal the three of us sat out in the garden, and the Rimpoche explained certain fundamentals of Vajrayāna meditation, so far as those related to the visualization of the figure of Padmasambhava. On his departure I gave him a large bag of oranges to take with him back to Pemayangtse – oranges that had been gathered from the Vihara's own trees that very morning.

Yogi Chen did not come to see me. He lived as a hermit in a small bungalow at the bottom end of the lower bazaar, never went outside his front door, and rarely received visitors. During my latter years in Kalimpong, however, I had been allowed to visit him from time to time, and this privilege was now extended to include Terry. A short, plump, round-faced man in his middle or late fifties, the yogi had an ebullient manner not usually associated with a hermit, least of all one who spent the greater part of each day engaged in various forms of meditation. Nor was he without his eccentricities. Sometimes he wore the traditional dress of a Chinese scholar, complete with black skullcap, sometimes an anorak and baseball cap. Despite his eccentricities, he possessed a thorough knowledge of the Buddhist scriptures (he had twice read through the entire Chinese Tripiṭaka), a comprehensive grasp of Buddhist doctrine, and a rich and varied inner life which included in its gamut not only insights and ecstasies of a more spiritual nature but also strange psychic experiences. Over the years I must have asked him hundreds of questions about the Vajrayāna, about Chan, and about Chinese Buddhism in general; and many were the times he had clarified a philosophical doctrine, or explained a meditation practice, in a way no one else had been able to do. For this reason I had come to regard Yogi Chen as one of my teachers, though he absolutely refused either to consider himself a guru or to allow others to speak of him as such. But he was always ready to share his knowledge and experience with the few who were allowed to visit him.[430] He certainly shared them very readily with Terry and me, and on one of our visits discoursed to us at length on Vajrayāna *sādhana* or spiritual practice. He also allowed Terry to take pictures of his thangkas, which for the most part depicted esoteric Tantric divinities of the wrathful kind, many of them in sexual union with their consorts.

Whether Terry and I happened to be on our way to see Dhardo Rimpoche or Yogi Chen, or were walking through the High Street, or investigating the Tibetan pavement stalls at the top end of the Lower Bazaar, we could not go more than a few yards without my bumping into, or being accosted by, someone I knew or who, at least, knew me. I was particularly glad to meet my old protégé Budha Kumar, now a civil engineer in Gangtok after making a romantic runaway marriage; and loyal, devoted Mrs King, a Tamang Buddhist married to a Chinese, with whom I had to have tea, and at whose house I met Durga's pretty young wife Meera, whom I had once taught English and who had not been the brightest of my pupils. People also came to see me at the Vihara. They included Joseph E. Cann ('Uncle Joe'), the prickly, chain-smoking Canadian Buddhist, now in his seventies, who had arrived in Kalimpong shortly after me, and who according to my diary 'talked almost without stopping for about two hours';[431] worried-looking Dawa Tsering, one of the most faithful and helpful of my old students; the plump, teenage Sogyal Rimpoche;[432] monks from the Tharpa Choling Gompa at Tirpai; and the head of the local branch of the Central Intelligence Bureau, one Mr Das Gupta. Terry and I also paid several more visits to Chakhung House. On one occasion the Kazini insisted on giving gruesome details of the Delhi communal riots of 1947, which rather upset Terry, while Uncle Joe, who also happened to be there, was no less negative. 'Both seemed to enjoy the horrors they were denouncing,' my diary comments.

Meetings with my friends and teachers thus occupied much of my time, as to a lesser extent they did Terry's likewise, so that within ten or twelve days of my return to Kalimpong I had seen practically all those who were not 'out of station', as the phrase went. But precious as these occasions were, and greatly as I appreciated being with my teachers and friends again, the thought of Goulstone's letter, and of what I should say by way of reply, was never far from my mind, especially as other letters were arriving from London as well as from other parts of the little world of British Buddhism. These letters were of a very different kind. From them it was evident that word of the Trust's decision to replace me as incumbent of the Hampstead Buddhist Vihara had somehow leaked out and that members of the Sangha Association had reacted to the news first with incredulity and then with mounting astonishment and indignation. 'Why did they have to behave in such an underhand manner?' wrote one correspondent, 'Could they not have talked to you while you were here?' There was also a sad, affectionate letter from Ruth Walshe, and a personal one from Maurice in which he sought to justify the action the Trust had taken on the grounds that like Caesar's wife I had to be above suspicion[433] and that, despite my talents, I was emotionally unbalanced and immature and in need of psychological and spiritual help. Though I had originally intended to reply to Goulstone at length, making the points that had occurred to me when I first read his letter, after several abortive attempts along these lines I realized that trying to rebut charges that had not been made in good faith, and of which in any case I had already been found guilty, was really a waste of time. I therefore wrote him a short letter, but not before I had consulted Dhardo Rimpoche and Yogi Chen (Kachu Rimpoche was consulted later), as well as the Kazi and Kazini. They agreed in thinking that I should return to England as planned, and there continue working for the Dharma, though probably only the Kazini understood the kind of difficulties I would have to face. My letter read, in part, as follows:

Dear Goulstone,

Having considered the contents of your letter dated 1st November, I do not propose to deal with spurious accusations through the medium of correspondence. My main concern at this juncture is to safeguard the Buddhist activities at Hampstead, which the Trust has now placed in an extremely difficult and unfortunate position. The charges you mention are so easily refuted as to suggest the possibility of their having been fabricated with an ulterior motive. Even if the Trust withdraws its support from me, my own allegiance to and responsibility towards the Buddhist movement in

England does not permit me to retract promises made or – more disastrous still – to abandon Buddhism to those incapable of recognizing the promising nature of the movement which has been built up at the Vihara during the last two years....

Having now lived with your letter for a few days, and having received from various prominent members of our movement letters protesting against the Trust's behaviour and promising support, I am not sufficiently alarmed to curtail my stay here and will return as planned early in the New Year.

Yours sincerely,
Sangharakshita

Once the letter had been sent I realized that the die had indeed been cast and that there would be no turning back, even if I wanted to do so.

48

THE MAN IN THE PIT

Since my arrival in India three months earlier my life had been predominantly one of travel (including pilgrimage), sightseeing, lecturing, and meeting people of many different kinds, from the Dalai Lama to illiterate villagers and convicted criminals. In other words, I had been living very much on the first of the three levels recognized by Tibetan Buddhists, the level of the outer life, and comparatively little on the second level, that of the inner life of reflection and meditation. As for my secret life, the life I led on the third level, this had continued, as usual, to look after itself in its own mysterious way, without having direct contact with the two other levels. Once while I was in Kalimpong, however, it broke through into those levels and I had an experience that had no connection with anything I had been doing or thinking the previous day. The experience happened at the Vihara, and though of a different kind from the one that had befallen me in Glasgow the previous year, it was hardly less intense, and no less memorable.

One night I awoke to find the whole room filled with light. Between my bed and the mattress on which Terry lay sleeping there was a deep pit, and in the pit there was a man standing. His hands were joined in supplication, and he was looking upwards with a piteous, imploring expression as if begging to be delivered out of the pit. It was Jivaka, the English doctor who, then bearded and pipe-smoking, had turned up at the Vihara one morning in 1958 with one of the oddest requests I had ever received: that I should teach him how to read people's thoughts and how to see what was happening at a distance. He had been directed to me by Dhardo Rimpoche whom he had met in Bodh Gaya and who had assured him that the English monk who lived in Kalimpong was the best person to help him in this connection. The Rimpoche had worn a skirt, he added, laughing uproariously at the recollection, as if the idea of a man wearing a skirt was the funniest thing in the world. In view of his own history this was ironic. He was in fact a woman. Born in 1915, he had been orphaned at an early age, had been brought up by two maiden aunts, had gone to Oxford, and between 1945 and 1948 had undergone a series of operations that had given him the outward appearance, at least, of a man, thus enabling him to pass as such. He had then qualified as a doctor, and until recently had worked as a ship's doctor on a British liner, resigning only when the discovery of his change of sex by a reporter had led to its extensive coverage in the press. All this I learned from the newspaper cutting which, within minutes of his arrival at the Vihara, he produced from his wallet and silently handed me. Later he told me he had been greatly impressed by the fact that I had read it without turning a hair, as he put it, as well as by the readiness with which I agreed to his staying at the Vihara. He stayed for more than a year, studying the Dharma, learning to meditate (though not how to read people's thoughts or how to see what was happening at a distance), and writing his autobiography. To make it difficult for the press to track him down he shaved off his beard, and I gave him the name of Jivaka, after the Buddha's personal physician.

The fact that he was the first female-to-male transsexual to have modern surgery and hormone treatment was not the most interesting thing about the Vihara's new inmate, at least so far as I was concerned. He was also a disciple of the notorious Lobsang Rampa, author of the best-selling *The Third Eye*, who was not a Tibetan lama at all but a plumber from Plympton with a vivid imagination and a racy style. A few weeks after his arrival at the Vihara Jivaka confided to me, with a solemn air, that Lobsang Rampa had initiated him into the Secret Order of the Potala and invested him with its robe and girdle. There were only thirteen members of the Order, he had told him, including the Dalai Lama, and any Tibetan who saw him wearing the robe – even the highest dignitaries – would immediately prostrate himself before him. He had worn the robe when he went to see Dhardo Rimpoche, he added, but strange to say the Rimpoche had not prostrated himself. Perhaps he was a low-ranking lama who had not heard of the Order. Naturally I wanted to know if he had brought the robe with him. He had brought it, and not only showed it to me but demonstrated how it was to be worn, wrapping it round himself in the most extraordinary fashion and tying it with what appeared to be a length of dressing-gown cord. 'But Jivaka, it's an ordinary Burmese monk's robe!' I exclaimed. 'No, it's not!' he retorted angrily. 'It's the robe of the Secret Order of the Potala.' Fortunately I had just such a monk's robe in my cupboard. It was of the same yellowish-brown colour as the one Jivaka was wearing, consisted of the same number of patches, and bore in one corner the same manufacturer's label – in Burmese script. Jivaka was dumbfounded by the discovery. Even so, I had a hard time convincing him that Lobsang Rampa was not, as he claimed, a lama who had spent many years in Lhasa and had been initiated into the deepest mysteries of Tibetan Buddhism, and that the Secret Order of the Potala existed only in his fertile imagination. Eventually, however, I did convince him, whereupon he wrote to Rampa, who was then living in Ireland in a house bought for him by Jivaka, a letter of indignant remonstrance. To this the supposed lama only replied that evidently some evil person had been undermining his faith.

Jivaka's faith in his erstwhile master was indeed undermined, but not his faith in his own high spiritual destiny – a faith that had enabled him to regard membership of the Secret Order of the Potala as being no more than his due. 'I *know* that I am a teacher, a teacher with a capital T,' he once told me. I had responded by saying that in that case he ought to have something to teach, and it was this remark that had led to his spending so much of his time studying the Dharma. Besides being spiritually ambitious, he was headstrong, wilful, and by his own admission a great believer in the fait accompli. He could also be high-handed in his dealings with people. While I was away on one of my preaching tours he took it upon himself to chastise one of the younger inmates of the Vihara with a slipper, a terrible indignity by local standards. I therefore made arrangements, soon afterwards, for him to continue his studies at Sarnath. There he quickly got himself ordained as a Theravādin novice, though without revealing to Sangharatana and other monks his true sexual identity. Later he spent five months at a monastery in Ladakh, where he became a novice in the Tibetan monastic tradition and started calling himself Lobsang Jivaka. He died suddenly in Dalhousie in 1962.[434]

This, then, was the unfortunate being whom I saw standing in the pit, his hands joined in supplication, and clearly wanting to be delivered. I felt an intense desire to deliver him, and was wondering how this was to be done when I suddenly remembered an incident that had occurred in the course of my connection with Jamyang Khyentse Rimpoche, whom I regarded as my principal teacher or 'root lama', as a Tibetan Buddhist would have said. I had met the Rimpoche in 1957, shortly after his arrival from Tibet, where he was widely regarded as one of the very greatest of living lamas. We met in the bungalow I had once occupied as the guest of Prince Latthakin of Burma, the son-in-law of the exiled King Thibaw. He was then about sixty, and though he wore the usual maroon robes he at once struck me as being more like a Burmese *mahāthera* or 'great elder' than a Tibetan incarnate lama.[435] A few months later, having seen more of him, I asked Jamyang Khyentse, through Kachu Rimpoche, for the Mañjughoṣa *abhiṣeka* or consecration, which he gave me on 24 October 1957, together with the consecrations of Avalokiteśvara, Vajrapāṇi, and Green Tārā.

The ceremony took place in Darjeeling, in the presence of Jamyang Khyentse's youthful *ḍākinī,* the Maharani of Sikkim, Kachu Rimpoche, and a few other friends. Partly because it was in Tibetan, and partly because I was unwell at the time, (as was Jamyang Khyentse, he died in 1959), I remembered little of what happened that morning. I did, however, remember offering Jamyang Khyentse a mandala or symbolic representation of the universe, and noticing with what reverence a disciple offered him the pointed red pandit cap which he donned at certain key points in the ceremony. Above all, I remembered the rapt, beatific expression with which he looked up as he was invoking Mañjughoṣa and the other bodhisattvas, as if he actually saw their diaphanous, rainbow-like forms floating in the air before him. He subsequently commissioned a thangka depicting Mañjughoṣa and the three other bodhisattvas together with the nineteen great teachers who were his main spiritual ancestors and whose different sectarian lineages he united in his own person. When I next visited Gangtok, where he was then staying, he handed me this thangka, at the same time explaining that in conferring the *abhiṣekas* he had transmitted to me the essence of all the teachings of all the gurus depicted therein.[436]

It was on the occasion of another visit to Gangtok, where Jamyang Khyentse was now settled, that there had taken place the incident which

I suddenly remembered when I saw Jivaka standing in the pit. The Rimpoche's quarters were on the upper floor of the magnificent building that was the royal chapel. On my arrival there I was asked to wait. I waited for about half an hour. On his emerging from an inner room, my venerable teacher apologized for having kept me waiting for so long, saying that a lama friend of his had recently died and in order to help him he had been reciting the hundred-syllable mantra of Vajrasattva, the Diamond Being who delivers from hell.[437] No sooner did I remember these words than I knew what I had to do to help Jivaka. I started reciting the mantra. As I did so I saw the letters of the mantra coming out of my mouth, one after another, and forming a chain or garland that went down into the pit and came up out of it in a continuous circular motion. On seeing the garland, Jivaka caught hold of the letters as they ascended and with their help hauled himself out of the pit and disappeared. At that instant the room was plunged into darkness and in the distance I heard the horn of the Jogi, the collector of the souls of the dead. I looked at my watch. It was two in the morning.

49
PACKING AND PRINTING

> Fine clear weather, not very cold.... Took photographs of Kanchenjunga. Climbed up to Observatory Hill. Took more photographs, though on the whole Mahākāla shrine etc. rather disappointing.

Thus my diary. Terry and I were not in Kalimpong but in Darjeeling, having arrived there early that morning. Darjeeling was 8,000 feet above sea level, as compared to Kalimpong's 4,000 feet, and the visitor who had the good fortune to be there on a clear day had an unobstructed view of the glittering wall of perpetual snow that was Kanchenjunga. The weather being clear that morning, Terry and I lost no time in walking up to the Chowrasta and thence to the Mall, from where we climbed to the top of Observatory Hill, stopping on the way from time to time to get our breath and to photograph the white mass that towered 20,000 feet above us, majestic against the blue. Having circumambulated the untidy Mahākāla shrine, sacred to Buddhists and Hindus alike, we made our way back to the Chowrasta, to the bookshops and curio stores, and so to the GPO,[438] for while we were glad to have had a better view of Kanchenjunga than was possible from Kalimpong, it was not really for the sake of the view that we were in Darjeeling that day.

We were there to send a cable to Christmas Humphreys. I had written to Toby shortly after replying to Goulstone's letter, assuring him that I would be returning to England despite the Trust's decision regarding me, and asking for his comments or advice. He had replied at once, and at some length,[439] and my cable was in response to his letter, which had reached me the previous day. I was sending the cable from Darjeeling because I did not want its contents to become common property, as would certainly have been the case had I sent it from Kalimpong, and because I wanted to make sure that it would reach Toby before the Sangha Association's AGM, which he had said he would be attending, and at which his was bound to be an influential voice. The cable did not say everything I wanted to say, but it made my position sufficiently clear.

> THANK YOU SUPPORT STOP GLAD YOU REALIZE NO EVIDENCE MAIN ALLEGATION STOP NOT INTERESTED IMAGE INTERESTED ENLIGHTENMENT SUPPORTERS LIKEWISE STOP BETTER SPLIT THAN UNITED MEDIOCRITY STOP VIHARA TACTICS DISGRACEFUL STOP AGM OPPORTUNITY GOOD PURGE STOP WONDER IF YOU DARE STOP NO INTENTION BEING SACRIFICED COMBINATION HINAYANA STERILITY BRITISH RESPECTABILITY STOP NOT ALL YOUR FACTS CORRECT WRITING IMMEDIATELY STOP GOOD LUCK

As was evident from the tenor of my cable, Toby's letter had been concerned mainly with the question of my 'image'. After acknowledging that the situation was 'tragic in the extreme', he had gone on to say that the trustees' decision was final, that it would not be affected by the views of the Sangha Association, that the magnificent work I had done for the Dharma was not enough, and that I had to face the depth and power of the English middle-class mind and its abhorrence of homosexuality. There was no question of any 'offences'. It was the image I had created that was the real cause of the present crisis. This was the clearest indication I had yet received that the Trust's decision had something to do with my friendship with Terry, for I could not but assume that it was to this that Toby was alluding when he spoke of the image I had created.[440] There was little doubt that he was in a position to understand the depth and power of the English middle-class mind and, in particular, its abhorrence of homosexuality. Had not his father been junior prosecuting counsel at the trial of Oscar Wilde in 1895?[441] Not that Toby himself was a man of illiberal views. There were homosexuals of high character and ability in the Buddhist movement in England, his letter continued, but the Buddhist public did not notice them as such and were no more offended by them than by the presence of someone they were privately informed to be an alcoholic. In my case, however, it was my public image, my *visible* way of life, that was in question. A fair analogy would be the behaviour of a vicar in a small Church of England parish. Suppose he were often drunk on church occasions, or spent most of his time in bookmakers' offices, or flaunted a mistress, or were known to show 'blue' films to his friends in private, the *scandal* would mean that he *had* to go, on the ground that his congregation was gravely upset by his conduct.

I had been astounded when I came to this part of Toby's reply, and told him as much in the letter which I sent from Darjeeling along with the cable. There was not the remotest resemblance between my behaviour and that of his Church of England vicar. The worst that could be said of me was that I handled money, that I sometimes took solid food after midday, and that I wore my hair a little longer than was customary. Toby subsequently had the grace to retract the analogy, in effect admitting that he had allowed words to run away with him, as I had bluntly told him was the case. Nonetheless, I could not help wondering what kind of stories Walshe, and perhaps others, had been circulating about me.

The cable having been sent, and my letter posted, Terry and I walked round the Chowk Bazaar, bought some cloth for the woodblock prints we had started making, and visited the Tibetan Self-Help Centre, where we saw some very beautiful but very expensive handmade rugs. Our day in Darjeeling ended with tea at Keventer's, a popular local rendezvous, after which we returned to Kalimpong and to a week of packing and printing and to what De Quincey would have called 'a thousand final or farewell farewells'.[442]

According to the Vinaya, the individual monk might possess only eight things: his three robes, a bowl, a razor, a needle, a girdle, and a water-strainer. In the course of my fourteen years in Kalimpong, however, I had managed to accumulate a couple of hundred books on Buddhism and other subjects, as well as various images, thangkas, ritual bells, etc. These would all be of use to the new Buddhist movement I would now be starting in England, and for the last week or more Terry and I had been packing them into the black steel trunks Lobsang had bought in the bazaar, together with such diaries and notebooks as I thought worth keeping. On top we placed, partly by way of filling, the woodblock prints we had been making and which we continued to make almost until the day of our departure. I had four or five such woodblocks, depicting White Tārā and other divinities, and it was from these that Terry and I had made our first, rather experimental prints on Tibetan handmade paper and on the brightly coloured cloths we had bought. We had also borrowed Dhardo Rimpoche's woodblocks. The prints would make good presents for our friends in England, we thought. It might also be possible for us to sell them at the Buddhist groups we would be visiting, along with the *mālās* and other religious requisites we had been buying in Varanasi and other places along the way, as well as in Kalimpong itself.

One day I remembered that the local Gelug monastery had a large collection of woodblocks of various kinds, and that for a small fee it was possible to get prints made from them. My connection with the monastery went back to 1951, when in the company of Marco Pallis, the author of *Peaks and Lamas*, I had called on the aged *khenpo* or abbot and invited him and his monks to collaborate in the reception I was organizing for the relics of the *arhants* Śāriputra and Maudgalyāyana, the Buddha's chief disciples, which were then touring India and the Buddhist countries of South-East Asia.[443] That collaboration had been gladly given, and over the years my relations with the monastery had become increasingly cordial. They had been particularly cordial since 1961, when I had organized the first public celebration of Tsongkhapa's death anniversary to be held in Kalimpong. The celebration was a great success, including as it did a grand procession through the town and a public meeting at which the principal speaker was Tijang Rimpoche, the Dalai Lama's Junior Tutor. This resulted in my becoming very much *persona grata* at the monastery, as well as with the wider Tibetan community, while the Tsongkhapa anniversary became a regular feature of the town's religious calendar.[444]

On my return I was pleased to find that during my absence the anniversary had been celebrated, albeit on a reduced scale, and that this year, too, there was to be a procession and a public meeting in honour of the great Tibetan reformer. The celebration was held two weeks later, enabling Terry to see something of the more popular, colourful side of Tibetan Buddhism. The procession followed the same route as in previous years. Starting from the monastery, which was situated a mile or more from the town, it made its way down the hill to the upper bazaar, circumambulated the Mela Ground, and returned to the monastery by the back road. Terry and I had stationed ourselves at a spot half a mile below the monastery, from which we could see the procession as it passed down the winding, dusty track. First came two eight-foot copper trumpets, each of them blown by one monk and supported on the shoulder of another. After the trumpets came a long line of monks wearing ceremonial robes of rich brocade, some carrying banners of victory, others playing drums, oboes, and conch shells. These were followed by monks wearing the usual maroon robes, lay devotees in traditional dress, and Tibetan schoolchildren. Lastly, borne in a golden palanquin under a huge umbrella of yellow silk, came the famous gold image of Tsongkhapa, which reputedly had the power to speak. An hour and a half later, the procession having arrived back at the monastery, the public meeting was held in the courtyard in front of the main building. The monks chanted verses of blessing and I spoke about Buddhism in England, at the same time announcing that I would shortly be leaving Kalimpong again, this time for good.

Terry had taken many pictures of the procession. On our arrival at the monastery in quest of woodblock prints, therefore, the monks were not surprised to see him with me, and we were both given a warm welcome. It was not long before the woodblocks were brought out, or before four or five monks were busy inking them, placing a sheet of paper or a length of cloth on the inked surface, and pressing it evenly against the woodblock with the aid of a heavy wooden roller. The print was then peeled off and hung up to dry. The monastery's woodblocks were of many shapes and sizes and depicted not only Buddhas and bodhisattvas but the wheel of life, mandalas of various kinds, and magic diagrams, while some also contained mantras and prayers in bold Tibetan script. After a while Terry and I noticed that not all the prints that were being produced were good enough either to give as presents or to sell. Some were smudged, some unevenly inked, and some not properly aligned with the paper or cloth on which they were printed. Terry therefore suggested that he should try his hand at producing a few prints, to which the monks laughingly agreed, obviously thinking that it would be a great joke to see what a mess the inexperienced Englishman made of the job. To their amazement Terry smilingly produced print after perfect print, so that in the end the laugh was very much on them rather than on him. Thereafter my friend and I paid several more visits to the monastery, each time taking with us a fresh supply of coloured cloth. The result was that thanks to the combined efforts of the monks, as well as to Terry's more skilled exertions, we eventually had over a hundred good prints to take with us back to England.

Terry enjoyed making the prints at the monastery, and enjoyed the company of the monks, with whom he seemed to be quite at home. Indeed, these sessions at the Gelug monastery were probably the happiest part of his time in Kalimpong, even as our stay in Kalimpong itself was probably for him the happiest part of our whole India tour. Only once during those four or five weeks did he become seriously depressed, despite the fact that his *ḍākinī* had proved to be no less elusive there than elsewhere. 'Do you think I shall meet my *ḍākinī* today?' had been his frequent cry during the early weeks of our tour, but now he was silent on the subject as if realizing that his hope of meeting her was an impossible dream.

A few dozen yards from the main building, half screened by trees, there stood a cottage that seemed to be part of the monastery and yet not part of it. This was the abode of Tomo Geshe Rimpoche, whom Terry and I had already met and who on the day of the Tsongkhapa anniversary had given us lunch. The Rimpoche was short and slightly built, and although then in his late twenties he had the physique of a boy of twelve or fourteen. At the same time, his bearing and manners were those of an old man, while his pale face had a waxen look. A slight smile, as if of amusement, usually hovered about his lips, and when he spoke it was in a low voice but with a quiet authority that commanded instant obedience from servants and disciples alike. Around him there was a certain atmosphere, almost an aura. This was perhaps due not so much to his own mysterious personality as to his having inherited the reputation and prestige of the previous Tomo Geshe Rimpoche, the celebrated yogi about whose wonder-working powers I had written, briefly, in *A Survey of Buddhism*.[445] I had known Geshe Rimpoche, as he was generally called, since 1961. Imprisoned by the Chinese in the aftermath of the 1959 Lhasa uprising, he had been released thanks to the intervention of the Government of India, and after a short stay in Gangtok had settled in Kalimpong. Soon he was studying English with me at the Vihara, and in this way we had become good friends.[446] Terry took a liking to the Rimpoche, and the Rimpoche seemed to take a liking to him, and we spent many pleasant hours in his company. Besides showing us the inner room where his renowned predecessor had been accustomed to meditate, he allowed Terry to take pictures of his most sacred images, as well as of himself.

Our last week in Kalimpong was a busy one. By the end of it, however, Terry and I had finished packing the last of the black steel trunks, had produced the last of our prints, and had paid farewell visits to Dhardo Rimpoche and Yogi Chen, as well as to Geshe Rimpoche, the Kazi and Kazini, and other friends. I was particularly sorry to be parting from Dhardo Rimpoche, and he, I believe, was sorry to be parting from me. At all events, in the course of the week he came to the Vihara twice, the first time being to attend the farewell tea party I was giving. Geshe Rimpoche, Sherab Nangwa, the Kazini, Uncle Joe, and Mrs King were also present on this occasion, as were several of my Nepalese former students. 'Quite a pleasant little gathering,' my diary records, 'though Kazini as usual struck a rather jarring note.' Dhardo Rimpoche stayed behind after the others had gone, and gave me a thousand small prints of the Three Long-Life Divinities, the Buddha Amitāyus, White Tārā, and the goddess Vijaya. Two days later he came again, bringing more presents: two fox tails for me (a traditional Tibetan gift); and a silk appliqué picture for Terry. The following day, Wednesday 28 December, was the day of our departure. In the morning we went and paid our last visit to Dhardo Rimpoche and I bade him a final farewell. Though I was sorry to leave him, I knew that I could never really be parted from him, any more than I could be parted from Yogi Chen, or Kachu Rimpoche, or any of my other teachers. Spiritually speaking, they would always be with me, and I with them, and I would always have their protection and blessing.[447]

A few hours later, Terry and I were on our way.

50
THE VALEDICTION THAT FAILED

The journey down to Siliguri and the plains was uneventful, as was the flight to Calcutta the following day. On our arrival at the Maha Bodhi Society in the early afternoon Terry and I found Thubden already established there. I had sent him on ahead of us by train, as he was eager to serve me for at least a few more weeks. Veronica was also staying at the Society. She was evidently on the friendliest terms with Venerable Jinaratana, who had installed her in the Welfare Home adjacent to the headquarters building, in a room next to the one he himself sometimes used. After I had talked with her, and she had told me about her unfortunate experience in Kalimpong, the four of us went out together. We walked all the way to Chowringhee, where we had a meal and where Veronica bought two books on witchcraft.

In the morning I awoke feeling unwell, and for a few days did little except work on the January number of the *Maha Bodhi*, talk with Terry and Veronica, read *The Meaning of Evolution*,[448] and have lunch in the Sri Dharmarajika Vihara shrine-room with the thirty or forty Sinhalese monks who were then staying at the Society before proceeding to Bodh Gaya on pilgrimage. I was not impressed by the monks. My first diary entry regarding them describes them as 'a rabble', while the second comments 'as motley a collection of rogues in yellow robes as I have seen for a long time'. When I felt better, Terry and I started spending part of each day exploring the curio shops, handicrafts emporia, and *khadi* or 'handloom cloth' stores of Chowringhee, as well as of those of the nearby New Market, in search of such Buddhist requisites as were not easily procurable in England, especially outside London. Before long we had quite a stock of sandalwood *mālās*, bundles of good quality incense sticks, and small images and heads of the Buddha, so that it was necessary to add another black steel trunk to the four we had bought in Kalimpong, which Thubden had lately collected from the Air Carrying Corporation. In some of the curio shops we saw exquisitely beautiful images of various Buddhas, bodhisattvas, and Tantric divinities, many of them gilded and studded with jewels, and all evidently of Tibetan provenance. Chowringhee being in the heart of the city's tourist district, they were extremely expensive, and we bought only one such image: a four-armed Avalokiteśvara which we took the precaution of sending to England by registered insured post. The Nepalese bronze images, on the other hand, were quite affordable, and of these we eventually bought seven or eight. We bought most of them at two curio shops in the New Market, where we spent so much time deciding what to buy and haggling over the prices that we came to be on friendly terms with the proprietors.

One day they showed us their respective storerooms. To our astonishment, both were filled with Tibetan images of every description, some of them several feet high, and many still wearing their brocade robes. They had been brought to India by Tibetan refugees who, being destitute and perhaps starving, had disposed of them for a fraction of their true value. In one of the storerooms we were shown a solid gold disc, about a foot in diameter, which was inlaid with several hundred turquoises of a lustrous sky-blue colour, those in the centre being exceptionally large. It was one of the most beautiful examples of the jeweller's art I had ever seen, and I found it difficult to take my eyes off the glorious creation, which until recently must have lain on the breast of some giant golden figure of Tārā or Avalokiteśvara, or have hung from one of its ears.

When Terry and I had been less than two weeks in Calcutta, however, we were obliged to curtail our expeditions to Chowringhee and the New Market, at least for the time being. Letters for us had started arriving at the Society in ever-increasing numbers, some of them straight from England, others redirected from Kalimpong, and I had to spend much of my time responding to such as were addressed to me. There were letters from Minh Chau, Viriya, and Francoise, letters from each of the Three Musketeers, and letters from scores of other members of the Sangha Association, particularly from Mike Rogers, Emile Boin, and John Hipkin, who with Mike Ricketts, Sara Boin, and René Rudio were campaigning vigorously for my reinstatement as incumbent of the Hampstead Buddhist Vihara. Some of the letters contained copies of the letters Mike Rogers and his colleagues had sent to various people who had somehow been drawn into what was becoming an increasingly complex situation, from the Thai ambassador to a wealthy and eccentric former benefactor of the Sangha Trust. From these letters, some of which were extremely lengthy, I learned something of what had been going on at the Vihara during the last few weeks. My locked cupboards had been broken into and their contents thrown into another room. Viriya had been told that if he wanted to remain at the Vihara he would have to be re-ordained under the auspices of the Thai Sangha. Walshe had been telling people that I had been dismissed for reasons much more serious than those that had been given out, but that they were to 'keep it dark'. Nor was this all. The Vihara had a new incumbent! 'New leader for the Buddhists', ran the heading of an article in the *Hampstead and Highgate Express* of 30 November 1966, a cutting of which was sent to me. The new leader was a 30-year-old Thai monk who had been three months in England, and of whom English Buddhists, at least, had not heard before.

Many of the letters reaching me at this time contained references to, or accounts of, the events of the Sangha Association's AGM, which Christmas Humphreys had said he would be attending. The fullest account came from John Hipkin, in a 2,500-word letter written on 1 January 1967, the day after the AGM. He began by assuring me that Maurice Walshe, and to a lesser extent Toby Humphreys and Tom Harris, had experienced a crushing defeat. My good name had not only been restored but strengthened, and there had been the strongest possible feeling among an overwhelming number of those present that I should return to England, be reinstated at the Vihara, and continue my work along the lines already started so hopefully and competently. It had fallen to him, he said, to represent my case at the AGM, to cross-examine Walshe and Humphreys, and to formulate the four important motions that had been put to the meeting. He was very happy that he had been able to play the part that he had done and that the outcome had been so entirely satisfactory.

The letter continued with an account of the events of the AGM in their sequential order. The Thai monks having all arrived, and the seniormost monk having led the meeting in two short sessions of meditation, the secretary had read the minutes of the last AGM and Walshe, as chairman of the Sangha Association, had given his report for 1966. The report was in two parts, he had said, the first outlining general matters and the second discussing in full the reasons for my dismissal. According to other accounts, the first part of the report dealt at some length, and in considerable detail, with the Vihara's activities during the period under review, though without my name being once mentioned in that connection; but John said nothing of this, going on, instead, to give me the gist of the second part of the report. Walshe had begun by saying that the Trust's decision regarding me was a regrettable one but that it was irrevocable (he stressed the irrevocable character of the decision on at least half a dozen occasions, John observed). Whatever my qualities, and they were considerable, I had not comported myself in a manner becoming a Head of the Sangha. I had given a number of people the impression that I was behaving indiscreetly. I slept out at night, young men were seen coming and going from the Vihara, one young man I had admitted as a novice saw fit to leave after only two weeks. Even before I had come to England there had been rumours of my alleged homosexuality. In any event, whether these charges were true or not a distinctly unsavoury atmosphere now surrounded the Vihara and it was better that I stayed away. My conduct since the decision was made was further proof that I was an unsuitable incumbent.

All this was heard in silence, John said. Someone – it may have been Humphreys – moved the adoption of the report. He (John) had opposed the adoption immediately. He had sprung to his feet because he feared that they might all be procedurally steam-rollered. He was familiar with the devices a chairman could employ to get his way even against the wishes of a meeting. From that moment the initiative had been his, he declared, and he had kept it.

He had then made a speech lasting twenty-five minutes. These were the points he made. First, he could not believe what had happened. That they should be gathered in that very room where they had so often listened to me now to consider my removal, expulsion, and banishment was unthinkable and horrible. The whole affair was ignominious. He urged everyone present to assure themselves of the true nature of the decision. I was a unique figure in the world of Buddhism – a man of undoubted and distinguished intellectual powers, of supreme efficiency and advanced spiritual awareness. That the Head of the Sangha should be endowed with these triple qualities was their extreme good fortune. They should be clear whom they had rejected: one who was beginning to devise an authentic Western Buddhism with its own distinctive idiom, and one who could bring to this task the most complete understanding of the indigenous context in which Buddhism had arisen and still evolved. That they should have removed such a man without the slightest evidence on the basis of rumour, gossip, and hearsay was shameful folly. Next he had spoken at length about my friendship with Terry. This I must forgive, he said. My personal relationships were of course best understood by me and those with whom I shared them, but Walshe had made great play of the fact that I and Terry had been away together for so long 'in a caravan'. (Wasn't that sweetly picturesque!) He (John) had spoken of the friendship as one he had seen at close quarters. We had both been to his house (but had not actually spent the night under his roof, he had added, to loud and sustained laughter). We were both sensitive and serious young men with a common concern for spiritual matters. Mine, as Head of the Sangha, was a lofty and isolated position. I was surrounded by people who drew upon me for advice, comfort, and support. I too needed replenishment and affection. Did the spiritual man become inhuman? Or more human? Whatever might be said about appearances my friendship was not an exclusive one. He and others had found me accessible at all times and he thought the quality of my concern and compassion had deepened since my friendship with Terry had started. 'Friendships often have that effect!' He had concluded his speech by asking what would be the effects of that abhorrent decision. Schism, dissent, and conflict! But if all that was necessary they would have to endure it. A great injustice had been committed. A man's reputation had been sullied. It was monstrous to suggest, as Walshe had done, that a *bhikkhu* was immune from the effects of salacious rumour and calumny. There was of course a core of my being that was unassailable but I had to function in the world of men, in a society, and in these circumstances a man's reputation meant a very great deal. They owed it to me to restore that reputation, to remove the blemishes, and to see me fully reinstated at the Vihara where I belonged.

This was a much abbreviated account of what he had said, John wrote, but the tenor must be clear. His speech had been greeted with long and sustained applause, as they said in the People's Republics, though he fancied it was a bit more spontaneous than was often the case in those particular polities!

Humphreys had then been called upon by Walshe to speak, the letter continued. (He had asked Humphreys in the course of his speech, John said, whether he, as a distinguished lawyer, would condemn a man on the sort of flimsy allegation which had been brought against me.) He was grave and serious. I was his friend. He had known me for twenty years. I had great ability, etc., etc. He then read the letter which he had sent me in reply to my request for his comments or advice. I would no doubt have a copy of that letter. His remark that I had to respect the middle-class abhorrence of homosexuality seemed to him of historic significance. Humphreys had largely defended my dismissal on the grounds that middle-class susceptibilities were offended by the appearance of my activities. I was like a parish priest who had to comport himself appropriately. In private and heated discussion with him later, John added, he had again referred to the Buddhist Society as a parish. It was now quite evident, and on the man's own admission, that Humphreys regarded the Buddhist Society not only as a primarily secular institution but as one that must be respectable and that according to the dictates of the English middle classes.

The remainder of John's long and circumstantial letter was occupied with the results of the various motions put to the meeting, and with the question of what should be done next. At the end of the briefest discussion the motion that the chairman's report be rejected had been passed and carried by 28 votes to 8 (or thereabouts), Walshe having ruled 45 to 50 proxy votes out of order. A motion rejecting the second part of the chairman's report on the grounds that the charges against me had not been substantiated had been passed by a similar majority, as had a further motion requesting the Sangha Trust in the strongest terms to reverse its decision to dismiss me. What John described as the *coup de grâce* had occurred at the end of the AGM. After further protestations of friendship, Toby had proposed sending me a motion expressing the Association's deep gratitude for the work I had done in the past on behalf of the Buddhist movement in England. To John this had sounded too much like a valediction, and he had proposed that the motion should go on to say that they looked forward to my return in the future to carry on the work I had begun. Toby had objected, shouting, 'No! That only brings back the hate.' 'Not to me it doesn't,' John had retorted, whereupon his proposal was carried overwhelmingly. The meeting had then broken up. Groups had stood on the pavement outside the Vihara for several minutes discussing what had happened. Many of those present had expressed themselves pleased with the course of events at the AGM. Viriya had been particularly heartened.

I replied to John's letter immediately. Much of my letter was taken up with the question of what should be done next. In general, I agreed with his suggestion that an Extraordinary General Meeting of the Sangha Association should be called before my return, that it should consider the whole question of the relationship between the Association and the Trust, and that if my complete reinstatement was prevented the Sangha Association should sever its links with the Trust. Action should also be taken in other ways, five of which I proceeded to tabulate. One of them was that a letter should be sent out over Mike's signature, informing members of our victory at the AGM, and giving the full text of the resolutions passed in my support. Another was that steps should be taken to ensure that a garbled version of the AGM proceedings was not published in *The Buddhist*. The opening paragraph of my reply struck a more personal note, however. After thanking John for his letter, written when the details of the AGM were still fresh in his mind, I wrote:

> My only real fear, that our case would go by default for want of a good spokesman, has been shown to be baseless. Clearly it was your sincerity, courage, and above all sheer ability, that carried the day, thus demonstrating once again how much even one committed individual, functioning under democratic conditions, can achieve, especially when he is backed up, as you were, by a strong body of staunch adherents. Emile writes that your oratory was brilliant and memorable and will not soon be forgotten by those present. It must have given you intense satisfaction, amounting to a sense of real fulfilment, to have been able to function, in a situation of this kind, in a manner that was so entirely adequate even by your own exacting standards of performance. Warmest congratulations from us both!

Towards the end of my letter I adverted to the subject of Toby, and the part he had played in the proceedings of the AGM.

> As for Toby, he has burnt his fingers badly, having been publicly defeated, perhaps for the first time in forty-odd years, on a major policy issue. Perhaps we should give him time to lick his wounds and think things over. In any case, I shall be writing to him again. There is much good in him, and given time he may come to see the absurdity of an exponent of Zen Buddhism burning incense at the shrine of the British Middle-Class Mind and murmuring 'Mrs Grundy Saranam Gacchami'. If he did, it would not be the first time he had performed a complete volte-face when confronted by serious opposition. Only he must be allowed to do so as though on his own initiative, and with complete consistency. In any case, however, he emerges from the AGM with diminished stature. What you did should really have been done by him. Instead, he had to taste the bitterness not only of having to make common cause with Walshe, in itself bad enough, but of being defeated with him too.

I concluded by striking a note of optimism regarding the future.

> In the midst of all these negations, however, let us not lose sight of the positive side of things. As a result of what has happened, English Buddhism may well thrive as never before. Let us act vigorously, but without personal enmity, confident that in the long run truth and justice will triumph.

Though John spoke of Walshe and Humphreys as having experienced a crushing defeat, I knew as well as they did that the Trust was in a strong position, in as much as it was legally entitled to say who should or should not stay at the Hampstead Vihara. At the same time, I appreciated the efforts he and his friends were making to have me reinstated, and was willing that they should continue with those efforts, if only to expose the intransigence of Walshe and his fellow trustees, and to make it clear to everyone that if I were to return to England at all, it could only be in order to start a new Buddhist movement. One of the most remarkable features of the situation was the fact that apart from John Hipkin, and perhaps Mike Rogers, none of those who had been at the forefront of the campaign for my reinstatement had had much personal contact with me. They had been content simply to attend my Sunday lectures and my meditation classes, and to absorb what they could of the Dharma. Yet it was they that had circularized the members of the Sangha Association, alerting them to the Trust's intentions regarding me, who had rallied my supporters, and who had done their best to restore my good name, and I was greatly indebted to them for their loyalty and resourcefulness. Mike Hookham and Alf Vial, on the other hand, who together with Jack Ireland had had more personal contact with me than almost anyone else, had shown no such loyalty, despite the fact that I had explained to them the four *mūla* or 'foundation' yogas of the Vajrayāna, taken them through certain forms of deity yoga, and given them the bodhisattva ordination. True, they had resigned from the Trust when the motion for my dismissal was carried by a majority of three to two against them, but now Mike wrote to say that they had become disciples of Trungpa Rimpoche, at the same time making it clear that even if I returned to England they wanted nothing more to do with me. Indeed, Mike urged me in the strongest terms not to return. If I returned, the present gossip of my critics would become more intense, and some of the mud would stick. All the societies and viharas would close their doors to me, literally refusing me admittance, let alone allowing me to speak or conduct meetings on their premises. No magazines would accept my articles, and I would have no facilities for talks or meditations, except in so far as I might be able to make private arrangements with individuals, which would be chancy, or hire a public hall, which would be expensive. There would also be the problem of advertising my activities, also a costly business since none of the societies would put them on their noticeboards. He also claimed that I would have little support from the provincial groups. They were mainly Theravādin in outlook and would easily be swayed by the pressures that would be brought to bear upon them. Mike did not know that many of the scores of letters of sympathy and support I had received were from members of these same provincial groups. They may or may not have been Theravādin in outlook, but they had a British sense of justice and had been appalled by the Trust's treatment of me.

Despite Mike's letter, which could hardly have been more discouraging, what kind of reception I would meet with on my return to England remained to be seen. Meanwhile Terry and I were in Calcutta, and were to be there for two or three more weeks. Once the flood of letters had abated, and I had finished replying to the more important of them, we were free to resume our expeditions to Chowringhee and the New Market, and before long Thubden had to be sent out for more black steel trunks. In the end we had altogether ten such trunks, the increase in their number being due not so much to the bulk of our new purchases as to our having had to redistribute my Kalimpong books and thangkas and pack them more securely for their long journey. All this took time, as did the typing in triplicate of a detailed list of the entire contents of each trunk, one copy for placing in the trunk itself, one for handing over to the shipping agent, and one for retention by me. But at last the work was done, and we had the satisfaction of seeing the shipping agent's van come and take all the trunks away. When I was not exploring the curio shops with Terry or repacking my trunks, I worked on the January and February numbers of the *Maha Bodhi*, talked with Jinaratana, and took part in some of the functions organized by the Society. Thus I attended the reception given for a party of Japanese Buddhists, made a speech at the Welfare Home on Netaji Day,[449] and spoke a few words at the Ceylon Independence Day celebrations in the Society's hall, besides meeting two Buddhist scholars from an East German university, and spending time with one B. R. Barua, an elderly Bengali Buddhist who had known both Anagarika Dharmapala and Dr Ambedkar. I also went to see Devapriya Valisinha, who was now back in hospital, having been obliged to return there shortly after our last meeting. Though he was able to move his arms more freely, his eyes had the same tragic haunted look as before, and I felt sorrier for him than ever.

I had a much happier meeting with Dilgo Khyentse Rimpoche, one of my teachers, who had not been in Kalimpong while Terry and I were there. He was staying at the Dharmankur Vihara, the headquarters of the Bengal Buddhist Association, and I went to see him after breakfast one morning, taking with me Terry and Thubden, as well as Sherab Nangwa, who was passing through on his way to Bodh Gaya. Like Kachu Rimpoche, Dilgo Khyentse was a follower of the Nyingma school, and like Jamyang Khyentse he was a *tulku* of the great nineteenth-century lama of that name (a lama could 'reincarnate' in more than one body at a time). He had arrived in Kalimpong as a refugee in 1959, together with his wife and his two grown-up daughters, and I had got to know him shortly afterwards when he was living in a cottage in the grounds of a Bhutanese monastery. I invariably found him sitting cross-legged on a bed in the tiny front room, a bulky Tibetan xylograph volume on his lap. Looking up from his book, he would welcome me with a smile of great sweetness, his wife would bring tea, and soon we would be deep in discussion, Sherab Nangwa usually translating. In the course of these meetings I learned much, and in 1963 he introduced me to the *sādhanas* of Jambhala and Kurukullā, besides giving me important teachings regarding the transference of one's consciousness from the mundane world to the transcendental realm of Amitābha, the Buddha of Infinite Light.[450] In 1964 I went to see him on the eve of my return to England (he was then staying in Darjeeling) and asked for his blessing. This he readily gave, and his wife, who had grown quite fond of me, presented me with a bone-handled Tibetan knife in a filigreed copper sheath. On my unexpected arrival at the Dharmankur Vihara, he welcomed me and my three companions with his usual easy dignity, and for the first time in our tour Terry had the experience of meeting someone who towered over him as much as he himself towered over others. I told my teacher about my work in England, and about the difficulties that I would have to face on my return, and once more he gave me his blessings. The difficulties were of little importance, he assured me with a smile, and would soon pass away.

The day after my meeting with Dilgo Khyentse I received a visit from Dorothy Carpenter, whom I had met in Dalhousie three months earlier. She was accompanied by a young Gelug monk named Saltim Tendzin, and I arranged for them to be lodged near Terry and me. They had just spent a week in Kalimpong, staying at the Triyana Vardhana Vihara, and they came with a proposal, namely, that four or five monks from the Lower Tantric College should be installed at the Vihara, there to be looked after by Lobsang and Thubden while they pursued their studies and meditations. In the course of the next few days we had several lengthy discussions, and in the end I agreed to accept the proposal and wrote a formal letter of invitation for Dorothy to take back to Dalhousie for delivery to the College authorities. I was pleased by the turn events had taken. I could now leave Calcutta and India with an easy conscience, knowing that my peaceful hillside hermitage would be in good hands and that some, at least, of the purposes for which it had been established would be fulfilled.

51
AGRA – ALMORA – CAIRO

The New Delhi branch of the Maha Bodhi Society was located at the Buddha Vihara, the Buddhist annexe to the very much larger Laksminarayan temple, a grandiose structure which, though dedicated to the second member of the Hindu trinity and his consort,[451] also had room for a host of lesser divinities. Both places of worship had been built by a Hindu multimillionaire philanthropist, and the difference of size no doubt reflected the relative importance of the two faiths in the eyes of a good Hindu. The Buddha Vihara occupied a special place in my personal history. I had first seen it in 1944, shortly after my arrival in India, and its modest shrine was the first Buddhist temple I had been inside. Next door there was a no less modest bungalow, on the lawn in front of which yellow robes were spread out to dry on that first occasion; but the door was locked and there was no sign of any monk.[452] In later years, when I was myself a monk, I had stayed there more than once, and had got to know the resident *bhikkhu*, Venerable Ariyawamsa. It was he who now welcomed Terry and me on our arrival from the airport and who, after giving us tea, arranged for us to be accommodated in the library.

There was much to see in New Delhi, but though my friend and I visited several handicrafts emporia and made a few purchases, our principal concern during our first two days in the city was to arrange for the dispatch of our unaccompanied luggage and to make enquiries about buses to Almora and trains to Agra. Almora was where my friends Lama Govinda and Li Gotami lived, while Agra was the city of Shah Jahan and the Taj Mahal. Owing to the possibility of strikes, there was no certainty about buses to Almora. We therefore decided to go to Agra first, and accordingly caught the fast Delhi–Agra tourist train early the following morning.

I had visited Agra – and seen the Taj Mahal – once before, in the course of my 1956 Buddha Jayanti pilgrimage with Dhardo Rimpoche. On that occasion I had been afraid that the beauty of the famous monument might be spoiled for me by all the photographs and paintings I had seen of it, not to mention the plastic models that were on sale everywhere; but in the event my fears had proved to be groundless.[453] This time, therefore, there was no question of my being disappointed, and I looked forward to seeing the Taj Mahal again as much as Terry did to seeing it for the first time. On reaching Agra station, however, we did not go straight to the Taj Mahal. Instead, we decided to catch the coach to Fatehpur Sikri, twenty-five miles away, and afterwards to see the Agra Fort, keeping the Taj Mahal for the conclusion – and culmination – of the day's sightseeing. The guidebook described Fatehpur Sikri as a ghost city, but it was a ghost city only in the sense that it had no inhabitants. There were many buildings of red sandstone which, in the brilliant sunlight, beneath a sky of cloudless blue, gave it a far from ghostly look. The city had been built by the emperor Akbar, the greatest of the Mughal rulers of India, in the latter half of the sixteenth century. Originally it was to have been joint capital with Agra, but the water supply soon dried up, the inhabitants left, and for more than 400 years Fatehpur Sikri had lain deserted. Starting from the Shahi Darwaza, or Martyrs Gate, Terry and I spent a couple of hours wandering from courtyard to spacious courtyard, and from palace to palace, admiring the red sandstone pillars and arches, and the white marble lattices, all intricately carved. Eventually we came to the Gate of Victory and the great Jamma Masjid, or Friday Mosque, within which was the white marble tomb of Sheikh Salim Chishti, the Sufi saint who had predicted the birth of Akbar's three sons.

Much of the Agra Fort was out of bounds to the public, the place being a military headquarters of some kind, but we were nonetheless able to see the greater part of Shah Jahan's palace, with its halls of public and private audience, its baths, its little marble Gem Mosque, built for the ladies of the zenana, and the pavilions that clustered round the high terrace overlooking the River Jamna. We also saw the famous tower from the top of which Shah Jahan, shortly before his death, had taken his last look at the monument he had erected for his beloved wife and where he himself was to be laid to rest. After seeing the fort, we visited the beautiful tomb of Mirza Ghiyath Beg,[454] and from there made our way to the Taj Mahal.

The entrance to the gardens in which the monument was situated lay through a massive arched gateway of red sandstone. Once inside, Terry and I saw a long avenue of dark cypresses, down the centre of which ran a waterway. At the far end of the avenue, flanked by its minarets, the world famous building showed dazzlingly white against the blue sky. From where we were standing, it looked quite small, but from previous experience I knew this to be no more than the effect of distance, and indeed, as we walked towards the platform on which it stood the rectangular frontage and surmounting dome rose ever bigger and grander before us. After climbing the steps leading to the platform and entering the deeply recessed archway in the front of the monument, we found ourselves in the high octagonal chamber containing the richly decorated cenotaphs of Shah Jahan and Mumtaz Mahal. The empty tombs lay side by side in the centre of the chamber, surrounded by a delicately carved marble screen. The actual tombs, simple and unadorned, were in the crypt immediately below, a smaller, much darker place which we also visited. On regaining the platform and the bright afternoon sunshine, we walked round the outside of the building admiring the fine relief carving, then descended into the Mughal-style gardens where, as we wandered about, Terry took a number of photographs. Later, when they were developed and printed, we agreed that no photograph could possibly do justice to Shah Jahan's masterpiece. The beauty of the Taj Mahal, like the beauty of Helen of Troy in Homer, could not be described but only inferred from the effect it had on the beholder.

Two days after our visit to Agra, we left for Almora, in the meantime having bought pottery and basketware and the cheese Lama Govinda wanted. We travelled the whole way by bus. The journey up into the Kumoan foothills took exactly twelve hours, with one change, and it was not until eight o'clock that night that we arrived in Almora. With a coolie carrying our bags, we started climbing the hill behind the town to Haimavati, the bungalow where the Govindas had made arrangements for us to stay. We reached it at ten o'clock, having passed the place in the dark and been obliged to retrace our steps.

In the morning, after the caretaker had given us breakfast and I had inspected the contents of the bookshelves, we made our way up the rough track to the Kasar Devi Ashram, three miles away. The isolated stone cottage was situated at the end of a ridge, and commanded a fine view of the snow peaks of the western Himalayas. My two friends had lived at the ashram for the last ten years or more, and I had visited them there on two separate occasions.[455] On our arrival they welcomed us – and the cheese – with open arms, and I soon perceived that Lama Govinda's kindly, unassuming manner and Li Gotami's more expressive friendliness had made Terry feel quite at home with them.[456]

At the Kasar Devi Ashram, Almora. l–r: Li Gotami, Lama Govinda and Terry (behind)

We spent five days in Almora, not including the days of our arrival and departure. On the third day we went down into the town for a few hours, principally in order to check the departure time of the Delhi bus and to visit the post office. The remaining four days were all spent at the Kasar Devi Ashram with Lama and Li, as the couple were affectionately known to their friends. Each morning we arrived at the cottage at about eleven o'clock, having breakfasted at Haimavati and read for a while, and stayed until the late afternoon or evening. 'As yesterday, spent the day in discussion, with refreshments in between,' reads one entry in my diary. Another entry reads, 'Li showed her photographs. This took more than two hours. Discussed my future literary work and other matters.' Li's photographs were those she had taken in the course of the Tsaparang Expedition, the eventful journey she and Lama had made in 1948–9 to the ruined temples of Tsaparang, the former capital of Western Tibet, a journey vividly described in Lama's book *The Way of the White Clouds*, then recently published. The discussion of my literary work was probably concerned more with the future than with the past. Lama had more than once strongly advised me to spend less time giving lectures and more writing books, and on this occasion he no doubt repeated the advice. *Littera Scripta Manet*. The written word *remains*. As for the 'other matters' discussed, I must have included my difficulties with the English Sangha Trust and my plans for a new Buddhist movement in England, and I must have received a sympathetic hearing. On the last day that we spent with them, our kind hosts performed for us the puja of the Arya Maitreya Mandala, the Vajrayāna order Lama had founded some years earlier, which had members in West Germany and Hungary and (I think) the United States. Besides making the customary offerings, they chanted the Refuges and Precepts and recited Pāli devotional verses with which I was already familiar. Thus Terry and I left them with the words of the sacred texts – and their own warm good wishes – ringing in our ears.

Our last days in Delhi – and India – were spent visiting the national museum, where there was little of Buddhist interest to be seen, and the Ladakhi Vihara, which was quite dirty, as well as in writing a large number of letters. Among the dozen or so written by me, there were letters to the Kazi and Kazini, and to Lobsang and Thubden, informing them of the arrangements I had made regarding the future of the Triyana Vardhana Vihara. On Sunday 19 February, shortly after nine o'clock in the evening, we left for Cairo.

Cairo, with Terry

In Cairo we stayed with Apa Saheb Pant,[457] who was now India's ambassador to Egypt. Since I was feverish, and Terry more depressed than he had been for a long time, we did not do much sightseeing. However, we did visit the Egyptian Museum, where we saw the gold mummy mask and other treasures from the tomb of Tutankhamun; and we did drive to Giza in order to see the pyramids and the sphinx. I had imagined these latter to be situated out in the desert, miles from anywhere, but Giza was now part of Cairo and as we drove through the suburb the Great Pyramid rose from behind the houses at the end of the street. Apart from a meal at the home of the Minister to the Embassy, these were our only outings. While Terry closeted himself in our room, I passed the time either talking with Apa Saheb and his wife Nalini, or reading about the civilization of Ancient Egypt, or simply sitting in the garden. On Wednesday 22 February, at seven-thirty in the evening, I gave a lecture at the Nile Hall. With Apa Saheb in the Chair, I spoke on 'Characteristics of Indian Spiritual Thought'. The audience was not a large one, as President Nasser happened to be making an important speech that evening at exactly the same time.

By midday on Friday 24 February Terry and I were back in London.

52
WHAT THE DISPUTE WAS ABOUT

My diary entry for Friday 24 February, 1967, reads in part as follows:

> Reached London 11.30 local time. Delayed going through customs, as one piece of baggage had been mislaid. Eventually found it. Then spent an hour collecting unaccompanied baggage. Did not leave airport till 1.30. Airline bus to Knightsbridge, then taxi to Centre House. Kathy and Marvin out, but shown our room by young Christopher. Half an hour later Kathy and Marvin came. Overjoyed to see us.

Centre House was home to a New Age group known simply as Centre. Terry and I had first become aware of the group's existence in Kalimpong, Dhardo Rimpoche having received a copy of its publicity brochure through the post. Though the group's nebulous ideology did not appeal to us, we found the brochure interesting. Not only did Centre House have a resident community; it also had rooms to let, and it was as a result of this circumstance that my friend and I now found ourselves taking a taxi to the large Victorian building at the top of Campden Hill Road and being shown our room there. Young Christopher, as my diary calls him, was the teenaged son of Christopher Hills, the founder of Centre and director of Centre House. Kathy and Marvin were a married couple who had attended my lectures at the Hampstead Vihara and the Buddhist Society. They planned to start a community of their own in

Cornwall, but were spending a few days at Centre House before their departure in order to help us settle in.

The day after our return was a busy one for both Terry and me, as were the days that followed. In the morning we discussed future plans with Kathy and Marvin, in the afternoon we met Christopher Hills and other members of the Centre House community, and in the evening we had dinner with Emile and Sara Boin and the rest of my more active supporters at the Boins' tiny flat near the British Museum. Mike Ricketts and his wife Anne were already there when we arrived, as were René Rudio and John Hipkin, and Terry and I received a very warm welcome. Mike Rogers came later. The last time I had seen any of them was at the reception the Sangha Association had given on the eve of my departure for India with Terry, five months earlier. We now met in very different circumstances. The relationship between us, too, had changed dramatically. Emile and the rest – Anne alone excepted – had been at the forefront of the campaign for my reinstatement, and a strong bond now existed between us. Though united by their devotion to the Dharma, their loyalty to me, and their determination that justice should be done, the six campaigners were of very different backgrounds. Emile, the cheerful proprietor of Sakura, the Japanese shop in Monmouth Street, was by trade a restorer of Japanese lacquer, while Sara did translation work at home.[458] René I remember only as a friend of Emile's, Mike Ricketts was an illustrator of books for children, John an up-and-coming young educationalist, and Mike Rogers a company secretary. In the course of the evening Terry and I learned a lot about what had been going on at the Hampstead Vihara, within the Buddhist Society, and among the provincial Buddhist groups while we were away. Evidently there had been quite an upheaval in the little world of British Buddhism once the contents of Goulstone's letter to me – and Walshe's underhand tactics – became generally known. In fact there had been something resembling a storm, even if it was a storm in what after all was a rather small teacup – a storm that had not yet abated and the reverberations of which would be heard for a long time. Before Terry and I left it was agreed that the following afternoon we should drive down to Crowborough in Sussex with Mike Rogers in order to meet Mr Newlin, the Sangha Trust's former benefactor, whom I had once met in Bombay, many years ago, and whom I remembered as a small, excitable man who was anxious to give money to Tibetan refugee monks. It was also agreed that we should have lunch with John in Cambridge, where he was now living, in two days' time.

The drive to Crowborough, deep in the stockbroker belt, was a pleasant one for the time of year. On the way Mike told us what he knew about H. J. Newlin. An inventor and businessman who had made his money in the City, he was now more or less retired, lived alone with his dogs and his library, and occupied himself forming and dissolving companies, moving his capital around, and carrying on a running battle with the Inland Revenue, a battle that involved an enormous amount of correspondence and which he seemed thoroughly to enjoy. He was interested in Buddhism, as his benefactions to the Sangha Trust showed; but he was also interested in Hinduism, and had developed idiosyncratic views regarding both faiths. Indeed he took himself very seriously as a thinker, and believed he had succeeded in reconciling the conflicting claims of science, philosophy, and religion. So much was this the case, Mike said, that he was trying to persuade an Oxford college to let him endow a chair for the propagation of his ideas, one of the conditions of the endowment being that the college should erect a life-sized statue of him, on the pedestal of which would be inscribed the words 'Henry John Newlin: Scientist, Philosopher, Theologian'. It was therefore not surprising that his residence, which we had difficulty finding, should be called Little Potala, or that in the course of our visit he should have treated Mike, Terry, and me to a rambling, not very coherent account of the nature and significance of his ideas. We were able, nonetheless, to discuss with him what further action should be taken with regard to the Sangha Trust. As I knew, he had already written to the trustees protesting strongly against my dismissal, and at Mike's suggestion he now agreed to write to them demanding to see their accounts. He also promised to write to the Board of Trade about the state of the Trust's finances and its failure, for many years, to submit returns to the Charity Commissioners. On the whole it was a satisfactory visit. Newlin seemed pleased that we had taken the trouble to come and see him, and despite my having been unable to agree that there was no difference between Buddhism and Vedanta, a trust he controlled subsequently made me a small allowance.

In Cambridge we had lunch with John Hipkin, as previously arranged, but not with him alone. Also present at the meal was Carmen Blacker, the University's lecturer in Japanese, who in the spring of 1965 had helped overcome the opposition on the part of the followers of Ananda Bodhi to my being invited to address the Cambridge University Buddhist Society. Though the four of us naturally discussed the way the Sangha Trust had behaved towards me ('Carmen intelligently sympathetic', my diary records), Terry and I did not spend our time in Cambridge dwelling on the subject. After lunch John took us to his new home, where we met Bronwyn and where Lodro Thaye, a red-robed English disciple of Trungpa's, came to see me. Later we went to hear F. R. Leavis speak on T. S. Eliot.[459] The famous critic's delivery was poor, and the lecture itself did not live up to his great reputation. The audience listened with rapt attention nonetheless, and I had the impression that for many of them it was enough simply to be sitting at the feet of the master. In the evening, after dinner at John's place, we made our way to the Guildhall, where we saw the Oxford versus Cambridge judo and karate competitions, which proved to be quite interesting. During the interval I spoke with Jack Austin, who was also now living in Cambridge, and who, as usual, was busy representing Buddhism on the committees of a variety of interfaith bodies.

The remainder of the week – our first week back in England – was no less fully occupied, and passed quickly. Besides spending time with Kathy and Marvin, telephoning some of my closest supporters, and (on my part) reading Neumann's *The Origins and History of Consciousness*,[460] Terry and I had a number of visitors. Prominent among the visitors were Alan – Terry's friend and former colleague – Francoise, and Thich Thien Chau, all of whom were very glad to see us. Tender-hearted Thien Chau indeed was quite overcome with emotion. We also saw Vivien in her office and visited Emile at Sakura, going our separate ways only when Terry called on his old landlady, Mrs Hartmann, and when I went to see Gerald Yorke at his Mayfair flat. As I climbed the stairs leading to the flat, there took place an amusing – and revealing – incident. Having let me in via the intercom, Gerald was leaning over the banisters and looking down into the stairwell. The instant he saw me he ran back into the flat calling out, 'Angela, Angela, he's here! *He's all right*!' It was as though he had expected to see me with my arm in a sling and a bloodstained bandage round my head. After assuring himself that I was indeed all right, and that far from being affected by the attacks of the Sangha Trust, I was in good spirits, he told me he had news for me. Rider and Co. had accepted one of Alan's designs for the dust jacket of *The Three Jewels*, and the book would be out within the next few months. There followed three hours of discussion about literary matters and about Hampstead Vihara affairs, towards the end of which we were joined by Angela. As I knew, Gerald had been one of the first to protest against my dismissal as incumbent of the Vihara (he had also taken Toby to task for having compared my conduct to that of a drunken clergyman), and while still hoping that the Sangha Trust could be persuaded to reinstate me, he was confident that inasmuch as there was a lot of good will towards me, among both Buddhists and friends of Buddhism, I would have little difficulty functioning independently, outside the framework of the existing Buddhist organizations.

That there indeed was a lot of good will towards me was demonstrated when, a few days later, I attended – and spoke at – the inauguration of Hannyakai, a new Zen group with which I had been in correspondence while still in India. The inauguration took place at the Alliance Hall, Westminster, in the presence of more than a hundred people, many of whom had come specially to hear me speak, and with Jack Austin – in his Sōtō Zen robe – occupying the chair. Besides the Marquess of Queensberry's appeal for funds and my own address the lengthy programme included a demonstration of *ikebana* – the Japanese art of flower arrangement – and demonstrations of judo and kendo. Afterwards many people came and spoke to me. Not all of them were known to me, but they all seemed very glad that I was back.

By this time I had composed a circular letter to all members and friends of the Sangha Association, and this had been sent out together with a covering letter of their own by Mike Rogers and his five fellow campaigners for my reinstatement. The letter was concerned mainly with the events of the last two and a half years, particularly those of the last few months, and it opened with a brief explanation of why I had written it.

> As it is impossible for me to reply individually to all the friends and well-wishers who have written welcoming me back to England and pledging their support for my work, and as a word from me seems called for at the present juncture, I have decided to write to you all collectively. At the same time, in view of the bond that lectures, classes, and personal interviews have established between us, I feel that I am addressing each one of you personally.

As most of you know, I went to India in 1944, subsequently spending there two years as an Anagarika (homeless wanderer), one year as a Sramanera (novice monk), and fourteen years as a Bhikshu (fully ordained monk). In 1957 I founded the Triyana Vardhana Vihara, Kalimpong, as the centre of my activities, which by this time extended over the greater part of India. I had no thought of ever returning to the West. It was my intention to live and die in the East. In 1963, however, Maurice Walshe, as chairman of the English Sangha Trust, urgently requested me to come to England and take charge of the Hampstead Buddhist Vihara. The invitation was strongly supported by Christmas Humphreys and other friends. After consulting my various gurus and spiritual teachers, and receiving their blessings on my mission, I accepted the invitation. In so doing, I made two conditions: that I would come for an initial period of six months, and that my mornings would be kept free for my own literary work.

After my arrival in August 1964 I received something like a shock. The Buddhist movement in England was far smaller and more insignificant than I had been led to believe, and both intellectually and spiritually quite mediocre. Too many of the wrong sort of people seemed to be in it for the wrong reasons. The Sangha Association and the Buddhist Society were at each other's throats, and the most alarming rumours were, I found, circulating about almost everybody of prominence. Moreover, wrong methods of meditation had seriously disturbed the mental balance of more than a dozen people. Organizationally, there was chaos. As for the psychic atmosphere, it was bad, and at the Hampstead Buddhist Vihara worse than anything I had previously encountered.

Nevertheless – indeed, all the more determinedly – I set to work. Organizational reforms were made, regular lectures given and classes held. Despite extremists, the various segments of the English Buddhist movement started becoming integrated into a recognizable whole, and gradually a more cheerful, friendly, and spiritually purposive atmosphere prevailed. All this is of course known to you. Indeed, it is the point at which many of you entered the Buddhist movement. Hence I need not elaborate. Six months went by, a year, two years. Whenever I spoke of returning to India there was a chorus of protest. Indeed, having realized the vast potential interest as yet untapped, I myself eventually decided that, as the seniormost and most experienced member of the English Sangha, my true place was in this country. When, therefore, I left for India in September last year, it was only for a short visit. At the request of the Trust, and the repeated insistence of Christmas Humphreys and other friends, I made it clear that I would be returning to England early in the New Year. A statement to this effect appeared in the October issue of the Buddhist.

The five months which I spent in India were extremely busy ones. Apart from touring among the ex-Untouchables, I had a long talk with the Dalai Lama, visited Sarnath, Buddha Gaya and other sacred places, worked with the Maha Bodhi Society of India in Calcutta and, finally, went up to Kalimpong to renew contact with friends and teachers and see what was happening at the Triyana Vardhana Vihara.

It was then that I received from George Goulstone, Administrator of the English Sangha Trust, a letter informing me of my dismissal from the Incumbency of the Hampstead Buddhist Vihara. Apart from a vague reference to 'unbecoming' behaviour no reason for this totally unexpected action was given. Friends have understandably reported me as 'shocked and distressed'. It would be truer to say that I was surprised and concerned – surprised at the depth of human perfidy and concerned for the religious life of the Vihara, which the three trustees who (I subsequently learned) had voted for my dismissal had so cynically and violently disrupted. Messrs Walshe, Goulstone, and Marcus had, apparently, hoped that the fact of my dismissal could be covered up with a bland announcement that I had decided to remain in India. But this was not to be. To me it was clear that my work in England must continue, and that I could not disappoint those who had placed their trust in me and whom I had promised I would return. My teachers, whom I consulted, were quite unimpressed by the 'difficulties' which had arisen, and calmly said, 'Return. You can work much better independently.' Moreover, as news of my dismissal leaked out a movement of massive discontent with the Trust's action and attitude began to make itself felt. Many of you wrote letters of protest. Frightened by the storm it had raised, the Trust dug its heels in and insisted that its action had the support and approval of all sections of the Sangha – a statement now known to be completely false. Even when the Buddhist Sangha Association, in a series of resolutions passed at its AGM, demanded my reinstatement, the Trust remained obdurate.

Despite the upheavals of the last few months, I remain optimistic about the future of Buddhism – properly understood – in this country. My determination to continue my work here is unshaken. The question of my Incumbency at the Hampstead Buddhist Vihara is, of course, one of the matters under dispute at the present time. But even if I do not return to Hampstead the position I occupy in the Buddhist movement in this country is quite independent of my place of residence. The Trust has constantly referred to 'the Buddhist authorities'. Who or what this expression refers to I do not know. However, I should like to make it clear that if there is any such thing as an authority in the English Buddhist movement it can only be the seniormost English-born member of the Sangha.

Whether my work in England continues to take the form it did before or whether a new departure will be necessary will be determined by the events of the next few weeks, perhaps days. You will be kept informed. But whatever the form of the work may be, the spirit remains unchanged: to make known the Buddha's Path to Enlightenment and to co-operate, in love and understanding, with all who truly seek the same goal.

With Metta and blessings,

Yours in the Dharma,
SANGHARAKSHITA
(Sthavira)

The question of whether my work in England was to continue along the previous lines, or whether a new departure would be necessary, was indeed determined by the events of the next few days. It was determined in effect by what happened – or rather did not happen – at the Emergency General Meeting of the Sangha Association which was held on 11 March at the Hampstead Vihara and which I did not attend, and could not have attended even if I had wanted to, as while I was still in India

Goulstone had written to me prohibiting my setting foot in any of the Sangha Trust's properties. The covering letter which had gone out with my own circular letter, and which was addressed to all members of the Association, was on the subject of this meeting. It was a deeply serious letter. I had returned to a sorry, even tragic state of affairs. There had been disputes in the English Buddhist movement before, but seldom had it been rent by dissension as sharp as that which now divided it. It was not a disagreement about the length of a man's hair or what he ate after midday. Basically the dispute concerned the right of a *bhikkhu* to be free of the burden of other men's projections and to lead a life authentically attuned to the different and complex conditions of Western life and thought. It further concerned the question of ownership: should English Buddhism belong to an esoteric coterie who viewed with suspicion the wider social and philosophic context in which we lived and thought – or should it be free to take hold of men and women and radically change the course of their lives? Was Buddhism in the West to continue as a 'fringe' cult with its parish priest and compliant parishioners or should it become the singular and developing centre of ordinary people's lives? *That was what the dispute was about.* There were times when to choose was imperative, the letter continued, and when the failure to choose became the cardinal existential sin against our humanity. In the face of injustice, arbitrariness, and victimization were we to resist or to succumb, to act or to acquiesce? That too was what was at stake. It was therefore most important that all those anxious to see justice done should attend the further General Meeting of the Sangha Association on 11 March. The 'Agenda' would comprise three important matters:

1. A Report of the Trust's response to the express wish of the Association that they reverse their decision dismissing the Ven. Sthavira Sangharakshita.
2. To consider the next stage in the Sthavira's restitution.
3. To consider the relationship between the Association and the Trust.

The letter concluded by declaring that the *sthavira*'s friends were anxious that the discussion should not degenerate. They would strive to remain mindful and free of anger. They had an interest in seeing that there was the fullest consideration of the facts in an atmosphere of calm objectivity.

The signatories were convinced that any open-minded observer would come to be persuaded of the gross injustice that had been committed and of the imperative need to learn the lessons of that sad and regrettable episode.

Members who were anxious to see justice done did attend the EGM, just as they had attended the AGM, but on this occasion, too, justice was not done. Though Walshe was voted from the chair (he resigned as chairman of the Sangha Association soon afterwards), he repeated all the old allegations regarding my personal conduct, adding a few more, and insisted that there was no question of the English Sangha Trust reversing its decision to dismiss me. The offensive and belligerent tone of his remarks was hardly conducive to the atmosphere of calm objectivity for which my supporters had hoped, and after an inconclusive and at times acrimonious discussion the meeting broke up. The future course of my work in England had been determined.

53
A BASEMENT IN MONMOUTH STREET

Monmouth Street was situated in the heart of London's West End, midway between Charing Cross Road on the one hand and Drury Lane and Covent Garden on the other. It was a narrow street of small, seedy shops, a café or two, and a hotel; Sakura, the Japanese shop, was located halfway down on the right as one looked towards Trafalgar Square. Previous to my departure for India I had visited the place only once (this was in the summer of 1965 when I discovered that its proprietor had been attending my lectures at the Hampstead Vihara), but after my return I was often there, sometimes with Terry, and the little shop was the scene of many a discussion between me and cheerful, loyal, Emile. The most important of these discussions, perhaps, was the one that took place two days after the EGM, when we discussed the formation of a meditation group. But where would the group meet? A new Buddhist movement might indeed be needed in England, but such a movement was as yet only an idea, even a dream. It had no premises of its own, and was not likely to have for years to come. But Emile had already given thought to the matter. Sakura had a basement, he explained. Perhaps the meditation group could meet there. The basement proved to be small and dark, and full of junk, but I thought it might serve our purpose, at least for the time being, and Emile undertook to ask his landlord if we could rent it from him. Four days later it was ours, and Emile and a few friends at once set about transforming the place into a shrine and meditation centre.

While this work was going on Terry and I were busy transferring ourselves from Centre House to my friend's old flat in Lancaster Grove, the former Other Vihara, and getting settled into our new abode. The rent at Centre House was high, and it was clear that Christopher Hills expected us to be part of Centre and its activities. During the two weeks we spent there Terry was very depressed, as indeed he had been ever since we left India. His depression had, of course, a long history, going back as it did to his unhappy childhood, the shattering of his illusions regarding marriage, his inability to re-enter the pure white light, whether through meditation or by any other means, and finally the circumstances of his divorce, including its consequences for his access to his daughter. More recently, there was his failure to meet his *ḍākinī* and the fact that now that we were back in England he would sooner or later have to resume his regular visits to his parents. He had been to Ilford once already, just to collect the Little Bus, and the thought of spending a whole weekend there made him feel physically sick. We talked about all this a lot, sometimes at great length, but our time together was by no means wholly spent in this way. We renewed our acquaintance with the Hampstead Public Library, walked in the grounds of Kenwood House, where the daffodils and crocuses were already out, and did a fair amount of reading. While Terry read Reich's *The Function of the Orgasm*, I pursued my Johnsonian studies and read, among other things, Porphyry's *On Abstinence from Animal Food* and Plutarch's *Isis and Osiris*.[461] We also listened to a good deal of music, mostly Haydn, Mozart, and Beethoven. Apart from Jack Austin, our only visitors at this time were Thien Chau and Phra Maha Prasit, my replacement at the Hampstead Vihara. The Buddhists' new leader, as the local press had dubbed him, was anxious to assure me that prior to his arrival at the Hampstead Vihara he had been ignorant of what was going on there, and that he had taken on the incumbency only because he had been asked to do so by Vichitr and the other Thai monks. Moreover, he would shortly be returning to Thailand, where he planned to give up the yellow robe and be a layman again. In these circumstances it was not surprising that there was now little activity at the Vihara, or that when Terry wanted to collect some belongings, one evening a few days after our return, we should have found the place in darkness.

After my satisfactory meeting with Maha Prasit, I spent the rest of the morning preparing the lecture I was to give at the Reading University

Buddhist Society that evening. Mike Rogers, who was an alumnus of the university, drove me there, and at eight o'clock, having met the Society's office-bearers, I spoke on 'Mind – Reactive and Creative'. In the years to come this was to prove one of my most popular lectures, being reprinted many times and translated into a number of languages. The starting point of Buddhism was the mind, which was twofold. On the one hand there was absolute mind, which was beyond the subject–object polarity; on the other, relative mind, or individual consciousness, which functioned within the framework of that polarity. Relative mind was of two kinds, reactive and creative. The reactive mind – the ordinary, everyday mind most of us used most of the time – did not act, but only *re*acted to external stimuli. It was therefore the conditioned mind inasmuch as it was dependent on, even determined by, its object. Being conditioned, it was mechanical, repetitive, and above all unaware. The creative mind, on the contrary, was not dependent on, or determined by, external stimuli. It *responded* rather than reacted, functioning out of the depths of its own intrinsic nature. It loved where there was no reason to love, was happy where there was no reason for happiness, and created where there was no possibility of creativity. Thus the creative mind was independent, spontaneous, and aware. When functioning on the highest possible level, at its highest pitch of intensity, the creative mind was identical with the Unconditioned – which was to say, it coincided with absolute mind. Not that there were literally two relative minds, one reactive and the other creative. There was only one relative mind, one individual consciousness, which was capable of functioning either reactively or creatively. Every event and every experience therefore presented us with a choice: we could *act* or we could *re*act. The spiritual life was one in which we consistently chose to be creative – to be independent rather than dependent, spontaneous rather than mechanical and repetitive, aware rather than unaware. Such was the gist of my lecture, which lasted for well over an hour and was followed by a lively discussion, as a result of which I was back at Lancaster Grove not much before midnight.[462]

A few days later I took the Tube to Holland Park, where I spent the afternoon with Adrienne Bennett, the *Maha Bodhi*'s faithful representative in Europe and the Americas. I was still having to edit the journal, and she was still helping me with articles and translations, so we discussed what should go into the next number. Except for a visit to Sakura to see how the work on the basement was progressing, my only other outing that week was to Rayleigh, where I had tea with my mother and gave her the Indian handloom silk she had wanted. Afterwards Joan came round to the bungalow with three-year-old Kamala, and Eddie soon followed. On Thursday 6 April, in the intervals between other work, I composed a kind of service for the dedication of the new shrine and meditation room, which was to take place that evening.[463] Succinct as ever, my diary describes the occasion in these words:

> At 6.10 drove round to Vihara with Terry. Picked up Thien Chau and Jack Ireland. Down at Sakura soon after 6.30. Put finishing touches to Shrine. Function started at 7. Spoke for 15 minutes, then all recited Dedication together, followed by Sevenfold Puja. Finally 20 minutes meditation. Finished 8 o'clock. Very good atmosphere. More than two dozen people present, by invitation, including Jack Austin, Graham Petchey, Anne Lobstein, Mrs Phillips, Kim Well. Gave Thien Chau and Vivien a lift back.

Emile's account of the ceremony, written for the information of our friends and well-wishers, was more expansive. Under the heading 'A Buddhist Dedication Ceremony in London' he wrote:

> An event which may turn out to be a landmark in the further development of the Buddha Dharma in Great Britain took place on the evening of the 7th April. This was the dedication ceremony of the new Triratna Meditation and Shrine Room.
>
> The ceremony was conducted by the Venerable Sthavira Sangharakshita, together with the Venerable Thien Chau from Vietnam, the Rev. Jack Austin and the Rev. Graham Petchey, both representing Sōtō Zen. The invited guests, numbering about twenty-five, were able to participate in the ceremony, which had been especially devised by the Venerable Sthavira Sangharakshita for the occasion. The ceremony started with a short talk by the Sthavira, and then proceeded with readings from Buddhist Scriptures and Puja; those attending also took the Refuges and the Precepts – a simple but very moving occasion.

Triratna shrine-room: the first Wesak celebration

The room itself has been designed, decorated, and paid for by voluntary contribution, without any connection with any official organization or society. It is somewhat in the Japanese style, the predominant colours being white, gold, rust and natural wood. There is a lacquered shrine, lit from behind by a paper-covered, Japanese shoji window, and the Teacher has a slightly raised platform, where he can use either a cushion or a chair. There are both cushions and chairs available for the participants. The atmosphere of this room is warm and quiet, most conducive to stilling the mind. An additional advantage is that, being on the premises of London's Buddhist shop, it is open during the day to individual meditators.

Initially, two meditation classes, conducted by the Venerable Sthavira Sangharakshita, will be held each week: one for beginners, and one for those who have already practised under his guidance. Further classes projected consist of a Zen Study Class, to be taken alternately by the Venerable Sangharakshita and the Rev. Jack Austin, and a fortnightly discussion meeting. Puja will also take place periodically.

The establishment of the Triratna shrine and meditation room marked the birth of the Friends of the Western Sangha which was to become, with the founding of the Western Buddhist Order a year later, the Friends of the Western Buddhist Order.[464] The new Buddhist movement was no longer just an idea, much less still only a dream. It had begun to be a reality.

54
CUI BONO?

How had the trouble started? What had led to the Trust's decision to dismiss me as incumbent of the Hampstead Vihara, so soon after my departure for India? And why was Walshe so opposed to my reinstatement? I could not help asking myself these questions as I reflected on the events of the last five or six months, as well as on all that had happened during the two years of my incumbency. So far as I could make out the trouble had started, as trouble so often does, with gossip, in this case gossip about my relationship with Terry. Dr Edward Conze, who had his own sources of information, later told me that the gossip had originated with 'the old ladies of Kensington', and I had no reason to dispute this. The ladies in question, as I well knew, were a group of some four or five middle-aged women, all of them staunch Theravādins, who lived in West London and were connected either with the Chiswick Vihara or with the Pali Text Society. Some of them regularly attended the Buddhist Society's annual summer school, and the gossip seems to have started at the summer school of 1966, which Terry and I had both attended, and to have reached Walshe not long after our departure for India.

By what means the gossip of the old ladies had reached Walshe, and whether they had gone so far as actually to slander Terry and me, was not clear. What was clear was that Walshe had panicked, as he tended to do in a crisis, that he had called a meeting of the Trust, and that he had proposed that I be dismissed as incumbent of the Hampstead Vihara. Alf Vial and Mike Hookham had, of course, objected to this high-handed and unjust proceeding, and on being out-voted by Walshe, Goulstone, and Marcus, had resigned in protest. Walshe was thus able to assure Humphreys that the trustees had voted for my dismissal unanimously and that, in any case, their action was justified by my behaviour. In these circumstances it was not surprising, perhaps, that Toby had agreed, albeit with genuine regret, that it would be better if I did not return to England. Both he and the three remaining trustees evidently assumed that in the absence of any support from either the Sangha Trust or the Buddhist Society it would be impossible for me to continue my work in England and that I would have no alternative, therefore, but to accept the face-saving formula that Goulstone's letter was shortly to offer me. They assumed, in other words, that I would agree to 'go quietly', thus enabling the Trust to announce that I had resigned as incumbent of the Hampstead Vihara, and would be staying in the East, without anyone knowing what had really happened.

These tactics having failed, and opposition to my dismissal having steadily grown among members of the Sangha Association, Walshe had dug in his heels, insisting on the Trust's legal right to dismiss me, which was incontestable, and covertly assuring people that I had been dismissed for reasons much more serious than those that had been made public. By the end of the year, however, he had become quite isolated, support for him probably being limited to a few former disciples of Ananda Bodhi. He also seems to have been apprehensive of what might happen once Terry and I were back in England, as we had originally planned. Be that as it may, in January he had agreed to publish in *The Buddhist*, of which he was now editor, a statement in which the trustees appeared to retract the charges levelled against me in Goulstone's letter. The idea of the statement had originated with Toby, who by this time was ready to dissociate himself from Walshe, and the exact wording had been hammered out in discussions between him and John Hipkin. As published in the February 1967 issue of *The Buddhist*, shortly before my return to the scene, the statement read as follows:

> The Directors of the English Sangha Trust Ltd., wish it to be known that in deciding to replace the Ven. Sthavira Sangharakshita in the office of Chief Incumbent at the Hampstead Buddhist Vihara they are not making any charge of impropriety or misconduct against him. The Directors hope that whatever may

have been said to the detriment of his character in the course of recent speculation and gossip may now be withdrawn, and that all concerned may turn their energies to the study and practice of the Dhamma.[465]

Although Toby, John Hipkin, and Walshe were collectively responsible for this statement, their reasons for wanting it to be published in *The Buddhist* were by no means the same. Toby was concerned, as ever, to protect the good name of the Buddhist movement, or rather, its reputation for British middle-class respectability. It was very regrettable that charges had ever been made against me, he had told John in the course of their discussions, and he now hoped that with the publication of the trustees' statement the fuss about me and my alleged homosexuality would die down. John himself was concerned to clear my name, a step he saw as essential to my eventual reinstatement as incumbent of the Hampstead Vihara. Toby, for his part, regarded my reinstatement as an impossibility in view of the fact that the Trust was acting within its rights. 'If you and your friends don't like its decision,' he had asked John, referring to my dismissal, 'why not get out of the Sangha Association and form a new group?' As for Walshe, so far as I could tell his reasons for wanting the Trust's statement to be published in *The Buddhist* were strictly legal, he and his two fellow trustees no doubt having realized that what he had been saying about my relationship with Terry was probably defamatory and that Terry, at least, might be thinking of taking action against him.

Whatever Walshe's reasons may have been for wanting the trustees' statement published, its appearance in the February *Buddhist* put him and his fellow trustees in a curious position. On the one hand, they denied that in deciding to replace me they were making any charge of impropriety or misconduct against me; on the other, they continued to resist the Sangha Association's demand for my reinstatement. Indeed, within a month of the statement's publication, Walshe was not only insisting, at the EGM, on the Trust's right to dismiss me, but also repeating the old allegations. Why was he so against me? Was it because I was in favour of closer cooperation between the Sangha Association and the Buddhist Society and he was not? Or was it because I had serious reservations about the 'insight meditation' with which, according to Ruth, his whole emotional security was bound up? Then there was my article 'The Meaning of Orthodoxy in Buddhism: A Protest', serialized in the January, February, and March issues of *The Buddhist*, in which I ventured to criticize an assertion by Miss I. B. Horner, the president of the Pali Text Society, that the Theravāda was 'certainly the most orthodox form of Buddhism'.[466] Were *these* the reasons why Walshe was so against me, I asked myself, and so opposed to my reinstatement as incumbent of the Hampstead Vihara? And how big a part had they played in my dismissal? Though Walshe had panicked when the gossip of the old ladies reached him, the gossip and the fact that I was out of the country may well have given him and Goulstone the opportunity to do what they had been wanting to do even before my departure. Had there, then, been a conspiracy to replace me with a Thai monk, and had Vichitr, whom Walshe saw regularly, perhaps been a party to that conspiracy? It was not easy to tell. Events had moved rapidly, a number of people had been involved, and men's real motives were in any case difficult to fathom. Perhaps instead of inquiring too closely into motives I should ask, as the lawyers sometimes did when seeking an explanation for a crime, *cui bono*? To whose benefit was the crime?

Clues were to be found in the January, February, March, and April issues of *The Buddhist*, especially in Walshe's editorials. His January editorial was entitled 'New Beginnings'. In Hampstead they had started the New Year with a new incumbent, he announced, after a few generalities, and they would be making a new beginning by going back to the fundamentals of Buddhism, in other words, by going back to the Theravāda. Evidently he believed that during the period of my incumbency there had been a distinct move in the direction of the Mahāyāna and, to that extent, a move away from the Theravāda. In this there was an element of truth. Though I had regularly lectured on the principal Theravādin teachings, teachings that were in fact common to all forms of Buddhism, I had not lectured on the Theravāda *exclusively*. I had also spoken on, or referred to, the teachings of some of the Mahāyāna schools, besides once presenting the Buddhist spiritual path in 'evolutionary' terms. In my meditation classes I had confined myself to teaching respiration-mindfulness (*ānāpānasati*), and the development of loving-kindness (*mettā bhāvanā*), both of which were regarded as Theravādin methods. Only to the Three Musketeers had I taught any distinctively Mahāyāna (Vajrayāna) practices, and Alf, Mike, and even quiet and unobtrusive Jack may well have been among those whom *The Buddhist*'s new editor described as seeking 'to run before they can walk, or even to fly before they can run'.[467] In his February editorial, entitled 'What is the Sangha?', Walshe was concerned to emphasize two things: that apart from the community of 'Noble Ones' the Sangha consisted exclusively of fully-ordained monks (there was no such thing as a 'lay sangha'), and that, basically, the monks were the preceptors of the lay people and the lay people the supporters of the monks. This was, of course, the traditional Theravādin position, the rigidity of which I had sought to moderate in my February 1965 editorial entitled 'Sangha and Laity', and Walshe may have had it in mind when writing his own editorial exactly two years later. In any case, he took occasion to remind the reader that according to one of the rules of the Sangha Association members should honour their obligations to support the Sangha, by which he meant support it financially on a regular basis, which not all those attending my lectures and classes at the Vihara had been doing.

An announcement elsewhere in the March issue drew the reader's attention to other rules. The meetings of the Association were to be concerned solely with the Buddhadhamma; speakers had to have the prior authority of the Sangha; meetings and classes, with the exception of those specifically stated to be public meetings, were to be open only to members of the Association, and members had to produce their membership cards when asked to do so. These rules had fallen into abeyance long before my arrival in Hampstead, and it was obvious why Walshe had decided to reinstate them. He wanted to make it clear that members of the Association should regard themselves as being 'lay people' in the traditional Theravādin sense, that they should be subordinate to the monks, and that the Association itself should be under the control of the Sangha Trust. An article in the April *Buddhist* suggested that it was 'back to the Theravāda' at the Biddulph meditation centre too. The article was by John Garrie, a Mancunian 'insight meditation' evangelist whom I had met once or twice, and who was now in charge of activities at Old Hall. In recent months, a programme of decoration and alteration had been completed, he declared towards the end of his article, and in fact Biddulph could well have a sign outside its door saying UNDER NEW MANAGEMENT. As Garrie was a former disciple of Ananda Bodhi, like other members of his team of 'Biddulph enthusiasts', new management naturally meant Theravādin management. The team, he moreover went on to say, was the management board of a completely new organization which had no connection with any other society or association and was only responsible to the English Sangha Trust. Thus the Sangha Association was now a Theravāda-type lay body, as was Garrie's team at Biddulph.

To whose benefit, then, was my dismissal as incumbent of the Hampstead Vihara? Evidently it was to the benefit of the Theravāda, or rather, to the benefit of the Theravādins as represented by Walshe, Goulstone, Vichitr, a minority within the Sangha Association and, no doubt, the old ladies of Kensington. Whether or not there had actually been a conspiracy, it was *they* who were responsible, directly or indirectly, for my being replaced by Phra Maha Prasit.

Yet much as my dismissal was to the benefit of the Theravādins, it was also of unintended benefit to me. Now that I was no longer incumbent of the Hampstead Vihara I was free to devote myself to the creation of a new Buddhist movement – free to devote myself to the creation, eventually, of the FWBO and the WBO. In the meantime there were lessons to be drawn from the events of the last six months. Two of these lessons were to be of particular significance for the new movement.

Though Walshe had taken the lead in the business, it was not Walshe but the Sangha Trust that had dismissed me as incumbent of the Hampstead Vihara. There were at that time five trustees, of whom four were Buddhists (if one included Goulstone), and one a non-Buddhist. Walshe and Goulstone had voted for my dismissal, Alf and Mike against it, and Marcus, the non-Buddhist trustee, had voted with Walshe and Goulstone, so that there had been a 3 to 2 majority in favour of Walshe's proposal. This meant that my dismissal, together with all the consequences of that dismissal for the religious life of the Vihara, had been the result of a deciding vote cast by a non-Buddhist member of what was ostensibly a Buddhist body. The lesson I drew from this circumstance was that a Buddhist organization had to be controlled by Buddhists, and that it was not possible for it to be controlled by Buddhists unless all its members were Buddhists. But who *was* a Buddhist? The traditional answer to the question was that a Buddhist was one who went for Refuge to the Buddha, the Dharma, and the Sangha, and to them alone. But *who* was the Buddha, *what* was the Dharma, and *who were* the members of the Sangha, and in any case, what did 'going for Refuge' to them mean? These were questions with which I had long been concerned, and in the years to come they were to occupy an increasingly central place in my own spiritual life and in the spiritual life of the movement of which I was the founder.

The second lesson to be drawn from the events of the last six months had reference to a matter that was of more general interest. The trouble, as I have called it, had started with gossip about my relationship with Terry. That relationship, it was alleged, was of a homosexual nature, and as Toby had pointed out the English middle-class mind had an abhorrence of homosexuality. So great was that abhorrence that even the *appearance* of homosexuality was sufficient, it seemed, to warrant a man's banishment from decent society or, as I had found, his removal from the position he occupied. What this meant in effect, at least in England, was that it was difficult for men to develop more than ordinarily close friendships without incurring the suspicion of homosexuality and, in some cases, the unpleasant and even painful consequences of such suspicion. But friendship occupied an important place in Buddhism, the Buddha having gone so far as to declare, on one occasion, that spiritual friendship (Pali *kalyāṇa-mittatā*, Sanskrit *kalyāna-mitratā*) was not the half but the whole of the spiritual life (*brahmacariya*).[468] Middle-class fear or hatred of homosexuality thus stood in the way of the full practice of the Dharma. The lesson I drew from *this* circumstance was that our new Buddhist movement would have to be free from homophobia, as it came to be called, if spiritual friendship was to flourish within it. Indeed it would have to be free from homophobia if it was to be truly Buddhist. Buddhism was a universal teaching, and as such its attitude was one of good will (*mettā*) towards all living beings, irrespective of race, nationality, social position, gender, or sexual orientation.

EPILOGUE

My prediction regarding Christmas Humphreys, that given time he would see the absurdity of his position and perform a volte-face, did not have to wait long for its fulfilment. Within weeks of my return to England he was making friendly overtures to me – overtures to which I did not immediately respond. Early in the 1970s I was once again lecturing at the Buddhist Society's premises in Eccleston Square under his chairmanship. During the last five or six years of his life Toby and I met fairly regularly and he assured me on more than one occasion that he had always been my best friend. In his autobiography *Both Sides of the Circle*, published in 1978, he spoke in highly complimentary terms about me and about the Western Buddhist Order, to which, he said, he gave his full support. Maurice and Ruth Walshe I saw only once more. Along with six or seven other monks I had been invited to the Vietnamese Embassy for a meal. When Maurice and Ruth entered the room and saw me chatting with the monks they were extremely confused and embarrassed, and at once retreated. Ruth died not many years later and Maurice soon remarried. After his retirement he spent the rest of his long life producing a scholarly new translation of the *Dīgha Nikāya* and campaigning against me and the FWBO. The monk who conducted his funeral service humorously remarked that he knew he was dead because when he bent over him and whispered 'Sangharakshita' in his ear, he did not react. Goulstone and Marcus I neither saw nor heard of again.

Alf Vial and Mike Hookham continued to tread the path of Tibetan Buddhism, though under the direction of another guru, Trungpa having departed for the greener pastures of the United States, while Jack Ireland pressed on with his Pāli studies, eventually producing a useful new translation of the *Udāna* and *Itivuttaka*. Ananda Bodhi travelled widely, transformed himself first into Namgyal Rimpoche and then into Star One, and developed his own 'Holistic Cleaning' method of meditation. Mangalo stayed in England and became a Church of England clergyman. Both Ratanasara and Vichitr followed Trungpa's example and betook themselves to the United States, where the latter returned to lay life and married. Viriya was not long at the Hampstead Vihara. Shortly before my return to England he left for Vietnam, Thien Chau having arranged for him to study at the Vanhanh University under my old friend Thich Minh Chau. Later he settled in Japan and married a Japanese woman. Thien Chau himself moved to Paris, where I stayed with him in 1970 and where he arranged for me to give a few lectures – my first on the Continent. Activities at the Vihara having virtually ceased, Francoise soon found herself out of a job and went to work at John Watkins, the famous oriental bookshop just off Charing Cross Road.

John Hipkin, Mike Rogers, Emile and Sara Boin, and Mike Ricketts were among the twelve founding members of the Western Buddhist Order, all of whom I ordained at Centre House on Sunday 7 April 1968, after I had given them their private ordinations, and their new names, at the Triratna meditation and shrine room in the course of the previous ten days.

And what of Terry Delamare? In August 1967 he and I moved into a bigger flat, on the third floor of an old terraced house at the lower end of Highgate West Hill. He had continued to be very depressed, and even before we moved had started seeing Dr David Cooper, the psychiatrist at whose Villa 21 he had undergone his ether abreaction – or seen the pure white light – four years earlier. Soon he was seeing him twice a week, but neither his sessions with Cooper nor the antidepressants he was now taking did him much good, and in the course of the next few months his condition grew steadily worse. My diary for these months is full of such entries as 'Terry very low all day', 'Terry extremely low again ... collapsed on the stairs', and 'Terry very low. Had quite a terrible hour.' By the end of the year he was talking of suicide and in January told me he had 'reached rock-bottom'.

Sara Boin receives her kesa during the first ordinations into the Western Buddhist Order, 7 April 1968

During this period I was busy taking meditation classes at Sakura, giving lectures in various public halls, and visiting the provincial Buddhist groups, which did *not* close their doors to me, despite Walshe's efforts to persuade them to do so. I was thus in the unenviable position of having to live in or at least commute between two very different worlds, and I often felt the strain. This was particularly the case after Terry started talking of suicide, as I took such talk seriously. More than once, having taken the meditation classes at Sakura that evening, I walked up the hill from the bus stop not knowing whether, on my arrival at the flat, I would find Terry alive or dead. The strain was exacerbated by the fact that I was unable to share my concern for Terry with any of our friends, as he was adamant that no one should know he was a victim of depression. Indeed, he put on such a good front whenever he drove me to Sakura or attended my lectures that it was a long time before Emile, Sara, and the rest suspected that there was anything wrong. The only person with whom I was able to discuss Terry's condition was Cooper, whom I met twice. I formed an unfavourable impression of him (he was to die of chronic alcoholism) and moreover found his therapeutic commonplaces unhelpful.

It was about this time that Terry wrote his parents a letter in which he told them, as tactfully as he could, that his childhood had not been a happy one – a claim to which they responded with hurt and incredulity. They were in any case quite worried about him already, the more especially as they had not seen him for nearly a year and had no idea what he was doing. Terry therefore asked me to go and see them and assure them that he had not gone mad, as they seemed to think. His father was a tall, powerfully built man who evidently had a temper, while his mother, no less obviously, was a chronic depressive. Both parents, I soon found, were convinced that the study of philosophy had affected their son's brain and that if he would only give it up and go back to his job in advertising all would be well. 'We can understand him wanting a change from work sometimes,' his mother told me, 'but he can always come and help his dad in the greenhouse on a Saturday afternoon.' Terry must have gone in fear of his father, I thought, and have sucked in depression with his mother's milk. When, therefore, he started going to pottery classes and made a black pottery head with round staring eyes and a hole of a mouth lined with jagged teeth, I was not surprised to learn that he proposed to call the hideous object 'Mother', or 'Woman', or perhaps 'Death'.

Unfortunately, I stopped keeping a diary after 15 April 1968, so that for the last year of Terry's life I have no written record but only memories. He was now living with Mafalda, a gentle, dark-haired Portuguese divorcee who had been attending my meditation classes and lectures. In January 1968 he had taken a room in a friend's house at Chalk Farm but communal living proved uncongenial to him and after a few months he had moved into Mafalda's flat in Islington. He came to see me almost every day. Some days he came twice, and sometimes he brought Mafalda with him. He continued to be deeply depressed, though he hid it from the world, even from Mafalda, and when we were alone together he talked with ever-increasing desperation of suicide. There was only one alternative, he declared: that he should be enabled to re-enter the pure white light and in this way transcend the pain of existence, which had become unbearable. With this end in view he asked Cooper to give him LSD (he had previously given him marijuana, to no effect).

Cooper agreed, but insisted that he took it under medical supervision. Terry therefore found himself taking the drug not at Mafalda's flat, and in her company, as he had wanted, but in the office of a white-coated woman doctor whose telephone kept ringing and who spent most of her time answering it. The result was that he experienced nothing. This finally convinced him that he could hope to see the pure white light only at the moment of death and that he had no choice, therefore, but to commit suicide.

In April came the FWBO's Easter Retreat, which I led and which Terry and Mafalda also attended. John Hipkin and our other friends were shocked to see how depressed and ill Terry looked, for by this time he had given up trying to conceal his condition. The retreat ended on Sunday 13 April, and after the concluding puja and meditation Terry, Mafalda, and I left for London in the Little Bus, Mafalda and I sitting beside Terry in the front seat. Halfway through the journey Terry suddenly declared that he felt like driving at top speed into the nearest brick wall and killing all three of us, and for a few minutes it seemed that he might actually do this. After dropping me at Highgate West Hill he drove on to Islington with Mafalda.

At ten o'clock the next morning I received a visit from two uniformed police officers. I knew at once what this meant. Terry had died two hours earlier, they informed me. He had died at Kentish Town Underground station, having apparently thrown himself under an approaching train, and my address had been found on his body. In response to their enquiries I told them that my friend had left nine months ago, and gave them his parents' address, as well as Mafalda's. When the officers had gone I noticed that on my desk there was a small pile of letters that had not been there the night before. Terry had come very early in the morning, while I was asleep, and left them. Two of the letters were for me.

'I must be brief for I am too upset,' the first letter began. '*My greatest fear is that I shall live after* this event, *if this should happen, please make something possible*, but I hope my remarks are superfluous.' His biggest regret, Terry went on to say, was that he never lived to bring all his energy and love – which he believed to have been quite considerable – into being. He also asked me to look after Mafalda as best I could, expressed his conviction that we could have worked miracles together on this earth, and maybe would do so another day, and reflected on the paradoxical split in his nature which had, he believed, torn him apart. He concluded, 'We will always be together. What happiness! Yours ever. T.' The second letter was much shorter and dealt with various practical matters.

A few hours later Terry's parents came to see me. They came straight from the mortuary, and reported that Terry had a slight bruise on one side of his head but looked peaceful. I gave them the letter he had left for them. In it he asked that he should be given a Buddhist funeral, that he should be cremated, and that I should be invited to conduct the funeral. He also asked that I should be given £1,000 out of his estate and Mafalda £500. His father's face darkened as he read the letter. It was not a legally valid will, he told me, and he proposed to ignore it. Terry would be given a Christian funeral and be buried in the local cemetery, so that his mother could visit the grave and change the flowers every Saturday afternoon after doing her shopping.

The next day they came again. This time it was to collect Terry's suits. There were three or four of them, and his mother insisted on my pinning sheets of newspaper round each one. 'What would the neighbours think,' she asked, 'if they were to see us coming out of the house carrying men's suits?'

'For two and a half days after Terry's death heard him calling me and felt him pulling,' I subsequently wrote in a notebook. 'Could not bear the thought of his suffering under the wheels of the underground train *alone*. Strong wish to follow. Kept seeing him standing on the edge of the platform, waiting.... Sense of waste.' Perhaps it was because of my wish to follow Terry that at some point during those two and a half days I went to Kentish Town Underground station, stood on the edge of the platform as Terry had done, and tried to imagine what it had been like for him as he waited for the train. I also attempted to describe Terry's last hours in a poem. The poem was entitled 'For the Record', and was addressed to him.

You wrote four letters, one
To your parents, one
To the girl who looked after you, one
To your accountant, and one
To your best friend
Me,

Sealed them neatly.
You wrote out
Two cheques in settlement of small
Debts,
Walked around
Here and there
Came in, went out
Two or three times
Returned my typewriter
(It was early morning,
I was in bed, asleep, did not hear you)
Felt a little uneasy,
Perhaps, for a minute or two
Parked your bus
Down at Kentish Town
In front of an old brick wall
Where it would not be in anybody's way
(After drawing the faded red
Curtains) bought a ticket
To somewhere, anywhere
Rode
Down the escalator
Stood
Heron-hunched in your old black duffle-coat
Hands thrust deep in pockets
Brooding, thinking,
Meditating,
Watched, waited
Anticipated
And when the train came
Heavily lumbering along the platform
Slowly gliding along the smooth shining rails
Suddenly threw yourself under, and in a moment
Found what you had been seeking
All your life.[469]

Under the heading 'Obituary', *FWBO Newsletter 5* carried the following report:

It is with very deep regret that we record the death of Terry Delamare on Monday, 14th April. He was born in 1934, and gave up a successful career in advertising three years ago to devote himself fully to the study of philosophy, religion and psychology. In October 1966 he accompanied the Ven. Sthavira Sangharakshita to India, where he took the remarkable series of colour slides entitled 'Buddhism in India' which has given pleasure to so many of our friends.

On Monday, 21st April a memorial service was held at 52, Noel Road, Islington, the residence of Mrs Mafalda Reis. The simple but moving ceremony was conducted by the Ven. Sangharakshita, and was attended by many friends who had not only known Terry but loved him for his great qualities of head and heart.[470]

But though I missed Terry, and wept every day for six months, what he had called 'this event' was not an unrelieved tragedy. The day after his death I took the classes at Sakura as usual. While meditating I heard these words:

Pain shall be transmuted into joy, suffering into ecstasy,
When to the eternal life of Buddhahood
We all awake.

I wish to acknowledge, with feelings of deep gratitude, the crucially important part played by Dharmachari Sarajit in the production of the last ten chapters of this book.[471]

Sangharakshita

1970 – A RETROSPECT

Throughout one's life periods of contraction tend to alternate with periods of expansion, either of which may last for months or for years. During a period of contraction one husbands one's resources, meets fewer people, reflects rather than acts, and follows well trodden paths rather than striking out in new directions. During a period of expansion, on the contrary, a spendthrift prodigality is the rule, personal contacts are multiplied, reflection finds fruition in practical achievement, and unknown dimensions are explored. Coming as it did after a long period of contraction, the year 1970 was for me on the whole a period of expansion, or at least the beginning of expansion, both geographically and spiritually.

At the invitation of French and Vietnamese Buddhists living in Paris, at the beginning of January I visited France, spending four days in Paris with my old friend Thich Chien Chau and two days at Luynes, in the Loire Valley, as the guest of Antoinette Willmott, who is translating *A Survey of Buddhism* into French. The object of the visit was both religious and cultural, 'official' and personal. In addition to lecturing on Buddhism, and meeting both foreign and native-born Buddhists and students of the Dharma, thanks to the kindness of Vietnamese friends I saw a good deal of Paris and visited a number of places of cultural and historical interest, including the Louvre, the Musée Guimet, Notre Dame, and Les Invalides. On the banks of the Seine, in the Latin Quarter, and in Montmartre, I felt particularly at home.[472]

We visited Montmartre at midnight. It had been snowing, and a brilliant full moon cast black shadows across the narrow snow-covered streets, through which blew a chill wind. On our way to Sacré Coeur we passed the brightly lit windows of ancient taverns from which, despite the lateness of the hour, there came the sound of revelry and the rich warm smell of cooking. Our way led through a tiny square in which stood two or three small leafless trees. Despite the bitter cold, a few artists were still sitting by their paintings, or walking up and down in front of them, in hope of a sale. A number of visitors to the quarter were, in fact, drifting from one group of paintings to another.

At the Louvre I was disappointed by the *Venus de Milo* and failed to see the *Mona Lisa*.[473] The Musée Guimet was much smaller and less rich in content than, from its reputation, I had been led to suppose; but the Khmer sculptures more than made up for any disappointment. The interior of Les Invalides seemed coldly pompous, lacking any true dignity and grandeur. From the Eiffel Tower, which I ascended on the day after my arrival, it was noticeable that the skyline of Paris, unlike that of London, was not rendered unsightly by blocks of flats or modern office buildings. Here culture had not been forced to yield to commercialism: the fact impressed me deeply.

While staying with Antoinette at Luynes I spent an afternoon in the ancient town of Tours, associated with the names of Ronsard and Balzac,[474] and visited the cathedral. The stained glass, said to be the second finest in France, was magnificent. The building itself, however, was badly in need of restoration. Driving into Tours along the snow-filled country roads I noticed enormous bunches of mistletoe hanging from almost every tree. Next day, on our way to the railway station, I saw a sight of even greater interest. For a distance of several miles the limestone cliffs overlooking the River Loire were honeycombed with dwellings, apparently all inhabited. It was fascinating to speculate that some of them might have been under continuous occupation since prehistoric times. All the dwellings had brightly painted doors and window frames, which gave them a neat and homely look. Most were double-storeyed, and of roughly the same height, but having been hollowed out of the rock at different levels they presented a picture of pleasing irregularity. Antoinette's husband remarked that some of the excavations were enormous, with vaults going miles back into the hillside, and that the biggest of them was said to house a top secret military establishment. Even here one was not allowed to forget that one was in the France of Charles de Gaulle.[475]

Though more significant in every way, and though taking me much further afield for a much longer time, my visit to the United States was of the same general character as my visit to France. Strictly speaking, it was a visit to New England, as I spent most of my time in Newhaven, Connecticut, with brief visits to Massachusetts, Rhode Island, New Jersey, and New York. The visit was organized by Tom Kasulis, a Senior of Berkeley College, Yale, who had attended my meditation classes in London the previous year, as well as participating in the summer retreat at Haslemere, and who had thought it would be a good idea if I could be 'let loose on the Yale campus'. With commendable efficiency, he had set up a Hall Seminar on 'Buddhism and the West' at Berkeley College and persuaded the authorities to invite me. I did not know it at the time, but a number of academic and administrative hurdles had to be surmounted before this could be done. Eventually, however, the official invitation was issued, was accepted, and on a crisp sunny afternoon in January I found myself, for the first time, in the United States of America.

From the first the visit was full of minor surprises. Instead of being detained, possibly interrogated, I went through customs and immigration control in a matter of minutes. In the arrival hall of the airport I saw a white woman rushing forward and greeting a black woman with rapturous embraces. A less welcome sight was that of two beefy policemen swaggering through the crowd swinging their batons and looking provocatively from side to side as if in search of trouble. Despite surprises, however, and despite certain differences between the American and the English way of life, I felt completely at home in America from the very first. On my return to England friends enquired, with solicitude, how long it had taken me to adjust. But there was really no question of adjustment at all. Admittedly, this was in great part due to the warmth and friendliness of my reception at Yale, or rather, at Berkeley College. The question of how and where I was to be accommodated had been the subject of anxious consultation between Tom and the College authorities, as well as correspondence with me, but soon after my arrival I was comfortably installed in the heart of the College in rooms overlooking the courtyard.

Excluding the two weeks of the Easter holiday, for which I flew back to England to conduct the Easter retreat, I spent three months at Yale. During this time all that was expected of me, in my official capacity as Visiting Lecturer in Philosophy, was that I should teach once a week for two hours, the way in which I organized the seminar being otherwise left entirely to my own discretion. As much ground had to be covered in a short time, and as some of my students had no previous acquaintance with Eastern thought, I decided to devote half the time at our disposal each week to a formal lecture and half to a discussion. I also decided to divide the whole course into two parts. In the first part I dealt with the Three Jewels, with the triad of morality, meditation, and wisdom, with the development of Buddhism, and with karma and rebirth. Having prepared the ground in this way, in the second part, coming to the meat of the seminar, I dealt with archetypal symbolism in the biography of the Buddha, with Karl Jaspers and Buddhism, with Zen and psychotherapy, and with evolution, lower and higher. To me all this was of course familiar ground. To my students, however, it was not only unfamiliar, not to say strange, but for the most part highly stimulating, and after each lecture they bombarded me with questions so vigorously, and I responded with such zest, that discussion usually lasted for two hours instead of for one, while some of the things they heard struck certain of the students with the force of a revelation.

With the seminar itself accounting for so small a portion of my week, I had ample time for extra-curricular activities, as well as for a limited participation in the social and cultural life of the Yale community. On Sunday evenings I held a meditation class in the Berkeley College common room, which willing hands transformed into a temporary Buddhist shrine complete with image, lighted candles, and incense. Before many weeks had passed this class was attracting upwards of eighty people, the majority of them students, but including a sprinkling of faculty members and friends from off campus. Half a dozen enthusiasts also met in my study for meditation every afternoon. Due to the influence of Zen, as well as to a recent visit from the Maharishi[476] and other factors, meditation was in fact rather in the air at Yale. Once I estimated that between five and ten per cent of the student population had at some time practised it in one form or another. Most of those who attended my class seemed to derive definite psychological benefit from the practice. A few made astonishing progress in a short time. Beyond a certain point, however, meditation seemed incompatible with normal student life. For several of my pupils this fact constituted a real problem.

From meditation it was only a step to human communication. Having already conducted a number of mixed communication courses in England,[477] I thought it might be a good idea to take advantage of the still predominantly masculine membership of the College and experiment with an all-male course. Friends to whom I mentioned the idea received it with enthusiasm. Twenty-six students enrolled for the course, which consisted of three sessions held late at night on three consecutive evenings of the week. The absence of women seemed to make no difference. The amount of negative emotion released in the exercises was indeed so extraordinary, and the resultant uproar so loud, that at one point one of the College guards looked in to see what was wrong. As I remarked afterwards, I felt as though I was in charge of a herd of stampeding young bulls. Two or three pairs of students

At Yale with Ben Guntersame

succeeded in breaking through into, and for a time experiencing, authentic human communication to an almost transcendental degree. On nearly everybody who participated the course had a highly tonic effect. Plans for a second course, this time a mixed one, were frustrated by stirring events inside and outside the University over which we had no control.

Since it was my first visit to the United States, the temptation to see as much of the country as possible while I was there was a strong one, especially as invitations reached me from as far afield as California. My commitments at Yale being what they were I could easily have spent the greater part of my time looking up personal friends (people who had visited me in India, or in England), inspecting Buddhist centres, and sightseeing. After thinking the matter over, however, I decided to stay where I was. Better to experience a small section of America in comparative depth than to skim the surface of a much larger area. Three months was in any case not too long a time to devote to a place like Yale, or even to Berkeley College. I therefore stuck to my rooms, cultivated the friendship of the students, got to know some of my colleagues, joined a poetry seminar, and in short tried to get as much as I possibly could out of life on the campus. A few short excursions, however, I did make. These were to Cape Cod; to Amherst, Massachusetts; and to Freemantle, New Jersey. On my way back to England at Easter I also spent four days in New York.

Cape Cod lies at the end of a long peninsula that curves up from the coast of North America just below Boston. On this occasion I went not for the sake of seeing the marvellous natural beauty of the area, where iron suspension bridges link fairy islands in an archipelago of loveliness, but to watch a total eclipse of the sun, of which from that longitude one would be able to have an almost perfect view. On our arrival in the middle of the morning of 8 March (we had left New Haven by car the previous evening, and spent the night at the Fantastic Umbrella Factory, a rural hippy commune) we found the broad white sands covered with about two thousand people, all shivering in the brilliant winter sunshine and waiting for the eclipse to begin. Some of them were trying to warm themselves round bonfires of driftwood. Dan and Randy and I, and the friends who had accompanied us, soon had a bonfire of our own blazing, and while the rest improvised a game of baseball I prepared a kind of vegetable stew. Presently it grew dark. It also grew very much colder. Dogs howled. Pieces of smoked glass, or exposed film, were passed from hand to hand. It was shortly after noon, and a shadow had appeared on one side of the sun's disk, as though an enormous bite had been taken out of it. Within an hour the shadow had grown much bigger, had in fact almost totally obscured the sun. By this time everybody's eyes were fixed on the battle that was taking place, as it seemed, in the heavens. The sun appeared to be struggling in the grip of some gigantic adversary. It was being overpowered. It was appealing to us for help. Between the struggling luminary in the sky and the human spectators on earth flashed an electric current of sympathy. We knew that the sun was in danger, we wanted to help him, and he knew that we knew. Suddenly, at the very moment that the shadow covered him completely, and defeat seemed imminent, the sun seemed to wrench himself free from his opponent's grasp and leap in the air. On the side on which the shadow had first been there appeared a crescent of dazzling gold. The instant it appeared an inarticulate roar of relief and triumph burst from the throats of the crowd. The sun was free! The forces of light had triumphed over the forces of darkness. Life could go on.

In Amherst I spent two days as the guest of Joe and Teresina Havens, with whom I had become acquainted in London two years before, when they were enjoying a sabbatical, and who had invited me to accompany them to the Victoria and Albert Museum to look at the Tibetan Mandala paintings there, in the symbolism of which they were both deeply interested and which they wanted me to explain. Joe, a Jungian analyst specializing in work with groups, also spent a few days at one of our retreats. By the time I visited Amherst spring had come and it was warm and sunny enough for us to be able to have lunch in the garden. Sitting in a deckchair, I inhaled the perfume of the violets that looked up at me from the long grass. But I was not allowed to sit there for long. Teresina, a woman of the indefatigable New England breed who taught comparative religion and English literature, was determined that I should get as much as possible out of Amherst and that Amherst should get as much as possible out of me. Besides giving the four lectures that had been arranged for me at the University of Massachusetts, Smith College, and elsewhere, I visited museums and art galleries, met a number of Teresina's friends, students, and colleagues, listened to some young jazz musicians, explored the beautiful riverside campus with its green lawns and flowering trees, and attended a lecture by Buckminster Fuller when the old gentleman spoke for two hours and twenty minutes without stopping and ended up fresher and livelier than he had begun.[478] After the leisured pace of Yale I found this whirlwind of activity quite exhilarating. We even had time to sit by a waterfall listening to the roar of the water as it fell and feeling the cold spray on our faces. While others drowsed, Teresina practised t'ai chi ch'uan movements on the grass.

On my visit to New Jersey I was accompanied by a member of the American Buddhist Order, a student at Yale. After the Second World War a number of Kalmyk Buddhists, originally refugees from Soviet Russia, had found refuge in the Garden State and had settled down there as farmers. Their spiritual head was Geshe Wangyal, a Mongolian lama whom I had known in Kalimpong in the early fifties.[479] Now well stricken with years, being over seventy, he was delighted to see me. For my part, I was happy not only to meet him once more but to see the Buddhist monastic centre which, almost single-handed, he had created in the heart of rural America. Standing in the shrine, with its painted scrolls, images, prayerful atmosphere, and special throne for the Dalai Lama, one was immediately transported to pre-communist Tibet. Unfortunately Geshe Wangyal was a disappointed man. His efforts to ensure the survival of the centre and the continuation of the work after his death had failed. Young refugee monks whom he had brought from India, he explained, had no interest in Buddhism and the spiritual life; as soon as they had learned English they got jobs, left the Order, and married. All that he wanted to do was to retire to a hermitage he had built eighty miles away, in an isolated spot, and tell his beads in peace. With tears in his eyes he begged me to stay and take charge of the centre. Almost with tears in my own I had to refuse, explaining that I was in the United States only on a visit, and that having started a new Buddhist movement in England I had there responsibilities which it was impossible to abandon.

Due to the imposing height of its principal buildings and the enormous length of its broad avenues, like Rome and New Delhi, but unlike London, New York had about it a faintly imperial air. Contrary to what I had been told, even in the heart of the megalopolis traffic was no faster, and the crowds no more dense, than in central London. Many of the huge apartment buildings were in a semi-derelict condition, garbage flowed from rows of unemptied dustbins (there may have been a strike that week), while even main roads were paved with cobbles, as in Paris. All the same New York was New York. Everything was on a bigger scale than anywhere else. There was more space in which to move – as it were more air to breathe. Life was real, life was earnest, and a sense of excitement, of exhilaration, filled the air. Until I was able to find my way round on my own, Dan, with whom I was staying, acted as my companion and guide. In the four days at my disposal I saw places of interest of all kinds, from the Metropolitan Museum of Art to McSorley's, and from Wall Street to Greenwich Village. At the Metropolitan, Rembrandt's paintings in particular arrested my attention, especially *Aristotle Contemplating a Bust of Homer*,[480] recently acquired, which seemed to have an unfathomable depth of meaning, and from which I had difficulty in tearing myself away. On my last evening Dan and his brother Steve and I spent a couple of hours sitting on a rock in Central Park. It was strangely silent. In the black waters of the lake at our feet sparkled the lighted windows of a row of inverted skyscrapers. On the other side of the park, looming up against the blackness of the sky, stood the skyscrapers themselves, brilliant with ten thousand eyes. Gazing up at them, I saw that America is not just another continent, but a new civilization, alien to that of Europe as the stars are to the Earth.

During the second half of the term the peaceful life of the campus was disrupted, and the town disturbed, by the same stirring events that made it impossible for me to hold a second communication course. So far Yale had not been touched by the wave of violence which, in the course of the last few years, had swept so many American universities, but it seemed that now it was about to engulf us. The immediate cause of the trouble was the trial, in New Haven, of the Black Panther leader Bobby Seale on a charge of murder.[481] As Seale was a negro, and moreover the leader of a paramilitary organization that did not disbelieve in violence, it was widely felt that he would not receive a fair trial. Demands were therefore made that the trial should be called off. This the authorities refused to do. Demonstrations accordingly took place outside the courthouse, a huge neo-classical building whose pillared façade fronted the Green, only a couple of hundred yards down the road from Berkeley College, and a potentially explosive situation developed. Most student and faculty members only wanted justice to be done, and to be seen to be done; but for a handful of extremists this was the opportunity for which they had been looking, and they collaborated with Black Panther Party workers in trying to stir up trouble. For two whole weeks the trial, and the implications of the trial, were the sole topic of conversation. Each day brought its teach-ins, its dining hall meetings, its propaganda films, and its shower of printed matter. Classes were boycotted, students and faculty members went on strike, and the academic life of the University came to a standstill. But for the tactful way in which the situation was handled by the President of Yale, Kingman Brewster Jr., things could have been far worse. As it was, one student was killed, and several others injured, while thousands of books were burned when, in a senseless act of incendiarism, the Law School Library was set on fire.

With the approach of May Day, for which a huge demonstration had been planned, rumours multiplied and tension greatly increased. Demonstrators were reported to be pouring into New Haven from all over America, and the extremist leaders predicted a turnout of at least a hundred thousand, possibly a quarter of a million. A thousand Weathermen were on the march, it was said, and two thousand Minutemen, and an armed clash between the two groups was expected that would lead to general violence and drench the whole campus in blood.[482] At their downtown headquarters, members of the Black Panther Party and their extremist white supporters devoted several hours a day to revolver practice. Across the corridor from my bedroom, a right-wing Senior oiled and cleaned his own weapon in readiness. I remained aloof. The negro community undoubtedly had ample cause for complaint, but the tactics of the Black Panthers seemed calculated to alienate, rather than to conciliate, the sympathy and good will of the white American majority with whom, after all, they had to live as fellow citizens. Throughout the disturbances, I therefore held my seminar as usual. When I asked my students why they did not boycott my classes they replied that they were not classes in the ordinary sense of the term. My sole concession to the situation was to allow my students to discuss it one evening in class after we had disposed of the lecture. Some of them were puzzled and confused, not sure what was the right thing to do in the circumstances, and beginning to tire of all the excitement. When they asked me for my opinion, I replied that I was not on principle opposed to external action, including political action, but that I gravely doubted the value of any such action that did not proceed from awareness. So far as I had observed, the majority of the activists were quite unconscious of their real motives. The Black Panthers, in particular, seemed blinded by hatred of a quite pathological degree of intensity. Indeed the student body as a whole seemed to be influenced much more by emotion than by reason. At a meeting at which I had been present, the four-thousand-strong audience had applauded enthusiastically when the Chaplain of the University, a noted liberal, appealed to them to make the demonstration a non-violent one. They had applauded with equal enthusiasm, and apparently equal conviction, when subsequent speakers made a no less impassioned plea for violence. I was reminded, I said, of the fickle behaviour of the Roman mob in Shakespeare's *Julius Caesar*.

By the time May Day weekend came, special security arrangements were in force in all the colleges. In Berkeley, two thirds of the students had left, or been withdrawn by their parents, while of the fellows and faculty members only the Master, the Dean, and I were left. Casualties being expected in large numbers, hundreds of medical orderlies had been recruited and hastily trained. In New Haven, police were very much in evidence, and gangs of negro youths roamed the streets. Four thousand National Guards had been stationed on the outskirts of the town and an unknown number of troops held in reserve. The great day itself, which fell on a Sunday, dawned fine and clear. Demonstrators in colourful garb, some of them gentle young women with babies, started arriving at the College, where arrangements had been made for their reception. At about noon I strolled down to the Green with the Master's wife and a few other friends to see what was happening. Thousands of youthful demonstrators were lying on the grass, some of them sunbathing. Tape-recorded speeches, interspersed with announcements, blared from the loudspeaker system. Black Panther buttonhole badges and Party literature were being hawked about, as well as Coca-Cola, ice-cream, and coloured balloons, and a festive, almost holiday atmosphere prevailed. On the way back to College I saw a pleasant-faced youngster sprawling on the steps. He was wearing buttercup-yellow flared pants and a bright pink shirt and was barefoot. On his head, tilted at a rakish angle, was a wreath of white flowers. As I passed him, we could not help smiling at each other. That night thirty thousand people took part in the demonstration. There was no violence. Scuffles were immediately suppressed by the student marshals, and the police had to intervene with tear gas bombs only twice. Next morning, with a sigh of relief that it was all over, the University went back to work. Apparently the fine weather had saved the situation. Angry and disappointed, the extremists complained that the students, seduced by the sunshine, had treated the occasion as a picnic rather than as a demonstration.

What with preparations for departure, and the inevitable leave-takings, my final week at Yale passed quickly. On the last night, Dan and Randy took me down to the beach, where we made a bonfire of driftwood and sat round it till two o'clock in the morning. In New York I went to the Ballet Joubert and saw an impressive performance of *Petroushka* and other works.[483] Late that night Dan and I climbed up to the flat roof of the twelve-storey apartment house where we were staying. All around us, like petals around the calyx of a gigantic flower, half a dozen skyscrapers, brilliantly lighted up, rose hundreds of storeys above us into the sky. Next morning I said goodbye to America.

During my absence from England the responsibility for conducting regular meditation classes had devolved on a few of the more active and experienced members of the Order. On my return I was pleased to find that, far from there having been any falling off while I was away, attendance at these classes had actually increased, each of them now containing a sprinkling of faces that to me, at least, were entirely new. Indeed, I was not only pleased by this fact but enthused, for one of the main reasons for my accepting the invitation to Yale had been that this would give me an opportunity of finding out whether or not the movement in London, to which I had devoted three years of my life, was capable of standing on its own feet for three months. Being now assured that it could not only stand but even walk, I returned with renewed enthusiasm to the accustomed routine of meditation classes, meetings of the Order, public lectures, council meetings, seminars, and retreats. No sooner was I back in harness, however, than I became aware that, in comparison with what I had experienced in the States, everything seemed smaller in scale and driven by a less dynamic impulse. People seemed less interested in things, less enthusiastic, *less alive*. At first I thought that this prevailing dullness and lethargy was a malaise afflicting the entire British people, perhaps consequent upon their losing their dominating position in world affairs. But then I thought that perhaps it was peculiar to English Buddhists, some of whom did seem to be below rather than above the average in liveliness and intelligence. Eventually I came to the conclusion that there was something to be said for both views, and that the general lifelessness of most of the people with whom I was associating was due to both social and individual factors. Nevertheless, I did not despair, and by way of both precept and example strove to infuse new life and energy into the movement. In the case of a few of those most closely associated with me, I knew that their lifelessness represented a definite stage in their development and that as such it was more apparent than real. Increased awareness had dissolved the old unconscious, conditioned motives for action, but new ones – freer, more spontaneous – had not yet emerged.

Among the most important of the activities to which I again devoted myself were the autumn lectures at Centre House and the two annual retreats at Haslemere in Surrey. Ever since my original return to England in 1964 it had been becoming increasingly clear to me that all my lectures, but more especially the different series given since 1967 under the auspices of the Friends, together constituted not only a systematic exposition of the fundamentals of Buddhism, interpreted from a non-sectarian point of view, but at the same time a total synthesis of traditional spiritual wisdom and modern scientific knowledge as represented, in particular, by biology, anthropology and psychology. The fullest and most detailed exposition of this synthesis was contained in the eight lectures on 'The Higher Evolution of Man' which I gave in the autumn of 1969. In this series I dealt with the subject in a very general manner, that is to say, in terms of biology, history, art, comparative religion, Hīnayāna and Mahāyāna Buddhism, and Modern Thought (Nietzsche). In the autumn of 1970 I gave a corresponding series of eight lectures on 'The Higher Evolution of the Individual'. Here the subject was dealt with in terms of the psychological and spiritual development, here and now, of the individual human being, with special reference to various problems arising in the course of this process. This series was consistently well attended, from seventy to eighty people being present at every lecture. Several members of the audience were on occasion in a state of evident shock, having only now realized that the light-hearted spirit in which they had taken up Buddhism, or the spiritual life, or the Higher Evolution, was in no way justified by the seriousness of the enterprise. It was as if they had awakened from a dream and now saw, for the first time, how precipitous was the ascent, how lofty the peaks they proposed to scale, and how terrifying the abysses that yawned on every side.

For some Friends the easter and summer retreats are the most important event of the year. With the help of meditation, lectures, discussion, communication exercises, and chanting, those present try to create for a few days, or even a few fleeting minutes, the nucleus of a spiritual community. This year's retreats not only fulfilled this purpose but had, as usual, a character of their own. The Easter retreat, indeed, fell in the middle of the spring term at Yale, and I flew back to England specially to take part in it. My evening in Central Park with Dan and Steve, as well as a short walk through the rain from Grand Central to the air terminal next morning, had given me, however, a severe chill. The fact would not be worth mentioning but for its consequences, which brought me nearer to death than I had ever been in my life. Indeed, it would almost be correct to say that I died.

Having tried to make up for my initial neglect of the infection by spending two days in bed, I arrived at Keffolds on the Friday evening,[484] and despite a painful cough felt well enough to conduct the puja and deliver a short address. At ten o'clock, thinking discretion the better part of valour, I retired for the night. At eleven o'clock, however, in response to an irresistible inner compulsion, I got out of bed and sat up cross legged in an armchair. I knew that if I continued lying down, or dropped off to sleep, I might well never open my eyes again. Kevin, who had wrapped me in blankets, and who was sitting up with me, lit a stick of incense, and for some reason gave it to me to hold. As I sat holding it, something strange in my expression, or attitude, made him ask me what I was thinking. I said I was thinking of the Tibetan custom of mourners carrying sticks of incense in funeral processions. This alarmed him, and he went and roused Brenda and asked her to come and take my temperature. It was 104°.[485] Brenda looked thoughtful, and said we would have to call the doctor in the morning. After making me comfortable she returned to her room. It was by that time about one o'clock. Kevin continued sitting up with me, and at intervals I told him how I felt. Though feeling physically very unwell, I was in a deeply meditative mood. Body and mind seemed to have separated and the latter to have withdrawn to a distance of thirty or forty feet. Observing this (I seemed to be neither the body nor the mind), I noted that so far as my experience at that moment went, the old dualistic way of speaking of death as a departure of the soul from the body seemed perfectly in accordance with the facts. Though I saw that I could easily die, this consideration did not disturb me in the least. Like the two empty pans of a scale, desire for life and desire for death hung exactly balanced, without even the shadow of turning in either direction. My mood was one of profound tranquillity. Though aware of work unfinished, and friends who still depended on my guidance, I viewed the prospect of departure from it all with absolute unconcern. My usual attitude being one of wanting to finish whatever I had begun, I could not help noticing the difference, though without surprise. Strangest of all, I felt no need whatever for any kind of religious support or consolation, and my mind did not once advert to the Buddha or Buddhism, or to spiritual principles or symbols of any other kind. I felt perfectly self-contained and self-sufficient. When I tried to give Kevin some idea of my state of mind, he not unnaturally became upset, and I asked him to put his arms around me. As he did so, crying, 'You mustn't go away yet, I need you too much!' it was as though a hair had been placed in the pan of life, so that, by an infinitesimal fraction, desire for life outweighed desire for death. From that instant I felt energy beginning to flow into me. A slight perspiration came on, and by two o'clock I felt well enough to send Kevin to bed. After sitting up alone till four o'clock, still in a meditative mood, I went back to bed and slept soundly.

When the doctor came next morning he diagnosed bronchial pneumonia, and said that I had had a lucky escape. Whether on account of the medicines he prescribed, or because of what happened that night, I recovered rapidly, and a few days later was well enough to conduct the communication exercises. The experience left me with permanent impressions. I am convinced that dying is, or at least can be, a pleasant rather than an unpleasant experience. I also feel that I may not have as much time in which to finish my work as I had, perhaps, previously supposed, and that it therefore behoves me to make the best possible use of every hour still remaining to me.

The experience of physical death, whether complete or only partial, resembles not only the state of heightened consciousness loosely termed meditation but also, to some degree, the 'psychedelic' condition, and of this too I had some experience in the course of the year. On the eve of my departure for Yale, Kevin and I, and another friend (one other being present who did not take the drug)[486] swallowed a moderate quantity of a blue powder and awaited results. It was my second such experience, the first having occurred ten months earlier. Though simple

With Kevin Brooks

curiosity had also played a part, my principal reason for undertaking the experiment was that with so many people asking me what I thought of the use of drugs, and even looking for personal guidance on the subject, I had come to feel, with increasing clarity of conviction, that it was incumbent upon me to speak, if I spoke at all, from experience rather than from hearsay.

About half an hour after our ingesting the drug, and before it had properly taken effect, Kevin suggested that the two of us go out for a walk. It was a fine day, cold, but with sunshine and blue sky. On Hampstead Heath, to which we directed our steps, a number of people were taking the air. As we skirted Highgate Ponds, passed through a grove of leafless oaks, and climbed the westward slope of Parliament

Hill, the drug started taking effect. Rainbows appeared at the edges of gnarled trunks and along the branches and delicate twigs of trees, and I began to feel as though I was losing control of my limbs. There was also, I think, a slight sensation of nausea. Kevin placed his hand against the trunk of a tree. The rough texture of the bark, and its mottled greens and browns, stood out with extraordinary vividness. Corrugations seemed like mountain ranges; vertical cracks had the mysterious depth of ravines. On the top of the hill, which commands a view of practically the whole of London, men and boys were launching kites into the stiff breeze, and we sat down on a bench for a few minutes and watched them. Descending the hill on the other side, and passing through the gloom of more trees, we made our way back to the main road. By this time my legs were moving mechanically, and I felt as though I was floating rather than walking. Faces loomed upon us with frightful intensity. Colours flashed and exploded. When a clergyman with a ghastly yellow face and grin of utter insanity shot past us with his wife and five children the realization that this bundle of neuroses was actually functioning as a religious teacher had a nightmare quality about it. People seemed caricatures of themselves, except that the caricatures were the people.

Having crossed the main road, as Kevin wanted to buy some tobacco, we were faced with the problem of crossing back to the Parliament Hill Fields side so as to be able to proceed homewards up Highgate West Hill. The effect of the drug was nearing its peak. Objects were now not only unbearably brilliant in colour but fast losing their solidity. Everything was floating, transparent, diaphanous, like soap bubbles. We could pass through everything; everything could pass through us. Stepping off the pavement as cars were speeding past, Kevin remarked that it was as though there was no danger of being run over, as even if he walked straight into a car it would simply pass through him. Seizing his arm, I steered him across the road to the pavement on the other side. With the fast vanishing remnants of my practical consciousness, I realized that we ought to get home without delay. My legs were functioning quite smoothly without me. We floated rather than walked up West Hill, floated in through the front door and up the stairs, floated into the sitting room of my second floor flat, where our friends were waiting for us (we had been out half an hour) and where I at once stretched out full length on the divan. The face of one of our friends loomed up close to my own like some gigantic billboard face. Behind the billboard was another, behind that another. There was a whole series of billboards.... Presently a voice seemed to come from somewhere behind them. It came from the depths, and every word had the resonance of infinite space and lasted for ages....

Everything now seemed not only diaphanous, not only bubble-like, but in movement. It was like the waves of the sea. The waves were all rising and falling, rising and falling. Every wave was a flower, a flower with a million petals, a flower that was the universe, and every flower was opening up from a centre, unfolding from infinite depths, unfolding in a timeless explosion of stars, lights, and jewels.... Everything was rising and falling, flashing and shining, opening and flowering, and now, from the heart of everything in the universe, as it unfolded, came a wondrous sound, the sound *oṃ*, came with absolute inevitability, came like music, came sonorous and infinitely prolonged, yet at the same time rising and falling, expanding and contracting, coming and going.... *Oṃ* was coming from the depths of our being too, we too were unfolding, we too were chanting *oṃ*. *Oṃ*, *oṃ* we said softly, with incredible satisfaction and delight, as we moved about the room, *oṃ*, *oṃ*, *oṃ*.... All ordinary sense of time had disappeared, but when, by the clock, about an hour had passed, *Oṃ* changed to Yes.... 'Yes, yes,' we said, slowly and wonderingly, in one long continuous blissful affirmation of existence. Yes ... yes ... yes ... yes ... yes ... yes....

Eventually I became aware that I was again lying on the divan. Four or five hours had passed. There seemed to be a disturbance in the corner – the friend who was tripping with us was crying, and Kevin was having to talk to him. Presently I heard Kevin telling me that they were going in to the other room.... Later, when the trip was drawing to a close, we turned on the radio. Someone was being interviewed about his life and career. Both questions and answers seemed so unspeakably fatuous, so stilted and pompous and empty, that at every few words all four of us burst into roars of laughter. Next came some classical music, but it seemed tinny and artificial.... At two o'clock our two friends went to bed, while Kevin and I lay down fully dressed on the divan with my cloak over us, and remained there talking, and occasionally dozing, until nearly five o'clock. During our walk on Hampstead Heath we had passed near Boadicea's barrow,[487] and we were now two Roman soldiers on guard duty. At five o'clock, when it was still dark, we went out for a walk on the Heath. We felt fresh and calm, and the air was cold in our faces.

Whether a psychedelic experience helps unfreeze the springs of human creativity I do not know, but as far as literary work is concerned 1970 was a more productive year for me than any other since my original departure from India in 1964. I also took up painting and colour photography. For a long time I had been haunted by the ghost of my unfinished autobiography, laid aside when I started writing *The Three Jewels*, and wanted to bring it to a conclusion as soon as possible.[488] So big a responsibility once discharged, I would be free to devote myself to more important projects. Not only was the whole subject of the Higher Evolution of Man, in all its aspects and ramifications, increasingly claiming my attention, but there was an enormous backlog of lecture notes waiting some kind of reduction to literary form. I have never found it difficult to write, only difficult to begin writing, and after so long a period of inactivity it was proving more difficult than ever. The visit to Yale, I hoped, would give me an opportunity of getting started again.

Before my departure from England Kevin and I agreed to correspond regularly, and at some length. This would enable him to give expression to his thoughts and feelings, in this way coming to a better understanding of them, besides obliging me to exercise myself in what I had begun to feel was for me the hopelessly intractable medium of prose. Both of us kept to our agreement. So well did the arrangement work, indeed, that in addition to showering Kevin and other friends with accounts of my life at Yale I wrote out for publication one of the most popular of my lectures, on *Mind – Reactive and Creative*, and for good measure produced half a dozen poems. After my return to England, I was, of course, kept busy by classes and other activities of the Friends, but towards the end of the summer, after moving from Highgate to Muswell Hill, I at last got back to the unfinished autobiography and in a couple of weeks wrote practically a whole chapter. Though perforce interrupted by the summer retreat and the two series of lectures, the momentum gained will not, I think, be lost. In the course of the year I also translated three more chapters of the *Dhammapada*[489] for publication in the *FWBO Newsletter*.[490] In November Doubleday brought out *The Three Jewels* as a paperback in their Anchor Books series,[491] while December saw the appearance of my poem 'On Glastonbury Tor' in a private edition of 300 copies.[492]

My reasons for taking up colour photography and painting were not, at first, aesthetic. They were practical. In the case of colour photography, all I wanted to do was to take a few pictures of Yale that would give friends in England some idea of what the place looked like. Terry's Yashica-Mat was still lying in a drawer, unused since his death, so that when I returned to the States after the Easter retreat I took it with me. The results were so much better than I expected that my interest was aroused and I felt encouraged to explore the medium for its own sake. Painting, or rather colour drawing, I took up at the summer retreat. Kevin had found that by doing a spontaneous drawing whenever he felt possessed by a particular mood he was able to objectify the mood, thus not only coming to a better understanding of it but also freeing himself from it to some extent. Most of the pictures he produced in this way were of human faces and these, we soon noticed, fell into three or four distinct groups, each representing a similar type of 'person' or mood. One day, at his suggestion, I tried my hand at the same technique. Amateurish though they were, especially in comparison with Kevin's accomplished work, the results were not without interest. Besides awaking my long dormant feeling for the visual arts, they helped me to realize how atrophied my colour sense had become since my return to England. A few days after the retreat we left for a fortnight's holiday in Cornwall. Both at St Mawes, where we eventually took refuge from our rain-sodden tent in a trim bed-and-breakfast bungalow, and at Millbrook, where we hired a caravan, we devoted a good deal of time to working on our colour drawings, besides doing a certain amount of colour photography. By the time the flow had dried up, which was not until after our return to London, I had produced about thirty such drawings and Kevin more than fifty. Both of us learned a lot from doing them, though probably in different ways.

Looking back over this development, I cannot help recalling how in my early teens I was as much interested in the visual arts as in literature. Indeed, I wanted to be an artist. Probably it was only the war, evacuation, and the army that finally stifled this ambition. Pens, pencils, and writing paper were easily available; artists' materials were not. I became exclusively a writer. During the years that I spent in Kalimpong my colour sense was satisfied, at least deeply gratified, by the brilliant hues of the Himalayan landscape in the midst of which I lived – by deep blue skies, gleaming white snow-ranges, blue woodsmoke over the

Camping in Cornwall

mottled sage green and Indian red of precipitous mountainsides, as well as by emerald rice-fields, orange bamboos, crimson poinsettias, yellow and purple orchids, black-white-and-blue butterflies, and the blaze of the multicoloured zinnias that environed the house for the greater part of the year. When I settled in England it was as though the colour had gone out of my surroundings. Perhaps it was this lost ingredient of my existence that I recognized in painting and colour photography.

Perhaps I recognized it in the art of film as well. At any rate, during 1970 I saw more films than during the whole of the rest of my life. As a Buddhist monk in India my attitude towards the cinema had been negative and ascetic, not to say puritanical. In view of the poor quality of Indian films this was probably not surprising.[493] Only after I had seen Antonioni's *Red Desert* in 1968, at the instigation of a friend, did my attitude really change.[494] I saw at once that film was a major art form, and that it could be an important vehicle for psychological, even of spiritual, insight. At Yale, where every college had its film society, I had the opportunity of seeing a number of outstanding films, including Ken Russell's *Women in Love*[495] (which at Dan's insistence we sat through twice), and since my return to London I have tried to see at least two or three films every month.

That I had succumbed to the glamour of the visual arts did not mean that I had become less susceptible to the magic of the written or spoken word. For a considerable period prior to 1970 I had been overwhelmed by a feeling that words had no meaning whatever. It was not simply that they were imprecise, or clumsy, or inept to express eternal verities, but quite literally that they were devoid of any meaning. Besides making the writing of letters virtually impossible, this feeling made it difficult for me even to speak. When asked a question about, for example, Buddhism, I would see quite clearly that the question was utterly meaningless, that in reality nothing had been asked at all, and that all that had happened was that, activated by certain psychological conditionings, someone had produced a series of completely meaningless sounds. During 1970, however, this feeling of the meaninglessness of words diminished in intensity – or perhaps I was able to cope with it better. Not only did I write more during this period than for some time previously, but I read more as well. At Yale, where I had a good deal of leisure, I made extensive use of the University library, besides buying between fifty and sixty books, a number of which were not readily obtainable in England. Among my new discoveries were the stories of Anaïs Nin and the poems of Cavafy.[496] Revealing as they do a literary individuality distinctively feminine, the former struck me as being without parallel in Western literature, though I suspect that the East may have a parallel in Murasaki Shikibu's *The Tale of Genji*.[497] Besides being enjoyable for its intrinsic poetic value, her delicate and sensitive writing makes one more deeply aware of the extent to which women writers have tended, as writers, to express themselves in terms of masculine psychology rather than in terms of their own feminine mental makeup, thus falsifying their experience and stultifying their creativity. Much of my reading had a bearing, in some cases a rather indirect one, on my preoccupation with the subject of the Higher Evolution of Man. Indeed I seemed to discover connections and illustrations in all sorts of unlikely places. J. Middleton

Murry's *Son of Woman*, a study of D. H. Lawrence, threw a great deal of light on the role of sex in human development, while the first chapter of H. G. Wells' fascinating *Experiment in Autobiography*[498] provided a trenchant statement of some of the more general aspects of the process. Towards the end of the year I became deeply immersed in a study of the life and writings of Goethe, who, ever since I first read Eckermann's *Conversations* in 1960 or thereabouts, had increasingly impressed me as one of the noblest examples of self-discipline and self-development in the history of Western culture. From *Italian Journey*, in particular, I gleaned a number of remarkable passages illustrative of the degree of awareness with which the great poet addressed himself to this greatest of all human enterprises.[499]

The year did not close without a change not only in the direction of my interests but also in the outward circumstances of my life. Having lived in the same flat for more than three years, I wanted a change. At the beginning of August, therefore, I removed from Highgate, with its associations with Bacon, Marvell, Coleridge, A. E. Houseman, and John Betjeman,[500] to Muswell Hill, which so far as literature is concerned seems to be virgin territory. As previously arranged, Kevin moved in with me after ten days, Graham after five or six weeks.[501] By the autumn the three of us had settled down in our new abode and were living as a mini-community. Kevin, a third year art student at St Martin's College of Art, attended classes during the day and worked on his thesis on 'Art and the Higher Evolution' in the evening and at weekends. Graham divided his time mainly between a part-time hospital job and classes at the North London College of Further Education. As for me, besides taking meditation classes three evenings a week at Sakura, I was working on my lectures on 'Aspects of the Higher Evolution of the Individual'. Our relationships with one another were also explored. While we were thus engaged, Christmas came and went, and in the silence of the night the Old Year expired and the New Year was born.

NOTES AND REFERENCES

FOREWORD

1 Chapter 25, p. 183.

2 Chapter 47, p. 377.

3 The movement Sangharakshita founded in 1967 was initially called the Friends of the Western Sangha. It was renamed Friends of the Western Buddhist Order after the founding of the Western Buddhist Order the following year. Much later, having developed into an international movement with centres throughout the world, it became (in 2010) the Triratna Buddhist Community.

4 William Wordsworth (1770–1850) in *The Prelude* (1805). Wordsworth was writing about the early period of the French Revolution.

5 Quoted in chapter 20, p. 144.

6 'Going for Refuge' in *The Meaning of Conversion in Buddhism*, *Complete Works*, vol. 2, p. 248.

7 Chapter 14, p. 90.

8 'Mind – Reactive and Creative' was a talk given in 1967. An edited transcript was included in *Buddha Mind*, published by Windhorse Publications in 2001 (*Complete Works*, vol. 11).

9 Ibid., p. 44.

10 S. Dhammika, *The Broken Buddha*, Nimmala Group, Singapore 2006, p. 159.

11 Chapter 36, p. 256.

12 Chapter 19, p. 132.

13 *Dhammapada* 27. See Sangharakshita (trans.), *Dhammapada: the Way of Truth*, Windhorse Publications, Birmingham 2001, p. 20 (*Complete Works*, vol. 15).

14 Chapter 39, p. 314.

15 *The Whole Works of Homer*, a translation by George Chapman of the *Odyssey* and the *Iliad*, was published in

1616. It was later made famous by John Keats' sonnet, 'On First Looking into Chapman's Homer'. Sangharakshita writes about reading Chapman's work and the effect it had on him in *The Rainbow Road from Tooting Broadway to Kalimpong*, *Complete Works*, vol. 20, p. 49.

16 'The Six Distinctive Emphases of the FWBO': Sangharakshita gave a number of talks on this theme in the years 2002–2008 (*Complete Works*, vol. 12).

17 Chapter 14, p. 94.

18 Chapter 15, p. 103.

19 John Hipkin, a disciple of Sangharakshita, speaking at a meeting of the English Sangha Trust in 1967. See p. 403.

20 Chapter 45, p. 364.

MOVING AGAINST THE STREAM

21 According to a letter written to his friend Dinoo Dubash dated 10 May 1964, Sangharakshita was expecting to fly from Calcutta. See *Dear Dinoo: Letters to a Friend*, in *Complete Works*, vol. 21, p. 588.

22 Andrew Lang (1844–1912) was a Scottish poet, novelist, and literary critic. The *Fairy Books* contained stories adapted and translated from various European languages and were in fact mostly the work of his wife. The first in the series, *The Blue Fairy Book*, was published in 1889.

23 The *Wizard* was a weekly story magazine launched in 1922. Its features included 'Wilson the Wonder Athlete' and 'The Wolf of Kabul' whose main character, Bill Sampson, also appeared in the *Hotspur*, another weekly adventure magazine, founded in 1933.

24 1. *Pickwick Papers* (original title, *The Posthumous Papers of the Pickwick Club, Containing a Faithful Record of the Perambulations, Perils, Travels, Adventures and Sporting Transactions of the Corresponding Members*) was written by the great and prolific Victorian novelist Charles Dickens (1812–1870) and published in 1837.

2. *Jane Eyre* by Charlotte Brontë (1816–1855) was first published in 1847 under the pseudonym Currer Bell. The novel is about the childhood and young adulthood of the eponymous heroine, a central theme being her love for Mr Rochester and the ethical dilemma that brings her.

3. *Hypatia, or New Foes with an Old Face* by Charles Kingsley (1819–1875) was published in 1853, a fictional account of the life of Hypatia, the Greek Neoplatonic female philosopher.

4. *The Last Days of Pompeii* by Edward Bulwer-Lytton (1803–1873) was published in 1834, its tale inspired by a painting of that name.

A reference to these and other books and the

impression they made on the young Sangharakshita can be found in *The Rainbow Road from Tooting Broadway to Kalimpong*, *Complete Works*, vol. 20, pp. 18–20.

25 Sangharakshita writes about reading the *Children's Encyclopaedia* in its sixty parts (sixty-one with the index) in *The Rainbow Road from Tooting Broadway to Kalimpong*, *Complete Works*, vol. 20, pp. 22–4.

26 Sangharakshita's more detailed account 'My First Eight Years: A Mosaic of Memories' can be found in *A Moseley Miscellany*, Ibis Publications, Ledbury 2015, pp. 17–42 (*Complete Works*, vol. 26).

27 Sangharakshita writes about the years following his confinement to bed in *The Rainbow Road from Tooting Broadway to Kalimpong*, *Complete Works*, vol. 20, chapter 3 et seq.

28 Samuel Johnson (1709–1784), was one of England's great men of letters. He was a poet, playwright, essayist, moralist, literary critic, biographer, editor, and lexicographer, and is one of Sangharakshita's 'five literary heroes' found in *A Moseley Miscellany*, Ibis Publications, Ledbury 2015, pp. 111–12 (*Complete Works*, vol. 26). Dr Johnson is known especially for his annotated edition of Shakespeare's plays, biographies of the English poets, and his *Dictionary of the English Language* published in 1755, which remained the pre-eminent English dictionary for 150 years.

29 Helena Petrovna Blavatsky (1831–1891) was the Russian-born co-founder in 1875 in the USA of the Theosophical Society (see note 76). She saw Theosophy as 'the synthesis of science, religion and philosophy'. *Isis Unveiled: A Master-Key to the Mysteries of Ancient and Modern Science and Theology* was published in 1877.

30 *The Diamond Sūtra* or *Vajracchedikā Prajñāpāramitā Sūtra* was composed in Sanskrit. It is one of the most influential and widely studied Buddhist scriptures. The date of its composition is uncertain but it first appeared in Chinese translation in the early fifth century CE. The first English version appeared in 1894, translated by F. Max Müller, which Sangharakshita read after reading William Gemmell's 1912 translation.

31 For detailed accounts of these very formative years, and the impact of the two works referred to in this paragraph, see *The Rainbow Road from Tooting Broadway to Kalimpong*, *Complete Works*, vol. 20, chapters 5–8, especially pp. 63–4 and p. 85.

32 See ibid., chapters 9–10, pp. 91–115.

33 The years in the army and experiences in India, Ceylon, and Singapore are recounted in ibid., chapters 9–13, pp. 91–145.

34 Ibid., chapter 15, pp. 152–7.

35 UP stands for United Provinces, at that time a large state in northern India whose borders were roughly equivalent to the Uttar Pradesh of today (2019). The Kishengunj (also written Kishenganj) referred to here was a suburb of the city of Dehra Dun – not to be confused with the district and city of the same name in the state of Bihar.

36 The experiences in Calcutta and Ahmedabad, the time spent with Anandamayi in Raipur and Kasauli, and the rainbow-spanned road of the Going Forth are described in *The Rainbow Road from Tooting Broadway to Kalimpong*, *Complete Works*, vol. 20, chapters 16–24, pp. 158–226.

37 1. Śāntarakṣita (725–788) was abbot at the monastic university of Nālandā. He was the first Indian pandit to take the Dharma to Tibet and his syncretic Yogācāra-Madhyamaka approach dominated Tibetan Buddhism until the arrival of Tsongkhapa (1357–1419). His *Tattvasaṃgraha* is an overview of the philosophies of his day. Much later it influenced the rise of the Rimé movement.

2. Mrs Rhys Davids' 'meaty little book' was probably *Buddhism: A Study of the Buddhist Norm*, Home University Library of Modern Knowledge, William & Norgate, London 1870.

38 *The Rainbow Road from Tooting Broadway to Kalimpong*, *Complete Works*, vol. 20, p. 302.

39 William Shakespeare (1564–1616), Sonnet 30.

40 Some of these thoughts were expressed in articles written at this time. See 'Wanderer in India' in *Early Writings 1944–1954*, pp. 157–94, Ibis Publications, Ledbury 2014 (*Complete Works*, vol. 7).

41 Sangharakshita visited Swami Ramdas (1884–1963), a Hindu mystic, at the Anandashram, Kanhangad, in 1949. See *The Rainbow Road from Tooting Broadway to Kalimpong*, in *Complete Works*, vol. 20, pp. 319–34.

42 Swami Ramana Maharshi (1879–1950) settled at Arunachala after a vital spiritual experience in his teens. Sangharakshita spent several months at his ashram and in the cave on Mount Arunachala the year before Ramana Maharshi died. The experiences Sangharakshita had at this time were crucial to his life and work. See *The Rainbow Road from Tooting Broadway to Kalimpong*, *Complete Works*, vol. 20, chapters 38 and 39, pp. 328–48.

43 A *gopuram* is a monumental tower set at the entrance to a Hindu temple.

44 *The Rainbow Road from Tooting Broadway to Kalimpong*, *Complete Works*, vol. 20, p. 345.

45 The experiences after leaving Arunachala are recounted in ibid., chapters 40–2, pp. 349–74.

46 120° Fahrenheit is about 49° Celsius.

47 A fuller account of the disappointment at Sarnath, ordination at Kusinara, and the preaching tour in Nepal can be found in *The Rainbow Road from Tooting Broadway to Kalimpong*, *Complete Works*, vol. 20, chapters 43–7, pp. 381–441.

48 A more detailed account of the 'academic interlude', the pilgrimage to Bodh Gaya, and arrival in Kalimpong is given in ibid., chapters 48–50, pp. 442–71.

49 These experiences are recounted in Sangharakshita's second volume of memoirs, *Facing Mount Kanchenjunga*, *Complete Works*, vol. 21, which covers the period March 1950 to early 1953. The Bangalore lectures took place the following year (1954) and are described in *In the Sign of the Golden Wheel*, *Complete Works*, vol. 22, chapter 9, pp. 142–6.

50 Śāntideva was an eighth-century Indian monk and scholar of the monastic university of Nālandā, an adherent of Madhyamaka philosophy, and a man devoted to the practice of the bodhisattva ideal, as he expresses in his *Bodhicaryāvatāra* or *Bodhisattva's Way of Life*. His *Śikṣā-samuccaya* or Training Anthology is a collection of quotations from mostly Mahāyāna works.

51 Sangharakshita's first meeting with Dhardo Rimpoche is described in the last chapter of *Facing Mount Kanchenjunga*, *Complete Works*, vol. 21, pp. 451–3. In the following volume, *In the Sign of the Golden Wheel*, *Complete Works*, vol. 22, Dhardo Rimpoche appears many times. An account of Sangharakshita's bodhisattva ordination conferred by Dhardo Rimpoche is given in *Precious Teachers*, *Complete Works*, vol. 22, pp. 541–3.

52 The Buddha Jayanti year was an *annus mirabilis* in Sangharakshita's life and work as recounted in *In the Sign of the Golden Wheel*, *Complete Works*, vol. 22, chapters 21–4, pp. 304–80.

53 Sangharakshita's book *Ambedkar and Buddhism*, in *Complete Works*, vol. 9, tells of the life and extraordinary achievements of Dr Bhimrao Ambedkar, who came from an 'untouchable' background, and against all odds rose to become chief architect of the Indian Constitution and Minister of Law under Independent India's first prime minister, Jawaharlal Nehru. He left the political world disgusted with politics as a means for radical change of society, and in the historic event

referred to here, on 14 October 1956, embraced Buddhism. In *Ambedkar and Buddhism* Sangharakshita charts the milestones that led to his conversion and makes clear its far-reaching significance.

54 Sangharakshita's experiences at the time of Dr Ambedkar's death are told in more detail in *In the Sign of the Golden Wheel*, *Complete Works*, vol. 22, pp. 361–4, and described in a letter written shortly after the event. See *Dear Dinoo: Letters to a Friend*, in *Complete Works*, vol. 21, p. 523.

55 For more on the publication of *The Three Jewels* and *The Eternal Legacy* see chapter 31, pp. 223–7 in this volume. *The Three Jewels* is included in *Complete Works*, vol. 2; *The Eternal Legacy* in *Complete Works*, vol. 14.

56 The friend who suggested Sangharakshita write his memoirs was Jivaka (the first female to male transsexual to undergo reassignment surgery), who turned up at Sangharakshita's vihara in Kalimpong in 1958. The story of Jivaka's stay in Kalimpong is told in *Precious Teachers*, *Complete Works*, vol. 22, pp. 434–45.

57 *Precious Teachers*, in *Complete Works*, vol. 22, gives some detailed accounts of Sangharakshita's meetings with his Vajrayāna teachers and the initiations he received. The bestowal of the name 'Urgyen' is related in ibid., p. 473.

58 The English Sangha Trust was founded in July 1955 by Bhikkhu Kapilavaddho, formerly William Purfurst and later known as Richard Randall. He had received Theravādin ordination in Thailand and his aim in setting up the Trust was to create a monastic community for Westerners in Britain. The supporting body for lay followers was called the English Sangha Association.

59 The last seven years that Sangharakshita spent in Kalimpong (1957–1964) are covered in *Precious Teachers*, in *Complete Works*, vol. 22.

60 According to the monastic rules or *prātimokṣa*, a *bhikkhu* should not eat food 'at the wrong time ... [which] means after noon has passed until sunrise'. *Pacittiya* 37 at Vinaya Piṭaka iv.85–6 (*Mahāvagga* 1.6), in I. B. Horner (trans.), *The Book of the Discipline*, part 2, Pali Text Society, Oxford 1996, p. 336.

61 *The Book of Common Prayer* was first published in 1549 and then revised a number of times, the 1662 version remaining the official prayer book of the Church of England. As well as the Thirty-nine Articles, *The Book of Common Prayer* contains prayers, forms of service for marriage, baptism, Holy Communion, etc.

62 Meister Eckhart (c.1260–c.1328) was a German monk, a Christian Neoplatonist philosopher and mystic, whose unorthodoxy led him to be tried for heresy by the Roman Catholic Church. His writings and outlook were rediscovered by the German Romantics and Idealists in the nineteenth century.

63 *Sangha*, vol. viii, no. 10 (October 1964), p. 16.

64 John Blofeld (1913–1987) was an English writer on Buddhism and Taoism who travelled extensively in the East and lived for some years in China. His autobiography, *Wheel of Life*, was published in 1978. The Vajrasattva initiation referred to here took place in April 1959. See *Precious Teachers*, in *Complete Works*, vol. 22, pp. 503–6.

65 'Summer School 1964' in News and Notes, *The Middle Way*, vol. 39, no. 3 (November 1964), p. 126.

66 'Twenty Years After' in the *Middle Way*, vol. 39, no. 3 (November 1964), pp. 118–20 (*Complete Works*, vol. 11).

67 Ibid., pp. 119–20.

68 Recounted in *The Rainbow Road from Tooting Broadway to Kalimpong*, *Complete Works*, vol. 20, p. 103.

69 An account of Clare's life can be found in Philip Pegler, *Hidden Beauty of the Commonplace*, Changemakers, Winchester 2013.

70 Clare Cameron, *Rustle of Spring: An Edwardian Childhood in London's East End*, Skilton & Shaw, London 1979.

71 1. Wei Lang, more commonly known as Huineng (638–713) is regarded as the founder of the Southern Chinese Chan school. The *Sūtra of Wei Lang* or *Sūtra Spoken by the Sixth Patriarch on the High Seat of the Treasure of the Law* (also known as the *Sūtra of Huineng* or *Platform Sūtra)*, was translated into English by Wong Mou-Lam, and published in Shanghai by the Yu Ching Press in 1930. It was this edition that Sangharakshita read in the summer of 1942 and which, along with the *Diamond Sūtra*, made such an impact upon him.

2. *Tao, the Great Luminant* by Evans S. Morgan, was published in Shanghai in 1933. It contains a series of essays on the Huainanzi or 'Writings of the Huai Nan Masters', an ancient Chinese collection based on scholarly debates held in second century BCE concerning the creation of a perfect socio-political order.

3. The German philosopher Georg Hegel (1770–1831) gave a number of lectures at the University of Berlin in the years 1822–1830 which were published in 1837 with the title *Vorlesungen über die Philosophie der Weltgeschichte* (*Lectures on the Philosophy of World History*). Hegel aimed

to show how history has a natural progression according to the workings of absolute spirit. An abridged version appeared in 1840 which was translated into English by J. Sibree in 1857 and published in London by Henry G. Bohn.

72 Ananda Metteyya, originally known as Allan Bennett (1872–1923), was trained as an analytical chemist. He joined the Hermetic Order of the Golden Dawn and was later ordained as a Theravādin monk in Burma. He established the first Buddhist mission to the United Kingdom. A friend wrote on his death:

> The work he began, that of introducing Buddhism to the West, he pushed with enthusiastic vigour in pamphlet, journal and lecture, all masterly, all stimulating thought, all in his own inimitably graceful style.

Although there is no full-length biography, an outline of his life can be found in Elizabeth J. Harris, *Ananda Metteya, the First British Emissary of Buddhism*, Wheel Publication No. 420/422, Kandy 1998. His approach to the Dharma can be read in his own words in Allan Bennett, *The Wisdom of the Aryas*, Kegan Paul, London 1923.

73 In Sri Lanka (formerly Ceylon) a *pirivena* is a college primarily for the training of Buddhist monks. Over the centuries they have also provided education for lay people.

74 Sangharakshita's taking of the Refuges and Precepts from U Thittila is recounted in *The Rainbow Road from Tooting Broadway to Kalimpong*, *Complete Works*, vol. 20, pp. 102–3. U Thittila's translation of the *Vibhaṅga*, the second volume of the *Abhidhamma*, was published by the Pali Text Society in 1968.

75 The English Civil War (1642–1651) was fought between monarchists ('Cavaliers') and parliamentarians ('Roundheads'), who wanted to do away with monarchy and were led by Oliver Cromwell (1599–1658). With the victory of the parliamentarians, Cromwell became Lord Protector of the Commonwealth of England, Scotland, and Ireland from 1653 until his death. The monarchy was restored in 1660.

76 The Theosophical Society was founded in New York in 1875 by Russian-born Helena Blavatsky (1831–1891), American Henry Steel Olcott (1832–1907), and Irish-born William Quan Judge (1851–1896). It was to be an 'unsectarian body of seekers after Truth, who endeavour to promote Brotherhood and strive to serve humanity' through the study of occultism and world religion. Blavatsky's

The Secret Doctrine (1888) gives an idea of the basic theosophical outlook and ideas. Blavatsky and Olcott went on to establish a headquarters in Adyar, India. In 1895 the Society split with a separate American section led by Judge. In 1913 the Anthroposophical Society was formed from a breakaway group of German-Austrian theosophists led by Rudolf Steiner (1861–1925).

77 Jiddu Krishnamurti (1895–1986) was born to an Indian family that moved to Adyar in south Chennai (then called Madras) when he was fourteen. He was 'discovered' by theosophists Charles Leadbeater and Annie Besant and groomed to be the 'World Teacher'. He later rejected this role but went on to give many lectures and publish books on religious and philosophical themes.

78 1. Travers Christmas Humphreys (1901–1983) – known to friends as 'Toby' – was educated at Malvern College where he became interested in theosophy and Buddhism. He went on to study law and became a barrister and later a judge at the Old Bailey where he was involved in a number of highly controversial cases. He was assistant prosecutor in the war crimes trials in Tokyo. The Buddhist Society, which he founded in London while still in his early twenties, was one of the first Buddhist societies outside Asia. He was a prolific writer, publishing many books on mainly Mahāyāna and Zen Buddhism. His *Buddhism: An Introduction and Guide*, was published by Pelican Books in 1951.

2. Sir Edwin Arnold (1832–1904) was an English poet and journalist. His epic poem recounting the life of the Buddha, *The Light of Asia: the Great Renunciation*, is based on the *Lalitavistara Sūtra*. It was first published in London in 1879.

79 Daisetsu Teitaro Suzuki (1870–1966) was born in Japan and was author of many books on Zen and Shin Buddhism, as well as a translator from Chinese, Japanese, and Sanskrit. His work was highly influential in bringing Zen to the notice of Westerners.

80 The *Middle Way* was the Buddhist Society's quarterly magazine. It was founded in 1926 as *Buddhism in England*. Ananda Bodhi's portrait photograph was published in volume 37, no. 1 (May 1962), facing p. 217.

81 Robert Stuart Clifton (1903–63) was born in Birmingham, Alabama. His interest in Buddhism took him to the Far East. He was ordained in Japan as a Zen priest named Sumangala and set up his Western Buddhist Order in 1951, styling himself the 'Superior-

General'. He is mentioned in *Facing Mount Kanchenjunga, Complete Works*, vol. 21, pp. 339–42 and p. 428. When Sangharakshita received the newsletter, *The Western Buddhist*, in Kalimpong – long before he actually met Jack Austin, its editor – he welcomed it warmly in a short piece written under the pseudonym Himavantavasi and published in the *Maha Bodhi* in November 1953 with the title 'Welcome, "Western Buddhist"!' See *Anagarika Dharmapala and Other 'Maha Bodhi' Writings*, Ibis Publications, Ledbury 2013, pp. 101–2 (*Complete Works*, vol. 8). After Clifton's death, claims made by him were refuted, including that he had been authorized by the Supreme Patriarch of Sōtō Zen to confer ordinations in the West. See note in ibid., p. 139.

82 How Sangharakshita became editor of the *Maha Bodhi* and his fight to make it a truly Buddhist organ with a truly Dharmic message – it eventually became the leading English-language Buddhist publication of its time – is related in *In the Sign of the Golden Wheel, Complete Works*, vol. 22; see especially chapters 5 and 8. The monthly editorials he wrote for the magazine are collected in *Beating the Drum*, Ibis Publications, Ledbury 2012 (*Complete Works*, vol. 8). The introduction to *Beating the Drum* gives a full history of the *Maha Bodhi* and Sangharakshita's involvement with it, as well as a history of the Maha Bodhi Society founded by Anagarika Dharmapala.

83 *Maha Bodhi*, vol. 62, no. 5–6 (May/June 1954), p. 215.

84 This Sevenfold Puja, whose verses are taken from Śāntideva's *Bodhicaryāvatāra*, was first published in *FWBO Newsletter* 4 (March 1969) with the explanation that the verses had been 'translated by Mrs A. A. G. Bennett. Selected and arranged by Ven. Sthavira Sangharakshita'. The Sevenfold Puja is now celebrated all over the Triratna world both in its original English and translated into other languages. See *Puja: The Triratna Book of Buddhist Devotional Texts*, seventh edition, Windhorse Publications, Cambridge 2008, pp. 7–27.

85 'Home of lost causes, and forsaken beliefs, and unpopular names, and impossible loyalties!' Lines from the Preface to *Essays in Criticism*, First Series (1865) by Matthew Arnold (1822–1888).

86 William Shakespeare (1564–1616), *Julius Caesar*, Act III, Scene i.

87 Edward Conze (1904–1979) mastered some fourteen languages including Sanskrit and was one of the first Western scholars to actually

practise the Dharma. Although Sangharakshita met him only after his return to England in 1964, the two men had already long been in contact through Sangharakshita's magazine *Stepping-Stones*. (See *Facing Mount Kanchenjunga*, *Complete Works*, vol. 21, pp. 314–5.) The association of the two men continued with Conze submitting articles to the *Maha Bodhi* which from 1954 for more than ten years was under Sangharakshita's editorship.

88 These cities changed their names subsequent to the era of which Sangharakshita is writing. Calcutta became Kolkata in 2001; Bombay became Mumbai in 1995; and Poona became Pune in 1978.

89 There all is order and beauty,
Luxury, peace, and pleasure.

From 'Invitation to the Voyage' ('L'invitation au voyage') in *Flowers of Evil / Fleurs du Mal* (1857) by the French poet Charles Baudelaire (1821–1867).

90 During the years I worked with Sangharakshita producing the Ibis Publications I often noticed that when he spoke of some friend or relative on whom I was to write a note, that person did indeed seem to be vividly before him as he spoke. He spoke of them with feeling and with an astonishing memory for details of their lives that would perhaps have surprised them.

91 See *The Rainbow Road from Tooting Broadway to Kalimpong*, *Complete Works*, vol. 20, chapter 8, pp. 75–90.

92 1. Lewis Carroll was the pen name of Charles Dodgson (1832–1898), a lecturer in mathematics at Christ Church, University of Oxford, but more famous as the author of *Alice's Adventures in Wonderland* (1865) and *Through the Looking-Glass, and What Alice Found There* (1871).

2. John Tenniel (1820–1914) was renowned as a political cartoonist for *Punch* magazine as well as an illustrator of children's books.

93 Maurice O'Connell Walshe (1911–1998) was born in London, studied in Germany, and became Deputy Director of the Institute of Germanic Studies in London. His interest in and engagement with Buddhism led him to become chairman of the English Sangha Trust and to publish articles on Buddhism. His best known publication is his translation of the *Dīgha Nikāya* under the title *The Long Discourses of the Buddha*, Wisdom Publications, Somerville 1997.

94 Ruth Walshe was also the writer of short articles on Buddhism. 'Coming to Terms With One's Shadow' and 'Buddhist Therapy' are included in *Collected Bodhi*

Leaves, vol. i, Buddhist Publication Society, Sri Lanka 2011. 'Coming to Terms With One's Shadow' was originally published in the *Middle Way*, vol. 49, no. 2, August 1964, pp. 78–81.

95 *A Survey of Buddhism*, sometimes regarded as Sangharakshita's *magnum opus*, was first published in 1957 to considerable acclaim. It is included in *Complete Works*, vol. 1, pp. 1–454.

96 E. Graham Howe (1897–1975) was one of the founders of the Tavistock Clinic and an early writer on psychotherapy, influencing R. D. Laing, Alan Watts, and others. *Invisible Anatomy: a Study of Nerves, Hysteria and Sex* was published by Faber & Faber, London 1944.

97 See Sangharakshita's 1970 lecture 'From Alienated Awareness to Integrated Awareness' (*Complete Works*, vol. 12).

98 Mahasi Sayadaw was the honorific title (meaning the head abbot of Mahasi monastery) of the Burmese monk whose ordained name was Sobhana. He was born in 1904 and died in 1982, having established meditation centres in Burma and other Eastern countries. His Western students included the founders of the Barre Massachusetts Insight Meditation Society, Joseph Goldstein, Sharon Salzberg, and Jack Kornfield.

99 See *Precious Teachers*, in *Complete Works*, vol. 22, p. 491.

100 Sangharakshita's commentary on the stories involving the relationship between Milarepa and Rechungpa can be found in volumes 18 and 19 of his *Complete Works.*

101 'I teach the Dhamma under the figure of a raft'. See the *Alagaddūpama Sutta*, *Majjhima Nikāya* 22, verses 13 and 14 (i.134–5); Bhikkhu Ñāṇamoli and Bhikkhu Bodhi (trans.), *The Middle Length Discourses of the Buddha*, Wisdom Publications, Boston 1995, pp. 228–9; or I. B. Horner (trans.), *The Collection of the Middle Length Sayings*, vol. i, Pali Text Society, London 1976, pp. 173–4. The symbol of the path is used in very many places in both the Pāli scriptures of the Theravāda tradition and the Mahāyāna *sūtras* – for example the threefold path of ethics, meditation, and wisdom; the Noble Eightfold Path; and the bodhisattva path of the ten *bhūmis*.

102 See Sangharakshita, *The Buddha's Noble Eightfold Path* in *Complete Works*, vol. 1, pp. 469–591.

103 As reported in *The Buddhist*, vol. 9, no. 2 (February 1965), pp. 54–5.

104 The circumstances of the lectures given in Bangalore are recorded in *In the Sign of the Golden Wheel*, *Complete*

Works, vol. 22, chapter 9, pp. 133–50. They were later written up as *A Survey of Buddhism*, see *Complete Works*, vol. 1, pp. 1–454.

105 These lectures, given at the Hampstead Buddhist Vihara in 1965, were subsequently transcribed, edited, and published as a booklet, *The Meaning of Conversion in Buddhism*, Windhorse Publications, Birmingham 1994. See *Complete Works*, vol. 2, pp. 233–85.

106 Ibid., p. 465.

107 Dag Hammarskjöld (1905–1961) was a Swedish economist and diplomat, and Secretary-General to the United Nations from 1953 to 1961. He died in a plane crash under suspicious circumstances on his way to negotiate a ceasefire in the Congo. He was posthumously awarded the Nobel Peace Prize. The situation of Indian 'untouchables' and what Dr Ambedkar and Buddhism was able to do to free them from 'the hell of caste' is described by Sangharakshita in *Ambedkar and Buddhism*, *Complete Works*, vol. 9, pp. 1–159.

108 How the Triyana Vardhana Vihara came to be established, and how Chattrul Sangye Dorje gave it its name, is related in *Precious Teachers*, chapter 1, *Complete Works*, vol. 22, pp. 387–95.

109 Sangharakshita took over the editing of *Sangha* magazine in September 1964. The name was changed to *The Buddhist* for the January 1965 issue (vol. 9, no. 1). Sangharakshita explained that there was a 'need for a title that will be immediately comprehensible to those knowing little, if anything, about Buddhism.' (p. 3).

110 Diedeircus 'Dick' van Buren (1921–2003) was born to Dutch theosophist parents though much of his early life was spent in the East, including a period as prisoner of the Japanese. After the Second World War he moved to England and trained in osteopathy, naturopathy, and homeopathy. He later became a leading figure in the introduction of acupuncture to the West, including setting up acupuncture colleges in several western countries.

111 See 'The Unacceptable Face of Communism' in *In the Sign of the Golden Wheel*, chapter 14, *Complete Works*, vol. 22, pp. 208–18, where Sangharakshita discusses his attitude towards communism as well as the tricks played on him by those who wished to make it seem he had communist sympathies. The effect on the little township of Kalimpong of Communist China's military crossing of the border with India in October 1962 is described in *Precious Teachers*, chapter 14, *Complete Works*, vol. 22, pp. 545–52.

112 1. Harold Wilson was Labour Prime Minister from 1964 to 1970 and again from 1974 to 1976. His reference to the 'white heat of technological revolution' came in a speech delivered at the 1963 Labour Party Conference which has been described as 'one of the most memorable political speeches of the twentieth century.'

2. Harold Macmillan was Conservative Prime Minster from 1957 to 1963. His assertion that Britain had never had it so good came in a speech given at a Tory rally in Bedford six months after becoming Prime Minister.

113 The American Christian evangelist Frank Buchman (1878–1961) launched the Moral Re-Armament movement in 1938 at a meeting in East London attended by 3,000 people. His message was that for economic recovery there needed first to be moral recovery. The idea appealed to many at that time.

114 For more on Dr Dinshaw Mehta, his life and friendship with Sangharakshita, especially during the 1950s, see 'The Monk and the Prophet' in *Dear Dinoo, Letters to a Friend*, *Complete Works*, vol. 21, pp. 599–619.

115 1. George Canning (1770–1827), a Conservative politician, held a number of cabinet offices including Secretary of State and Chancellor of the Exchequer. He was elected Prime Minister in 1827 but died the same year.

2. Richard Cobden (1804–1865) was an independent Member of Parliament, a radical reformer who, with John Bright, founded the Anti-Corn Law League. The Corn Laws sought to protect the price of domestic cereals and imposed high tariffs on imported grains, which led to hunger when domestic crops failed.

3. John Bright (1811–1889) was likewise a radical Member of Parliament who joined in the battle against the Corn Laws, promoting free trade.

4. William Gladstone (1809–1898) was a Liberal and four times Prime Minister between 1868 and 1894. During his time in office the Church of Ireland was disestablished and secret voting was introduced.

5. Benjamin Disraeli (1804–1881) was Conservative Prime Minster in 1868 and again from 1874 to 1880. He is remembered for his support of Queen Victoria and the growth of the British Empire.

6. David Lloyd George (1863–1945) was a Welsh liberal politician who held a number of cabinet posts and was Prime Minister of the United Kingdom 1916–1922.

7. Winston Churchill (1874–1965) was Conservative Prime Minister from 1940 to

1945 when he brought Britain through the Second World War. He was again Prime Minister from 1951 to 1955.

116 The Trappist monastic order, a branch of the Cistercian Order of the Roman Catholic Church, was founded in 1664 in La Trappe, France. A well known Trappist of modern times was Thomas Merton (1915–1968).

117 Khantipālo (born Laurence Mills in 1932) was an Englishman ordained within the Thai monastic tradition who studied Pāli and wrote books and articles on Buddhism. He disrobed after thirty years and explored Tibetan and other forms of Buddhism, going on to found Buddhist centres in Australia. Early on he spent time in India including a year in Kalimpong with Sangharakshita in the early 1960s, accompanying him on preaching tours. He was present with Sangharakshita at talks given by Yogi Chen, see *Buddhist Meditation, Systematic and Practical. A Talk by the Buddhist Yogi C. M. Chen, written down by B. Khantipālo*, published in Kalimpong in 1967. See also Khantipālo, *Noble Friendship: Travels of a Buddhist Monk*, Windhorse Publications, Birmingham 2002, pp. 140–8, where a main theme is his friendship with Sangharakshita. See also *Precious Teachers*, chapter 13, in *Complete Works*, vol. 22, pp. 525–44.

118 Sangharakshita visited Poona with Khantipālo in the early 1960s. Using Dr Mehta's Nature Cure Clinic as a venue, he held a month-long seminar. About forty people attended each day from 7 p.m. to 'take' the Refuges and Precepts, meditate, and study the *Dhammapada*. Three of those attending were later ordained as members of the Trailokya Bauddha Mahasangha, as the Triratna Buddhist Order was known during its first years in India.

119 The forty meditation exercises referred to here are the *kammaṭṭhānas* described in detail by Buddhaghosa in part 2 of his *Visuddhimagga*. They are summarized in *A Survey of Buddhism*, *Complete Works*, vol. 1, pp. 154–161.

120 *The Tibetan Book of the Dead* is the title given by W. Y. Evans-Wentz to his 1927 edition of Kazi Dawa Samdup's translation of the Tibetan *Bardo Thödol*, which means 'Liberation Through Hearing During the Intermediate State'. It comes from a larger corpus of teachings, *Profound Dharma of Self-Liberation through the Intention of the Peaceful and Wrathful Ones* said to have been discovered by the *terton* Karma Lingpa (1326–1386).

121 1. Edmund Spenser (1552/3–1599) is best known for his epic allegorical poem *The Faerie Queene* but he also published collections of shorter poems including, in 1595,

Amoretti and *Epithalamion*, poems of love and longing.

2. Barbara Cartland (1901–2000) was a prolific and hugely popular writer of romantic novels. According to one source she wrote 723 novels which were published in 38 languages.

122 1. Alfred Lord Tennyson (1809–1892) was a much read English poet whose popularity has continued to the present day, his 'The Lady of Shalott' being one of Britain's all-time favourites. He married Emily Sellwood in 1850, the same year he was appointed Poet Laureate.

2. Dean William Inge (1860–1954) was an Anglican priest, writer on Plotinus, Christian mysticism, and other topics, Professor of Divinity at the University of Cambridge, and Dean of St Paul's Cathedral. He married Mary Catherine Spooner in 1904.

123 *The Bible*, Philippians 4:7.

124 1. Ronald David Laing (1927–1989) was a Scottish psychiatrist who pioneered treatment of mental illness counter to the electroshock and chemical treatments that were in use at the time. He saw family dynamics, and social conditions and conditioning, as crucial causes in behaviour generally ascribed to mental illness. Along with Cooper, he was dubbed 'anti-psychiatry'.

2. Psychiatrist Aaron Esterson (1923–1999) published a number of books with R. D. Laing, and with him and others founded the Philadelphia Association, a UK charity dedicated to the understanding and relief of mental suffering.

125 David Cooper, *Psychiatry and Anti-psychiatry*, Paladin, London 1970, p. 16.

126 There is in God, some say,
A deep but dazzling
Darkness...

lines from the poem 'The Night' by the Welsh poet Henry Vaughan (1621–1695). The great mystical theologian of the sixth century, usually referred to as Pseudo-Dionysius the Areopagite, wrote of God's mystery as 'hidden in the darkness beyond light', in *Treatise De Divinis Nominibus* (On the Divine Names).

127 1. The Fabian Society was founded in London in 1884 to promote democratic socialism. Early members included George Bernard Shaw, Annie Besant, and for a short time Bertrand Russell.

2. The Personalist Group promoted a philosophy known as 'Personalism'. It developed through the nineteenth century in reaction to depersonalizing elements of Enlightenment rationalism, Hegelian idealism, and so on. A notable Personalist was Scottish philosopher John MacMurray (1891–1976).

3. The Gurdjieff Society sought to promote the teachings of the Russian mystic and philosopher George Ivanovich Gurdjieff (c.1866–1949). It was formed in London in the year of Gurdjieff's death. See also note 128(1).

4 .The College of Psychic Science was formed after the First World War to further the studies of spiritualism and mediumship. Its first president was Sir Arthur Conan Doyle (1859–1930), more famous as the creator of Sherlock Holmes. See also pp. 90ff. above.

128 1. George Ivanovich Gurdjieff (c.1866–1949) was born in Armenia (then in the Russian empire) and grew up among people of many ethnic and religious backgrounds. After a period of wandering he arrived in Moscow and began to teach his 'Fourth Way'. He established small communities in southern Russia, and later set up his Institute for the Harmonious Development of Man near Paris. He visited America many times and had many pupils there. His teachings concern the development of the body, the emotions, and the mind.

2. Pyotr Demianovich Ouspensky (1878–1947) studied mysticism and esotericism, searching for a new wisdom. He met Gurdjieff in 1915 and became his disciple. He separated from him in 1924, but continued to teach the Gurdjieff system in England and the USA.

3. Advaita Vedanta is a sub-school of the Vedanta, one of the six orthodox schools of Hinduism. Advaita literally means 'not two' and refers to the idea that the true self (*ātman*) is identical to the highest reality (*brahman*). The spiritual path consists in coming to a realization of this truth. The school is associated especially with the Indian philosopher Śaṅkara (c.788–820).

4. Maharishi Mahesh Yogi (1918–2008) was an Indian guru who taught a meditation technique known as transcendental meditation (TM) which has been practised by millions of people all over the world. He rose to fame in particular when the English pop group the Beatles became his disciples in the 1960s. His teachings derived from the Hindu tradition.

129 The Shankaracharyas (Sanskrit *śaṅkarācāryas*) were the heads of the four *maths* (also written *mathas*) or monasteries established by non-dualist philosopher Śaṅkara (see note 128(3)). The *maths* were built at the four cardinal points of India: Puri in the east, Sringeri in the south, Dwaraka in the west, and Uttarakhand in the north. Sangharakshita met the Shankaracharya of Puri more than once (see *The Rainbow Road from Tooting Broadway*

to Kalimpong, *Complete Works*, vol. 20, pp. 175–7 and 343–4). The strange story of his visit to the Sringeri *math* and his meeting with the Sringeri Shankaracharya is told in ibid., pp. 367–73.

130 Plato (c.427–c.347 BCE), the great Athenian philosopher and founder of the Platonic school of thought that has so influenced western civilization down to the present day, wrote *The Republic* around 380 BCE. It takes the form of a dialogue looking at the questions of what is a just man, and what is a just state. Its ten books include themes such as his theory of ideal forms and the role of the philosopher in society, including the philosopher-king.

131 'As the hart panteth after the water brooks, so panteth my soul after thee, O God.' *The Bible*, Psalm 42, King James Version.

132 Wilhelm Reich (1897–1957), the Austrian psychoanalyst, coined the term 'character armour'.

133 From 'The Solitary Reaper' (1807), a ballad by William Wordsworth (1770–1850).

134 Timothy Leary (1920–1996) was an American psychologist who researched the therapeutic use of psychedelic drugs. T. Leary, R. Metzner, and R. Alpert, *The Psychedelic Experience: a Manual Based on the Tibetan Book of the Dead*, was published in the USA in 1964.

135 How Sangharakshita received these initiations from the great Rimé teacher, Jamyang Khyentse Rimpoche (also known as Dzongsar Khyentse Chökyi Lodrö, c.1893–1959) is related in *Precious Teachers*, in *Complete Works*, vol. 22, pp. 401–2.

136 *The Rainbow Road from Tooting Broadway to Kalimpong*, *Complete Works*, vol. 20, p. 85.

137 These are themes explored in *The Buddha's Noble Eightfold Path*, in *Complete Works*, vol. 1, pp. 469–591; and *Transforming Self and World: Themes from the Sūtra of Golden Light*, in *Complete Works*, vol. 16, pp. 225–435.

138 Colin Wilson (1931–2013) was an English writer and, in the 1950s, aligned with the group known as the 'angry young men'. He wrote many books on themes such as the paranormal, psychology, and existential philosophy. His most widely read publication is *The Outsider* (1956) which explored the role of the outsider as evoked in works of philosophy and literature.

139 Hans Jonas (1903–1993) was a German-born American philosopher. His *The Gnostic Religion: The Message of the Alien God and the Beginnings of Christianity* was published in 1958.

140 A reference to Plato's *Symposium* (written c.385–370 BCE), in which a number

of friends, who have gathered together for a drinking party, discourse on the topic of Eros or love. Aristophanes, famous as a comic playwright, tells a creation myth in which the original people of the world had round bodies with dual sex organs, front and back. When they try to climb Mount Olympus, the seat of the gods, Zeus splits them in half so that the two halves endlessly seek after one another.

141 This was the *Maha Bodhi*. See note 82.

142 The eight precepts taken by lay Buddhists are listed in *Complete Works*, vol. 2, p. 654. In traditionally Buddhist countries these precepts are observed by the laity on festival days. They are based on the ten *śrāmaṇera* precepts observed by the novice monk.

143 *In the Sign of the Golden Wheel*, *Complete Works*, vol. 22, pp. 34–7.

144 Marco Pallis (1895–1989), also known as Thubden Tendzin, was a British-born writer. He was also a teacher of early music at the Royal Academy of Music, and a performer himself. He travelled in Tibet as recorded in *Peaks and Lamas* (1939) which Sangharakshita read in Singapore in 1946. He lived in Kalimpong for four years during which time he became a good friend, a contributor to *Stepping-Stones* and the *Maha Bodhi*, both of which Sangharakshita edited, and acted as interpreter when Sangharakshita had dealings with local Tibetans. See *Facing Mount Kanchenjunga*, *Complete Works*, vol. 21, pp. 159ff and 176ff. He hurriedly left for England in 1951 because of his activities connected with the Tibetan resistance movement. Before he left he gave Sangharakshita a number of presents including three beautiful thangkas. See ibid., pp. 228–30.

145 René Guénon (1886–1951) was a French writer on philosophy and esotericism. He was initiated into a Sufi order in 1912. He is considered the first of the thinkers and writers of the Traditionalist School whose central tenet is that there are primordial and universal spiritual truths that are the foundation of all major world religions.

146 This was the occasion when the young Dennis Lingwood 'took' the Refuges and Precepts from the Burmese monk U Thittila thus formally and publicly declaring himself a Buddhist. See *The Rainbow Road from Tooting Broadway to Kalimpong*, *Complete Works*, vol. 21, pp. 102–3.

147 'Wesak 1965' in the *Middle Way*, vol. 40, no. 1, p. 73.

148 Douglas Harding (1909–2007) taught a spiritual path based on looking and seeing one's true nature which he declared to be 'No-thing and Everything'. *On Having No Head: Zen and the*

Rediscovery of the Obvious was published in 1961.

149 'The medium is the message' is a phrase coined by Canadian philosopher Marshall McLuhan (1911–1980) and introduced in his book *Understanding Media: the Extensions of Man*, published in 1964.

150 See 'With Allen Ginsberg in Kalimpong', in *Complete Works*, vol. 22, pp. 563–8.

151 The famous Royal Albert Hall poetry reading took place on 11 June 1965 when Allen and other poets read to a crowd of some 7,000 people in an auditorium filled with marijuana smoke and flying paper darts.

152 The Peanuts Group formed in 1962, when the Labour Party leader, Hugh Gaitskell, had been booed and heckled at a May Day rally in Glasgow for defending the Polaris nuclear missile system based at Faslane. He had described the hecklers as 'pro-Soviet peanuts'. The group met in the King's Arms, Bishopsgate, London, and consisted of young anti-nuclear, anti-apartheid supporters who liked to meet and talk, tell jokes, recite poetry, and make music.

153 See *Tibetan Buddhism*, chapter 2, in *Complete Works*, vol. 13, pp. 15–34.

154 1. Milarepa (c.1052–c.1135), one of Tibet's greatest Buddhist teachers, is associated with the Kagyu school. He abandoned the black arts and turned to the Dharma finding a teacher in Marpa the Translator (1012–1097). He went on to become a yogi, living in the mountains and communicating his profound realizations through songs. For Sangharakshita's seminars on some of the Songs of Milarepa see *Complete Works*, vols. 18 and 19.

2. Hanshan (lit. 'Cold Mountain') flourished in ninth-century China. He was a recluse, writing his hundreds of poems on bamboo, wood, stones, and cliffs.

155 Three editorials written for the *Maha Bodhi* at this time comment on the events in Vietnam. The editorial for June 1963 is included in *Beating the Drum*, Ibis Publications, Ledbury 2012, pp. 261–2 (*Complete Works*, vol. 8). See also *Precious Teachers*, in *Complete Works*, vol. 22, pp. 516–17.

156 1. Jagdish Kashyap (1908–1976) was an Indian *bhikkhu* and scholar of Buddhist philosophy and Pāli who translated portions of the Pāli canon into Hindi and later brought out a complete *devanāgarī* edition of the Pāli canon. He held, among other posts, those of professor at Benares Hindu University and at the Nava Nalanda Mahavihara. He was Sangharakshita's first Buddhist teacher with whom he lived in Benares for seven months in

1949, and who afterwards took him to Kalimpong, leaving him there with the injunction to 'stay here and work for the good of Buddhism'. See *The Rainbow Road from Tooting Broadway to Kalimpong*, *Complete Works*, vol. 20, chapters 48–50 and p. 470.

2. The Nava Nalanda Mahavihara was established in 1951 at Nalanda, Bihar, near the site of the ancient Buddhist monastic university.

157 The Ashmolean is the University of Oxford's museum of art and archaeology, founded in 1683. Christ Church and St John's are two of the many colleges that make up the University of Oxford.

158 Chögyam Trungpa (1939–1987) was a Tibetan *tulku* who, along with Akong Rimpoche (1939–2013), escaped Chinese occupation and persecution in Tibet by fleeing to India. They went on to found Samye Ling in Scotland, the first Buddhist monastery in the West. In 1970 Trungpa, now a married layman, moved to the USA where he became a foremost teacher of the Vajrayāna, creating the Shambhala training. He founded scores of meditation centres, several retreat centres, and Naropa University in Boulder, Colorado, the first Buddhist university in America. He was a controversial figure owing particularly to his promiscuity and consumption of alcohol. His students included Allen Ginsberg and Pema Chödrön.

159 These initiations and practices are the subject of *Precious Teachers*, in *Complete Works*, vol. 22, pp. 383ff.

160

> The night is chill, the cloud is gray
> 'Tis a month before the month of May,
> And the Spring comes slowly up this way.

From part 1 of Samuel Taylor Coleridge's ballad poem 'Christabel' (1797).

161 *The Buddhist*, vol. 9, no. 10 (October 1965), pp. 253–5.

162 1. Rodney Collin (1909–1956) was a British disciple of P. D. Ouspensky (1878–1947). See note 128(2). *The Theory of Eternal Life* was published in 1949 and *The Theory of Celestial Influence* in 1954.

2. Iamblichus (245–325 CE) was a Syrian Neoplatonist philosopher. His *De Mysteriis Aegyptorum* (*The Egyptian Mysteries*) was a reply to criticisms made by Plotinus' pupil Porphyry of an earlier book.

163 The BBC (British Broadcasting Corporation) inaugurated the radio programme *The Brains Trust* in January 1941. Five experts formed a panel to answer questions sent in by listeners. At its peak the programme attracted twelve million listeners.

164 *The Buddhist*, vol. 9, no. 10 (October 1965), p. 255.

165 1. Samuel Johnson (1709–1784) was born in Lichfield, a small cathedral city in Staffordshire in the English Midlands. For more details of his life and work see note 28.

2. James Boswell (1740–1795) was a Scottish lawyer who became Dr Johnson's companion. His famous *Life of Samuel Johnson*, whose details of the great man's conversations and habits brought him vividly to life, was published in 1791.

166 Carl Gustav Jung (1875–1961) was a Swiss psychoanalyst and psychiatrist who was a pupil of and collaborator with Sigmund Freud before striking out on his own path. His writings on anima and animus are to be found in C. G. Jung, *Collected Works*, vol. ix, part 2, chapter 3.

167 The visualization and mantra-recitation practice centred upon the figure of Vajrasattva is one of the four *mūla yogas* or foundation meditation practices of the *Tharpe Delam* of Tantric Buddhist tradition. See chapter 6, 'The Four Foundation Yogas', in Sangharakshita, *Tibetan Buddhism*, *Complete Works*, vol. 13, pp. 82–5. Sangharakshita was introduced to the *mūla yogas* in 1962 by his friend and teacher Kachu Rimpoche. See *Precious Teachers*, in *Complete Works*, vol. 22, pp. 473–5. He also received the Vajrasattva *abhiṣekha* or initiation from Dudjom Rimpoche. See ibid., pp. 503–6.

168 This is echoed in *Aṅguttara Nikāya* i.10: 'This consciousness (*citta*) is luminous, but it is defiled by adventitious defilements.' See F. L. Woodward (trans.), *The Book of the Gradual Sayings*, vol. i, Pali Text Society, Oxford 2000, p. 8; or Bhikkhu Bodhi (trans.), *The Numerical Discourses of the Buddha*, Wisdom Publications, Somerville 2012, p. 97.

169 'Ordination and Initiation in the Three Yanas', *Dhammamegha*, no. 49, July 1992, Sinhanad Publications, Pune (*Complete Works*, vol. 7).

170 *The History of My Going for Refuge*, in *Complete Works*, vol. 2, p. 448.

171 *The Buddhist*, vol. 9, no. 2 (February 1965), p. 29.

172 Ibid., p. 30.

173 On 12 August 1965 Anna Phillips was ordained as a 'Lay Sister observing the Eight Precepts'. See report in *The Buddhist*, vol. 9, no. 10 (October 1965), p. 257.

174 Sangharakshita writes about the relationship between commitment and lifestyle in *The Ten Pillars of Buddhism*, *Complete Works*, vol. 2, pp. 351–3.

175 The *Karaṇīyamettā Sutta* (or simply *Mettā Sutta*) can be found at *Sutta-Nipāta* 1.8. See H. Saddhatissa (trans.), *The Sutta-Nipāta*, Curson Press, London 1985, pp. 15–16 for

one of many translations into English. Sangharakshita's commentary on the *sutta* is published as *Living With Kindness*, Windhorse Publications, Birmingham 2004 (*Complete Works*, vol. 15).

176 *The Buddhist*, vol. 9, no. 10 (October 1965), p. 257.

177 Rayleigh is a town in Essex, some thirty miles east of London.

178 William Shakespeare (1564–1616), *As You Like It*, Act III, Scene v, line 82.

179 *The Buddhist*, vol. 9, no. 10 (October 1965), pp. 258–9.

180 Most of the well known Socratic dialogues were composed by the great Greek philosopher Plato (c.427–c.347 BCE) in which Socrates – who historically had been Plato's teacher – becomes the main interlocutor.

181 Lance Cousins (1942–2015) studied history and oriental studies. He went on to become a scholar of Pāli and Buddhist studies, lecturing in comparative religion at the University of Manchester, publishing books and many articles, and was briefly president of the Pali Text Society (2002–3). He was instrumental in setting up the Samatha Trust in 1973, which went on to become one of the largest Theravāda organizations in the UK.

182 The Buddhist Society of Great Britain and Ireland came into being in 1907 with the Pāli scholar T. W. Rhys Davids as president. Ananda Metteyya played a crucial part in helping the Society to grow. See Christmas Humphreys, *Sixty Years of Buddhism in England*, Buddhist Society, London 1968. After Ananda Metteyya's death in 1923, the Society's assets were eventually inherited by the Buddhist Society. See John L. Crow, 'Allan Bennett & the Emergence of Buddhism in the West' in *Insight*, the magazine of the Theosophical Society in England, vol. 28, no. 3 (Summer 2008).

183 The World Fellowship of Buddhists was founded in 1950 with representatives from twenty-seven nations, though it has been predominantly Theravādin. Its five 'aims and objectives' refer to the promotion of the practice and propagation of the Dharma, as well as humanitarian and cultural activities. Sangharakshita's editorial in the *Maha Bodhi*, vol. 69, no. 10 (October 1961) exhorted the WFB, then about to hold its sixth council, to do more to spread the Dharma; it is included in *Beating the Drum*, Ibis Publications, Ledbury 2012, pp. 247–8 (*Complete Works*, vol. 8).

184 The attack from the *Buddhist World* with its repercussions is recounted in *In the Sign of the Golden Wheel*, *Complete Works*, vol. 22, pp. 168–78.

185 Gunapala Piyasena Malalasekera was born in 1899 and died in 1973.

186 See Vinaya Piṭaka i.9–14 (*Mahāvagga* 1.6), in I. B. Horner (trans.), *The Book of the Discipline*, part 4, Pali Text Society, Oxford 1996, pp. 13–21.

187 *Both Sides of the Circle: the Autobiography of Christmas Humphreys*, George Allen & Unwin, London 1978, p. 224.

188 Christmas Humphreys, 'The Seventh Conference of the World Fellowship of Buddhists' in the *Middle Way*, vol. 39, no. 4 (February 1965), pp. 150–2.

189 In fact Buddhists from various eastern and western countries visited or lived with Sangharakshita during the years he lived in Kalimpong. See *In the Sign of the Golden Wheel* and *Precious Teachers* in *Complete Works*, vol. 22.

190 See *The History of My Going for Refuge* in *Complete Works*, vol. 2, pp. 397–503, which explains the development of Sangharakshita's understanding of this vital topic, and the events and people that influenced it.

191 'Report of the Fifth General Conference of the World Fellowship of Buddhists, Bangkok, Thailand, 24–30 November BE2501 (1958)' is a review in the *Maha Bodhi*, vol. 68, no. 10 (October 1960), pp. 321–2. In fact the Sixth Conference did not take place that year at all but twelve months later.

192 'The World Fellowship of Buddhists' in *Maha Bodhi*, vol. 69, no. 10 (October 1961), p. 308; and *Beating the Drum*, Ibis Publications, Ledbury 2012, pp. 247–8 (*Complete Works*, vol. 8).

193 Maurice Walshe, 'Not All is Zen in Japan' in the *Buddhist*, vol. 9, no. 12 (December 1965), pp. 303–316.

194 Peggy Kennett (1924–1996) was an English student of Zen. She spent a number of years in Japan training in the Sōtō Zen school before moving to the USA where she founded the Zen Mission Society (later the Order of Buddhist Contemplatives) and Shasta Abbey in California where she lived and was the abbess until her death. She was one of the first women to hold the title of roshi or authorized teacher.

195 Sangharakshita was ordained as a *bhikkhu* or monk in the Theravādin tradition in 1950 (see *Facing Mount Kanchenjunga*, *Complete Works*, vol. 21, pp. 107–9). One of the rules of conduct for *bhikkhus*, established at the time of the Buddha, is not to eat after noon. See note 60.

196 Yogi C. M. Chen (1906–1987) was one of Sangharakshita's eight main teachers. Born in China, he lived as a hermit in Kalimpong for twenty-five years and later moved to the USA to spread the Dharma. Sangharakshita spent many hours learning about and discussing all kinds of meditation practices with Yogi Chen. See *Precious Teachers*,

chapter 13, *Complete Works*, vol. 22, pp. 525–44. See also note 117.

197 Sangharakshita writes about his meetings with, initiations, and the gifts he received from Jamyang Khyentse Rimpoche in *Precious Teachers*, in *Complete Works*, vol. 22, pp. 399–407 and of the relationship between the Rimpoche and his *ḍākinī* in ibid., pp. 404–6.

198 For further reflections on the place music played in his life, see Sangharakshita's 'And On His Dulcimer He Played' in *A Moseley Miscellany*, Ibis Publications, Ledbury 2015, pp. 136–46 (*Complete Works*, vol. 26).

199 Richard Wagner (1813–1883) was a German composer of opera. *Lohengrin*, first performed in 1850, and *Tannhäuser*, first performed in 1845, are Romantic operas set in medieval times. *Der Ring des Nibelungen* (*The Ring of the Nibelung*) consists of four operas based on the Norse sagas and a medieval German epic.

200 *Kūṭadanta Sutta*, *Dīgha Nikāya* 5; see M. Walshe (trans.), *The Long Discourses of the Buddha*, Wisdom Publications, Boston 1995, pp. 133–141; or T. W. Rhys Davids (trans.,) *Dialogues of the Buddha*, part 1, Pali Text Society, London 1973, pp. 173–185.

201 *The Persecution and Assassination of Jean-Paul Marat as Performed by the Inmates of the Asylum of Charenton Under the Direction of the Marquis de Sade* is a play by German-born Peter Weiss (1916–1982).

202 The departure for India in 1944 is recounted in *The Rainbow Road from Tooting Broadway to Kalimpong*, *Complete Works*, vol. 20, p. 106.

203 For a full exposition by Sangharakshita of the twelve positive *nidānas* see *The Three Jewels*, chapter 13, in *Complete Works*, vol. 2, pp. 101–18, and *What is the Dharma?*, chapter 7, in *Complete Works*, vol. 3, pp. 258–79. For a canonical source see the *Nidānavagga*, *Saṃyutta Nikāya* ii.29–32 in Bhikkhu Bodhi (trans.), *The Connected Discourses of the Buddha*, Wisdom Publications, Boston 2000, pp. 553–6; or C. A. F. Rhys Davids, *The Book of the Kindred Sayings*, part 2, Pali Text Society, Oxford 1997, pp. 25–27.

204 These ideas are explained in 'Mind – Reactive and Creative', in *Buddha Mind*, Windhorse Publications, Birmingham 2001, pp. 55–61 (*Complete Works*, vol. 11).

205 For further explanation of the fetters that bind us to conditioned existence see *The Taste of Freedom*, chapter 1, pp. 16–36 (*Complete Works*, vol. 11).

206 See, for example, *Dhammapada* chapter 26: 'The Brāhmaṇa'.

> I call him a brāhmaṇa by whom no evil is done by the body, by speech, (or) by the mind.... One is not a brāhmaṇa on account of matted hair, or (one's) clan, or birth. He in whom there exists both truth and principle (*dhamma*), *he* is pure, *he* is a brāhmaṇa.

Sangharakshita (trans.), *Dhammapada: the Way of Truth*, Windhorse Publications, Birmingham 2001, verses 391–3, pp. 128–9 (*Complete Works*, vol. 15).

In the *Vasala Sutta* (*Sutta-Nipāta* 1.7) the Buddha redefines the meaning of *vasala* or outcast. See H. Saddhatissa (trans.), *The Sutta-Nipāta*, Curzon Press, London 1995, pp. 13–15.

207 These ideas were further explored in Sangharakshita's 1969 lecture, 'Religion: Ethnic and Universal', the fourth in the series 'The Higher Evolution of Man' (*Complete Works*, vol. 12).

208 For further exploration of the Buddha being neither 'God' nor 'man', see *Who is the Buddha?*, *Complete Works*, vol. 3, pp. 139–53.

209 Joseph Butler (1692–1752) was an influential theologian and philosopher and a Christian apologist. He was bishop of Bristol from 1738 to 1750.

210 The Glasgow Razor Gangs were notorious, especially in the 1920s and 1930s, for violent clashes between themselves and with the police, and for their weapon of choice.

211 '*Je suis un homme pour qui le monde visible existe*' (I am a man for whom the visible world exists) is a remark made by Pierre Jules Théophile Gautier (1811–1872), a French writer, poet, and painter. See Joanna Richardson, *Théophile Gautier: His Life & Times*, Max Reinhardt, London 1958, p. 14.

212 See note 60.

213
> If one who is richly adorned lives in tranquillity, is calm, controlled, assured (of eventual enlightenment), and devotes himself to the spiritual life, laying down the stick with regard to all living beings, then (despite his being richly adorned), he is a brāhmaṇa, he is an asketic, he is an almsman.

Dhammapada 142. See Sangharakshita (trans.), *Dhammapada: the Way of Truth*, Windhorse Publications, Cambridge 2008, p. 54 (*Complete Works*, vol. 15).

214 Sangharakshita's Going Forth took place in August 1947 when he and his friend Robin Banerjee dyed their shirts and sarongs the traditional saffron of the world-renunciant. After his *śramaṇera* ordination in May 1949 Sangharakshita wore the robes of the Theravādin monk. See *The Rainbow Road from Tooting*

Broadway to Kalimpong, Complete Works, vol. 20, pp. 225 and 408–11.

215 Sangharakshita's Bengali brahmin friend Robin Banerjee (1922–2013) who, as a wandering ascetic with Sangharakshita, took the name Satyapriya, was ordained as Buddharakshita. He is a significant figure in the memoir *The Rainbow Road from Tooting Broadway to Kalimpong, Complete Works*, chapters 16–47. He went on to found the Bangalore Maha Bodhi Society, and helped establish schools and hospitals. He published many books on Buddhism under the name Acharya Buddharakkhita, including a translation of the *Dhammapada*. See *The Dhammapada: The Buddha's Path of Wisdom*, Buddhist Publication Society, Kandy 1998.

216 Sangharakshita writes about Thich Thien Chau in *In the Sign of the Golden Wheel, Complete Works*, vol. 22, p. 515.

217 Dr Johnson decided he should cease backstage visits at the Drury Lane theatre during the performance of his play *Irene* since 'the silk stockings and white bosoms of your actresses excite my amorous propensities.' James Boswell, *The Life of Samuel Johnson L.L.D* , 1749: Aetat. 40.

218 The life of Dr Mehta and his friendship with Sangharakshita is told in 'The Monk and the Prophet' in *Dear Dinoo: Letters to a Friend*, in *Complete Works*, vol. 21, pp. 599–619.

219 See *Facing Mount Kanchenjunga*, in *Complete Works*, vol. 21, p. 108. Hammalawa Saddhatissa (1914–1990) left his native Ceylon (Sri Lanka) at the request of the Maha Bodhi Society to work as a *dharmadūta* in India. In 1957 he moved to Britain where he studied and lectured, writing books and translating, including a well known translation of the *Sutta-Nipāta* (1985). He went on to become head of the London Buddhist Vihara and Sanghanayaka (head of the *bhikkhu* sangha) in Britain.

220 1. In the *Kevaddha Sutta* a monk visits the Great Brahmā whom lesser *brahmās* believe to be 'All-Seeing, All-Powerful, the Lord, the Maker and Creator,... Father of All that Have Been and Shall Be.' But the Great Brahmā, finding himself unable to answer the monk's question about the origin of the elements, takes the monk aside, and tells him that in fact he is not what the lesser *brahmās* believe him to be! See *Dīgha Nikāya* 11.80–83 in M. Walshe (trans.), *The Long Discourses of the Buddha*, Wisdom Publications, Boston 1995, pp. 178–9.

2. 'The world does not proceed from a single cause that is called God, or Puruṣa or Pradhāna or any other name...' Vasubandhu, *Abhidharmakośabhāsya*, vol. i, translated from the French of Louis de La Vallée Poussin by Leo M. Pruden, Asian Humanities Press, Berkeley 1988, p. 306.

3. 'A certain school holds that there is a God ... this theory is illogical for the following reasons...' Xuanzang in his *Cheng Wei Shi Lun (Doctrine of Mere-Consciousness)*, trans., Wei Tat, Ch'eng Wei-Shih Lun Publication Committee, Hong Kong 1973, p. 39.

221 I have heard it contended times without number and I have read in books also claiming to express the spirit of Buddhism that Buddha did not believe in God. In my humble opinion such a belief contradicts the very central fact of Buddha's teaching.

From Gandhi's English-language magazine, *Young India*, 24 November 1927, quoted in M. K. Gandhi, *My Religion*, compiled and edited by Bharatan Kumarappa, Jitendra Desai, Ahmedabad 1968, p. 393.

222 Maurice Walshe, 'Annual General Meeting Report' in *The Buddhist*, vol. 10, no. 1 (January 1966), pp. 39–42.

223 Lal Bahadur Shastri (1904–1966) was a member of the Indian National Congress and second prime minister of India. He died of a heart attack whilst in Tashkent having just signed a peace agreement between India and Pakistan.

224 1. Harold Wilson (1916–1995) was at this time (1966) Labour Prime Minister, the Labour party having won the 1964 General Election. He remained in office until 1970 and was again Prime Minister from 1974 to 1976.

2. Lord Mountbatten (1900–1979) was the last Viceroy of India and Governor-General of India from 1947 to 1948. He was Chief of the Defence of Staff, i.e. head of the British Armed Forces, for six years until 1965. He was assassinated at the hands of the Irish Republican Army (IRA).

3. Selwyn Lloyd (1904–1978) was a Conservative politician who held many cabinet posts including Foreign Secretary during the Suez Crisis of 1956. He was Shadow Leader of the House of Commons from 1964 to 1965.

4. Lord Sorensen (1891–1971) was a Labour politician and Unitarian Minister. He was made a life peer in 1964.

5. Jeremy Thorpe (1929–2014) was a Liberal politician who had been returned to parliament with a huge majority after the October 1964 General Election. In 1967

he would become leader of the Liberal Party until 1976 when scandals that led to a much publicized court case put an end to his political career.

6. Clement Attlee (1883–1967) was leader of the Labour Party for twenty years from 1935 and, replacing Winston Churchill after the Second World War, was Prime Minister from 1945 to 1951.

7. Kingsley Martin (1897–1969) was a journalist with left-wing sympathies. For thirty years he had been editor of the *New Statesman*.

8. Dame Sybil Thorndike (1882–1976) was a renowned British actress. In 1965 she starred in a televised version of E. M. Forster's *Passage to India* (1924) playing the character Mrs Moore.

9. Arnold Toynbee (1889–1975) was a journalist, historian, scholar, and expert on international affairs. In 1961 he had published the last of his twelve-volume *Study of History*.

225 Ignatius Timothy Trebitsch-Lincoln (1879–1943) was born of Jewish parents in Hungary. He later moved to England and became an Anglican priest, a Liberal Member of Parliament, a spy and collaborator with the Nazis, and, after moving to China and converting to Buddhism, a monk, setting up his own monastery with himself as Abbot Chao Kung. After the death of the Thirteenth Dalai Lama he proclaimed himself the new Dalai Lama.

226 1. Palden Thondup Namgyal (1923–1982) was the last king or *chogyal* of the Kingdom of Sikkim. (Sikkim became a state of India in 1975 and the monarchy was abolished.) He followed his father, Sir Tashi Namgyal, whose funeral Sangharakshita attended in December 1963. (See Letter 24 and note 1 in *Dear Dinoo: Letters to a Friend*, *Complete Works*, vol. 21, pp. 583–4.)

2. Hope Cooke was born in the USA in 1940. Her much publicized marriage in 1963 to the Maharaja of Sikkim made her 'Queen Consort'. They divorced in 1980. In the lead up to the marriage Sangharakshita wrote to his friend, then still the Crown Prince, protesting at the number of animals that were to be killed and the amount of alcohol expected to be consumed at the wedding (the Crown Prince was a Buddhist). See *Precious Teachers*, *Complete Works*, vol. 22, pp. 485–6.

227 1. Sangharakshita first visited Gangtok in 1951 when he accompanied the sacred relics of Maudgalyāyana and Śāriputra and gave discourses on the Dharma. As a result there was an upsurge of interest in Buddhism and a branch of the Young Men's Buddhist Association was

formed with the Crown Prince as President – though it did not prosper long. See *Facing Mount Kanchenjunga*, *Complete Works*, vol. 21, p. 190.

2. The Crown Prince met personally with Sangharakshita in Kalimpong in 1954, seeking his advice on matters concerning the Maha Bodhi Society of which the Crown Prince was by then President. See *In the Sign of the Golden Wheel*, *Complete Works*, vol. 22, p. 240.

3. The Crown Prince invited Sangharakshita to the Sikkim capital, Gangtok, where in June 1955 he gave a series of lectures (ibid., chapter 16, pp. 240–9). He was also there in 1958 (ibid., p. 470).

4. Sangharakshita had two meetings with Jamyang Khyentse Rimpoche at the palace temple in Gangtok. See *Precious Teachers*, *Complete Works*, vol. 22, pp. 406–7.

228 See 'A Damsel in Distress' in *Precious Teachers*, *Complete Works*, vol. 22, pp. 408–18.

229 Sonam Topgay was one of those 'Eminent Buddhists' – likewise Sangharakshita and Dhardo Rimpoche – who were invited by the Indian government to tour the Buddhist holy places in the Buddha Jayanti year 1956. During the tour he acted as translator into Tibetan and Nepali and helped organize various private meetings for Sangharakshita including with Lama Tenzin Gyaltsen and the Dalai Lama. He was present at Sangharakshita's last meeting with Dr B. R. Ambedkar (*In the Sign of the Golden Wheel*, chapter 22, *Complete Works*, vol. 22, pp. 329–55). It was from Sonam Topgay that Sangharakshita first heard about Chattrul Sangye Dorje (ibid., pp. 372–3; and *Precious Teachers*, *Complete Works*, vol. 22, pp. 390–1). Sonam Topgay also acted as interpreter when Sangharakshita first met Jamyang Khyentse Rimpoche, and during the subsequent initiations (ibid., pp. 399; and p. 402 where Sonam Topgay is referred to as 'my good Dharma-friend'). He also told Sangharakshita stories about his own teacher, Dudjom Rimpoche (ibid., p. 502).

230 Sangharakshita explains *paramārtha-satya* (Pāli *paramattha-sacca*) and *saṃvṛti-satya* (Pāli *sammuti-sacca*) or absolute and relative truth in *A Survey of Buddhism*, chapter 2, section 7. See *Complete Works*, vol. 1, pp. 264–71.

231 Sangharakshita writes about his Aunt Jessie in *The Rainbow Road from Tooting Broadway to Kalimpong*, *Complete Works*, vol. 20, pp. 10–11.

232 Laurence Olivier (1907–1989) was an English actor and director. He performed many roles on film and stage. He was both director and acted the title role in the film of Shakespeare's *Henry V* (1944).

233 D. T. Suzuki, *The Zen Doctrine of No Mind* was subtitled *The Significance of the Sutra of Hui-Neng*. It was first published in 1949. For more on D. T. Suzuki see note 79.

234 Erich Fromm (1900–1980) was of German-Jewish origin. He emigrated to the USA after the Nazi takeover in Germany. A neo-Freudian psychoanalyst whose ideas extended beyond the individual to society, his seminal book *Fear of Freedom* was published in 1942. *The Heart of Man* bore the subtitle, *Its Genius for Good and Evil* and was first published in 1964.

235
> I thought of Chatterton, the marvellous Boy,
> The sleepless Soul that perished in his pride.

from William Wordsworth's poem 'Resolution and Independence' (1802). Thomas Chatterton was a poet. He was born in 1752 near to St Mary Redcliffe and poems and prose written by him were inspired by it. His suicide in 1770 at the age of seventeen made him a heroic tragic figure of the Romantic movement.

236 See 'The Enemy of the Church', *Facing Mount Kanchenjunga*, chapter 17, *Complete Works*, vol. 21, pp. 345–66.

237 *The Rainbow Road from Tooting Broadway to Kalimpong*, *Complete Works*, vol. 20, pp. 63–4.

238 Ibid., p. 85.

239 1. Augustine of Hippo (354–430 CE), one of the foremost church fathers of Christianity, was a bishop in North Africa. His autobiography, *Confessiones*, was written (in Latin) between 397 and 400 CE, amounting to some thirteen books.

2. The great mystical theologian of the late fifth and early sixth century CE used the name of the Athenian Christian convert of St Paul as a pseudonym. He is thus sometimes referred to as Pseudo-Dionysius the Areopagite.

240 This article was called 'Brother Lawrence: A Study in Mysticism, Eastern and Western' and was published in two parts in the *Vedanta Kesari*, vol. 33, nos. 1 & 2 (May and June 1946). See *Early Writings 1944–1954*, Ibis Publications, Ledbury 2014, pp. 109–122 (*Complete Works*, vol. 7).

St Lawrence of the Resurrection (c.1614–1691) was a lay brother of the Carmelite Priory in Paris where he worked in the kitchen. (He lacked the education to become a full cleric.)

241 John Henry Newman (1801–1890) was a theologian, philosopher, and poet. He was ordained as a priest of the Church of England in 1825. He was ordained as a priest in the Roman Catholic Church in 1837. In 1879 he was made a

cardinal by Pope Leo XIII. In 2010 he was beatified by Pope Benedict XVI.

242 1. Timothy Ware (b. 1934) was brought up in the Anglican church. He embraced Orthodox Christianity when he was twenty-four, and went on to become a monk at the monastery in Patmos, Greece, when he received the name Kállistos. He lectured at the University of Oxford for thirty-five years, publishing many books. In 1982 he was consecrated as a bishop, and later a metropolitan (or archbishop). *The Orthodox Way* was published in 1963.

2. Arthur Penrhyn Stanley (1815–1881): *Lectures on the History of the Eastern Church*, John Murray, London 1861.

3. Nicholas Arseniev (1888–1977) wrote a number of books on the subject including *Russian Piety*, Faith Press, London 1964.

243 Sangharakshita writes of the consciousness that characterizes true spiritual community as,

> not the sum total of the individual consciousnesses concerned, nor even a kind of collective consciousness, but a consciousness of an entirely different order for which we have no word in English but to which the Russian word *sobornost* perhaps gives a clue.

The History of My Going for Refuge, *Complete Works*, vol. 2, p. 474.

244 Vladimir Solovyov (1853–1900) was a Russian theologian, philosopher, and poet, a man with broad interests and concerns from his response to German idealist dualism to defending Jewish Civil Rights. *Lectures on Godmanhood* describe and explore his mystical encounters with Sophia, the Divine Wisdom.

245 The Second Vatican Council (1962–1965) was called by Pope John XIII to look at the role of the Roman Catholic Church in the modern world and other matters. As a result some changes were introduced including the use of vernacular languages instead of Latin in celebrating mass.

246 John Robinson (1919–1983) was a priest of the Church of England and Bishop of Woolwich from 1959 to 1969. He was a lecturer and later Dean of Trinity College, Cambridge. *Honest to God* was published in 1963. (See *Complete Works*, vol. 11.)

247 Dietrich Bonhoeffer (1906–1945) was a German pastor, theologian, and anti-Nazi dissident who was executed by the Nazis. The idea of Christ as a man for others is mentioned in his 'Outline for a Book' in *Letters and Papers from Prison* (abridged), SCM Press, London 2001, p. 143.

248 1. Socrates (c.470–399 BCE), the great Athenian philosopher, was put to death by poison after a trial in which he was found guilty of corrupting the minds of Athenian youth and not believing in the gods of the state. Plato (see note 130), in his *Apology of Socrates*, speaks of him as having been the 'gadfly' of the state, questioning its morals and justice.

2. Edith Cavell (1865–1915) was an English nurse and hospital matron who worked in Belgium during the First World War. She helped soldiers from both sides, including helping Allied soldiers to escape for which she was executed by firing squad. She is remembered for her words: 'I must have no hatred or bitterness towards anyone.' Sangharakshita writes of her in *A Moseley Miscellany*, Ibis Books, Ledbury 2015, p. 119 (*Complete Works*, vol. 26).

3. The first Vietnamese monk to self-immolate in protest at the persecution of Buddhists by the Vietnamese government led by Ngô Đình Diệm was Thích Quảng Đức. It took place on 11 June 1963 at a busy crossroads in Saigon. He was 66 years old. David Halberstam, a *New York Times* journalist who witnessed the event, wrote in *The Making of a Quagmire*, Random House, New York 1965:

> As he burned he never moved a muscle, never uttered a sound, his outward composure in sharp contrast to the wailing people around him.

Sangharakshita writes about the events in Vietnam in *Precious Teachers*, *Complete Works*, vol. 22, pp. 516–17. The situation was of such concern to him that three *Maha Bodhi* editorials written at this time were on this theme. The editorial for June 1963 is included in *Beating the Drum*, Ibis Publications, Ledbury 2012, pp. 261–2 (*Complete Works*, vol. 8).

249 Mrs Proudie is the unpopular (with the clergy) but influential wife of the Bishop of Barchester in Anthony Trollope's *Barchester Towers* (1857).

250 Don Cupitt (b. 1934) was ordained as an Anglican priest, although he later ceased to be a member of the church. He was a writer and broadcaster. In 1984 he presented a six-part television series called *The Sea of Faith*, named after a line from 'Dover Beach' (1867), a poem by Matthew Arnold:

> The Sea of Faith
> Was once, too, at the full, and round earth's shore
> Lay like the folds of a bright girdle furled.
> But now I only hear
> Its melancholy, long, withdrawing roar,
> Retreating,...

The series looked at Western thought about religion; and proposed that religion is a human creation. A Sea of Faith network with local groups grew up as a result of the series.

251 Sangharakshita describes dreams from this and other times in 'Dreams Old and New I and II' in *Adhisthana Writings*, *Complete Works*, vol. 26.

252 Agnolo di Cosimo, called Bronzino, (1503–1572) was a leading Florentine painter. *Venus, Cupid, Folly and Time (An Allegory of Love)* was created between 1540 and 1545. It shows Cupid kissing his mother, Venus – both are naked – whilst other figures look on. An old woman with contorted features rends her hair, a man, who may be Time, stands before an hourglass.

253 Śāntideva, *Bodhicaryāvatāra* 7.65:

> So, even at the conclusion of one task, one should plunge straight away into the next, as does a tusker, inflamed by the midday heat, immediately on coming to a pool.

K. Crosby and A. Skilton, *The Bodhicaryāvatāra*, Windhorse Publications, Birmingham 1995, p. 73.

254 'Ven. Sthavira's Literary Work' in *The Buddhist*, vol. 10, no. 4 (April 1966), p. 153.

255 *The Three Jewels* appeared in five editions, the most recent being for the *Complete Works*, where it is one of the main texts included in Volume 2. There is a brief history of its publication, ibid., pp. 3–4.

256 *The Eternal Legacy* was first published by Tharpa Publications in 1985, and a second edition by Windhorse Publications in 2006. It is included in *Complete Works*, vol. 14, pp. 1–284.

257 These editorials were subsequently published in *Crossing the Stream*, Windhorse Publications, Birmingham 1996 (*Complete Works*, vol. 7).

258 *The Meaning of Orthodoxy in Buddhism: A Protest* was serialized in *The Buddhist*, in three parts, January–March 1966. It was afterwards published as a pamphlet by Windhorse Publications (1987) (*Complete Works*, vol. 7).

259 Isaline Blew Horner (1896–1981) was an English Pāli scholar and president of the Pāli Text Society from 1959 to 1981. Her first book was *Women Under Primitive Buddhism* (1933). She went on to translate Pāli texts which were published by the Pali Text Society, including the Vinaya Piṭaka in six parts (published as *The Book of the Discipline*); the *Majjhima Nikāya* (*The Collection of the Middle Length Sayings*); and the *Milindapañha* (*Milinda's Questions*).

260 Maurice Walshe, 'Orthodoxy and Fundamentalism' in *The Buddhist*, vol. 10, no. 5 (May 1966), p. 171.

261 The poem 'Waiting in the Car' begins,

> How beautiful is Berkeley Square!
> Sunlit in the Spring air...

See *Complete Poems 1941–1994*, Windhorse Publications, Birmingham 1995, p. 252 (*Complete Works*, vol. 25, p. 303).

262 A series of lectures on the same subject given in 1968 were later transcribed, edited, and published as *Tibetan Buddhism*, *Complete Works*, vol. 13, pp. 1–112.

263 From 'Letter to Dr Zaehner', printed as an appendix to *The FWBO and 'Protestant Buddhism'*, *Complete Works*, vol. 13, p. 517. Robert Charles Zaehner (1913–1974) was a British scholar of Eastern religions. Sangharakshita's letter to him was a response to his book, *Evolution in Religion: Study in Sri Aurobindo and Pierre Teilhard De Chardin*, Oxford University Press, Oxford 1971.

264 The Vietnam War (1955–75) was fought between the Vietcong Communists of South Vietnam, backed by the Communist forces of North Vietnam, and the anti-Communist forces of the government of South Vietnam backed by the USA. There were hundreds of thousands of casualties.

265
> Thou, light-winged Dryad of the trees
> In some melodious plot
> Of beechen green, and shadows numberless,
> Singest of summer in full-throated ease....

John Keats (1795–1821) wrote his 'Ode to a Nightingale' after hearing the bird sing in a garden in Hampstead where he lived, not far from Lancaster Grove.

266 Sangharakshita had himself taken bodhisattva ordination from Dhardo Rimpoche in 1962. See *Precious Teachers*, *Complete Works*, vol. 22, pp. 542–3. For the arising of the will to Enlightenment see 'The Awakening of the Bodhi Heart' in *The Bodhisattva Ideal*, *Complete Works*, vol. 4, chapter 2, pp. 27–54.

267 Henry Miller, *The Colossus of Maroussi*, Penguin, London 2016, p. 162. It was first published in San Francisco in 1941.

268 'Vaisakha Celebrations in England' in *The Buddhist*, vol. 10, no. 6 (June 1966), pp. 205–7.

269 Ibid., p. 205.

270 *The Buddhist*, vol. 10, no. 5 (May 1966), p. 159.

271 For Khantipālo, see note 117.

272 Rechung Rimpoche, said to be the latest incarnation of Milarepa's wayward disciple, was one of the *tulkus* whom

Sangharakshita came to know in Kalimpong. He writes about him in *Precious Teachers*, *Complete Works*, vol. 22, pp. 491–2.

273 AA stands for Automobile Association. The AA would give advice about driving in mainland Europe.

274 Kenwood House is a seventeenth-century former stately home on the northern edge of Hampstead Heath.

275 Sangharakshita writes about his holidays in Shoreham in *The Rainbow Road from Tooting Broadway to Kalimpong*, *Complete Works*, vol. 20, p. 33.

276 1. Euripides c.480–c.406 BCE was one of the great Athenian tragic playwrights. *Iphigenia in Tauris* dates from c.414 BCE.

2. Iphigenia is the daughter of Agamemnon and sister to Orestes. In this play she is a priestess on the island of Tauris, years after escaping being sacrificed by her father in order to appease the goddess Artemis who was withholding the winds that would enable the Greek ships to sail home after the Trojan War. When the Greeks eventually returned, Agamemnon was killed by his wife Clytemnestra and her lover. Orestes then killed his mother to avenge their father's murder. In this play he finds his way to Tauris not knowing he will find his sister there.

3. *Hecuba* is an earlier play, dated to c.424 BCE, whose story is of Hecuba, Queen of Troy, her grief over the death of her daughter, and revenge for the murder of her son Polydorus.

4. *The Plays of Euripides in English* was published in two volumes in the Everyman Series by J. M. Dent and Sons, Ltd., London 1908.

5. *The Bacchae* was written towards the end of Euripides' life and performed posthumously in 405 BCE. The play was an innovation in that the god Dionysus was the protagonist. Gilbert Murray (1866–1957) was a classical scholar. His translation into English rhyming verse was first published in 1902 in a volume containing two other works, Euripides' *Hippolytus*, and Aristophanes' *The Frogs*.

277 Hail to thee, blithe Spirit!
Bird thou never wert,
That from Heaven, or near it,
Pourest thy full heart
In profuse strains of
unpremeditated art.

Percy Bysshe Shelley (1792–1822) completed 'To a Skylark' in 1820.

278 Plutarch (46–120 CE) was born near Delphi and educated in Greece, then under Roman rule. In the later part of his life he was a priest at the temple of Apollo at Delphi. His *Lives of the Noble Greeks and Romans* (commonly called *Parallel Lives* or *Plutarch's Lives*), is a series of biographies of famous

men, arranged to illuminate their common moral virtues or failings.

279 Aristides (530–468 BCE) was an Athenian statesman and general known as Aristides the Just.

280 Later, on seeing Tuscan huntsmen shooting songbirds for sport, Sangharakshita wrote a poem, 'Hercules and the Birds'. See *Complete Poems 1941–1994*, Windhorse Publications, Birmingham 1995, pp. 459–68 (*Complete Works*, vol. 25, pp. 512–20).

281 David of Dinant (c.1160–c.1216) was a French medieval scholar and teacher, probably at the University of Paris. He studied Aristotle whose works had only recently been translated from Ancient Greek into the Latin familiar to medieval European scholars. David's *Quaternuli* (*Little Notebooks*) contained ideas offensive to the Roman Catholic Church. His books were banned and he was forced to flee Paris.

282 Johann Wolfgang von Goethe (1749–1832) was one of the greatest figures of German culture. He wrote novels, plays, poetry, and literary criticism as well as carrying out scientific research including investigating the phenomenon of colour. In his *Italienische Reise* (*Italian Journey*), based on diaries and letters to friends, he describes his travels in Italy between 1786 and 1788 when he slipped away from his court duties as Privy Councillor in the Duchy of Weimar and went on a kind of quest. It was first published in 1816–7.

283 John Addington Symonds (1840–1893) was an English poet, literary critic, cultural historian, and correspondent of Walt Whitman. He was an advocate of Greek Love and may have been the first to use the term 'homosexual'. His *Renaissance in Italy*, a series of extended essays on the subject of the title, was published between 1875 and 1886.

284 *The Idler* was a series of 103 essays, all but twelve by Samuel Johnson, published in a London weekly magazine, the *Universal Chronicle*, between 1758 and 1760. No. 97 (23 February 1760) bore the title, 'Narratives of travellers considered'.

285 When he was eleven, Sangharakshita joined the local Boys' Brigade which was affiliated to the Baptist Church. The captain of the Brigade (who was also superintendent of the Sunday School) worked for a shipping company, attending conferences in Rome and elsewhere. *The Rainbow Road from Tooting Broadway to Kalimpong*, *Complete Works*, vol. 20, pp. 40–1.

286 Smooth the descent, and easy is the way;
But to return, and gain the cheerful skies,

Therein the toil and mighty labour lies...

Virgil (70–19 BCE), *Aeneid*, book 6, lines 124–6, trans. John Dryden (1631–1700).

287 Leonardo da Vinci (1452–1519) was an Italian Renaissance polymath known for science and engineering, architecture and invention, but most of all for his painting and drawing. *The Last Supper*, painted in the 1490s, shows Jesus and his apostles at the moment when Jesus foretells that one of them will betray him.

288 1. Antonio di Puccio Pisano known as Pisanello (c.1395–c.1455), one of the most accomplished early Italian Renaissance painters of frescoes, murals, portraits, and drawings, and creator of medallions.

2. Andrea Mantegna (c.1431–1506) who painted religious subjects and landscapes, experimented with the representation of perspective.

3. Tiziano Vecelli (1488/90–1576), known as Titian, was the leading painter of the Venetian school of art. Very versatile, he painted portraits, landscapes, and mythological and religious subjects. See also note 346(4).

4. Jacopo Comin known as Tintoretto (1518–1594), called for his phenomenal energy 'Il Furioso'. Another Venetian, he was known for painting muscular figures with dramatic gestures, and for his bold use of perspective.

5. Paolo Veronese (1528–1588) was also based in Venice and is known for his paintings of large canvasses showing scenes from the Bible and classical mythology. See also note 297.

289 The Basilica of San Zeno is the main church of Verona. Andrea Mantegna (see notes 288(2) and 291(1)) painted this triptych c.1457–1460. In the centre is the Madonna with child. They are surrounded by angels. On each of the panels to the right and left are four saints.

290 William Shakespeare (1564–1616) wrote his famous tragedy about the star-crossed young lovers whose death finally reconciles their feuding families, probably in the first half of the 1590s.

291 1. Andrea Mantegna (c.1431–1506) see notes 288(2) and 289(1) above.

2. Giovanni Battista Tiepolo (1696–1770) was a Venetian painter and printmaker in the rococo style.

3. Hans Memlinc (c.1430–1494) was a German painter who settled in Bruges and became a leading painter of portraits and diptychs. His painting of Christ Crucified is in the Palazzo Chiericati.

292 *Herodias with the Head of John the Baptist* by Francesco Cairo (1607–1665);

St Sebastian by Pietro della Vecchia (1603–1678); *The Ecstasy of St Francis* by the Venetian Giambattista Piazzetta (c.1682–1754).

293 Andrea Palladio (1508–1580) was a Venetian architect of great influence. The Basilica Palladiana of Vicenza, built in Gothic style, was originally known as the *Palazzo della Ragione* and served as the seat of government.

294 David Herbert Lawrence (1885–1930) was an English poet and writer of novels and essays whose themes include the effects of industrialization and modernization, Mexican culture, sexuality, spontaneity, relations between men and women, and male friendship. Sangharakshita writes about him as one of his five literary heroes in *A Moseley Miscellany*, Ibis Publications, Ledbury 2015, pp. 117–18 (*Complete Works*, vol. 26). Lawrence, he says, 'touched nothing which he did not bring to life'.

295 1. Johann Wolfgang von Goethe (1749–1832) had his first glimpse of the sea when he arrived in Venice on his Italian Journey in September 1786. He writes about his impressions of Venice in *Italienische Reise* (*Italian Journey*). See note 282.

2. George Gordon, Lord Byron (1788–1824) is famous as an English poet though he was also a politician. He spent seven years in Italy where he lived in Venice, Ravenna, and Pisa after being forced to leave England because of debts and scandals. His 'Ode on Venice' (completed 1819) begins

> Oh Venice! Venice! when thy marble walls
> Are level with the waters, there shall be
> A cry of nations ...

3. John Ruskin (1819–1900) was an English art critic and patron of the arts, painter, social commentator, and essayist on many subjects. He first visited Venice with his parents in 1835, and again in 1844, and four years later with his wife, Effie. His famous work, *The Stones of Venice*, examines Venetian architecture, including a description of over eighty churches. It also gives a general history of the city. It was published in three volumes from 1851 to 1853.

4. Frederick Rolfe (1860–1913) is known by several pen names including Baron Corvo. He was an English writer, artist, and photographer whose later years were spent in Venice, where he died. His *The Desire and Pursuit of the Whole* contains many beautiful descriptions of Venice. It was written between 1910 and 1913 but then lost. It was found and published in 1934.

296 Giorgio Barbarelli da Castelfranco (1477/8–1510), known as Giorgione, was an Italian painter and one of the

founders of the Venetian school whose works emphasized colour and mood. *The Tempest* (also known as 'The Gypsy and the Soldier') dates to 1506–8. It depicts a woman sitting to the right, suckling a baby; to the left a man who could be a soldier or a gypsy looks on.

297 Paolo Veronese (1528–1588) (see note 288(5)). *The Feast in the House of Levi* (1573) shows Christ surrounded by other figures at a banquet. Originally it was called *The Last Supper* but after interrogation by the Inquisition of the Roman Catholic Church, Veronese changed the title.

298 The doge was chief magistrate and leader of the Republic of Venice 726–1797 CE. Each year a ceremony took place in which the doge dropped a consecrated ring into the sea saying 'Desponsamus te, mare, in signum veri perpetuique domini' (We wed thee, sea, as a sign of true and everlasting governance), thus declaring Venice and the sea to be indissolubly one.

299 Marco Polo (1254–1324) was a Venetian explorer and writer who famously travelled across Asia to the court of Kublai Khan in China. He wrote about his travels in his *Book of the Marvels of the World* (also known as *The Travels of Marco Polo*), which was published c.1300.

300 1. Donato di Niccolò di Betto Bardi (c.1386–1466), known as Donatello, was one of the most renowned sculptors of Renaissance Italy. He worked in stone, bronze, wood, clay, stucco, and wax. His bronze 'Equestrian Statue of Gattamelata' dates from 1453.

2. Erasmo of Narni (1370–1443), known as 'Gattamelata' meaning 'Honeyed Cat', was an Italian general or *condottiero* who led military campaigns for the expanding Republic of Venice. He died in Padua.

301 Giotto di Bondone (1267–1337) was a Florentine painter and architect. He moved away from stylized painting to drawing accurately from life. The Cappella degli Scrovegni, also known as the Arena Chapel, was consecrated in 1305. Its walls are covered with Giotto's frescoes of the Life of Christ, the Last Judgement, and the Life of the Virgin.

302 Henry James (1843–1916), brother of philosopher and psychologist William James, and diarist Alice James, was born and grew up in the USA but lived most of his adult life in England and for a shorter time in Paris. In both countries he came to know many great literary figures. *The Bostonians* was first published as a serial in *The Century Magazine* 1885–1886, and as a book in 1886. The main characters include a political conservative and two feminists through

whose interactions James explores the role of women in society and other themes.

303 See note 278 for Plutarch's *Lives*. Pericles (c.495–429 BCE) was a statesman of Ancient Athens and an orator of great influence.

304 1. 'Sheep may safely graze' (German: *Schafe können sicher weiden*) is a soprano aria from the 1713 cantata, *Was mir behagt ist nun die muntre Jagd*, ('The Lively Hunt is All My Heart's Desire'), BWV 208. Often played at weddings, it was written for the birthday of the Duke of Saxe-Weissenfels by the great German composer, Johann Sebastian Bach (1685–1750).

2. George Handel (1685–1759) was a German composer who settled in England. He composed operas and oratorios, as well as anthems and concertos. His oratorio *The Messiah*, composed in 1741, is one of the best-known and most frequently performed choral works in all of Western music.

305 1. Hyperion was one of the twelve Titans of Classical Greek mythology, offspring of Gaia (Earth) and Uranus (Sky), who overthrew Cronus and who were themselves overthrown by the Olympians. In later Greek literature Hyperion was regarded as the god of watchfulness, wisdom, and light. He was father of Helios, the sun.

2. Apollo is the Greek god of music and poetry, truth and prophecy – he is the prophetic deity of Delphi – and healing. He was associated especially with the sun and light.

3. Aton (or Aten) in Ancient Egyptian mythology was the disk of the sun, an aspect of the god Ra. Aton was the focus of the quasi-monotheistic religion established by the pharaoh Amenhotep IV or Akhenaten (died c.1335 BCE).

306 Homer was the author (thought by some to be legendary) of the two early Ancient Greek epic poems, the *Odyssey*, which tells how Odysseus returned from the Trojan War to his homeland in Greece through many perils and adventures, and the *Iliad* whose main subject is the quarrel between King Agamemnon and the warrior Achilles during the Trojan War. The poems were composed in the late eighth or early seventh century BCE. Their influence on all that came later in western civilization has been immense.

307 Lines from D. H. Lawrence's 'The Argonauts' in *Last Poems*, published posthumously in Florence in 1932.

308 Jean-François Millet (1814–1875) was a French painter and founder of the Barbizon school which valued realism. His *Angelus* is an oil painting completed 1859. It depicts two peasants in a field bowing over a basket of potatoes to say a prayer. The signal to recite the Angelus prayer was

sounded by the local church bells. The prayer begins, 'Angelus Domini nuntiavit Mariæ' (the Angel of the Lord declared unto Mary).

309 The Shell Oil Company, founded in 1912 and based in the USA, is one of the largest oil companies in the world.

310 The *Iliad* and the *Odyssey* (see note 306) were translated into English by poet and dramatist George Chapman (1559–1634) (see note 15). Sangharakshita writes about his first encounter with Chapman's translation of the poem in *The Rainbow Road from Tooting Broadway to Kalimpong*, *Complete Works*, vol. 20, p. 49.

311 *Iliad*, book XVI, lines 233–8. See *The Iliad of Homer*, Richard Lattimore (trans.), University of Chicago Press, Chicago 1951, p. 336.

312 Euripides (c.484–c.406 BCE) together with Aeschylus and Sophocles was one of the great tragedian dramatists of Ancient Athens. He wrote more than ninety plays.

313 'Hercules and the Birds', in *Complete Poems 1941–1994*, Windhorse Publications, Birmingham 1995, pp. 459–68 (*Complete Works*, vol. 25, pp. 512–20).

314 Euripides, *The Madness of Herakles* in *Euripides: Plays*, trans. A. S. Way, vol. ii, J. M. Dent & Sons, London 1956, p. 68.

315 'The wonderful Avalokita, who labours for the weal of all beings' from *Devotion to Tārā: the 108 Names of Tārā* quoted in E. Conze (ed.), *Buddhist Texts Through the Ages*, Harper & Row, New York 1964, p. 196.

316 Byron became involved in the movement for Greek independence from the Ottoman Empire, spending large amounts on refitting the Greek navy, and narrowly avoiding being taken by an Ottoman warship on his way to Missolonghi. He sought to reconcile factions among the Greeks and was involved in a plan to attack the Turkish-held fortress of Lepanto. In February 1824, before the expedition could set sail, Byron fell ill in Missolonghi. Within two months he was dead. See also note 295(2).

317 G. K. Chesterton (1874–1936) was a journalist, novelist, essayist, and poet. He composed 'Lepanto' in 1911. It tells of the defeat of the Ottoman fleet by the Christian Don John of Austria and begins:

> White founts falling in the courts of the sun,
> And the Soldan of Byzantium is smiling as they run.

318 Delphi is the last of the places described by Henry Miller in *The Colossus of Maroussi* (1941). His description of Delphi can be found in the 2016 Penguin edition on pp. 159–163.

319 And while the bubbling and loud-hissing urn
Throws up a steamy column, and the cups,
That cheer but not inebriate, wait on each,
So let us welcome peaceful evening in.

William Cowper (1731–1800), 'The Task: A Poem in Six Books' (1785).

320 From John Keats (1795–1821), 'Ode to a Nightingale' (1819).

321 Henry Miller, *The Colossus of Maroussi*, Penguin, London 2016, p. 162.

322 John Milton (1608–1674), *Paradise Lost*, Book IV, line 845. The description is of the Cherub Zephon as he rebukes Satan.

323 John Keats (1795–1821) 'Ode to Psyche' (1819).

324 *The Pelican History of Greece* by A. R. Burns (1902–1991), a senior lecturer in Ancient History at the University of Glasgow, had just been published (1966). The book has been described as

> Readable, erudite, enthusiastic and balanced, it sweeps the reader along from the days of Mycenae to the splendors of Athens and to the conquests of Alexander and the last dark ages.

325 1. Richard Lattimore (1906–1984) was an American classical scholar, translator, and himself a poet. His *Odes of Pindar* (1947) is a collection of translations of lyric poems by the Ancient Theban poet, Pindar (c.518–c.438 BCE). See also note 333.

2. Benjamin Rogers (1828–1919) was an English classical scholar who translated all the surviving plays of Aristophanes into English, reproducing the Greek metre in the English version. *Five Comedies of Aristophanes: The Birds, The Frogs, The Clouds, The Wasps, Lysistrata*, was published by Doubleday, New York 1955. Aristophanes (c.446–c.386 BCE), the great comic dramatist of ancient Athens, wrote some forty comedies, eleven of which have survived complete.

3. *The Essential Works of Stoicism*, edited by Moses Hadas, was published by Bantam Books in 1965. It included works by the Stoic writers, Diogenes Laertius, Cleanthes, Seneca, Epictetus, and Marcus Aurelius.

326 1. Goethe's views are expressed in *Goethe Gespräche* 2.157 and 3.2.603–4 quoted by W. Daniel Wilson in his article '"Höhere Begattung," "höhere Schönheit": Goethe's Homoerotic Poem "Selige Sehnsucht"' in Daniel Purdy (ed.), *Goethe Yearbook 20*, Boydell & Brewer 2013, pp. 124–5.

2. Schopenhauer expresses such an idea when he says that the beauty of a young man

compared to that of a young woman is like an oil painting in comparison to a pastel ('Jünglingsschönheit verhält sich zu Mädchenschönheit wie Ölmalerei zu Pastell'), *Neue Paralipomena* §480.

327 Aristophanes, *The Frogs*, lines 455–9. Translator unknown.

328 These events form the backdrop to Aeschylus' *Oresteia* trilogy: *Agamemnon*, *The Libation Bearers*, and *The Eumenides.*

329 'One Sunday I read ... all seven of Aeschylus' tragedies.' *The Rainbow Road from Tooting Broadway to Kalimpong*, *Complete Works*, vol. 20, p. 51.

330 Pausanius (c.110–c.180 CE) was a geographer and traveller who described the sites of Ancient Greece in ten travel books. Of Epidaurus he wrote: 'What architect could seriously rival Polycleitus in symmetry and beauty? For it was Polycleitus who built both this theatre and the circular building.' *Description of Greece*, 2.27.5.

331 1. Lycurgus (fl. c.820 BCE) was the quasi-legendary lawgiver of Sparta who reformed Spartan society in accordance with Apollo's oracle at Delphi and promoted the virtues of equality among citizens, military fitness, and austerity, for which Sparta became famous.

2. Leonidas was a warrior king of Sparta who died 480 BCE when leading the Greek forces against the Persians at the Battle of Thermopylae.

332 1. Hesiod (fl. around 750–650 BCE) was a poet. Two works generally agreed to be authored by him have survived: *Works and Days* and *Theogony.*

2. Homer, the great blind poet, perhaps legendary, of late eighth and early seventh century BCE composed the *Odyssey* and the *Iliad.* See note 306.

3. Pindar (c.518–c.438 BCE) was a lyric poet from Thebes, the first Greek poet to reflect on the role of poet and poetry.

4. The Attic Dramatists are the tragedians Aeschylus, Sophocles, and Euripides, and the comic playwright Aristophanes, all from the fifth century BCE.

5. Socrates (c.470–399 BCE), the Athenian philosopher and teacher of Plato.

6. Plato (428/7–348/7 BCE) was a pupil of Socrates and founder of the Platonist school of philosophy whose unparalleled influence has been felt throughout western civilization. His Academy in Athens was the first university of the western world. See also notes 130 and 140.

7. Aristotle (384–322 BCE) was a pupil of Plato who later founded his own Lyceum in Athens attracting students from all over Greece. He lectured or wrote on many themes including logic,

metaphysics, mathematics, physics, biology, botany, ethics, aesthetics, politics, agriculture, medicine, dance, and theatre. Aristotle's works became lost in the western world but continued to be read in the Islamic world until translated into Latin and reintroduced into the West in the thirteenth century.

8. Herodotus (c.484–c.425 BCE) dubbed 'The Father of History'. His *Histories* were an inquiry into the origin of the Greco-Persian Wars.

9. Thucydides (c.460–c.400 BCE) was an Athenian historian and general. His *History of the Peloponnesian War* recounts the war between Sparta and Athens.

10. Demosthenes (384–322 BCE) was an Athenian statesman and orator.

11. Pericles (c.495–429 BCE) was also a statesman of Athens and an orator of great influence.

12. Phidias (c.480–430 BCE) was a sculptor and architect who, among many works, designed the statues of Athena at the Acropolis.

13. Myron of Eleutherae (active c.480–440 BCE) was also an Athenian sculptor whose works included statues of Apollo and Hercules.

333 1. Pindar (c.518–438 BCE) wrote fourteen Olympian Odes to glorify the victors of the Olympic games.

2. Thomas Gray (1716–1771) was an English poet, known for his 'Elegy Written in a Country Churchyard'. He was also a classical scholar and composed a number of Pindaric Odes in one of which he refers to Pindar as the 'Theban eagle'.

334 Praxiteles was the most renowned of the Greek sculptors of the fourth century BCE. He was the first to sculpt a life-size female nude. His statue of Hermes Carrying the Infant Dionysus was rediscovered in 1877.

335 The traditional attribution of the authorship of the play *Rhesus* to Euripides has been disputed since antiquity.

336 The *Gorgias* of Plato (written c.380 BCE) is a Socratic dialogue on the subject of rhetoric.

337 Walt Whitman (1819–1892), the American poet, essayist, and journalist. 'A Passage to India' is a long, free-verse poem which was included in the 1872 edition of *Leaves of Grass* and was the inspiration for the title of E. M. Forster's 1924 novel of that name.

338 Rodolfo Alfonso Raffaello Pierre Filibert Guglielmi di Valentina d'Antonguella aka Valentino (1895–1926) was an Italian who emigrated to the USA and became a popular idol of the silent movies.

339 Aristotle (384–322 BCE): *The Nicomachean Ethics* is in ten books based probably on lectures given by Aristotle at the Lyceum he founded.

Its central theme is how individuals should best live.

340 After his *śrāmaṇera* ordination in 1949, Sangharakshita and his friend Buddharakshita went on the traditional almsround of the Buddhist monk. See *The Rainbow Road from Tooting Broadway to Kalimpong*, *Complete Works*, vol. 20, pp. 414–18. He also went on the almsround with his teacher, Jagdish Kashyap, in Bihar (ibid., p. 459), and for a short time in Kalimpong (*Facing Mount Kanchenjunga*, *Complete Works*, vol. 21, pp. 11–15).

341 Sangharakshita first met Arjundev Rashk in Sanchi in 1952 when the young scriptwriter was working for Bombay film star Raj Kapoor. Sangharakshita became their advisor for a proposed film involving a Buddhist monk. See *Facing Mount Kanchenjunga*, *Complete Works*, vol. 21, pp. 399–417. He stayed with Rashk at his residence in Bombay (late 1955 and early 1956) while writing up *A Survey of Buddhism* when he experienced a mysterious 'presence in the corner', and heard a strange and memorable story of escape from Rashk. Among the books he discovered in Rashk's bookcase was *The Story of San Michele*; see *In the Sign of the Golden Wheel*, *Complete Works*, vol. 22, pp. 275–80.

342 Sangharakshita writes about this legend in *From Genesis to the Diamond Sūtra*, chapter 9, *Complete Works*, vol. 13, pp. 653–64. See also David Marshall Lang, *The Wisdom of Balahvar – A Christian Legend of the Buddha*, George Allen and Unwin, London 1957, which Sangharakshita reviewed for the *Maha Bodhi*, October 1961. This review can be found in *Anagarika Dharmapala and Other 'Maha Bodhi' Writings*, Ibis Publications, Ledbury 2012, pp. 172–3 (*Complete Works*, vol. 8).

343 1. The marble, life-sized *Laocoön* or *Laocoön and His Sons* shows the Trojan priest Laocoön and his two sons attacked by sea serpents. It was excavated in Rome in 1506.

2. The *Apollo Belvedere* is thought to be a marble copy from c.120–140 CE of a bronze original made between 350 and 325 BCE by the Greek sculptor Leochares. It was rediscovered in central Italy in the late fifteenth century and was copied by Albrecht Dürer for his Adam in the famous engraving *Adam and Eve* (1504). In the eighteenth century the Apollo Belvedere was regarded as an example of the Greek aesthetic perfection; though in the nineteenth century John Ruskin was disappointed by it.

3. Raffaello Sanzio da Urbino known as Raphael (1483–1520) painted his famous fresco, the *School of Athens*, between 1509 and

1511. Plato and Aristotle are the central figures, surrounded by other philosophers.

344 Stefano Maderno (1576–1636) was a foremost sculptor of his time. He sculpted the *Martyrdom of St Cecilia* in marble in the years 1599–1600.

345 Gian Lorenzo Bernini (1598–1680) was an architect, writer, and director of plays, but more famous as a leading sculptor of his day. His marble statue of the biblical *David* shows the young man half turned to the right, preparing to release from his sling the stone that will kill Goliath. It was created 1623–1624. Bernini's *Apollo and Daphne* (1622–1625) is also of marble and shows the god Apollo in the act of seizing the nymph Daphne whose prayers are answered as she turns into a laurel tree. The *Rape of Persephone* (1621–1622) shows the goddess as she is abducted by Pluto who will take her down to the Underworld.

346 1. Lucas Cranach the Elder (1472–1553) was a German painter and printmaker. His *Venus and Cupid* (1531) illustrates a fable from ancient Greece in which the boy Cupid (in the painting a mere toddler), having been stung by bees when stealing a honeycomb, complains to his mother Venus, the goddess of love – who stands naked in the painting – about the pain produced by such small animals. She replies that he, too, is small but the wounds occasioned by his arrows are much more painful.

2. Michele Angelo Merigi (or Amerighi) da Caravaggio (1571–1610) was active in many of the great cities of Italy. He is known for the accuracy of his observation of both physical and emotional states of being, and a dramatic use of lighting. His oil painting *St Jerome* (1605–1606), also known as *St Jerome Writing*, shows the elderly saint at his desk reading and writing – engaged presumably in translating the Bible – with a skull before him.

3. Giovanni di Niccolò de Luteri (1489–1542), known as Dosso Dossi, was court artist in Ferrara, Italy. He painted mythological and allegorical subjects. *Circe* is a beautiful sorceress who is shown casting a spell in a beautiful landscape while her faithful dog looks on.

4. Tiziano Vecelli (1488/90–1576) known as Titian, see note 288(3). *Sacred and Profane Love* (c.1514) shows a woman – possibly a bride – dressed in white, seated beside a child sometimes thought to be Cupid, while another woman, maybe Venus, sits naked, looking on. There have been many interpretations including those referring to Titian's Neoplatonic interests.

347 The Pyramid of Cestius was built 18–12 BCE as a tomb for

Gaius Cestius, magistrate and member of one of the four great religious corporations of Rome. Percy Bysshe Shelley (1792–1822) described it as 'one keen pyramid with wedge sublime' in *Adonaïs* (canto 50), his 1821 elegy for the poet John Keats.

348 'Butchered to make a Roman holiday...' from George Gordon, Lord Byron (1788–1824), *Childe Harold's Pilgrimage*, canto 4.

349 Claudius Ptolemy (c.100–c.170 CE) was a Greco-Roman mathematician, geographer, astronomer, and astrologer who wrote a number of highly influential treatises including the *Algamest* on astronomy. In the Ptolemaic model the Earth was the unmoving centre of the universe. The fixed stars did not change their positions relative to one another, but lay on the surface of a single starry sphere which rotated. The Empyrean was the outermost region (identified in the Christian cosmology as the dwelling place of God).

350 'The dark backward and abysm of time' from William Shakespeare (1564–1616), *The Tempest*, Act I, Scene ii.

351 1. A. H. Armstrong (1909–1997) known as a foremost authority on Plotinus, published *An Introduction to Ancient Philosophy* in 1947. The work looks at philosophical thought from pre-Socratic days in Greece, through Plato and Aristotle, to the Roman philosophers and schools, Plotinus and the Neoplatonists, and the Christian philosophers up to St Augustine.

2. Karl Jaspers (1883–1969) was a German-Swiss psychiatrist and philosopher, sometimes regarded as an existentialist. *Way to Wisdom: an Introduction to Philosophy* was published in 1951. For Jaspers the source of philosophy is to be found 'in wonder, in doubt, in a sense of forsakenness,' and the philosophical quest is a process of continual change and self-discovery.

3. Plato's *First Alcibiades* is a Socratic dialogue (formerly disputed as to its Platonic authenticity) in which Socrates persuades the ambitious Alcibiades, who wants to enter into public life, that he needs Socrates as mentor. They discuss war and peace, justice, and the meaning of the Delphic inscription, 'Know Thyself'.

4. The Upanishads are religious and philosophical texts written in India between c.800 BCE and c.500 BCE. *Śvetāśvatara* is a foundational text of Shaivism. Metaphysical questions are explored and the unity of the individual self and the Ultimate Self is asserted. The *Kaivalya Upanishad* has some similar themes.

352 *Śvetāśvatara Upaniṣad*, 8.iv. See Paul Deussen, *Sixty Upanisads*

of the Veda, vol. i, Motilal Banarsidass, Delhi 1980, p. 315.

353 The baptistery with its octagonal dome is one of the oldest buildings in Florence, constructed 1059–1128 in Romanesque style. Lorenzo Ghiberti (1378–1455) was trained as a goldsmith and sculptor. His bronze-gilt east doors for the baptistery consisted of ten panels each showing a scene from the Old Testament. They were later described by Vasari as 'the finest masterpiece ever created'.

354 1. Jacob Burckhardt (1818–1897) was a Swiss historian of art and culture. His *Civilization of the Renaissance in Italy* was first published in 1860.

2. Luigi Barzini Jr. (1908–1984) was an Italian journalist, writer, and politician. *The Italians: a Full-Length Portrait* (1964) described Italian life and culture, and the Italian national character.

355 William Wordsworth (1770–1850) 'Composed upon Westminster Bridge, September 3, 1802', a Petrarchan sonnet.

356 Benvenuto Cellini (1500–1571) was a Florentine goldsmith, sculptor, and painter – also a draughtsman, poet, and musician. His bronze *Perseus with the Head of Medusa* (1545–1554) shows the youthful Perseus standing on the body of the gorgon, Medusa. He holds up her head with his left hand, in his right is his sword.

357 1. Sandro Botticelli (1445–1510) was a Florentine painter. His *Primavera* or *Allegory of Spring* is a large panel painting with figures including Zephyrus, the wind god, the nymph Chloris, Flora, Venus, the three Graces, and Mercury who raises his caduceus towards the heavens. Botticelli did not leave an explanation of his allegory though many have been given, including a Neoplatonic interpretation.

2. The *Birth of Venus* shows the newly-born goddess standing naked on a scallop shell arriving from the sea. Zephyrus, the wind god, who carries a female figure, blows the wind from the left. A female figure stands waiting on the right to welcome Venus with a cloak.

358 Dante Alighieri (1265–1321) was an Italian poet best known for his *Divine Comedy*. *La Vita Nuova* (*The New Life*) is a piece in both prose and verse telling the story of his love for Beatrice, from their first meeting, through Dante's sufferings, to his overwhelming grief at her death, and the transformative vision of her in heaven. *La Vita Nuova* was published in 1295. Penguin Books brought out a translation by William Anderson in 1964.

359 To give the reader a very simple overview of these extraordinary men of Renaissance Florence, they are listed below with

dates and a brief reminder of the field in which they excelled – though many, as Renaissance men, excelled in several fields. Giorgio Vasari (1511–1574), himself a painter and architect, included many of these in his *Lives of the Most Excellent Painters, Sculptors, and Architects* (1550, enlarged 1568).

1. Dante Alighieri (1265–1321), poet; author of the *Divine Comedy*.

2. Giotto di Bondone (1267–1337), painter of the frescoes in the Cappella degli Scrovegni (Arena Chapel) of Padua, and (disputed) painter of the frescoes of Francis of Assissi in the Upper Church of Assissi.

3. Tommaso di Ser Giovanni di Simone known as Masaccio (1401–1428), a painter chiefly of scenes from the Bible, one of the first to use linear perspective.

4. Donato di Niccolò di Betto Bardi (c.1386–1466), known as Donatello, sculptor. His works in bronze include *David*.

5. Andrea del Verrocchio (1435–1488), painter and sculptor whose works include a bronze *David*, and a painting of *Tobias and the Angel*.

6. Leonardo da Vinci (1452–1519), a polymath known for science and engineering, architecture and invention, but most of all for his painting and drawing such as the *Mona Lisa* and *The Virgin of the Rocks*.

7. Leon Battista Alberti (1404–1472), Roman Catholic priest of many talents, known chiefly as poet and architect.

8. Filippo Brunelleschi (1377–1446), architect, considered a founding father of Renaissance architecture.

9. Guido di Pietro, known as Fra Angelico (c.1395–1455), Dominican Friar and painter who specialized in scenes from the Bible such as the annunciation; in 1982 beatified as a saint.

10. Sandro Botticelli (1445–1510), painter, including *Primavera* or *Allegory of Spring* and *The Birth of Venus*.

11. Michelangelo di Lodovico Buonarroti Simoni (1475–1564), sculptor in marble, painter, architect, poet. Among his sculptures are his *Pietà* and *David*; and among his paintings the frescoes of the Sistine chapel.

12. Cosimo de' Medici (1389–1464) was a banker and first of the Medici dynasty to rule Florence. He was a keen supporter of philosophy and the arts, a patron of Fra Angelico, Donatello, and others. Lorenzo de' Medici 1449–1492) was likewise a ruler of Florence who greatly patronized the arts, including Michelangelo, Botticelli. Leonardo da Vinci and others.

13. Girolamo Savonarola (1452–1498) was a Dominican

Friar who preached repentance and renewal to huge crowds. He sought to bring about reform in Florence. He was eventually put to death as a heretic.

14. Marsilio Ficino (1433–1499) was a priest and humanist philosopher, a reviver of the Neoplatonic tradition, and founder of the Florentine Academy.

15. Galileo Galilei (1564–1642) is known as the father of observational astronomy or father of modern science. His scientific interests were wide and he championed Copernicus' view of the solar system in which the planets rotate around the sun. For this heretical view he was tried by the Inquisition of the Roman Catholic Church and spent the rest of his life under house arrest.

360 Jacob Burckhardt, *Civilization of the Renaissance in Italy*, Random House, New York 1954, p. 245.

361 Ronald Segal, *The Crisis of India*, Penguin Books, Harmondsworth 1965.

362 Plotinus (c.204/5–270 CE) was a Greek-speaking philosopher of the Roman empire.
He studied philosophy in Alexandria, and spent his later years in Rome where he had many pupils. His writings have inspired and influenced mystics and metaphysicians of Islamic, Jewish, Christian, and Gnostic backgrounds. *The Essential Plotinus: Representative Treatises from the Enneads*, translated by Elmer O'Brien, was published by Hackett Publishing in 1964.

363 The *Enneads* are the collection of writings by Plotinus put together by his student, Porphyry (c.270 CE) in groups of nine (nine is the literal meaning of the Greek 'Ennead'). Thomas Carlyle (1795–1881) was a Scottish essayist and satirist, historian and mathematician. He wrote of Time as the Conflux of Eternities.

364 1. Dean William Inge (1860–1954) was an Anglican priest, writer on Plotinus, Christian mysticism, and other topics; professor of divinity at the University of Cambridge; and Dean of St Paul's Cathedral.

2. Thomas Whittaker (1856–1935), *The Neo-Platonists: a Study in the History of Hellenism* was first published in 1901.

3. Henry G. Bohn (1796–1884) was a British publisher who inaugurated the *Bohn's Libraries* editions of classic works of theology, science, classics, archaeology, and history. *Select Works of Plotinus translated from the Greek with an introduction containing the substance of Porphyry's life of Plotinus by Thomas Taylor*, edited by G. R. S. Mead (private secretary to Madame Blavatsky) was published by George Bell and Son in 1895.

4. Thomas Taylor (1758–1835) was an English translator and Neoplatonist, the first to translate into English the complete works of Plato and Aristotle, as well as works by Neoplatonists Proclus and Iamblichus. His own original writing includes *A Vindication of the Rights of Brutes* (1792).

365 Porphyry of Tyre (c.234–c.305 CE) collected and edited the work of his teacher, Plotinus, with an introductory biography; as well as writing himself an influential introduction to logic and philosophy and many other works. His *Against the Christians* fuelled debate and was banned by emperor Constantine the Great.

366 The Shrine of Wisdom is the publishing imprint of the Fintry Trust which from 1919 published mystical texts and commentaries with the aim of showing that there is one universal teaching behind all philosophies and religions.

367 1. Plato (c.427/c.424–c.348 BCE) composed the *Symposium* c.385–370 BCE. A number of friends who have gathered to drink together discourse on the topic of Eros or love. The crux of the piece comes when Socrates gives his speech, reporting the words of a wise woman, Diotima, who showed how love is in truth desire for the Beautiful.

2. Percy Bysshe Shelley (1792–1822), *Prometheus Unbound* (1820) is a drama in four acts and concerns the Greek mythological figure of Prometheus who, defying Zeus, gives fire to humankind, and as a consequence is condemned to eternal punishment and torture.

368 Elmer O'Brien, *The Essential Plotinus*, Hackett Publishing, Indiana 1984, p. 34.

369 Nanda is a young monk who has followed the Buddha, leaving behind the girl he might have married. When he begins to pine the Buddha takes him to a heavenly realm where he sees nymphs of far greater beauty. The Buddha promises Nanda that if he continues on the path he can win these beautiful nymphs for himself. Nanda goes back to his meditation but is teased by the other monks until, determined to reach the goal, he achieves 'the taintless mind-deliverance' and realizes he has no need of pink-footed nymphs! See Eugene Watson Burlingame (trans.), *Buddhist Legends* (*Dhammapada* Commentary), part 1, Pali Text Society, Luzac, London 1969, pp. 218–23; and *Udāna* 3.2 in John D. Ireland (trans.), *The Udāna and the Itivuttaka*, Buddhist Publication Society, Kandy 2007, pp. 35–9.

370 Elmer O'Brien, *The Essential Plotinus*, Hackett Publishing, Indiana 1984, pp. 37–8.

371 Sangharakshita writes about the Padmasambhava initiation and the name he received from

Kachu Rimpoche in *Precious Teachers*, *Complete Works*, vol. 22, pp. 472–4.

372 Nāgārjuna (flourished in India between 150 and 250 CE) is regarded as the founder of the Madhyamaka school. His *Mūlamadhyamaka-kārikā* (*Fundamental Verses of the Middle Way*) is a Sanskrit text, in part a commentary on discourses of the Buddha, to demonstrate the futility of metaphysical speculation and to affirm the Middle Way the Buddha taught as a direct perception of *śūnyatā* or the 'emptiness' of all things.

373 K. Venkata Ramanan, *Nāgārjuna's Philosophy, As Presented in the Mahā-Prajñāpāramitā-Śāstra*, Motilal Banarsidass, Delhi 1998, pp. 328–9.

374 The *Daily Telegraph* is a widely read British newspaper founded in 1855, which supports conservative or centre-right politics. The *New Statesman* is a widely read weekly magazine founded in 1913 by leading members of the Socialist Fabian Society. Today (2019) it characterizes itself as having a 'liberal, sceptical political position'.

375 'Stay here and work for the good of Buddhism' was the parting injunction to the twenty-four-year-old Sangharakshita as his teacher, Jagdish Kashyap was driven away, leaving him in the Himalayan hill station of Kalimpong in north-eastern India. See the final paragraph of *The Rainbow Road from Tooting Broadway to Kalimpong*, *Complete Works*, vol. 20, p. 470; and the opening paragraph of *Facing Mount Kanchenjunga*, *Complete Works*, vol. 21, p. 7.

376 See p. 224 and note 256.

377 Walpola Rahula's book was published in English as *The Heritage of the Bhikkhu*, Grove Press, New York 1974. It had first appeared in Sinhalese in Sri Lanka in 1946. Sangharakshita later wrote a review of the book. After giving a detailed chapter by chapter account of its contents, he applies himself to Walpola Rahula's views as he had found 'much that is muddled in Rahula's thinking, and much, indeed, that is ambiguous in his own position.' The review was published in the *FWBO Newsletter*, no. 28 (Autumn 1975), pp. 22–33; and appears as 'Religio-Nationalism in Sri Lanka' in *Alternative Traditions*, Windhorse Publications, Glasgow 1986, pp. 69–71, (*Complete Works*, vol. 26).

378 Sangharakshita met Tsering Chodron, Jamyang Khyentse Rimpoche's consort, at the time he visited him in Darjeeling to receive initiation in 1962, and again in Kalimpong. He discusses the nature of her relationship with Jamyang Khyentse Rimpoche in *Precious*

Teachers, *Complete Works*, vol. 22, pp. 404–6.

379 *The Observer* is a weekly newspaper published on Sundays. Founded in 1791, it is the world's oldest Sunday newspaper. Its views tend towards the social-democratic end of the political spectrum.

380 'Editorial: Message From the Head of the English Sangha' in *The Buddhist*, vol. 10, no. 10 (October 1966), pp. 300–2.

381 Sangharakshita first met the Dalai Lama in Delhi during the Buddha Jayanti celebrations in 1956 when both the Dalai Lama and the Panchen Lama were able to enter and leave India (see *In the Sign of the Golden Wheel*, *Complete Works*, vol. 22, pp. 354–5); and again at the Grand Hotel, Calcutta (ibid., pp. 365–6). The Dalai Lama also visited Kalimpong and a reception was held for him at Everton Villa, Sangharakshita's residence and venue for local Buddhist activities. The following day Sangharakshita visited him at Bhutan House when the Dalai Lama bestowed on him a number of gifts (ibid., pp. 368–71). In 1959 Sangharakshita met the Dalai Lama as he arrived as a refugee in India when his train stopped at Siliguri for an hour – he was on his way to Mussoorie. See *Precious Teachers*, *Complete Works*, vol. 22, p. 488.

382 Vijaya Dasami (literally 'the ten-day victory') is known more widely as a Hindu festival that commemorates the victory of the god Rama over the demon Ravana – the triumph of the forces of good over the forces of evil – as told in the Sanskrit epic *Ramayana*. In 1956 Dr Ambedkar chose the Vijaya Dasami celebration day – which that year fell on 14 October – for his historic conversion to Buddhism, along with hundreds of thousands of followers, which took place in Nagpur, and which is commemorated there and elsewhere each year. (October 14 was also the date on which in c.261 BCE the great Mauryan emperor Aśoka converted to Buddhism. To the Buddhists of India, therefore, 14 October is also known as Ashok Vijaya Dashami.)

383 'Letter from India I' in *The Buddhist*, vol. 10, no. 11 (November 1966), pp. 324–8.

384 Sangharakshita writes about his time staying with Dr Mehta at his Nature Cure Clinic in Poona in *In the Sign of the Golden Wheel*, *Complete Works*, vol. 22, chapter 20, pp. 291–303. Their friendship is discussed in 'The Monk and the Prophet' in *Dear Dinoo: Letters to a Friend*, *Complete Works*, vol. 21, pp. 599–619.

385 Between 1979 and 1992 Sangharakshita was to return to India for several lecture tours among the Ambedkarite Buddhists. These lectures are

collected in *Complete Works*, vols. 9 and 10.

386 See note 381.

387 Mohandas Karamchand Gandhi (1869–1948), often given the honorific 'Mahatma' (great-souled), led the Indian movement for independence from British rule. It was from the Sabarmati Ashram that he set out in March 1930 on the twenty-four-day Salt March (also known as the Dandi March) in protest against the British salt monopoly.

388 The Jain doctrine of karma differs from the Buddhist one. In ancient times the Buddha encountered Jains who came to dispute with him, including about the doctrine of karma. See the *Upāli Sutta*, *Majjhima Nikāya* 56. Bhikkhu Ñāṇamoli and Bhikkhu Bodhi (trans.), *The Middle Length Discourses of the Buddha*, Wisdom Publications, Boston 1995, pp. 477–92; or I. B. Horner (trans.), *The Collection of the Middle Length Sayings*, vol. ii, Pali Text Society, Oxford 1994, pp. 36–54.

389 Sangharakshita writes about Hilla Petit and her friend Maurice Frydman in 'Some Bombay Friends', *Adhisthana Writings*, *Complete Works*, vol. 26.

390 For more on Gulbehn Mehta see *Dear Dinoo: Letters to a Friend*, *Complete Works*, vol. 21, pp. 615–16.

391 Poona (Pune) was the seat of the Peshwas (or Prime Ministers) of the Maratha Empire 1674–1818. The empire extended to much of the Indian subcontinent.

392 At the second ceremony of mass conversion, held in Nagpur on 15 October 1956, Dr Ambedkar declared that through his conversion he felt that he had been delivered from hell, the hell of caste, and he wanted all his followers to share that experience. *Ambedkar and Buddhism*, *Complete Works*, vol. 9, p. 134; and Bhagwan Das (ed.), *Thus Spoke Ambedkar*, vol. ii, Bheem Patrika Publications, Jullundur n.d., p. 147.

393 One 'useful paper' published by Adele Fiske is 'Caste among the Buddhists,' in Harjinder Singh (ed.), *Caste among Non-Hindus in India*, National Publishing House, Delhi 1977, pp. 91–106. Also of interest is Adele Fiske and Christoph Emmrich, 'The use of Buddhist Scriptures in B. R. Ambedkar's *The Buddha and His Dhamma*' in Surendra Jondhale and Johannes Beltz (eds.), *Reconstructing the World: B. R. Ambedkar and Buddhism in India*, Oxford University Press, Oxford 2004.

394 Father Mascarenhas appears in *In the Sign of the Golden Wheel*, *Complete Works*, vol. 22, p. 286.

395 Camp is a district in Poona (Pune) that once accommodated British Indian Army troops.

396 Gulbhen Mehta was diagnosed with cancer in 1974 and died within a year.

397 The conversion to Buddhism of Dr Ambedkar and his followers on 14 October 1956 is recounted in *Ambedkar and Buddhism*, chapter 7, *Complete Works*, vol. 9, pp. 120–35.

398 This meeting with Dr Ambedkar in Delhi is described in *In the Sign of the Golden Wheel*, *Complete Works*, vol. 22, pp. 352–3; and *Ambedkar and Buddhism*, *Complete Works*, vol. 9, pp. 19–21.

399 Sangharakshita recounts in detail the events subsequent to Dr Ambedkar's death in *In the Sign of the Golden Wheel*, *Complete Works*, vol. 22, pp. 360–4, also quoting from a letter to his friend, Dinoo Dubash, which was written just over a week after the event. See *Dear Dinoo: Letters to a Friend*, *Complete Works*, vol. 21, p. 523. See also *Ambedkar and Buddhism*, *Complete Works*, vol. 9, pp. 21–3.

400 Lewis Carroll, *Alice's Adventures in Wonderland* (1865), chapter 7 is entitled, 'A Mad Tea-Party.'

401 The People's Education Society was founded by Dr Ambedkar in 1945. Its first educational institution was Siddharth College, founded the following year in Bombay (Mumbai).

402 The Buddha tells Ānanda of the four places that can 'arouse emotion in the faithful' in the *Mahāparinibbāna Sutta*, *Dīgha Nikāya* 16 (ii.141). See M. Walshe (trans.), *The Long Discourses of the Buddha*, Wisdom Publications, Boston 1995, pp. 263–4; or T. W. and C. A. F. Rhys Davids (trans.), *Dialogues of the Buddha*, part 2, Pali Text Society, London 1971, p. 154.

403 Rummindei was the name of the village when it was visited by King Aśoka in 249 BCE. A pillar was set up to mark the place of the Buddha's birth, since when it has been associated with the name of Lumbinī, the place, according to the Buddhist scriptures, where the mother of the future Buddha, Māyādevī, gave birth.

404 The disappointment at Sarnath is described in more detail in *The Rainbow Road from Tooting Broadway to Kalimpong*, *Complete Works*, vol. 20, pp. 388–92.

405 It was with Sangharatana that Sangharakshita first visited Bodh Gaya in 1949. See *The Rainbow Road from Tooting Broadway to Kalimpong*, *Complete Works*, vol. 20, pp. 453–6; and Sangharatana who invited Sangharakshita to the celebration of the anniversary of the opening of the Mulagandhakuti Vihara: *Facing Mount Kanchenjunga*, *Complete Works*, vol. 21, p. 97; and was present at his ordination (ibid., p. 108). Later Sangharatana invited Sangharakshita to join him and Jagdish Kashyap as the official

delegation accompanying the Sacred Relics of Śāriputra and Maudgalyāyana to Sikkim. See ibid., p. 173 and chapter 11, pp. 189–215.

406 *Mahāmaṅgala Sutta*, *Sutta-Nipāta* 2.4;. *Karaṇīyamettā Sutta*, ibid., 1.8; *Ratana Sutta*, ibid., 2.1. See H. Saddhatissa (trans.), *The Sutta-Nipāta*, Curzon Press, London 1985.

407 Sangharakshita mentions Kusho Bakula, 'an aloof, mysterious figure with a strangely triangular face and an expression of remarkable thoughtfulness and refinement', in writing about his *bhikṣu* ordination in *Facing Mount Kanchenjunga*, *Complete Works*, vol. 21, p. 107.

408 *The Rainbow Road from Tooting Broadway to Kalimpong*, *Complete Works*, vol. 20, pp. 453–6.

409 Bhikkhu Vivekananda, 'a short Thai of indeterminate age' who had once been a kick boxer, is introduced in *Precious Teachers*, *Complete Works*, vol. 22, p. 525.

410 *Saṃyutta Nikāya* i.138. See Bhikkhu Bodhi (trans.), *The Connected Discourses of the Buddha*, Wisdom Publications, Boston 2000, p. 233; and C. A. F. Rhys Davids (trans.), *The Book of the Kindred Sayings*, part 1, Pali Text Society, London 1979, p. 174. See also *Ariyapariyesanā Sutta*, *Majjhima Nikāya* (i.167–70) in Bhikkhu Ñāṇamoli and Bhikkhu Bodhi (trans.), *The Middle Length Discourses of the Buddha*, Wisdom Publications, Boston 1995, pp. 261–2.

411 Repairs and restoration of the temple were undertaken by J. D. Beglar, an appointment authorized by Sir Ashley Eden, Lieutenant-Governor of Bengal, in 1880.

412 Vinoba Bhave (1895–1982) established his Samanvaya Mandir as a centre for 'religious, cultural and racial synthesis' in 1954. The quote is from a report of the opening published in an Indian newspaper. Sangharakshita's scathing response to the idea of an inter-religious institution to 'increase the importance of Bodh Gaya in the eyes of the world' can be found in an editorial written for the May–June 1954 issue of the *Maha Bodhi*, vol. 62, nos. 5–6, pp. 224–7. See *Beating the Drum*, Ibis Publications, Ledbury 2012, pp. 111–13 (*Complete Works*, vol. 8). He was always alert to the tendency of Hinduism to destroy Buddhism. He had often heard Hindu swamis quoting Swami Vivekananda: 'Hinduism killed Buddhism with a loving embrace.' The newspaper reported Vinoba Bhave as saying that Buddhism could not exist without the Vedanta for '*Satya* (truth) was revealed in all its glory only in Vedanta.'

See *In the Sign of the Golden Wheel*, *Complete Works*, vol. 22, p. 127.

413 In the autumn of 1952 Sangharakshita spent some weeks in Calcutta immersed in the diaries of Anagarika Dharmapala in order to write a biographical sketch. See *Facing Mount Kanchenjunga*, *Complete Works*, vol. 21, chapter 18, pp. 367–89. On how Anagarika Dharmapala dedicated himself to the rescue of the Maha Bodhi temple and his many other works to spread the Dharma, see *Anagarika Dharmapala, a Biographical Sketch*, Ibis Publications, Ledbury 2013 (*Complete Works*, vol. 8).

414 For a short history of Anagarika Dharmapala and the founding of the Maha Bodhi Society and the *Maha Bodhi*, see *Beating the Drum*, Ibis Publications, Ledbury 2012, pp. 9–33, especially pp. 15–17.

415 For a short history of Sangharakshita's involvement with the *Maha Bodhi*, see ibid., pp. 61–77.

416 See 'Proof-Reading at 110°F' in *In the Sign of the Golden Wheel*, *Complete Works*, vol. 22, chapter 8, pp. 120–32. This includes a detailed description of the contents of the first Vaiśākha number brought out under Sangharakshita's editorship (ibid., pp. 122–7).

417 This was Kantaraj, 'a diminutive South Indian with a dark bearded face and an astonishingly bass voice' whose 'sole passion was service'. *The Rainbow Road from Tooting Broadway to Kalimpong*, *Complete Works*, vol. 20, pp. 130–1.

418 1. Alfred Adler (1870–1937) was an Austrian doctor and psychologist, founder of the School of Individual Psychology. *Understanding Human Nature* was published in 1927.

2. Edmund Husserl (1859–1938) was a German philosopher and a founder of phenomenology. His *Phenomenology and the Crisis of Philosophy*, translated by Quentin Lauer, was published in 1964.

419 1. David Lack (1910–1973) was a British evolutionary biologist whose research on birds and their egg clutches supported the theory of evolution by natural selection. He had been a religious agnostic but converted to Anglicanism in 1948. In his *Evolutionary Theory and Christian Belief* (1957) he gave expression to his view that evolution could not account for morality, truth, beauty, free will, self-awareness, and individual responsibility.

2. Julian Huxley (1887–1975) was a British evolutionary theorist who popularized science through books and articles, and presentations on radio and

television. He was a founding member of the World Wildlife Fund (WWF), and first director-general of UNESCO (United Nations Educational, Scientific and Cultural Organization). His *The Living Thoughts of Darwin* was published in 1939.

3. George Bernard Shaw (1856–1950) was an Irish playwright, the writer of more than sixty plays. He was also a literary critic and political activist. *Back to Methuselah: A Metabiological Pentateuch* consists of a preface called 'The Infidel Half Century', and a series of five plays: *In the Beginning: B.C. 4004 (In the Garden of Eden); The Gospel of the Brothers Barnabas: Present Day; The Thing Happens: A.D. 2170; Tragedy of an Elderly Gentleman: A.D. 3000; As Far as Thought Can Reach: A.D. 31,920*. They were first performed in 1922 in New York.

420 Devapriya Valisinha (1904–1968) was born in Ceylon. He was adopted by Anagarika Dharmapala, and brought up by the Anagarika's mother. He studied in Calcutta and at Shantiniketan. He became recording secretary and treasurer of the Maha Bodhi Society in 1927 and after the death of Anagarika Dharmapala in 1933 its general secretary, continuing the Anagarika's work for Buddhism and for the control of the Maha Bodhi temple. He was arrested in 1941 because of his (Buddhist) connections with the Japanese with whom the British, still rulers of India, were at war. His harsh treatment during the weeks of his arrest led to a nervous breakdown. Several years elapsed – during which time Jinaratana was acting secretary – before he could resume his work for the Society. Sangharakshita first met him in Gangtok in 1951 but their acquaintance flourished when Sangharakshita went to Calcutta in the autumn of 1952 at Devapriya Valisinha's request to write a biographical sketch of Anagarika Dharmapala. See *Facing Mount Kanchenjunga*, *Complete Works*, vol. 21, chapter 18, pp. 367–89.

421 *The Rainbow Road from Tooting Broadway to Kalimpong*, *Complete Works*, vol. 20, p. 166.

422 The Inner Line Permit was introduced by the British in 1873 as a demarcation beyond which the British government could not guarantee protection of its subjects. It related to areas in the north-east which were partly populated by tribal peoples. The requirement for the ILP continued after Indian Independence and Partition.

423 Monks, a (formal) act of censure or guidance or banishment or reconciliation or suspension should not be carried out against monks who are not present.

Whoever should carry one out, there is an offence of wrong-doing.

Vinaya Piṭaka ii.73 (Cullavagga 4.1). See I. B. Horner (trans.), *The Book of the Discipline*, part 5, Pali Text Society, London 1975, p. 96.

424 Sangharakshita tells the story of the Kazini's arrival in Kalimpong as a newly-wed and the friendship that arose with her and the Kazi in *Precious Teachers*, *Complete Works*, vol. 22, chapter 3, pp. 408–18; and of the politics in Sikkim with which they were involved in chapter 9, pp. 478–86.

425 Durgaprasad was a cousin of Sangharakshita's close friend Sachin who appears many times in the pages of *In the Sign of the Golden Wheel*, *Complete Works*, vol. 22.

426 Sangharakshita writes of this tour in 'Holy Places and Eminent Buddhists', *In the Sign of the Golden Wheel*, *Complete Works*, vol. 22, chapter 22, pp. 329–55.

427 Sangharakshita took bodhisattva ordination, including the sixty-four bodhisattva precepts, from Dhardo Rimpoche on 12 October 1962. See *Precious Teachers*, *Complete Works*, vol. 22, pp. 541–3. The sixty-four precepts are listed as an appendix in *Complete Works*, vol. 2, pp. 657–9.

428 *Precious Teachers*, *Complete Works*, vol. 22, p. 562.

429 The initiations bestowed on Sangharakshita by Kachu Rimpoche are related in *Precious Teachers*, *Complete Works*, vol. 22, pp. 472–4; and the vision which led to the banner of victory on the roof of the Triyana Vardhana Vihara is described in ibid., p. 477.

430 Sangharakshita writes about his contact with Yogi Chen in *Precious Teachers*, *Complete Works*, vol. 22, chapter 13, pp. 532–43.

431 Joe Cann helped with the setting up of the Young Men's Buddhist Association soon after Sangharakshita's arrival in Kalimpong in 1950 and features in *Facing Mount Kanchenjunga*, *Complete Works*, vol. 21 as well as in *In the Sign of the Golden Wheel*, *Complete Works*, vol. 22.

432 Sogyal Rimpoche (1947–2019) would go on to become highly influential in the West through his book *The Tibetan Book of Living and Dying*, published in 1992, and the Rigpa movement which he set up which now has centres and groups all over the world. In 2018 he stepped down from his position as Rigpa's spiritual advisor in the wake of allegations of sexual and physical abuse by some of his students.

433 Julius Caesar divorced his wife, Pompeia, because although no fault against her had been proven 'she ought to be above suspicion'. See Plutarch, *The*

Parallel Lives: The Life of Julius Caesar, 9.10.

434 Sangharakshita writes about Jivaka, and the time Jivaka spent with him in Kalimpong, in *Precious Teachers*, *Complete Works*, vol. 22, chapter 5, pp. 429–45.

435 Sangharakshita writes about his first meeting with Jamyang Khyentse Rimpoche in *Precious Teachers*, *Complete Works*, vol. 22, pp. 399–400.

436 Sangharakshita writes about the initiations he received from Jamyang Khyentse Rimpoche in *Precious Teachers*, *Complete Works*, vol. 22, pp. 402–3; and about the thangka the Rimpoche gave him in ibid., pp. 406–7.

437 Ibid., p. 407.

438 GPO stands for 'General Post Office'. Founded in 1660 in England, The GPO came to deal not only with mail but also telecommunications including telegrams. Branches of the GPO were established all over the British Empire.

439 Christmas Humphreys' letter begins 'Dear Bhante' and is signed 'Toby'. It is dated 10 December 1966. It reads, in part, 'It is the image you have created which is the real cause of the present crisis, even though no "offence" has been committed by you or anyone at any time.'

440 Sangharakshita made it clear in conversation with two senior disciples, Subhuti and Mahamati, posted online as *Conversations* (2009): 'There was never any question of sex between Terry and I. He would simply not have been interested and that was not the nature of our friendship.'

441 Oscar Wilde (1854–1900) was an Irish writer of plays, poems, short stories, a novel (*The Picture of Dorian Gray*), and literary criticism. During his lifetime he was one of London's most popular playwrights. Sangharakshita includes him as one of his 'five literary heroes' (*A Moseley Miscellany*, Ibis Publications, Ledbury 2015, pp. 116–17. Also *Complete Works*, vol. 26). Wilde was tried and convicted by an English court for 'gross indecency with men' and given a prison sentence of two years with hard labour. Owing to the climate of British opinion, after leaving prison he was forced to live as an exile in France. He died there, destitute, at the age of 46. It was not until 1967 that the Sexual Offences Act – applicable to England and Wales – decriminalized sexual acts between men. In Wilde's native Republic of Ireland sexual acts between men were decriminalized only in 1993. Currently (April 2019) there are seventy-three countries in the world that have anti-homosexual laws and twelve in which a person may be executed for homosexual acts.

442 Thomas De Quincey (1785–1859) *Confessions of an Opium-Eater: Being an Extract from the Life of a Scholar* (1822). Sangharakshita may be thinking of the passage near the end of the book; his entry for June 1819 reads: 'the sound was reverberated – everlasting farewells! And again and yet again reverberated – everlasting farewells!'.

443 Sangharakshita's visit in the company of Marco Pallis to the *khenpo* of Tharpa Choling Gompa, the Gelug monastery in Kalimpong, is described in *Facing Mount Kanchenjunga*, *Complete Works*, vol. 21, pp. 176–8.

444 An account of this celebration of Tsongkhapa's death anniversary can be found in *Precious Teachers*, *Complete Works*, vol. 22, pp. 510–11.

445 *A Survey of Buddhism*, *Complete Works*, vol. 1, pp. 342–3.

446 Sangharakshita writes about his friendship with Tomo Geshe Rimpoche, and the story of his life, in *Precious Teachers*, *Complete Works*, vol. 22, pp. 492–7. There is a photograph of the Geshe in ibid., p. 496, taken by Terry.

447 Sangharakshita later told how, during the week immediately preceding the handing on of the headship of the Order he had founded in 1968, which took place on his seventy-fifth birthday, 26 August 2000, he had dreamt of his teachers.

> Each night I dreamt of several of them and in the course of the week I must have dreamt of each and every one of them a number of times. These dreams were very, very powerful and of a sort of visionary brotherhood. I took them to mean that in handing on responsibility for the Order I was doing the right thing and that, in fact, what I was doing had the blessing of all my teachers.

See 'Recollections of my Early Life – and some Reflections on Rebirth', a talk given at the Sheffield Buddhist Centre, 8 July 2008 (*Complete Works*, vol. 12).

448 George Gaylord Simpson (1902–1984) was an American paleontologist, an expert on extinct mammals and their migrations. *The Meaning of Evolution* (1949) 'follows the rise and fall of the dynasties of life through the 2,000,000,000 years of the history of earth'.

449 Netaji, meaning 'respected leader', was the honorific bestowed on Subhas Chandra Bose (1897–1945) the Indian nationalist leader who sought to rid India of British rule during the Second World War with the help of Nazi Germany. Sangharakshita had listened to Bose's 'bloodthirsty tirades' while in the army. See *The Rainbow Road from Tooting Broadway*

to Kalimpong, *Complete Works*, vol. 20, p. 141–2. His friend, Robin Banerjee (later Buddharakshita) had as a young man worked for Bose for a while as a volunteer (ibid., p. 146).

450 Sangharakshita writes about his contact with Dilgo Rimpoche and the initiations he received from him in *Precious Teachers*, *Complete Works*, vol. 22, pp. 553–7.

451 The Hindu 'Trinity' or *Trimūrti* refers to Brahma the Creator, Vishnu the Preserver, and Shiva the Destroyer. Vishnu's consort is Lakshmi, the goddess of wealth, fortune, and prosperity.

452 *The Rainbow Road from Tooting Broadway to Kalimpong*, *Complete Works*, vol. 20, p. 115.

453 Sangharakshita writes about his first visit to the Taj Mahal in the company of Dhardo Rimpoche, and the poem he wrote subsequently (partly as a consequence of the visit taking place at the time of the 1956 Suez Crisis) in *In the Sign of the Golden Wheel*, *Complete Works*, vol. 22, pp. 340–1.

454 Mirza Ghiyath Beg (d. 1622) was a Persian official of the Mughal Empire who emigrated to India and served under the Mughal emperor Akbar and his successor, Jahangir. Mumtaz Mahal (1593–1631) was the beloved chief consort and confidante of Shah Jahan (1592–1666, reigned 1628–1658). She died giving birth to their fourteenth child. It was for her that the Taj Mahal was built as a mausoleum and monument to undying love.

455 These visits are not recorded in his memoirs. However, in an unpublished letter from Lama Govinda to Sangharakshita dated 6 March 1961 the Lama writes, 'Your and Bhikkhu Vivekananda's visit gave us much pleasure'.

456 Sangharakshita came into contact with the German-born lama in 1950 through the magazine he founded soon after arriving in Kalimpong. 'Lama Govinda ... hailed the appearance of *Stepping-Stones* with great enthusiasm, sending me letters of advice and encouragement after every issue, and promising support and cooperation' (*Facing Mount Kanchenjunga*, *Complete Works*, vol. 21, p. 87). Articles for publication followed; and then a visit to Kalimpong from the lama and his Parsi wife, Li. Sangharakshita found in Lama Govinda 'a kindred spirit' (ibid., chapter 13, pp. 243–62). They remained in contact for the rest of Lama Govinda's life. His final letter to Sangharakshita, from America where he spent the last years, was written just four days before he died in January 1985.

457 Sangharakshita met Apa Saheb Pant (1912–1992), also known as Parashuram Rao Pant, in Gangtok in 1955 at which time

he was the Political Officer and representative of the Indian government to the principality of Sikkim. Although he was a staunch Hindu and a Brahmin, Pant invited Sangharakshita to give lectures on Buddhism and to stay with him at his home – a relic of the British Raj. See *In the Sign of the Golden Wheel*, *Complete Works*, vol. 22, pp. 246, 261–2, 319.

458 Sara Boin (1937–2008) (after her second marriage, Sara Boin-Webb) translated from the French a number of scholarly books by Étienne Lamotte, as well as two Mahāyāna *sūtras* which Lamotte had rendered into French from the Sanskrit: *The Teaching of Vimalakīrti* (*Vimalakīrtinirdeśa*), Pali Text Society, London 1976; and the *Śūraṃgamasamādhisūtra* (*Concentration of Heroic Progress*), Curzon Press, Surrey 1999. She was the first of the twelve Order members ordained by Sangharakshita in 1968 (see p. 440) when she received the name Sujata.

459 Frank Raymond Leavis (1895–1978) was a renowned literary critic, for three decades a lecturer at Downing College, Cambridge. His first book, *New Bearings in English Poetry* (1932) identified the achievements of a number of new poets including T. S. Eliot and W. B. Yeats.

460 Erich Neumann (1905–1960) was a German-Jewish analytical psychologist who emigrated to Israel after Hitler's rise to power in 1933. His *Ursprungsgeschichte des Bewusstseins* (1949) charts the mythological stages in the evolution of consciousness. It was published in English as *The Origins and History of Consciousness* in 1954.

461 1. Porphyry (c.234 CE–c.305 CE), *De Abstinentia ab Esu Animalium* translated from Latin into English as *On Abstinence from Animal Food* in which Porphyry argues for vegetarianism on spiritual and ethical grounds. (See also note 365.)

2. Plutarch of Chaeronea (46–120 CE) drew on the Egyptian myth for his *On Isis and Osiris* which is included in the seventy-eight essays and speeches of his *Moralia*. In this way the myth became widely known in the Graeco-Roman world. (For more on Plutarch see note 278.)

462 'Mind – Reactive and Creative' in *Buddha Mind*, Windhorse Publications, Birmingham 2001 (*Complete Works*, vol. 11).

463 This dedication ceremony continues to be used to this day (2019) to dedicate shrine-rooms, retreats, and even projects to the Three Jewels. It can be found in *Puja: The Triratna Book of Buddhist Devotional Texts*, seventh edition, Windhorse Publications, Cambridge 2008, pp. 36–7.

464 In 2010 the movement founded in 1967 (which in the West was known as the Friends of the Western Buddhist Order and in India as Trailokya Bauddha Mahasangha Sahayak Gana) was renamed by Sangharakshita the Triratna Buddhist Community. The early years of the FWBO are described by Buddhadasa in *On the First Rung: Reminiscences of the Early Years of the Triratna Buddhist Order 1969–1974*, Ola Leaves, Ledbury 2014.

465 'The Ven. Sthavira Sangharakshita: A Statement' in *The Buddhist*, vol. 11, no. 2 (February 1967), p. 13.

466 *The Meaning of Orthodoxy in Buddhism: A Protest* was published in *The Buddhist* in three parts (January–March 1966) and later by Windhorse Publications, Glasgow 1987 (*Complete Works*, vol. 7).

467 Maurice Walshe, 'New Beginnings' in *The Buddhist*, vol. 11, no. 1 (January 1967), p. 2.

468 *Upaḍḍha Sutta*, *Saṃyutta Nikāya* v.2; see Bhikkhu Bodhi (trans.), *The Connected Discourses of the Buddha*, Wisdom Publications, Boston 2000, pp. 1524–5; also F. L. Woodward (trans.), *The Book of the Kindred Sayings*, part 5, Pali Text Society, London 1979, p. 2.

469 *Complete Poems 1941–1994*, Windhorse Publications, Birmingham 1995, pp. 270–1 (*Complete Works*, vol. 25, pp. 314–15).

470 'Obituary' in *FWBO Newsletter*, no. 5, June 1969, p. 12.

471 In the summer of 2001 Sangharakshita suffered sudden and serious impairment to his vision and was no longer able to read or write. Neal Warren, a Mitra from the USA who was visiting England at the time, was invited to Birmingham to help him. His first task was to put archival papers in order, in particular original Tibetan *sādhanas* that Sangharakshita had brought back from India. They then turned to *Moving Against the Stream* which Sangharakshita wanted to complete in the same literary style in which he had been writing before the deterioration of his eyesight. Neal became amanuensis, working daily with Sangharakshita. The book was completed in 2002. Neal was ordained in 2003 and given the name Sarajit, which means 'essence-conquered'. He returned to the USA in 2006 to take up the life of a 'yogi-householder'. He and Sangharakshita remained in touch until Sangharakshita's death in 2018.

1970 – A RETROSPECT

472 1. The Louvre is the largest art gallery in the world, situated on the banks of the river Seine. It opened in 1793.

2. The Musée Guimet was founded in 1879 by Émile Étienne Guimet, a French industrialist who travelled in the Far East and brought back many Buddhist, as well as non-Buddhist, images and artefacts which became the foundation for the museum.

3. Notre Dame de Paris is a cathedral built in the Gothic style dedicated to Our Lady of Paris. It was built mainly 1160–1260, and is one of the city's great landmarks.

4. Les Invalides (formerly Hôtel National des Invalides or the National Residence of the Invalids) includes a military museum, mausoleum, and a church with tombs including that of Napoleon Bonaparte.

5. Montmartre is a hill in the northern part of Paris known for the Basilica of Sacré-Coeur and for its association with artists who have lived and worked there, especially in the nineteenth century.

473 1. The *Venus de Milo* is a marble statue from Ancient Greece, from the period 130–100 BCE. It is named after Milos, the Greek island on which it was discovered.

2. The *Mona Lisa* or *La Gioconda* is the famous painting of the woman with the 'enigmatic' smile by Leonardo da Vinci (1452–1519).

474 1. Pierre de Ronsard (1524–1585) was one of the great French poets, writer of Odes, love poems, and other verse.

2. Honoré de Balzac (1799–1850) was a French novelist – also playwright – best known for his series, *La Comédie Humaine (The Human Comedy)* which includes ninety-one completed stories, novels, and essays, plus others left unfinished.

475 Charles de Gaulle (1890–1970) was a French army officer and later a statesman. He led French Resistance against Nazi Germany in the Second World War and went on to found the Fifth French Republic with himself as president. He had resigned in April 1969.

476 Mahesh Prasad Varma (1918–2008) was known as Maharishi Mahesh Yogi. See note 128(4).

477 Sangharakshita first came across communication exercises in India. They were invented by educationalist Muriel Payne OBE, author of *Creative Education* (1958), whom Sangharakshita met in the 1950s. See 'Some Bombay Friends' in *Adhisthana Writings (Complete Works*, vol. 25).

478 Buckminster Fuller (1895–1983) was an architect, systems theorist, writer, and inventor. Among his many original ideas and designs was the geodesic dome.

479 Geshe Ngawang Wangyal (1901–1983) was of Kalmyk origin. He had studied at Drepung monastery in Tibet, spent time in China, and worked as translator for the British Political Officer, Sir

Charles Bell. After the Chinese invasion of Tibet in 1950 he escaped to India. In 1955 he went to America where he established the Labsum Shedrub Ling monastery in New Jersey, teaching many Western students. He is mentioned in *In the Sign of the Golden Wheel*, *Complete Works*, vol. 22, pp. 119 and 192.

480 Rembrandt van Rijn's (1606–1669) *Aristotle Contemplating a Bust of Homer* dates to 1653. The oil painting shows a bearded Aristotle wearing a gold chain with his right hand on the head of a bust of Homer.

481 Bobby Seale (b. 1936) created the Black Panther Party for Self-Defense in 1966 after the assassination of Malcolm X. It was to be 'a righteous revolutionary front against this racist, decadent, capitalistic system'.

482 Weathermen – later the Weather Underground Organization – was an American left-wing terrorist organization responsible for bombings, jailbreaks, and riots from 1969 through the 1970s. The Minutemen was a right-wing anti-communist organization founded in the early 1960s who were stockpiling weapons in the belief that there would be a communist bid to take over the USA.

483 The ballet *Petroushka* was choreographed by the great dancer Michel Fokine (1880–1942) with music by the Russian composer Igor Stravinsky (1882–1971). It was first performed in Paris in 1911.

484 Keffolds is a large house, just outside Haslemere, which was then owned by the Ockenden Venture and rented out. Haslemere is 45 miles (72 kilometres) south-west of central London.

485 104° Fahrenheit = 40° Celsius.

486 The person who did not take the drug was Eric Wright, who three years later was ordained as Mangala.

487 Boadicea or Boudicca was the queen of the Iceni tribe who led an uprising of native Britons against the occupying Roman forces in c.60 CE. The barrow, to which local tradition has given her name in the belief that it was here that she was buried, dates back to the Bronze Age.

488 This was the first volume of memoirs, *The Rainbow Road from Tooting Broadway to Kalimpong*, *Complete Works*, vol. 20.

489 Sangharakshita eventually translated the whole of this text which was published as *Dhammapada: the Way of Truth*, by Windhorse Publications in 2001 (*Complete Works*, vol. 15). He bought a copy of the scripture shortly after arriving in India in 1944 and had learnt its verses by heart. *The Rainbow Road*

from Tooting Broadway to Kalimpong, *Complete Works*, vol. 20, pp. 115 and 328–9.

490 The *FWBO Newsletter* was a quarterly magazine which ran from May 1968 until winter 1985/6 when it was superseded by *Golden Drum*. Early on it was edited mainly by Dharmachari Ananda, also by Padmaraja and Marichi. Nagabodhi became editor in summer 1975 and brought out all the subsequent numbers.

491 Doubleday was an American publishing company, founded in 1897, which within fifty years had become the largest in the USA. The Anchor Imprint produced quality paperbacks.

492 The private edition of 300 copies was printed on A4 paper and included two black-and-white illustrations by Richard Caston and Bob Chaplin. On the back page we are informed: '"On Glastonbury Tor" was written during the summer of 1969, after a visit which he [Sangharakshita] paid to Glastonbury in the company of about three dozen friends, and describes actual happenings.' (See *Complete Works*, vol. 25, pp. 499–504.) Later he wrote of it as 'an expression of much that was happening in the 1960s, especially among the younger generation.' See 'Living With Carter' (*Complete Works*, vol. 26).

493 Sangharakshita's attitude towards making films during his time in India was not always 'negative' as can be seen by the article published in 1953 under the pseudonym Himavantavasi, 'To Film or Not to Film?' which looked at how making a film on the life of the Buddha was being discussed by different parties. See *Anagarika Dharmapala and Other 'Maha Bodhi' Writings*, Ibis Publications, Ledbury 2012, p.104 (*Complete Works*, vol. 8).

494 *The Red Desert* (*Il Deserto Rosso*) was a 1964 film by the Italian director and screenwriter Michelangelo Antonioni (1912–2007).

495 Ken Russell (1927–2011) was a British film director. His *Women in Love*, first shown in 1969, was based on the famous novel of the same name by D. H. Lawrence, first published in 1920.

496 1. Anaïs Nin (1903–1977) was born to Cuban parents in France, though her later years were spent in the USA. She was a diarist, essayist, novelist, and writer of short stories and erotica. Her many lovers included Henry Miller and Otto Rank.

2. Constantine P. Cavafy (1863–1933) was born in Egypt to Greek parents. He became one of the leading poets of his time. Writing in Greek, his poems revivified Greek poetry. There are many volumes translated into English.

497 Murasaki Shikibu (c.973 or 978 – c.1014 or 1031) was a

Japanese poet and a lady-in-waiting at the Imperial Court. She wrote only one novel, *The Tale of Genji* (*Genji Monogatari*), which is not only the first novel ever written but also widely regarded as one of the finest. It deals with the lives of courtiers during the Heian period. The complete novel was first published in English translation by Arthur Waley in 1933.

498 1. John Middleton Murry (1889–1957) was an English writer on social issues, politics and religion, and literary criticism. He married the writer Katherine Mansfield and was a close friend of D. H. Lawrence. His *Son of Woman* was written in 1931, the year after Lawrence's death.

2. Herbert George Wells (1866–1946) was an English writer of imaginative science fiction novels such as *Journey to the Centre of the Earth*, and a historian whose best-known work, *The Outline of History*, was published in 1920. His *Experiment in Autobiography: Discoveries and Conclusions of a Very Ordinary Brain (since 1866)* was published in 1934.

499 1. Johann Peter Eckermann (1792–1854) was Goethe's personal secretary for the last nine years of the great man's life. His *Conversations with Goethe in the last years of his life* (*Gespräche mit Goethe in den letzten Jahren seines Lebens*) was published in three volumes, two in 1836, the last in 1848. The conversations are not simply records of interviews but an artistically selected arrangement of information about Goethe's life and thought. The first volume was translated into English in 1839.

2. *Italian Journey*: see note 282.

500 1. Francis Bacon (1561–1626) was a philosopher and statesman who served as Lord Chancellor of England under James I. He died in Highgate after contracting pneumonia: he had been carrying out an experiment with snow.

2. Andrew Marvell (1621–1678) was a metaphysical poet, a satirist and politician, a supporter of Oliver Cromwell, and a friend and colleague of John Milton. He spent some years living in Highgate.

3. Samuel Taylor Coleridge (1772–1834), one of the great English Romantic poets, also literary critic, philosopher, and lecturer, lived in Highgate from 1816 as house guest of Dr and Mrs Gillman and it was from here that he published his *Biographia Literaria* (1817).

4. A. E. Houseman (1859–1936) was a poet and classicist, best known for *A Shropshire Lad* which was written in his cottage in Highgate.

5. John Betjeman (1906–1984) was an English poet and Poet Laureate from 1972 until his death. His childhood home

was in Highgate and he later returned to live there.

501 Graham Sowter continued living in the Muswell Hill community after Sangharakshita left for a sabbatical in 1973. He went on to be ordained in 1975 as Siddhiratna ('Magic Jewel'). Kevin Brooks never joined the Western Buddhist Order but he maintained his contact with Sangharakshita until the latter's death in 2018.

APPENDIX: LECTURES BY SANGHARAKSHITA

Throughout Moving Against the Stream and 1970 – A Retrospect we find Sangharakshita teaching meditation, and communicating the Dharma through lectures given in Britain, India, Egypt, and the USA. Comparatively few are referred to by title, but the following list, gleaned from the text, gives an indication of the themes that interested him and which he felt would most interest and benefit his audiences. From early on, at least in Britain, some lectures were recorded. Recordings from these early years that have survived, as well as hundreds of later ones, can be listened to online at freebuddhistaudio.com.

INDEX

A GUIDE TO THE COMPLETE WORKS OF SANGHARAKSHITA

Gathered together in these twenty-seven volumes are talks and stories, commentaries on the Buddhist scriptures, poems, memoirs, reviews, and other writings. The genres are many, and the subject matter covered is wide, but it all has – its whole purpose is to convey – that taste of freedom which the Buddha declared to be the hallmark of his Dharma. Another traditional description of the Buddha's Dharma is that it is *ehipassiko*, 'come and see'. Sangharakshita calls to us, his readers, to come and see how the Dharma can fundamentally change the way we see things, change the way we live for the better, and change the society we belong to, wherever in the world we live.

Sangharakshita's very first published piece, *The Unity of Buddhism* (found in volume 7 of this collection), appeared in 1944 when he was eighteen years old, and it introduced themes that continued to resound throughout his work: the basis of Buddhist ethics, the compassion of the bodhisattva, and the transcendental unity of Buddhism. Over the course of the following seven decades not only did numerous other works flow from his pen; he gave hundreds of talks (some now lost). In gathering all we could find of this vast output, we have sought to arrange it in a way that brings a sense of coherence, communicating something essential about Sangharakshita, his life and teaching. Recalling the three 'baskets' among which an early tradition divided the Buddha's teachings, we have divided Sangharakshita's creative output into six 'baskets' or groups: foundation texts; works originating in India; teachings originally given in the West; commentaries on the Buddhist scriptures; personal writings; and poetry, aphorisms, and works on the arts. The 27th volume, a concordance, brings together all the terms and themes of the whole collection. If you want to find a particular story or teaching, look at a traditional term from different points of view or in different contexts, or track down one of the thousands of canonical references to be found in these volumes, the concordance will be your guide.

1. FOUNDATION

What is the foundation of a Buddhist life? How do we understand and then follow the Buddha's path of Ethics, Meditation, and Wisdom? What is really meant by 'Going for Refuge to the Three Jewels', described by Sangharakshita as the essential act of a Buddhist life? And what is the Bodhisattva ideal, which he has called 'one of the sublimest ideals mankind has ever seen'? In the 'Foundation' group you will find teachings on all these themes. It includes the author's *magnum opus, A Survey of Buddhism*, a collection of teachings on *The Purpose and Practice of Buddhist Meditation*, and the anthology, *The Essential Sangharakshita*, an eminently helpful distillation of the entire corpus.

2. INDIA

From 1950 to 1964 Sangharakshita, based in Kalimpong in the eastern Himalayas, poured his energy into trying to revive Buddhism in the land of its birth and to revitalize and bring reform to the existing Asian Buddhist world. The articles and book reviews from this period are gathered in volumes 7 and 8, as well as his biographical sketch of the great Sinhalese Dharmaduta, Anagārika Dharmapala. In 1954 Sangharakshita took on the editing of the *Maha Bodhi*, a journal for which he wrote a monthly editorial, and which, under his editorship, published the work of many of the leading Buddhist writers of the time. It was also during these years in India that a vital connection was forged with Dr B. R. Ambedkar, renowned Indian statesman and leader of the Buddhist mass conversion of 1956. Sangharakshita became closely involved with the new Buddhists and, after Dr Ambedkar's untimely death, visited them regularly on extensive teaching tours.

From 1979, when an Indian wing of the Triratna Buddhist Community was founded (then known as TBMSG), Sangharakshita returned several times to undertake further teaching tours. The talks from these tours are collected in volumes 9 and 10 along with a unique work on Ambedkar and his life which draws out the significance of his conversion to Buddhism.

3. THE WEST

Sangharakshita founded the Triratna Buddhist Community (then called the Friends of the Western Buddhist Order) on 6 April 1967. On 7 April the following year he performed the first ordinations of men and women within the Triratna Buddhist Order (then the Western Buddhist Order). At that time Buddhism was not widely known in the West and for the following two decades or so he taught intensively, finding new ways to communicate the ancient truths of Buddhism, drawing on the whole Buddhist tradition to do so, as well as making connections with what was best in existing Western culture. Sometimes his sword flashed as he critiqued ideas and views inimical to the Dharma. It is these teachings and writings that are gathered together in this third group.

4. COMMENTARY

Throughout Sangharakshita's works are threaded references to the Buddhist canon of literature – Pāli, Mahāyāna, and Vajrayāna – from which he drew his inspiration. In the early days of the new movement he often taught by means of seminars in which, prompted by the questions of his students, he sought to pass on the inspiration and wisdom of the Buddhist tradition. Each seminar was based around a different text, the seminars were recorded and transcribed, and in due course many of the transcriptions were edited and turned into books, all carefully checked by Sangharakshita. The commentaries compiled in this way constitute the fourth group. In some ways this is the heart of the collection. Sangharakshita often told the story of how it was that, reading two *sūtras* at the age of sixteen or seventeen, he realized that he was a Buddhist, and he has never tired of showing others how they too could see and realize the value of the '*sūtra*-treasure'.

5. MEMOIRS

Who is Sangharakshita? What sort of life did he live? Whom did he meet? What did he feel? Why did he found a new Buddhist movement? In these volumes of memoirs and letters Sangharakshita shares with his readers much about himself and his life as he himself has experienced it, giving us a sense of its breadth and depth, humour and pathos.

6. POETRY, APHORISMS, AND THE ARTS

Sangharakshita describes reading *Paradise Lost* at the age of twelve as one of the greatest poetic experiences of his life. His realization of the value of the higher arts to spiritual development is one of his distinctive contributions to our understanding of what Buddhist life is, and he has expressed it in a number of essays and articles. Throughout his life he has written poetry which he says can be regarded as a kind of spiritual autobiography. It is here, perhaps, that we come closest to the heart of Sangharakshita. He has also written a few short stories and composed some startling aphorisms. Through book reviews he has engaged with the experiences, ideas, and opinions of modern writers. All these are collected in this sixth group.

In the preface to *A Survey of Buddhism* (volume 1 in this collection), Sangharakshita wrote of his approach to the Buddha's teachings:

> Why did the Buddha (or Nāgārjuna, or Buddhaghosa) teach this particular doctrine? What bearing does it have on the spiritual life? How does it help the individual Buddhist actually to follow the spiritual path?… I found myself asking such questions again and again, for only in this way, I found, could I make sense – spiritual sense – of Buddhism.

Although this collection contains so many words, they are all intent, directly or indirectly, on these same questions. And all these words are not in the end about their writer, but about his great subject, the Buddha and his teaching, and about you, the reader, for whose benefit they are solely intended. These pages are full of the reverence that Sangharakshita has always felt, which is expressed in an early poem, 'Taking Refuge in the Buddha', whose refrain is 'My place is at thy feet'. He has devoted his life to communicating the Buddha's Dharma in its depth and in its breadth, to men and women from all backgrounds and walks of life, from all countries, of all races, of all ages. These collected works are the fruit of that devotion.

We are very pleased to be able to include some previously unpublished work in this collection, but most of what appears in these volumes has been published before. We have made very few changes, though we have added extra notes where we thought they would be useful. We have had the pleasure of researching the notes in the Sangharakshita Library at 'Adhisthana', Triratna's centre in Herefordshire, UK, which houses his own collection of books. It has been of great value to be able to search among the very copies of the *suttas*, *sūtras* and commentaries that have provided the basis of his teachings over the last seventy years.

The publication of these volumes owes much to the work of transcribers, editors, indexers, designers, and publishers over many years – those who brought out the original editions of many of the works included here, and those who have contributed in all sorts of ways to this *Complete Works* project, including all those who contributed to funds given in celebration of Sangharakshita's ninetieth birthday in August 2015, and to a further outpouring of generosity after Sangharakshita's death in October 2018. All these donors have made the publication of this series possible, and we are very grateful. Many thanks to everyone who has helped; may the merit gained in our acting thus go to the alleviation of the suffering of all beings.

Vidyadevi and Kalyanaprabha
Editors

THE COMPLETE WORKS OF SANGHARAKSHITA

I FOUNDATION

VOLUME 1 A SURVEY OF BUDDHISM / THE BUDDHA'S NOBLE EIGHTFOLD PATH
A Survey of Buddhism
The Buddha's Noble Eightfold Path

2 THE THREE JEWELS I
The Three Jewels
The Meaning of Conversion in Buddhism
Going for Refuge
The Ten Pillars of Buddhism
The History of My Going for Refuge
My Relation to the Order
Extending the Hand of Fellowship
Forty-Three Years Ago
Was the Buddha a Bhikkhu?

3 THE THREE JEWELS II
Who is the Buddha?
What is the Dharma?
What is the Sangha?

4 THE BODHISATTVA IDEAL
The Bodhisattva Ideal
The Endlessly Fascinating Cry (seminar)
The Bodhisattva Principle

5 THE PURPOSE AND PRACTICE OF BUDDHIST MEDITATION
The Purpose and Practice of Buddhist Meditation

6 THE ESSENTIAL SANGHARAKSHITA
The Essential Sangharakshita

II INDIA

7 CROSSING THE STREAM: INDIA WRITINGS I
Early Writings 1944–1954
Crossing the Stream
Buddhism in the Modern World: Cultural and Political Implications
The Meaning of Orthodoxy in Buddhism
Buddhism in India Today
Ordination and Initiation in the Three Yānas
A Bird's Eye View of Indian Buddhism

VOLUME 8 BEATING THE DHARMA DRUM: INDIA WRITINGS II
Anagarika Dharmapala and Other 'Maha Bodhi' Writings
Dharmapala: The Spiritual Dimension
Beating the Drum: 'Maha Bodhi' Editorials

9 DR AMBEDKAR AND THE REVIVAL OF BUDDHISM I
Ambedkar and Buddhism
Lecture Tour in India, December 1981–March 1982

10 DR AMBEDKAR AND THE REVIVAL OF BUDDHISM II
Lecture Tours in India 1979 & 1983–1992
Other Edited Lectures and Seminar Material

III THE WEST

11 A NEW BUDDHIST MOVEMENT I
Ritual and Devotion in Buddhism
The Buddha's Victory
The Taste of Freedom
Buddha Mind
Human Enlightenment
New Currents in Western Buddhism
Buddhism for Today – and Tomorrow
Buddhism and the West
Aspects of Buddhist Morality
Buddhism, World Peace, and Nuclear War
Dialogue between Buddhism and Christianity
Buddhism and Blasphemy
Buddhism and the Bishop of Woolwich
Buddhism and the New Reformation
Great Buddhists of the Twentieth Century
Articles and Interviews

12 A NEW BUDDHIST MOVEMENT II
Previously unpublished talks

13 EASTERN AND WESTERN TRADITIONS
Tibetan Buddhism
Creative Symbols of Tantric Buddhism
The Essence of Zen
The FWBO and 'Protestant Buddhism'
From Genesis to the Diamond Sūtra

IV COMMENTARY

VOLUME 14 THE ETERNAL LEGACY / WISDOM BEYOND WORDS
The Eternal Legacy
The Glory of the Literary World
Wisdom Beyond Words

15 PĀLI CANON TEACHINGS AND TRANSLATIONS
Dhammapada (translation)
Karaṇīyamettā Sutta (translation)
Living with Kindness
Living with Awareness
Maṅgala Sutta (translation)
Auspicious Signs (seminar)
Salutation to the Three Jewels (translation)
The Threefold Refuge (seminar)
Further Pāli Sutta Commentaries

16 MAHĀYĀNA MYTHS AND STORIES
The Drama of Cosmic Enlightenment
The Priceless Jewel (talk)
Transforming Self and World
The Inconceivable Emancipation

17 WISDOM TEACHINGS OF THE MAHĀYĀNA
Know Your Mind
Living Ethically
Living Wisely
The Way to Wisdom (seminar)

18 MILAREPA AND THE ART OF DISCIPLESHIP I
The Yogi's Joy
The Shepherd's Search for Mind
Rechungpa's Journey to Enlightenment

19 MILAREPA AND THE ART OF DISCIPLESHIP II
Rechungpa's Journey to Enlightenment, continued

V MEMOIRS

20 THE RAINBOW ROAD FROM TOOTING BROADWAY TO KALIMPONG
The Rainbow Road from Tooting Broadway to Kalimpong

WINDHORSE PUBLICATIONS

Windhorse Publications is a Buddhist charitable company based in the UK. We produce books of high quality that are accessible and relevant to all those interested in Buddhism, at whatever level of interest and commitment. We are the main publisher of Sangharakshita, the founder of the Triratna Buddhist Order and Community. Our books draw on the whole range of the Buddhist tradition, including translations of traditional texts, commentaries, books that make links with contemporary culture and ways of life, biographies of Buddhists, and works on meditation.

To subscribe to the *Complete Works of Sangharakshita,* please go to: windhorsepublications.com/sangharakshita-complete-works/

THE TRIRATNA BUDDHIST COMMUNITY

Windhorse Publications is a part of the Triratna Buddhist Community, an international movement with centres in Europe, India, North and South America and Australasia. At these centres, members of the Triratna Buddhist Order offer classes in meditation and Buddhism. Activities of the Triratna Community also include retreat centres, residential spiritual communities, ethical Right Livelihood businesses, and the Karuna Trust, a UK fundraising charity that supports social welfare projects in the slums and villages of India.

Through these and other activities, Triratna is developing a unique approach to Buddhism, not simply as a philosophy and a set of techniques, but as a creatively directed way of life for all people living in the conditions of the modern world.

For more information please visit thebuddhistcentre.com